ACKNOWLEDGMENTS

I get by with a little help from my friends.
The Beatles

I would like to acknowledge Toby Trowt-Bayard for her foresight and initiative in writing the first edition of this video communications treatise in the early days of video communications technology. I would like to thank Toby for inviting me to co-write the second edition, and for solely entrusting me with the stewardship of this book once the second edition was complete. I hope that I have maintained, in the view of you, the reader, the high standards that Toby alone set in the first edition, and that we together set in the second edition.

I would like to thank the love of my life, Susie, for her support and patience throughout this very demanding period of our lives. I would like to acknowledge my hero, Dick Wilcox for inspiring me and teaching me, among other things, that we do our most worthwhile work with the help of others. And, finally, I would like to thank my favorite people, Bailey and Evan, for delivering hugs to their dad in the dungeon and motivating him to get out and play.

I would like to acknowledge Matt Collier and the other accommodating people at Polycom, Kevin Flanagan at PictureTel, and Michael Russell and Susie Capozza at VTEL for their assistance. I would like to acknowledge Christine Perry for her keen market analysis, and Chuck Grandgent at Octave Communications for sharing his passion for, and knowledge of, videoconferencing. I would like to acknowledge Jill Adams at the Multnomah County Library for her research assistance and enthusiasm. Thanks to Toby Bayard, David Gibson, Claude Chauveau, Justin Radke, Cliff Bihl and other patient souls who have helped me to understand how this stuff *really* works.

The many contributors to the standards organizations (whose work I have spent many late nights reading) are the unsung heroes and pioneers who, along with the early adopters of the technology, deserve credit for removing barriers to worthwhile communications. It is a thrill to learn about and to report on their work.

James R. Wilcox, CISSP

VIDEOCONFERENCING & INTERACTIVE MULTIMEDIA: THE WHOLE PICTURE

By
James R. Wilcox

Illustrations by
Laura Long
and
Michel L. Bayard

Published By Telecom Books
An imprint of CMP Media, Inc.
12 West 21st St., NY, NY., 10010
http://www.telecombooks.com

ISBN: 1-57820-054-7

For individual orders, and for information on special discounts for quantity orders, please contact:
Telecom Books
6500 Silacci Way
Gilroy, CA 95020
Tel: 800-LIBRARY or 408-848-3854
Fax: 408 848-5784
Email: telecombooks@rushorder.com

Distributed to the book trade in the US and Canada by:
Publishers Group West
1700 Fourth St., Berkeley, CA 94710

Manufactured in the United States of America

Third edition, February 2000.

Illustrations by Laura Long & Michel Bayard
Copy editing: James R. Wilcox
Text design and layout: Jon Lee and Associates
Set in 10 point Times

PREFACE

"The hinge of radical change almost always swings on new information systems."

James Champy, Chairman CSC Consulting Group

This book is about an emerging communications tool; videoconferencing, and the applications that are built upon it. Videoconferencing and interactive multimedia represent an aggregation of technologies that includes information coding and compression, telecommunications and networking, broadcasting, and end-user presentational and data manipulation tools. The field of interactive multimedia and videoconferencing is not new, but it is rapidly evolving.

In preparing this book, I seek to present clearly and concisely the complex subject of videoconferencing. It is helpful but not necessary that the reader know a little about videoconferencing and about networking. I start with the basics to build a foundation with which the reader can grasp the elementary issues. My intent is to spend equal time on technology, standards, and applications. In all cases, I want the reader to understand the business implications of interactive multimedia and videoconferencing. Selling a solution, even if it is in an organization's best interest, requires that. It is my position that the purpose of technology, as fascinating as it is, is to serve human needs.

For those who are new to the topic, this book will serve as a good introduction to the various forms of video communications. For the technically advanced, it will provide information for understanding and assessing new products, staying abreast of standards, and refining expertise. In any case, I encourage the reader to explore ways to implement video communications to enhance collaboration, facilitate competitive strategies, improve information delivery, and increase efficiency.

Interactive video communications strategies can be significant enablers in the construction of applications that span multiple geographic locations, and even organizational (e.g., corporate or governmental) boundaries. These applications include group-to-group meetings, person-to-person desktop, videophone, one-to-many broadcasts and multicasts, point-to-point and multipoint data collaboration, and variations thereof. One should adapt combinations and implementations of these applications to suit specific organizational or personal needs. Some of the more successful application categories include telemedicine, distance learning, telecommuting and site-to-site collaboration, legal and judicial, joint engineering, diplomatic relations, and negotiations and more additional examples than one can list! Strong needs-analysis, ingenuity, and senior management support can make practically any video communications application successful.

For videoconferencing to deliver on its promise, a strong interoperability model is required. In this area, recent developments have been particularly favorable. With the adoption of numerous global standards, videoconferencing applications can traverse a wide variety of networks including analog *POTS*, circuit-switched digital (ISDN, T-1, switched 56), and packet-switched (primarily IP-based networks such as corporate intranets and the Internet). Interoperability is nearly universal, and the level of cooperation between industry leaders is unprecedented. This is a welcome development, given the industry's earlier tendency toward proprietary implementations. I admire those who can profit by developing technologies that address human needs; I applaud even more those who adopt rather than impede better technologies that serve the public good.

A standards-based approach integrates tools from multiple sources. It is scalable, flexible, and based on best-of-breed components. Videoconferencing system implementations that pursue this strategy are more likely to deliver an application-responsive, manageable, and cost-effective solution. When properly executed, users can exchange information with correspondents regardless of what system they use.

I believe that people will increasingly leverage the power of standards-based videoconferencing and interactive multimedia to address important business processes that directly relate to organizational success or competitive advantage. Video communication facilitates teamwork. Many of the ways in which one can leverage it to respond quickly to changing business conditions between remote regions of the earth are unimaginable. Systems based on such architecture can break through organizational barriers, and thereby provide links that bind trading partners in a flexible, personal, and highly efficient manner.

Although my focus in this book is on corporate enterprises, I must emphasize that interactive video communications can help individuals complete ordinary tasks. Many valuable videoconferencing applications provide breakthrough solutions for individuals and small organizations. Network choices abound such that anyone anywhere in the world can deploy conferencing solutions.

Small or large, the principles that underlie videoconferencing systems architecture remain the same. Standards-based systems are always better than closed ones (although proprietary solutions may provide needed functionality in the absence of a standard). By promoting standards and supporting the efforts of groups such as the ITU-T, the IMTC, the IETF and the ISO we will overcome barriers to worthwhile work. The promise of such standards is any-to-any videoconferencing with the same seamless connectivity that we have come to expect of the telephone.

I hope that you enjoy this book. If you have questions or comments, please exchange electronic mail with me at the following Internet address:

James R. Wilcox, CISSP jim_wilcox@uswest.net jwilcox@iprg.nokia.com

TABLE OF CONTENTS

LIST OF FIGURES

PART ONE

VIDEOCONFERENCING: TERMS, CONCEPTS AND APPLICATIONS

1

AN INTRODUCTION TO VIDEOCONFERENCING

Vision is the art of seeing things invisible.
Jonathan Swift

WHAT IS VIDEOCONFERENCING?

What is videoconferencing? Although it is common to hear videoconferencing referred to as a "technology," it is not a technology. Rather, it is a collection of technologies that form the foundation for a wide variety of applications. The term videoconferencing refers to these applications and, to a lesser degree, the technologies that support them.

One can trace the term videoconferencing to two Latin words--videre which means, "I see," and conferre that means, "to bring together." Videoconferencing unites meeting participants such that they can share visual information. It overcomes distance as a barrier to collaborative work.

The combination of the words videre and audio (which, in turn, stems from the Latin audire: "to hear") gives us the word video. One can define video as a system that records and transmits visual information by conveying that information using electrical signals. Although the term video, in its strictest sense, refers only to images, common vernacular reflects the assumption that audio is synchronized with these images.

For the purposes of this book we will define videoconferencing as an exchange of *digitized* video images and sounds between conference participants at two or more separate sites. The transferred images may be pictures of the participants themselves, but they may also include video clips or other material such as still pictures of objects or information that is stored on a computer (e.g., graphics, data files, applications). Likewise, the sounds that are conveyed between sites in a videoconference could be discussions between meeting participants in different sites, but they could also be any other form of digitized audio that is, in some manner, synchronized with the video. Video and audio generally share the same communication path in our definition of a videoconference, but they can also be transmitted separately.

One can apply videoconferencing to coalesce separate gatherings of individuals into a single multi-site meeting. They can also link two people through dissimilar personal computers, videophones, or other intelligent devices.

Both group-system-based and personal videoconferences can take place as point-to-point or multipoint events. Point-to-point, as the name implies, links participants in only two sites. Multipoint arrangements join more than two sites. The device that links three or more locations in a single conference is called a multipoint control unit (MCU).

Group-system multipoint conferencing has historically been more common than personal multipoint conferencing, but significant changes are occurring in this area. The local area networks that link workstations, servers, and other intelligent devices within a limited geographic area also permit connections to the corporate wide area network and points outside. Organizations are upgrading their LANs to support the bandwidth-intensive demands of videoconferencing. When the networking infrastructure is in place, individuals in disparate sites will participate in a wide variety of multipoint videoconferences. The powerful applications that will result from this capability are both diverse and exciting; indeed, they will eventually transform historic notions of teamwork.

One of the stimulants to the videoconferencing market has been the adoption of widely accepted interoperability standards. Until recently, construction of a videoconference always required all participants to use the same manufacturer's equipment, and to connect by a compatible network. Standards are easing these restrictions, and soon they will eliminate them. Arranging a videoconference will be much like sending a fax: all one has to know is the address.

The era of any-to-any videoconferencing has dawned, but there is much more to come. Standards have provided the boost that videoconferencing and interactive multimedia long needed, and market growth is the result. Just as the value of telephone service grew as organizations and individuals subscribed to it, the value of videoconferencing will grow as organizations and individuals install end points.

As these end points continue to proliferate, the day will come when adding a visual component to a distance communication is an ever-present option. This ability (to enjoin a shared visual experience that spans distance) will change the sociodemographics of the workplace by, at last, enabling telecommuting.

Cultural shifts take time but, as we have seen with the almost overnight acceptance of the Internet and its hypertext-linked subset, the World Wide Web (WWW), these shifts eventually reach critical mass. In the late 1990s, interest in personal computing tools and applications is practically a national obsession. Moreover, as new applications appear on our desktops and our mobile computing devices, they become successively less intimidating. Aided by the graphical user interface (GUI)

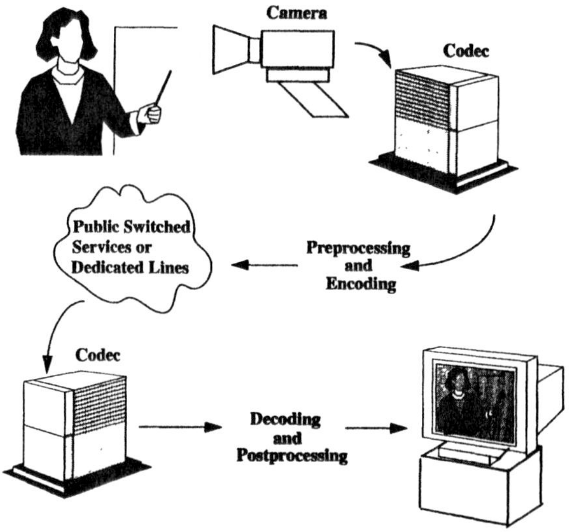

Figure 1-1. How Videoconferencing Systems Work.

and on-line help utilities, we gain expertise with increasing confidence and speed. In this fertile environment, we see videoconferencing becoming a basic tool, just one of many communications options that are as easy to use as they are powerful.

Videoconferencing was not always an accessible, low-cost option for anyone who owned a computer or workstation with a reasonably powerful processor. Until 1990, videoconferencing was a tool for the business-elite. Moreover, until early 1994, when Intel introduced their ProShare family of personal conferencing products for Windows™ PCs, videoconferencing was almost non- existent on the desktop. The history of videoconferencing, how it progressed from a tightly-engineered, customized boardroom implementation that cost as much as $1 million per site to be a low-end "freebie" bundled in with a PC's operating system is an interesting tale.

Market advancement has been less a continuous progression of enhancements than a random string of breakthroughs. It has been more revolutionary than evolutionary.

THE HISTORY OF VIDEOCONFERENCING

Bell Labs produced the first few demonstrations of videoconferencing in the U.S. In the 1920s, scientists demonstrated a very crude videoconferencing application between Washington DC and New York City. Others were engaging in experiments in Europe in the 1930s, where television technologies and systems were more mature than in the U.S. World War II intervened and, for almost two decades nothing further was done with videoconferencing. In the late-1940s, Bell Labs commenced to revisit videoconferencing by embarking on a series of research projects. After researching for a decade and a half, the Labs, in 1964, rolled out the Picturephone. It was the world's first digital, interactive video-enabled telephone. Launched at the World's Fair in Flushing Meadow, New York, it weighed 26 pounds and sat on a nickel-plated pedestal with a base that measured about 10 inches in diameter.

Picturephone compressed a video signal; it squeezed it down so it could be carried over the digital equivalent of 100 telephone lines. They transmitted the audio signal separately. Images were a bit blurry (displayed using less than one-half the resolution of a North American television picture) and the screen was notably small (5.25 inches wide by 4.75 inches high). Nevertheless, it was a well-designed and engineered system.

Picturephone was a personal conferencing tool. In the 1970s, attention shifted to a different implementation of audiovisual conferencing technologies that could be used by a group. Nippon Electric Corporation (NEC) became the first company in the world to produce a group-oriented videoconferencing system. British Telecom (BT), another pioneer, introduced their own version of a videoconferencing system shortly thereafter. BT persuaded the telephone companies that various European countries owned to conduct country-to-country trials of videoconferencing using facilities that they opened to the public. The efforts to render these first videoconferencing public rooms operational paved the way for the videoconferencing interoperability standards that exist today.

Early videoconferencing systems used television technology in its raw, analog form. Progress was delayed in the area of digital transmission because networks could not provide the requisite bandwidth. It was not until low-cost, large-scale solid state memory became available in the early 1980s that videoconferencing advances began in earnest. The key was to store picture information during the processing sequence. Once very large scale integration (VLSI) technology appeared, it was harnessed with amazing results. One early videoconferencing project was commissioned by the US Defense Advanced Research Projects Agency (DARPA). DARPA wanted an inexpensive, small profile system. The resulting product, Widcom, used VLSI to consolidate large numbers of circuits on a single chip. The approach reduced the required bandwidth for image transmission to the digital equivalent of a telephone line. Consequently, it transmitting a single image took quite some time, a while to transmit a single image and Widcom, which was introduced in 1983, faded into obscurity for lack of a commercial application.

Figure 1-2. Picturephone (AT&T)

In the late 1970s and early 1980s, the installation of a corporate videoconferencing network required a true leap of faith. At the time, the substitution paradigm (pay for videoconferencing with travel dollar savings) was used to make a business case for the strategic application. The cost of a videoconferencing system was $250,000—and that bought only the codec.

The codec is the heart of a videoconferencing system. A codec adapts audiovisual signals to the requirements of the digital networks that transport them. As the term implies, compression/decompression and coding/decoding are a codec's four most important jobs. A codec must first turn analog signals into a continuous stream of zeros and ones (coding or digitizing), and then select only the bits necessary to send meaningful audio and video information (compression).

One begins to appreciate the job performed by a codec when one considers that an uncompressed digitized telephone signal requires a network transmission speed of about 90 million bits per second (Mbps) or more. Even after discarding the vertical and horizontal synchronization information required by analog television signals, an uncompressed digitized television signal still requires 45 Mbps or more. Contrast this with the capabilities of the Integrated Services Digital Network (ISDN) bearer or B channel that offers a transmission speed of 64 Kbps (in which K is kilo, or thousand). Even when two B channels are combined, as they are with ISDN's Basic Rate Interface (BRI), the resulting 128 Kbps of capacity comes no where near to satisfying the uncompressed signal's bandwidth requirements. In short, if one wants to transmit full-motion video plus audio from home (having captured that signal using some type of standard camera and microphone) one must discard 99.99% of the information to get it to fit over the line. Even when one uses ISDN's Primary

Rate Interface (23 B channels) for transmission, the compression burden is enormous.

Today we can squeeze a reasonable quality videoconference over two ISDN B channels. We can squeeze a somewhat degraded version of the same signal over a plain old telephone service (POTS) line, the type of line that connects the vast majority of residential and business telephone users to the telephone network. In 1978, the same degree of picture resolution and motion handling required 6 Mbps of bandwidth. Along with the $250,000 codec we mentioned earlier, a company, in the late 1970s and early 1980s had to buy cameras, microphones, and speakers and prepare the conference facility to offer acceptable acoustics and lighting. In short, early adopters of videoconferencing built broadcasting studios at a cost of $500,000–$1,000,000 or more. A coast-to-coast line that connected corporate videoconferencing facilities rented annually for about $35,000.

Unless organizations conducted videoconferences all day, every day, the videoconferencing projects of yesterday were not often economically feasible. Implementation depended on senior management's belief in the strategic value of the technology. A few forward-thinking companies were up to the challenge. Early adopters of videoconferencing include Aetna Life and Casualty, Atlantic Richfield, Boeing, Citibank, Chrysler, DEC, Eastman Kodak, Federal Express, Ford, Hewlett-Packard, J.C. Penney, Merrill Lynch, MONY, Proctor and Gamble, and Texas Instruments. Only 187 of the Fortune 500 companies listed in 1970 still existed in 1993; all the videoconferencing early adopters on this list were among the survivors.

Nearly all these early adopters used group-oriented, room-based videoconferencing systems that were manufactured by Compression Labs, Incorporated (CLI) of San Jose, California. CLI was founded in December 1976; it was initially dedicated to developing facsimile and video compression technologies. A CLI founder, Dr. Wen-hsiung Chen, will go down in history as one of the great pioneers of video compression. In 1963, Dr. Chen emigrated from Taiwan to the U.S. where he pursued his Ph.D. in mathematics. While at the University of Southern California, he discovered a compression technique that became a fundamental part of CLI's first commercial system: the low bit-rate (compared to previous methods) VTS 1.5. The first VTS 1.5 reached the market in September 1982. It required the equivalent of 24 telephone lines for signal transmission, and provided very good picture quality, considering the bandwidth. T-1 carrier, the basis of the North American digital hierarchy, is composed of 24 channels, each of which is the equivalent of a telephone line. CLI's system allowed companies to move from satellite-based videoconferencing to terrestrial transmission—the "T" in T-1 means terrestrial. Consequently, the transmission costs associated with videoconferencing plummeted.

In 1984, CLI began to face competition from a Massachusetts company called PictureTel. A team of Massachusetts Institute of Technology (MIT) engineering students and their professor founded PictureTel (Danvers, Massachusetts). The group had invested a great deal of time researching low-bandwidth digital video signal processing. After a lot of trial and error, they developed a way to reduce the bandwidth requirement for transmitting an acceptable-quality videoconference to an amazing 224 Kbps — the equivalent of four telephone lines. Overnight, group-system videoconferencing became economical at low data rates.

PictureTel's product was the first software-based videoconferencing system to become commercially available. It became the cornerstone of a planned migration strategy that led from a build-your-own product to an integrated system in which all the necessary components were packaged in a single chassis. CLI responded with a similar product, and the race began. The two firms began gràppling for control of an exploding market in a competition that still exists today. While the two were busy working magic in their laboratories, a third company, VTEL (formerly VideoTelecom Corporation) challenged the competition. Founded in 1985, VTEL was the first company to offer a videoconferencing product that ran on a DOS-based PC. For the first time, customers could upgrade their videoconferencing systems by simply downloading new sets of manufacturer-provided floppy disks. In 1980, only a few companies knew how to code and compress a video signal to affordable bandwidths. Manufacturers produced codecs at a rate of 100 per year.

Today, a codec just as powerful as a good 1980 model (which required a refrigerator-sized cabinet) can be implemented in software only. These software-based codecs are being packaged as enhancements to high-end personal computers. They are also based on standards, and thereby pave the way for any-to-any communications, regardless of the platform on which they run.

From the Boardroom to the Desktop

As we stated, videoconferencing applications began with Picturephone, a personal conferencing product, and moved on to group-oriented systems. The migration was driven by economies of scale. The tremendous cost of early codecs and, that of the bandwidth required to move a compressed audiovisual signal, had to be amortized across a group. The economics have changed but the market is still lagging.

Figure 1-3. Custom Boardroom System (courtesy of AT&T).

The legacy of boardroom videoconferencing lingers. Because early installations were so costly, the first applications of videoconferencing often reflected their boardroom environment. Housed in custom-designed and engineered studios, videoconferences were formal events that were often exclusively attended by senior managers and executives. These conference attendees were often so senior that another person, someone not really part of the meeting, was present to operate the equipment. To recover productive time that was lost to travel, executives and other highly valuable and scarce human resources were leveraged through videoconferencing. They generally did not, however, inconvenience themselves with the technical complexities that such systems presented.

This paradigm is changing, albeit more slowly than many would like. The ease-of-use challenges posed by videoconferencing are being addressed. Powerful processors make quick work of compression. The cost of the codec and other peripherals (cameras, microphones, and speakers) is plummeting. Digital bandwidth is generally abundant, and the cost of that bandwidth has dropped significantly. Competition, as a result of a newly deregulated telecommunications market, will drive transmission costs even lower and increase the number of carriers that offer digital service. Fast processors, cheap bandwidth, simplicity in system operation all suggest a market that is poised to skyrocket. The real market driver is consumer demand for useful tools that allow people to lead just-in-time lives in an era in which they have scant time to respond.

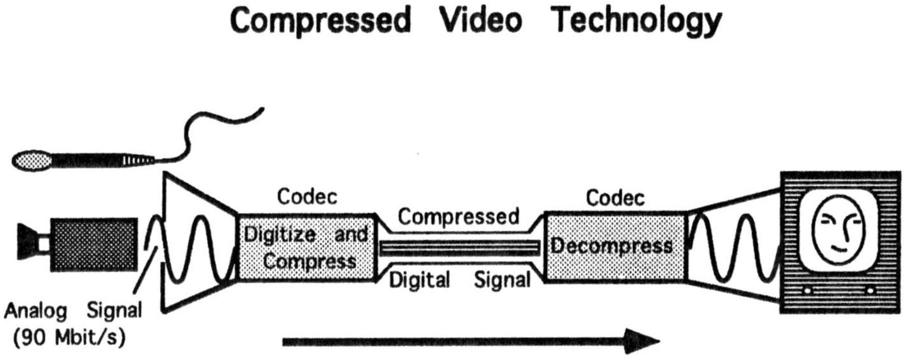

Figure 1-4. Compressed Video Technology (Michel Bayard).

In this very competitive, highly-dispersed global economy, every competitor struggles to capture market share. Markets fragment and shift, and niches repeatedly emerge for firms that act quickly before the opportunity is lost. We are *all* scarce human resources in today's environment. Our productivity is key to the survival of the enterprise for which we work. Furthermore, because there is so much to know and so much to do, we are forced to specialize. As the challenges intensify, each person's focus becomes smaller. Teamwork and collaboration, whether on a personal level or an enterprise level, are mandatory.

Visual communications enhance collaborative activities. However, not every work environment is the same; each has adapted to its special needs. That is why another form of collaboration, that which leads to interoperability standards, is key to the survival and prosperity of videoconferencing. In December 1990, an international telecommunications standards organization, part of the United Nations, voted to accept a videoconferencing interoperability standard. This standard allowed codecs that were manufactured by CLI, PictureTel, VTEL and many others to negotiate technically compatible sessions over variable bandwidth channels. The standards-making process did not end in 1990, it began. Today audiovisual standards exist for every application. They share many common attributes. All are designed for digital networks, and all share the goal of a reduction in the amount of information that must be transmitted. While the 1990 standard was aimed at group-system video, those ratified in 1996 were more inclusive; they clearly reflected that PC-based personal conferencing is the next frontier.

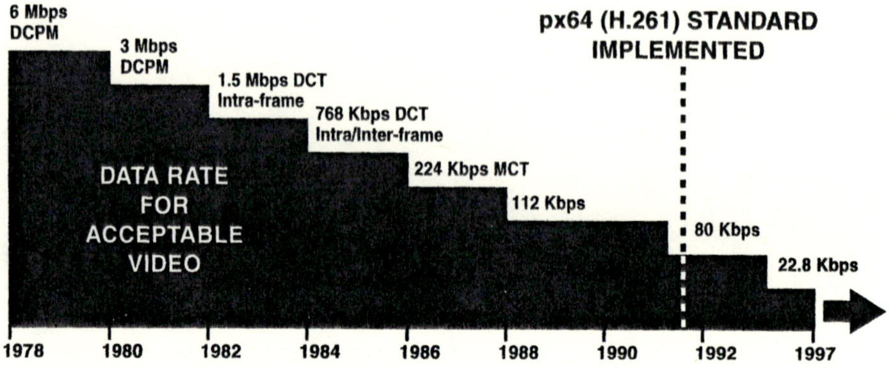

Figure 1-5. Bandwidth Needed for Business-Quality Video (Laura Long).

It was inevitable that videoconferencing would arrive at the PC. In 1989, only VTEL was shipping a PC-based product and, at five feet tall and 200 pounds (including the packaging), it was not invited to sit on many desktops. Three years later, several true desktop systems were introduced but, with prices at $10,000–15,000, few organizations could afford them. In 1993, more than 20 new desktop products entered the market. Most sold for $5,000–8,000 (including the requisite computer), and several were in the $3,000 range. One of the companies that offered a product in 1993 was ShareVision of Milpitas, California.

ShareVision's ShareView product ran on an Apple Macintosh computer and transmitted video, voice, and computer data over ordinary telephone lines—POTS lines. The package, which consisted of a combination video capture board and codec, and a network interface board, also included a color camera, a handset, a headset, and software. At initial introduction, the system sold for $4,499, but the price later dropped to under $4,000. ShareView enhanced mere file transfer and image sharing, however, by offering document conferencing. A ShareView user could launch an application and share it with another party even though the second user did not have it running on their system. This feature made ShareVision one of the pioneers in the area of visually assisted collaborative tools. Throughout this book, we will refer to this area as *personal conferencing*. Many competitors have followed where ShareVision led.

In January 1994, almost exactly one year after the introduction of ShareVision, Intel introduced their ProShare family of personal conferencing (desktop) products. One ProShare family member, the Video System 200, allows conferees to see each other in a quarter-screen window on their PC monitor while sharing a computer application. Other members of ProShare forgo the face-to-face altogether, in favor of document conferencing and voice exchange. Intel owns the term document conferencing; in 1993, it bought the rights to use it from VTEL.

Critics of ProShare emphasized, at the time of its introduction, that it required the local telephone company to furnish ISDN BRI services. Such services consist of two B channels that are melded into a 112/128 Kbps aggregate channel. The problem with ISDN was, and still is to some extent, availability. Although almost all telephone companies are moving to offer some form of high-bandwidth digital transmission service to business and residential consumers, not all offer ISDN. Intel can take much the credit for a surge in ISDN deployment by the Regional Bell Operating Companies (RBOCs) and GTE; they worked cooperatively with them to demonstrate that customers are anticipating such networks. ISDN applications are, of course, not limited to videoconferencing. Remote access to enterprise network services and telecommuting (replacing the physical commute with a telecommunications-based alternative) provided many ISDN market opportunities.

Besides complaining that ProShare required network services that were not always available, Intel's competitors criticized them for not embracing the international standard for videoconferencing that the International Telecommunications Union's Telecommunications Standardization Sector (CCITT/ITU-T) ratified in 1990. Without support for standards, ProShare could not interoperate with other systems.

Intel's response was rational: the standard in question, known as H.320, was overkill for the desktop, and too expensive to implement. Intel had managed to keep the ProShare Video System 200 priced at under $1,500 for most installations; that price has since dropped dramatically. Although H.320 required expensive hardware codecs, ProShare compressed using software only. Intel eventually implemented the mandatory portions of the standard, but only after making their point. The desktop videoconferencing market, and personal conferencing, would not happen until the ITU-T ratified a new standard that was aimed at the desktop.

In 1996, the new personal conferencing standard appeared. Known as H.324, it was aimed at videoconferencing over POTS. Even before H.324, another standard, aimed only at graphics conferencing, was ratified by the ITU-T. This standard is formally known as Transmission Protocols for Multimedia Data, but is better known by its ITU-T Recommendation number, T.120. T.120 is an umbrella standard. Under the T.120 umbrella is an applications template, a specification for how multipoint audiographics conferences can be set up and managed, a specification for how binary file transfers are to be accomplished, and a few other technical provisions.

At the same time that the ITU's H.324 standard for videoconferencing over POTS was completed, yet another personal conferencing standard was completed. The H.323 standard defines how videoconferencing systems communicate over local area networks (LANs) to integrate real-time voice, data, and video into networked devices such as PCs, workstations, and video telephones. Other umbrella standards are being developed by the ITU-T. They include H.321, a standard for videoconferencing over fast-packet Asynchronous Transfer Mode (ATM) networks, H.322, a standard for videoconferencing over LANs that can guarantee the low latency (minimal time delays) required for moving frames of video in rapid succession, and other supporting standards. Clearly the ITU, always the most prescient of organizations, sees desktop videoconferencing as a very strong market. Moreover, inspection of many of the standards that fall under the H.321, H.322, H.323, and H.324 umbrellas show a great deal of commonality. This commonality will lead to interoperability between systems that are connected to diverse networks, including LANs, the Internet, telephone lines, and super-fast ATM-based networks.

THE MARKET FOR VIDEOCONFERENCING

Largely as a result of the developed world's omnipresent fascination with the Internet, the market for videoconferencing is greater than it has ever been. However, it is time to discard the historic distinctions between conventional videoconferencing, application sharing and whiteboarding, and store-and-forward video communications. Publishers, manufacturers, and service providers fashioned these distinctions at a time when videoconferencing was a series of technologies that were looking for applications. That time has passed. Now that the applications are defining video communications, the myriad combinations and variations make those distinctions unhelpful. For instance, live streaming is both videoconferencing and store-and-forward. Many new applications employ various video communications on demand depending upon the needs or desires of the users.

In his speech, "The Future of Collaboration on the Net," Dr. Norm Gaut, chair of PictureTel Corporation, stated that three drivers have been changing the entire IT industry: development of the Internet, the growing power of PC processors, and the deployment of new high-bandwidth networks. Dr. Gaut defined four waves of visual communication. Respectively, the first and second are dial-up room conferencing, and ISDN-based desktop conferencing. The third wave is videoconferencing over LANs (including LAN-multicast in which multiple users receive a broadcast signal over a single *channel*). The last wave is videoconferencing over the Internet. Modern PCs are integrated videoconferencing-ready packages that include H.323 LAN-based video, H.324 codecs, video-ready modems, speakers, cameras, and microphones. These multimedia PCs are capable of videoconferencing, Web surfing, DVD recording and playback, and interactive games. The technology works and it is ubiquitous; that doesn't mean that people are using it.

The challenge now is to reduce significantly the complexity of conference calling, and to improve the network so that the quality of the user's videoconferencing experience is as reliable as the one he enjoys with his telephone. Rather than a complex process of a pre-scheduling a call with an operator, customers must be able to arrange a conference call on the fly as they do audio-only conference call. They must be able to videoconference with anyone as easily and as spontaneously as they send or receive Email or that they surf the Internet. Users want to use the Internet to incorporate interactivity, multimedia, security, manageability, and all the functionality of a conventional telephone.

TeleSpan Publishing proclaims that mergers and acquisitions, the consequences of corporate downsizing, the trend toward geographically diverse teamwork, the drive to control costs, and the need to decrease response times the are driving the conference calling market. While the Internet is itself an enabler, its popularity is a driver, something to use in every way possible. It is an infrastructure and a technology to which Hambrecht & Quist LLD/IDC projects 800 million users will be connected by 2002. There is little doubt that the Internet is becoming the predominant data, voice, and videoconferencing platform.

However, the Internet, as a network, is not as mature or reliable as the video communications technologies that people would like to use over it. It is no coincidence that the most powerful companies in the world are rising to the occasion. The aggregate of AT&T's $100 billion investment in cable TV and its existing fiber optic backbone network is an unprecedented network to which a variety of devices can attach. Qwest Communications, by buying US West, expanded its worldwide fiber network with DSL service to homes in fourteen states. Level 3 Communications and Enron Corporation are deploying IP networks with Wave Division Multiplexing (WDM). IP Security (IPSec) enables users to maintain confidentiality and to verify message integrity in a standards-based interoperable method. IP protocols 802.1q and 802.1p offer a methodology for service level agreements (SLAs) and virtual LANs (VLANs), respectively, so that users can share IP networks reliably for interactive multimedia applications. Unfortunately, these technologies are complex and difficult to manage. Overall, the Internet is still not a reliable teleconferencing network. Nevertheless, companies want to use the Internet to converge video, voice, and data traffic. The benefits include avoidance of long-distance charges, the ability to manage fewer networks, presence management, and unified messaging.

Unfortunately, converging networks is not easy; it involves programming PBXs and routers (or Layer 3 switches) to interoperate. Nevertheless, corporations big and small are breaking the ice by converging inter-branch voice traffic onto private T-1 data links. They want never to buy another conventional PBX. Private communications exchange (PCX) systems are beginning to displace conventional key telephone systems (KTS) and PBXs (Private Branch Exchange). PCXs combine dissimilar architectures in a single communications system that employs a high-bandwidth backbone to connect switching nodes and applications. The next generation of this will be distributed communications exchange systems (DCX), that evolve the KTS, the PBX, and the PCX into a truly converged network system architecture. Replacing those proprietary PBXs and KTSs will take time, but the cost will be lower. Dataquest forecasts the average price of conventional PBX systems to decrease only by 5–10% per year, so they will have a hard time competing with server based systems on price, much less on features. Programming conventional PBXs and KTSs to interoperate with retrofitted routers for such use is complex. Troubleshooting such configurations ranges from difficult to insufferable.

Historically, data networks and voice/video networks have been separate and have, therefore, been managed independently. Management packages, such as Cisco's CiscoWorks that only recognize devices from a single manufacturer are of value only in completely homogenous networks (apparently there are some). Products such as Lucent's Navis at least recognize data devices from a variety of data products manufacturers. However, they were not designed to recognize PBXs or KTSs, much less PCXs or DCXs. Fortunately, X.500 directory standards are facilitating a tendency for manufacturers and users to adopt *resource systems configuration-management systems* such as Hewlett-Packard's OpenView. This will be important as data and voice resellers adopt support and systems integration strategies to sell, implement, and manage converged network solutions. Convergence will require those with expertise in conventional voice and video, and those with expertise in data networking to overcome their historic cultural and ideological conflict.

Network Analyst Christine Perry asserts that the market has outgrown earlier distinctions between videoconferencing, interactive multimedia, and store-and-forward video communications. Whereas, in the past, video communications represented a technology that was looking for applications, applications are now appearing that may use a combination of video communications technologies. Any communications in which the observance of visual queues may provide insight are good candidates for videoconferencing; one can not predict which meetings those will be. Therefore, the market is growing. While conventional group system end point sales are growing about 42% each year, commercial personal system are growing 80% per year, and personal systems are growing at about 50% per year. PC camera sales are expected to double each year through at least 2001.

Improvements in videoconferencing standards and in hardware such as codecs, MCUs, cameras, and PCs are enabling real-time VCR quality video at 30 frames per second (FPS). Emerging technologies such as USB and Firewire will increasingly simplify installation and reduce desktop and compact videoconferencing costs. Such systems are eroding the conventional ISDN system end point market, which declined about 12% in market share to 93,600 units in 1998. As WANs become more robust, they are making packet-switched videoconferencing more practical.

The market research firm, Frost & Sullivan, anticipates that the IP-based desktop videoconferencing systems market will hit wide-scale deployment between 2001 and 2002. The videoconferencing systems market generated $811 million in revenues in 1998, and desktop and compact videoconferencing alone accounted for $511 in revenue. IDC (International Data Corporation) projects desktop and compact videoconferencing revenue to grow from about 400,000 end points in 1999 to about 2.1 million end points in 2003. IDC expects that the number of desktop and compact videoconferencing systems will increase from 622,000 end points in 1998 to more than 4.2 million end points in that same period. By then, the average price of a commercial desktop videoconferencing system is expected to drop to $850. Teleconferencing commentator Elliot Gold predicts that, "Videoconferencing will enter 50% of conference rooms by 2010."

Appliance-based videoconferencing systems are storming the market in the wake of PictureTel's pioneering SwiftSite Suitcases, and Polycom's perfection of the idea with their ViewStation product line. Polycom went so far with ViewStation as to provide a color-coded back panel and corresponding color-coded cables. Polycom's product is small and quiet, but includes H.262+ compression, and supports up to four sites with simultaneous display. By 2001, Don Lies, CEO of RSI Videoconferencing Systems, expects the market to buy more than 100,000 appliance-based systems. Laptop computer based systems will comprise 10–15% of that. Examples of such applications include professional conferences, telemedicine, sales kiosks, employment interviews, legal proceedings, product support, and financial services.

Market researcher, Roopam Jain, at Frost & Sullivan estimates that group systems sales (including the entire range of systems) will grow from $616.9 million in 2000 to $1.4 billion by 2005. She expects U.S. business desktop videoconferencing to grow from $67.3 in 2000 to $438 million by 2006. As videoconferencing systems have evolved from the $70,000 room-based systems to the latest generation of desktop, set-top, and compact systems, they have grown more affordable and more appealing to a broad range of commercial customers. IDC expects the worldwide price of commercial desktop videoconferencing systems to fall to $850 by 2003. Forward Concepts concludes that set-top and PC-based group systems will grow at a compound annual growth rate of more than 40% to represent $639 million in revenue in 2003. The firm expects unit growth to grow by 60% over that period. Forward Concepts expects set-top boxes to dominate the compact room system segment, and that PC-based systems will account for a 28% market share. Consumer oriented videoconferencing kits have fallen by nearly half, have become easier to use, and have thereby become more commonplace in homes. IDC reports that 964,000 consumer PC cameras shipped worldwide in 1998, and it expects the worldwide price of consumer grade desktop videoconferencing systems to fall to $150 by 2003.

Nevertheless, although market analysts seem to agree that the future of videoconferencing is IP at the desktop, conventional ISDN-based group videoconferencing still dominate the market. In 2000, Frost & Sullivan estimated that 94% of all videoconferencing was still ISDN based. Roughly, group systems at that time made up 72% of the market in terms of revenue and business desktop systems trailed a distant second with about 8% of the market. The other 20% was fairly evenly divided between consumer videoconferencing systems and multiple control units (MCUs). Unit growth rates for small group systems with a manufacturer's selling price of $12,000 or less averaged 50–60% per year between

1997 and 2000. Unit growth rates for large group systems with a manufacturer's selling price of more than $12,000 averaged only 4–6% per year in the same period.

The fact that numerous equipment manufacturers vie for a comparatively small market underscores the potential and the importance of videoconferencing. That potential includes an installed base of more than 300 million PCs and more than 100 million new PCs every year. To tap that market, manufacturers know that they must simplify videoconferencing systems installation. To that end, by 2001, 80% of the PC camera market is expected to migrate from the parallel port to USB technology. At that point, the market will begin moving to Firewire (IEEE 1394), and entry level cameras should cost about $40.

At the other end of the spectrum, two-way broadband videoconferencing will see similar extensive growth. Although the 1998 market for broadband videoconferencing systems and services was a mere $740 million, Frost & Sullivan expects it to grow more than 27% per year to $4 billion by 2005. The resultant bandwidth and QoS of the installation of fiber and the deployment of ATM in the core will enabled this. Carrier integration of video, voice, and data on broadband networks will also be a significant enabler. TDM (time division multiplexing) based systems, although reliable, have not given way to usage based pricing offerings. Therefore, carriers are deploying ATM to foster broadband level video, voice, and data convergence. Because it is a cell-based technology, ATM offers a much better base over which to deliver the IP (Internet protocol) based traffic. All things equal, IP is clearly the choice for videoconferencing.

CONCLUSION

The Picturephone, so far ahead of its time that it was considered a failure, was far more important than anyone realized. Its developers recognized that people naturally communicate not just aurally but also visually. The market today is proving that those Bell Labs pioneers did not labor in vain, and that their vision simply transcended the environment in which they lived. Successful technology applications are not possible without pioneers: the scientists, the engineers, and the human factors specialists (including marketers and sellers). As important as their work is, however, it would all be for naught if it were not for the early adopters who try their products.

Eventually, successful applications achieve broad-based acceptance and move into the corporate mainstream. A typical conclusion to the cycle of research and development finds these applications delivered to and embraced by the casual consumer. With market growth comes acceptance, and with acceptance comes greater demand for ease-of-use, new capabilities, and lower cost. At some initial point, those who would benefit overlook the brilliance of every technological development.

The state of the videoconferencing industry is somewhere in the middle of the adoption continuum. It is a market that promises to grow dramatically over the next five years. The stigma of videoconferencing is that, throughout its history, *next year* has always been the year it was going *to really take off*. However, with the advent of the Internet and the Internet protocol, the future of videoconferencing is finally clear.

We dedicate the remainder of this book to fostering in the reader an understanding of videoconferencing applications, the technologies they depend upon, and the key decision points one must consider when making a product or service selection. Once mastered, we firmly believe that most readers will extol the benefits of videoconferencing, and will want to gain first-hand experience.

Chapter 1 References

O'Brien, Jennifer M. "IDC predicts bright future for videoconferencing." Computing Canada, October 29, 1999 v25 i41 p7.

"Videoconferencing for 2000." Communications News, October 1999 v36 i10 p64.

"Desktop Videoconferencing Shipments to Hit 2.1 Million by 2003, IDC Says New Technologies Make for Better Viewing Experience." PR Newswire, August 23, 1999 p4456.

"Corporate buyer demand for group videoconferencing systems is rising, while sales of desktop systems have yet to take off." Purchasing. October 21, 1999 v127 i6 p82.

"Videoconferencing Forecast: PC Camera Market to Reach $1 Billion by 2003." EDGE: Work-Group Computing Report, April 19, 1999.

Wittmann, Art "Is Video Broadcasting Coming to Your Network?" Network Computing, April 19, 1999 p152.

"Say Cheese: PC Camera Market to Reach $1 Billion by 2003." Business Wire, April 13, 1999 p1144.

"Videoconferencing: New Study Predicts over 40 Percent Growth for New Product Segment in Videoconferencing Industry." EDGE, March 1, 1999.

Emmerson, Bob. Back in the game.(innovations on videoconferencing) Communications International, March 1999 v26 i3 p20.

"Astronomical Growth Expected For Broadband Video Market." Communications Today, January 8, 1999.

"Astronomical Growth Expected For Broadband Video Market." Broadband Networking News, January 5, 1999 v9 i1.

Smulders, Charles, Dexter, Kathy, Thompson, Christopher. "Voice and Data Convergence: The Impact for Resellers," Dataquest Incorporated, 1999.

Anderson, J., Fralick, S.C., Hamilton, E., Tescher, A.G., and Widergren, R.D. "Codec squeezes color teleconferencing through digital phone lines," Electronics 57: 1984 pp. 113-115.

Barnard, Chester I. "The Functions of the Executive," Harvard University Press

Cambridge, Massachusetts, 1979 p. 217.

Levy, Steven D. and Yuen, Randall A. "The Visual Communications Market: A View into the Future," Hambrecht & Quist March 5, 1993.

Lowenstein, Mark. "Videoconferencing: Directions for Group and Desktop Systems," Yankee Group, Boston, Massachusetts. Keynote presentation at Video-Enabled Workplace (VIEW '93), Atlanta, Georgia, November 1, 1993.

Lowenstein, Mark. "Videoconferencing: The Future of Group and Desktop Systems," The Yankee Group: Boston, Massachusetts, December, 1992.

Portway, Patrick and Lane, Carla, Ed.D. "Technical Guide to Teleconferencing and Distance Learning," Applied Business teleCommunications. San Ramon, California. 1992 p. 4.

Whitmore, Sam. "Do not sell any new product before its ripped to shreds," PC Week February 21, 1994 p. A10.

2

VIDEOCONFERENCING APPLICATIONS

Nothing in the world is single,
All things by a law divine
In one spirit meet and mingle
Percy Bysshe Shelley

VIDEOCONFERENCING IN THE REAL WORLD

After a slow start in the 1980s, video communication has gained broad support. Videoconferencing is an invaluable human resource management tool. It fosters collaboration, increases scheduling flexibility, shortens response times, and provides access to specialists and experts.

Manufacturing companies leverage it for comprehensive quality assurance and real-time process and equipment monitoring. Healthcare providers employ videoconferencing to enhance continuity of care, and legal teams use it to standardize and, therefore, streamline casework. As a result of dramatic declines in network and equipment costs, cultural changes, and standardization, videoconferencing is solving a wide range of business problems. Advances in group system, application sharing, LAN, and even POTS standards have advanced interoperability such that it has transcended the confines of intra-organizational communications.

Public videoconferencing rooms abound. One can find and reserve a nearby Kinko's Copy Center videoconferencing room by simply dialing 1-800-254-6567. By pointing one's web browser to http://www.kinkos.com/ and typing in one's address, one can even obtain a map. Once there, one will find a room based videoconferencing system and accommodations that rival those in many corporations' conference rooms. Personal Conferencing is even easier. Manufacturers bundle increasingly adequate personal conferencing capabilities in the consumer PCs they sell through retail outlets. If that is not enough, consumers can buy more sophisticated systems from the same retailers.

Businesses use personal conferencing to save time and money by linking employees, customers, suppliers, and strategic partners. Legislators encourage it by rewarding organizations that adopt telecommuting initiatives and thereby reduce the number of vehicles on the roads. Moreover, the Telecommunications Act of 1996 is motivating competitors to upgrade bandwidth to the desktop to accommodate multimedia traffic. Cable television service (CATV) providers, inter-exchange carriers (IXCs), and new entrants such as utilities and wireless service providers are frenetically seeking ways to compete in the local loop that Local Exchange Carriers (LECs) historically considered their exclusive domain. This is great for videoconferencing.

Any organization that relies upon geographically separated resources can benefit from videoconferencing. Apparel makers use videoconferencing to review concepts, artwork, type proofs, and sales and marketing collateral. Retailers use it to display merchandise and thereby specify color and style, and recommend price and advertising messages. Pharmaceutical companies use videoconferencing technology to develop new products. Chemical companies, railroads, and jewelers all employ videoconferencing. It is even credited with developing U.S. customers for companies in formerly communist countries.

Videoconferencing is valuable for reducing travel expense. It is even more valuable as a cost-effective tool for improving productivity and communication. It is vital to many organizations' success. Many successful organizations find it indispensable for managing resources (such as the time of strategic personnel) and for accelerating business cycles. They also find that videoconferencing facilitates meetings that travel might preclude.

Moreover, criticism of political party convention press coverage sets the stage for videoconferencing to assume an increasingly important role in government. Live videoconferences could displace prearranged conventions as a medium for open discussion and debate. The 1996 conventions laid the groundwork for this trend by sponsoring Worldwide Web sites and chat rooms on the Internet. Both parties also provided delegate groups with personal computers, and provided strategic individuals with personal hand-held communications systems.

With increasingly fast and increasingly inexpensive network bandwidth to offices and to homes, videoconferencing technology is becoming the basis for countless new products and services. 512 Kbps is no longer an unusually fast connection for individuals who are reaching the Internet from their homes. Home users can already view MPEG2 streams while simultaneously browsing the Internet and making an Internet-based telephone call. Considering the markets that the videocassette inspired, one can only speculate on the potential new markets that ubiquitous videoconferencing will engender. It is already common in many applications such as:

Figure 2-1. Videoconference With Set-top System (courtesy of Polycom).

- Executive, task force, and board member meetings
- Project management
- Desktop-to-desktop communications; personal conferencing
- Merger and acquisition management
- Collaborative-engineering, product development, and product review
- Product Support
- Legal protocol (depositions, testimony, and remote arraignment)
- Surveillance
- Emergency Response
- Distance Learning
- Distance Training
- Large multi-site meetings
- Key personnel recruitment
- Telemedicine and health care provisioning
- Consulting
- Inter-company meetings with customers, suppliers, and partners
- New product announcements to restricted audiences

Although people generally associate videoconferencing with business meetings, its applications are quite diverse and, ideally, creative. Following are some examples:

- One dedicated violin master in Manhattan uses room based videoconferencing technology to instruct financially and physically challenged students in New Jersey, Minnesota, and Georgia.

- To alleviate traffic during the 1996 Olympics in Atlanta, some local companies provided their workers with ISDN lines and videoconferencing systems so they could telecommute.
- Some upscale hotel chains are equipping rooms with videoconferencing systems.
- In 1996, the US Navy broadcast an interview with then Secretary of Defense, William Perry, using its tactical satellite communications and teleconferencing system. A major television network intercepted the signal with satellite trucks that it parked outside the Navy's Norfolk, Virginia center.
- A broker of videoconferencing public room service tells of a videoconference in which pairs of twin girls auditioned for a spot in a television advertisement that was cast on a very short schedule.
- While participating in the Biosphere Project in Arizona, Allison Alling interviewed for admission as a doctoral candidate at a Virginia university. The Biosphere participants had agreed to remain sealed inside the self-sustaining ecosystem for a set duration, and admission necessitated the interview conducted before the experiment ended. The school admitted Ms. Alling to the program as the result of a videoconference.
- One company uses video communications between employees in a cleanroom, and their co-workers outside. Feet, not miles, separate the two groups. However, suiting up is a time-consuming barrier to communication. Videoconferencing allows managers to monitor activities in the lab and to keep projects on schedule without suiting-up. Moreover, online images of defects do not introduce contamination, as does airborne-particulate-producing paper.
- A Detroit automobile manufacturer uses PictureTel systems to virtually co-locate two engineering groups that are an hour apart. Together, the groups hold design reviews and evaluate tests. They show video of durability tests, vehicle crashes, and product demonstrations over videoconferencing. They also expedite the process by sharing engineering drawings and 3-D models from their CAD/CAM system.
- Also using a PictureTel videoconferencing system, flight test engineers share results with design engineers who are thousands of miles away. Video of the flight is captured by a trailing aircraft, and is examined by all parties with video. Real-time discussion and analysis instantly after the flight tests, when pilots are fresh, allows test engineers to schedule test flights more quickly.
- A real estate and financial services firm leverages a Panasonic videoconferencing system for its weekly staff meetings. Each week, 6–8 people in each office discuss new listings and previous sales. Using a split-screen feature and a personal computer, the regional sales manager details highlights of each listing, points out the financial highlights, and trains salespeople. Most

important, the firm shows videos of properties using a *voice-over* feature to emphasize key points.

- The Joint Warfare Center (JWC) in Hurlburt, Florida uses videoconferencing to coordinate data transfer and information exchange between isolated locations in Florida. The United States' Navy Fleet Combat Training Center in Virginia Beach, Virginia uses videoconferencing to teach soft-skilled courses to naval students. Though satellite videoconferences, NASA provides an in-service program to educators throughout the school year that features NASA scientists, astronauts, program managers, and education specialists.
- The Federal Health and Human Services Department (HHS) is planning for regular inter-departmental videoconferences in which regional and central office personnel will discuss top agency issues. It is also planning to leverage its videoconferencing infrastructure to sponsor nationwide community issue forums and thereby solicit responses from its customers.

SENIOR MANAGEMENT APPLICATIONS

Building a cohesive team in a global environment is a challenge. Through videoconferencing, executives can include more team members in the strategic planning process, and effectively create a global campus. Downsized companies must often accomplish more work with fewer executives; videoconferencing allows executives to simultaneously manage field and headquarters operations.

Several investment firms use videoconferencing for *crisis management* (e.g., a major swing in the financial market). Bear Sterns and Company in New York City uses video to allow traders who work on the floor to receive up-to-the-minute financial reports from various news networks such as CNN and CNBC.

Executives and senior managers also use videoconferencing to maintain rapport with important customers, partners, distributors, and suppliers. They meet with Wall Street analysts, legal experts, and consultants.

Executive applications are easy to cost-justify even though they may require premium facilities. Travel savings are usually a secondary objective. Typically, the real issues are saving time, bolstering productivity, and fostering opportunities—areas in which one can express improvements in financial terms. One firm factored into their business case the creative potential lost due to excessive travel fatigue; no-one disputed the assertion.

Senior managers usually warrant high-quality transmission, multiple large monitors, premium audio, and facilities that correlate to the size of their audiences.

Figure 2-2. Boardroom System (courtesy of VTEL).

PROJECT MANAGEMENT AND CONSULTING

Videoconferencing is an ideal tool for managing projects over distance. It unites team members and subject-matter experts for prompt collective decision-making (or troubleshooting) for joint or distributed undertakings. It improves the frequency and the efficiency of communications; direct cost savings are often secondary to accomplishing the job.

In the mid-1980s, the aerospace industry discovered that inter-company videoconferencing was valuable for managing contractors and subcontractors who cooperated on large projects. Many more companies are now using video for similar applications. Videoconferencing works well in the management of construction projects. Experts at remote sites can inspect footage captured at the construction site, as can distant customers who are paying for the project.

Air Products and Chemicals is one firm that has benefited from the use of videoconferencing in project management. The company is a major international supplier of industrial gases and related equipment, chemicals, and environmental, and energy systems. It maintains project management control through a communications system that links their Allentown, Pennsylvania location with Bechtel in Pasadena, Texas.

Throughout one project, Bechtel provided engineering support to Air Products for a new plant that they were constructing at Air Products in Pasadena. The project team received project status updates through regularly scheduled video meetings. The Project Forum team met every other week to discuss project designs with engineers in Texas. The Project Steering Committee met every other week with the entire project team. Every six weeks, formal project review meetings were presented on behalf of senior managers. Videoconferencing allowed greater staff and senior management participation in the project; it even allowed controllers to join, for the first time, in discussions. Models, blueprints, and 35mm slides provided additional information about the project during meetings. The use of videoconferencing saved more than $100,000 and eliminated more than 30% of the travel.

FINANCIAL SERVICES

A Michigan based wholesale mortgage lender has improved the way it receives and processes loan applications from more than 4,400 loan originators and mortgage brokers nationwide. The system allows officers to complete 8–10 mortgage applications each day rather than, as had been the case, only one. Videoconferencing enables loan applicants, loan officers and underwriters to meet, and thereby eliminate approval steps and avoid delays. In such meetings, underwriters input and make judgments about information, reconcile it, and verify it with the correct documentation. One company officer declares that the only alternative to the videoconferencing system would have been to hire 25,000 geographically dispersed loan underwriters.

Nationwide, more than 500 institutions installed more than 600 sites between March 1995 and September 1996. Consequently, a typical time for processing a loan is five hours. The process begins when a loan originator faxes the applicant's completed loan forms to the mortgage center, calls the center to confirm receipt of the application, and requests the assignment of a loan underwriter. The underwriter calls the originator's office to arrange a videoconference and to designate a conference time. At the end of the videoconference, loan information is entered into the computer system for final processing and approvals.

The system incorporates Intel's ProShare videoconferencing software, Madge Networks' wide-area Access Switches, and Sprint's 800-Video call service. The incoming call is received over an ISDN network by the WAN switch, which assigns the call to the first available loan officer, and thereby eliminates the need to pre-arrange the video call. The Madge Access Switch uses each call's automatic number identifier to match it to the appropriate conference.

MANAGEMENT OF MERGERS AND DECENTRALIZATIONS

An effective tool in encouraging post-merger communications between two disparate workgroups, videoconferencing allows companies to quickly establish a management team and to keep that team communicating regardless of distance. A successful merger requires integration at all levels of a company; videoconferencing is ideal in these situations because it promotes comprehensive team participation. The tool helps companies overcome the challenges of coordinating activities between two formerly unaffiliated companies that are not only separated by culture, but also by hundreds or thousands of miles. It is particularly valuable for merging engineering, management information systems (MIS), legal, accounting, and human resources workgroups.

Visual communications tools are equally valuable in managing a decentralization project. When a department is split into multiple groups, video can foster a sense of teamwork intact, and facilitate regularly scheduled meetings.

JOINT-ENGINEERING AND PRODUCT DEVELOPMENT

Review and in-depth focus meetings often involve numerous people. Video enhances the exchange of graphical and textual information with the conventional *talking head*. Computer aided design (CAD) conferencing has emerged.

Technical people are not often demanding of motion video quality as long as they receive good audio and graphics support. One early-adopter that began using video in 1979 employed two 4.8 Kbps modems to send and receive data. This restricted the firm to the exchange of freeze-frame images—video frames sent sequentially but not fast enough to convey a sense of realistic movement. Nevertheless, the system enabled engineers in New Jersey to supervise a design process that took place at an elevator manufacturing plant in Pennsylvania. The group credited video with saving the company from paying late penalties on the contract.

Video has an excellent track record for reducing product time-to-market intervals. Delivering a high revenue-generating product ahead of schedule can pay for an entire videoconferencing system. In one instance, Boeing simultaneously reduced the development time of their 767 by one full year, generated revenues much sooner than anticipated, and cornered the market for a new generation of airplane. A manager at Boeing estimated that the accelerated development process resulted in profits that exceeded "every dollar ever invested" in video.

BancTec, a company that builds, markets and services financial document processing equipment for companies in the financial industry uses video to shorten product development and delivery cycles. By linking the company's Texas headquarters to manufacturing facilities in Oklahoma, research and development teams develop rapid solutions to product quality issues. One problem with a new product was demonstrated to a distant BancTec research and development team with the aid of a document camera. Remote visual inspection allowed the team to immediately implement corrective action.

Videoconferencing is beneficial for engineering and design applications even when coworkers are not in different states. For instance, NASA's Jet Propulsion Labs (JPL) installed, on an evaluative basis, 40 desktop videoconferencing units that connected various departments throughout its 200 buildings—all of which fall within a 20-mile radius. The systems, which used the public switched digital network, enabled JPL designers (even those in the same building) to collaborate on engineering drawings. It also allowed JPL employees to present lectures and to "meet" with colleagues in Washington, D.C., Canada, and New Hampshire without the time and expense of traveling.

Engineers, architects, and other technically oriented professionals collaborate and make technical presentations during videoconferences. They commonly require systems that offer sophisticated audiographics—including high-resolution capabilities. They may also require the ability to store documents and images as electronic files for recall during a conference. Some need computer aided design (CAD) system interfaces. Customers often incorporate ceiling-mounted cameras into their systems to provide sufficient depth of field for capturing large documents and blueprints.

CUSTOMER SUPPORT

A manufacturing company in the southeastern region of the U.S. integrates videoconferencing technology into its product support strategy. The company designs and manufactures packaging machinery that automates its customers' packing processes. It is machinery represents the last step in its customers' production lines. To ensure reliability, and thereby establish a market advantage, the company employs PictureTel conferencing systems at their own site, and at those of their customers.

Because an inoperable machine arrests an entire production line, assisting customers with maintenance of its sophisticated packaging machinery is a crucial part of the company's business. Therefore, if a machine breaks down, customers place a video call to the manufacturer's technicians. A camera that is positioned over the factory floor allows a technician to see the machine while talking directly to the customer. Collaboratively, they identify the problem and develop a solution.

Videoconferencing allows the manufacturer to resolve 80% of its customer service calls remotely. The system includes a wireless remote camera with a 24-hour battery and a RF system that transmits the video signal to an antenna. It also employs a wireless headset. With high resolution monitors (450 lines), 384 Kbps bandwidth, and 30 Fps the system offers ample clarity for technicians to diagnose most problems.

As a result, the company simultaneously limits the chances of stopping a production line, reduces the cost of service interruptions, maintains machines, and improves equipment performance and life span. It also gains a strategic advantage over its competition; through videoconferencing, the manufacturer reduces its own costs and those of its customers.

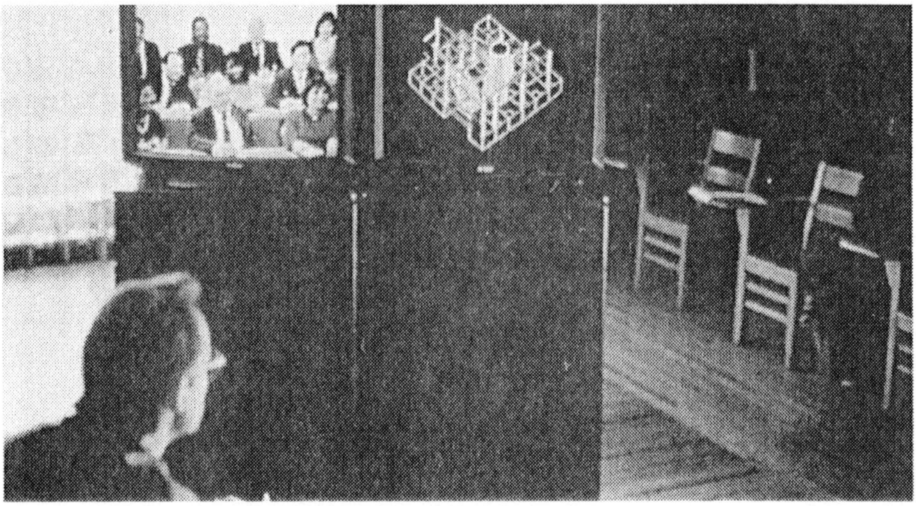

Figure 2-3. Dual Monitor System (courtesy of CLI).

BCA Corporation (Los Angeles, California) sells computer chips and circuit boards. The company uses videoconferencing to share plans and finished products with a factory in Taiwan. BCA uses Panasonic's Vision Pro system to ensure that each product's design meets each customer's specific expectations. BCA eliminates surprises by allowing customers to scrutinize finished product over video before mass productions begins; doing so without video would add significant time.

LEGAL AND JUDICIAL APPLICATIONS

Many states and counties now use videoconferencing for applications such as the remote arraignment of prisoners. San Bernardino (California) County Municipal Court finds remote arraignment valuable in reducing or eliminating the cost, time, and security risks associated with transporting prisoners. Sheriff's deputies are free to enforce laws rather than drive buses. Moreover, the technology expedites arraignment time to just minutes. Proceedings can even be recorded for subsequent viewing. When used to conduct remote arraignments, a video screen is often divided into quadrants. The prisoner appears in one quadrant, the district attorney in a second, the judge in a third, and the date, time, case number and information appear in the fourth quadrant for archival.

On the other side of the bench, clients are not always satisfied with local legal resources; they want the best-qualified attorney to represent them. Although communications by telephone, voice mail, email, and fax bridge much of this gap, they do not supplant face-to-face meetings. One law firm that serves large high-profile clients links 120 lawyers in six U.S. cities using Intel ProShare Personal

Conferencing Products. Attorneys collaboratively draft documents in real time, interactively discuss legal briefs, and conduct face-to-face meetings despite the thousands of miles that separate them.

Videoconferencing is also useful for taking depositions over distance. Legal Image Network Communications (LINC) in Dallas provides attorneys with an opportunity to obtain depositions that travel might render prohibitively expensive. The visual component of a deposition is critical to attorneys who are skilled at reading body language and facial expressions. The service is available in more than twenty U.S. cities. Videoconferencing also allows remote and sensitive witnesses (e.g., children or battered or mentally abused victims) to testify without being physically present in the courtroom. Many legal and judicial applications require large monitors, as well as VCRs, faxes, and *flatbed scanners* (cameras designed to capture an entire page of printed text). Many legal applications rely on videoconferencing public rooms to provide distant-end facilities.

SURVEILLANCE

Video surveillance supports the ability to remotely view a location without establishing a physical presence. Surveillance applications often incorporate lower-quality cameras and monitors. Applications include monitoring parking lots, corridors, and entrances. Some surveillance applications allow guards to press a button to unlock a door, and thereby remotely allow admission to a building. Amtrak incorporates a unique video surveillance application to control and manage movable bridges in Atlantic City, New Jersey from a control center in Philadelphia, Pennsylvania. Four cameras, two on each side of a moveable bridge, relay pictures of the bridge to the control center. When a boat approaches the bridge, the control center performs a visual check for trains before remotely opening the bridge only long enough to let the boat pass. Before the use of surveillance technology, a bridge keeper was on location at all times. The installation pays for itself, and provides better visibility—the cameras provide four views of the bridge rather than the former bridge attendant's single view. Amtrak has since expanded the use of surveillance to Connecticut.

A Houston, Texas company offers continuous surveillance services to its customers without the high cost of security guards. Its Intel ProShare based system remains dormant until someone either passes through a photoelectric or infrared beam or until someone manually presses an alert button. Then, the system notifies an operator at the company's control center. The operator may use the audio function of the system to advise the intruder to retreat, or she may notify local police. The system allows operators to identify false alarms. Moreover, since the system captures intruders on videotape, it thoroughly serves the interests of justice.

Federal, state, and local law enforcement agencies used videoconferencing codecs to conduct security surveillance of both internal and external grounds during the

1996 Republican National Convention in San Diego. Stationed at the San Diego City Emergency Operations Center, the Joint Incident Command Post, and the San Diego Convention Center, law enforcement agencies simultaneously observed strategic areas, and surveyed the convention site and adjacent areas. Employing interactive, encryption-based codecs through a spread spectrum microwave system, law enforcement agencies incorporated a helicopter-mounted camera and seventy land-based cameras. On the ground, the network leveraged a T1 connection to transmit video signals at 768 Kbps. Authorities employed similar strategies to assist state and federal disaster field centers with emergency operations in south Sacramento and again in Southern California during the January 1994 Northridge earthquake.

EMERGENCY RESPONSE

Duke Power Company, in North Carolina, leverages videoconferencing technology to enable immediate communication between emergency-response personnel. At two of its three nuclear power plants, Duke provides a network of desktop videoconferencing systems that instantly allow face-to-face communication.

At two plants (that generate more than half of the electricity it supplies) Duke relies on videoconferencing systems to improve its responsiveness and, therefore, its Nuclear Regulatory Commission (NRC) ratings. One system is located in each plant's technical support center that links two other desktop systems in each plant's operations support center. Duke uses Incite's Desktop Multimedia Package that includes voice and video dialers, programmable buttons, shared whiteboard, and tones to alert users to incoming calls.

Each system connects to the power company's fiber backbone network with an Incite Multimedia Hub that integrates voice, video, and data. Duke dedicates six ISDN B channels (384 Kbps per second) of the network to videoconferencing. The company equips each of the three sites with server software to manage the desktop; the system requires one server, but Duke configures the other two for redundancy.

When a potentially dangerous event occurs, the 800 members of the Emergency Response Organization report to their stations. In seconds, the videoconferencing systems link the two support centers. A technician at the technical support center (TSC) evaluates the problem and collaborates online with a user at the operations support center to solve the problem. The TSC also calls the videoconferencing unit at the Charlotte facility to inform outside agencies that decide whether to alert communities. Duke Power Company is exploring the use of the videoconferencing system to communicate during other serious situations such as natural disasters.

Figure 2-4. Surveillance Application (courtesy of Intel).

In February and March of 1996, the Army's 3rd Signal Brigade, in Fort Hood, Texas, created a tactical LAN that permitted communications over a 20- by 30-mile area during its 10-day battlefield exercise. The Army unit also constructed an encrypted videoconferencing network in the field to synchronize activities between units. Remarkably, the soldiers who did so were largely untrained, and constructed the network using nothing more than a ten-page user's manual.

The National Education Association (NEA) conducted its first videoconference, in 1982, to alert NEA members about the Reagan Administration's proposed cuts in educational spending. After the budget became public, the NEA had little more than a week to rally its membership to protest the cuts before members of Congress traveled home for Easter recess. Organized in only eight days, the NEA's "crisis conference" was an enormous success. Satellite transmission allowed the presenters to reach more than 3,000 NEA members in all 48 contiguous states.

DISTANCE LEARNING

Videoconferencing is used extensively in the delivery of educational services and programs. Tens of thousands of students receive their education with the aid of videoconferencing. Distance learning is not a replacement for, but rather an extension of, classroom learning. In distance learning, instructors' roles do not change, but the audiences those instructors reach significantly increase. Consequently, videoconferencing is not a method of instruction, but a medium for delivering instruction. The success of distance learning correlates directly to the ability of students to assume responsibility for their own academic experience.

Therefore, distance learning is more promising for higher education than for primary education in which students require more personal attention. With distance learning, the success of a learning institution is relating less to proximity and more to their ability to conveniently provide relevant curricula.

The move to use video technology in education started in the 1950s, when the City Colleges of Chicago began using television to deliver for-credit courses. In 1950, Iowa State University went on the air with WOI-TV. According to Dr. Carla Lane, a distance education consultant and an internationally recognized authority on distance learning, WOI-TV was the "world's first non-experimental, educationally owned television station."

In 1963, the FCC allocated a portion of the microwave spectrum to Instructional Television Fixed Service (ITFS); the California State University System was the first to apply for a license. In 1971, the British Open University began offering courses over television. Designed to offer students non-traditional opportunities for education, it enrolls approximately 40,000 students annually.

In 1987, the Mind Extension University (ME/U) was formed. An education network that focuses on higher, for-credit courses ME/U is a division of the Jones Cable network and is carried on a cable television channel. Instructors teach for-credit college courses from colleges and universities around the country. As with other college courses, all classes include tests and assignments. Students contact instructors by mail, telephone, and even videoconference. The ME/U now offers an MBA program and has extended service to elementary and secondary school students.

An experiment in video-enabled distance learning shipped videoconferences over the Internet using *FrEdMail* (Free Educational Electronic Mail). The *Global Schoolhouse Project* linked students in Tennessee, California, Virginia and London, England and was part of a six-week joint-study curriculum about the environment. During the project, students read Vice President Al Gore's book, Earth in the Balance. At the end of the project, the students presented the information they had compiled to each other and, again, to governmental officials over the Internet. Funded in part by the National Science Foundation, the experiment was so popular that it has become an ongoing experiment that links an expanded group of students. Increasing numbers of schools from Australia, Canada, Japan, Mexico, and European countries are participating in Global Schoolhouse (http://k12.cnidr.org/gsh/gshwelcome.html).

Figure 2-5. Emergency Response Application (courtesy of Intel).

DISTANCE TRAINING

Training Magazine's 1995 Industry Report estimated that about 48% of companies that have more than 100 employees make use of computer-based training. As the term *distance learning* describes video-enabled instruction in an academic environment, the term *distance training* connotes video-enabled instruction in an organizational environment. Global competition and the increasing rate of change combine to make training workforces increasingly difficult for business, industry, and government institutions alike. Many organizations find traveling-shows an efficient way to train employees in remote cities except that reaching all cities in this manner often takes months. However, through videoconferencing, they can simultaneously train everyone in a matter of days.

One of the nation's largest freight rail operators, Conrail, uses videoconferencing to train a management team that is dispersed across five states. Training that used to take two days now takes two hours and includes valuable interactive discussion between instructors and employees. Wilson Learning (Eden Prairie, Minnesota) uses videoconferencing equipment to offer its suite of corporate training courses (including sales and sales management, customer service, and supervisory skills) to nearly any point in the world.

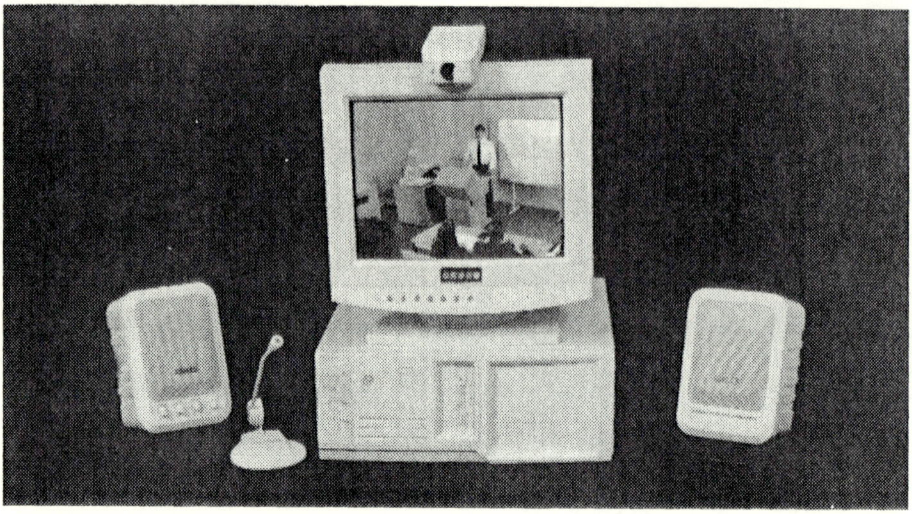

Figure 2-6. Distance Learning System (courtesy of Canvas).

In yet another example of distance training, The World Bank conducts *virtual seminars*. Through videoconferencing on the Internet, the organization unites individuals who are addressing similar or related issues but are in such geographically separated locations as South Africa, Russia, and Egypt. The World Bank has installed numerous room-based videoconferencing systems. However, administrators have found desktop video to be not only less expensive, but also more convenient and adaptable, and better suited for communications between very small groups. The World Bank relies largely on ISDN lines and fairly direct connections to the Internet to provide up to 25 Fps.

Videoconferencing, especially with the aid of video on demand (VOD) through a video server, provides *just-in-time* education and training. An AMR Training & Consulting Group study found that interactive multimedia training has resulted in returns on investment as high as 400%. Increasing network bandwidths and interface speeds improve the conditions for leveraging a variety of geographically dispersed sources of data and information to run distributed object-oriented multimedia training applications. Video on demand increases productivity, and improves resource management and availability by fostering flexibility in terms of distance, schedule, and learning pace. Like broadcast based distance learning, VOD also reduces or even eliminates commuting time. Because the focus of this book is two-way real-time interactive video communications, we will not explore video server based training on demand any further.

PRODUCT ANNOUNCEMENTS

Many companies use videoconferences to introduce products to their sales forces before the products hit the market. In 1982, Champion Spark Plug used videoconferencing to introduce a new product in what was, at the time, the largest business meeting ever held. Approximately 30,000 automotive parts sales representatives in 181 Holiday Inns throughout the U.S. participated in the event.

Companies often conduct regular meetings in which remote territory sales managers participate by telephone and videoconferencing. Subsequently, those companies introduce those products and services to resellers through live nationwide multipoint videoconferences. Video is delivered through a one-way broadcast, and participants at remote sites ask questions through two-way audio-only connections.

TELEMEDICINE

Telemedicine includes many applications. It is used to enhance military health care for patients who are on remote bases where not all areas of medical specialty are represented. One very popular application is the provision of health services at correctional facilities. The cost of providing health care services to prison inmates is very high. Treatment sometimes poses security risks and few doctors want to go into prisons to provide such service. Prisoners receive better health care when physical visits can be reinforced with Telemedicine. For example, fitted scopes allow doctors to see a patient's inner ear or the back of a retina. Cameras can zoom in on a skin cancer, electronic stethoscopes can magnify a heartbeat and machines, can rapidly transmit digitized X-rays and lab results. These off-the-shelf tools help doctors diagnose and treat prisoners over distance at much less expense to taxpayers.

Telemedicine offers many advantages. As the abundance of aging baby-boomers stresses the already overburdened health care system, Telemedicine tools will allow physicians to remotely monitor and treat numerous patients. This will, most likely, decrease the number of days that patients must remain hospitalized. It will also permit *visiting nurses* who, in the past, personally called on every patient, to provide services to a larger segment of the population. For instance, a visiting nurse could visually examine a group of patients before deciding which are in the greatest need of in-person care.

Videotaping doctor-patient consultations can even decrease malpractice exposure. The process the physician uses to diagnose and prescribe treatment can be reliably evaluated after the fact. Many health care professionals prefer the process because a doctor on tape is a polite and courteous doctor.

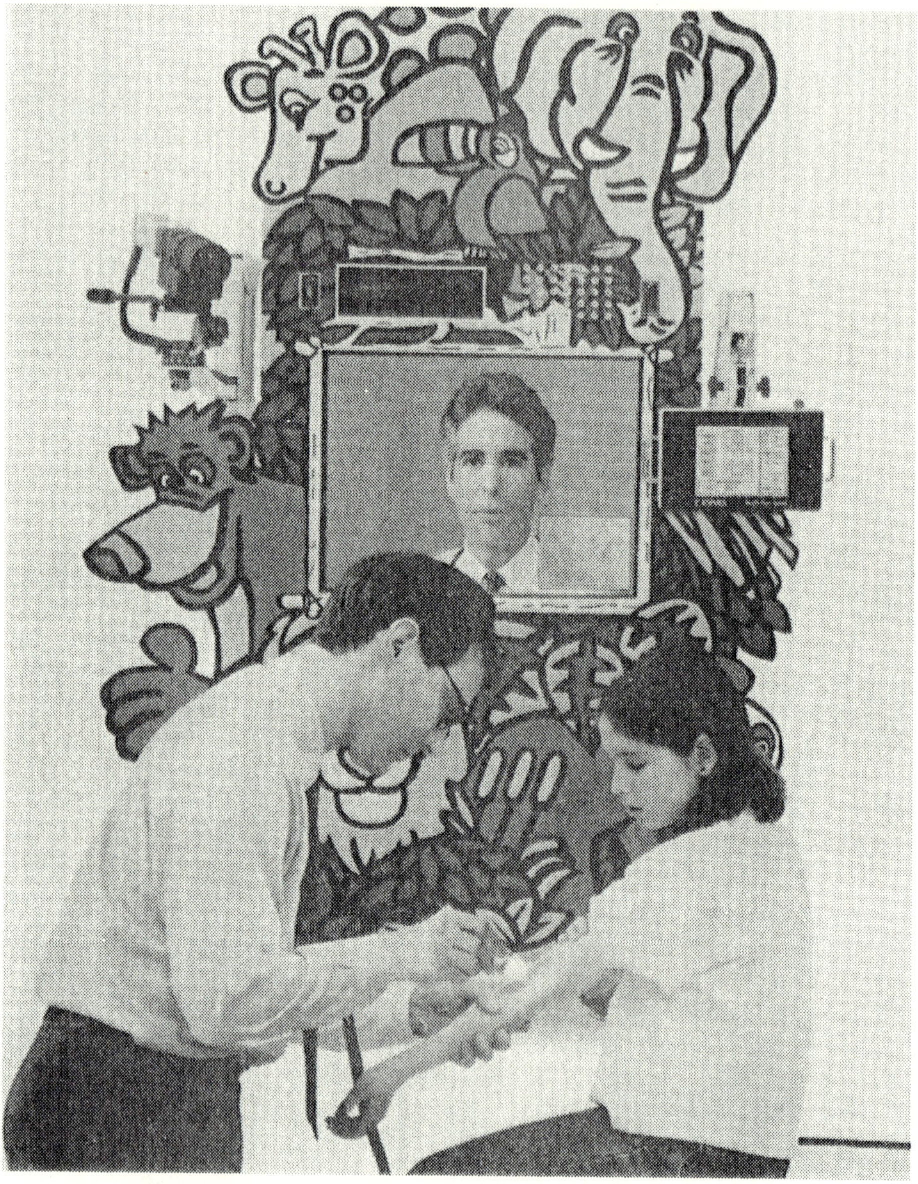

Figure 2-7. Pediatrics Application (courtesy of Canvas).

CONCLUSION

As no spice suits every dish, videoconferencing may not suit every situation. For instance, learning how to operate and maintain machinery requires the assistance of an on-site instructor. Moreover, the larger the audience, the easier it is to cost-justify videoconferencing infrastructure.

Nevertheless, time spent commuting is, for the most part, time wasted. Many people who drive to an office or a classroom could, with a computer and a telephone line, perform their work at home, at a remote office, or on the road. Workers can be geographically dispersed across cities, states, or countries. In addition, schools and colleges can disregard time and distance limitations by delivering education through audioconferencing, audiographics, video, and computer-mediated communication.

Furthermore, if one can shed the preconceptions that distinguish videoconferencing from broadcast media and store-and-forward video one can combine a variety of technologies to remove barriers to worthwhile work... which is what it is all about. When one focuses on the needs, discards stereotypes, and applies the necessary technologies to solve communications challenges, the possibilities are practically endless.

Through the remainder of this section, we will detail videoconferencing cases.

CHAPTER 2 REFERENCES

Frentzen, Jeff. "A path to understanding online videoconferencing," PC Week September 16, 1996 v13 n37 p. 133.

Gardner, W. David. "A maestro fiddles with videoconferencing," Electronic Engineering Times August 26, 1996 n916 p. 26-27.

Girard, Ken. "Bank tries ISDN two-way video," Computerworld August 12, 1996 v30 n33 p. 53.

Hamblen, Matt. "Desktop video surge forecast," Computerworld October 14, 1996 v30 n42 p. 85.

Hayes, Mary. "Face To Face Communication–Desktop videoconferencing helps utility respond to potential nuclear emergencies," Information Week December 9, 1996, Issue 609.

Lach, Eric. "Flagstar's Snappy Solution—Videoconferencing Helps Mortgage Banker Speed Loans," Communications Week September 18, 1996 Issue 629.

Lazar, Jerry. "Feds get the picture on videoconferencing," Federal Computer Week August 26, 1996 v10 n25 p. 53-59.

Petropoulos, Gus, and Vaskelis, Frank. "College piggybacks video network on phone system," Communications News February 1996 v33 n2 pp. 24-25.

PictureTel Corporation. "This Way to an Eye-opening Exhibit of Creative Uses for Videoconferencing," 2268/APPS/496/15.

Pietrucha, Bill: "Videoconferencing Played Security Role at Republican Convention," Newsbytes August 20, 1996.

Riggs, Brian. "Team spirit guides WAN; Northrop Grumman picks SMDS for videoconferencing and document-conferencing apps," LAN Times July 22, 1996 v13 n16 p. 37-39.

"Soldiers Take Their Offices to the Battlefield," Government Computer News April 15, 1996.

3

CASE STUDIES

Sometimes you can tell a large story with a tiny subject.
Eliot Porter

AMERICA TRUE TEAM NAVIGATES COMMUNICATIONS CHALLENGE

As the crew of America True made a run at the America's Cup, videoconferencing kept the team on course. The physical process of racing is just one aspect of what makes a successful America's Cup team; races require months of preparation. Complicating preparations for America True team members in San Francisco and Auckland was a vast body of water and some 6,513 miles. San Jose-based Polycom signed on as a corporate sponsor and exclusive videoconferencing supplier to America True. The team leveraged Polycom's ViewStation MP multipoint videoconferencing systems to navigate its communications challenge.

America True used Polycom ViewStation systems to maintain communication between the team headquarters in San Francisco and the racing team in Auckland, New Zealand, where preliminary races began in fall 1999. The value of ViewStation quickly became apparent to America True CEO and Captain, Dawn Riley, the first female skipper of an America's Cup syndicate, and the first skipper of a co-ed America's Cup team. Riley used ViewStation regularly to communicate with the entire America's Cup team. Every Wednesday morning, she would host a staff meeting that included 25 people who were scattered across two separate continents, as well as corporate sponsors and community supporters.

Riley claims that the ViewStation systems allowed her to sail with the team in New Zealand, and still maintain communication about the critical day-to-day operations at our Pier 17 headquarters in San Francisco. She proclaims, "When we're discussing pivotal subjects, such as sponsorships, upcoming events in both California and New Zealand, and sailing updates, it's critical that we are all in the same room, so to speak… that way, no details go unnoticed, we can keep everyone in the loop, and we stay on course to win the America's Cup."

America True held a video press conference on September 24, 1999 using their Polycom ViewStation videoconferencing systems. This allowed the press an opportunity to meet the crew, get caught up on how the team is doing, and to tour the America True boat and the compound in Auckland. Polycom's ViewStation videoconferencing products have made videoconferencing affordable and have dramatically improved the video quality and functionality. Phil Kaiko, America True's principal designer, used videoconferencing to assist in faster decision-making on boat designs. Kaiko declares, " When I used videoconferencing about five years ago, the transmission was broken up and the camera angle wasn't wide enough to capture the whole room, so it was really a waste of time. Now, with the Polycom ViewStation, I'm seeing videoconferencing in a whole new light for enhancing our team productivity."

Kaiko asserts that the video quality that the ViewStation provided enabled the team to exchange ideas between California and Auckland, to make timely decisions on designs and, subsequently, to get the boat in the water faster. Therefore, the America True team credits videoconferencing not only with providing convenience, but also with saving time and money. Without videoconferencing, the travel costs to accomplish the same tasks would have reached the tens of thousands of dollars. Said Chuck Riley, America True's vice chairman, "Using Polycom ViewStations, we have been able to connect potential donors to the program with our Auckland activities and let them see the set-up there first hand; this would have been impossible without videoconferencing."

Schenectady Schools Multicast

In November 1999, the Schenectady School District selected InfoValue Computing's QuickVideo OnDemand (QVOD) and QuickVideo Multicast (QVMC) systems for its Distance Learning Program. Approved by the New York State Education Department earlier in the year, the program employed the software to distribute academic video content to more than 3,000 PCs in eighteen different schools in the Schenectady area. The District planned to expand the project throughout New York State once Schenectady had completely implemented its program.

Streaming video cost-effectively provides students on the network with simultaneous access to smooth, high-resolution video and eliminates the need special hardware. QVOD can deliver video streams at speeds of 800 Mbps (500+ simultaneous MPEG1 videos), and InfoValue claims that it is the industry's fastest video-on-demand software for Microsoft NT networks. The implementation provides high-quality network video for conventional applications such as encyclopedias and classroom software. The Schenectady School District's distance learning program will also be used to deliver an outreach program for challenged students and small rural schools where it is currently impossible to offer such specialized courses to students.

In addition to delivering video playback capabilities to the district's 9,500 students and teachers, the distance learning project supports one-way broadcasting. For live broadcasts, the District uses QuickVideo Multicast with instant replay. With QVMC, the District can broadcast live MPEG2 video at up to sixteen Mbps to any number of PCs without overwhelming the network. The QuickVideo systems eliminate the complicated tasks and costs of distributing, duplicating, and sharing video files, and provide an open architecture that helps the school district protect its investments in existing platforms and applications. Fully compatible with any IP network, the InfoValue solutions deliver educational videos and live broadcasts to virtually any off-the-shelf PC hardware over the Schenectady School District's existing ATM network.

Program head, Sal Deangelo, is Director of Technical Services for the Schenectady School District. He proclaims, "By using high-bandwidth networks to take advantage of the embedded video in new academic applications such as World Book, Science Discovery, Amazonia and CCC, we can deliver multimedia-enhanced content directly to the desktop. Information that combines action, sound and video is not only more interesting, it's more memorable and it really enriches the learning experience." For multicasting, the review team wanted an advanced, platform-independent solution that would allow the school district to multicast TV-quality video to the desktop without disrupting district network activities. For the video-on-demand applications, the review team needed a solution that would provide students with simultaneous access to high-quality video without special hardware. Clearly, the District believes that it achieved its goals.

PREVENTING NUCLEAR DESTRUCTION

The U.S. Department of Energy (DOE) and Russia's atomic energy ministry constructed a videoconferencing link that provided a key part of the communications infrastructure between the two countries' energy departments during the year 2000 date rollover. U.S. Energy Secretary Bill Richardson and Russia's Minister of Atomic Energy Yevgeniy Adamov demonstrated the videoconferencing equipment that linked the DOE's Emergency Operations Center in Washington to a MinAtom Situation and Crisis Center that was dedicated October 2, 1999 in Moscow.

The videoconferencing system used a T1 line and off-the-shelf switches, codecs, and LCD video projectors. Unix-based routing software developed by the DOE was used for the internal routing of video signals. Videoconferencing allowed officials in Moscow and Washington to view graphics and stored pictures simultaneously to address issues that arose. Russia and the U.S. exchanged personnel on December 31. Russian experts were in the DOE's emergency center and U.S. experts were in the MinAtom center to monitor and to provide advice on year 2000-related issues regarding Russia's electricity grid and nuclear power plants. U.S. experts were also stationed in Ukraine, the site of the 1986 explosion and fire at the Chernobyl nuclear power station, to monitor the situation there.

The DOE began working on the videoconferencing link in March after Richardson and Adamov signed a report that the nuclear committee of the U.S.-Russian Joint Commission on Economic and Technological Cooperation prepared. The two countries agreed to establish a working relationship within their respective emergency centers, and the Department of Energy agreed to provide MinAtom with emergency management training and exercise assistance. The Department of Energy also agreed to provide future assistance for technology and engineering at the Situation Crisis Center. In preparation for the date rollover, the DOE helped to monitor all 29 nuclear power reactors in Russia, and provided hardware, software, training, and assistance with contingency plans.

TELEPAROLE & TELEJUSTICE: THE IOWA PAROLE BOARD

The Iowa Board of Parole began applying video communications technology in 1994 to manage the state's prison population. The Iowa Communications Network (ICN) provides the infrastructure for two-way distance communications for the Iowa Board of Parole, and thereby saves the county time and money, and reduces risk. Operational in the fall of 1993, the ICN is a statewide two-way full-motion fiber optic communications network that connects sites in Iowa's 99 counties. The Board uses the distance learning system for their parole interview process, for their registered victim input process, and for parole revocation hearings. Recently, it also began leveraging the system to allow college level students of the judicial process to observe parole interviews in real time.

The Teleparole system enables interaction between the parole board and registered victims, and thereby simplifies the jobs of many people in the process. The network links the parole board at an ICN classroom with the Mount Pleasant and Oakdale correctional institutions. The two-way network connects the board, the inmate, and registered victims even though miles of distance often physically separate the participants.

Before the Iowa Board of Parole created its Televictim program, registered victims endured significant inconvenience. Upon notice that the board would interview an inmate, victims would travel to isolated correctional facilities. After rigorous security checks, they would tolerate the hostile, tense experience of sitting next to the inmate's family and friends. The ICN allows the board to isolate victims from such situations. In the initial case, the inmate participated from the Mount Pleasant Correctional Facility, the board participated from the STARC Armory classroom in Johnston, and a registered victim participated from the Iowa Valley Community College District classroom at Marshalltown.

The Iowa Board of Parole's Telejustice program saves the county time and money in parole revocation hearings. Previously, parole judges traveled as much as four hours to counties where alleged parole violations occurred. After conducting a hearing, making a determination, and rendering a sanction, a judge would make the return journey. Telejustice allows a parole judge to conduct numerous hearings from a proximate ICN classroom without wasteful travel. One judge can now perform as much as three times the work in the same amount of time.

The ICN system also provides a basis by which students witness parole hearings in real time, and by which instructors analyze hearings in real time without disrupting them. The Iowa Board of Parole intends to increase its use of Teleparole, Televictim, Telejustice, and distance learning programs through the ICN system.

North Slope Borough School District: A Big Cold Classroom

Distance education has been of particular benefit to rural communities that often find it difficult to attract teachers in specific areas of the curriculum. Low demand for particular courses, and difficulty in meeting state-mandated requirements compound the problem of delivering rural education. Barrow, Alaska's North Slope Borough School District provides K–12 service to one such rural community.

The North Slope Borough School District is the largest in the United States. Equal in size to the state of Minnesota, it measures 650 miles from east to west and covers 88,000 square miles. All points are above the Arctic Circle. Eighty-six percent of the 1,700 students within the district are Alaskan natives who are scattered among eight villages. Of these students, more than 1,000 attend school in Barrow. Others attend village schools where, with only few high school students and very harsh climatic conditions, it is hard to find and retain trained professional staff schooled in all subjects. Most teachers are generalists, and some high schools have only two or three seniors.

The North Slope Borough School District began using a particular form of videoconferencing that the codec provider, VTEL, dubbed Media Conferencing. PC-based multimedia conference systems that offer both face-to-face video communications and the ability to create and store slide-based presentations (computer graphics and text files) were placed in village schools. A multipoint bridge allowed simultaneous conferencing among three or more sites. Students and teachers can converse between sites; contrast this with an older satellite system (which the project replaced) that provided receive-only video and two-way audio.

Instructors using the system are finding that students enjoy education over videoconferencing. The medium allows increased social interaction between students that might otherwise meet only once or twice a year. Videoconferencing allows students at the smaller schools to leverage resources and develop relationships that would otherwise not be available. Eleven interactive videoconferencing sites, 650 computer workstations, and more than 2,500 users make use of the system. With the advent of the distance learning curriculum, national achievement test scores have improved steadily throughout the borough.

ESCAMBIA COUNTY SCHOOL DIST.: DISTANCE LEARNING ON THE PANHANDLE

Extending more than one hundred miles between the Gulf of Mexico and the state of Alabama, Florida's Escambia County School District is responsible for educating more than 43,000 students. Retaining instructors to provide students at each of Escambia's eight high schools with diverse elective courses, such as Russian, Latin, and calculus (much less night school curricula) was challenging and, in some cases, unfeasible. Providing in-service training and conducting administrative meetings was equally difficult.

To provide two-way interactive video, audio, and multimedia capabilities, the school district equipped each of its eight sites with two monitors up front and two in the back. In each classroom, it installed VTEL QuickFrame, Pen Pal Graphics, fax capabilities, TrueTalk, and two SmartCam pan/tilt/zoom cameras, along with an Elmo document stand. The Escambia School District created a single extended classroom in which all students can interact as if they were in the same room. Students hear each other with the aid of ceiling microphones, and teachers speak into cordless microphones. Teacher's aides at each location provide such administrative support as preparing handouts, operating a SmartCam, supervising students, and faxing quizzes.

During the 1995-96 school year, the district delivered a total of sixteen courses including calculus, numerous foreign languages, and speech communication. Of those classes, thirteen were limited to two total sites, but three included at least three sites. Prior to the implementation of the distance learning program, teachers attended a one-week training session taught by peers who had participated in a two-site pilot network since 1993.

As a result of the distance learning program, students are taking elective courses that better prepare them for college. Moreover, they are exposed to technology they will certainly encounter in their careers. Teachers use the technology for administrative meetings, and to further their own education with University of West Florida courses.

WESTERN ILLINOIS EDUCATION CONSORTIUM: EXTENDING EDUCATION

To improve regional economies and overall quality of life, the State of Illinois formed ten regional affiliations of universities, community colleges and school districts, and government and business organizations to collaboratively serve citizens' diverse education and training needs. One of these is the 17-member Western Illinois Education Consortium (WIEC), which spans a geographic area that is bordered by Wisconsin, Iowa, and Missouri. The education of the vast region's sparse population was encumbered with long, often impractical, commutes.

To provide underserved areas with graduate and undergraduate curricula, supplement the workforce training options of businesses, and reduce travel expenses overall, WIEC worked with VTEL to build a strategy of consolidating technologies into an integrated system that would support instruction. In 1993, WIEC establish an extensive distance-learning network by obtaining Higher Education Cooperative Act (HECA) grants through the Illinois Board of Higher Education and Community College Board. One of 39 nodes on the Illinois Video Network (IVN), WIEC also offers connections to State agencies and to the Sprint Meeting Channel. Additionally, WIEC coordinates programming with the University of Illinois' Chicago, Champaign, and Springfield campuses.

The 29-site WIEC network incorporates VTEL 227 and 235 systems and eight 20-port multipoint control units. The WIEC network transmits video at 384 Kbps over dedicated fractional T1 lines. A proprietary bulletin board system (BBS) supports instruction and administration.

In WIEC's *regional degree program*, students can use interactive videoconferencing to attend courses at multiple campuses. The University of Illinois also leverages the videoconferencing system by contracting with community colleges to provide students with lower-division courses, and provides upper-division courses to students in remote regions.

Extension sites (e.g., medical centers and businesses) allocate nine or more hours each week for community education centers to schedule their video rooms. One extension site, Trinity Hospital, serves as the originating location for a region-wide mammography course, and as a receiving location for a drug education course that originates at Western Illinois University. Member institutions save thousands of dollars and numerous hours per year in travel by using videoconferencing for region-wide meetings. College students fulfill course work and access senior instructors from colleges throughout the region without squandering time commuting. In addition, seniors at about a dozen high schools that have joined the network now participate in college and university curricula, and courses offered by other participating high schools.

MEDICAL COLLEGE OF GEORGIA: HEALTHCARE & EDUCATION OVER DISTANCE

Even the best of physicians occasionally need a second opinion. When appropriate help is in another town, the solution used to be to fax X-rays and attempt to describe the circumstances of the case over the telephone. Videoconferencing provides a better alternative for the Medical College of Georgia (MCG).

Dr. Jay Sanders took a leading role in one of the country's first Telemedicine applications, at Massachusetts General Hospital in Boston. Subsequently, as Director of Telemedicine for MCG, Dr. Sanders' vision was to build, "A system that electronically transports a consulting physician from a medical center complex to a patient at a distant health care facility. "The MCG's system integrates interactive video communications with remote controlled biomedical telemetry to allow a consulting physician to examine a patient at a satellite location as if the patient were in the physician's office.

The lack of access to specialty care is often a disadvantage of living in an isolated community. Rural hospitals require a minimum number of full beds to support doctors, nurses, technicians, and administrators. Therefore, every patient counts in the hospital's struggle to survive; each time a patient is transported to an urban hospital for specialty treatment, the bed census statistics of the small rural hospital are adversely affected. In addition, transportation of fragile patients presents health risks, and discontinuity of care can result. Rural doctors often suffer from professional isolation, and find continuation of their medical education difficult. A highly specialized form of videoconferencing, Telemedicine, allows rural physicians to almost instantaneously access the specialized medical expertise of university doctors. It decreases the recurrence of referrals, provides immediate attention to life-threatening problems, establishes an integrated care network, and provides enhanced quality of care in rural situations. Even so, the cost to the patient is significantly reduced.

Videoconferencing enables the MCG to improve care and delivery of medical services, and to reduce travel time and expense for hospital staff. It enhances patient referrals, consultations, and post-operative examinations. MCG is preparing for emergency room to emergency room support, emergency psychiatric consultation, supervision at community hospitals, benefits consultations, recruitment, administrative meetings, and clinical research collaborations. Specialties such as cardiology, dermatology, neurology and ophthalmology all employ telemedicine.

MCG will soon overcome even the limitations of touch by using tactile electronic gloves with sensors. Such gloves will permit examining physicians to electronically convey the sense of touch to medical specialists at main or hub sites who simultaneously wear identical gloves.

Figure 3-1. Distant Learning Application (courtesy of CLI).

Through videoconferencing, interns, residents, fellows and students exchange published papers, discuss patient cases, and analyze prognoses throughout patients' illnesses. In this way, videoconferencing improves the quality of patient care by fostering new relationships. Moreover, by using the system to provide staff with information on such diverse subjects as women's health issues and financial planning, the institution believes videoconferencing has improved morale and saved more than $10,000 for every twelve hours that it is used. In addition, referring physicians earn credit for participating in tutorials with consulting physicians who are also members of the institution's faculty. Consultations are recorded on videotape for subsequent observation by review panels.

Through distance learning and individualized laboratory work, MCG allows remote medical professionals to participate in classes without forfeiting their homes and jobs, or even traveling. This is important to Georgia hospitals because state law requires a medical technologist to be on duty on the hospital premises at all times. Cameras placed throughout classrooms at both remote and primary sites capture and transmit images across special cabling. Instructors provide personal attention by scheduling time after lectures or answering toll-free telephone calls. Personal Interactivity between students is fostered by promoting competition between groups of students at remote sites; as little as half a given class may participate at the primary site.

With state and federal funding, each facility has been furnished with videocassette recorders, motion cameras, auxiliary cameras, and ELMO EV-308 graphics cameras. The graphics cameras provide whiteboard and transparency projection capabilities, and record live or still graphics for broadcast. Users control the video system, audio system, and the codec (including camera pan, tilt, zoom, and focus functions, as well as transmission of motion and still video) with a touch screen control panel. Using Sony wireless microphone systems with lavaliere lapel microphone and separate clip-on transmitters, a receiving unit, and an antenna, presenters move freely within classrooms. The total cost is estimated at $90,000 per site. MCG leverages a sophisticated network of T1 lines, satellite dishes, and microwave and cable systems to examine real-time images through viewers that interoperate with microcameras and to broadcast live, real-time, interactive health programming from the MCG campus to distance learning facilities throughout the state. It will soon broadcast nationally from its own satellite uplink facility.

The State of Georgia had to work with five LECs and two IXCs (AT&T and Sprint) to bridge all service boundaries. The state required vendors to provide an automated scheduling system so it could efficiently manage the system. Instructors simply fax their schedules to DOAS, which programs the system to connect appropriate sites at set times; teachers do not personally make the various connections. The state also required vendors to provide a flat billing structure for every location in the state, a point-to-point or multi-point environment, and the capability of any site to talk to any other site.

THE ABORIGINAL PEOPLES VIDEOCONFERENCE

In the fall of 1991, the remote Aboriginal communities of the Tanami, consisting of Yuendumu, Lajamanu, Willowra and Kintore, made a decision to install a six-point videoconferencing network to link their villages to each other, to Darwin and Alice Springs and to points beyond. The Tanami Network consists of PictureTel codecs linked via Hughes earth stations to the AUSSAT 3 satellite that serves Australia.

Dating back more than 50,000 years, the Aboriginal is the oldest surviving culture. In the early 1940s, the Australian government established Aboriginal communities in the desolate outback region known as the Tanami desert. Unfortunately, outside intervention began to disrupt the complex network of information and personal contacts that, for thousands of years, had existed between the area's people. Aboriginal law and traditions started to erode. Young people turned from their elders and family members to television. Alarmed, the Tanami community employed videoconferencing to resurrect tribal tradition in which culture and knowledge passed from the elders to the young. The Tanami Network is now used to preserve the age-old culture and heritage by remotely conducting ceremonial activities and other Aboriginal business.

The development of the videoconferencing network began in 1990 with a successful trial of systems that connected Lajamanu, Yuendumu, and Sydney. Over the links, students received education. Community spokespeople, for the first time, gained a voice in their government. Aboriginal artists discovered the system could be used to negotiate art and craft sales directly with buyers all over the world. This eliminated a chain of go-betweens that had, for years, exploited the Aborigines' isolation.

After a successful trial, videoconferencing was widely deployed. The philosophy behind the $200,000 project consists of three aspects. First, the Aboriginal people will have local control of the systems and network. Second, the project will be but one part of an attempt to enhance ceremonial and family links. A program of community visits, workshops that are conducted by elders, and proactive government involvement, will also further social communication, vital to the Aboriginal community. Other technologies such as telephone, facsimile, radio, local video production, and regional broadcasting will be integrated into the solution. Finally, the cost of the project will be spread across as many applications as possible. This includes the display and promotion of arts and crafts directly to overseas markets, the delivery of educational, medical and governmental services from remote locations, support of community detention and bush and urban court proceedings, and the strengthening of community, family and ceremonial links.

MANAGEMENT RECRUITERS INTERNATIONAL: RECRUITING OVER DISTANCE

Cleveland, Ohio-based Management Recruiters International (MRI) is the world's largest search and recruiting organization, with approximately 600 offices and 2,000 employees in 46 states, the District of Colombia, Puerto Rico and Canada. MRI, in the late 1980s, began investigating videoconferencing and video-enabled training applications to increase its ability to interact with field office personnel. It conducted live training through satellite broadcast video with incoming audio lines. MRI's Vice President of Franchised Operations instructed, "We considered two-way video through terrestrial lines, but quickly discovered that the cost of creating a national network was prohibitive." By 1991, however, the price of videoconferencing had dropped substantially, from both an equipment and transmission standpoint. MRI initiated another investigation.

The second study was prompted by changes in the executive search industry. The recession of the late 1980s, combined with a trend toward downsizing, caused the industry to shrink considerably. Competition intensified for every customer. MRI strategically leveraged videoconferencing to provide service in a way that gave it a competitive edge.

Of the 22,000 people that MRI places every year, approximately 9,000 are what it calls *long distance placements*. In such a case, a candidate must fly in for an interview with the hiring authority. MRI arranges over 90,000 such interviews each year (a ratio of ten for every one placement). After an extensive investigation, MRI discovered that its customers were spending, on average, between $1,600 and $1,700 for the related travel costs. Since interviews are typically scheduled with very little notice, airfares are almost always high. For about $250 per half-hour, the MRI service offered customers a significant cost reduction. MRI calculated that if its hiring authorities used videoconferencing instead of fly-ins for all initial interviews, these customers could save more than of $135 million per year. In early 1993, Compression Labs, Incorporated (CLI), announced a new low-end roll-about called eclipse (CLI spelled "eclipse" without a capital "e"). Eclipse was what MRI had been waiting for; they installed one unit in each of the top 50 markets in the United States. Assuming that candidates would be willing to drive up to two hours for a face-to-face interview over videoconferencing, MRI calculated that over 90% of America's population was within range of the service.

Creating its videoconferencing infrastructure was eventful. A company spokesperson proclaimed,

> *What transpired between the first and the fiftieth site is enough to fill a technical manual. The lessons we learned in dealing with local telephone companies and the variations (on switched digital services) alone could fill volumes. Out of the first fifty units, there was not one easy installation.*

Nevertheless, when asked what videoconferencing had done for MRI, he declared,

More than we ever imagined. MRI is now the only search firm in the world that can offer this kind of service. And, it is a valuable service that our client companies appreciate. We have had some surprises, too. We always considered videoconferencing as acceptable for the initial interview. We anticipated that, once the videoconferencing phase of the interview process was complete, the companies would fly their first-choice candidate in for the final interview. Imagine our surprise when, on the second videoconference interview ever conducted on the MRI videoconferencing network, our client company extended an offer to the candidate over the network and the candidate accepted on the spot!

MRI points out that the ideal candidate is rarely looking for employment. When the candidate is not convinced that she is interested in the position, it is difficult to disrupt her busy routine with an interview that requires travel. Interviews that substitute videoconferencing for travel are more likely to occur. MRI is emphatic when discussing the role of videoconferencing in interviewing, and the company expects utilization to increase. Moreover, it regards its videoconferencing infrastructure as a strategic advantage for expanding his company worldwide. Again, a company spokesperson pronounces, "All things considered, having our own network, in spite of the cost and the problems inherent to it, has been one of the smartest strategic moves in the history of our company."

MRI hopes to utilize its network (ConferView) to enable small companies to perform on-campus recruiting at colleges. Since today only the largest firms can send recruiters directly to campuses, videoconferencing should help the smaller firms compete for top candidates. MRI will also rent excess system capacity to customers and others who wish to use videoconferencing but lack facilities.

Figure 3-2. Business Conferencing Application (courtesy of CLI).

XEROX PARC EXPERIMENT: MEDIA SPACES

According to Sara Bly, Steve Harrison and Susan Irwin, the authors of Media Spaces: Bringing People Together in a Video, Audio and Computing Environment, a media space is a "Technologically created environment" that emerges from a "Concern for both the social and technical practices of collaborative work and from an effort to support those practices." In the mid-1980s, XEROX PARC's System Concepts Laboratory (SCL) was geographically split between Palo Alto, California and Portland, Oregon. The intent was to "maintain a single group and explore technologies to support collaborative work." The media space had to support not only cross-site work but also provide the necessary social connections between workers to allow them to "be together."

At the time of the media space experiment, the SCL had a hierarchical management structure, but lab members "regularly attended staff meetings and most decisions were made by consensus." SCL's way of working was acknowledged to be both professional and social. The group accepted the split as a challenge to integrate access across distance, to information, computing, and social interaction including "Casual interrupting, gossiping and brain-storming."

Media space put cameras and microphones in offices and common areas on both ends (Portland and Palo Alto). A fixed two-way 56 Kbps video link connected the sites. The link included video compression equipment, an audio teleconferencing system, and consumer-quality video cameras and monitors in the commons area of each site. Microphones were interspersed throughout each building. The link was dedicated and was, therefore, always active. The portable video equipment was sometimes moved from the commons into individual or private offices.

Eventually the Design Methodology researchers expanded on the initial prototype by adding the ability to reconfigure the cameras, monitors, and microphones in each office using a crossbar switch. Participants could walk to a panel and push a button to change the audio and video arrangement to match their current need and activity. Just as often, participants would change the arrangement at random so that anyone might be seeing and talking to anyone else on the other end. The goal was to approximate the casual encounter and move through a range of socially significant contacts in any given day.

Users controlled their availability across the medium by controlling cameras (on, on but focused on something other than the person in the office, and off). Microphones were either on or off. Individuals were expected to take responsibility for controlling their own boundaries of personal and private space.

What did the media space project learn about work over distance? First, that technology can enable the social relationships of workers separated by space. The Frequent and regular use of the media space for awareness, informal encounter, and culture sharing indicate that technology can support more than task-specific communication. The media space project showed that a group could and did maintain itself as a single community that was separated only by distance. Participants routinely referred to all members across sites as, "We."

The group learned that different settings require different media spaces. During design, thought should be given to "not only the objects of the system but also to their placement," how they are accessed and how well they are integrated into the ongoing organization of work life. Open, continuously available video and audio is not appropriate for every environment or culture. The challenge is to build systems that reflect the changing needs of user communities. One size does not fit all when it comes to electronically-mediated connections.

The unique needs of the SCL led the researches to uncover a need for a shared drawing surface. Users not only wanted to see what their coworkers had written, but also wanted to amend what had been written or drawn, to collaborate on problems and solutions. This aspect of the project resulted in Xerox's LiveBoard, which it introduced in 1993. It is a 3- by 5-foot backlit active-matrix liquid crystal display (LCD) powered by an Intel processor. LiveBoards allow workers in different locations to simultaneously view and edit the same document.

The group also noted that typical "marketplace technological offerings" including videoconferencing and desktop video devices did not offer the flexibility of media spaces because they were not integrated into a computing environment. "Most videoconferencing requires that one 'go' someplace; it is not an integrated part of the office itself." The study went on to note that it would be "interesting to explore the possibilities for desktop video in supporting activities like peripheral awareness, chance encounters, distributed meetings, and discussions and envisionment exercises."

The researchers of the project noted the importance of media literacy and how participants progressed from computing to computing augmented with video and audio. This progression illustrates an evolution "toward a unified field of audio, video and computing." Finally, the project led the research team to consider whether "awareness of people and activities in a working group had value independent of other mechanisms that might be available for collaboration." In other words, just thinking about co-workers in another area or department might be the first step toward working together; and seeing and hearing them from time to time might stimulate thinking.

Chapter 3 References

Johnston, Margret. "U.S., Russia Set Up Y2K Video Link." Computerworld, December 3, 1999 04:24 PM

"InfoValue Video-on-Demand, Multicasting Solutions Chosen for New York State School System." Business Wire, November 22, 1999 p0039.

Baard, Mark. "CNN News Hounds Use Digital Technology To Report, Edit, Produce," Macweek June 3, 1996 Volume 10 Number 22.

Bly, Sara A. Harrison, Steve R. and Irwin, Susan. "Media spaces: bringing people together in a video, audio and computing environment," Communications of the ACM, January 1993 pp. 28-50.

Chute, Alan G., Ph.D. and Elfrank, James D. "Teletraining: Needs, Solutions..." International Teleconferencing Association 1990 Yearbook, June 1990.

EDGE on & about AT&T. "Videoconferencing: SunSolutions unveils industry's first complete desktop product for workstations," November 1, 1993 p. 7.

Fogelgren, Stephen W. "Videoconferencing at Management Recruiters," A document provided courtesy of MRI, Cleveland, Ohio, 1993.

Gold, Elliot M. "Industry-Wide Video Networks Thrive," Networking Management November 1991 pp. 60-64.

Halhed, Basil R. and Scott, D. Lynn. "There Really Are Practical Uses for Videoconferencing," Business Communications Review June 1992, pp. 41-44.

Hayes, Mary. "Face To Face Communication–Desktop videoconferencing helps utility respond to potential nuclear emergencies," Information Week December 9, 1996, Issue 609.

Lach, Eric. "Flagstar's Snappy Solution—Videoconferencing Helps Mortgage Banker Speed Loans," Communications Week September 18, 1996, Issue 629.

Lane, Carla, Ed.D. Technical Guide to Teleconferencing and Distance Learning Applied Business teleCommunications San Ramon, California, 1992 pp. 125-193.

McMullen, Barbara E. and McMullen, John F. "Global Schoolhouse," Newsbytes April 29, 1993, p. NEW 04300011.

Newcombe, Tod. "Georgia Spans Education, Medicine Gap with Two-Way Video,"
Government Technology 1995.

Persenson, Melissa J. "Electronic field trips for the '90s," PC Magazine February 8, 1994 p. 30.

PictureTel Application Notes and VTEL and Panasonic User Profiles were used to develop several of these applications.

PictureTel Corporation. "This Way to an Eye-opening Exhibit of Creative Uses for Videoconferencing," 2268/APPS/496/15M.

Pietrucha, Bill: "Videoconferencing Played Security Role At Republican Convention," Newsbytes August 20, 1996.

Rash, Wayne. "Virtual meetings at the desktop. (Fujitsu Networks Industry... " Windows Sources January 1994 p. 235.

Sanders, Dr. Jay. "Three Winning Videoconferencing Applications," Advanstar's VIEW '93 Conference, Videoconferenced between Houston, Texas and Atlanta, Georgia, November 1, 1993.

"Soldiers Take Their Offices To The Battlefield," Government Computer News April 15, 1996.

Toyne, Peter. "The Tanami Network," As presented to the Service Delivery and Communications in the 1990s Conference, Sydney, Australia, March 17-19, 1992.

"United States Largest School District Uses Videoconferencing to Bridge Gaps," Business Wire (an Information Service of INDIVIDUAL, Incorporated) October 26, 1992.

"Wilson Learning and PictureTel Join to Deliver Professional Training Courses," Business Wire (an Information Service of INDIVIDUAL, Incorporated) October 26, 1992.

4

THE BUSINESS CASE

Talk of nothing but business and dispatch that business quickly.

Placard on the door of the Aldine press, Venice (1490)

In his IBM Systems Journal article setting forth a process for senior managers who must deal with the challenge of ensuring that business processes, people, and technology are meshed within an organization, Peter G. W. Keen notes that an executive's most important contribution to the organization is to, "Clarify the firm's business imperatives that are based on knowledge anchors and linked to its vision and strategic intent." Keen, in his discussion of information technology (IT) continues, "The key step in the business and technology dialog is to link business imperatives to IT imperatives." It is on this note that we will begin our chapter on making the business case for videoconferencing.

To sell a technical concept to senior management, one must link that concept to business imperatives. Therefore, one must explicitly interpret how the technology can provide a competitive edge, reduce costs, or provide the business with some other significant, tangible benefit. The business case will probably consist of a combination of these three elements.

Although this point is not a new one, it is repeatedly overlooked. To those who are familiar with it, a technology's benefits are conspicuous. A common mistake is to assume that others will immediately see the value of the technology, embrace the concept, and readily pursue those benefits. To those who daily address the realities of business, there are too many valuable projects and too few dollars to accommodate all, or even most of them. Consequently, if videoconferencing is to become a vital part of the communications infrastructure, one must describe it in terms of how it can enable business imperatives.

The best business case for video communications is not based on *technology* because technology has no inherent value. One must present technology as an extension to the organization's communications infrastructure, an IT platform (foundation) upon which the business will improve its processes. In the vernacular of the sales profession, one can note the features and advantages, but one must emphasize the benefits. A feature might be a video communications system itself, and a benefit might be the improved availability of human resources that system enables. However, the benefit might be the business opportunities gained (expressed in dollars) by making those resources available.

Just as a company's mission statement and culture provide a basis for its objectives, infrastructure is the foundation on which a company builds its information technology-dependent business applications. Infrastructure links all parts of the business and provides a mechanism for sharing common business constructs such as policies, customers, products, markets, and regulatory requirements. Infrastructure enables the business to operate as a coherent whole. Therefore, the basis of one's project vision must be an active business model; technology and its applications are merely layers of the overall infrastructure.

Because the priorities of senior managers include increasing market share, improving efficiency, reducing operating costs, and fostering agility in a rapidly changing economic climate, one must frame one's video communications proposal in those terms. Many top-level managers have experienced disappointment in IT investments and are, consequently, skeptical. The business case for video must clearly inform these executives of cost reductions or markets gained. They will want to know whether other companies (competitors and key customers, for instance) are making similar infrastructure investments.

Government and public sector enterprises, like their private sector counterparts, are now, more than ever, focusing on strategic and market issues. The emphasis on improving the quality of service to the public and service to the citizen is likely to endure as a popular topic. For government IT or information resources management (IRM) managers, this means that technology projects will be funded based on how well they improve service and reduce costs. A number of agencies are using, and many more are considering the use of, video communications as a service delivery tool. Government agencies at the federal level have, for years, used FTS 2000-based video for internal communications. Now the Social Security Administration plans to use video communications in the resolution of claims disputes and disability cases. Other agencies, such as health and human services, are similarly interested in extending its use to meet face-to-face with the public, either through kiosks, over the Internet, or through other configurations.

When developing a business case for and selling any technology with which one's company has little or no experience (and about which it probably entertains numerous misconceptions), one must hone one's skills in areas such as:

- Understanding of the enterprise's market, industry and challenges
- Knowledge of standard business concepts and accounting practices
- Internal partnering, investigation, and needs-analysis
- Grasp of how video communications can enhance competitive position
- Vendor alliances and support from key business partners

Know Your Business

The first step in implementing videoconferencing as a business solution is becoming familiar with the organizations' market, industry, and challenges. IT professionals only increase their stature by putting business first and technology second. The key to success is thinking strategically, thoroughly understanding the enterprise and its market, and developing strong relationships with managers in functional groups outside IT. Enthusiasm for a technology will rarely compensate for overlooking any of these fundamental issues. A prepared IT professional will study her company's prospectus, annual report, or SEC filing (in the case of a publicly held organization). She will scan trade magazines and publications for articles about the company, and she will interview administrative staff and others to understand the executive agenda. She will base her business case on the company's mission, value statements, strategic goals, and business objectives.

Nearly all organizations promote mission and values, strategies, goals and objectives. Goals and strategies provide one with the most leverage for selling technology. Objectives enable one to think in the same way that end users (we will call them customers) think—in terms of results.

An organization's mission describes its reason for being; the kind of business the firm should be in and what its performance objectives should be. Values, the general abstract ideas that guide thinking, provide the basis for the mission statement. Competitive strategy is determined by finding the right product-market sales approach to accomplish the economic mission. Goals develop from strategy and differ between the business's various functional areas. Goals are future states or outcomes that the organization desires. An organizational goal might be to increase market share or to improve customer service. An objective is a well-specified target that is measurable and which should be attained by a specified point in time.

To help in distinguishing between goals and objectives, following are some sample goals:

- Goal: Improve ABC's communications to enhance competitive position
- Goal: Improve quality standards on a global (national, regional) basis
- Goal: Increase the global market share of product X
- Goal: Improve product time-to-market schedule
- Goal: Improve productivity within the corporation
- Goal: Get closer to the customer/ improve customer service
- Goal: Retool the organization in response to our changing market

And here are some sample objectives:

- Objective: Include European management in '95 strategic planning process
- Objective: Reduce customer complaints by 20% by year-end
- Objective: Establish operations in Singapore and Australia by Q4
- Objective: Get FDA approval on projects X and Y within nine months
- Objective: Improve the output of widgets per worker by 10 % by June, 1996
- Objective: Establish programmed account sales plan by Q3. Hire managers
- Objective: Train X% of our personnel on Y by March 1995

In most companies, a needs-analysis and a project proposal are prerequisites to a capital expenditure. Part of preparing these documents is working formally with customers, and interviewing various functional groups, departments, or teams. In the needs-analysis phase, it is important to keep the discussion focused on the customer, their situation, and the problems they face. It is especially key to listen for a manager's dissatisfaction with a current manner of achieving a goal. One will develop an understanding by exploring their objectives and the yardsticks by which they measure their success. It is best to not suggest solutions at this point.

In interviewing each client group, one should develop a matrix of objectives and problems that videoconferencing might solve, and pay particular attention to issues related to time, distance, teamwork, and collaboration. One should also listen closely when discussing project management or heightened demands on scarce human resources. Another area to explore is communication difficulties between distant workgroups (headquarters and the field, marketing and engineering, engineering and service). One must probe plans for training and retooling. Any obstacle that relates to getting the job done over distance is of interest.

Note that there are two kinds of objectives: mandatory and desirable. Mandatory objectives, as James Harry Green points out in his "Irwin Handbook of Telecommunications Management", "are the conditions that an alternative must satisfy in order to be acceptable." On the other hand, desirable objectives are "the conditions we would like the alternative to satisfy, but their lack will not disqualify." For example, it might be mandatory that a video communications system interoperates with a system installed at a customer's location. A desirable objective might be that establishing a connection would be as easy as dialing a telephone, when a more complicated method of connection might be acceptable under certain circumstances. One should develop one's matrix of problems and objectives with a focus on critical problems and attributes that an acceptable solution must have, and note characteristics that are valuable but not compulsory.

At the end of the needs-analysis phase, one will have a catalog of problems to which one can begin to attach visual communications solutions. For a small, centrally-located team that provides sales, training, or engineering support to a large number of field offices, one can offer a productivity-enhancing tool that can also minimize "burnout." Clients in highly competitive or volatile environments might find that video communications improves their response time to fast-breaking events. Channel managers might use it to maintain and improve customer, distributor, partner or value-added reseller (VAR) relations. Sales may use video to make product demonstrations and to bring executives into the presentation process. Video Communications can involve a broader base of people in strategy setting and decision making. It has a track record of reducing product time-to-market and helping to avert late penalties in a contract. Video communications is *a solution looking for a business problem.*

Because video communication is such a powerful tool, it is a mistake to place one's focus on reducing travel expense unless one's customer emphasizes that as a priority. Senior managers are not often concerned with the cost of a plane ticket. They are concerned with business results, productivity, and human resource management. When it comes to spending scarce capital funds, they will not invest funds just to reduce their travel budget unless savings are exorbitant. They will invest in technology that enables them to succeed in their core areas of focus.

THE PROJECT PROPOSAL

Proving-in and selling video communication is a fairly routine exercise. One will probably develop a business case or project proposal. The document outlines the project vision in terms of a project overview, customer description, justification, and goals. It proposes a solution and describes the result of the solution's implementation, offers a plan of action (the tasks that must be carried out in order to implement the solution), considers the technical impact (not dependencies upon existing hardware or network) and provides a cost-benefit analysis.

The cost-benefit analysis documents the project's total development cost, which typically has several components: the purchase cost of the equipment, the installation cost for the network required to support video communication, the cost of any outside consulting required to make it operational, and the user and the IS personnel cost. Personnel costs include installing and operating the equipment and should be broken down by department or cost center. One should provide a total figure that includes all departmental costs. Using a company's own project cost worksheet is ideal; using some form of cost estimate worksheet is essential.

The proposal should include a statement about net gain in operations. This figure is the difference between current annual operating cost and future annual operating cost gained by the implementation of video communication. Operating costs are not limited to the IT organization, but include all direct cost savings to the corporation. Revenue saved by improving productivity and revenue gained by taking product to market early and eliminating travel could be included in this category.

The proposal should also list additional indirect benefits. These might include improved service and account management for a key customer, more up-to-date product information, or training to a distributed group of employees, enhanced decision making through the ability to include more people in the decision-making process, and other *soft-dollar* benefits. It is not always possible to attach a dollar value to these intangible advantages.

One should also include any specific evaluation criteria, the Chief Information Officer (CIO) or other senior executives will use to assess the impact of video communication on the organization. Those criteria will include outside influences. Several different types of outside influences apply to video communication. For instance, the federal Clean Air Act, American Disabilities Act, and Family Leave Act could all prompt implementation of visual communications tools within a company, particularly in support of telecommuting activities. Competitive pressures can also prompt the installation of video communication. Recall how Management Recruiters Incorporated (MRI) used video to reduce costs associated with executive search activities. MRI has stated that this action has proven to be a significant competitive advantage; its competitors may be considering the use of similar technology as a result of MRI's success. In still other cases, a key customer or business partner may request that an organization install video communication. In presenting video communication, one should identify outside influences, and detail the demands of each.

In evaluation criteria, one should also include the cost recovery period. Dividing total development cost by the net gain in operations derives this figure. From a financial perspective, a good investment is one with a positive net present value—that is, one whose value exceeds its costs. Most companies will not consider a project if they can not recover costs in a particular period of time—typically, 18 months or less. However, an organization may require video communication just to maintain market share (defensive investments), or to execute a critical transformation —although it may be hard to prove this beforehand.

A project proposal or business case should end with a statement of recommended action. That statement should reflect IT assessment of all the known facts and corporate activities. If video communication is viable, this section should present a recommendation that upper management approve funds and schedule the project. Some authorities suggest that an IT manager should prepare a purchase order in advance so she can implement the project without delay.

When presenting a recommendation, it is the very specific business benefit that has the most punch. For instance, rather than saying:

> *We recommend the purchase of video communication. Video communication can increase the number of contacts between marketing and engineering and reduce travel expense by $76,000. Travel savings will pay for all costs related to video communication within 14 months...*

it is better to say:

> *We recommend the purchase of video communication. It can increase the number of contacts between the marketing group in Georgia and the engineering group in Minnesota by 30% (80 additional group contacts per year) while improving productivity by 22% (38 trips eliminated with each representing 10 hours of lost productive time). This will allow the introduction of product X to be accelerated by nine months, and represent anticipated revenues of $78,000 per month. In addition, the tool will reduce travel expense by 12% ($76,000). Travel savings will pay for all costs related to video communication (capital and operational) within fourteen months, and ongoing savings will be approximately $50,000 annually.*

SELLING A RECOMMENDATION

Some video communication *sales* require little effort on the part of the IT professional: A senior-level project sponsor understands, and is ready to defend, the need for video. It is easy to articulate how the technology will be applied to solve one or more business problems; the company has evolved to the point that managers perceive the value of strategic investments.

However, most cases are a little more challenging. Perhaps mid-level managers realize there is an application and a need for video communication, but key decision-makers remain unconvinced. A critical step in the justification process might be familiarization through video communication trials and demonstrations. In all cases, it is best to use video communication to support actual business meetings rather than using canned demonstrations. One should test everything, and conduct at least one "dry-run" before "going live"—resolve lighting and audio issues, and become adept at moving cameras. The more mission-critical the meeting, the greater the risk. Therefore, if you are going to take risks, take measured risks. Presenting to every potential project champion at once is dangerous; the consequence of a calamity is too high.

As key individuals become comfortable with the technology and understand the potential benefits, they often become enthusiastic supporters. One is more likely to experience success if one addresses the technology only as it accomplishes the business at hand; the more transparent the technology is the better. Video communication technology must appear quite mature; it should appear as an "everybody is doing it" device. On the other hand, honesty is crucial. Do not demonstrate a boardroom system and recommend a rollabout. Managing expectations is a part of maintaining integrity.

Some video communication sales require an extended period of time. For instance, some companies are slow to change, or place a high value on "pressing flesh" and communicating face-to-face. Some corporate cultures simply do not embrace technology. Moreover, some companies foster a very strong bias toward *proving in* projects based on their internal rate of return (IRR). In a situation such as this last one, it might help to make the following point,

Although companies use diverse methods for evaluating strategic projects, one tenet holds true for all organizations. Methods for measuring financial performance are far more sophisticated and deeply entrenched than those used to measure strategic value. Since double-entry bookkeeping was developed, in the fifteenth century, accountants have been perfecting the art. Today, general accounting principles are codified and enforced by a vast institutional infrastructure that consists of public accounting firms, educators, and the government.

In contrast, methods for measuring customer satisfaction, market share, innovation, quality and organizational teamwork are much less well-defined. Metrics are infrequently generated; improvements are hard to document. Being competent in these areas is, however, widely recognized as critical to organizational survival. We simply have not yet turned that art into science. Performance measurements are still evolving.

By presenting video communication as a business enabler—much like telephone systems and fax machines—one can sometimes get past the initial reluctance to *bring in more technology*. Most senior managers would agree that telephone systems, computers, and fax machines are necessary. Video will be, in a very short period of time (it already is) another *must-have* communications tool. Seventy-two percent of companies with 1000 or more employees already use room-based systems; sixty percent of all companies use personal video systems. Video communication has moved to the mainstream.

TIPS FOR COLLECTING DATA

Bell Labs, the research arm that the seven RBOCs previously owned (now owned by Lucent Technologies), conducted early studies to determine how video communication can improve communication and, by extension, work. Although the findings were not conclusive, the Association of Computing Machinery published them in 1994 and they can provide valuable insight. A copy of the report, which can be obtained by calling the ACM in New York, New York, could provide some helpful insights into the business value of video communication.

Although we downplay travel as part of a business case for video communication, we should note that a good working relationship with one's travel department or travel agent could be extremely valuable. Most travel professionals are people-oriented service providers who know much about the organization. They know not only who travels most frequently (individuals and departments), they also know why they travel. They can prepare data on frequently traveled "city-pairs" and impart the average per-trip cost of air travel, lodging, car rental, and incidentals. In-house travel departments almost always know the size of the entire travel budget, and can usually attribute it by department. One must, however, recognize that video communication is *competition* to travel and that it is threatening to some travel professionals. This is particularly true of travel representatives who work on a commission-basis. In-house travel departments are usually compensated differently and can, therefore, afford to be helpful.

Knowing the total amount spent on travel, one can calculate direct savings. Savings will invariably result and should be represented in the business case. Often, such savings will cover system depreciation and operating costs. The many business benefits that come along with video communication can be "had for free." It is risky, however, to promise more than 15% travel reduction without flawless historical data and a senior-level manager who is committed to using it whenever possible.

Once travel savings are identified, one can engage with functional managers to formulate assumptions about the value of any productive time recovered. How can the organization reinvest salvaged time? Could people meet more often if meetings were electronically mediated? If so, could projects be completed more quickly? What is the financial implication of accelerating a project or process? What is the cost of *not* meeting?

Is there a high concentration of centrally-located employees who possess key skills that are in demand in remote locations (e.g., trainers, sales support, engineers, project managers)? What is the monetary value of increasing their reach? How could the organization invest reclaimed travel time to increase revenue and save money? Could one use video communication to spend more time in front of more customers? What is the return on responding more quickly to problems and opportunities?

Trade shows are a great source of information, especially such shows as Telecon or Computer Telephony. These events allow one to quickly gather a wealth of information and to meet resourceful people who have a vested interest in the success of video communication efforts.

In constructing a business case, one can start planning for the procurement of video communication. Contacting prospective suppliers early is useful as most actively gather and disseminate genuine applications information. Nearly all track the success of their customer's projects. PictureTel sponsors a "Best Practices" contest where customers submit detailed information on their projects and the results.

Some suppliers have innovative tools; for instance, Intel's Web site has many white papers that address the value of personal conferencing and it also offers a ProShare Conferencing Benefits Calculator. VTEL's Web site also includes a great deal of information on how to prove-in videoconferencing and interactive multimedia (VTEL's specialty). The Web site addresses of all suppliers mentioned appear in Appendix I of this book.

To conclude, suppliers are usually great allies; obviously they want such efforts to succeed. For that reason, an applications statement is a crucial component of any structured procurement document (e.g., request for proposal or request for information). The degree to which one clarifies and emphasizes objectives (to customers as well as suppliers) is the degree to which one will succeed in a video communication project. It is worth the effort.

CHAPTER 4 REFERENCES

Camp, Robert C. Benchmarking: The Search for Industry Best Practices that Lead to Superior Performance Quality Press, Milwaukee, Wisconsin, 1989 pp. 17-21.

Caruso, Jeff. "Mission: impossible?" CommunicationsWeek July 1, 1996 n617 p. 29.

Dickinson, Sarah. "Videoconferencing: hard sell, soft dollars," Data Communications May 1996 v25 n6 p. 35.

Dudman, Jane. "Have you been framed?" Computer Weekly February 8, 1996 p. 38.

Eccles, Robert G., "The Performance Manifesto," Harvard Business Review January-February, 1991, pp. 131-137.

Gilder, George. "Into the Telecosm," Harvard Business Review March-April, 1991 pp. 150-161.

Green, James Harry. The Irwin Handbook of Tele-Communications Management. Dow Jones-Irwin, Homewood, Illinois, 1989, 68-78.

House, Charles H. and Price, Raymond L., "The Return Map: Tracking Product Teams," Harvard Business Review January-February, 1991, pp. 92-100.

Porter, Michael E. "Competitive Strategy; Techniques for Analyzing Industries and Competitors," The Free Press, A Division of Macmillan Publishing Co., Incorporated pp. 7-83.

Robinson, Teri. "Where it all begins: desktops: end-user applications drive the technology," CommunicationsWeek March 18, 1996 n601 p. S7.

Simon, Alan R. How to be a Successful Computer Consultant, 2nd Ed. McGraw Hill, San Francisco, California, 1990, pp. 101-114.

Smith, Laura B. "By the numbers," PC Week June 17, 1996 v13 n24 p. E1.

Synnott, William R. The Information Weapon John Wiley and Sons, Incorporated 1987, 93-122.

Portway, Patrick. "Videoconferencing Market Forecasts," Teleconference: Telecon XVI Show Issue, October 1996 Volume 15, Number 5.

PART TWO

TECHNOLOGIES AND STANDARDS FOR VIDEO COMMUNICATIONS

5

THE HISTORY AND TECHNOLOGY OF ANALOG VIDEO

When we stop talking about the technology, that's when it will be here.

Dr. Norman Gaut

In this chapter we will summarize the significant events that paved the way for videoconferencing. Those who are not interested in history may want to skim through the first part in which we trace the development of television. In the latter part of chapter (the part one should not skip) we explain how broadcasting techniques evolved, why there are different television systems in different parts of the world, and what those systems are. We also examine how visual communication technologies "trick the eye," how cameras work, what scanning is, and how, together, the technologies capture and display an analog video communications signal.

To people born after World War II, television is not a marvel of technology but a simple fact of life. It is an object of fascination only when we see ourselves on it and, when we do, our experience with the technology causes us to want TV quality; this provides a distinct challenge for today's video communication systems that use only a fraction of television's bandwidth. First demonstrated in the 1920s, television is the predecessor of video. As is true with most technology, it is nearly impossible to establish the precise time at which TV was "invented." Centuries of experiments combined successively to produce the telegraph, the radio, the television and, now, two-way interactive video communications.

We are still living in the age of discovery, and gifted engineers and scientists in all parts of the world are pushing the limits of video compression, transmission, and applications. This golden age of technology began when early scientists applied the principles of electromagnetic waves to communications over distance.

RADIO—SOMETHING IN THE AIR

The Europe of the nineteenth century was the center of the developed world. Commerce was controlled via communications between the great cities of Europe—London, Paris, and Berlin. Moving information faster between these centers meant achieving great competitive advantage. When Samuel Morse, in 1842, devised the telegraph code, it was immediately heralded as a tool for accelerating trade. Almost overnight, people were transmitting intelligible coded messages between Berlin and Paris over the world's first long-haul telegraph system. By the end of the nineteenth century, all the continents were linked by telegraph networks that were owned and operated by huge companies, the first of the global corporations created to operate for a profit across national boundaries.

Wires were expensive to place, however, and cable costly to maintain. A wireless transmission method was soon introduced. In the late 1860s, James Clark Maxwell, a Scot, used mathematics to prove that electromagnetic waves should exist and that they should travel at approximately the speed of light. Twenty years later, a German, Heinrich Hertz, demonstrated the validity of Maxwell's theory when he devised an apparatus for detecting and producing electromagnetic waves. An electromagnetic wave is characterized by its frequency that is commonly diagrammed as a sine wave (Figure 5-1). Sine waves are portrayed as a continuous series of S-shapes placed on their sides. A conceptual base line, (zero crossing point), bisects the "S." One such "S" is a wave cycle. Each cycle has a positive polarity when the wave rises above the zero crossing point and a negative polarity when it drops below.

The breakthrough Hertz made was enormously important to electronic communications. For a period after he introduced his scientific work, electromagnetic waves were called Hertzian waves. The frequency of their oscillations was measured in cycles. Later, in the 1960s, the term hertz replaced the word cycles in describing the number of complete cycles occurring in a second. Throughout this book we will use terms such as kHz (in which 'K' means kilo, or thousand) and MHz (mega, or million Hz).

In 1891, an Irish-Italian, Guglielmo Marconi, began experimenting with the newly discovered potential of Hertzian waves. He proceeded to explore antennas or, what he called, "aerials," and proved the importance of a grounded connection to a complete wireless transmission system. The French joined the effort the same year when Edouard Branly perfected an apparatus for intercepting wireless impulses. The device intercepted Hertzian waves in the air and caused them to ring an electric bell. The English made a contribution when Sir William Crookes proved the theoretical feasibility of "telegraphy through space" in an article published in the "Fortnightly Review." In 1895, Thomas Edison patented a system of induction telegraphy that included elements that later advanced wireless communications. In 1831, Michael Faraday (an Englishman) discovered induction by showing that a current

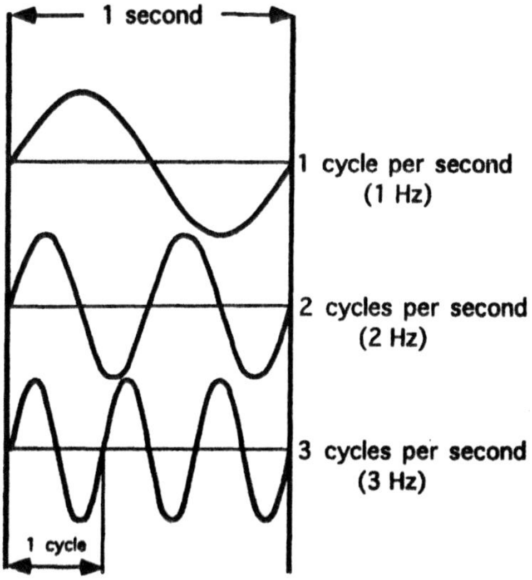

Figure 5-1. Sine Wave (Michel Bayard)

in one wire could produce a current in another wire.

Finally, in 1895, Marconi amalgamated all the principles just mentioned, added some of his own science and applied for the first patent for a wireless telegraph. Once granted, it became the basis for his Marconi Wireless Telegraph Company, the world's first commercial radio service. In 1901, Marconi was able to receive the three dots of the letter 'S' in a transoceanic broadcast between England's Cornwall coast and Canada's Newfoundland. He went on to establish the first regular commercial transatlantic wireless telegraph service in 1907.

In 1901, Dr. Reginald Aubrey Fessenden, a professor at Pittsburgh's Weston University, took another huge stride forward when he succeeded in transmitting and receiving the human voice without wires. Fessenden, instead of interrupting a wireless wave with signal bursts, decided to alter the inherent characteristics of a sine wave (in this case, its amplitude), by superimposing another signal over it. The carrier or sideband, over which the second signal travels, is a wave of extremely accurate frequency. Fessenden's approach, today called amplitude modulation (AM), became the foundation for broadcast technologies.

Fessenden filed a series of patents that described continuous transmission and formed the National Electric Signaling Company. In 1906, working with a Swedish-born scientist, Ernst F. W. Alexanderson, he created an alternating current generator and used it to power a radio transmitter located at Brant Rock, Massachusetts. From that location, the first broadcast of sounds, not letters, was transmitted on Christmas Eve, 1906. It started when Fessenden tapped out a series of CQ signals used to gain the attention of radio operators. Once done, he broadcast a live Christmas concert complete with music and readings from the Bible. At the end of the historical broadcast, Fessenden requested that anyone receiving the signal contact him. Many did, including representatives of the United Fruit Company. Its wireless operators on banana boats in the West Indies heard the broadcast. United Fruit, impressed with the possibilities of ship-to-shore communications, immediately placed an order for a system.

A month later an American, Lee De Forrest applied for a patent on his three-element amplifier that he called the Audion tube. An improvement on an earlier two-element tube, it had the power needed to push a radio or television signal over great distance. De Forrest and his assistant were in a Manhattan laboratory testing the Audion when they decided to conduct an experiment. At random, they broadcast the William Tell overture. An astonished wireless operator in Brooklyn Naval Yard four miles away who could not understand why he was getting music through his headset intercepted the transmission. The radio tube was born.

By the end of World War I radio tubes were being mass-produced. The term "radio" derived from the fact that signals from transmitters radiate out in all directions and, by 1912, the term replaced the word "wireless." It was around that time that David Sarnoff, the legendary promoter of American television, began his rise up through the ranks of the Marconi Wireless Company.

Sarnoff, a Russian immigrant, arrived in the U.S. in 1900. In 1919, Sarnoff left Marconi to join the newly formed Radio Corporation of America (RCA). By 1920, RCA had launched two radio stations, KDKA of Pittsburgh and WWJ of Detroit; they were soon making regular broadcasts. Within the next two years, radio experienced explosive growth that was only surpassed by that of its cousin, television.

SPINNING DISKS AND SHOOTING ELECTRONS

During this same era, the foundation was being laid for today's visual communications systems. No one individual can be credited with inventing the television—as was true with radio, it was a collective, though not always cooperative, effort. It might be said that the process started when a couple of British telegraphy engineers discovered, in the 1870s, some interesting properties of the element selenium. Selenium conducted electricity better when it was exposed to a light source than when it was left in darkness. This discovery was developed into a system in which a source of light was placed at one end of a circuit and selenium at the other. If an object passed between the light and the selenium, it would interrupt the flow of electricity. When a group of these circuits was combined, it could create a mosaic of light.

Many inventors began experimenting with selenium—Alexander Graham Bell was one. In 1880, Bell invented something he called the photophone. It used selenium to transmit a visual display of the frequencies that comprised the human voice. Today, it seems astonishing that Bell ignored the potential of image transmission unless one understands that Bell's priority was to leverage another medium to simulate sound so that his deaf wife could better communicate.

Others had different priorities. Paul Nipkow, a German university student in Berlin, became entranced with the idea of image scanning. He developed a spherical disc that he perforated with holes. The apertures of the disk were positioned such that, as the disc revolved at a specific speed, each hole swept over a segment of a picture (Figure 5-2). When rotated between an object and a light source, it reproduced a crude electrical representation of the original object by responding to variations in light. The concept provided a framework for image reproduction by using electrical signals, but was far too slow to offer any picture quality. Nevertheless, Nipkow's German patent No. 30,105, which was awarded in 1883, was termed "the master patent in the television field."

In 1893, Archibald Campbell-Swinton, a Scottish engineer, made an address to the Roentgen Society. In his address, he outlined plans for an electronic television system that was remarkably similar to that which the British Broadcasting Company (BBC) later adopted, in 1937. Campbell-Swinton never made a television or similar apparatus; his work was purely theoretical.

In 1907, a German professor, Boris Rosing of the Technical Institute of St. Petersburg, became interested in understanding how images could be produced using electrical means. His research led him to develop a prototype device—the first cathode ray tube or CRT. It produced crude outlines of shapes using a rotation-mirror image to transmit a signal received by a cold-cathode picture tube. Magnetic coils generated the scanning signals the tube required. It was the world's first glimpse of television.

Although Rosing's CRT produced only faint patterns with no light or shade, it attracted the attention of one of his students, Vladimir Kosma Zworykin. Fascinated with the CRT, Zworykin continued to perfect it after immigrating to America in 1917. While employed at Westinghouse, in 1923, he filed a patent for a television receiver. By 1924, he was able to demonstrate the technology—a seven-inch CRT that used electrostatic and electromagnetic deflection to steer an electron beam. This first picture tube was so crude that it could basely transmit a single character. It was, however, a fundamental component of the television system that Zworykin proceeded to invent.

Next, Zworykin developed an improved image-scanning device. It replaced Nipkow's disc, which was mechanical, with an electronic technique. Combining the Greek words "icon" (image) and "scope" (to watch), Zworykin called the invention an iconoscope (Figure 5-3). It was a CRT with a lens on an angled shaft. At the back of the device, an electron gun focused a beam of electrons on a target that consisted

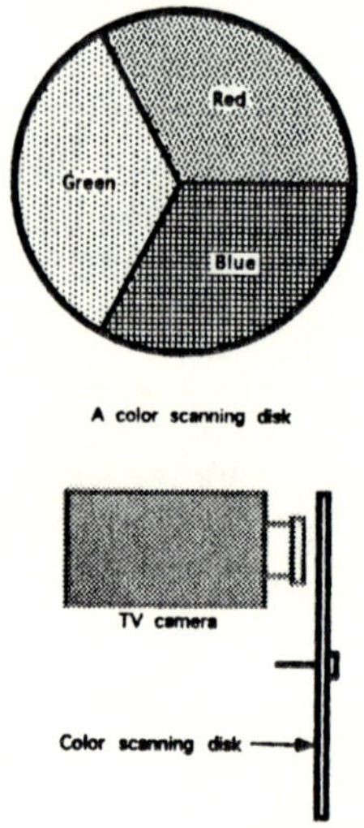

Figure 5-2. Nipkow Disk (Michel Bayard).

of a mica plate that was covered with tiny photosensitive cesium-silver droplets. The beam of electrons varied in accordance to the light captured from the original image. As the beam passed over the cesium-silver droplets, it energized them. The change in their charge induced a current in the signal plate, and varied in relation to the lights and shadows along each line of the picture. The result was a coded signal that was passed along a transmission path and decoded by a television's picture tube. The original image was recreated from behind, and appeared on the screen as a series of glowing dots that formed a picture.

In 1925, Zworykin filed a patent application for his electronic television system. That same year, an American inventor named Charles Jenkins used mechanical means (Nipkow's disc) to produce a system that transmitted a picture of a waving hand. The signal was carried via radio between Washington D.C. and Philadelphia. RCA acquired the rights to most of Jenkin's inventions when the Great Depression, in 1930, claimed Jenkins Television Corporation as one of its many casualties.

Across the ocean, a Scot, John Logie Baird, was also experimenting with television. In April 1925, he exhibited a working prototype that produced a decidedly low-definition picture with eight lines of resolution. The demonstration featured two images: a wooden ventriloquist's dummy named Bill (who did little but sit quietly for the event), and the live moving head of His Royal Highness, the Prince of Wales, the future King Edward VIII. As was true of Jenkins' television, Baird's system relied on Nipkow's disc to produce electro-mechanical images. What it lacked in electronic sophistication, it compensated for with results. Unlike Zworykin's transmissions that were crude outlines of a scanned object, Baird's system transmitted images complete with gradations of light and shade.

Thus began the race for television. Baird was often at the head of the pack. In 1926, he offered the first formal public broadcast of his television system. Viewers could clearly see the head of Bill the dummy, back on the set for another go. It was a higher-definition Bill; Baird's screen now boasted 30 resolvable lines. Moreover, having just secured a radio license from the Post Office (which was also in charge of broadcasts), Baird was transmitting from his own experimental television station, 2TV, that was based in Harrow, England.

With the help of an investment firm, Baird formally launched the Baird Television Development Company in 1927. Investors were told Baird had a monopoly on television. Meanwhile, in America, researchers at Bell Labs had developed an electromechanical television using motor-controlled scanners to capture images. An array of neon tubes collectively formed a display. On April 9, 1927, they presented the technology to the public across a distance of over 200 miles in a transmission between Washington D.C. and New York. Word of the demonstration reached England on April 28, the day after Baird's public offering had closed.

Shareholders furiously claimed that they had been misled, but Baird redeemed himself when he sent pictures by telephone line over a distance of 435 miles between London and Glasgow. Although the images flickered and some were unsteady, it was a major achievement. In 1928, Baird dispatched 30-line pictures between England and New York through an amateur short-wave radio station with a35 foot antenna. The New York Times proclaimed: "Baird was the first to achieve television at all, over any distance. Now he must be credited with having been the first to disembody the human form optically and electrically, flash it piecemeal across the ocean and then reassemble it for American eyes. His success deserves to rank with Marconi's sending of the letter S."

In 1928, Baird demonstrated color television by transmitting images of blue flowers and red berries in a white basket. To do this, he used a transmitter with three interlaced spirals, one with a red filter, another green, and a third blue. The first transmission of RGB (red, green, blue) component television signal was achieved. Next, Baird recorded video frequencies, noting the distinctive "sound" of a subject. He eventually filed a British patent for his "Phonovision." The device incorporated discs and played like a record to produce a recognizable picture—it foreshadowed the VCR and the videodisk.

In 1928, Baird astonished the public by demonstrating a three-D color television. On the receiving screen, two images were displayed that were separated by one-half an inch. One corresponded to objects as seen by the right eye, the other as seen by the left. When viewed through a stereoscopic device the two images merged.

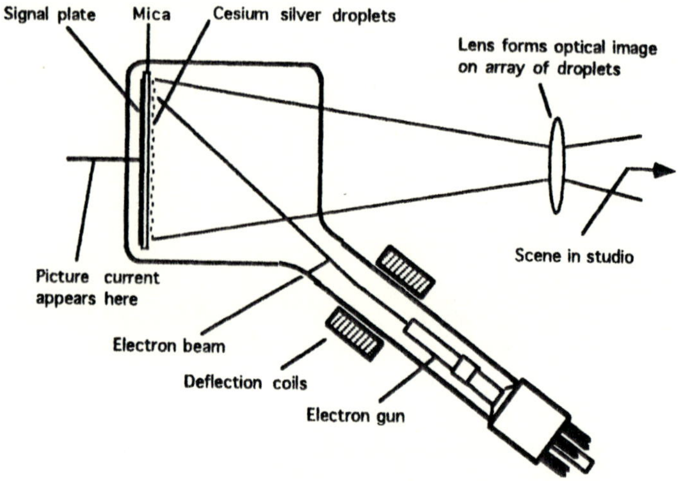

Figure 5-3. Iconoscope (Michel Bayard)

The BBC, still focused on radio, reacted negatively to Baird's new technology that complicated their existence. However, in 1929, they allowed Baird to use their medium-wave transmitters to broadcast experimental television programs. The morning broadcasts each lasted thirty minutes. Sound and vision alternated every two minutes. In 1930, Baird and the BBC achieved simultaneous transmission of picture and sound. In 1931, Baird helped the BBC make their first-ever-scheduled outdoor transmission. Viewers in a London theater saw the Derby broadcast direct from Long Acre, filmed from a van situated next to the finish line. As the winner, Cameronian, galloped past the post, viewers heard the roaring crowd, almost as if they were there themselves. The event, a huge success, was repeated in 1932.

On August 22, 1932, the BBC inaugurated a 30-line television system. It produced a pinkish picture that was received horizontally. A lift-up lid, with a mirror on the underside, displayed the image. One was installed at 10 Downing Street and, by 1933, almost 10,000 TV receivers had been sold in the UK. Nevertheless, Baird was frustrated with TV's general progress. He was restricted by British regulations to the use of medium-wave transmission. This limited him to thirty lines of resolution with only 12.5 frames sent each second. Later, as ultra short waves were introduced, he increased his resolution to 600 lines with a higher frame rate.

In the U.S., television was still very experimental; no sets were installed in homes. In 1930, RCA demonstrated large-screen television at a theater in New York. The screen consisted of over 2,000 small lamps that each contributed to a particular element in the picture. Elsewhere, the big news was radio. Its popularity had exploded, and stations proliferated. Transmissions began to encroach on one another. All the activity over the airwaves prompted Congress to create the Federal

Radio Commission through passage of the Radio Act of 1927. In 1928, the FRC established classes of stations by geographic zone. It was too little too late. General Electric was operating what could be described as an experimental TV station, WGY that was based in Schenectady, New York. It broadcast the first TV drama that year. However, the Act neither addressed television broadcast, nor asserted jurisdiction over telegraph and telephone carriers.

In 1929, Vladimir Zworykin and David Sarnoff, both born in Russia, met for the first time. Zworykin was interested in joining RCA to pursue television technology. However, as a condition of employment, he required Sarnoff to renounce electro-mechanical television and commit to electronic methods, even though they still faced many unsolved problems. Sarnoff asked Zworykin to estimate RCA's cost to prepare electronic TV for commercial use. Zworykin placed it at $100,000, and Sarnoff consented. Over a 12-year period, RCA's development of television exceeded Zworykin's estimate and cost nearly $50 million. Nevertheless, Zworykin prospered at RCA, and basked in the luxury of a large research budget and supportive executives. In that fertile environment, he perfected his science. There was only one real problem. In Provo, Utah, a youth named Philo T. Farnsworth was far ahead of everybody. He was busy filing important patents.

Farnsworth, unlike Zworykin, did not have a sponsor with deep pockets. Self-taught but brilliant, he received sporadic funding from small investors. In 1928, he demonstrated the world's first all-electronic television system. It was based on a camera that Farnsworth called an "image dissector." By 1939, he had coupled the camera with a sophisticated picture tube to intensify the dissected image.

The system was far more sensitive than was anything RCA could conceive and develop, but Farnsworth would not sell his patents. RCA took to the courts in a strategy that eventually cost more than $2 million. Another $7 million went for research in an effort to get around Farnsworth's technology. Eventually, aware that they would fall behind in the global race for television, RCA gave Farnsworth his price. At age 34 he retired to a farm in Maine. Zworykin and Sarnoff, both Russians, went down in history as the fathers of American television. At the 1939 New York World's Fair, the first RCA "high-definition" television set was inaugurated; it had 441 lines of resolution. The National Broadcasting Company (NBC) provided the broadcast.

In 1933, Franklin D. Roosevelt requested that his Secretary of Commerce convene an inter-agency committee to study how the U.S. should regulate electronic communications. The airwaves of the day were awash with signals. The committee recommended that Congress establish a single agency to regulate all interstate and foreign wire and radio communications including television, telegraph, and telephone. Congress, in turn, passed the Communications Act of 1934. It created the Federal Communications Commission (FCC) that began operation on June 11, 1934. One of its important tasks was to manage the airwaves; it did so by allocating the spectrum among companies wishing to use it. The FCC also inherited the task of approving television standards.

TELEVISION STANDARDS AND TECHNOLOGY

The year 1934 marked the beginning of the standards wars. England was in the process of investigating a new television system—something with more than Baird's 30 lines of resolution. There were two contenders: Baird's system, now producing a mechanically-scanned non-interlaced 240-line television picture, and Marconi-EMI's all-electronic system that interlaced two fields to produce 405 image lines. The BBC placed the two systems in direct competition in a series of trials. In May 1937, it selected Marconi-EMI's system as its standard, and broadcast George VI's coronation to 60,000 people.

By 1937, RCA had rectified their television system but faced new problems. The television industry could not agree on a common standard. In 1936, the Radio Manufacturers Association (RMA), which was backed by RCA, set up a committee to approve a system. In 1937, they rubber-stamped RCA's 441-line 30 frames per second (fps) proposal. However, RCA's iron grip on the industry inspired controversy and, in 1940, the FCC chairman intervened to order additional study. NBC, which had been broadcasting since the 1939 World's Fair, was downgraded from a licensed to an experimental station until the difficulties could be resolved.

A flurry of hearings ensued. On April 30, 1941, the FCC approved an amplitude-modulated monochrome television system. A video frame, by definition, contained 525 scanning lines. Each second, thirty such frames were to be transmitted and synchronized with frequency-modulated audio. The system was analog; the electron flow that was sent as a signal was analogous to the original waveform.

As part of the standard, the FCC determined the range of frequencies to allocate to each television channel. They specified that monochrome television signals be modulated onto radio frequency (RF) carrier waves with bandwidths of 4.2 MHz. Each channel would occupy 6 MHz of bandwidth. Starting at 4.5 MHz, audio information would be transmitted above video. Unused bandwidth above the audio and below the video would protect the signal from interfering with other channels.

On July 1, 1941, the FCC licensed NBC and the newly formed Columbia Broadcasting System (CBS) to operate commercial television stations in the U.S. They promptly began broadcasting.

In 1945, the FCC allocated spectrum space for 13 television channels, all of which were assigned in the very-high frequency (VHF) band occupying the spectrum between 54 and 216 MHz. Also interspersed in this band were FM, mobile and emergency radio, and air navigation signals. When channel one was eventually deleted, only 12 channels remained. Soon afterward, U.S. entry into World War II arrested all television progress. A ban was placed on manufacture because it siphoned resources away from the war effort. It was only after the war ended, in

1946, that television broadcasting resumed in earnest.

In 1952, the FCC established the ultra-high frequency (UHF) television with UHF channels; they were numbered 14 through 83, and extended from 470 to 890 MHz. The FCC also reserved TV channels for non-commercial educational stations, specified mileage separation distances for TV stations to reduce the potential of interference, and made city-by-city television assignments.

The monochrome image on the TV sets of the 1950s needed frequent adjustment. Viewers had to fiddle with vertical and horizontal hold, twist knobs to juggle light-dark contrast and fuss with the antennae to eliminate ghost-like images and snow. Even so, television achieved overnight acceptance. Market penetration accelerated from 6% in 1949 (in which 100% equaled the total number of households in America), to 49% by 1953. This was an average growth rate of over 300% for the first five years of commercial operation.

In the post-war U.S., the viewers' real preference was not monochrome, however, but color. It had been available in Europe for some time. Americans were not to be outdone. The FCC started exploring ways of adding color to the existing monochrome system and, in 1950, tentatively endorsed a solution developed by CBS. Called a field-sequential system, it worked as follows: a monochrome camera scanned an image—just as with black-and-white TV. But, unlike monochrome filming, a color wheel that was divided into transparent RGB sectors was placed in front of the lens (see Figure 5-4). The timing of the rotation was such that a colored sector appeared in front of the lens for exactly one field. The resulting sequence of fields corresponded to the color components in the image. At the television receiver, another color-filter disk that was synchronized exactly with the color field rotated in front of the picture tube.

The system was bulky, noisy, and prone to wear. It required exact synchrony between the rotating filter and the fields presented on the picture tube—if the timing was off, color shift would take place. But the biggest problem with field-sequential color was incompatibility with the monochrome system of the day. The color system generated 24 fps—not 30. Scanning lines were likewise reduced—instead of 525, the system offered 405, as did European TV systems.

The FCC could have ignored the incompatibility and introduced color television as a separate system. In 1967, the English began the laborious process of converting from their 405-line color system to a 625-line color system that was compatible with their monochrome system. The changeover required considerable investment in new broadcast and studio equipment. English broadcasters were required to transmit programs that conformed to both standards until dual-standard receivers could be developed. The FCC avoided this by rescinding their endorsement of the field-sequential system in anticipation of a system that would enable the coexistence of color telecasting on the same channels with monochrome TV. To identify a solution, they established, in 1950, the National Television Systems Committee (NTSC). Three years later, in December 1953, the NTSC defined a color-telecasting

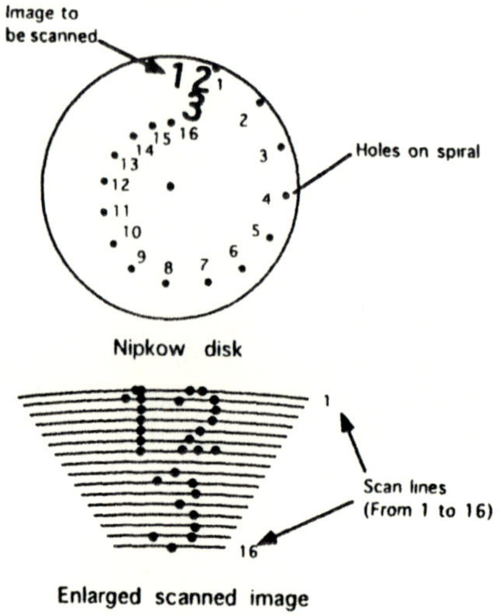

Figure 5-4. Field Sequential System (Michel Bayard).

FROM LIGHT WAVES TO BRAIN WAVES

To understand the NTSC system of color telecasting, it is helpful to understand how eyes process light. Simply stated, eyes capture patterns of light and send them to the brain for interpretation. Television exploits the eyes' properties and is patterned after them.

The human eye's structure parallels that of a camera. At the front of the eye is the transparent cornea. It captures a picture of the outside world and forms an image. Behind the cornea is the iris, a circular muscle that expands and contracts to control the amount of light that enters the eye. It is similar to an automatic exposure system in a camera. The lens focuses an image by changing shape to accommodate differences between close and distant subjects. Behind the lens is a fluid-filled compartment on the surface of which is the retina. This is made up of over one hundred million tiny photoreceptors called rods and cones. Rods, which are exceedingly sensitive, respond to brightness only, and thereby describe an image to the brain in shades of gray. Cones, on the other hand, are concentrated toward the center of the retina. They respond to color, specifically, light of three different wavelengths that we know better as red, green, and blue. Blending these three colors in the brain derives all other colors.

Each rod and cone are connected to an individual fiber in the optic nerve. When we scan an image, the messages sent by the rods and cones create in the brain a very

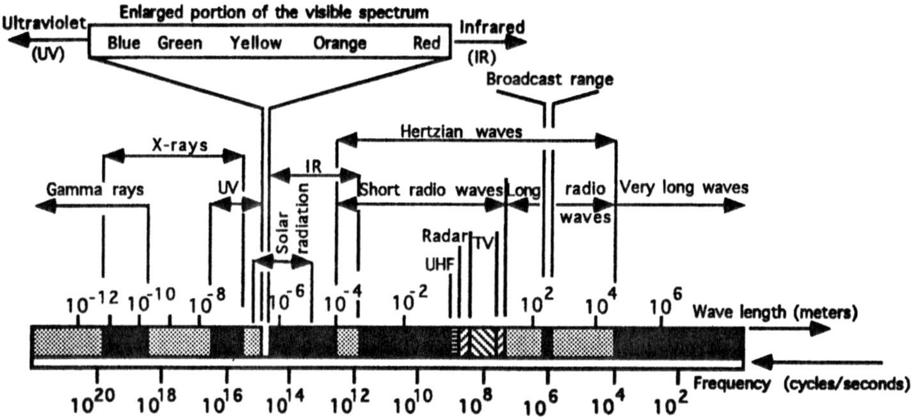

Figure 5-5. Frequency Chart: From X-rays to Radio Waves (Michel Bayard)

high-resolution light "mosaic" that the brain interprets as an image.

Visible light—color—is but a small interval in the spectrum of electromagnetic radiation. This radiation, which fills the universe, possesses dual characteristics of waves and particles. The particles, called photons, contain energy. It can be expressed in any unit from calories to kilowatt-hours although, for the purposes of video communications, energy is measured in electron volts (ev). The energy of visible light varies from two to four ev.

The particles that comprise electromagnetic radiation are assembled in waves. A particular signal's frequency can be determined by measuring the number of wave-crest cycles that pass a fixed point in one second. Although frequency is typically measured in hertz, it is not practical to use the traditional system to measure light—the frequencies we are dealing with are too high. Therefore, we discuss these waves in terms of their lengths. Light waves have lengths of between 380–770 nanometers (10–9 meters), in other words, between 16 and 28 millionths of an inch. We describe these various wavelengths by giving them color names—violet, blue, green, yellow, orange, and red.

The exact length of a wave determines its color, but most visible lights we see are blends of three primary colors—red, green, and blue (RGB). These colors are referred to as additive primaries—in contrast to the subtractive primaries cyan, yellow, and magenta (because the printing process also requires black ink, these are commonly referred to as CMYK). Additive color is that which emanates directly from a light source, and subtractive color is that which reflects off a surface (e.g., a sheet of paper, a sweater, or a blade of grass). In the case of subtractive color, an object possesses no actual color properties until a white light shines on it, and the

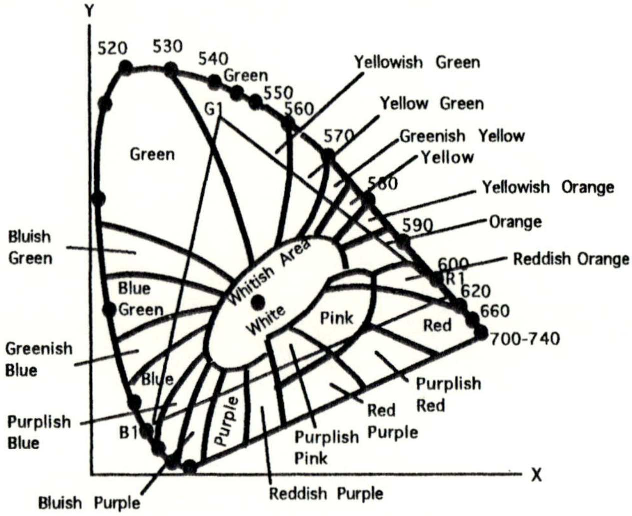

Figure 5-6. Chromaticity Chart (Michel Bayard).

pigments in its surface selectively reflect or absorb wavelengths. The light waves reflected are those we perceive to be an object's color: the paint covering a yellow car absorbs all frequencies except those with wavelengths that we know as yellow. In video communication, we are primarily concerned with additive primaries.

In 1931, the Commission Internationale de l'Eclairage (CIE) set forth international standards for color measurement. They defined the actual wavelengths of colors. Red has a wavelength of 700 nanometers, green, 546 nm, and blue, 435.8 nm. In 1950, the FCC redefined the standard to better adapt it to the phosphors used in TV picture tubes. The FCC's red is 610 nm, green is 534 nm, and blue is 472 nm. The NTSC recognized the FCC's color definitions when they developed the 1953 standard for color telecasting.

A chromaticity chart, shown in Figure 5-6, demonstrates that blending the primary colors in various combinations can produce any color used in television. However, it is not possible to create primaries themselves from other primaries. They are unique.

Scanning and Framing

Of course, the process of capturing an image for a television or video application involves the use of a camera. Cameras work much like eyes. They scan a scene to detect, capture, and transform light waves into electricity.

The first all-electronic camera was the image-orthicon tube that RCA introduced in 1941. The more compact and simple vidicon tube was developed in 1951. It trained

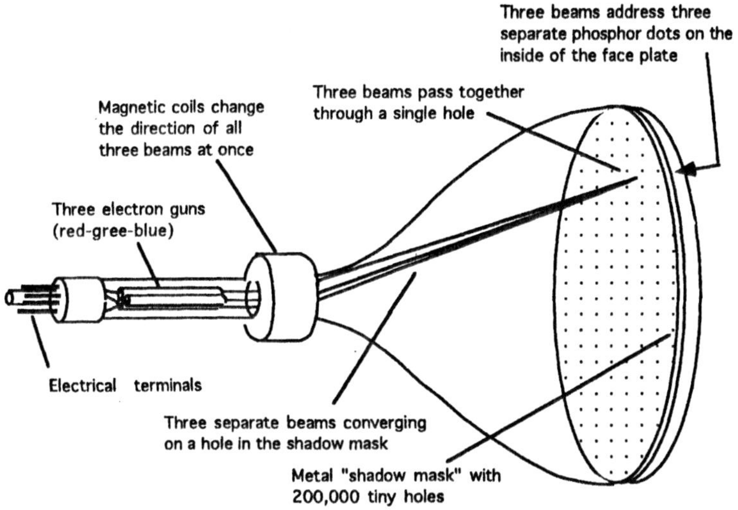

Figure 5-7. Scanning in the Picture Tube (Michel Bayard).

an electron beam, a scanning point, on an image. The beam swept the image left-to-right and top-to-bottom, measuring the scene's photosensitive surface.

Conventional optical techniques are used to focus the light onto a target area at the rear of the tube's faceplate. The back of the target is coated with a transparent, electrically-conductive substance, and a photoresistive coating. The light of an image passes through the transparent conductor and strikes the photoresistive coating, and thereby produces a charge that varies in proportion to the light that strikes it. An electron beam behind the target measures the fluctuating charges and translates them into a series of voltages that are proportional to the changing light intensity. Heating a cathode creates the electron beam that does the measuring. It is focused using principles of static electricity. Electromagnetic deflection coils that are placed around the neck of the vidicon tube move the beam vertically and horizontally.

Color cameras separate light waves into RGB components using prisms, color filters, or dichroic mirrors. Once RGB signals were separated, older systems used multiple camera tubes to apply these principles. Today's cameras utilize solid state chips known as charge-coupled devices (CCDs) to store the electrical charges that make up the light's intensity. The charges are transferred to another layer called a frame buffer where they are formatted. Next, a formatted electrical signal, with an amplitude directly proportional to the amplitude of the light, is sent across some type of transmission medium or network. It is received and displayed on a viewer's screen or monitor.

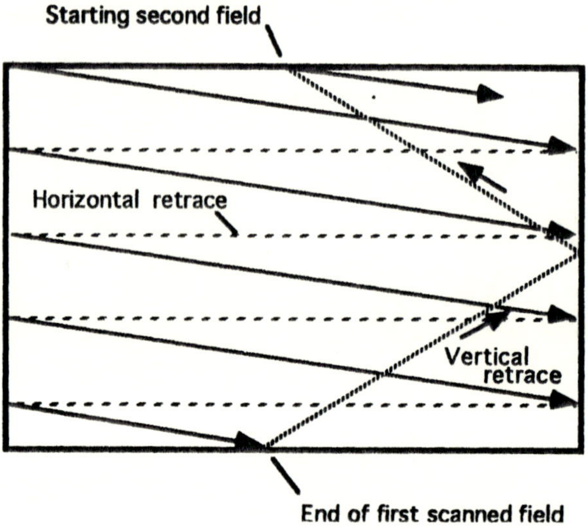

Figure 5-8. TV Raster Scan (Michel Bayard).

Video transmission networks are not like the optic nerve. The nerve is a huge number of separate fibers that each carries a minuscule part of the image to the brain. All operate in parallel and the brain receives a single image made up of many, many parts. Video communication networks could never cost-justify parallel communications. Processing images with human vision techniques would require hundreds of thousands of channels. Each would have to be synchronized with all the others. Parallel communication is not feasible over distance—it is too complex and costly to have separate paths for each information bit.

Video communications technologies rely on dividing an image into lines containing picture bits and transmitting them serially—one after the other. The video image is, therefore, a mosaic of light, and the "tiles," or points of light, are called picture elements (also called *pixels*). The term is abbreviated to *pel* in broadcast TV parlance. In the fields of telecommunications and computing (and, therefore, throughout this book), they are called pixels.

The image on a video monitor is constructed before our eyes one pixel at a time. What looks like a continuously moving picture is actually a series of still images called frames. If a series of still image frames is sent fast enough, they fuse in our minds and appear to be moving. The faster the frame rate, the better the fusion, and the smoother the motion will appear to be.

In the early 1820s, Peter Mark Roget, a doctor who specialized in vision (and the father of the Thesaurus) began to experiment with the properties of human vision. In 1824, he delivered a paper to the Royal Society in which he introduced the concept of "persistence of vision." It can be defined as the brain's ability to retain the impression of light after the original stimulus has been removed. The brain

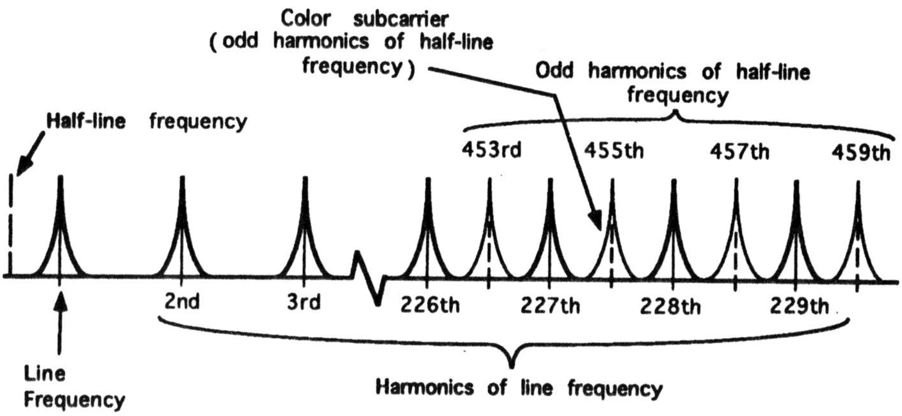

Figure 5-9. Color Television Spectral Detail (Michel Bayard).

holds the light for about one tenth of a second, although it starts to fade almost immediately upon receipt. Therefore, if images are sent at a rate of at least 10 fps, they appear to be continuous, though somewhat jerky. Somewhere between 10 and 20 fps the jerkiness completely disappears. A new image is presented long before the old one fades appreciably. The brain fails to see that the video monitor is "blinking" images.

Different video applications use different frame rates. Television standards specify that video frames be sent at a rate of between 25 and 30 per second, depending on which standard is being applied. Scanning systems reflect the electrical systems that exist in a country. In Europe and other parts of the world that Europeans colonized, the national electrical system operates at 50 Hz. In the U.S. and most of the rest of the world, the electrical system delivers alternating current at a rate of 60 Hz. These differences caused television systems to evolve dissimilarly. The U.S., Mexico, Canada, and Japan (and 19 other countries) use the NTSC system. Europe, Australia, Africa and parts of Asia and South America, use a television system that specifies 25 fps. The number of lines of resolution varies from 625 in England and much of Western Europe, to 819 in France, Russia and Eastern Europe.

A frame of video is displayed by reversing the camera's scanning process. Images are painted on a screen using a process called raster-scan. The process starts with heat. The cathode gets hot and thereby causes electrons to stream from a device called an electron gun. The beam of electrons, sometimes referred to as a reproducing spot, continuously bombards the inside surface of a monitor. The beam traces its course in a series of thin lines, striking phosphor dots that coat the inside of the monitor. When hit with an electron, an individual phosphor emits light.

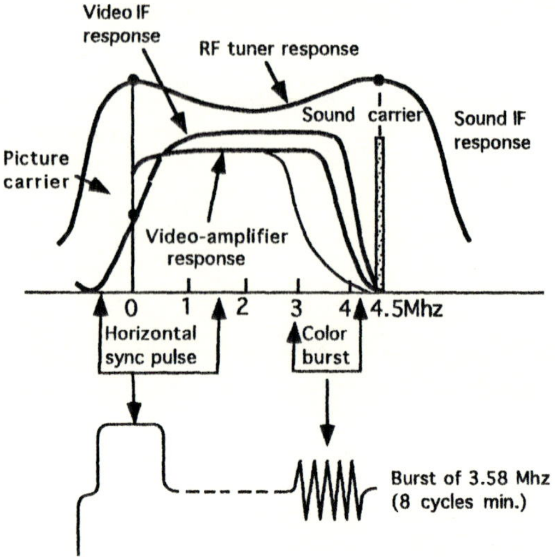

Figure 5-10. Color Burst (Michel Bayard).

Starting at the top-left, the spot sweeps horizontally to the right, and completes the task in about 50 microseconds (μs). At that point, for 10 μs, the beam shuts off and the electron gun executes a carriage return that is referred to as the *horizontal blanking interval.* After the blanking interval, the beam starts up again on a new line. The process continues until the spot reaches the lower right-hand corner of the screen where it shuts off again during the vertical blanking interval. Next, *retrace* occurs as the reproducing spot returns to the top of the screen. This process continues left to right, top to bottom, synchronized by oscillators that keep the electron operating strictly on schedule. As the horizontal oscillator drives the electron stream laterally, the vertical oscillator moves slowly downward. In that manner, the illusion of motion is produced using still-image frames.

Although we have just asserted that North American television incorporates a frame rate of 30 per second, adding color to the television signal requires that the rate be dropped to 29.97 fps (although most people round it to 30). Each 525-line video frame is divided into two halves, each of which is called a field. One of the 262.5-line fields contains the odd scan lines, and the other contains the even ones. During display, first the odd-line field then the even field is painted in a process called field-interlacing. Interlaced fields of video are sent at a rate of 59.94 fps. Why divide an image in half? Why not send complete frames with the odd and even lines combined? The answer is in the eye of the beholder. Although the brain retains the perception of light for one-tenth of a second, the image starts to fade instantly. If complete video frames are sent at a rate of 30 per second, the eye senses the change in light intensity and images appear to flicker. For most people, images fuse at frame rates faster than 40 per second. To solve flicker problems, each image is displayed twice using a shutter speed of 60 images per second.

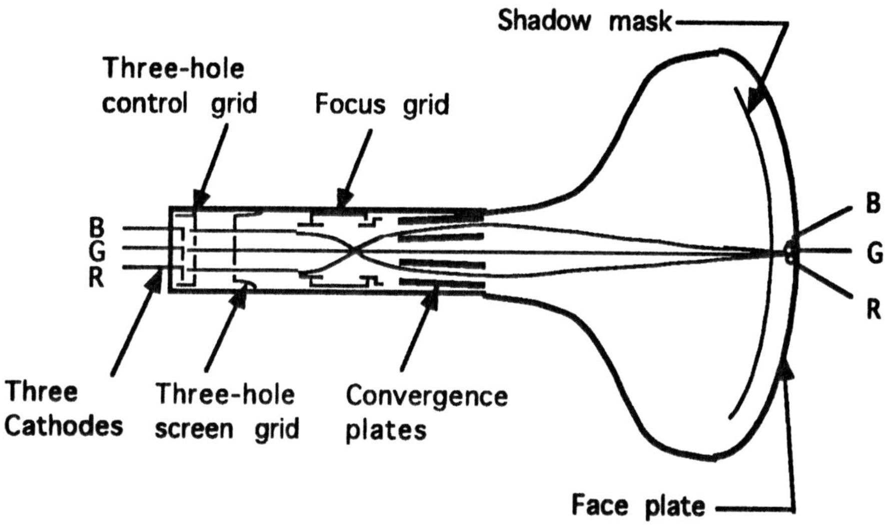

Figure 5-11. Color Picture Tube (Michel Bayard).

Interactive videoconferencing frame rates vary enormously—we will explain why in later chapters. Suffice it to say that, the more the video frames viewed during a given period of time, the smoother and more natural motion sequences will appear to be. Also suffice it to say that the goal of video communications systems is to come as close as possible to the frame rates offered by television.

In Living Color—NTSC

Television System A good understanding of video communication requires knowledge of the color television system approved by the NTSC in 1954. Before it came up with what is today known as the NTSC system of color telecasting, the committee considered various solutions. Members soon realized they could not expand on the existing monochrome approach by using separate RGB subcarriers.

This would have been a synchronization nightmare and would have required that the bandwidth allocated to each TV channel be greatly expanded to convey not only luminance but also red, green, and blue signals. It was not practical or acceptable. Nor was it acceptable to simultaneously broadcast a program in both monochrome and color. What was needed was a hybrid system that superimposed color information (chroma) over the brightness (luma) signal.

The system finally selected by the NTSC used this approach, adding hue (the identifiable color) and color saturation (color intensity, e.g., pastel pink, bright red, rose) to the luma signal. It did this by leveraging the fact that luminance occupies the 4.2 MHz subcarrier in bursts of energy at harmonic multiples of the horizontal scanning rate. This creates frequency clusters with empty spaces in which hue and

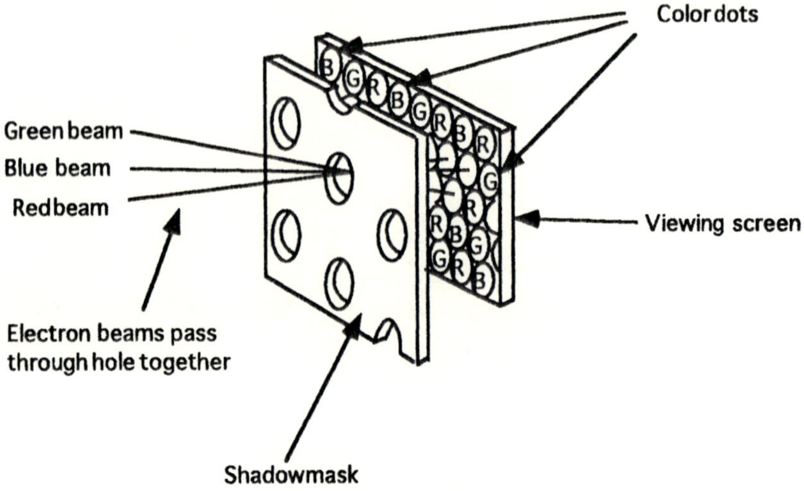

Figure 5-12. Shadow Mask (Michel Bayard).

saturation signals can be inserted. Hue and color saturation are thus inserted in these empty spaces using a technical concept described as frequency interleaving. The frequency of the color subcarrier 3.579545, rounded 3.58 MHz, was selected to achieve compatibility with the installed base of monochrome television sets.

The U.S. NTSC color television system is detailed in a document prepared by the Electronics Industries Association (EIA). This highly technical document, known as RS-170A, describes how color is added to the monochrome signal.

The NTSC system, and any other system that combines luminance and chrominance to represent images, is called composite video. In the case of NTSC, the composite signal is achieved not only by frequency interleaving but also through three different modulation techniques (phase, amplitude, and frequency). Each of the three conveys different elements of the signal. Audio is frequency-modulated, as is the luminance information contained in the signal.

Briefly, color television is encoded through a process of *color differencing*. Subtracting luminance information, referred to as "Y, from each of the primary color signals, R, G and B, forms signals. Only two of the three color difference signals are needed; the third is redundant. NTSC uses (R-Y) and (B-Y) that are combined to create two new signals, I and Q. The formula for deriving I and Q is:

$$I = 0.74(R-Y) - 0.27(B-Y)$$

$$Q = 0.48(R-Y) + 0.41(B-Y)$$

The I and Q signals are used to modulate two color subcarriers at the same frequency but 90 degrees out of phase—an approach that is also referred to as *quadrature modulation*. This technique exploits the fact that the polarity of an alternating current is constantly reversing. Phase is measured in degrees. The full cycle of a sine wave describes a 360-degree arc. The sine wave crosses the base line at zero volts, achieves its highest positive voltage at 90 degrees, dips down to touch the base line again at 180 degrees, achieves its lowest negative voltage at 270 degrees and finally returns to the zero volt base line at 360 degrees. Phase-modulation electrically alters this pattern of positive and negative undulation to convey information—in this case, the color of a pixel. Phase is hard to determine without a phase reference. Such a phase reference is obtained by a short eight-cycle burst of the 3.58 MHz color subcarrier frequency. This color burst, which is transmitted during horizontal blanking as a reference for establishing the picture color, keeps everything synchronized. The luminance and the modulated color signals are added to produce a final signal. This YIQ signal modulates the RF carrier for broadcast over the air.

When received at the set, the YIQ signal has no color content. The receiver's electronics translate it back into the three different wavelengths that comprise the RGB signal. Each color signal charges a separate electron gun. The aim of the three guns is varied by the application of magnetic deflection coils. The coils control the vertical and horizontal stream of electrons. In addition, another method is used to control which phosphor dots are energized by which gun. A metal plate, pierced with more than 200,000 tiny holes, is positioned between the electron guns and the viewing screen. Known as the shadow-mask, it conceals the two unwanted dots in each triangular group of three so that they converge on only one hole. This confines the beam to the phosphor dots of the proper color—for instance, the red signal strikes only the red dots and the blue signal strikes only the blue dots. "blending" the output of multiple electron guns produces colors other than pure red, green, and blue. Red and green, for instance, produce yellow. Blue and green combine to produce cyan. Red and blue produce magenta. Red, green, and blue can also be blended to produce white (all colors present) and gray. Black is the absence of light, and white is the presence of all colors in equal volumes.

The NTSC system allowed coexistence of monochrome and color television. Both receive luminance information, but the chrominance information is lost to monochrome sets.

Today, the NTSC system is derided as "kludgey" and unduly complex. A common joke is that NTSC stands for *Never The Same Color*. Certainly, the NTSC system is an awkward method for adding color to a video signal, but the approach was born of necessity. The committee had to live within the constraints of the existing television system and they did so by fitting color into the frequency band used for the monochrome signal. With television still a new technology, they were not prepared to pay for progress with obsolescence. Instead, they found a way to preserve the existing installed base of monochrome sets.

In Germany, the Telefunken found that the NTSC standard resulted in uneven color reproduction as a result of phase errors introduced during signal propagation. To cancel out the phase errors, the Germans inverted the color signal by 180 degrees on alternate lines. Phase alternate line (PAL) is now used by more than 40 countries including the U.K., Germany, and Western Europe (except France). The French adopted an FM system to transmit color television information that eliminated the phase error problem. Under the French system SECAM (Sequential Couleur Avec Memoire), color information is separated into red and blue and sent by two alternating carriers. A memory circuit within the TV set remembers the signals and uses them for faithful color reproduction.

Few changes have been made to the NTSC system since 1953. The problems inherent to the system are amplified when the already compromised signal is modulated onto an RF subcarrier. Once propagated in free space, it is fair game for interference from a wide variety of random signals—a phenomenon known as radio frequency interference or RFI. Most RFI problems are eliminated in cable television that, perhaps, explains why the system has lasted as long as it has.

In spite of its glitches, the NTSC system will have to satisfy our needs for color TV for some time. That's because the United States was slow to approve a new, digital television (DTV) standard, which will eventually replace the NTSC system.

HDTV

By the year 2010, the FCC may ban all analog TV transmitters from the airwaves. This is contingent upon how soon the 98% of Americans, who own most of the world's 600 million television sets, either upgrade to HTDV or buy digital adapters for their conventional TVs. HDTV sets display engaging wide-screen, high-definition images with approximately twice as many scanning lines as NTSC offers. Moreover, HDTV offers the ability to broadcast six channels of Dolby sound at the same time. Throughout the foreseeable future, they will continue to be popular consumer products that offer unprecedented image and sound, and interactivity through an on-screen program menu.

HDTV is a logical successor to NTSC in part because it offers the sense of involvement that audiences in wide screen theaters enjoy. When the screen occupies our periphery, we feel more involved. Although HDTV offers greater visual detail, it achieves much of its effect from its wider horizontal field of view. Moreover, because HDTV offers almost twice as much detail, it allows viewers to sit closer and thereby sense even more of a peripheral visual field.

Japan was the first country in the world to transmit high definition television. It did so in the early 1980s, after which it reported its success at an international meeting of telecommunications engineers in Algiers. The Japanese system was known as MUSE (Multiple Sub-Nyquist Encoding), and was a variant of its NHK HDTV standard for direct broadcast satellite service. Although MUSE is analog, it still worried the U.S. to think that Japan might overtake it in global market for broadcasting equipment. In spite of its fears, the FCC was slow to endorse any specific HDTV format. It was not until the Japanese actually demonstrated MUSE HDTV to American broadcasters, who had assembled in Washington DC for the showing, that the broadcasters themselves asked the FCC to develop a HDTV system for the U.S.

The FCC responded by creating the FCC's Advanced Television Systems Committee or ATSC in 1987. The ATSC oversaw the competition to create a domestic HDTV system. A variety of companies worked on their version of the specification; all were analog. Then, without warning, General Instruments announced they had developed a digital system—and then demonstrated it. Shortly thereafter, the ATSC asked the HDTV competitors to cooperate. Although they were reluctant, they agreed out of sheer necessity. The costs of going it alone were enormous. There was also a very real risk of losing the entire investment, were the FCC to approve another vendor's strategy. Finally, the contenders really needed to share technology, for although each of the four systems had its strong points, there was no clear technology leader. The cooperative effort, formalized in May 1993, became known as the Grand Alliance. From the time of its formation until April 1995, the group (which included AT&T Corp., General Instrument, MIT, Philips Consumer Electronics North America, the David Sarnoff Research Center, Thomson Consumer Electronics, and Zenith Electronics Corporation) worked cooperatively on a specification.

The Grand Alliance defined the conventions for HDTV, and based them on the International Standards Organization (ISO) Motion Picture Experts Group (MPEG) specification known as MPEG-2. The scanning formats they selected drew from a combination of computer-friendly progressive scanning and television-friendly interlaced scanning modes that broadcasters have historically embraced. MPEG-2 transport and compression technologies were also a part of the specification, as was quadrature amplitude modulation (QAM) or a variant, vestigial-sideband (VSB) modulation. The system used an error correction system known as Reed-Solomon Forward Error Correction (RSFC), that is also used in Compact Discs (CD), hard drives, telephone modems, and digital transmission systems. Audio was encoded using six-channel, CD-quality digital surround sound technology.

With the completion of a specification, the Grand Alliance (GA) began laboratory tests. They found VSB superior to QAM, and modified the specification accordingly. At the end of all their proof-of-concept testing, the GA documented their HDTV specification and submitted it to the ATSC for approval. On April 12, 1995, the ATSC approved the GA's Digital Television Standard for HDTV Transmission (formally known as ATSC A/53.) ATSC A/53 uses AT&T's and General Instrument's video encoder, Philips' decoder, Sarnoff/Thomson's transport subsystem and system integration expertise, and Zenith's modulation sub-system.

In July 1995, the computer industry belatedly noticed that ATSC A/53 was not computer-friendly. It was biased toward interlace scanning (as opposed to a PC screen's progressive scanning method), used an aspect ratio that was not compatible with computer monitors (16:9), and formatted pixels in an awkward fashion. In a last-minute effort to stop the FCC's final approval of ATSC A/53, Microsoft, Apple, Compaq, and others formed the Computer Industry Coalition for Advanced Television Service (CICATS.) CICATS led the charge against interlace, and submitted a standard that was based on the work of Gary Demos, a winner of an Oscar for technical excellence in filmmaking. Progressive scanning offers an observed resolution of about 70% of maximum vertical resolution as a result of pixels falling between the (three) scanning lines. Interlaced scanning offers only 50% of maximum vertical resolution unless the image is still. Moreover, interlacing produces serrated edges, and flicker along horizontal edges and improperly aligned frames.

From July 1995 until November 1996, the Grand Alliance and CICATS remained at a standoff. Finally, when it appeared that the FCC was prepared to do nothing rather than approve a standard that was so hotly contested, the broadcasters compromised. The Grand Alliance agreed to include progressive scanning in with the interlace specification. The FCC approved the modified HDTV standard in December 1996. In April 1997, it adopted an expedited timetable, ground rules, and a preliminary channel allocation; in February 1998, it approved a final channel plan. At that point, the FCC mandated that all HDTV outlets be broadcasting by 2003, and announced that it would repossess all analog channels by 2006. By the end of 1999, the number of HDTV stations grew to nearly 100.

What does HDTV mean to digital videoconferencing? Much of its technology will be interchangeable. We will want to use components of one for the other (e.g., cameras, monitors, chips and transmission systems.) The interest that HDTV will generate will do wonders for the acceptance of videoconferencing. To lay the foundation of what digital television will do for digital videoconferencing, we will, in the following chapter, address the basics of digital coding and compression.

CHAPTER 5 REFERENCES

Abramson, Albert. "Pioneers of Television—Vladimir Kosma-Zworykin," SMPTE Vol. 90, July 1981 pp. 580-590.

Bussey, Gordon and Geddes, Keith. "Television, the First Fifty Years," Philips Electronics and the National Museum of Photography, Film and Television (Prince's View, Bradford, West Yorkshire, England), 1986, pp. 2-5.

Frezza, Bill. "Digital TV limps to the starting line," Network Computing Oct 15, 1996 v7 n16 p. 35.

Fink, Donald G. and Lytyens, David M. The Physics of Television Anchor Books Doubleday & Company, Incorporated Garden City, New York, 1960 pp. 17-82.

Herrick, Clyde. "Principles of Colorimetry," Reston, Virginia. Reston Publishing, Incorporated A Prentice-Hall Company 1977, pp. 12-65.

Leopold, George. "Fate of HDTV is now in lawmakers' hands," Electronic Engineering Times March 25, 1996 n894 p. 1.

Leopold, George. "First HDTV broadcast studio set," Electronic Engineering Times April 1, 1996 n895 p. 1.

Leopold, George. "New HDTV format offered," Electronic Engineering Times March 11, 1996 n892 p. 22.

McArthur, Tom and Waddell, Peter. "Vision Warrior," A Scottish Falcon Book; The Orkney Press Kirkwall Orkney, Scotland, pp. 6-164.

Noll, A. Michael. Television Technology: Fundamentals and Future Prospects Artech House, Incorporated Norwood, Massachusetts, 1988 pp. 9-151.

The National Geographic Book Service. Inventors and Discoverers Changing Our World Washington D.C. National Geographic Society 1988.

Yoshida, Junko. "HDTV's story: fits, starts and setbacks," Electronic Engineering Times May 27, 1996 n903 p. 20.

Yoshida, Junko. "High definition still elusive," Electronic Engineering Times June 10, 1996 n905 p. 35.

6

CODING AND COMPRESSION

"God made integers, all else is the work of man."

Leopold Kronecker, 1823 - 1891

We experience the natural world by way of our senses. Our eyes and ears capture light and sound and then pass the sensations to our brains for processing. Cameras and microphones do much the same thing. They detect and respond to the electromagnetic waves associated with light and sound and pass them, in analog form, for manipulation by audiovisual processing systems. Some audiovisual processing systems are analog (conventional broadcast television) while others are digital. The primary concern of this book is *digital* video communications; hence, this chapter begins with a discussion of digital encoding techniques.

We refer to the process of converting a signal from analog to digital as *encoding*. For years, telephone companies have been encoding analog signals to digitally transmit them. Digital transmission systems have replaced most analog telephone networks in the industrialized world. The reasons include improved transmission quality, cost, increased bandwidth, and efficiency. By efficiency, we mean that when a signal is converted to a stream of bits, that stream can be easily shuffled with other bit streams, regardless of source or content.

Video and audio signals benefit greatly from analog-to-digital conversion. The universe contains innumerable electromagnetic waves—not all of them relate to any particular signal. That so many frequencies exist in free space does not matter to human eyes and ears that can only detect a limited range of sights or sounds. However, it does become a problem when these sights and sounds are electronically modulated onto a carrier wave.

A carrier wave is an electrically constant energy path that one uses to transport a signal from one place to another. Modulation is the process of altering this stable carrier wave in response to fluctuations in the signal being carried. Analog modulation techniques perform well in controlled environments or over short distances. The signal, when it is first superimposed onto the carrier, is strong and unadulterated. However, because travel steadily weakens a signal, a signal that travels any distance requires amplification. If amplification were to restore the signal to its original pristine state, it would effect no harm. Unfortunately, frequencies abound and, unless a transmission system is shielded, interference contaminates the signal. The original envelope, which once contained only the signal, accumulates random waveforms that are not associated with the original signal, but which occupy the same frequency band. Amplification boosts both the signal and these random waveforms, which we refer to as *noise*.

Noise affects video signals. They may arrive on a screen full of *artifacts* (undesirable elements or defects in a video picture). Image aliasing (subjectively intolerable distortions in the picture) is another noise-related problem. Unlike analog signals, digital ones are somewhat immune to noise. The signal is coded and sent as a string of zeros and ones. Sufficiently distinct phenomena (the absence or presence of light—positive or negative voltage levels) distinguish these binary values. In digital systems, a repeater (that replaces the amplifier that is used in analog systems), exhibits a high degree of accuracy in distinguishing between a zero and a one. The integrity of the signal is extremely high because, with today's transmission systems, bit errors are quite rare.

Digital transmission preserves the quality of an original signal. However, that is not the only reason digital technology is so widely accepted today. A bigger reason — the real reason — is that computers are inherently digital. They do not process analog data. To leverage the enormous power that computers can offer practically every application, one must convert sounds and pictures from their natural analog state to a digital (or binary) one. Once they have been digitized, these streams of audio and visual information can be compressed, and thereby moved economically across telecommunications networks.

Audio Encoding

Like conventional television, digital video consists of a series of image frames that are synchronized with an audio track. The sounds are interleaved with the video data during the process of capture and transmission.

Audio and video must each be digitized. Digitizing a signal is a multi-step process that starts with sampling. Sampling is the process of measuring slices of an analog signal over time, and at regular intervals. Typically "X" represents the number of samples taken in a second; X is defined as a number that is twice the highest frequency of the analog signal.

In 1928, a Bell Labs engineer named Harry Nyquist presented a paper that laid out a technique for sampling an analog signal in such a way that its digital representation would be *lossless*—that is, functionally identical to the original waveform.

Nyquist's Theorem, the gospel of digital encoding, states that the sampling rate must be twice that of the highest frequency present in the analog waveform. When Nyquist's Theorem is not followed during the analog to digital (A/D) conversion process for digitizing video, aliasing often results. Aliases show up as moiré (wavy patterns that look like plaid or watered silk) and color shifts (where rainbow hues appear in an object of supposedly uniform color).

In the analog world, the bandwidth of a signal is the difference between its highest and its lowest frequencies. It is the highest frequency with which sampling is concerned. The frequency of sound waves is measured in hertz (Hz); an expression of the number of complete cycles that occur in one second. Although those with the most acute hearing can perceive frequencies as high as 20 kHz (20,000 hertz), the public telephone network does not convey them because they do not occur in speech. The human voice typically produces frequencies between 50 Hz and 4 kHz. Since this range is where most of the information in human speech is concentrated, telephone networks were specifically designed to carry those frequencies. Thus, the analog local loop—the connection between an end-user and the telephone company—has a bandwidth of 4 kHz. According to Nyquist's Theorem, this signal must be sampled at a rate of 8,000 samples per second. The device that does the sampling is called a codec (coder-decoder) and it forms the basis for much of today's digital telephone network.

The basis of the North American public switched telephone network is an extremely precise 8 kHz (Stratum) clock. This clock produces reference pulses that are distributed across all networks in North America. This clock determines how samples are pulled from analog signals, in accordance with a digital modulation technique known as Pulse Code Modulation (PCM).

In 1938, Alec Reeves, an English employee of ITT, developed the concept of PCM. Unfortunately, in the 1930s, PCM was not deployable in the public network. The pulse generation equipment of the day relied on vacuum tubes that were too large and power-hungry to make wide-scale implementation feasible. In 1947, a group of Bell Labs physicists were experimenting with a germanium crystal they had placed between two wires. Unexpectedly, a signal that was traveling across the wires began to amplify to 40 times its original strength. This discovery of the transistor—from which all integrated circuit technology evolved—paved the way for the digital world in which we now live.

PCM is the most common method used to convert an analog audio signal to a digital one. An audio channel is sampled at uniform intervals 8,000 times per second. As a sample is taken, its voltage is compared to a set of numeric values. Since the sample is going to be encoded using eight bits, one of 256 integers can be used to represent it. The integer most closely resembling the sample is used to represent it. This step

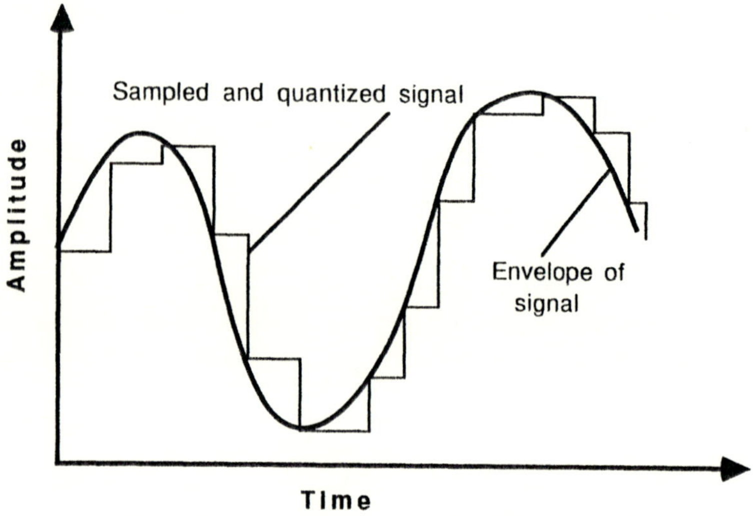

Figure 6-1. Pulse Code Modulation (Michel Bayard).

is called quantizing. Encoding follows quantizing. In this step, the selected integer is expressed as an eight-bit word, a BYTE Streams of bytes are transmitted across networks at a rate of one every 125 microseconds. As each byte reaches its destination, a codec reconverts it to its analog form.

PCM-encoded voice requires a transmission line with a speed of 64 kilo-bits-per-second (Kbps). The signal is sampled 8,000 times per second and each sample is encoded using eight bits (8,000 x 8 = 64,000). This 64 Kbps channel is the fundamental building block of digital networks, although many telephone carriers rob 8 Kbps from a circuit and use that 8 Kbps to carry timing information.

The 64 Kbps data rate forms the basis of the Integrated Services Digital Network (ISDN) bearer (B) channel. It is multiplexed with 23 other PCM-encoded channels into a wide pipe known as a DS-1 or a T-1. DS-1, by definition, is a digital transmission link with a capacity of 1.544 Mbps (in which M represents million). The bandwidth of a DS-1 is sub-divided into channels using a technique called time division multiplexing (TDM).

The North American digital hierarchy multiplexes or *muxes* four T-1 signals together to derive a T-2 or DS-2 (6.312 Mbps channel) and seven DS-2 pipes together to create an even higher-speed multiplexed signal called a DS-3. DS-3 is the term most commonly used to refer to the 44.736 (usually rounded to 45) Mbps pipe that is used for high-capacity transmission. The digital multiplex system we have just described is being replaced by Synchronous Optical NETwork (SONET) transmission systems (we will describe SONET) later in this book.

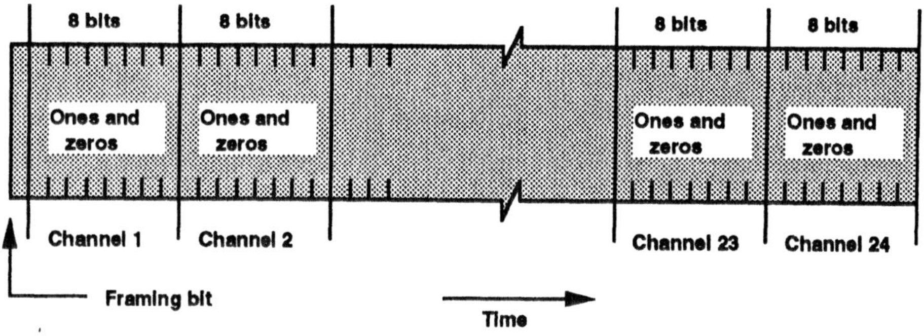

Figure 6-2. T-1 Frame Including Framing Bit (Michel Bayard).

In Europe, T-1 is replaced with E-1/CEPT (typically referred to as E-1). E-1 is a 32-channel pipe in which two channels (13 and 30) are reserved for network signaling and synchronization. Phone companies base their networks on digital carrier. That is to say, they connect their switching centers together using channels packaged in accordance with the digital hierarchy specification. The specification for all digital networks is D4 framing; it describes the basic DS-1 signal including the framing bit.

We digress from audio and video coding specifically into networks for good reason. T-1 pipes are often installed in conjunction with videoconferencing *room* systems when T-carrier is not already installed for voice or data services. Multiples of the 24 channels (six is typical) are commonly used for videoconferencing applications. The remainder can be used for other services such as outbound and inbound long distance or access for various data communications services.

The public switched telephone network was designed for audio signals. Dealing with audio is easy; human speech is endowed with characteristics that permit efficient coding. The range of frequencies is narrow and sounds occur at the lower end of the electromagnetic spectrum. Coding audio information is easy in comparison to coding video signals.

VIDEO ENCODING

Video consists of patterns of light. This light is a manifestation of energy that occurs at the upper end of the human-defined electromagnetic spectrum. In this sphere, waves are very short, frequencies are very high and encoding techniques must be very sophisticated.

The human eye, as we said in the last chapter, incorporates photoreceptor cells (cones) that capture this light. There are three types of cones; hence the human visual system exists in a *color space* that recognizes brightness, hue, and saturation.

Because the human visual system is three-dimensional, we must use three different components to describe a video image. This three-dimensional representation of light also expresses images in terms of their brightness, saturation, and hue. This video color space can be depicted as follows. A center dividing line or brightness column is the axis. Along that line, no color exists at all. Hues (colors) form circles around this axis. A horizontal axis describes the amount of saturation—the depth of color. Highly saturated colors are closest to the center and less saturated colors are arranged toward the outer edges. Chrominance is the combination of hue and saturation that, taken together with luminance (brightness), define color.

Color encoding systems used for video must transform color space; they must change it into a different format so that it can be more readily encoded and compressed. This conversion of color space exploits the characteristics of the human visual system. The human eye accommodates brightness and color differently. We perceive changes in brightness (luminance) much more readily than we do fluctuations in chrominance. Hence, video-encoding systems devote more bandwidth to the luminance component of a signal. The symbol Y represents this *luma* component. White light is the composite of equal quantities of red, green, and blue light. Therefore, to determine how much red, green or blue light is present in an image, one can develop a system that subtracts color (chrominance) information from luminance information. This is exactly what video coding systems do. There are many different variations but, essentially, they all rely on *color differencing*.

Color differencing is the first step in encoding the color television signal. Subtracting the luminance information from each primary color forms the color difference signals: red, green, or blue. Color difference conventions include the SMPTE format, the Betacam format, the EBU-N10 format and the MII format. Color difference signals are not component video signals—these are, strictly speaking, the pure R, G, and B waveforms.

There are two types of video signals, component and composite. In component video, the Y or luminance signal is recorded and transmitted separately from the C (hue and color saturation) signal. The luminance signal is recorded at a higher frequency and, therefore, more resolution lines are available to it. Because the eye is less sensitive to chroma signals, those signals are recorded at lower frequencies and transmitted using less bandwidth. Component video is not a standard, but rather a technique. It results in greater signal control (keeping signals separate makes them easier to manipulate) and higher image quality. Component video is often called Y/C video.

Composite video is used in NTSC and PAL television systems. In composite video, brightness, hue and saturation are combined into a single signal. In its analog form, the chrominance signal is a sine wave that is modulated onto the luminance signal, which acts as a subcarrier. In NTSC systems, the YIQ trichromatic color system is used. The two color differences are first combined, using a technique known as quadrature modulation. Next, this color information is modulated onto the 4.5 MHz Y subcarrier with the phase of the sine wave describing the color itself and the amplitude describing the level of color saturation. This technique is called frequency interleaving.

A digital image is a grid that contains a two-dimensional array of values that represent intensity or color. To achieve this format, an analog image must first be converted to this 2-D space, using pixels to convey its resolution. If the image is black and white, the values used might be 0 and 1. Eight bits might be used for a gray-scale image. True color requires at least eight bits each for R, G, and B; it also requires three frames of information, one for each color component.

Many different video-encoding schemes exist. Each has been designed to meet the needs of a unique application. Still video applications demand different requirements than do moving video applications. Digital video can be stored on a typical CD-ROM or on a powerful video server, and delivered in broadcast (one-way transmission) format. However, digital video is not always stored; videoconferencing is an interactive real-time digital video application.

COMPRESSION: KEEPING ONLY THE CRITICAL BITS

Compression, the art and the science of compacting a signal for transmission, is far more sophisticated today than it was ten years ago. Nevertheless, despite today's fast networks, a mismatch persists between the bandwidth needed to transport digitized video, and the bandwidth available to carry it. Different approaches to encoding a video signal produce different results, but virtually all techniques result in uncompressed bandwidth requirements of 25 Mbps or more. Networks that offer this capacity are rare and expensive.

Compression would be superfluous if bandwidth were available in limitless quantities and at extremely low cost—but it is not. Economy mandates compression. If the additional cost to compress is lower than the price of the additional bandwidth required to carry an uncompressed signal, customers will compress. In the early 1980s, both costs were very high and, consequently, videoconferencing was not very popular. As time went by, video codecs became more powerful. By the mid-1980s, they reduced the bandwidth required for a conference to below T-1 speeds.

Visual compression techniques usually involve manipulating pixels—the medium of exchange in video communications. As a codec compresses, it replaces the data of the original signal with complex mathematical models. The goal is to eliminate as much of the signal as possible without destroying its information content.

Compression involves two-steps. Anything that is compressed must be decompressed. A trade-off exists between the time it takes to compress an image and how much compression one achieves. Time-consuming compression techniques do not work for videoconferencing applications, which must move quickly to produce the illusion of fluid motion.

In videoconferencing, there are two primary methods for categorizing compression. One technique, redundancy elimination, is based on eliminating signal duplication. The other is based on degrading the picture and sound slightly, preferably in areas where the human eye and ear are not particularly sensitive. It is called quality reduction. Before we get into the nuts and bolts of these techniques, we must introduce some new terms.

One fundamental way to categorize compression is to look at the result. After decompression, are the data identical to those that constitute the original signal? If so, the compression is said to be *lossless*. If compression is achieved by permanently discarding parts of the signal—ideally, components not critical to its interpretation—the technique is said to be *lossy*. When reversed, lossy compression does not produce a signal that is identical to the original but, rather, approximates it. Lossy techniques can produce very high ratios of signal compression, but do so at a considerable price. That price is reduced image quality or sound fidelity (or a combination of both). Generally, signals degrade as compression increases. Both lossy and lossless techniques are used in interactive video compression, although lossless methods usually take place at the end of the process, and involve expressing strings of zeros and ones using "shorthand" codes.

Another method for categorizing compression is based on the methods used for decompression. Is decompression an exact reverse of the compression process? If so, the compression is said to be *symmetric*. If the techniques used to compress are more compute-intensive than those used to decompress, compression is *asymmetric*. Symmetric techniques are used for real-time, interactive videoconferencing applications. Asymmetric compression is commonly used for video playback applications. Most of the resource goes into compression so that receiving devices of limited sophistication can cheaply and easily decompress.

Even with symmetric compression, the work is not equally divided. Real-time encoding requires complex math, so the sending codec does more work. However, in interactive videoconferences, both codecs are simultaneously sending and receiving.

Intraframe and Interframe Compression

Frames of motion video are full of duplication, as one can demonstrate with a strip of movie film. One will discern little difference between the successive frames. The background is static, and action takes place incrementally. Moreover, within a single frame exist many long sequences of constant pixel value—walls, tables, clothing, and hair tend to be of uniform color. Efficient codecs do not waste bandwidth on repetitive information. They code the unique parts of the signal and describe, using an algorithm, how patterns repeat.

Video codecs that compress data within a single frame of video are known as *intraframe* codecs. They commonly divide a video frame into blocks and then look for redundant data. When they find it they eliminate it; they attempt to reduce the content of that frame to *entropy*. Other types of codecs compare multiple frames of data. These are known as *interframe* codecs. They, too, try to achieve entropy through compression.

What is entropy? It is a scientific term that refers to the measure of disorder, or uncertainty, in a system. Good compression techniques eliminate signal duplication by using shorthand methods that are readily understood by the coding and decoding devices on each end. The only part of the signal that must be fully described is the part that is random, and is thereby impossible to predict.

Redundancy-elimination compression first worked on achieving entropy in text messages. Text files consist of only about 50 different characters, some of which appear often. The letters E, T, O, and I, for instance, collectively account for 37% of all character appearances in an average text file. David Huffman, a researcher at MIT, noted and subsequently exploited their repetition. In 1960, Huffman devised the first text compression algorithm. The idea behind Huffman encoding is similar to that of Morse code. It assigns short, simple codes to common characters or sequences and longer more complex ones to those that appear infrequently. Huffman encoding can reduce a text file by approximately 40%. A lossless compression technique, it is used to reduce long stings of zeros in many standards-based video compression systems including H.261, H.263, and MPEG.

Other lossless compression techniques followed Huffman coding. Developed in the 1970's, Lempel-Ziv-Welch (LZW) compression focused not on the characters themselves, but on repetitive bit combinations. LZW coding builds a dictionary of these commonly used data sequences and represents them with abbreviated codes. Originally developed for text, another technique called run-length coding, compresses at the bit level by reducing the number of zeros and ones in a file. Sending only one example, followed by a shorthand description of the number of times it repeats, indicates a string of identical bits. LZW and run-length coding can be used in video compression, but are usually performed after lossy techniques have done their job.

Compressing moving images is much more demanding than compressing text. A frame of video contains vastly more information. Fortunately, there is usually a correlation between neighboring pixels. Collocated pixels can be neighbors in terms of space (they sit adjacent to each other) or time (they occupy the same space but in different frames). Intraframe compression techniques eliminate spatial redundancy. Interframe techniques eliminate temporal redundancy. Intraframe compression relies on transform coding (DCT, for instance). Interframe compression is largely a subtractive process: pixels contained in a frame of video are subtracted from a previous frame's pixels. The difference is information—the entropy that results from the interframe coding process.

Early forms of video compression relied solely on interframe coding. In the 1960s, Bell Labs began experimenting with a variation of PCM called differential pulse-code modulation (DPCM). DPCM uses "differencing" to compare successive video frames. Codecs (one transmitting, one receiving), use identical methods to predict, using a past frame, what the pixel composition of a present frame will be. The transmitting codec, after making its guess, checks its accuracy by comparing its prediction, (stored in memory array), with reality. It subtracts reality from its prediction, encodes the *errors* and transmits them to the receiving codec. Because the receiving codec is making identical predictions, it knows what to do with errors, which it interprets as corrections. It makes the changes, displays the signal, and then stores the amended frame as the basis for the next prediction. The prediction and correction process is continuous; each new frame updates the previous one.

DPCM is still used in standards-based videoconferencing compression, although it is generally optional (by optional, we mean that a decoder must decode a DPCM compressed image, but a coder is not required to encode it). DPCM works because, on average, only about 9% of the pixels in a moving sequence change between frames. In 1969, a process known as conditional frame replenishment (CFR or CR) was developed. CR recognizes that information (something that is not already known) is present in a scene only when motion occurs. Moreover, information is present only in the part of the frame that contains motion. CR compression techniques transmit only the changes in the part of the frame that comprise motion. It works well when the motion in a scene does not exceed 15% between frame intervals.

In 1972, two engineers recognized that, in a moving sequence, there is less correlation between pixels that occupy the same place in subsequent frames than there is between pixels that are close to each other but shifted to a different position. After reflection, it became clear that motion vectors play a significant role in pixel prediction. As objects move, pixels shift left, right, up, or down. If a codec were prepared to recognize the direction and rate of pixel motion, it would do a much better job of predicting where each pixel might end up in successive frames. This discovery led to another form of interframe compression called motion compensation. It improved the image compression factor by 50–100% when compared to CR.

Motion compensation is based on the observation that moving objects are most efficiently described by re-mapping their original position to a new position. For instance, a pointer used to call attention to a figure on a whiteboard moves in a predictable fashion. Only the motion vector requires retransmission because the receiving codec already possesses a mathematical representation of original object.

In other words, in motion vector prediction, the codec must send information about the position of a subject, but not about the subject itself.

Intraframe encoding came along in the mid-1970s. It is fairly compute-intensive; and uses more sophisticated algorithms than all but a few interframe codecs. Two different intraframe coding techniques are typical today. One, which is common to almost every standards-based video encoding technique today, is the discrete cosine transform, better known as DCT. The other, which is more prevalent in proprietary codecs, is known as vector quantization (VQ).

DISCRETE COSINE TRANSFORM

Any student of image compression will encounter DCT; it forms the basis for three very important video communications compression standards. One is the Joint Photographic Experts Group (JPEG) standard, which is used for still-image compression. Another is the Moving Picture Experts Group (MJPEG) standard that is used to compress TV-quality or near-TV-quality moving pictures (typically for playback applications). Furthermore, DCT is used for two very important standards-based videoconferencing codecs, the ITU-T's H.261 and H.263 Recommendations.

The DCT is a technique that converts pixel intensities into their frequency-based equivalents. To do this, it applies numeric transformation to the data contained in a pixel block. After the DCT is complete, a block of video data is described in terms of frequencies and amplitudes rather than a series of colored pixels. Frequencies describe how rapidly colors shift. For instance, high frequencies denote very rapidly shifting colors such as edges where one color stops and another starts. Amplitudes describe the magnitude of a color change associated with each shift.

To understand DCT, one must possess some knowledge of sines and cosines. In trigonometry, the sine is the ratio between the side opposite an acute angle in a right triangle and the hypotenuse (the side of a right-angled triangle opposite the right angle). Examine Figure 6.3 for a straightforward picture. A sine wave is a graphical representation of the sine ratio. Remember that the polarity of an AC power source is constantly changing from positive to negative. The waveform produced from alternating current can be plotted. The result is a sine wave that undulates with shape of the wave as it continues from zero polarity to its peak positive value, then back to zero and beyond, to its peak negative value and then back to zero.

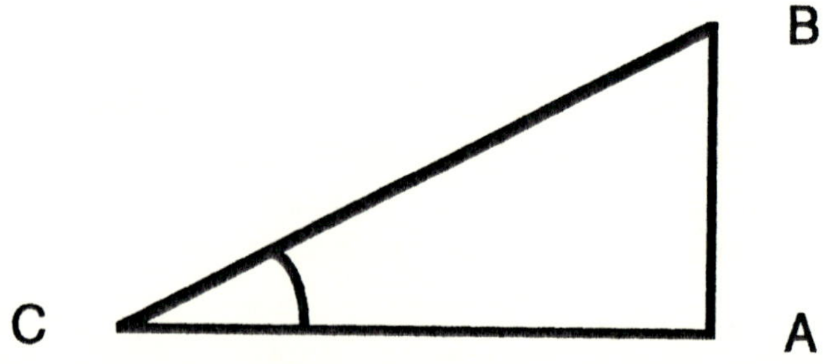

Sine of angle ACB = AB/BC

Figure 6-3. Sine (Michel Bayard).

Webster describes a cosine as "the sine of the complement," the ratio between the side adjacent to a given acute angle in a right triangle and the hypotenuse, as depicted in Figure 6.4. It is the reciprocal of a sine. How does discrete cosine transform work? When the information in a picture is processed, using a technique called spatial filtering, it is transformed into a series of frequencies that mimic the eye's perception of light and color. The high-frequency portions of the picture are the areas of greatest change; for instance, complex patterns in clothing and black letters on a white page. The low frequency elements are the parts with relatively little change across an area such as blank walls and other objects of uniform color and shape. The DCT uses the reciprocal of those frequencies to describe a pixel block.

The DCT process begins by dividing a video frame into eight-by-eight pixel blocks that are each comprised of a set of waveforms of different horizontal and vertical frequencies. These waveforms, when scaled by numbers called coefficients and added together, can be used to represent any of the 64 sample values (a coefficient is nothing more than a multiplier). For instance, in the formula a(y + z), "a" is the coefficient. Y could be the sine and z the cosine. A coefficient could also be thought of as the least common denominator, and that is how it is used in DCT.

After dividing a picture into blocks of pixels, the DCT scanning procedure starts in the upper left-hand corner of a block and finds the average luminance for the entire block. This value is known as the *DC coefficient*, and it is the first number produced by the transform. The DCT scanning process continues and as it does, 63 more values are produced. The second and third are expressions of the lowest frequency in the horizontal and vertical directions. As scanning proceeds, it

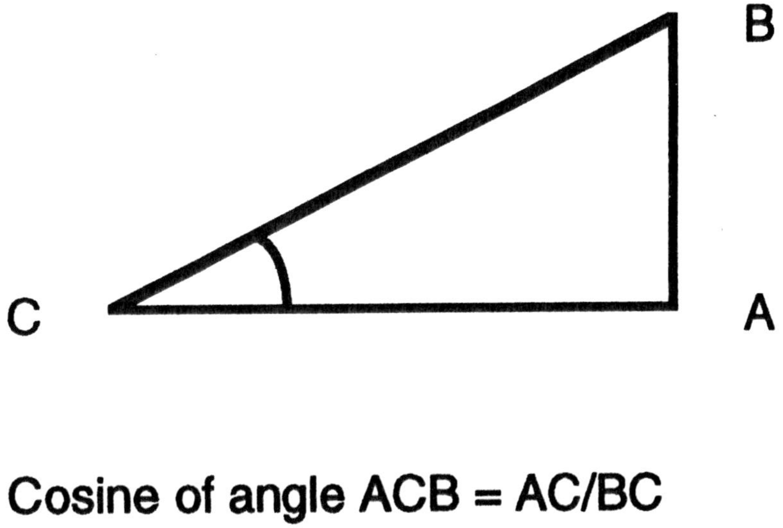

Figure 6-4. Cosine (Michel Bayard).

concentrates the low-frequency components, which describe large areas of uniform color, in the upper left corner of the array. The high-frequency components, describing detail shifts in the image (edges and color changes), are concentrated in the lower right.

Since there are usually more flat surfaces than sharp edges in a picture, the first few values will probably be non-zero. However, as the zigzag scanning continues the frequency increases. The coefficients produced become smaller and smaller. By the time the sixty-fourth value is measured, it is an expression of the magnitude of the highest frequency in both the horizontal and vertical planes—a value that tends to zero after the quantization process is applied.

The resulting 64 DCT values are arranged in a matrix. Compression has not been achieved at this point—what started as 64 eight-bit pixels resulted in 64 eight-bit coefficient values, most of which are zero or almost zero. In the process of quantization, the almost-zero values become zero; they are not important because the human eye would not perceive them anyway. The most important value, the DC coefficient, is quantized and coded using an 8-bit code.

After quantization, a bit stream is formed from the pixel block. This bit stream is ready for compression. Compression in H.261 and H.263 codecs takes the form of run-length and Huffman encoding. In run length encoding the codec compresses a string of identical bits by sending a bit pattern followed by a token that indicates the number of times the pattern repeats. Huffman encoding is then used to convert the most frequently repeated tokens into the shortest bit strings.

To summarize, the human eye, like the human ear, is more responsive to low frequencies than to high ones. In audio companding, PCM codes low frequencies with more precision than higher ones. DCT works the same way. The low frequencies in image encoding contain the picture's detail. DCT compresses by giving priority to that which humans need most for image processing.

VECTOR QUANTIZATION

Used in a number of proprietary compression techniques (most notably, Intel's Indeo) vector quantization is a less compute-intensive alternative to the DCT.

Vector quantization is a lossy compression method that uses a small set of data to represent a larger one. Stated differently, codecs that use vector quantization share a *codebook*. This codebook contains an array of possible values, and shorthand codes that can be used to convey them.

As the name implies, vector quantization quantizes vectors. A vector is a mathematical representation of a *force*. In video coding this force can be interpreted as a color (in other words, a frequency). Not only must we consider frequency when dealing with images, we must also consider the intensity of that frequency (its amplitude). Amplitude is determined by luminance, the relative saturation of a pixel's color.

In vector quantization, we analyze a block of pixels to discover its vector. This vector is then used to select a predefined equation that describes it in a more efficient way. Codecs can be tuned so that the quantization process considers not just a pixel block's vector, but also how this vector relates to those of surrounding blocks within the image. In most pictures, colors (and their corresponding saturation) are concentrated in certain areas. These colors are associated with objects (e.g., walls, white boards, clothing, and paper). A codec can select a relatively small subset of the representative vectors in an image and use this subset to approximate the vectors of all other pixel blocks. If a pixel block's vector, once measured, falls into the "red" codebook, it can be described using an abbreviated code. That code, which might be only a few bits long, is interpreted by the decoder as a "red" with a given hue and saturation.

VIDEO COMPRESSION

Unlike manufacturing processes that strive for total quality, video compression techniques are designed to settle for "good enough." Good enough, of course, depends on the application, and quality is, therefore, subjective. However, all types of lossy compression leverage the human tendency to consider context and thereby interpret what one sees or hears when minor bits of information are missing.

Video compression techniques are designed to exploit the functioning of the human eye. The eye-brain team is quite sensitive in some ways and quite tolerant in others. For instance, the eye adjusts very well to variations in relative and absolute brightness, but not to lack of focus. It is sensitive to distortions in familiar images (e.g., people's faces), but can tolerate minor flaws in motion handling as long as the overall movement looks realistic. Viewers want the parts of the picture that convey critical information—numbers, letters, and the eyes of other people—to be clearly discernible, but blurring in a picture's background is not distracting.

Techniques that sacrifice video quality for reduced bandwidth fall into two categories. One method is to approximate instead of sending the actual information. DCT is an approximation of luminance. Motion compensation uses motion vectors to approximate how an object will move from one frame to the next. Quality is technically reduced using these techniques, but the approximations are good enough and, since most humans can not perceive the loss, it is trivial.

Another method of quality reduction works on picture resolution. Resolution depends on pixels, which are the conveyers of video information. The more pixels, the more detail. Detail is, for some applications, critical. The more detail in an X-ray, the better. Other applications require less detail. Seeing the pattern on the tie worn by a person in a videoconference is not important. Capturing the messages conveyed through body language and gesture is important. As long as quality-reduction does not impair the conveyance of important information, we overlook it. Most participants in a videoconference become accustomed to the reduced quality image and cease to notice it—particularly if the audio quality is good.

Different video formats define different picture resolutions. For instance, color VGA video specifies a graphics mode that is 640 pixels wide by 480 pixels tall. Super-VGA is 1,024-by-768 pixels. In both formats, a colored pixel is defined using 24-bits. The CCIR (an international standards body that is part of the United Nations) defines a digitized version of NTSC in its Recommendation CCIR-601 in which 525 vertical lines are each painted with 720 horizontal pixels (For more on CCIR-601, please refer to Appendix C). HDTV in North America will have yet a different resolution, as will that little window on the PC that contains video clips downloaded from the World Wide Web.

To match image-sharpness with application requirements, one can use various pixel reduction techniques. One approach is to shrink the viewing window using a technique known as *scaling*. Scaling works because smaller viewing areas require fewer pixels. The image displayed in a quarter-screen PC monitor is painted with far fewer pixels than is required by the 27-inch monitor on a videoconferencing room-system.

Reducing the frame rate is another way to compress a motion video sequence. Although the NTSC standard calls for 30 frames per second, one rarely gets 30 in a videoconference, especially when using a desktop system. When there is little or no motion taking place on the distant end, one may receive 15 to 20 frames per second, possibly even more. However, the moment someone moves the camera, or gets up and walks across the room, a flood of new bits must be shipped to the receiving end and the frame rate drops substantially.

Dropping the frame rate allows transmission bandwidth to be significantly compressed with little corresponding degradation. Unlike a car race, most business related video applications include limited motion. Nevertheless, even business meetings can generate more motion than a low-bandwidth channel can accommodate. A person who is rising from a chair and walking to a whiteboard will translate to a large amount non-zero information that must be sent. It may begin to exceed the channel's bandwidth. At that point some of the signal must be discarded. As more and more people get up and walk around, the codec gets frantic. It eventually falls behind, discarding excessive numbers of frames. The picture degrades to a point at which it is annoying. This is a much greater problem at low bandwidths (POTS or ISDN BRI) than at speeds of 384 Kbps, or especially 224 Kbps, because the codec has less room to maneuver.

Other quality reduction techniques are sometimes used in video compression. One we have not yet mentioned has to do with color. If a color coding system were to represent a video image using only one bit per pixel, the picture would be monochrome. Bits could take only two values. A zero would represent an absence of light while a one would portray light of a single frequency, white or red, for instance. A coding system of this type is said to have a single bit plane.

Additional colors are added to the system through the use of multiple bit planes. The total number of planes used to represent an image is sometimes called a bit-map. The more bits in the map, the better the resolution. With a two-bit plane, four color values can be represented: 00, 01, 11 and 10. Bit planes containing eight bits can represent 256 discrete values. When R, G, and B are each assigned eight bits, millions of color combinations can be created (256^3). Each time an additional bit is added to a bit plane, the picture's resolution doubles. Unfortunately, so does the bandwidth required to transmit the uncompressed image.

AUDIO COMPRESSION

As we asserted earlier, human speech has attributes that lend themselves to efficient compression. Pauses between words can be eliminated through compression. Amplitudes rise and fall predictably. We also instructed that PCM coding results in eight-bit samples. While this is true, we have omitted a step. Samples are quantized at 2^{12} (4,096 values) and then compressed to eight bits (256 values) using logarithmic encoding. This process is called *companding*; it is a contraction of the word compress and the word expand. Companding is performed in accordance with either μ-Law (pronounced "mu-Law") or A-law; μ-Law is used in North America and Japan, and A-Law is used elsewhere. When compressing voice, logarithmic modeling works better than linear schemes. This is because humans are more sensitive to small changes at low volume than changes of the same magnitude at higher volumes.

The CCITT (now known as the ITU-T) has standardized PCM as G.711 audio.

Using G.711 coding, speech and sounds with bandwidths of approximately 3.4 kHz are converted to 56 or 64 Kbps bit streams.

A slightly more recent ITU-T standard, G.728, encodes 3.4 kHz audio frequencies into 16 Kbps bit streams. The technique used for compression is known as low-delay Code- that it encodes speech to fit a simple, analytical model of the vocal tract. It generates

ITU-T Number	Range of Compression	Description of Encoding Technique (Comments)	Used with ITU-T Codec Recommendations
G.711	56 – 64 Kbps	Pulse Code Modulation (PCM) of voice frequencies	H.320
G.722	64 Kbps	7 kHz audio-coding within 64 Kbps (PCM)	H.320, H.322, H.323
G.723	5.3 and 6.3 Kbps	Multipulse-Maximum Likelihood Quantization (MP-MLQ)	H.322, H.323, H.324
G.728	16 Kbps	Low-Delay Code Excited Linear Prediction	H.320, H.322, H.323
G.729	8 Kbps	Coding of speech at 8 Kbps using conjugate-structure algebraic-code-excited linear-prediction (CS-ACELP)	H.323

Figure 6-5. CCITT/ITU-T Audio Encoding Recommendations.

synthetic speech that is very similar to the original waveform. The *code excited* version LPC goes a step further to compute the errors between the original speech and the LPC model. It transmits both the model parameters and a highly-compressed representation of the errors. CELP results in compression that is remarkably faithful to the original signal. Indeed, G.728 audio virtually replicates G.711 quality at one-quarter the bandwidth.

There are many different audio-encoding standards. The ones that relate to videoconferencing are listed in the chart below, along with an indication of with which ITU-T video compression standard they are associated (for a thorough discussion of video compression standards, refer to Chapter 7).

DIGITAL SIGNAL PROCESSORS

Compression methods can be categorized in one additional way. Some do their work in software only, while others use a combination of software and dedicated processors. Hardware-assisted codecs have one significant advantage over their software-only cousins: they are much faster.

Codecs are usually implemented on digital signal processors (DSPs). In the past, DSPs were software-based algorithms that ran on mainframes. Engineers soon found ways to move these processors off the CPU and onto less expensive silicon. In the early 1980s, DSPs became available as specialized high-performance coprocessors. Today, DSPs are fine-tuned to the point that they can execute even complex multiply-accumulate (MAC) instructions in a single clock cycle. Because of DSPs, the cost of multimedia on the desktop has declined to the point that it is an attractive option. One multimedia application that makes heavy use of DSP chips is videoconferencing.

DSPs come in two flavors; function and applications specific integrated circuits (FASICs) and *programmable*. Programmable DSPs are multimedia-processing engines that can be harnessed to perform a number of tasks. For instance, they can be programmed to compress either audio or video, using a wide variety of proprietary or standards-based algorithms. Some programmable DSPs process millions of operations per second (MOPS) while others process billions (BOPS). The ability to process different media (audio, video, data) at high speeds is important in videoconferencing applications because, increasingly, a videoconference has video, audio, and graphics content. Moreover, POTS-based videoconferences also require modulation to convert from a digital to an analog format for transmission.

FASICs are also used in videoconferencing applications. They are referred to by the function/application for which they are designed. There are MPEG-1 FASICs, H.320 FASICs, and audio FASICs (e.g., G.723 or G.726 chips).

Many companies manufacture programmable DSPs and FASICs. These include (but are not limited to) C-Cube, IBM, Intel Corporation, and Lucent Technologies. There are many important software-only codecs on the market, too. These include White Pine's Enhanced CU-SeeMe, Intel's Indeo, H.324, and others.

At the time of this writing, the leading videoconferencing codec choices conform to the ITU-T's various codec recommendations. These recommendations are referred to as the H.32X family of videoconferencing codecs. They include compression algorithms that are designed for transmission over ISDN-B channels, over LANs, and over POTS. The ITU-T is working on others that are optimized for transmission over Broadband ISDN (B-ISDN) and Asynchronous Transfer Mode (ATM). The next chapter presents a thorough discussion of these codecs and the standards that define them.

Chapter 6 References

Brooks, John. "Telephone—The First Hundred Years," Harper & Row, Publishers, New York, New York, 1975, pp. 202-223.

DeBaldo, Paul. "Compression Technologies and Techniques," Teleconference Magazine (San Ramon, California) March/April 1983, pp. 10-11.

Green, James Harry. The Business One Irwin Handbook of Telecommunications, 2nd Ed., Business One Irwin, Homewood, Illinois, 1992, pp. 109-133.

Iinuma, K. and Ishiguro, T. "Television Bandwidth Compression Transmission by Motion Compensated Interframe Coding," IEEE Communications Magazine July 1982, pp. 24-30.

Lucky, Robert W. Silicon Dreams, Information, Man and Machine St. Martin's Press, New York, New York, 1989, pp. 37-348.

Mokhoff, N. "The Global Video Conference," The Institute of Electrical and Electronics Engineers, Inc., Spectrum November 1980 vol. 17, pp. 45-47.

Newton, Harry. "Newton's Telecom Dictionary," Flatiron Publications, New York, New York, 1991, p. 630.

Rocca, F. and Zanoletti, S. "Bandwidth Reduction Via Movement Compensation on a Model of the Random Video Process," IEEE Communications Magazine Comm. 20, 1972, pp. 960-965.

7

STANDARDS FOR VIDEOCONFERENCING

"The future of proprietary algorithms for videoconferencing is as bright as the future of EBCDIC for data exchange."

Dave Brown, Network Computing

THE ITU

To accomplish successful interchange, information must be represented in a mutually agreed-upon format. The process of defining the specifics of that format is known as standards-setting. Perhaps the most important international standards-setting body in the world is the United Nation's International Telecommunications Union (ITU). An intergovernmental treaty organization, the ITU was formed in 1865. Its objective was to publish telecommunications-oriented recommendations after studying technical, operational, and tariff-based issues.

The part of the ITU that promotes interoperability in wireline telecommunications networks is the Telecommunications Standardization Sector, or ITU-T (formerly the Comité Consultatif International Téléphonique et Télégraphique, or CCITT). A sister organization to the ITU-T is the ITU-R (in which R represents radio). The ITU-R (formerly the Comite Consultatif International des Radiocommunications—CCIR) coordinates wireless (mainly broadcasting) standards and is currently working to achieve global harmony in the area of HDTV, among other things.

Good things are happening within the ITU-T. The new name indicates an expanded interest—its orientation now plainly extends beyond Europe. Whereas the CCITT originally worked in four-year cycles, the ITU-T has adopted an accelerated standards-setting schedule. The approval process, formerly a face-to-face arrangement, can now be conducted via correspondence and e-mail. Provided a study group is in consensus, final approval can be achieved in a period of months. Also speeding things along are the efforts of non-accredited standards groups such as the International Multimedia Teleconferencing Consortium (IMTC). These ad-hoc bodies develop specifications and introduce them to the ITU-T for approval. This increase in global participation and in speed has helped speed many technologies to market. Videoconferencing is no exception, as we shall see.

THE HISTORY OF THE PX64 STANDARD

Europe was the first part of the world to embrace and implement videoconferencing as a tool for stimulating commerce. In 1979, British Telecom initiated the idea of a European visual service trial. The BT trial started in 1982 and ran concurrently with the European Visual-teleconference Experiment (EVE) that was promoted by the Conference of European Postal & Telecommunications Administrations (CEPT). Both projects required standards-based video codecs, and thereby prompted the CCITT, in 1980, to form the COST 211 Specialists Group. COST was an acronym for Co-Operating for Scientific and Technological research. In 1983, the Specialists Group defined a codec—a single chassis equipped with roughly 40 circuit boards. The specification was formally adopted by the CCITT in 1984 as Recommendation H.120 (Codecs for Videoconferencing Using Primary Digital Group Transmission). It incorporated the standard PAL television signal that most Western European countries embrace.

H.120 multiplexed audio, video, and signaling using the G.732 Recommendation (Characteristics of Primary PCM Multiplex Equipment Operating at 2048 Kbps). It offered interchangeable compression techniques: one optimized for normal face-to-face business meetings, and the other—that incorporated an approximately 1.5 second transmission delay—optimized for sending colored graphic images. H.120 provided for both monochrome and color operation, for multipoint switching between video codecs, and for signal encryption. Eventually, H.120 was expanded to include the SECAM broadcast standard. The new recommendation was named H.130 (Frame Structures for Use in the International Interconnection of Digital Codecs for Videoconferencing or Visual Telephony). Upon H.130's adoption, networks of standards-based publicly-available videoconferencing studios were constructed throughout Europe.

Unfortunately, the *international* H.130 standard fragmented the global videoconferencing market. European codec manufacturers embraced it, but U.S. manufacturers could not deploy it as it was developed for E-1 (as opposed to T-1) networks. To address the problem, the CCITT established, in 1984, a new specialists group. Dubbed the Specialists Group on Coding for Visual Telephony, it was a genuinely international effort that included North American members, enjoyed strong European support, and was chaired by a representative from Japan.

Working on two standards simultaneously, the group met more than ten times between late 1984 and 1988. One of the standards was referred to as Mx384; M stood for *multiples,* the x was pronounced *by* (i.e., M-by-384), and the 384 represented transmission speed in Kbps. The group expected Mx384 to leverage the internationally-available ISDN H0 standard for switched 384 Kbps digital dialing. The second standard was known as Nx64 in which "N" referred to a variable per-second frame rate from 1–30, and "64" referred to the 64 Kbps ISDN B-channel over which a compressed video signal would travel.

By September 1988, the Specialists Group had completed the Mx384 standard. Unfortunately, it was already obsolete. One year earlier, an American manufacturer had introduced a product that delivered adequate picture and sound quality at 224 Kbps. Although the Specialists Group recommended that the CCITT General Assembly formally ratify Mx384, none of the world's codec manufacturers ever built products that conformed to it. Instead, they waited for the Nx64 standard (which was later renamed Px64).

During the process of developing Px64 (pronounced "P times 64"), Study Group XV (the term Study Group had, by that time, replaced the term Specialists Group) had to consider many alternative compression algorithms. No single method offered the efficiency and flexibility to meet the group's goals, so they combined techniques. Unable to afford the time or expense required to model every coding iteration, the Group used computer-based simulation systems that consisted of digitally sampled video sequences. To simulate picture-coding algorithms, they applied various computer programs to the sequence. After compression, they viewed and evaluated the results, made changes, and re-applied the simulated coding process. Eventually, Study Group XV selected a hybrid-coding scheme that became the foundation for H.261, the "Video Codec for Audiovisual Services at Px64 Kbps." H.261, and five other recommendations, were submitted to the CCITT during its July 1990, meeting in Geneva. In December 1990, the CCITT approved all six recommendations, and formally declared them the H.320 family of standards.

H.261

Study Group XV considered many issues as they developed the H.261 specification. First, they recognized that the market for videoconferencing services would benefit from a global standard. Second, they identified that ISDN B channels were being internationally deployed; these digital circuits, used individually or aggregated, appeared to be the ideal transport mechanism. Third, they knew that a compression specification would not achieve broad acceptance if it were not adaptable. By adaptable we mean two things: flexible enough to permit various elaborate and inexpensive implementations and versatile enough to incorporate new technologies as they become available.

The H.261 standard meets these criteria. It accommodates globally-disparate digital network and television standards. Many, if not most, H.261-based implementations use ISDN B channels, just as the CCITT predicted. The products built on H.261 are diverse. Some implement the Recommendation's optional procedures for delivering superior resolution and motion handling while others omit them to reduce cost. H.261 has proven to be flexible enough to accommodate ongoing advances in technology. As chips get faster, frame rates can increase and motion handling can improve without imposing fundamental change on the standard.

H.261 can be a video system's sole compression method, or it can be ancillary, and thereby used as a substitute for a proprietary algorithm when two dissimilar codecs must interoperate. Although the ITU-T has since approved a more efficient codec H.261 is still the most widely implemented videoconferencing codec in the world.

H.261 and CCIR Recommendation 601

The Consultative Committee for International Radio developed Recommendation 601 as an international specification for the analog-to-digital (A/D) conversion of color video signals. An H.261 source coder manipulates non-interlaced pictures in accordance with a portion of that Recommendation. To understand H.261, one must possess some knowledge of CCIR-601's characteristics.

CCIR-601 Characteristics	NTSC 525/60	PAL/SECAM 625/60	CIF	QCIF
Scanning Technique	Interlaced	Interlaced	Non-Interlaced	Non-Interlaced
Fields sampled per second	60	50	30	30
Sub-sampling direction	Horizontal	Horizontal	Vertical and Horizontal	Vertical and Horizontal
Luminance resolution	720 H x 485 V	720 H x 576 V	352 H x 288 V	176 H x 144 V
Chrominance resolution	360 H x 485 V	360 H x 576 V	176 H x 144 V	88 H x 72 V
Chroma Sub-sampling	YCbCr 4:2:2	YCbCr 4:2:2	YCbCr 4:1:1	YCbCr 4:1:1

Figure 7-1. CCIR-601 Picture Formats.

CCIR-601 addresses the incompatibility of the world's three television formats (NTSC, PAL and SECAM) by defining two picture structures that will work with any of them. These are the Common Intermediate Format (CIF) and the Quarter Common Intermediate Format (QCIF). In Figure 7-1, the four CCIR-601 picture

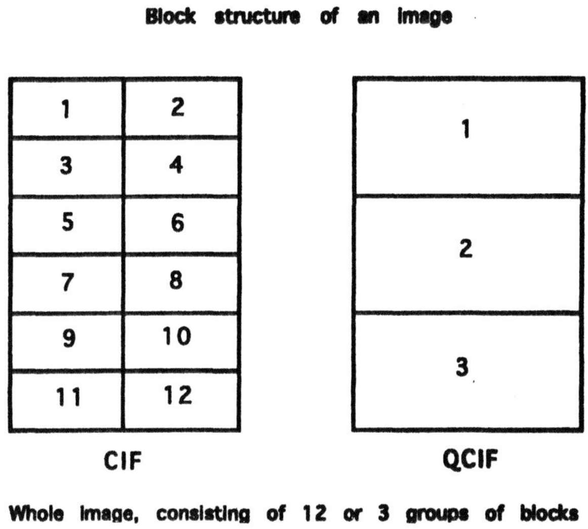

Figure 7-2. CIF and QCIF (Michel Bayard).

structures are presented, along with the techniques used to derive them.

Since H.261 is concerned only with CIF and QCIF resolutions, in our discussion of CCIR-601 we will address only CIF and QCIF image formats.

Both CIF and QCIF are compromises that use the frame rate of North American TV (30 fps), and a resolution that easily adapts to that of European television. Compliance with CIF (also called full-CIF or FCIF) is optional under H.261, while compliance with QCIF is mandatory. At one-quarter the spatial resolution of CIF, QCIF is best suited to small screen (20" and below) and "talking head" (PC window) videoconferencing applications. CIF is much more important to large screen (group system) applications.

The CCIR-601 A/D conversion process begins with frequency filtering. A loop filter separates the frequencies contained in non-interlaced CIF or QCIF images into horizontal and vertical functions. The output of the filter is a two-dimensional array of values.

The values that result from frequency filtering are of two basic types: luminance and chrominance. The human visual system is more perceptive to subtle changes in light than to subtle changes in color. For that reason, the CCIR-601 conversion process allots higher spatial resolution for luminance than for chrominance, specifically for every four luma (Y) samples, two color-differenced samples (Cb and Cr) are taken. This method, known as chroma subsampling, results in a format known as YCbCr 4:1:1.

As we discussed in Chapter 6, quantization follows sampling. Once scanned, the uncoded YCbCr data is quantized according to CCIR-601. Luminance (grayscale)

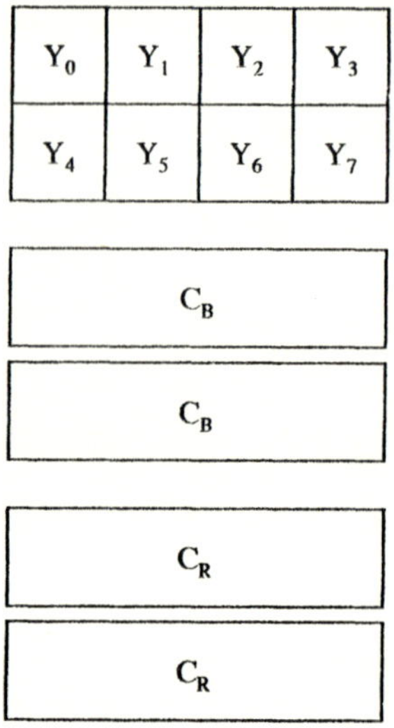

Figure 7-3. YCbCr 4:1:1 Format (Michel Bayard).

information is quantized using one of 220 different levels. Color-difference information is quantized as one of 255 different levels. These quantization levels are the same as those used in the DCT (which, in H.261 encoding, is the next step after quantizing).

One of two different types of compression is applied to the 8-by-8 pixel blocks: intraframe and interframe. It is possible to perform both intraframe and interframe coding on a pixel block but only intraframe coding is mandatory in H.261. Intraframe encoding relies on the DCT (see Chapter 6). Interframe encoding uses DPCM, and motion compensation techniques (also described in Chapter 6). H.261 codecs that perform both DCT and motion compensation are known as hybrid coders. Of course, H.261 codecs operate in pairs or multiples. Each has a coder and a decoder component. The coder on one end talks to the decoder on the other. Between them flows a bit stream that is arranged into 512-bit frames. Each frame contains two synchronization bits, 492 data bits that describe the video frame, and 18 error-correction code bits. These 512 bits are then interlaced with the audio stream and transmitted over Px64 channels in which "P" represents the number of 64 Kbps channels that are available for transmission.

H.261 Options

As we have stated, H.261 is a permissive standard. It allows for a great deal of flexibility. This flexibility can confuse videoconferencing system buyers (and, for that matter, videoconferencing system vendors).

Block structure of an image

1	2	3	4	5	6	7	8	9	10	11
12	13	14	15	16	17	18	19	20	21	22
23	24	25	26	27	28	29	30	31	32	33

Group of blocks, consisting of 33 macro-blocks

Figure 7-4. Subdivision Of A Frame Of Video Into GOBS (Michel Bayard).

As we mentioned above, QCIF, a lower-resolution picture format, is mandatory under H.261 and CIF is optional. CIF and QCIF can code at varying frame rates: 7.5, 10, 15, or 30 per second. As we said in the previous chapter, dropping frames is common as a means of compressing data for transmission. A codec that produces only 7.5 fps is, technically-speaking, just as "H.261 compliant" as a codec that produces 30 fps. This vagueness in the standard allows a manufacturer to slow the frame rate to deliver CIF resolutions (which come at the expense of motion handling).

On the other hand, no matter how many frames are sent in a given second, a receiving codec *must* decode up to and including 30 frames per second. Thus, to assess the end result of a coder's capacity, the evaluator must view it at the decoder. Stated another way, when one compares interoperating codecs, what one sees on the near end is the result of the work being done on the far end.

Motion Compensation

As we just said, H.261 specifies, as an option, motion compensation. Motion compensation is performed *in addition to* intraframe transform (DCT) encoding, which is mandatory. While intraframe coding removes an image's spatial redundancy, interframe encoding works on temporal (frame-to-frame) redundancy. In all cases, H.261 encoding will start out with an intraframe-coded image that has been compressed using a combination of DCT, Huffman and run-length encoding. It must do this in order to have an original frame of video that can become the basis for the motion compensation process.

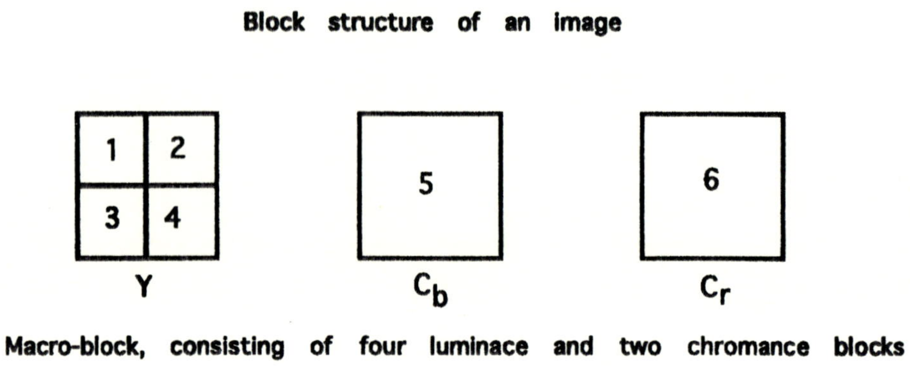

Figure 7-5. Macroblocks (Michel Bayard).

An encoder that compresses using motion compensation presumes that successive frames of video will contain similarities. Thus, it models current frames after previous ones. The codec, working at the macroblock layer, compares a previously encoded frame (a reference frame) to an actual one. As it does so, it looks for motion vectors (a directional movement of groups of pixels). Upon seeing movement, the coder tells the decoder about which pixels are moving and their line of direction. Both codecs then assume this motion will continue. The coder transmits only the prediction error—motion that did not correspond to what was predicted. When the prediction error is minimal, it is not transmitted at all.

When prediction error *is* transmitted, the decoder adds it to the previously coded image, and thereby creates a mathematical representation of the original block. The encoder stores this and uses it to predict the next image. If this were done indefinitely, it could result in cumulative error. For that reason, one out of every 32 blocks is encoded using intraframe techniques, and thereby provides a fresh image.

The requirement for an H.261 codec to decode motion vector information is mandatory, but an H.261-compliant codec does not have to send such information. Sending codecs that *do* use motion vectors often produce superior pictures at the receiving end, in comparison to sending codecs that do not. That is because they are generally three to four times more efficient (allowing better use of bandwidth).

Forward Error Encoding

The CCITT included forward error correction (FEC) as an option in H.261. Forward error correction can reduce the number of transmission errors in a video stream but it does so at the expense of an increase bit rate. The H.261 standard allows a decoder to ignore an encoder's FEC codes, which provide little value in instances in which H.261 applications traverse networks with very low bit error rates. FEC is rarely implemented in H.261 coders or decoders.

Video Multiplexing

Video multiplexing is integral to H.261. It allows a H.261 decoder to accurately scan and decode the flood of bits that represent video data. Multiplexing is performed as a step in the H.261 process by the video multiplex coder portion of the H.261 codec.

An H.261-compliant multiplex encoder must present its output bit stream in accordance with the requirements of a hypothetical reference decoder, described in Annex B of H.261. Various aspects of this hypothetical reference decoder (HRD) are set out in the standard: how it *clocks* to the encoder; what its buffer size is; how often the buffer is examined, what is stored in the buffer and precisely when stored data must be removed. The HRD's buffer size, by definition, depends on the bit rate of the connection. If the bit rate is relatively high, the buffer is relatively large.

Slower transmission speeds mean fewer frames are being delivered in a given second, thus the buffer can be smaller. A HRD is designed to accept the maximum flood of bits permitted in the H.261 Recommendation. The "high water mark" occurs when a high resolution (CIF-capable) codec is sending images over a very fast transmission link (30 B channels) at a rate of 29.97 per second. The HRD must buffer and decode this fast-moving bit stream without dropping frames. It must also be able to buffer reference frames used during motion compensation. All H.261-compliant decoders must conform to Annex B.

Layered Block Encoding

An H.261 encoder multiplexes the bits it passes to a HRD by breaking a picture into four hierarchical layers. A picture (a frame of video) represents the highest layer. This picture has been subdivided into groups of blocks (GOB). Each GOB is sub-divided into macroblocks and each macroblock contains 8-by-eight pixel blocks. Sub-dividing an image into successively smaller blocks permits orderly coding and orderly transmission. Start codes define the two highest layers: a picture is indicated by a 20-bit start code; a GOB is declared by a 16-bit code. At the macroblock layer and below, codewords are used.

A macroblock uses a variable length codeword to indicate where it sits within a GOB. A pixel block uses a codeword to indicate which coefficient is to be used during reverse-transform. At the end of each pixel block there is also an end-of-block marker.

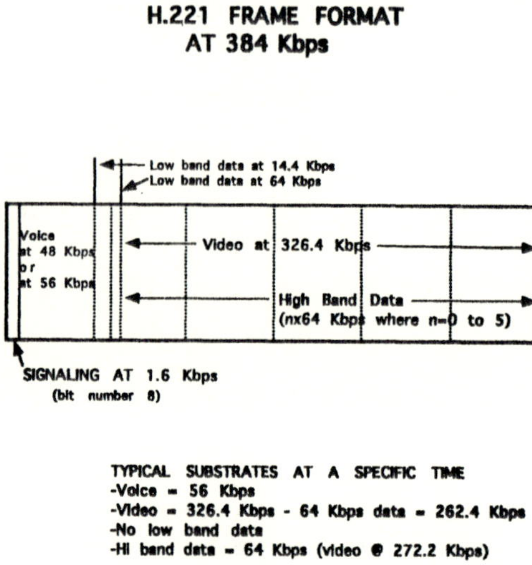

Figure 7-6. H.221 Frame Format at 384 Kbps (Michel Bayard).

A frame of video is broken into GOBs, each of which contains a specific number of luminance and color-differenced pixels. In a GOB, luminance is conveyed using 176 vertical pixels and 48 horizontal pixels. The pixels that convey color difference (Cb and Cr) are spatially arranged with reference to luminance. There are more GOBs in a CIF-resolved image than in one that is QCIF-resolved. The higher-resolution CIF picture requires 12 GOBs; QCIF needs only three.

A GOB is subdivided in to 33 macroblocks. A macroblock represents luminance using 16-by-16 pixel blocks (four 8x8 blocks). The four luminance blocks are overlaid with two color-differenced (CR and CB) chrominance blocks, which cover the same area as the luminance blocks but at half their resolution.

At the bottom of the hierarchy is the block layer. A block is comprised of eight-by-eight pixels. These pixel blocks are encoded using the DCT and, possibly, using motion compensation (predictive encoding).

We have taken the reader step-by-step through the coding specification laid out in the ITU-T's H.261 specification. We conclude our discussion with this final thought: Prior to the December 1990 approval of H.261, customers displayed unwavering brand loyalty to specific codec manufacturers. In 1991, the first H.261 compliant codecs made their debut. By June 1992, all major North American, European and Japanese codec manufacturers supported the standard. The H.261 codec is, today, the fulcrum of videoconferencing technology. Even at 112 Kbps or 128 Kbps speeds, H.261-based systems reliably interoperate. They yield acceptable resolution, audio, and motion handling with a degree of quality that is more than adequate for most business purposes.

As For The Rest Of The Family . . .

The formal title of the H.320 Recommendation is "Narrow-band Visual Telephone Systems and Terminal Equipment." The H.261 Recommendation is only part of the original H.320 family, which was ratified by the CCITT in December 1990. Also included in the original specification are H.221, H.230 and H.242—and two audio encoding specifications, G.711 and G.722.

In November of 1992, the ITU-T added several new recommendations to the H.320 standard. One is H.231, which defines a multipoint control unit for linking three or more H.320-compliant codecs. A second is H.243, which describes control procedures between H.231 multipoint control units and H.320-compliant codecs.

In March 1993, the ITU-T approved G.728, which defines how H.320-compliant codecs will handle 16 Kbps toll-quality audio. G.711, G.722 and G.728 are discussed in Chapter 6.

H.221

The formal name for this specification is "Frame Structure for a 64 to 1920 Kbps Channel in Audiovisual Teleservices." H.221 framing recommendation, probably the second most widely known of the ITU-T's H.320 family, defines the frame structure for a video bit stream across one or more 64 Kbps B channels. It also acknowledges the ITU-T's HO (switched 384 Kbps) dialing and other recommendations such as H11 (switched 1.536 Mbps) and H12 (switched 1.920 Mbps is available only in Europe). H.221 also defines a protocol that allows a single B channel to be broken down into sub-channels that can carry video, voice, data, and control signals.

H.221 specifies synchronous operation. The H.221 coder and decoder handshake and agree upon timing. Synchronization is arranged for individual B channels or bonded connections when contiguous B channels are combined. After synchronization has been established, H.221 sends fixed-size frames of 80 bytes across the network.

Information about synchronization is carried over a service channel. H.221 acquires framing at the start of a session by sending some number of bytes in a pattern. The "service channel" is a bit pattern that is spread-out bit-by-bit over dozens of bytes. Within the service channel are two signals, FAS and BAS. FAS stands for Frame Alignment Signal and is used to delineate H.221 frames.

BAS stands for Bit-rate Allocation Signal. BAS codes are used to indicate the capabilities of the audiovisual devices using the B channel's capacity. There are hundreds of BAS codes that define many different functions that are used to combine B channels into high-bandwidth services at H.0 and other rates. They allow a receiving device to inverse multiplex an incoming signal and to understand the control and indication information coming across the channel. They define how a channel is to be shared between audio, video, and signaling, and indicate how audio is being encoded.

H.230

The formal name for this specification is "Frame-Synchronous Control and Indication Signals for Audiovisual Systems." H.230 Recommendation defines how frames of audio, video, user data, and signal information are multiplexed onto a digital channel. It defines control and indication information for those various data types and supplies a table of BAS escape codes that define the particular instances when control and indication information must be exchanged between sending and receiving devices. The H.230 standard primarily addresses control and indication signaling. H.230 distinguishes four categories of control and indication information: video, audio, codec and MCU interoperation, and maintenance.

H.231

The formal name for this specification is "Multipoint Control Unit for Audiovisual Systems using Digital Channels up to 2 Mbps." H.231 defines the network configuration for an H.320-compliant multipoint control unit (MCU). The MCU is used to bridge three or more H.320-compliant codecs together in a simultaneous conference. The procedures and functionality of a H.231 MCU are defined in a companion standard, H.243.

H.242

The formal name for this specification is "System for Establishing Communication Between Audiovisual Terminals Using Digital Channels up to 2 Mbps." Recommendation H.242 defines the protocol for establishing an audiovisual session, and subsequently disconnecting that session. During an H.242 call set-up, a terminal indicates its capabilities to other terminals.

H.242 defines signaling procedures for identifying a compatible mode, for initiating a conference using that mode and for switching between modes throughout a call. Besides that very important exchange, H.242 covers basic sequences for in-band information exchange. It details procedures for recovering from faults; it specifies procedures for adding channels to, removing channels from, and transferring calls into the session. This Recommendation also works with H.221 to permit a digital channel to accommodate audio, video, and data across a range of data rates. Signaling procedures allow codecs to identify how different portions of the channel are allocated.

H.243

The formal name for this specification is "System for Establishing Communication Between Three or More Audiovisual Terminals Using Digital Channels up to 2 Mbps." Recommendation H.243 is a companion standard to H.231. It describes procedures and functionality for multipoint videoconferencing. Included in the features are chair control/directorship, determining which site will broadcast at any given time, muting video and audio from specific terminals as desired, etc.

THE H.32X FAMILY

The ITU-T has developed, and is continuing to develop, extensions to H.320. H.320 now belongs to a family of standards known as H.32X. In this family, along with H.320, are H.310, H.321, H.322, H.323 and H.324.

The H.32X family is truly a family. Each group of specifications recognizes the other members and each includes similar functionality, albeit with differences, which are largely due to the unique characteristics of the networks, they were designed to operate over.

H.310

H.310 targets HDTV-class video quality (e.g., CCIR-601 and above) using the International Standards Organization (ISO) Motion Picture Experts Group's MPEG-2 video compression algorithm (we address MPEG 2 in more detail in Appendix B).

The H.310 specification employs the MPEG-2 coding system to convert an analog video signal for transmission over a cell-relay-based digital network—in other words, a network based Asynchronous Transfer Mode (ATM). IBM did much of the preliminary work on the H.310 standard, and is working closely with the ITU-T to refine it to the point of approval.

H.310 is made up of three sub-parts. One is H.262 ("Information Technology – Generic Coding of Moving Pictures and Associated Audio Information") better known as MPEG-2. Another H.310 sub-part is H.222.0 ("Information Technology – Generic Coding of Moving Pictures and Associated Audio Information: Systems"). The MPEG-2 standard includes a system layer. The system layer allows MPEG-2 to keep data types synchronized and multiplexed in a common serial bit stream. H.220 adapts H.310 to work within the confines of that system layer. The third sub-part is H.222.1. The preliminary name for Draft Rec. H.222.1 is "Multimedia Multiplex and Synchronization for Audiovisual Communication in ATM Environments." The MPEG-2 system layer specifies a format for transmitting audiovisual information over a data communications network. The format, known as a transport stream, relies on clock reference information to maintain synchronization between related audio and video streams. H.222.1 describes how MPEG-2-encoded transport streams flow over ATM.

H.310 allows various G.7XX audio-quality standards—there are no constraints because ATM has plenty of bandwidth to accommodate any audio coding algorithm. The H.310 standard also references Rec. H.245. H.245 is a multimedia control protocol that permits H.310-aware audiovisual equipment to establish and maintain broadband audiovisual sessions.

As this book went to press, this specification was still under construction. For more information, refer to the IMTC's home page. Subscribers to the ITU-T publications can obtain the official specification directly.

H.321

The H.321 Study Group began developing standards for private ATM networks in 1996. H.321 is a companion standard to H.310. It preserves fundamental components of the original H.320 Recommendation including H.261 and, therefore, maintains a high degree of backward compatibility with it. H.321 functions extend the type of transmission networks that carry H.32X videoconferencing signals to include ATM and broadband ISDN.

As is true of H.310, this specification was still in ITU-T Draft status when this book went to print. For more information, contact the sources listed for H.310.

H.322

The formal name of H.322 is "Visual Telephone Systems and Terminal Equipment for Local Area Networks Which Provide A Guaranteed Quality of Service." Isochronous LANs that can guarantee the constant bit rate required for real time audiovisual exchanges can take advantage of H.322. It integrates components of H.320 and H.324 (see below) such as the H.263 video codec and audio algorithms that include G.722, G.723, and G.728. H.322 also includes the H.261 video codec and G.711 audio codec.

H.322 is widely recognized as Isochronous Ethernet. Developed by IBM and National Semiconductor, isoEthernet was ratified by the IEEE under the title 802.9. It superimposes 96 ISDN B channels on top of 10Base-T Ethernet by using special hubs and network interface cards to create an additional 6 Mbps of bandwidth. The overall 16 Mbps pipe is time division multiplexed into a traditional 10 Mbps Ethernet channel, the 96 ISDN B channels, one 64 Kbps ISDN D channel (used for signaling) and one 96 Kbps M (maintenance) channel.

Although Isochronous Ethernet is an elegant solution, it has not been well received. Perhaps the reason is that it requires a new adapter at the workstation and a special isoEthernet hub/switch. The added cost and effort, combined with the emergence of ATM as the future multimedia-networking standard, have discouraged the major hub and switch vendors from supporting it. This may change, but for now, isoEthernet is a beautiful solution designed for a time-gone-by.

H.323

The formal name of H.323 is "Visual Telephone Terminals over Non-Guaranteed Quality of Service LANs." It was approved by the ITU-T in October 1996. H.323 defines four components: terminal, a gatekeeper, a gateway and a multipoint controller.

H.323 Components

Terminals include devices such as PCs, workstations and videophones. All H.323-compliant terminals must support voice-data conferencing. Voice-data-video conferencing is optional. Multiple channels of each type are permitted.

A gatekeeper aids in call management. The gatekeeper is a utility that controls videoconference access on a packet-switched LAN. It requires that multimedia terminals register "at the gate," which is accomplished when the terminal provides its IP or IPX address. The gatekeeper translates network addresses and aliases to make connections. It can also deny access or limit the number of simultaneous connections to prevent congestion.

A H.323 gateway is different from a gatekeeper. The gateway allows LAN-based H.323 systems to interoperate with other H.32X products. For instance, the gateway could link the H.323 session with an H.320 (ISDN-based) system, an H.321 (ATM-based) system, an H.322 (isoEthernet-based) system, or a H.324 (POTS-based) system. At the present, most H.323 gateway implementations are concerned with linking H.323 and H.320 systems across a LAN/WAN connection.

A multipoint controller is built in to H.323 implementations (typically on the client-side) in which it works to establish multipoint conferences between disparate end points. It is the functional equivalent of the H.320's H.231 and H.243 specifications.

H.323 and Internet Protocols

In contrast to H.322, which deals with LANs that have been modified to provide circuit-switched service, H.323 faces the difficult challenge of providing adequate service in packet-switched environments in which latency characteristics are difficult to manage. It copes by borrowing several different protocols from the Internet Engineering Task Force (IETF). These include the Real-Time Transport Protocol (RTP), User Datagram Protocol (UDP), the Transmission Control Protocol (TCP) and the Internet Protocol (IP).

Although H.323 is not aimed exclusively at IP networks, implementations, for the most part, will run over IP-based LANs. This is because the other protocol mentioned in the standard (Novell's IPX) generally supports only point-to-point connections. Since H.323 multipoint connections are established using multicasting, IPX implementations are unlikely.

On IP LANs, H.323 audio and video uses the UDP. When compared to the

Transmission Control Protocol (TCP), UDP lacks sophistication. It is a unidirectional protocol that does little more than divide data into IP packets and send them, along with a checksum. But UDP is better suited to real-time data types than is TCP. TCP strives for reliable delivery and will retransmit if it detects corrupted packets or packets are not acknowledged. UDP does not retransmit. It discards packets that are corrupted; otherwise it simply forwards them.

To bolster the UDP's lack of reliability, H.323 uses RTP (RTP is also used on the Internet's Multicast Backbone—the MBONE). RTP appends a 10-byte header (that contains a time stamp and a sequence number) to each UDP packet. At the receiving end, H.323 implementations buffer and process UDP packets to capture timing and sequence information and to guard against duplicate and out-of-order packets. Thus, audio, video, and data are generally resynchronized and presented to the user in a coherent stream.

While audio and video use the UDP, H.323 does specify TCP for data conferencing, which is not time sensitive. H.323 also uses TCP for conference control and signaling.

Another IETF protocol, the Resource Reservation Protocol (RSVP), is not an official part of H.323 but products without it may suffer from network congestion problems. The RSVP allows a conference participant to reserve bandwidth for a particular real-time data stream. The reservation is made in the network (in which RSVP-compliant routers receive and grant requests). Although users can ask for bandwidth, there is no guarantee (at the time of this writing) they will get it.

H.323-Compatible Products

Since only the end-points of multimedia applications are impacted by H.323, there is no need to make changes to network interface cards, hubs, routers, or switches—except, perhaps, to upgrade routers and/or switches to make them RSVP compliant. Newer Cisco Systems and Bay Networks products support it, but a bottleneck may occur at any point along the data path at which a device does not.

H.323-compatible products began appearing on the market late in 1996. By the first quarter of 1997, there were many more implementations, which continue to evolve as a result of the rigorous interoperability tests that interested vendors sponsor and participate in.

In October 1998, the ITU-T ratified H.323 version two (H.323v2). The new version of the standard advances integration with T.120, resolves limitations in the original version, and specifies enhancements to the H.225, H.245, and Q.931 protocols. New features include:

GSM Compression Arbitration – New audio capabilities via H.245.

V.Chat Arbitration – V.Chat, a chat protocol, exchange.

Fast Connect or Fast Start – Decreases call setup time by reducing the number of round trip times necessary to establish a session.

Overlapped Sending – Allows connection to be established more quickly by enabling process routing to occur while the calling party is entering the address.

Security – H.235 Specifies enables Authentication, Integrity, Confidentiality, and Non-Repudiation.

Supplementary Services – H.450.1–3 defines the signaling protocol between endpoints for supplementary services, Call Transfer, and Call Diversion.

H.323v2 enhancements include:

Additional Alias Address Types – URLs, Email addresses, and public and private party numbers.

Call Identifier – Creates a unique global identifier to allow all messages associated with a call to be transferable between the RAS protocol in IP networks, and the Q.931 signaling protocol used in circuit-switched telephony networks.

Conference List – Allows a MCU to specify a calling endpoint by sending a Q.931 Facility Message, which contains a list of conferences, to that endpoint.

Conference Requests – Allows for the transmission of new control-oriented H.245 conference request packets.

Dynamic Channel Replacement – Provides a streamlined method of changing modes between codecs that does not require two media decoders.

Empty Capability Set – Enables gatekeeper to re-route connections to an endpoint that supports Supplementary Services (from one that does not).

Endpoint Redundancy – Allows an endpoint to specify an alternate network interface or H.323-defined interface.

Endpoint Type Prefixes and Data Rules – Enables gateways to specify data rates for each supported protocol, and to define prefixes for protocols.

Gatekeeper Redundancy – Enables gatekeepers to specify backup gatekeepers if the primary contact fails.

H.263 – Improves video capabilities and provides new structures to improve the H.263 video stream.

Keep Alive – Enables a gatekeeper to verify the status of a user and to act appropriately by allowing an endpoint to register with a gatekeeper and to inform the gatekeeper of all aliases.

Pre-Granted Admission – Decreases call processing time by enabling endpoint pre-verification.

QoS (Quality of Service) – Allows endpoints to set QoS parameters (e.g., RSVP) for media streams.

RAS Retry Timers and Counters – Enhances RAS transaction processing by ensuring that messages arrive within a specified period, that they are re-sent when needed, and that end-users are notified or delivery failure.

Reliable Information Request Response (IRR) – Introduces two new messages, IACK and INAK, to indicate whether messages were delivered.

Request in Progress (RIP) Message – Allows the receiver of a request to specify, when a message can not be processed before the initial timeout value expires, that a new timeout value should be applied.

Resource Availability – Improves gatekeeper performance by enabling a gateway to notify a it of the gateway's present call capacity.

Time to Live – The duration for which a gatekeeper should keep a registration active.

T.120/H.323 Integration – Requirement that endpoints that support both T.120 and H.323 must begin the call with H.323 to standardize and simplify the process.

Tunneling – Enables Q.931 channel to carry H.245 Protocol Data Units (PDUs).

User Input Indication (PDU) – Enables more inclusive DTMF signaling by providing new structures, such as length of tones.

H.324

The formal name of H.324 is "Terminal for Low Bit Rate Multimedia Communication." It was approved in May 1996 as the first standard to provide point-to-point video and audio compression over analog telephone lines (POTS). A shortcoming of H.320 is its requirement that customers use similar devices at all end points (e.g., V.90 modems or ISDN terminal adapters). H.324 allows users to interoperate across diverse end points (ATM, ISDN, POTS, or even wireless services). In July 1996, sixteen vendors participated in the first formal H.324 interoperability test. More than a dozen participated in subsequent testing.

Whereas H.320 is designed for use with multipoint control units (MCU), H.324 allows users to choose what party they want to see on their monitor through a feature called continuous presence. Continuous Presence allows images to be stacked; it is useful in videoconferences in which one camera can not adequately capture an entire group at one end. H.320 suffered from incompatibilities between systems that were only technically H.320 compliant. In contrast, H.324 allows users to share video, voice, and data simultaneously over high-speed (28.8 Kbps or faster) modem connections using the application interface, V.80. Within the V.80 standard, *voice call first* allows users with V.8 bis enabled modems to add video at any time during an audio only call. V.80 also allows the transmission of still photographs when a signal is inadequate to transmit motion video.

H.324 incorporates both DCT and pulse code technology to provide enhanced video performance at low bit rate transmission. The ITU-T updated the H.261 standard to H.263; H.263 is H.324's video algorithm.

H.223

The formal name for H.223 is "Multiplexing Protocol for Low Bit Rate Multimedia Communication." Within H.324, H.223 defines the multiplexing of the individual audio and video streams into a single synchronized data stream that suits the bandwidth constraints of POTS. To transmit digital data on analog telephone lines, synchronous modems transmit a High-level Data Link Control (HDLC) protocol that adds a framing protocol layer. Using a standard asynchronous interface, videoconferencing would add another framing layer. Because the H.263 codec performs framing, any additional framing the modem performs is redundant. The V.80 interface mediates by letting the host define the frame boundaries for the multiplexed video and audio signal, but allowing the modem to complete the bit-oriented framing.

H.263

The formal name for H.263 is "Video Coding for Low Bit Rate Communication." H.263 is one of two alternatives for video compression under H.324. The other is H.261, which we have already covered.

Although early H.263 drafts specified data rates of less than 64 Kbps, the final Recommendation included no such limitation. The coding algorithm of H.263 adds many performance and error recovery improvements to H.261. For instance, it incorporates half pixel precision for motion compensation; H.261 is limited to full pixel precision. H.263 codecs do not require a loop filter, which is required by H.261 codecs.

Like H.261, H.263 makes QCIF picture formatting mandatory. It provides support (as options) for additional frame sizes. One is the CIF, also used in H.261 codecs. Another is Sub Quarter Common Intermediate Format (SQCIF), which is used for very low-resolution images. And, H.263 compliant codecs can compete with higher bit rate video coding standards (such as MPEG) because of the standard's support for two other formats, 4CIF and 16CIF. 4CIF is four times the resolution of CIF, and 16CIF is 16 times the resolution of CIF.

H.324 implementations will most often use SQCIF because it is helpful for low bandwidth videoconferencing. SQCIF resolves an image at 128 horizontal pixels by 96 vertical pixels. Although this resolution is too low for use in many applications, it suffices for communicating over the PSTN with V.90 modems. SQCIF seems to be most useful for providing a brief sample of a more extensive video segment such as a movie or so-called *infomercial.*

H.324 also allows customers to dynamically choose between two low bit-rate audio codecs, Multi-Pulse Maximum Likelihood Quantization (MP-MLQ) or Algebraic Codebook Excited Linear Prediction (ACELP) and, therefore, to choose audio quality. The two standards feature 6.3 Kbps or 5.3 Kbps audio, respectively. The standard leverages T-84 for still-frame graphics.

Finally, H.263 codecs can be configured for a lower data rate or for better error recovery because parts of the data stream's hierarchical structure are optional. The H.263 standard incorporates four negotiable options to improve performance. One is P-B frames, which, much like MPEG frames, provide forward and backward frame prediction. The other three options are Unrestricted Motion Vectors, Syntax-based Arithmetic Coding, and Advance Prediction.

P-B framing allows two images to be coded as a single unit. The term "P-B" is derived from MPEG (see Appendix B). A P-B frame consists of one P (predictive) frame, which is created by using a past frame as a model and one B (bi-directional) frame that is interpolated (created through comparison) from a past P frame and the P-frame currently being computed. Computationally demanding, P-B framing can really compress a video stream down to a low bit rate. The technique works best for simple sequences; it starts to show stress when there is significant frame-to-frame motion.

When an H.263 codec is in the Unrestricted Motion Vectors mode, it can project motion outside the frame and use those vectors (associated with non-existent pixels) to predict movement along the edge of an image (or sequence of images). This mode also allows an extension of the H.261 motion vector range, and allows larger motion vectors to be considered. This is quite useful in the case of rapid camera movement.

Syntax-based Arithmetic Coding can be substituted in H.263 for Variable Length Coding. This allows the compression process that takes place after Huffman encoding to be based on unique aspects of the motion sequence, (rather than relying on a single "codebook").

Advance Prediction is an optional mode with which a codec can use overlapping block motion compensation for creation of P-frames. Four eight-by-eight vectors can be substituted for a 16-by-16 macroblock. The encoder must determine which type of vectors to use. Four vectors generate more bits but give much better prediction. Advance Prediction coding also results in fewer blocking artifacts.

H.324 Summary

In June 1996, at the H.324 interoperability test, 8x8, Incorporated performed the first two-way video call over POTS lines that met the ITU-T's H.324 requirements. Key to 8x8's H.324 success was the company's proprietary, dedicated Low bit rate Videophone Processor chip that, with hardware acceleration, enables the videophone to work on a PCI-based Intel 486 instead of demanding a 133 MHz Pentium with 16 Mb of memory.

Because of its flexibility and efficiency, H.324 is becoming a popular standard for use on wide area networks. Indeed, the H.324 standard and H.263 codec are likely to displace the H.320 and H.261 combination in many applications.

H.324/M

How low can one go? That might be a good question to pose to the ITU-T, in view of the fact that they are developing a variation of the H.324 standard for cellular telephone-based videoconferencing. The ITU anticipates that H.324/M, the existing videoconferencing suite with added forward error-correction and retransmission codes, will be approved sometime in 1997.

H.324/M permits a full-duplex connection for videoconferencing/multimedia exchanges over the cellular network. There is speculation that the first cellular videophone might resemble a Nokia 9000, which combines a cell phone with a personal digital assistant (PDA). The Nokia has a small LCD screen (now used to display alphanumeric data) that could be adapted to display images. Other cellular telephones offer a similar display.

The ITU-T H.324/M Study Group face a difficult task as they try to adapt the North American AMPS cellular network (which tops out at about 9.6 Kbps bit rates) to carrying time-sensitive streams of synchronized audio and video. The cellular network is full of noise that causes errors in transmission. Additionally, AMPS is used only in North America; most of the rest of the world uses Europe's Global System for Mobile Communications (GSM) standard. GSM is a much more capable architecture, which permits data rates up to about 28.8 Kbps. It may be that the ITU-T will wait for North American Personal Communications Service (PCS), or rather broadband PCS, which is aimed at higher-bandwidth data carriage.

H.235

The formal name of H.235 is "Security and encryption for H-Series (H.323 and other H.245 based) multimedia terminals." One of the improvements that is defined in Revision Two of Recommendation H.323, H.235 was developed to provide a security framework for H.323 and other multimedia systems. It addresses authentication and confidentiality. H.235 can leverage IETF security protocols such as IPSec (Internet Protocol Security) or TLS (Transport Layer Security).

Formerly H.SECURE, H.235 was developed to address the need for organizations to trust the integrity and confidentiality of H.323 calls as they have trusted circuit-switched voice calls. Securing H.323 involves not only protecting the audio or video stream, but also Q.931 (call setup), H.245 (call management), and Gatekeeper Registration/Admission/Status.

H.235 addresses the three fundamental goals of information security, confidentiality, integrity, and authentication. Authentication is the process of identifying and verifying a potential caller/callee, or a particular machine.

Authentication is critical in H.323 security since, without it, anyone can represent himself or herself as anyone else and can thereby enter a conference. Moreover, the execution of all other H.235 security options is contingent upon the authentication of nodes in an H.323 call.

To ensure integrity, H.235 validates a packet's data payload to ensure that the payload has not been corrupted or altered while in transit between endpoints during an H.323 call. The process employed in H.235 is similar to that used in other IP communications protocols. However, rather than using checksums and CRCs (cyclic redundancy checks), H.235 data integrity uses an encryption mechanism (a hash) to protect the packet's integrity value. In this approach, the integrity checksum value must be encrypted, but not the actual data payload. This reduces the necessary amount of encryption processing.

H.235's encryption techniques provide a mechanism to conceal data from eavesdroppers. Without the appropriate decryption algorithm and the key to unlock the encrypted packet, an encrypted packet cannot be viewed even if it is intercepted. However, encryption requires processor-intensive computation and thereby adds delay. Therefore, one must balance the risk that the H.323 call may be compromised against the need to emulate circuit-switching quality in the session. Of course, there is no practical way to make a session completely secure, so one must refer to security policies to determine an organization's risk tolerance before deploying H.323.

Non-repudiation is the prevention of any party from falsely denying that they have made a commitment or, in the case of H.235, denial that they participated in an H.323 session. The most conventional example of non-repudiation (repudiation prevention) is the requirement of a signature upon delivery of a package or acceptance of a credit card. This is important for service providers who must accurately charge for their services and validate those charges, but it is also important for any organization that desires to verify who participated in any given H.323 session.

There are two viable RAS authentication techniques: Symmetric Encryption-Based Authentication and Subscription-Based Authentication. Gatekeepers typically authenticate the client. However, clients can also request the Gatekeeper to authenticate itself. Symmetric Encryption-based Authentication is a one-way form of authentication that is used only by Gatekeepers. It requires no prior contact between endpoints. The Gatekeeper uses this form of authentication to validate subsequent Gatekeeper directed requests and to verify that the requests are from a registered node. Symmetric Encryption-based Authentication does not provide a mechanism for the endpoints to validate the Gatekeeper's identity.

Subscription-based Authentication requires prior contact or information exchange between the endpoints—usually through the use of passwords or signed digital certificates. Each endpoint identifies itself with a well-known text string identifier. Subscription-based Authentication allows both endpoints to be authenticated and is, therefore, bi-directional.

The Q.931 protocol uses a reliable IP transport-based mechanism to establish the first leg in a point-to-point session between two endpoints. The H.245 protocol is responsible for capability exchange communication and mode switching. H.235 integrity protection can enhance security by preventing tampering with the Q.931 and H.245 packets, by enabling complete encryption of the Q.931 streams, and by facilitating user authentication to verify end-points during the transmission of the call setup packets.

H.450

H.450 comprises three recommendations for implementation of *supplementary services* to H.323. The formal names of those standards are, "H.450.1 - Generic Functional Protocol For The Support Of Supplementary Services In H.323," "H.450.2 - Call Transfer Supplementary Service For H.323," and "H.450.3 - Call Diversion Supplementary Service For H.323." All were approved in February 1998.

These supplementary services are designed to enable IP networks to provide the telephony features that users have come to expect in conventional circuit-switched networks and, conversely, to enable conventional circuit-switched networks to provide non-conventional services that are offered on IP networks. H.450 enables hybrid IP/circuit-switched networks by enabling interoperability of IP networks with conventional (legacy) telecommunications equipment. Users can establish native H.323 data, voice, fax, or video sessions on a private network without a H.450 gateway as long as both endpoints support the H.450 protocols and the users subscribe to the services. However, the availability of such services in on calls between networks requires such capabilities across the entire signaling path of the call. Moreover, service providers may adopt business models in which they not only charge per call duration, but also per service. Users can attach legacy telephone and fax devices to an H.323 network with terminal adapters that provide similar functionality to the H.323 gateway. Such a device implements the H.450 supplementary services, and communicates with the legacy device with DTMF tones over the analog interface.

The H.450 protocols are simplifying the migration from proprietary PBX and service provider systems to server-based open standards based systems. Some of the basic services are as follows:

Multiple Call Handling – Enables a multimedia client to concurrently handle multiple calls.

N-way Conferencing – Enables establishment of multi-party conferences.

Call Transfer (H.450.2) – Enables manual forwarding of a call to a third party.

Call Forwarding (H.450.3) – Includes Call Forwarding Unconditional, Call

Forwarding Busy, Call Forwarding No Reply, and Call Deflection.

Call Hold (H.450.4) – Enables a user to transfer another user to a pending status and to resume the call at a later time. Allows for music or messages on hold.

Call Waiting (H.450.6) – Informs user, who is already on a call (or on multiple calls), that another call is coming in.

Message Waiting Indication (H.450.7) – Enables a user to choose from a variety of methods (e.g., email, voicemail, or page) to be informed that he has received a message.

Name Identification (H.450.8) – Provides the called party with the name of the calling party.

Call Completion on Busy Subscriber and on No Reply (H.450.9) – When a called party is engaged in another session, enables a caller to monitor that called party's endpoint to place the call when the called party becomes free.

Audiographic Conferencing Standards

The H.32X family relies on a series of audiographic standards for data sharing during a videoconference. Chapter 8 covers the ITU's T.120 family of Recommendations that provide audio graphic interoperability during H.32X videoconferences.

SESSION INITIATION PROTOCOL

H.323 does not efficiently accommodate Internet conferencing issues such as wide-area addressing and loop cancellation because it was primarily developed for use over a LAN. Even H.323 Version 2, that supports *zones*, does not scale adequately to the size of an IP-based public telephone network. Consequently, the Multiparty MUltimedia SessIon Control (MMUSIC) Working Group of the IETF has developed protocols to support Internet teleconferencing sessions. MMUSIC developed the Session Initiation Protocol (SIP) specifically as a teleconferencing protocol for the Internet, and Session Delivery Protocol (SDP) which SIP uses to convey which codecs an endpoint will support for a session. Concurrently, it developed the Media Gateway Control Protocol (MGCP) as a gateway-to-gateway protocol for use by carriers. Although MMUSIC designed them to support loosely-controlled conferences over the Internet, these three protocols are general enough to also be used in managing tightly-controlled sessions.

Like H.323, SIP provides mechanisms for call establishment and teardown, call control and supplementary services, QoS, and capability exchange. H.323 is less prone to interoperability issues because it more meticulously defines supplementary services, and is mandated to be backward compatible and to interoperate with the PSTN. However, SIP provides more flexibility for adding new features and easier implementation and debugging. Since both SIP and H.323 use RTP to carry media flows, the main difference between the two is their methods of handling call signaling and control.

SIP gained early support from Level 3 Communications, MCI WorldCom, and the cable TV industry for carrying IP services and interacting with the PSTN. Comcast, Cox Communications, MediaOne, Rogers Cablesystems Limited, Tele-Communications Inc. (now AT&T), Time Warner, and Le Groupe Vidéotron began sponsoring SIP/SDP interoperability efforts in 1999 in conjunction with CableLabs. CableLabs is a research and development consortium of cable television system operators that represents nearly 90% of the cable subscribers in the United States, 80% of cable subscribers in Canada, and 15% of cable subscribers in Mexico.

The family is comprised of the following protocols:

Session Initiation Protocol (SIP) – For initiating sessions and inviting users.

Session Description Protocol (SDP) and **Session Announcement Protocol** (SAP) – For distributing session descriptions.

SAP Security – For providing security for session announcements.

Real-Time Stream Protocol (RTSP) – For controlling on-demand delivery of real-time data.

Simple Conference Control Protocol (SCCP) – For managing tightly-controlled sessions.

Session Initiation Protocol (SIP)

The Session Initiation Protocol (SIP) is defined in IETF RFP 2543 and was ratified in February 1999. SIP is an application-layer control protocol for creating, modifying, and terminating sessions with one or more participants. It is targeted at Internet multimedia conferences, Internet telephone calls, and multimedia broadcasts.

H.323 was designed to extend H.320 to packet-switched local area networks. It depends upon H.245 for control, H.225 for connection establishment, and H.332 for large conferences. Furthermore, it leverages H.450.1–3 for supplementary services, H.235 for security, and H.245 for interoperability with circuit-switched services. The interrelations between these protocols can be quite complex. Call Forward, for instance, relies on components of H.450, H.225.0, and H.245. Consequently, H.323v1 call establishment may require as many as twelve packets and about 6–7 round-trip times (RTT). In contrast, SIP reuses many HTTP header fields, encoding rules, error codes, and authentication mechanisms to simplify multimedia conferencing over the Internet. Defined in 736 pages, H.323 defines hundreds of elements; defined in only 128 pages, SIP contains a total of 37 headers. One can implement a SIP call with only the headers *To*, *From*, *Call-ID*, and *CSeq*, and the request types *INVITE*, *ACK*, and *BYE*. While H.323 represents its messages in binary, SIP (like HTTP) encodes messages as text. Moreover, SIP allows for HTTP code reuse so that existing HTTP parsers can be quickly modified for its use.

H.323 was not designed to perform loop detection in multi-domain searches. It requires gatekeepers to maintain information about a session (referred to as *state*) for that session's entire duration. For service providers, this is impractical. SIP leverages a loop detection algorithm that is similar to that in BGP, that allows a gatekeeper to forget about an established session by using UDP. SIP also allows for *stateful* sessions over TCP. Therefore, SIP scales much more efficiently. Also, unlike H.323, SIP does not require a central control point that must remain in the session to provide functionality that the session requires.

Members in a SIP session can communicate via multicast, unicast, or a combination of the two. SIP can be used to initiate sessions, or to invite members (or to add media) to sessions that have been advertised and established by multicast protocols such as SAP, Email, news groups, web pages, or directories (e.g., LDAP). SIP does not require a session initiator to participate in any session that she (or it) initiates. SIP transparently supports name mapping and redirection services, and thereby allows the implementation of ISDN and Intelligent Network telephony subscriber services. SIP is an enabling technology for *personal mobility*, or the ability of end users to originate and receive calls and access subscribed telecommunication services on any terminal in any location, and the ability of the network to identify end users as they move. Called parties can redirect callers to any number of locations that are represented by URLs. H.323 can do this to a limited degree, but it does not allow a gatekeeper to proxy a request to multiple servers.

SIP supports establishment and termination of multimedia communications as follows:

User location – Determination of the end system to be used for communication

User capabilities – Determination of the media and media parameters to be used

User availability – Determination of the willingness of the called party to respond

Call setup – *Ringing*, or establishing call parameters for called and calling parties

Call handling – Such as transfer and termination of calls

SIP is part of the IETF multimedia data and control architecture. As such, it incorporates RSVP (RFC 2205) for reserving network resources, RTP (RFC 1889) for transporting real-time data and providing QoS feedback, RTSP (RFC 2326) for controlling delivery of streaming media, SAP for advertising multimedia sessions via multicast, and SDP (RFC 2327) for describing multimedia sessions. However, SIP's functionality and operation do not specifically depend upon any of these protocols and can be used in conjunction with other call setup and signaling protocols. An end system can use SIP exchanges as a protocol-independent method to determine, from a given address, the appropriate end system address and protocol. SIP can, for example, be used to determine that the callee is reachable via the PSTN, to indicate the phone number to be called, and to even suggest a viable

Internet-to-PSTN gateway. Similarly, SIP could be used to determine that a party can be reached via H.323, to obtain the H.245 gateway and user address, and then to use H.225 to establish the call. Although SIP does not offer conference control services (e.g., floor control or voting) and does not prescribe how to manage a conference, it can be used to introduce conference control protocols. SIP does not allocate multicast addresses. SIP does not reserve resources, but can convey to the invited system what information is necessary to do so. It can invite users to sessions with or without resource reservation.

SIP relies upon SDP for notifying an endpoint of which codecs another endpoint supports. Any one of a myriad codecs can be identified with a string name and registered with Internet Corporation for Assigned Names and Numbers (ICANN is the successor to IANA, the Internet Assigned Names Authority). As such, SIP allows for interoperability with any registered (either standards-based or proprietary) codec.

Although H.323 has a significant head start, it may favor to SIP because the latter is specifically designed for the application that is driving the teleconferencing market, Internet telephony. Anyone who is knowledgeable in HTTP will recognize much of SIP, and will find it intuitive. It seems likely that manufacturers will provide SIP as another option in their multiprotocol telephony gateway. If that is the case, the market will get to decide.

Chapter 7 References

Dalgic, Ismail and Fang, Hanlin. "Comparison of H.323 and SIP for IP Telephony Signaling," Photonics East, Boston, Massachusetts, September 20-22, 1999.

Schulzrinne, Henning, and Rosenberg, Jonathan. "A Comparison of SIP and H.323 for Internet Telephony," *Columbia University Technical Report CUCS-005-98*, January 1998.

Handley, M., Schulzrinne, H., Schooler, E., Rosenberg, J. "Network Working Group RFC: 2543 ACIRI Category: Standards Track SIP: Session Initiation Protocol," IETF March 1999.

Korpi, Markku. "Exploring H.450 Needs and Usability," Telecon West November 1999.

Brown, Eric. "ADSL Jumps Into the Race," New Media October 7 1996 volume 6, number 13.

Carr, Jim. "Solving Asynchronous Transfer Mode—A Practical Guide to Cell Relay," VAR Business March 1, 1996 Issue 1203.

Grunin, Lori. "Image Compression For PC Graphics: Something Lossed. Something Gained," PC Magazine April 28. 1992.

Hurtig, Brent. "A/V Streaming Brings the Web to Life... Almost," New Media October 28, 1996.

Johnson, Colin. "Tool Compresses Images; Fractal Aid Web Pages," Electronic Engineering Times March 25, 1996 Issue 894.

Mehrbians, Raphael. "Modems must provide V.80 support," Electronic Engineering Times November 25, 1996 Issue 929.

Morris, Tom. "Video standards compared," UNIX Review March 1996 v14 n3 pp. 49-55.

Murray, James D. "SPIFF: still picture interchange file format: JPEG's official file format," Dr. Dobb's Journal July 1996 v21 n7 p. 34.

Nolle, Thomas. "Reservations about RSVP," Network World October 28, 1996.

O'Malley, Chris. "The Big Picture," Computer Shopper April 1996 v16.

Ohr, Stephan. "ITU effort eyes mobile video phone," Electronic Engineering Times October 28, 1996 n925 pp. 1-2.

Semilof, Margie. "Users Cool to Network Video," Communications Week November 20, 1995 n585.

Strom, David. "Standards," Windows Sources September 1996. 1996 Ziff-Davis.

Tabaska, Steve as quoted by Rendleman, John. "Carriers Move Ahead With ATM," Communications Week October 14, 1996 Issue 633 Section: WAN Services & Equipment.

Wasserman, Todd. "Net phones rally around Wintel," Computer Retail Week August 5, 1996.

Wilson, Ron. "Designers find many roads to multimedia," Electronic Engineering Times January 29, 1996 n886 p. 47.

Yoshida, Junko. "Emphatically MPEG; MPEG Standard Taking Lead Role," Electronic Engineering Times November 1, 1995 Issue 876.

Yoshida, Junko. "IBM. LSI Logic Launch Full MPEG-2 Chip Sets," Electronic Engineering Times March 25, 1996 Issue 894.

8

STANDARDS FOR AUDIOGRAPHIC CONFERENCING

"Et loquor et scribo, magis est quod fulmine iungo (And I speak and I write, but more, it's with light that I connect)."

Giovanni Pascoli, 1911

In the previous chapter, we discussed the ITU-T standards that are oriented toward face-to-face videoconferencing. In this chapter, we will discuss another aspect of conferencing—audiographics conferencing. Originally, the term audiographics referred to facsimile, slow scan television, and 35mm slides. Today, it refers to applications that blend voice communications (point-to-point or multiparty) with PC-oriented graphics, data, and document sharing. The voice portion of the exchange takes place over ordinary telephone lines; the data portion occurs over LANs, WANs, ISDN, the Internet or POTS. The result is a visually enhanced teleconference in which high-resolution images can be created, exchanged, shared and discussed.

When conference participants can conveniently access and share PC-resident documents, group collaboration is a more rich experience. Audiographics conferencing (better known as *document conferencing* or *data conferencing*) provides the ability for two or more users to *gather around* a virtual conference table to observe and collaborate on documents. Regardless of geographic location or computer operating system, conference participants deploy an array of software- and hardware-based tools and utilities to simulate co-location. The emphasis of audiographic applications is on computer documents and data. For that reason, we will use the term data conferencing (it is also slightly more concise than the term *audiographics conferencing* that the ITU-T uses in the specification for applications, services, and protocols).

Data conferencing eases the burden of preparing for a teleconference. Teleconferences are audio-oriented and are still quite common, notwithstanding the widespread acceptance of videoconferencing. Linking distant teleconference

The International Multimedia Teleconferencing Consortium (IMTC) is a San Ramon, California-based non-profit organization dedicated to the promotion of ongoing development and adoption of international standards for multipoint document conferencing (specifically the ITU-T's T.120) and videoconferencing (the H.32X series). At the time of this writing the IMTC (which is open to any interested party) had approximately 100 members. Neil Starkey of DataBeam is the long-standing president of the IMTC, and has been instrumental in its success.

The IMTC maintains an information-packed World Wide Web site, which can be reached at http://www.imtc.org. If you look around, you'll find an abundance of useful information on audiographic and videoconferencing standards and applications.

participants often requires a preliminary exchange of faxes, electronic mail messages, and overnight packages. Even with all the effort and expense that goes into preparation, teleconference participants often struggle to "stay on the same page" during a remote meeting. Document conferencing provides the missing link. People can coordinate their thoughts when they collaborate visually.

Many instances exist in which a comprehensive videoconference is overkill, and a telephone conversation is inadequate. The missing element is focal, not facial. Data conferencing provides a place to focus, collect, and store the ideas and experiences that result from a meeting. In practice, data conferencing is being used more in conjunction with audio conferencing than with videoconferencing.

THE HISTORY OF DOCUMENT/DATA CONFERENCING STANDARDS

Standards for document conferencing are relatively new. In November 1993, the Consortium for Audiographics Teleconferencing Standards (CATS), a coalition of sixteen founding companies, announced their intention to draft a suite of data and graphics conferencing standards that would compliment the ITU-T's H.320 videoconferencing interoperability standard. The CATS group, in early 1994, began to promote the ratification and adoption of the T.120 family of standards that the ITU-T was developing. CATS was primarily an U.S. oriented consortium.

A more internationally oriented group existed as the Multimedia Communications Community of Interest (MCCOI). MCCOI was principally concerned with promoting the widespread adoption of H.320 videoconferencing standards. However, a MCCOI committee was looking into the ITU-T's emerging T.120 document conferencing efforts. MCCOI and CATS had some common members and soon the two groups were engaged in informal collaboration.

In mid-1994, CATS merged with MCCOI. The combined group took on a new name—the International Multimedia Teleconferencing Consortium (IMTC). The IMTC pledged to continue pushing for standards, but to broaden their scope to include document and data conferencing.

Meanwhile, a group of 150 vendors from the computer software and hardware, telecommunications, and teleconferencing communities was pursuing a similar but somewhat less standards-oriented agenda. The group, spearheaded by Intel and formed in January of 1994, called itself the Personal Conferencing Working Group (PCWG). The PCWG quickly outlined a comprehensive set of specifications that addressed the special needs of desktop and document conferencing users. Called the Personal Conferencing Specification (PCS), it offered interoperability across a variety of hardware platforms, operating systems, and networks. Central to PCS 1.0 was support for Intel's Indeo compression algorithm and Microsoft's DVI graphics/video interface. The document conferencing specification mirrored the features offered by Intel's ProShare family of personal conferencing products. The PCWG came under fire by opponents (read Intel) who accused it for trying to derail the ITU-T's document conferencing standards effort. The IMTC launched an aggressive effort to force the PCWG to support the de jure standards-setting activities of the ITU-T. In response, the PCWG announced that PCS 2.0 would provide support for the ITU-T's Rec. H.320 and Rec. T.120.

Intel defended the PCWG's decision to ignore H.320 in favor of Indeo. It noted that H.320 was a room-system oriented compression algorithm that was too complex for many desktop systems to implement economically. Indeo, a compression-only codec, can be inexpensively added to desktops. This argument took a blow in February 1995, when Microsoft announced support for ITU-T standards.

In May 1996, the Personal Conferencing Work Group (PCWG) agreed to craft the PCS 2.0 specification such that desktop conferencing products initiate calls to other systems using H.320 and T.120. If, after call initiation, the PCS 2.0 software discovers that the called system also supports PCS 2.0 then the software would communicate in the PCS (Indeo/ProShare) mode.

The PCWG's acquiescence settled a long-standing battle on the desktop conferencing standards-front and cleared the way for wide acceptance of the ITU-T T.120 standard. A number of corporations, that had been waiting to see whether the PCWG or T.120 would prevail, signed orders.

Most desktop videoconferencing products on the market now support the T.120 family of data conferencing specifications.

T.120—AN INTRODUCTION

T.120 is an ITU-T standard that defines point-to-point and multipoint document conferencing over a variety of transmission media. Like H.320, T.120 is an umbrella standard. It is a model that defines a flexible communications infrastructure that enables participants in any teleconference (including an H.32X videoconference) to concurrently view, share and exchange computer files. T.120-based conferences do not rely on services from the H.32X family of recommendations and can just as easily stand on their own (although the T.120 standard does not address the audio aspect of a conference).

Using T.120, conference participants can share and manipulate information much as they would were they gathered around a whiteboard in the same room. Sessions can be point-to-point or multipoint. The data exchanged in a T.120 conference can travel between end-points across a variety of network choices. Connections can be established over dissimilar transport services. This allows a single T.120 conference to include consumers connected via POTS, corporate users supported by LANs/WANs, and small office/home office (SOHO) workers linked over ISDN BRI. The conference extends flexibility even further. T.120 conference participants can use virtually any type of desktop hardware and operating system commercially available. Many computer manufacturers now build T.120 support into their operating systems.

Although most people think of T.120 as being used for shared whiteboarding and multipoint file transfer, it is useful for many other applications including telemedicine, online chat sessions, on-line, multiparty game playing, and virtual reality simulations. While H.320 provides a basic means of graphics transfer (T.84, which is essentially JPEG), T.120 supports higher resolutions, pointing, and annotation. T.120 enables audio bridge manufacturers to add graphics to their products in support of a wide range of applications such as training, project management, brainstorming, and engineering.

T.120 is evolving. The ITU-T plans to extend it to include standardized reservation protocols, remote camera and microphone control, and management of the Quality of Service (QoS) delivered by transmission systems. Unfortunately, document conferencing systems manufacturers have stymied much of the progress of T.120 by putting profitability (market share) before interoperability. Therefore, although we address the potential of T.120, the reality is that most document conferences are between users with like software.

T.120

The formal title of the T.120 Recommendation is *Transmission Protocols for Multimedia Data*. T.120 was approved by the ITU-T in Q1, 1996. It contains a conceptual description of the T.120 series of recommendations that define multipoint transport of multimedia data in a conferencing environment. T.120

describes the interrelationships between the constituent standards that make up the Series. It also describes how the T.120 series can be used in support of other ITU-T standards, namely, the H.32X family of videoconferencing specifications.

T.120 encapsulates the concepts it expresses in six supporting ITU-T recommendations, arranged in a layered hierarchy. Each layer leverages its preceding layers to define protocols and service definitions.

T.121

The formal title of the T.121 Recommendation is "Generic Application Template." T.121 describes a conceptual model of a T.120 application and defines those operations that are common to most T.120 application protocols.

This portion of the series aims to facilitate the process of applications development. It does this by providing a common structure of protocols and services that underlie T.120 applications. This structure ensures a consistent approach to the development of T.120-compliant applications. The Generic Application Template does not impose rules on the structure of application software but rather defines what that applications that software might be called on to support.

T.122

The formal title of the T.122 Recommendation is *Multipoint Communication Service for Audiographics Conferencing—Service Definition*. The T.122 MCS is a generic connection-oriented service that collects point-to-point transport connections and combines them to form a Multipoint Domain.

T.122 supports highly interactive multimedia conferencing applications. It supports full-duplex multipoint conferencing among an arbitrary number of connected application entities over a variety of networks (as specified in T.123). T.122 assumes error-free transport connections with flow control. It uses these connections to provide broadcasts and to support multipoint addressing (one to all, one to sub-group, one-to-one). It also ensures selection of the shortest path to reach the receiver and uniform data sequencing. T.122 uses tokens to resolve resource contention—channel availability.

T.122 also works in tandem with T.125, a multipoint communication service protocol. Together, the two form Multipoint Communication Services, the regulative portion of T.120 conferences.

T.123

The formal title of the T.123 Recommendation is *Protocol Stacks for Audiographic and Audiovisual Teleconference Applications*. T.123 presents a uniform OSI Transport interface and services to the MCS layer above it. Essentially, it is comprised of numerous network-specific transport protocol stacks. Network categories are addressed in T.123 profiles and include ISDN B channels, POTS,

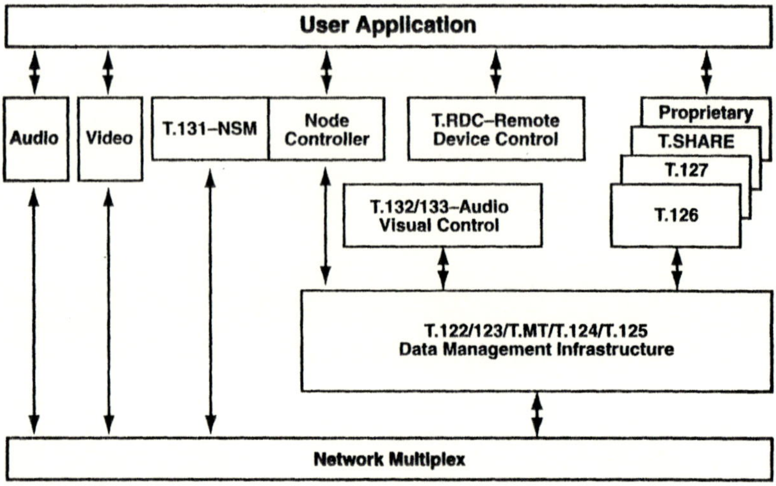

Figure 8-1. The T.120 Family of Recommendations (Laura Long).

packet-switched networks (IP and IPX), and others. Each profile may extend as high as layer seven in the OSI reference model, depending on the mode selected.

T.124

The formal title of the T.124 Recommendation is *Generic Conference Control.* T.124 provides a high-level framework for conference management and control. Generic conference control functions provide tools for the establishment and termination of sessions and the coordination of conference management. They also allow oversight of the nodes that are participating in a conference, and provide a registration directory to track them. A portion of the specification is devoted to managing the roster of application capabilities and the Application Protocol Entities that support them.

The services addressed by T.124 include:

- Conference establishment and termination
- Managing the conference roster
- Managing the application roster
- Application registry services
- Conference conductorship
- Miscellaneous functions

T.125

The formal title of the T.125 Recommendation is *Multipoint Communication Service Protocol*. T.125 defines a protocol that operates across layers of multipoint communication hierarchy. It specifies the format of messages that are passed between T.125 entities, and procedures that govern their exchange over a set of transport connections. The purpose of T.125 is to implement the services defined by ITU-T Rec. T.122.

T.126

The formal title of the T.126 Recommendation is *Multipoint Still Image and Annotation Protocol*. T.126 defines the protocol to be used by a wide array of user applications that require the exchange of graphical information in a heterogeneous (multi-vendor) environment. Applications include the annotation and exchange of still images, simple whiteboarding, screen sharing, and remote computer application piloting. T.126 uses services provided by T.122 and T.124.

The T.126 protocol permits conference-wide synchronization of multi-plane/multi-view graphical *workspaces*. An extensible set of bitmap, pointer and parametric drawing primitives can be directed to these workspaces. The protocol also supports advanced options (keyboard and pointing device signaling), and can be used in remote application piloting and screen sharing. T.126 also supports in-band facsimile exchanges. T.126 is deliberately extensible; it allows any new or extended capabilities that are not defined in the original specification to be added later. Information about these extended capabilities is passed in-band.

T.127

The formal title of the T.127 Recommendation is *Multipoint Binary File Transfer*. T.127 defines multipoint binary file transfer within an interactive conference. It provides mechanisms that facilitate simultaneous file distribution (broadcast) and retrieval. It also provides for private distribution of files to a selected subgroup. T.127 permits file distribution control by a chairperson.

T.127 protocols are simple and versatile. They provide a core functionality with the ability to extend that core to meet the demands of more sophisticated applications.

T.SHARE

The formal title of the T.SHARE Recommendation is *Multipoint Computer Application Sharing Protocol*. T.SHARE has not been adopted, but the work of its authors is worthy of reconsideration at a later date.

T.SHARE defines a cross-platform, multipoint computer application-sharing model. It allows a computer application hosted at one site to be viewed at all sites within a session. It includes provisions that arbitrate which site is currently in control of the session's pointing device and keyboard stream. The result of T.SHARE is that multiple sites can concurrently host one or more shared applications.

T.SHARE has two modes of operation. One, the *Legacy Mode* was designed to be compatible with Microsoft's NetMeeting and PictureTel's Group Share products. This was included to achieve industry compatibility in a market dominated by some very large companies. The Legacy Mode coexists harmoniously with all other T.120 application protocols, but no future enhancements will be made to it.

The Base Mode is modeled after the Legacy Mode but it makes more extensive use of generic conference control for capabilities negotiation and session management. Physical Data Unit organization and encoding has been brought in line with other T.120 application protocols. The Base Mode will provide the basis for future extensions to T.120's application sharing support.

T.SHARE does the following:

- Provides a protocol for font matching and text exchange
- Provides a protocol for basic window management
- Defines a protocol to manage shared pointers
- Supports compressed bitmap exchanges
- Supports rectangle, line and frame operations
- Defines caching policy for bitmaps, pointers, color tables & desktop save areas
- Defines protocol for the communication of keyboard & pointing device events

T-SHARE has been available on the Macintosh platform, on UNIX, and on various Microsoft Windows platforms (Microsoft's Remote Desktop Protocol, RDP, is a single-session extension of T.SHARE).

T.120 FUTURE ENHANCEMENTS

T.RES

The T.RES is concerned with Reservation Systems. This T.120-oriented set of specifications was designed to simplify the process of reserving a conference across product platforms. Like T.SHARE, T.RES deployment has suffered at the expense of manufacturers who do not necessarily consider cross platform interoperability to be in their interests. It is quite unfortunate.

There are four components to T.RES—T.RES.0, T.RES.1, T.RES.2 and T.RES.3. T.RES.0 provides a reservation system overview. T.RES.1 defines the user-to-reservation system interface. This protocol specifies how user terminals access conference reservation systems. T.RES.2 defines a reservation system-to-MCU interface. T.RES.3 defines a reservation system-to-reservation system interface.

T.MT

T.MT is a set of specifications that are designed to allow Multicast Transport—e.g., to enable the multipoint conference service (MCS) to ride on the top of IP-based networks. To accomplish this, T.MT relies on several different methods to transport data across IP-based networks. The first is UDP (see Chapter 9). The second is OSI end-to-end services on top of the Internet suite of protocols (TCP/IP). OSI over TCP relies on RFC 1006, an important IETF document ("ISO Transport Arrives on Top of the TCP/IP") co-authored by Dwight Cass and Marshall T. Rose. Additional transport techniques include Multicast Transport Protocol-2 (MTP-2), which is a revised version of MTP (originally introduced as RFC 1301) and Real-Time Multicast Protocol (RMP); T.MT also includes an *other* category for IP-based transport protocols as yet unspecified.

T.MT's deployment has been limited because Internet service providers do not want their already over-subscribed networks to have to support the additional traffic that Multicast introduces. As bandwidth becomes cheaper and, subsequently, as the backbones become more robust, T.MT may play an important role.

T.130

T.130 represents an entirely new family of ITU-T standards. T.130 (along with T.132) was determined in March 1997 and ratified in 1998. Like T.120 it is an overview document that incorporates subordinate recommendations. These provide a network-independent control service for Real-Time audio and video streams. Implementation of the completed standard will allow users to coordinate the audio and video components of a conference across diverse network boundaries. At the IMTC's Fall Forum in Sunriver, Oregon, Pat Romano, Director of Advanced Development, Polycom, Inc., delivered an update on the ITU-T's progress as it relates to T.130. Our discussion of T.130 is primarily based on this presentation. Even at the end of 1999, little exists on T.130 because it simply has not been deployed. Vendors all state that they are interested in T.130 and that they are following the standard.

The T.130 specifications are:

- T.130 Real Time Audio-Visual Control for Multimedia Conferencing
- T.131 Network Specific Mappings
- T.132 AVC: Infrastructure Management
- T.133 AVC: Conference Service Management
- T.134 Multimedia Application Text Conversation protocol (T.CHAT)
- T.135 Secure T.120 conferencing

- T.RDC Remote Device Control
- T.TUD Transportation of user-defined bitstreams between endpoints

T.130

The formal title of the T.130 specification is *Real Time Audio-Visual Control for Multimedia Conferencing*. T.130 and T.132 were determine by the ITU-T in March of 1997 and ratified in 1998. T.130 provides a description of how terminals with diverse capabilities can manage audio and video transcoding, continuous presence and other features in a conference. T.130, where possible, leverages existing ITU-T control protocols (H.242/3, H.245). It addresses virtual networks and virtual and distributed multipoint conferencing units—a concept that is new to the H.32X and T.120 family. In addition, T.130 allows a terminal to request and measure the network quality of service (QoS) with respect to Real-Time streams.

The T.130 series defines an architecture, a management and control protocol, and a combined set of services that constitute an Audio-Visual Control system (AVC). T.130 supports the use of Real-Time streams and services in a multimedia conferencing environment. T.132, outlines the protocol and services in terms of management and control. T.130 enables devices (e.g., conference server, gateway, or MCU) to provide endpoints with T.132 video and audio services. Such services include stream identification, on-air identification, video switching, audio mixing, continuous presence, and remote device control.

The T.130 series leverages H.320 and T.120. It is compatible with systems in which audio and video are transmitted independently of T.120. However, it is also compatible with systems that are capable of transmitting multiple media types within a common multiplex. T.130 is useful for any conferencing scenario that requires multipoint audio or video. Because of the transmission requirements of Real-Time dataflows, the audio and video streams are transported in independent logical channels. However, T.130 relies upon the services of GCC and MCS to transmit control data.

Although the T.130 suite addresses manipulation of real time streams within an established conference topology, it does not define mechanisms to set up that topology. Terminals are not required to implement the protocols referenced in T.130 to participate in the audio and video portions of a T.130-based conference. However, terminals that do not may have very limited options as they relate to audio and video control services.

T.131

The formal title of the T.131 is *Network Specific Mappings*. Each network requires unique control mechanisms that manage audio and video streams. T.131 specifies the mapping between the network-independent control mechanisms of T.132/3 audio video control (AVC) and that of the active network. Network specific mapping mechanisms reside in a node controller. Given that AVC depends on the data services provided by T.120, it must provide for the inheritance of audio and video streams that are activated prior to the start-up of T.120.

Networks supported by T.131 include:

- PSTN Defines interaction between AVC and H.245 in H.324 systems
- ISDN Defines interaction between AVC and H.242/3 in H.320 systems
- LAN Defines interaction between AVC and H.245 in H.323 systems
- ATM Defines interaction between AVC and H.245 in H.310 systems
- DSM-CC Defines interaction between AVC and DSM-CC DAVIC systems

T.132

The formal title of the T.132 is *Audio Video Control: Infrastructure Management.* The T.132 protocol performs operations that are needed by T.133, Audio-Video Control: Conference Services. T.132 specifies mechanisms for multimedia capabilities exchange (whereby terminals handshake and exchange information about the services that they support/require). It also defines procedures used to arbitrate access to the various channels and support mechanisms that, collectively, sustain a conference. T.132 characterizes the procedures used to configure and control the audio-visual infrastructure.

The T.132 specification introduces the concept of zones, whereby a zone is a group of terminals that share a common network type. For instance, videoconferencing terminals connected in a switched digital arrangement (e.g., via ISDN) might comprise Zone 1 while terminals connected to an H.323 LAN might constitute Zone 2. Zone 3 might contain terminals connected via POTS. A zone manager would represent each zone on behalf of the entire bridged connection (where all three zones are linked). T.132 defines procedures that arbitrate the access to audio-visual infrastructure across zones.

T.133

The formal title of the T.133 Recommendation is *Audio Video Control: Conference Services.* In the T.130 family, T.133 defines audio video control conference services. These include:

- Real Time Channel Management
- Video switching
- Video processing and transcoding (including continuous presence)
- Audio mixing
- On air indication

- Source identification and selection
- Floor control
- Privacy

T.133 relies on the services provided by T.132, which it uses to convey service-oriented capabilities across zones and between terminals.

T.RDC - Remote Device Control

The formal title of T.RDC is *Remote Device Control.* The T.RDC specification provides for remote control of cameras, VCRs, microphones and other peripherals. It defines a mechanism to select and configure audio and video sources. Using the T.RDC specification, T.130-compliant terminals can define the control of audio mixing, video switching and continuous presence facilities.

T.RDC is defined in the spirit of a T.120 application protocol that additionally uses the services of AVC (T.132/3). It attempts to define a number of standard device types (cameras, microphones, VCRs) with standard control attributes. This model accommodates network equipment and unmanned audio/video device paradigms in addition to conventional audio/video terminals. The technical direction of T.RDC is to endow T.130-compliant nodes with the ability to advertise attached devices and their associated attributes. A T.RDC protocol will be defined to control, configure, query status and receive event notifications from remote peripherals.

Development of T.120 Compliant Products

With the T.120 standards complete, third-party developers must now implement them. Several development environments are available for doing so. Perhaps the oldest and most widely used is DataBeam's T.120 toolkit for developing multimedia data-sharing applications. The toolkit encapsulates the complex T.120 specification into a development environment that can be used to create complex, standards-based point-to-point and multipoint applications. Others are following in DataBeam's footsteps. DataBeam deserves special mention because it has been involved in the T.120 process since its inception, and because it has displayed admirable restraint in avoiding any temptation to put its own particular spin on things. DataBeam has acted in the interests of the T.120 family of standards and, therefore, in the interests of users, vendors, and the market in general.

Using T.120 mature development environments accelerates the development of software applications and network infrastructure products (i.e., PBXs, bridges, routers, network switches, and LAN servers). T.120-based products can deliver industry-wide interoperability in the areas of data collaboration and document conferencing. For a complete list of companies that supply these products, refer to Appendix H, Interactive Multimedia Suppliers (by Category).

T.120 / T.130: A TRIBUTE TO THE ITU-T AND IMTC

To respond to proprietary audio video system, standards-based products must provide roughly equal capabilities. The argument that proprietary is better is only difficult to counter when standards bodies stop short of complete specifications that address real-world needs.

The ITU-T and the IMTC perform a tremendous service for the videoconferencing and data collaboration industry — and for the users of industry products. Their accomplishments, to date, reflect their pragmatism. Equally important is their ability to work quickly and thereby keep abreast of proprietary advances. Because of their diligence, these two groups have essentially discouraged even the largest players from *going it alone*.

All the goals that T.120 initially set out to accomplish are completed. Moreover, goals were added throughout the standards-setting process. Not only are most of the core standards stable and complete, they are already being revised after years of exhaustive effort.

The IMTC will continue to work on the T.120 and T.130 protocol suites; years will pass before they consider those standards complete, if they ever do. Technology marches along and those who draft standards must lock step. On the horizon are plans to extend the infrastructure standards to leverage new communications technologies as they emerge (e.g., ATM, wireless networks, and cable television networks). The IMTC will also work to expand the set of application protocols (e.g., chat, generic object management, and remote procedure invocation).

T.120 and Cable Television

The DSM-CC/T.120 coordination group (DTCG) was formed in February 1996. A specification being developed by the International Standards Organization (ISO) DSM-CC (Digital Storage Media-Command and Control) defines a user to network and user-to-user interface for digital television. An early version of it, in which a simple stream control protocol for MPEG-2 Transport Streams, is included in MPEG-2 ISO/13818-1 Standard for encoding/decoding of video streams. The DTCG is concerned with mapping between DSM-CC resources and T.120 transport systems. Provisions for T.120 multipoint bridging and conference directory services within the DSM-CC environment are specified. Descriptions of the technical details regarding DSM-CC and T.120 integration appear in draft T.130 Annex A. Now more than 400 pages in the current ISO/IEC 13818-6 International Standard, DM-CC provides the necessary protocols for such applications as home shopping or video on demand.

DSM-CC is a transport layer independent, generic client-server model. DSM-CC defines network session and resource control, configuration of a client, and downloading to a client so that a server can push the latest information and the latest software to the client. It also defines VCR-like control of the video stream, generic interactive applications services, and generic broadcast applications services such as data carousel, a user to user object carousel, and switched digital broadcast channel change (that provides VCR functionality). Fiber to the Curb (FTTC) and Hybrid Fiber Coax (HFC) each support DSM-CC.

The Digital Audio-Visual Council (DAVIC) has adopted DSM-CC in its DAVIC 1.0 Specification as the protocol for control of multimedia interactive sessions, the resources within sessions, and for service level interactions. DAVIC is also applying DSM-CC to Internet access. The ITU-T Study Group 8 is also applying DSM-CC as part of the T.120 Multimedia Conferencing Recommendations.

CHAPTER 8 REFERENCES

"A Primer on the T.120 Series Standard," DataBeam. December 1999. http://www.databeam.com/ccts/t120primer.html

"Ratification Schedule for the T.120 and H.323 Series Standards," DataBeam. December 1999. http://www.databeam.com/standards/schedule.html

Adams, Chris. "An Introduction to Digital Storage media – Command and Control," Nortel. 1996.

"T.120-Based Conferencing To Explode," Newsbytes September 25 1996 PNEW09250010.

Brown, Dave. "Bytes. Camera. Action!" Network Computing March 1, 1996 v7. n3 pp. 46-58.

Grigonis, Richard. "H.324 Video and T.120 Data Will Change Your Life," Computer Telephony October, 1996 pp. 122-131.

Halhed, Basil R. "Standard Extend Videoconferencing's Reach," Business Communications Review September, 1995 p52.

Knell, Philip D. "The Multipoint Revolution: Where We're Headed," Telecon XVI Show Issue October 1996 v15 n5 p. 13.

Labriola, Don. "The Next Best Thing," PC Magazine December 1995 v14 n21 pNE 1-9.

Lee, Yvonne L. "Videoconferencing Takes Off As Vendors Standardize Wares," InfoWorld June 3 1996.

Masud, Sam. "Conference server beams Internet users in real time," Government Computing News June 10, 1996 v15 n12 p. 55.

Romano, Pat. "T.120 Update," IMTC Fall Forum. Sunriver, Oregon, October 1996 (Courtesy of the IMTC and Polycom. Inc.)

Rose, Marshall T. "The Open Book," The Wollongong Group Inc. Prentice Hall 1990.

Schroeder, Erica. "PictureTel, Intel Deals Shape Future Of Videoconferencing," PC Week April 3, 1995 p97.

Semilof, Margie. "Intel Retreats on Conferencing Spec," Communications Week March 6, 1995 p. 157.

Sullivan, Joe. "How T.120 Standards Support Multipoint Document Conferencing," Business Communications Review December, 1995 p. 42.

9

STANDARDS FOR CONFERENCING OVER IP NETWORKS

The standards that have come out of the IETF have been impressive. They are produced quickly, and they work.

Carl Malamud

THE INTERNET AND INTERACTIVE MULTIMEDIA

Today's enterprise seeks out networks capable of transmitting all media—voice, still-image moving-image, and data. The goal is to find a single solution for all corporate information flows, to front-end it with a Web browser, and endow it with enough bandwidth so that the average corporate user never has to give the network a second thought.

With the rise in popularity of the Internet and its enterprise-adapted equivalent, the intranet, the direction of the enterprise network is now clear. Corporate America is migrating over to TCP/IP (Transmission Control Protocol/Internet Protocol)—leaving behind SNA, IPX/SPX and other proprietary networking protocols. While open-systems standards are great things, it's also true that they evolve in response to a particular need or application set. This holds true for TCP/IP, a set of Internet Engineering Task Force (IETF) protocols that are defined in a diverse group of Request For Comments (RFC) documents. RFCs are a series of notes that contain Internet-oriented protocols. RFC documents also set forth ideas, implementation techniques, observations, studies, measurements, and clarifications related to the diverse set of specifications that collectively run on Internet Protocol (IP) based networks.

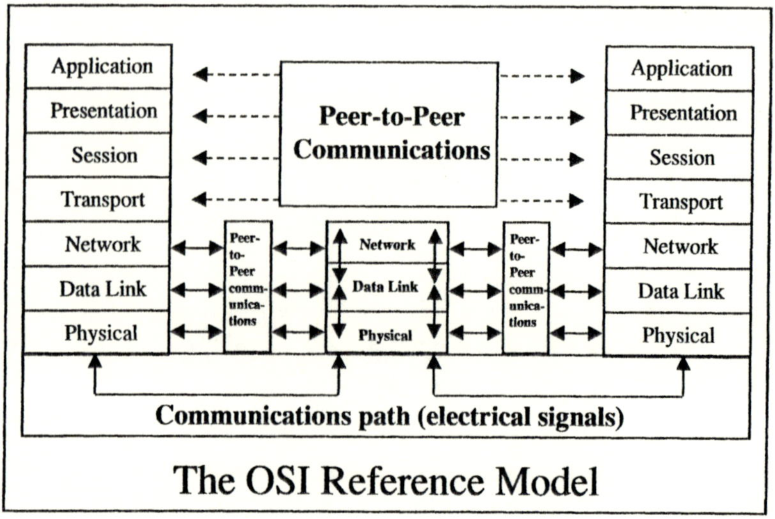

Figure 9-1. The OSI Model.

Before we can discuss videoconferencing over internets (a generic term which includes both the "capital I" Internet and corporate intranets), we must understand how certain IETF protocols function, and how those functions must be modified to meet the unique needs of real-time media streams.

IP-Based Networks

TCP/IP is a protocol suite. A protocol suite (also known as a "stack") is made up of a set of protocols that permit physical networks to interoperate. Protocol suites are layered in such a way that they break up the interoperability task into a set of services. These layers are often discussed in relation to the ISO's OSI Reference Model. The OSI model describes a conceptual seven-layer architecture that divvies up interoperability tasks. It does this by starting at the top, with an application (conferencing, for instance) working its way downward all the way to where the application's bits are placed onto a physical network.

In a layered protocol, higher-level protocols require services from protocols below them. In return, they provide services to lower-layer protocols. Each protocol in a "stack" also provides services to its peer on the other side of the connection.

TCP/IP conforms to the OSI reference model conceptually, but not precisely. It is has four conceptual layers. There is the Application Layer, which passes messages or streams between devices. There is the Transport Layer, whose primary duty it is to provide reliable, end-to-end communication across applications. There is the Internet Layer, which handles communications from one machine to another. This layer moves packets or datagrams, as they are known in IP networking terminology. Lastly, there is the Network Interface Layer. It is responsible for

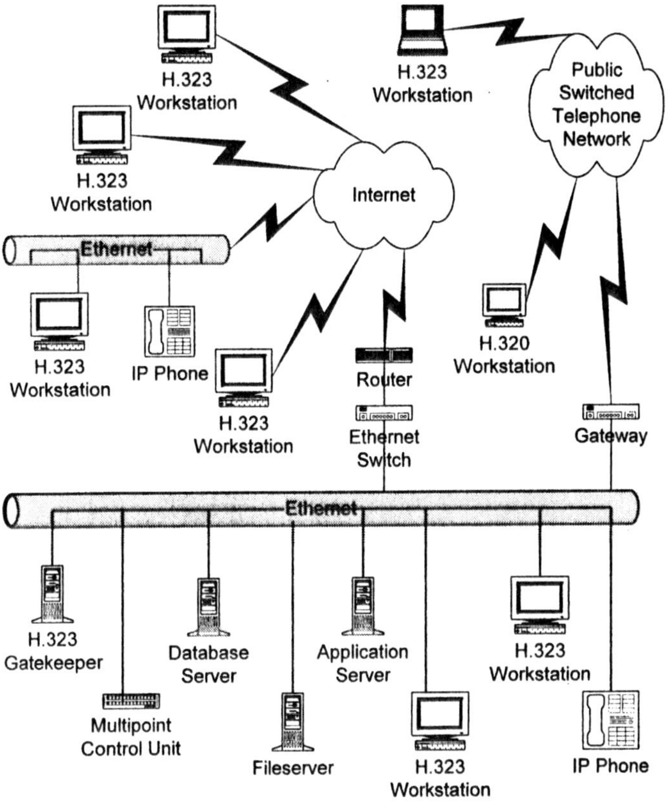

Figure 9-2. An H.323 Network.

accepting IP datagrams and transmitting them over a specific network. Using these four layers, TCP/IP forms a virtual network in which individual hosts are identified not by physical network addresses but by IP addresses.

The networks that comprise an inter-network (whether *the Internet* or an intranet) are physically connected by devices called routers. A router is a special computer that is designed to transfer datagrams from one network to another. The IP protocol routes datagrams by hopping from network to network. The router acts as a connection point between networks, or a *gateway*. Software hides the underlying routing process from the user and thereby makes the process transparent.

Routers perform their task by using IP addresses. IP addresses are actually 32-bit strings that identify specific network devices. To make them easier to remember and understand, people express IP addresses in dotted decimal notation, (e.g., 134.13.9.6). When conveyed across a network, these addresses are converted to hexadecimal notation (hence, the 32 bits). Special database servers, or DNS (Domain Name System, RFC 1034, 1035) servers, translate IP addresses into more

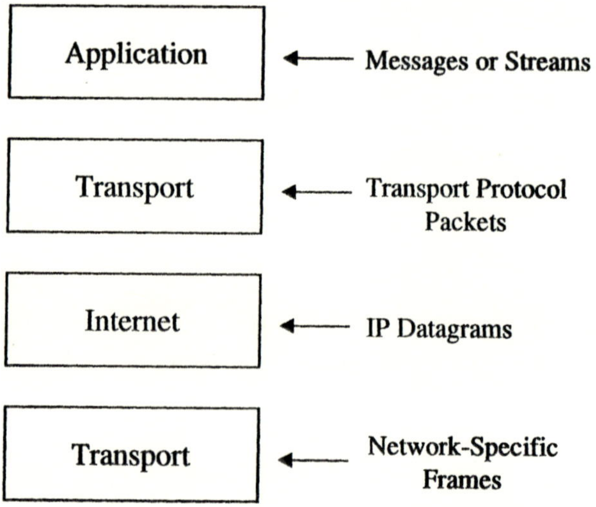

Figure 9-3. Layering in the TCP/IP Protocol Stack (Laura Long).

recognizable Internet addresses. An example of this is *name@company.com*.

The component of the address to the left of the @ character is the local part of an address, and identifies a user. The component to the right side of the @ character identifies the *domain*, or the name of the system (whether that person's company or an Internet service provider) that provides services for the user.

A domain name such as *company.com* refers to the company, *company*, in the commercial (*com*) sector. Other suffixes include *org* for non-profit organizations, *edu* for educational institutions, *gov* for government agencies, and *net* for network services providers. The domain *company.com* can be further subdivided in to sub-domains such as *eng.company.com* and *mkt.company.com*. The subdivision will distribute the site in to smaller sections to avoid network congestion and to simplify network management. The term *sub-networks*, or *subnets*, refers to these subdivisions or smaller network segments.

Through a global network of routers and DNS servers, computers anywhere in the world can communicate with any other host, as long as they have that host's Internet address and they have been granted privileges to do so. After DNS does its job at an Internet-wide level, a smaller version of DNS is applied to convert a human-friendly Internet address to a computer-friendly IP address. Lower in the stack, the network interface layer converts an IP address into a machine address (e.g., a 48-bit Ethernet ID).

Internetworking, specifically TCP/IP internetworking, was designed for the exchange of data and documents. It was never intended to meet the rigors of time-sensitive media streams. This becomes glaringly apparent when people try to conduct videoconferences over the Internet. Some desktop conferencing products have tried to deliver synchronized audio/video over the Net. But, most reviewers share the same opinion: these products deliver two results. First, they tend to wreak

havoc on the performance of other applications. Second, they produce only minimally-acceptable frame rates, with sound and pictures that are unstable, garbled and poorly synchronized.

The biggest obstacle to deploying Real-Time multimedia over the Internet is the lack of an appropriate infrastructure and interoperability between different schemes. TCP/IP protocols do what they are supposed to do: transmit data across a network reliably, and in a proper sequence. In theory, when network traffic is light, TCP/IP is capable of reliably transporting Real-Time, synchronized multimedia. But in the real world, most networks suffer from periodic congestion. Faced with contention, TCP/IP is not able to guarantee that Real-Time media will arrive properly timed, and with all audio and image packets intact.

The Internet Engineering Task Force's (IETF) Audio-Video Transport Working Group is adapting the IP protocol stack to the unique needs of interactive media streams. Several Internet standards have been the result, with more on the way. This chapter examines the most widely-implemented, the User Datagram Protocol (UDP), the Real-Time Transport Protocol (RTP), the Real-Time Transport Control Protocol (RTCP) and the Resource Reservation Protocol (RSVP).

In this chapter we will also discuss the Real-Time Streaming Protocol (RTSP), IP multicasting.

UDP

Overview of UDP

The User Datagram Protocol (UDP) is a streaming IP protocol that is being substituted for TCP in Real-Time multimedia applications. UDP is unidirectional; no mechanism is available at the sender to know if a packet has been successfully received. Thus, UDP does not wait for transmission acknowledgements. It carries the packets presented to it but, if those packets get dropped, are duplicated, or arrive out of sequence, UDP no corrective action is taken.

On the other hand, UDP increases the throughput of an IP network. Since there is no need to wait for acknowledgement by receivers, the UDP is an efficient mechanism for delivering multiple streams of information. TCP, on the other hand, has an inherent need to track and retransmit dropped or corrupted packets. The service that TCP provides has, unfortunately, no value for Real-Time applications. The sequence and timing of videoconferencing is such that if a frame of video or a packet or audio is lost, it can not be sent again and inserted somewhere else in the data stream.

Today, UDP provides the foundation for the other IETF protocols that are being developed to support videoconferencing over the Internet. These include the RTP, the RTCP, and RSVP. UDP is also being used for IP multicasting. Applications developed in accordance with the IETF protocols rely on codecs to detect and recover from packet loss, in conjunction with RTP.

UDP and Firewalls

Most organizations that deploy Internet audio and video technologies to conduct business and communicate with their global counterparts demand that these communications be secured through corporate firewalls. Firewalls are usually placed between internal LANs and WANs and external networks such as the Internet (they usually reside directly behind the router). Although it may provide reporting functions, a firewall's primary purpose is access control. Firewalls require configuration; the forfeiture in allowing a service (e.g., UDP) through the firewall is that one creates another door through which a hacker may intrude. Setting up firewall access rules on routers (what can pass through, what will be denied) is a time-consuming, error-prone process. However, it is generally accepted that static filters are not adequate for security, and firewalls are being designed to be simpler to configure. Still, network administrators generally adopt a "whatever is not expressly permitted is forbidden" approach to incoming Internet traffic.

Most Internet (and intranet) applications are delivered as connectionless streams over UDP sockets. Since firewalls approach security in connection-oriented terms, they do not permit packets that are associated with connectionless streams to penetrate the corporate network.

Different types of firewalls handle security differently, of course. There are four general categories: packet-level firewalls, circuit-level firewalls, proxy servers, and dynamic or intelligent packet filters (a well-known term for what this type of firewall performs is *stateful inspection*). Today most categories are combined into hybrid products that offer multiple security levels. At the lowest security level are packet-filtering routers; they are not truly firewalls, but they do examine each (or at least some) incoming IP packets. The router checks the packet's source, destination addresses, or services and, based on what it learns, decides whether or not to let the packet on to the corporate network. Packet filters are complex to maintain. They are also easy to penetrate.

Circuit-level gateways operate at the session level (as does UDP). They are host-based, and as such, act as a relay program. They receive packets from one host and hand them off to another. This design is more secure than that of packet-filtering routers, but less secure than application-level gateways. Circuit-level gateways are not often used as standalone firewalls, but are combined with application gateways to deliver a full suite of features for a robust firewall system.

Proxy-based firewalls have a detailed understanding of specific IP protocols and are extremely secure because they allow packet analysis at the application layer;

packets claiming to be of one type but carrying another type of data will be rejected. They are very good for security because they do not actually allow an outside host to connect to an inside host but, rather, relay information from one to the other. Unfortunately, a proxy firewall does not deal well with connectionless protocols such as UDP. Proxy servers can also add delay to connections if the computers on which they are running are slow or if the firewall code is not efficient (this increasingly becoming less of an issue).

Dynamic filtering firewalls offer sophisticated, customizable access-control schemes that allow network managers to granularly determine who they will allow to pass through the firewall onto the corporate network, and under what conditions. Firewalls in this category deal with packets at the applications-level. They are sometimes called *stateful* firewalls because they enhance packet-filtering with historical context to keep a history of all IP traffic that moves through the firewall. If a packet has gone from an intranet to someone on the Internet, it is generally assumed that it is acceptable to reverse the process, and thereby allow the host on the outside to return packets through the firewall. Application-level firewalls adapt best to UDP-supported media streams.

Protocols such as RTP (which attaches a header to UDP packets that can be used to detect packet loss), RTCP (which guarantees quality of service) and RSVP (which establishes service classes) are bringing streaming data to TCP/IP, as supporting router infrastructure is being deployed.

RTP

Overview of RTP

In January 1996, the IETF's Audio-Video Transport Working Group published RFC 1889, entitled, "RTP: A Transport Protocol for Real-Time Applications" and with it, a companion standard, RFC 1890, "RTP Profile for Audio and Video Conferences with Minimal Control." RTP and RTCP are part of the IETF's IIS (Internet Integrated Services) model, along with RSVP (described below). A second version of RTP and RTCP became available shortly thereafter. RTP bridges the gap between the lower-level UDP transport and a Real-Time multimedia application.

The RTP is a streams-oriented protocol. It provides end-to-end network transport services for Real-Time multimedia applications over IP based networks. It can be used in multicast (multipoint) or unicast (point-to-point) applications.

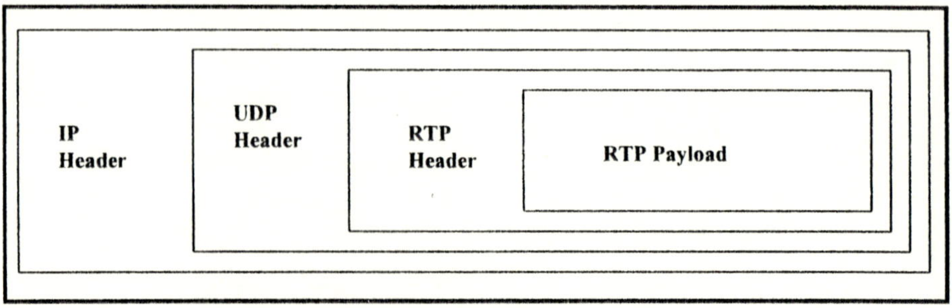

Figure 9-4. IP Packet Containing Real-Time Data

How RTP Works

RTP applications can compensate, to a degree, for the instability of UDP/IP networks by appending a 10-byte header onto each UDP packet. The header is designed with Real-Time transport in mind. It contains a time stamp and a sequence number to keep multimedia packets in the proper order during transmission. The time stamp is used to pace frame display and synchronize multiple streams (e.g., voice, video and data) while the sequence number is used to reassemble the data stream at the receiving end. The header also carries information about the information payload (in other words, the types of compression used to generate the media stream.)

Unlike the point-to-point TCP, only end-points (and not network devices) are required to support RTP. An interactive audiovisual application in an RTP-based conference must buffer data and examine the header's timing and sequence information. Using this information the application performs sequencing, synchronization, and duplicate packet elimination. The result is a coherent media stream within which varying degrees of network latency are compensated. The application may also use RTP payload information (also included in the header) to select a codec to be used for the exchange (e.g., MPEG or H.261).

The Future of RTP

RTP is being integrated into many videoconferencing and audio products. One of its shortcomings is that it is limited to IP networks. On the other hand, IP seems to be the direction in which the networking world is headed. Still, no single Real-Time protocol has emerged as the industry standard.

Nevertheless, RTP has gained a tremendous amount of attention as is demonstrated by the proliferation of RTP based IETF drafts:

RFC 2032: Describes a scheme to packetize an H.261 video stream for transport using RTP with any of the underlying protocols that carry RTP.

RFC 2190: Specifies the payload format for encapsulating an H.263 bitstream in the

RTP. Three modes are defined for the H.263 payload header. An RTP packet can use one of the three modes for H.263 video streams depending on the desired network packet size and H.263 encoding options employed. The shortest H.263 payload header (mode A) supports fragmentation at Group of Block (GOB) boundaries. The long H.263 payload headers (mode B and C) support fragmentation at Macroblock boundaries.

RFC 2198: Describes a payload format for use with RTP, version 2, for encoding redundant audio data. The primary motivation for the scheme is the development of audio conferencing tools for use with lossy packet networks such as the Internet MBONE, although this scheme is not limited to such applications.

RFC 2250: Describes a packetization scheme for MPEG video and audio streams. The scheme proposed can be used to transport such a video or audio flow over the transport protocols supported by RTP. Two approaches are described. The first is designed to support maximum interoperability with MPEG System environments. The second is designed to provide maximum compatibility with other RTP-encapsulated media streams and future conference control work of the IETF.

RFC 2343: Describes a payload type for bundled, MPEG-2 encoded video and audio data that may be used with RTP, version 2. Bundling has advantages for this payload type particularly in video-on-demand applications. This payload type may be used when its advantages are important enough to sacrifice the modularity of having separate audio and video streams.

RFC 2354: Summarizes a range of possible techniques for the repair of continuous media streams subject to packet loss. The techniques discussed include redundant transmission, retransmission, interleaving, and forward error correction. The range of applicability of these techniques is noted, together with the protocol requirements and dependencies.

RFC 2429: Specifies an RTP payload header format applicable to the transmission of video streams generated based on the 1998 version of ITU-T Recommendation H.263. Because the 1998 version of H.263 is a superset of the 1996 syntax, this format can also be used with the 1996 version of H.263, and is recommended for this use by new implementations. This format does not replace RFC 2190, which continues to be used by existing implementations, and may be required for backward compatibility in new implementations.

RFC 2431: Specifies the RTP payload format for encapsulating ITU Recommendation BT.656-3 video streams in RTP. Each RTP packet contains all or a portion of one scan line as defined by ITU Recommendation BT.601-5, and includes fragmentation, decoding, and positioning information.

RFC 2435: Describes the RTP payload format for JPEG video streams. The packet format is optimized for Real-Time video streams where codec parameters rarely change from frame to frame.

RFC 2508: Describes a method for compressing the headers of IP/UDP/RTP datagrams to reduce overhead on low-speed serial links. In many cases, all three headers can be compressed to 2-4 bytes.

RTCP

Overview of RTCP

The Real-Time Transport Control Protocol is a companion protocol to RTP. Like the RTP, it is also standardized in RFC 1889 and RFC 1890. The primary function of the RTCP is to provide feedback on the quality of a connection.

RTCP allows monitoring of multimedia data delivery in a manner scalable to large multicast networks. It provides minimal control and identification functionality to senders and recipients of a media stream. RTCP, like RTP, is simply data from the point of view of routers that handle packets on their way between senders and recipients. However, conferencing end-points can use RTCP to provide any-to-any feedback on current network conditions. Knowing something about network performance, and its impact on a conference, gives participants some options. The sender might reduce the video frame rate to conserve bandwidth. Another choice might be to switch from IP to ISDN transmission. If video is not critical to the collaborative process, the conference manager might elect to eliminate the picture portion of the conference altogether and rely strictly on voice and data.

How RTCP Works

RTCP works by periodically transmitting control packets to all participants in a session, using the same distribution method as the packets themselves. The underlying protocol must provide multiplexing of the data and control packets. One way of doing this is to use separate UDP port numbers.

RTCP carries a persistent transport-level identifier for an RTP source called the canonical name or CNAME. Receivers use the CNAME to keep track of each participant in a conference and to associate multiple data streams from a given participant in a set of related RTP sessions.

All participants in an RTP multicast must send RTCP packets to each other. Therefore the rate of the RTCP packet flow must be controllable to allow for a very large number of participants. RFC 1889 describes the RTCP and includes a discussion of the RTCP Transmission Interval. It includes an algorithm that calculates the interval between sending compound RTCP packets to divide the protocol's allowed control traffic bandwidth among participants.

RTCP can also be used to display the name of a participant at the user interface. This is most useful in loosely controlled sessions in which participants come and go at will, or when membership control features are not part of an application.

There are five types of RTCP packets. Type one is Sender Report or SR. It is used for transmitting and receiving reception statistics from all participants that are active senders. Type two is Receiver Report or RR. This type of packet is used to convey reception statistics from participants that are not active senders. Source-Destination packets comprise type three. CNAME is included in such a packet. Type four is used to indicate the end of a session and is aptly named BYE. There is also a fifth type, known as APP. It is used to carry application-specific functions.

RTCP is being implemented, along with RTP (whose services it uses), by a number of Internet videophone providers. It is becoming a popular and widely supported protocol, and is included as part of many Internet/intranet products.

RSVP: IETF RFC 2205

Overview of RSVP

The Resource Reservation Protocol (RSVP) relies on its companion protocols (UDP, RTP and RTCP) to promise Real-Time or near Real-Time transport over IP networks. In creating bandwidth-on-demand, it is RSVP's job to dynamically request that network bandwidth be set aside. Such bandwidth is required for building a Real-Time multimedia session between one or more devices.

RSVP acts on behalf of applications to request necessary bandwidth from devices throughout the network in accordance with priority. It allows a receiver to request a specific amount of bandwidth for a particular data stream, and to receive a confirmation or denial of that request. This protocol is the one necessary for guaranteeing QoS (quality of service) on the Internet. RSVP requests the bandwidth needed for a session; it does not have the authority to command that bandwidth and, therefore, can not guarantee that resource availability.

Standards Approval

RSVP was first outlined in 1994 in IETF RFC 1633, "Proposed extension to the Internet architecture and protocols to provide integrated services, i.e., to support real- time as well as the current non-Real-Time service of IP." It was approved as an IETF standard in October of 1996, and was revised again in 1997 as RFC 2205. Several key concerns remain even after the first version was approved.

How RSVP Works

RSVP includes two components—a client and a network device. The RSVP client is built into the videoconferencing application, which relies on it to request service priority levels from the RSVP network devices that support the transmission infrastructure. These network devices must, in return, recognize and respond to client requests. Upon receiving a request, an RSVP-enabled device considers network conditions and other factors to determine whether or not the request can be granted. If the situation looks promising, the router signals the application that it can proceed with its transmission.

RSVP requests theoretically result in resources being reserved in each node along the data path, but only in one direction (two-way traffic would require two RSVP flows). RSVP operates on top of IPv4 or IPv6, as a transport protocol in the protocol stack. Like ICMP, IGMP, or routing protocols, RSVP is a control protocol and does not transport application data. However, RSVP is designed to operate with current and future unicast and multicast routing protocols and is not a routing protocol. Routing protocols determine where packets get forwarded, and RSVP attempts to ensure the QoS of those packets that are forwarded. RSVP makes receivers responsible for requesting a specific QoS (RSVP93). Of course, RSVP's weakness lies in the fact that receivers tend to grant the highest QoS to every application that they use. The RSVP protocol carries the user's request to all the routers and hosts along the reverse data path to the data source, as far as the router from which the receiver's data path joins the multicast distribution tree.

RSVP Classes of Service

RSVP has four service classes, although only two are aimed at Real-Time multimedia. The two most common are Guaranteed Delay and Controlled Load.

As the name implies, guaranteed delivery specifies the maximum allowable transmission delay. Controlled load allows priorities to be associated with different streams of data and, in response to those priorities, tries to provide consistent service, even if network usage increases.

For applications that can tolerate the late arrival of some packets, two additional RSVP classes, Controlled Delay and Predictive Service are offered. They allow for specified bounds on delay.

Deploying RSVP on the Client

RSVP sits on top of IP in the protocol stack. Client applications will have to add it to use the services of RSVP network devices. Early implementations of RSVP shipped as middleware (Precept Software has a well-publicized one) but RSVP soon became an inherent part of the desktop operating system (e.g., Windows 98 and Windows 2000).

RSVP's Impact on Network Infrastructure

While RSVP does not require a wholesale overhaul of network infrastructure, it does require support by the switches and/or routers that make up a transmission path. If any device along the path fails to support RSVP, it can circumvent the efforts of the rest that do.

For switches and routers to become RSVP-enabled, they must be able to provide multiple queues. These queues buffer lower-priority data when higher-priority data is being transmitted. Some of today's routers do not have multiple queuing capability, but an increasing number do. Consequently, they must deal with traffic on a first-in, first-out (FIFO) basis. Here, RSVP faces a challenge. The frame format of Ethernet varies, with no frame smaller than 64 octets (bytes) and no frame larger than 1518 octets. If two bandwidth-reserved frames arrive at a single-queue router simultaneously, the first one to enter the buffer is the first in line for transmission. Because the whole frame must be sent, the second stream is held in queue. If the first frame comes close to Ethernet's maximum 1518 octet frame size, the second application's payload will be noticeably delayed. Because of this, RSVP-enhanced IP networks fare poorly in comparison to ATM, which uses very small cells (53 bytes), and thereby makes QoS guarantees more realistic.

The real-world effect is that many routers must be upgraded or replaced for widespread deployment of RSVP. The two largest router/switch manufacturers, Cisco (San Jose, California) and Bay Networks (Billerica, Massachusetts), have long since made their products capable of responding to RSVP requests. Cisco was first to market, with its IOS software that began shipping in September of 1996. The two groups most likely to buy and install those upgrades are private corporations and Internet service providers. The Internet service provider (ISP) BBN Planet (now GTE), Cambridge, Massachusetts offered the first commercial implementation.

In 1996, RSVP was largely a test-bed implementation. Vendors, working collaboratively, tried out many different implementations. Most early RSVP implementations left it up to the user to set load and delay parameters. This may work in an experiment, but when RSVP is widely deployed, this approach will quickly fall apart. Users, perennially bandwidth-starved, would promote their application to the front of the service line. In response, vendors are developing offerings in such a way that network administrators (often the decision makers when it comes to selecting products) have the ability to charge for higher-priority service and therefore, to limit congestion. As this book goes to press in 2000, RSVP is still not as widely deployed as one might have hoped. However, the IETF is still improving RSVP to fulfill its potential for supporting converged IP networks.

The Future of RSVP

The IETF is developing specifications to allow users to assign priorities to applications according to their business needs. Unfortunately, in the years that it has been perfecting RSVP, competing QoS standards MPLS (multiprotocol label switching), Diffserv (differentiated services) have evolved. It is likely to be 2005 before a system is in place for transmitting prioritized data across multiple IP networks and with which carriers can bill each other for premium service. In the meantime, customers will need to work with service providers who circumvent the problem by offering copious bandwidth. Moreover, they may need to load balance multiple links (perhaps from various providers) to ensure that they always have the bandwidth they need.

Proprietary implementations such as that offered by Packeteer or Xedia (now

Lucent) may provide the necessary prioritization, but they must be viewed as temporary solutions to fill a gap until a standards-based solution is ubiquitous. The market (other than carriers) is making it clear that it does not want the complexity of ATM. Unfortunately, it forfeits ATM's deterministic qualities and accepts a best-effort network. However, since the market and, therefore, the money is going into IP networks, it is only a matter of time until this inadequacy is overcome.

RTSP

The Real-Time Streaming Protocol (RTSP) is a streaming-media client/server-oriented protocol that was submitted to the IETF in draft form on October 9, 1996, and was defined by the IETF in RFC 2326 in April 1998. RTSP is an application-level protocol for control over the delivery of data with Real-Time properties. It provides an extensible framework to enable controlled, on-demand delivery of audio and video, whether live or stored. RTSP is intended to control multiple data delivery sessions, provide a means for choosing delivery channels such as UDP, multicast UDP, or TCP, and provide a means for choosing delivery mechanisms in conjunction with RTP.

The RTSP allows interoperability between client/server multimedia products from multiple vendors. It can be implemented across a broad array of client-side operating systems such as Macintosh and various flavors of Windows and Unix. It is supported by an equally large number of server-side platforms including Macintosh, Windows NT, and variations of UNIX.

Using RTSP, application developers can create products that will interoperate within the heterogeneous environment of the Internet and corporate intranets. The protocol defines how a server can connect to a client-side receiver (or multiple receivers) to stream multimedia content. Streaming multimedia can be anything that includes time-based information, such as on-demand multimedia playback, live Real-Time feeds, or stored non-Real-Time programming. RTSP is closely associated with the ITU-T H.323 protocol stack, and is thereby facilitating the merging of the separate spheres of telephony, conferencing, and multimedia broadcasting.

RTSP allows non-traditional broadcasters (computer and software manufacturers) to leverage IP networks (e.g., the Internet) to compete with television and radio programmers. The protocol allows data to be displayed as it is received, rather than requiring that it be first stored and processed. This makes RTSP ideal for developing network computer applications in which hard disks are either non-existent or very small.

Until now, each vendor of Internet multimedia systems has been developing applications independently or as part of a collaborative, but proprietary effort. This does not meet the needs of the Internet or of intranets, both of which use open protocols and support attachments of thousands of diverse clients and servers. Forty companies decided to cooperate on the development of RTSP, although Progressive Networks, Inc. (now RealNetworks) and Netscape Communications spearheaded the effort.

RTSP appeals to Internet content providers because it allows them to create and manage the delivery of their programs in a commercial environment. Content providers want to be compensated for their efforts, and the RTSP addresses their concerns in terms of delivery control and efficiency, quality of service, security, usage measurement, and rights management.

RTSP provides a mechanism for choosing IP-based delivery channels—UDP, IP multicast and TCP—and supports delivery methods based upon the RTP standard.

RealNetworks, one of the two RTSP sponsors, offers software developments kits for creating RTSP-compliant applications. In only four years, from 1995 to 1999, RealNetworks software systems became the most pervasive method of streaming media on the Internet and intranets. By 2000, the company claimed that more than 80 million unique users had been registered, its RealPlayer download rate had exceeded 175,000 per day, more than 145,000 hours of live entertainment had been broadcast over the Internet, and hundreds of thousands of hours of content were available on-demand.

IP Multicasting and its Protocols

IP multicasting (for that matter, multicasting in general) calls for the simultaneous transmission of data to a designated subset of network users. It exists somewhere between unicasting (sending a stream of data to a single user) and broadcasting (sending a data stream to everyone on a network.) Most frame-based networks (e.g., Ethernet) can communicate in all three modes.

Most applications incorporate unicasts. Examples of a unicast might include a client contacting a server or two users exchanging messages and files across the network. Broadcasts allow a single station to communicate simultaneously with all other devices on the network. Broadcasts must reach across subnets to reach all machines on an IP network. Broadcasts have their place in the corporate intranet, where they are useful for company meetings, product announcements and addresses by the chairman of the board. But broadcasts are not useful for delivering information to a sub-set of network users, for instance, a department, or a group of students who are registered for a particular training session.

IP multicasting is similar to a pay-per-view cable television channel. A viewer can tune if they are authorized to do so. To handle the invitation process, a sending computer specifies a group of recipients by transmitting a single copy of its multicast to a special IP address. Special protocols are employed to translate from the group address to the IP addresses or group members, and from there, to the MAC addresses of individual hosts. Multicasting also requires a special protocol that is used to manage group membership. Lastly, it requires routers that can interpret multicast protocols and use them to distribute packets only to the proper networks. These three special multicast-specific functions—address translation, dynamic management of group membership, and multicast-aware routing—are discussed in the next section.

Layer-3-to-Layer 2 Address Translation

The hosts that combine to make up a multicast group are assembled under a special class of IP address. This address category is known as a Class D address. There are also Class A, B and C addresses (used for unicasts and broadcasts) and Class E addresses (unassigned at present but reserved for the future.)

Class D addresses exist at the network-layer and are used exclusively for multicast traffic. These addresses are allocated dynamically; each represents a select group of hosts interested in receiving a specific multicast. The network-layer (Class D IP address) that is used to communicate with a group of receivers must be mapped over to the data-link layer (typically Ethernet MAC) addresses associated with each group member.

Translation between an IP multicast address and a data-link layer address is accomplished by dropping the lowest-order 23 bits of the IP address into the low-order 23 bits of the MAC address. In order for a host to participate in a multicast its TCP/IP stack must be IP-multicast aware — most, but not all, are. Network adapters must be multicast-enabled, too. Good ones allow several MAC addresses to be programmed in by the TCP/IP stack. This allows a host to monitor several multicast groups at once without receiving an entire general range of MAC addresses. Network adapters in this category use both hardware and software (drivers) to deliver their functionality.

Dynamic Management of Group Membership

IP multicasting works thanks to an extension of the IP service interface. This extension allows upper layer protocol modules to request that their hosts create, join, confirm ongoing participation in, or leave a multicast group. This process is known as dynamic registration. It is served within the IP module by the Internet Group Management Protocol (IGMP), which was defined by the IETF in RFC 1112.

IGMP provides the mechanism by which users can dynamically subscribe and unsubscribe to multicasts. It ensures that multicast traffic is present only on those subnets where one or more hosts are actively requesting it. Using IGMP, hosts inform their network or subnet that they are members of a particular multicast group. Routers use this registration information to transmit, or abstain from transmitting, multicast packets that are associated with specific groups.

There are three versions of IGMP. IGMPv2 lets a host tell a router that it no longer wants to receive traffic. The router will stop retransmission of traffic, based on a time-out parameter. This is not possible with IGMPv1. IGMPv3 adds source filtering ("only some" or "all but some" sources) to the host membership protocol. Routers merge requests from different hosts so that everyone gets at least what they want (but maybe more). IGMP versions one and two attempted to reduce the group membership protocol traffic by having hosts suppress group memberships that had already been reported. IGMPv3 transfers the burden of merging multiple requests from the hosts to the routers by eliminating the need for suppression by sending reports to the all-routers multicast group. There are three types of reports: *current state*, *filter mode change*, and *source list change*. The current state report is used in response to the router's periodic queries, and the filter mode change and source list change (collectively known as *state change records*) are used when the host's state changes in response to an application request. Queries are backwards compatible, so that an IGMPv3 router may send a single message and get responses back from IGMPv3, IGMPv2 and IGMPv1 hosts.

IGMP client support is offered in the TCP/IP stacks of most hosts, including most flavors of Windows. IGMP must also be supported at the router level; CISCO, Bay Networks and others offer routers that can cope with it.

Multicast-Aware Routing

There are several standards available for routing IP Multicast traffic. These are described in three separate IETF documents. RFC 1075 defines the Distance Vector Multicast Routing Protocol (DVMRP). RFC 1584 defines the Multicast Open Shortest Path First (MOSPF) protocol—an IP Multicast extension to the Internet's OSPF. The Protocol-Independent Multicast (PIM) Sparse Mode was defined by the IETF in RFC 2117; PIM-Dense Mode (PIM-DM) is, at the time of this writing, still a draft. PIM is a multicast protocol that can be used in conjunction with all unicast IP routing protocols.

DVMRP uses a technique known as Reverse Path Forwarding to flood a multicast packet out of all paths except the one that leads back to the packet's source. Doing so permits a data stream to reach all LANs. If a router is attached to a set of LANs that do not wish to receive a particular multicast group, it can send a *prune* message back up the *distribution tree*. The prune message stops subsequent packets from flowing to LANs that do not support group members. DVMRP refloods on a periodic basis in order to absorb hosts who are just tuning in to the multicast. The more often that DVMRP floods, the shorter the time that a new recipient will have to wait to be added to a multicast. Flooding frequently, on the other hand, greatly increases network traffic.

Early versions of DVMRP did not support *pruning*. Customers should not implement DVMRP for IP multicasting unless their routers support prune.

DVMRP is used in the Internet's multicast backbone (MBONE) which has a following in the academic community. The MBONE's primary application is the transmission of conference proceedings although a variation of it (CU-SeeMe) also supports desktop conferencing.

MOSPF was defined as an extension to the Open Shortest Path First (OSPF) unicast routing protocol. It will only work over networks that use OSPF. OSPF requires that every router in a network be aware of all of the network's available links. Each router calculates routes from itself to all possible destinations. MOSPF works by including multicast information in OSPF link state advertisements. An MOSPF router learns which multicast groups are active on which LANs, and then builds a distribution tree for each source/group pair. The tree state is cached and recomputed every time that a link state change occurs (or when the cache times out).

MOSPF works best when there are only a few simultaneous multicasts at any given time. It should be avoided by environments that have many, simultaneous multicasts or by environments plagued by link failures.

PIM works with all existing unicast routing protocols, and is usually more popular from both a customer and a vendor perspective because it is simpler to implement and to manage. PIM supports two different types of multipoint traffic distribution patterns: dense and sparse. PIM-Dense mode (PIM-DM), a proper subset of PIM-Sparse Mode (PIM-SM) performs best when senders and receivers are in close proximity to one another. It is also best adapted to situations where there are few senders and many receivers. PIM handles high volumes of multicast traffic and it also does well when the streams of multicast traffic are continual. PIM-DM uses Reverse Path Forwarding and resembles DVMRP. The most significant difference between DVMRP and dense-mode PIM is that PIM works with whatever unicast protocol is being used; PIM does not require any particular unicast protocol.

Sparse-mode PIM is optimized for environments with intermittent multicasts in with many multipoint data streams, and for senders and receivers that WAN segments separate. It works by defining a Rendezvous Point. When a sender wants to send data, it first sends to the Rendezvous Point. When a receiver wants to receive data, it registers with the Rendezvous Point. Once the data stream begins to flow from sender to Rendezvous Point, the routers in the path will optimize the path automatically to eliminate superfluous hops. PM-DM is simpler because it does not require the control overhead that is necessary for a Rendezvous Point, which is often not needed when leveraging the data-handling capacity in the switch infrastructure, and one is not running a connection oriented network (e.g., ATM). Another difference between PIM-SM and PIM-DM is that the latter does not transmit periodic *joins*, only explicitly triggered grafts/prunes. Although PIM-DM is not yet a RFP, it does work, and it is interoperable.

Sparse-mode PIM assumes that no hosts want the multicast traffic unless they specifically ask for it. It works well in corporate environments where multiple groups may need to multicast across WANs, but only occasionally.

Conferencing and the Internet

Enterprises will continue to seek networks that facilitate the transmission of every type of data, including Real-Time multimedia. A debate has subsided for now, and the enterprise network of choice is a refined set of IP protocols that runs over fat pipes. Companies could overcome IP's best-effort design limitations by moving from packet switching to cell-switching, and thereby make ATM their switching choice for both the LAN and the WAN? Deterministic ATM-based networks currently have the advantage in service quality, but IP protocols are widely implemented and are constantly evolving. Moreover, it is very difficult to find skilled resources with an ATM background (or to pay for them once one has found them). In contrast, IP-oriented network management expertise is prevalent. Right or wrong, the current Internet/intranet infatuation only strengthens the position of IP-networking. Still, IP was designed in the 1970s when interactive multimedia over packet-switched networks was hardly conceivable; no matter what tires, engine, and transmission one puts on a '62 Dodge Dart, it is still a '62 Dodge Dart.

ATM would seem to be the future. It apportions bandwidth in a connection-oriented arrangement, and thereby accommodates multiple streaming data flows. IP-based connectionless networks transmit in bursts and force video and audio streams to adapt, if not suffer. ATM has an inherent provision for service quality. IP-based protocols are being retrofitted to meet this requirement. ATM can support TCP/IP traffic and any other type of traffic, both gracefully and with applications-specific adaptation layering. IP-based protocols do their best to adapt, but their best is sometimes kludgey. ATM upgrades are expensive but applications such as Real-Time streaming media are motivating organizations to take a second look. Perhaps the good news is that the fiber that is now being strung to served today's needs with Gigabit or Ten Gigabit Ethernet will also be able to serve tomorrow's needs with ATM.

We will discuss ATM in greater depth in the following chapter as we move downward in the stack to look at physical and data-link layer transmission systems.

CHAPTER 9 REFERENCES

Bailey, Brian, "PIM-DM." Extreme Networks (internal document). November 12, 1999.

Baker, Richard H., "Fighting fire with firewalls," InformationWeek October 21, 1996 (Computer Select).

Comer, Douglas E., Internetworking with TCP/IP Volume I: Principles, Protocols and Architecture, 2nd edition, Prentice Hall 1991.

Coy, Peter, Hof, Robert D., Judge, Paul C. "Has the Net finally reached the wall?" Business Week, August 26, 1996 n3490 pp. 62-67.

Crotty, Cameron. "The revolution will be Netcast," Macworld October 1996 v13 n10 pp. 153-155.

Frank, Alan. "Multimedia LANs and WANs," LAN Magazine July 1996 v11 n7 pp. 81-86.

Fulton, Sean. "Steaming multimedia hits the 'net," CommunicationsWeek July 22, 1996 n620 p. 52-58.

Kosiur, Dave. "Internet telephony moves to embrace standards," PC Week November 18, 1996 v13 n46 p. N16.

Kosiur, Dave. "Supporting multimedia on the Internet," PC Week: November 11, 1996.

McLean, Michelle Rae. "RSVP: promises and problems," LAN Times October 14, 1996 v13 n23 p. 39-42.

Plain, Steve. "Streamlining," Computer Shopper December 1996 v16 n12 p 620.

RFC 2032, "RTP Payload Format for H.261 Video," IETF October 1996.

Rogers, Amy. "A blueprint for quality of service," CommunicationsWeek November 18, 1996 n638 p. 1.

Schulzrinne, H., Casner, S., Frederick, R., and V. Jacobson, RFC 1889, "RTP: A Transport Protocol for Real-Time Applications," IETF, January 1996.

Schulzrinne, Henning and Casner, Stephen, "RTP: A Transport Protocol for Real-Time Applications," Audio-Video Transport Working Group, Internet Engineering

Task Force, working draft, October 20, 1993.

Steinke, Steve. "Multimedia: the I-way drive-in," LAN Magazine August 1996 v11 n8 pp. 45-51.

Steinke, Steve. "The Internet as your WAN," LAN Magazine October 1996 v11 n11 pp. 47-52.

Streaming branches on the 'Net. CommunicationsWeek October 28, 1996.

Tannenbaum, Todd. "IP Multicasting: Diving Through The Layers," Network Computing November 15, 1996 pp. 156-160.

Wirbel, Loring. "Desktop ATM perseveres," Electronic Engineering Times June 10, 1996 n905 p. 78.

Yoshida, Junko. "Intel, Microsoft get behind Internet phone," Electronic Engineering Times July 22, 1996 n911 p. 14.

10

CIRCUIT-SWITCHED NETWORKS

"It's kind of fun to do the impossible."
Walt Disney (1901-1966)

Two types of networks can be used to transport video/data conferencing signals, circuit-switched and packet-switched. In this chapter, we will discuss circuit-switched networks; in the next, we will discuss packet switching.

Until Ethernet really became established, in 1979, the concept of packet switching was scarcely implemented anywhere. Today, packets traverse LANs and WANs all over the world; indeed, many people use the word networking to refer to packet-switched service exclusively, without acknowledging that circuit switching, a different type of networking, is older by almost a century.

Today, the bulk of video conferencing takes place over circuit-switched telephone lines, such as ISDN or Switched 56, or over dedicated lines, such as T-1 or fractional T-1. Even when the conference end points are workstations on the same LAN, they typically use telephone lines, not the LAN, for video conferencing traffic. For that reason, we will start our discussion of video/data conferencing networks with a look at the public switched telephone network (PSTN).

THE PUBLIC SWITCHED TELEPHONE NETWORK (PSTN)

When installing a videoconferencing system, it is important to understand the circuit-switched wide area network, better known as the PSTN (the term general switched telephone network, or GSTN, is increasingly, interchangeably appearing). The PSTN is the set of digital dial-up services offered by carriers. It includes network-based services and network-based switching.

The PSTN consists of analog and digital components. In order to identify what is analog and what is digital, we will divide the PTSN into three broad categories: *access*, *switching*, and *transport*.

Access is the portion of the circuit that connects the customer's premises to the first network switching point. Another term used to refer to access is *local loop*. A local loop has two ends, the one that connects to the customer's equipment and the one that connects to the telephone company's (carrier's) switching equipment. The switching equipment is said to reside in the carrier's *central office* or *CO*. Switching allows one node to be connected to another node and is accomplished via addressing (in which an address is a telephone number). A circuit-switched connection can be made directly within the serving central office (if the same CO also serves the called party) or carried across the PSTN to a distant CO.

The local loop is almost always conditioned to provide analog transmission service (POTS). Some customers in the United States can, as an option, buy digital local access. The remainder of the PSTN is digital. CO switches are digital and the trunks that connect them are high-capacity digital facilities.

Prior to 1996, only local exchange carriers (LECs), with a few minor exceptions, provided the local loop, in a monopoly arrangement. Although allowing monopolies to exist seems like a misguided practice, at the time that the U.S. PSTN was being constructed, this was really the only alternative.

The Old PSTN

In 1934, Congress passed the Communications Act. It created the Federal Communications Commission (FCC). The Act was intended to regulate the market for telecommunications services, and allow everyone to have a telephone. At the time that the Act passed, the U.S. was building its telecommunications infrastructure. The companies that supplied the funds (primarily AT&T) wanted to be assured of a reasonable return on their investment. Permitting the construction of competitive networks would jeopardize an investor's profitability. Moreover, duplicating infrastructure was wasteful. As long as regulation ensured that a single operator (carrier) did not engage in predatory practices, one network per area would suffice. The funds required to build regional telephone systems could be spread across more customers. Universal Service would be the result.

For more than sixty years, the structure held; the U.S. enjoyed (arguably) the best telephone system in the world. It benefited one organization enormously: AT&T. But in 1974, the Department of Justice filed an antitrust suit against AT&T in which it accused them of anti-competitive practices. After years of maneuvering, AT&T and the DOJ (Department of Justice) reached an out-of-court settlement. Dubbed the Modified Final Judgment, or MFJ, it became effective on January 1, 1984. It separated the Bell Operating Companies (BOCs) from AT&T and grouped them into seven holding companies. Today these holding companies (which now number five, not seven) are loosely referred to as the Regional Bell Operating Companies or RBOCs.

The MFJ permitted the RBOCs to provide local telephone service as monopolies, but precluded them from providing long distance service. AT&T became, exclusively, a long distance carrier; the MFJ banned it from providing any type of local service. To distinguish between long distance and local service, Local Access and Transport Areas (LATAs) were established. A RBOC or independent LEC could carry a call that originated and terminated within a LATA. Once a call crossed a LATA boundary, a long distance carrier (inter-exchange carrier or IXC) was required to haul it.

As a result of the MFJ, the RBOCs were highly regulated. Their activities were watched by the FCC, the DOJ and, above all, the state public utility commissions (PUCs are known by other names in some states). The PUCs were tasked with the dual responsibility of keeping phone rates affordable and telephone companies profitable enough to provide high-quality service. The goal of this delicate balancing act continued to be the provision of universal service.

Over the years, telephone service became truly universal. Over 96% of U.S. households have telephones. A new concern arose, however. In the process of making telephone service universally affordable, regulators had effectively discouraged the largest phone companies from investing in network upgrades. The local loop (POTS) was narrowband and analog. POTS service is not compatible with the requirements high-bandwidth applications (e.g., multimedia). Congress, the FCC, and other administrative branches of the U.S. government studied how to introduce competition to the local loop in order to stimulate a complete overhaul.

The New PSTN

On February 6, 1996 Congress passed the Telecommunications Competition and Deregulation Act of 1996. The Deregulation Act was aimed at promoting competition in local loop, cable television, and long distance service. It blurs the distinction between types of carriers (e.g., LEC, IXC, cable television, and electrical utility). Today anyone can file to be a competitive local exchange carrier (CLEC) and, in the future, local exchange carriers (the Regional Bell Operating Companies or RBOCs and independents such as GTE) will be able to provide long distance service. Cable television service is up for grabs since the act overturned restrictions that prohibit RBOC/cable television cross-ownership. Electrical utility (power) companies can also pursue the local access market. One popular method for merging telecommunications and electrical networks is to embed fiber optics technology (which uses optical signaling) into the core of an electrical cable. Electrical and optical signaling can coexist, so a power company can maintain a single, multipurpose infrastructure.

As competitors in pursuit of the lucrative local access market have three choices. They can buy from existing local loop services from the LEC at a discount and resell them at a profit; they can build their own up-to-date digital networks, or they can combine these two strategies. The third choice is a popular one. Most companies that are trying to grab a piece of the local access market (e.g., AT&T, Qwest/US West, or MCI WorldCom/Sprint) are pursuing the hybrid approach.

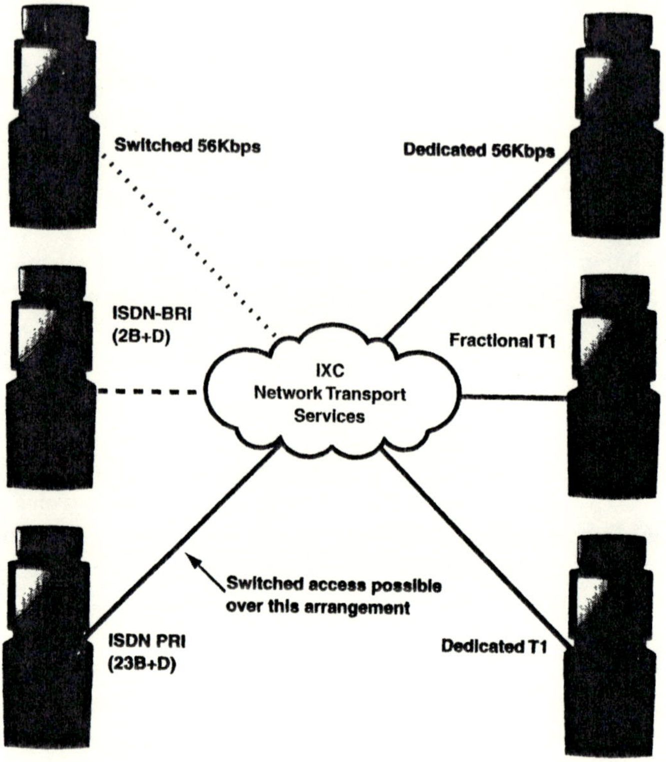

Figure 10-1. IXC Access Options (Laura Long).

Ramifications of the Telecommunication Act of 1996 (derisorily referred to as the Attorney Employment Act and other less delicate terms) can not be projected in the scope of a text such as this. Monthly, weekly, and daily publications are the best source for the most current information—many good sources are listed in the reference sections of this book. The Deregulation Act is relevant to video communication in that it is certain to change many aspects of the industry. It is already blurring the distinction between carrier types. For instance, when MCI provides local service, is it a LEC or an IXC? For simplicity, we will use terms such as LEC and IXC broadly throughout this text even though references may not be precisely accurate.

Two broad categories of digital circuit-switched WAN access services exist: dedicated and switched. In the following section, we will address the differences between these two categories.

DEDICATED ACCESS

In the past, customers usually connected a videoconferencing system to a long distance carrier's point-of-presence (POP) through a dedicated digital circuit (sometimes called a private line). A dedicated digital circuit is a permanent configuration that routes traffic exclusively across the network of the carrier to which one is connected. This approach is declining in popularity because it causes problems when a conferencing application involves external companies. Connecting through an IXC's POP is acceptable, however, when all videoconferences will be intra-company, or when all participants contract with the same IXC.

A dedicated access connection can be provided over a T-1 or lower speed digital circuits, depending on the application's bandwidth requirement. Most companies install a T-1 for other purposes (long distance service, data communications) and then segregate channels (typically between two and six) from the rest of the pipe for videoconferencing applications.

A survey of 75 telecommunications managers, performed by Personal Technology Research (Waltham, Massachusetts) in 1993, found that 77% of those interviewed used codecs requiring bandwidths of 384 Kbps or lower. An organization that falls into this category may want to consider Fractional T-1 (FT-1). Providers of FT-1 use a digital access cross connect system (DACS) to split a T-1/DS-1 signal into one or more DS-0s. IXCs package FT-1 differently, with the low-end speeds starting at 56 or 64 Kbps and ranging, in 64 Kbps multiples, through 768 Kbps. FT-1 terminates on a specially equipped multiplexer. Prices vary widely, depending on bandwidth.

When dedicated access is chosen over switched, the segregated T-1 approach is usually more cost-effective than the FT-1 approach. Sharing a dedicated access pipe among multiple types of traffic often allows a customer to cost-justify a T-1.

Not only can dedicated access be ordered in several different sizes but customers can also choose from whom to buy that access. The most costly approach is to procure access directly from an IXC, who leases the service used to connect the customer to its closest POP from a LEC. In this scenario, the customer pays the IXC a flat fee to provide end-to-end circuit reliability. The monthly charge covers the LECs' access charge and compensates the IXC for assuming responsibility for the performance of the entire circuit.

Another approach is to go directly to a LEC and request a dedicated connection to an IXC (Base Line Service). In this type of arrangement, a customer pays two bills: one to the LEC, and one to the long distance provider. It is possible that even more than two bills will be rendered: depending on how many LEC's areas the circuit passes through to reach the IXC's closest POP. The total cost for access is lower than with a dedicated connection because, in times of circuit malfunction, *the customer* is responsible for problem resolution.

Probably the least costly way to obtain access is to buy it from a competitor of the local telephone company, a local alternative carrier—also known as an alternate local exchange carrier (ALEC). Historically, these tend to specialize in digital access service. Managers who have the option of using ALECs often find that they are, in addition to being price-competitive, very service-oriented. Their networks tend to be newer, but many gain some depth-of-experience by hiring former telephone company employees. ALECs often offer faster response time for circuit installation and repair, and are flexible (and interested) enough to fill atypical customer requests.

Astute managers make sure that the telephone company delivers T-1 service over the shortest possible path. This is because T-1 billing takes into account how far a customer is from the CO. It is also prudent to weigh the discounts awarded for long term-commitments against the future pricing declines that a deregulated industry is certain to engender. Just as long distance rates dropped by 60% after competition was introduced, so local access rates will decline. How quickly this will happen is a topic of debate. We recommend that an organization pay the extra 5% to preserve its future flexibility.

The post-Deregulation Act environment offers other choices, too. In any given area there might be cable television operators, electrical utilities and others, all of whom are seeking to grab a piece of the local exchange market. Shopping around can be both confusing, and rewarding, depending on how the process is managed.

Signaling and Synchronization in the Digital Network

Carriers, when taking orders for T-1 service, always ask what type of signaling/framing should be used. The videoconferencing system provider usually knows what to ask for—that is, if they are to install a *turnkey* solution. There are two choices: Alternate Mark Inversion (AMI) and Extended Super Frame (ESF)/Binary Eight Zero Substitution (B8ZS).

The digital telephone network is synchronized, in order to manage the stream of zeros and ones that run across it. Synchronization relies on clocking, which uses cues from the bit streams to maintain order. Generally, a voltage indicates a one bit and no voltage indicates a zero bit. The network uses the voltages of the 1 bits as clocking pulses. In signaling, no more than eight bit times should pass without a signal. But it is not usual for a customer's data to have eight or more successive 0s and thus provide no heartbeat for clocking. Without synchronization, the network shuts down.

One solution has been to dedicate one bit out of every eight as a control bit. If all the other bits in an eight-bit string are 0s, then the control bit will be set to 1 and synchronization will be maintained. The need for this control bit is the reason that switched 56 service (discussed later in this chapter), which runs over 64 Kbps DS0 circuits, provides only 56 Kbps service to users. Synchronization borrows the eighth (least significant) bit to maintain clocking. Thus, only seven out of eight bits are available to users.

An alternate solution to the synchronization problem was developed in the mid-1980s. It involves forcing a deliberate violation (called a bipolar violation or BPV). The BPV is used to maintain network clocking, but networking knows not to interpret BPV pulses as data. This technique, binary eight zero substitution, is called B8ZS. DS0 circuits that support B8ZS from end to end can carry 64Kbps of user data—in other words, offer clear-channel service.

The point of this digression is this: if channels of a T-1 carrier will be used for some of the newer clear-channel digital services offered today (e.g., ISDN), it is best to order ESF/B8ZS. ESF/B8ZS also supports 56 Kbps service. If the T-1 carrier will be used for 56 Kbps service exclusively, AMI signaling is a safe choice.

Later in this chapter we will take the concept of network signaling one step further, when we introduce out-of-band signaling. ESF/B8ZS is not to be confused with out-of-band signaling, which uses an entirely separate packet-switched network overlay to pass network information.

Channel Service Units/Data Service Units

Leased line connections rely on special terminating equipment. When the leased line is a T-1, this equipment is of two types, a channel service unit (CSU) and a data service unit (DSU). In most cases, a CSU includes a DSU, providing the customer specifies this arrangement.

Customer premises equipment (CPE)—particularly equipment with a data rate lower than 56 Kbps—produces asynchronous bit streams. Asynchronous transmission relies on start and stop bits to distinguish between bytes of data. Furthermore, in asynchronous traffic, the interval between bytes is usually arbitrary. The digital signaling hierarchy, on the other hand, relies on synchronous signaling, in which senders and receivers exchange clocking information in order to identify the boundaries between units of data.

CSUs and DSUs are used to condition asynchronous bit streams, so that they can be passed over the synchronous network. DSUs connect to CPE via RS-232 or V.35 interfaces. They adjust between asynchronous and synchronous timing systems by putting bytes of data onto the network at precise intervals. This activity is known as rate adaptation.

Second, a DSU converts digital pulses from the format used by videoconferencing (or other computerized equipment) into the format used by the network. In computers and codecs, for example, ones are represented by a +5 volt charge and zeros are represented by the absence of voltage. This is called unipolar nonreturn to zero signaling. Carriers use bipolar signaling, in which a zero voltage level represents zeros and ones alternate between +3 and -3 volts. In networks, bipolar signaling is preferable to unipolar signaling, which tends to build up a DC charge on the line.

The CSU ensures that a digital signal enters a communications channel in a format that is properly shaped into square pulses and precisely timed. In addition, it manages other OSI layer one signal characteristics such as longitudinal balance, voltage isolation and equalization. Nearly all CSUs allow the carrier to test the line by performing a loopback test.

The customer is always responsible for buying, installing and maintaining both the CSU and the DSU (or a combined version of the two).

Carrier Gateways

Every carrier structures the signaling and management portion of their digital networks a little differently. These networks, after all, were developed during a time when competition was fierce. Carriers did not exchange network information because it was considered proprietary. The legacy of the 1980s lives on today, when it comes to digital network interconnection. If dedicated access service will be used for videoconferencing, bear this in mind: While the IXCs' analog networks are universally interconnected, their digital networks are not. This presents a problem when two different companies—both of who use dedicated digital access, but whom different long distance carriers serve—want to set up a videoconference.

Placing a call through a carrier gateway is still the most reliable way to bridge between carrier's digital networks when dissimilar dedicated access causes connection problems. The cost for using these gateways varies widely, based on speed, location, type of service, and carriers. All the major long distance carriers offer these gateways (AT&T, MCI WorldCom).

Some gateways are one-way. In other words, carrier A's customers may be able to gateway to the network of carrier B, but customers of the carrier B may not be able to gateway to the network of carrier A. When a customer of carrier B needs a videoconference with a customer of carrier A, he must arrange for that party to initiate the call. Since the customer of carrier B initiated the call, they are billed for it. Moreover, carrier A's customer *must* be registered with carrier B's videoconferencing network, even though that carrier does not serve them. Registration requires connectivity tests, a process that can take up to a week. In short, first time, spur-of-the-moment connections between dedicated access customers served by different carriers are almost impossible to arrange. Explaining this to a room full of executives, who are waiting for a videoconferenced connection to be established with an important customer, may be stressful.

SWITCHED ACCESS

The way to avoid this problem is to access an IXC's digital network using switched access service provided by the LEC. Switched access service is service that allows a customer to flexibly route calls across different long distance carrier's networks. To achieve this flexibility, a customer must generally buy their access service from a company that is *not* their long distance carrier. Since the distinction is blurring between long distance carrier and local access providers, it is important to ask the access provider if the switched connection being installed can be used to call anyone, on any other network, by simply dialing their telephone number.

Switched digital service choices for video and data conferencing include Switched 56, ISDN Basic Rate Interface (BRI), ISDN Primary Rate Interface (PRI), and asynchronous transfer mode (ATM). Switched access should not be confused with dedicated access service, which may also rely on ISDN PRI or ATM. In a switched access arrangement, channels can be assigned flexibly, to any long distance carrier *and* a customer can override the long distance carrier assignment by dialing a carrier access code.

Long Distance Carrier Access Arrangements

When ordering local service, customers are required to select a primary inter-exchange carrier (PIC). The LEC indicates the PIC choice by entering the selected carrier's access code in a routing table or database. When a " 1+" long distance call is made—in other words, a long distance call that is not specifically directed to a different long distance carrier—it defaults to the PIC. In a switched-to-switched connection, it does not matter what PIC the called party uses.

In a switched-to-dedicated access connection, an extra step may be required—but only if the called party uses an IXC different from the one used by the caller. When a difference exists, the caller dials a five-digit carrier access code, which forces the call over the long distance network that serves the called party. Examples of carrier access codes are as follows: dialing 10288 designates AT&T as the carrier; dialing 10222 designates MCI; and dialing 10333 designates Sprint. It is likely that carrier access codes will expand to seven-digits soon; there are many more carriers than there once were.

Switched access is easy to use but it has two cost-related drawbacks. First, IXCs typically offer lower rates for calls conducted over dedicated access arrangements that for switched access calls. The reason for this is simple. An IXC must pay the LEC a per-minute fee for long distance calls that pass over the local network. This fee does not apply when a call originates over a dedicated access connection—in that case, the LEC gets its compensation in the form of a *private line monthly rental charge*. IXCs pass the additional cost of switched access on to their customers. Consequently, the cost for switched-to-switched connections is higher than dedicated-to-dedicated connections.

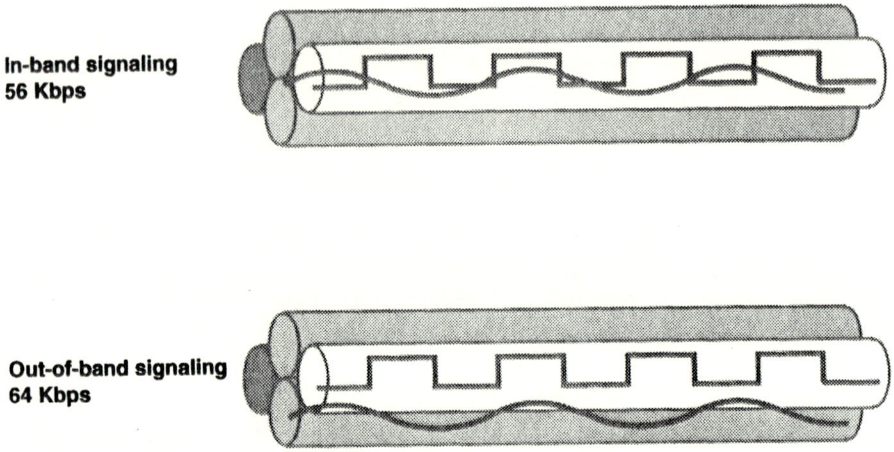

Figure 10-2. In-Band Vs. Out-Of-Band Signaling (Laura Long).

The second reason that switched access might be more costly is duplication. Most companies that are in the position to install videoconferencing have at least one, if not more, T-1 connections to an IXC. Often there are channels standing idle. It seems logical to use these channels for videoconferencing, and thereby eliminate a separate monthly cost for switched access. However, an IXC often charges a sub-multiplexing fee to split out videoconferencing channels from the rest of a T-1 pipe. That charge can, in some cases, equal or exceed the cost of separate switched digital access channels.

Several categories of switched digital access service exist. Before we can discuss them further we must further examine network signaling and control methods. Differences between signaling systems may impact the type of switched digital service offered.

Signaling: In-Band Versus Out-Of-Band

Network signaling is used to control the operations in a carrier's network and to establish connections between communication end points. The two categories of network signaling are *in-band* and *out-of-band*. The most noticeable difference between the two is the fast call setup times that out-of-band signaling delivers—often less than one second, compared to the 30 seconds (or more) setup time required to establish an in-band signaled connection.

Out-of-band signaling involves the separation of network signaling from customer data. This arrangement delivers the entire bandwidth of a digital channel for use by the customer. When signaling is separated from the transmission path, the result is clear channels, which are, by definition, 64 Kbps wide.

In-band signaling is an older method of establishing network connections. It requires that a customer relinquish some channel bandwidth to the carrier, who uses it for signaling. This technique of deriving bandwidth for network overhead is known as *bit-robbing*. A bit-robbed 64 Kbps line will only carry 56 Kbps of customer data.

In-band signaling not only steals valuable bandwidth from the customer's channel, it is also inefficient. Call set-up requests are routed progressively, from switching center to another, using the same circuit that the call will travel over after the connection is established. The method is slow and inefficient because each switching point introduces processing delays. A call could travel nearly all the way to its destination only to be blocked at a busy CO. During the time it took to reach its point of failure, the doomed call will have tied up circuits that other calls could have used.

Inside a carrier's network, out-of-band signaling methods are, almost exclusively, used to establish connections. Requests for call set-up and teardown are conveyed separately from the call itself, as are special messages that indicate caller-ID, class of service status, and other customer-specific data. The signaling portion of the network is packet-switched while the part that carries customer data is circuit-switched. Out-of-band signaling can be extended all the way to the customer's premise, but only if a special path is provided for its transit. If it is not, the carrier must use a portion of the line for signaling. The customer, who is able to transmit only 56 Kbps of data, pays the price.

Out-of-band signaling was first introduced by AT&T in 1976, when long distance competition forced it to become more efficient. Even in the '70s, AT&T's network was shared by millions of calls on any given day. Slow set-up times, and bandwidth wasted on failed calls, necessitated additional circuits. To streamline the process, AT&T devised a way to signal network status on a call-by-call basis. In order to identify available facilities, AT&T developed several huge databases of circuit inventories. These were accessed using a system known as Common Channel Interoffice Signaling (CCIS). CCIS circuit status requests were carried to replicated databases across a separate, analog packet-switched network, operating at speeds between 2.4 and 4.8 Kbps. Multiple routing-request packets streamed along the common highway, one after another.

In 1980, the CCITT approved an updated out-of-band signaling system. Known as Signaling System 7 (SS7), it also relies on a separate, packet-switched network. SS7 differs from SS6 in that it is digital and operates at either 56 or 64 Kbps. Call set-up times are significantly reduced because the network is so fast.

The SS7 protocol has gradually developed over the last decade to become the "nervous system" of the PSTN. Almost all modern carriers have migrated the *trunk side* of their networks to SS7 but the *line side* (the part that provides local access service to customers) sometimes uses bit-robbed signaling. Central offices must be retrofitted to accommodate clear channel service, and upgrades can be expensive.

Thus, bit-robbed (switched 56 and T-1) service is sometimes all that is available to customers wanting digital service.

Switched 56 Service

The IXCs and LECs offer *switched 56* dial-up digital service. It is a non-standards-based digital adaptation of a regular telephone line, which means it uses in-band signaling. As its name implies, it allows customers to call up and transmit digital information at speeds up to 56 Kbps, using regular dialing techniques. Switched 56 service is billed like a voice line—e.g., a monthly charge plus a cost for each minute of usage.

AT&T was first to offer switched 56, back in 1985. At the time, expensive dedicated arrangements were required to access it (T-1) because the LECs did not offer a comparable form of switched digital access. Now, nearly every telephone company sells switched 56. MCI, Sprint and LDDS WorldCom have tariffed it as well. Even though switched 56 is not standards-based, any two customers who use LEC-provided switched 56 service can call each other, even when an IXC's switched 56 product is used to cross a LATA line.

In most switched 56 videoconferencing applications, two channels are aggregated to yield one 112 Kbps circuit. This is bare-minimum bandwidth for group-system videoconferencing but many organizations get by with it.

Organizations that want the freedom to call anyone, regardless of which long distance carrier serves them, use the LEC's switched 56 lines (or, alternately, ISDN BRI) to reach their IXC's switched 56 service. Users of switched 56 (using either switched or dedicated access) can place calls to ISDN customers, as long as the ISDN equipment can accept switched 56 calls, as most can. Placing a video call to a customer using switched 56 service is much like making a long distance phone call. The caller dials two phone numbers, one for each channel. Placing a call using switched 56 is just as easy. One dials the telephone numbers associated with the channels that connected to the videoconferencing system on the other end. Because signaling is in-band, the connection may take a minute or more to establish. Part of the delay is usually associated with the codec handshaking process, however.

Switched 56 service is provided as either a two- or a four-wire arrangement. Four-wire service requires two cable pairs; two-wire requires only one. Generally, the packaging depends on the type of equipment located in the IXC's or LEC's switching center. Three different serving arrangements exist for switched 56: the four-wire variety (INC USDC) that AT&T developed, a two-wire version that Northern Telecom developed (Datapath), and Circuit Switched Digital Capability (CSDC), which is yet another two-wire version that few LEC's offer.

Two-wire switched 56 is actually transported at rates of 144 or 160 Kbps, and multiplexed using ping-pong modulation. Also called time-compression multiplexing (TCM), this technique supports transmissions from only one end of the connection at any given time, and simulates bi-directional (full-duplex) transmission by rapidly accepting signals from both ends on an alternating basis. Four-wire switched 56 provides a communications path for each end of the connection, with each pair of wires operating at only 56 Kbps. Two- and four-wire implementations of switched 56 are compatible. From a subscriber's point of view, there is really not much difference between the two except that four-wire service permits loops between the subscriber and the CO to span a greater distance.

Switched 56 service terminates in a DSU, which connects to CPE via an RS-232 or V.35 interface. Customers must be sure to buy the proper type of DSU: they differ, depending on whether the carrier provides two- or four-wire switched 56 service. The carrier should specify which type is required. Most manufacturers offer both varieties.

In switched 56 applications, DSUs not only manage clocking and bipolar conversions, they also signal the destination of the call to the telephone company switch. DSU dialing conforms to the Electronics Industries Association (EIA) RS-366 dialing standard. The RS-366 interface uses the AT command set that was originally employed by Hayes modems. The AT command specifies an auto-call unit (ACU) that takes a line off-hook, detects dial tone, dials a number, detects ringing, and recognizes call completion or failure.

Switched 56 service is reliable, universally available and painless to use. Its biggest drawback is that local access is expensive. Switched 56 access typically costs two to three times more than that of ISDN (Integrated Services Digital Network) Basic Rate Interface (BRI), despite the fact that ISDN BRI delivers 16 Kbps in additional bandwidth.

ISDN BRI

ISDN is an all-digital subscriber service—a single transport medium that can carry any type of information: voice, data, or video. The Basic Rate Interface, one of the two primary ISDN interfaces, relies on a single twisted copper pair of wires— the same two wires on which digital POTS service rely. Using this wired-pair, it delivers two 64 Kbps circuit-switched B channels and one 16 Kbps packet-switched *delta* (*data* or D) channel. The B channels can be aggregated. For instance, a videoconference can be carried over the 128 Kbps data stream derived by combining two B channels. Low-end videoconferencing applications (in which the need for motion handling and picture clarity is moderate) make extensive use of ISDN BRI service. Where it is offered, it is usually priced competitively, particularly in comparison to Switched 56 service. Not only are monthly rates low, installation charges are also reasonable. The biggest problem with BRI is that is not universally available.

If ISDN can deliver 144 Kbps of combined bandwidth, it would seem reasonable to expect POTS lines to do the same. Yet, even when POTS service is equipped with very fast modems, it can generate a maximum data transfer rate of only 33.6 Kbps (56 Kbps modems—that, at the time of this writing, require a number of caveats—eliminate digital-to-analog conversion and, therefore, do not provide analog service). The reason that ISDN is more than three times as fast as analog POTS is filtering. The PSTN uses filters to keep unwanted frequencies out of the 4 kHz analog voice pass band. Digital signals are not impeded by spurious frequencies, so the same twisted pair cable can, using digital modulation techniques, deliver much greater throughput.

Primarily, it is speed (and lack of an alternative) that has accounted for ISDN BRI's popularity. Approximately one million ISDN BRI lines existed at year-end 1995. This represents a 300% increase from the preceding year. It is estimated that, in 1996, this number more than doubled to 2.5 million. Although videoconferencing applications accounted for only a small portion of the installations (5–10%) ISDN BRI is particularly well-suited to interactive streaming media applications.

ISDN BRI service charges vary greatly, both within the United States and abroad. Rates fluctuate not only due to tariff differences, but also in relation to the distance between the customer and central office. On average, ISDN lines are priced about 1.5 to 2 times higher than POTS lines.

ISDN service has many advantages over POTS. ISDN data connections are set up in less than a second compared with over 30 seconds for POTS connections. ISDN can also be configured to provide enhanced Caller ID and other custom network features. There are many B and D channel configuration choices (although choices narrow when videoconferencing is passed over the B channel).

ISDN BRI can terminate up to 18,000 feet from a CO (in some areas, 24,000 feet), without signal reinforcement. COs have to be equipped for ISDN; if they do not have this capability, or if the customer is too far away from the CO, a telephone company may be able to provide ISDN BRI through the use of a Basic Rate Interface Terminal Extender (BRITE) card. BRITE technology uses T-1 carrier to transport up to 24 ISDN BRI channels. Since each BRI has three channels—two B and one D—this means that a BRITE card can support eight total ISDN BRI connections.

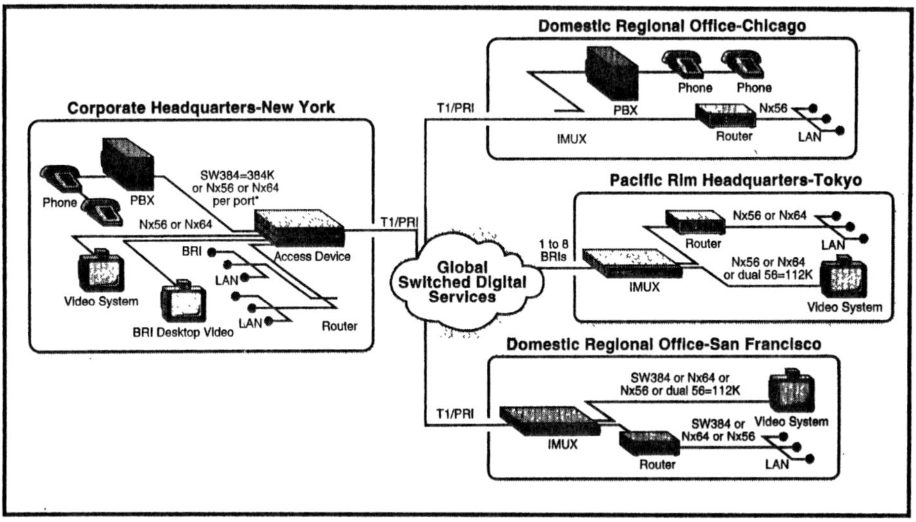

Figure 10-3. Global Videoconferencing (courtesy of Ascend Communications).

The ISDN NT-1

Eventually, ISDN BRI ends up at the customer's premises as a single twisted pair. These two wires terminate on a building block or protector and are then connected to an NT-1 (network termination, type one). As originally conceived by the CCITT, the NT is service-provider-owned equipment installed on the customer's premises. It establishes the point of telecommunications service delivery by a carrier. In the U.S. only, provision of the NT is the customer's responsibility (as mandated by the FCC's Network Channel Termination Equipment Order). On one side of the NT-1, circuit integrity is the responsibility of the carrier. On the other side, it is the responsibility of the customer. As such, the NT-1 is just like any other network demarcation (demarc) point.

The NT-1 is about the size of a stand-alone modem and requires a power supply. The power supply plugs into a commercial power outlet in the customer's equipment room. This is one drawback of ISDN when compared to POTS. POTS is powered by batteries in the CO. ISDN BRI requires more power than can be provided over the local loop. If an ISDN BRI-supported videoconferencing system must remain operational even during times of commercial power failure, a customer must provide a battery or uninterruptible power supply.

NT1 units allow up to eight different devices to be daisy-chained to the ISDN circuit, and thereby enable all eight to use it simultaneously or to contend for the circuit. Thus, as many as eight videoconferencing devices could share the same ISDN BRI line and contend with one other for the B channels as needed.

NT-1s and their associated power supplies vary widely in price; the cost difference correlates to capability. More expensive NT-1s can terminate ISDN offered by both AT&T and Northern Telecom. The cheaper ones are of switch-specific design. Some equipment vendors build the NTI-1 into CPE. The disadvantage to a built-in NT-1 is that it cannot be shared by other systems.

The ISDN Terminal Adapter

The ISDN specification also requires a terminal adapter or TA. ISDN TAs place calls, make connections and transfer digital data across the ISDN circuit. They consist of a call-control module and a B channel and D channel transport module. The call control module manages the resources of the ISDN line, using the Q.931 protocol to perform signaling functions. Q.931 is discussed below.

TAs can be internal (operate from the computer's local bus) or external (in which they are limited to the speed of the computer serial port—typically 115 Kbps. In videoconferencing applications, the TAs is almost always built in to software (in other words, it is internal).

Configuring a TA can be tricky. For instance, the person doing the set-up must know the type of CO with which the TA is communicating. Between North America and Europe, there are many different versions of the D-channel protocol. Some of these are based on standards (see National ISDN, below). Others are unique to a type of central office (e.g., AT&T 5ESS Custom, Northern Telecom DMS-100, European 1TR6, NET3, etc.).

One of the biggest configuration challenges in setting up the TA had to do with entering the proper Service Profile Identifier (SPID). The customer must enter the SPID into the ISDN TA before a device can, using the D channel, initialize at layer three of the OSI Reference Model.

A TA sends out its SPID each time it communicates with the CO—and each TA has a unique SPID. The SPID is associated with a set of ISDN features and capabilities. SPIDs can be assigned *only* after a customer has notified the LEC about what ISDN service and features are required. The carrier then translates this configuration into two or more SPIDs. Since eight TAs can share one ISDN NT-1, it is possible that eight SPIDs might be entered during an ISDN BRI configuration. Microsoft and others have tried to address the confusion over SPIDs in software (for instance, Microsoft released its ISDN Accelerator Pack for 1B connections. It can be found at www.microsoft.com/windows/software/isdn.htm. But configuring the SPID also involves the LEC and, until recently, their support has ranged from extremely helpful to moderately disinterested.

Some products offer TAs that support both POTS and ISDN. This allows a videoconferencing application to use ISDN B channels when the far-end can accommodate ISDN, and POTS when it can not. A good TA will adhere to the Multilink Point-to-Point Protocol (PPP), which defines a common method of negotiating a PPP session over two B channels. This is more important for data conferencing than for videoconferencing. When using external TAs, overhead and the speed of the computer's bus can severely limit bandwidth; although the BRI provides a potential 128 Kbps, the bus may limit bandwidth to as little as 70 Kbps. Small routers provide more bandwidth, but configuring them can be somewhat complex.

ISDN PRI

ISDN PRI consists of 23 B channels and a single 64 Kbps D channel. PRI is packaged much like North American T-1 carrier (24 total channels). ISDN, however, differs from T-1 in its signaling and synchronization methods. T-1 uses bit-robbing, and thereby results in a pipe made up of 24 channels, each of which offers 56 Kbps of bandwidth. PRI uses out-of-band signaling, and thereby results in a pipe with 23 B channels (each of which offers 64 Kbps of bandwidth) and one 64 Kbps D channel.

An ISDN PRI customer has exclusive use of the 23 B channels, which can be used separately or aggregated for data transport. Although PRI B channels are used for video and data conferencing, it is not common to dedicate an entire ISDN PRI pipe to a single videoconferencing system.

In both PRI and BRI arrangements, the ISDN D channel extends the intelligence of a carrier's SS7-based network beyond its traditional boundaries, and allow it to exchange signals with customer premise equipment. The customer and the carrier can share the D channel, (e.g., the customer can transmit packet-switched data over it) however this is very rare.

PRI terminates in a network terminal device called an NT-2. The NT-2 provides the same functions for ISDN PRI service as the NT-1 provides for BRI lines. In addition, the NT-2 performs switching (to route individual B channels) and bonding (to aggregate them into Nx64 pipes).

Although it is not always possible to access BRI from a LEC, ISDN PRI is generally available from an IXC. PRI is used for many things, including inbound and outbound long distance, remote LAN access, and videoconferencing. A PRI pipe typically terminates in a PBX or an ISDN hub.

In an ISDN-enabled PBX environment, the PRI comes in to the trunk side of the switch (the side leading to the telephone company) and videoconferencing CPE hangs off the *station side*. To make a video call, a station goes off-hook (perhaps using software) and dials a number. If there are ISDN B channels available on the PRI trunk, one or more are allocated to the station. Using the term *station*, we include both desktop video and data conferencing systems and group-systems.

Not all PBXs are ISDN-enabled and some that are do not conform to ISDN standards (see National ISDN, below). However, if the PBX is newer (built in 1993 or later) it probably offers ISDN PRI and BRI circuit packs. These can be installed so that individual desktop or group-system conferencing units can share ISDN PRI

B channels.

The alternative to an ISDN-enabled PBX is an ISDN hub. This can be installed if a PBX is not capable of supporting ISDN. An ISDN hub may already be in place—used, perhaps, for remote LAN access or other applications. The ISDN hub uses a separate wiring infrastructure to run BRI jacks to locations in a building where a need for service exists. One can envision the hub as a device similar to the ISDN-enabled PBX, but with voice-oriented features and capabilities.

Issues Related to ISDN

When the first set of ISDN standards was ratified in 1984, the CCITT (now the ITU-T), intended that it provide a migration path to move the historically analog PSTN to an end-to-end digital system. While the ITU-T was busy planning an evolution, customers were envisioning a revolution. It was expected that the PSTN would, overnight, move from analog to digital service. What was overlooked was the cost of upgrading a carrier's network to ISDN. The carriers that did deploy ISDN in the 1980s soon discovered that there was no demand for high-bandwidth (at the time) digital service. ISDN, it was said, really stood for "innovation subscribers do not need."

A decade after ISDN's introduction, several *killer applications* almost simultaneously emerged. Remote LAN access, telecommuting, Internet access, and low-bandwidth videoconferencing proved that the CCITT had been right—and visionary in their thinking. The problem today is this: ISDN deployment is by no means seamless. In the present competitive environment, telephone companies face revenue pressures; budgets are much tighter as a result. Aggressive customer demand can lead to upgrades or work-arounds (back-hauling from an ISDN-capable CO, for instance), but implementation takes time.

Even when ISDN is available, its clear channel capabilities may not extend beyond the LEC's regional boundaries. This is due to an oversight in the original CCITT specification. ISDN defines two interfaces, the network-to-user (N-interface) and the user-to-user (U-interface). It does not now, nor will it ever, define a network-to-network interface. This means that extending ISDN's clear-channel capabilities between carrier's networks requires negotiated agreements and special engineering. When the LECs and IXCs work cooperatively, ISDN can be arranged to offer end-to-end digital service on a clear-channel (64 Kbps) basis. The component that makes ISDN capable of offering end-to-end digital service is SS7; it *is* the network-to-network interface. However, D channel signaling has been implemented in various proprietary ways and one carrier's SS7 system might not be compatible with another one's.

The trouble with SS7 interoperability can be traced to a rather sluggish standards-setting process. In 1984, the ITU-T published the first ISDN specifications. Unfortunately, it was incomplete as it related to signaling over the D channel. Without a comprehensive standard, the switch manufacturers were left to their own devices to fill the holes in the D-channel protocol. AT&T and Northern Telecom, the two dominant CO manufacturers in North America, turned out proprietary interpretations. Since switching systems could not interpret each other's D-channel protocols, inter-network signaling had to be passed in-band. Even in 1997, it is very difficult to arrange for 64 Kbps clear channel endpoint-to-endpoint, using LEC access. This haphazard arrangement is ceasing with the advent of National ISDN and other concerted efforts made on behalf of ISDN.

National ISDN

In 1991, the Corporation for Open Systems (COS) and the North American ISDN User's Forum (NIUF) developed an initiative to standardize the implementation of ISDN within the United States. In November 1992, Bellcore, the COS, and the NIUF introduced National ISDN-1 (NI-1), a standard that aims to provide a consistent interface among LECs, IXCs, and equipment manufacturers. NI-1 was introduced at a week-long event called the Transcontinental ISDN project, or TRIP '92. The NI-1 standard, which precisely defines ISDN's Basic Rate Interface, has been widely implemented.

NI-1 is but the first step in developing a seamless national ISDN network. Judging from comments in a threaded series of e-mail messages, it has not entirely been embraced.

The second step, National ISDN-2, got underway in late 1993. In the NI-2 standard, Bellcore strengthened NI-1, and thereby provided for service uniformity and facilitating operations and maintenance. NI-2 also defines various PRI features, including circuit-switched voice and data call control, packet-switched data call control, switched T-1, fractional T-1 service, and D-channel backup. NI-2 did not address Non-Facility Associated Signaling (NFAS)—the ability for one D channel to provide signaling services for multiple PRIs. NFAS allows a customer with multiple PRI connections (typically 11, maximum) to allocate only one D channel to handle signaling for all of them. Each additional PRI, after the first, has 24 B channels.

The third iteration of National ISDN is NI-95. NI-95 improves the PRI and defines how ISDN is used for access to personal communications services (PCS) networks. The most recent iterative of National ISDN is NI-96. It lists new ISDN features and capabilities and gives references to Bellcore requirements documents for these services. Both ISDN-95 and ISDN-96 represent a change in the nomenclature for

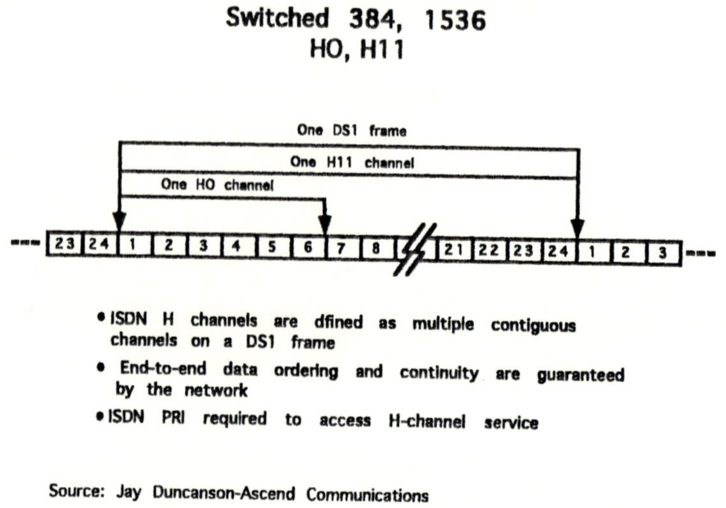

Figure 10-4. Switched 384, 1536 (H0, H11) Framing (Michel Bayard).

National ISDN. To get more information on National ISDN, customers may contact Bellcore via its National ISDN Hotline: 1-800-992-ISDN or at its web site:

In May 1996, the U.S.'s largest LECs, under the aegis of the National ISDN Council (Gaithersburg, Maryland), agreed to implement a standard procedure for a customer's establishment of ISDN service. These companies included all regional Bell companies, Cincinnati Bell Telephone Co., GTE Corporation, and Southern New England Telephone Co. The ISDN ordering standard includes codes, known as EZ-ISDN codes, that cover the two most commonly-ordered ISDN BRI configurations. Neither of the two EZ ISDN versions (EZ ISDN 1 and EZ ISDN 1a) are aimed at easing the ordering process for videoconferencing configurations (two circuit switched B channels configured for voice/data and a single packet-switched D channel).

The standard also includes a uniform SPID format. Under the new definition, a SPID is exactly fourteen digits in length whereas, in the past, SPIDs could be anywhere from 11 to 20 digits.

The video codec connects to the station side of the PBX with a BRI connection. Only a handful of switches offer a National ISDN-1 (NI-1) BRI interface (two that do are the NEC ICS and the Northern Telecom Meridian with Release 18 or newer software). Most switches require some type of adapter to be plugged into their regular digital station ports to support NI-1 connections. At any rate, the videoconferencing equipment, when placed behind a PBX, is assigned a DID (direct inward dialing) number, that makes it accessible through the PBX. The advantage to this scenario is that the videoconferencing system shares PRI channels on a call-by-call basis with other applications. The disadvantage is that the connection is essentially dedicated and, therefore, results in the same problems with inter-IXC calling that are encountered with other dedicated access methods.

ISDN H0, H1 AND MULTIRATE

In the future, customers will be able to easily select different videoconferencing bandwidths by combining, on a flexible basis, the number of ISDN B channels necessary to deliver a specified level of motion handling and picture resolution. Today a North American customer can decide to set up a videoconference at 384 Kbps or 1.536 Mbps using a long-distance carrier's H0- and H11-based products.

H0 and H11 service use several ITU-T protocols for call set-up. These are Q.920, Q.921 and Q.931. Link Access Protocol-D (LAPD) is formally specified in ITU-T Q.920 and ITU-T Q.921. LAPD is an OSI layer-2 protocol. The connection-oriented service establishes a point-to-point D channel link between a customer and a carrier's switch. Data is sent over the link as Q.921 packets. Whereas the D channel is packet-switched, B channel connections are circuit-switched and are established, maintained, and torn down using the Q.931 interface (also known as ITU-T I.451). In Q.931, the ITU-T specified how 'H' channels—multiple contiguous channels on T-1 or E-1/CEPT frames—can be bound together and switched across an ISDN network.

In addition to the switched 384 H0 standard and the switched 1.536 H11 standard, the ITU-T specifies H12 (European switched 1.920. All are part of Q.931, and all make it possible for high-bandwidth circuits to be created on-demand. The network guarantees end-to-end synchronization and clear-channel access. However, the customer's premise equipment must bond the channels and pass them to the network over PRI access.

H0 dialing calls for six contiguous DS0s to be combined into a single 384 Kbps channel. At 1.544, PRI can carry 4 H0 channels or 3 H0 + D; at 2.048 it can carry 5 H0 + D. H11 dialing combines 24 DS0s into a channel-less arrangement with an aggregate bandwidth of 1.536 Mbps. H12 combines 30 channels into a channel-less arrangement.

In 1991, AT&T became the first U.S. carrier to offer commercial H0 service, by making it available on a dedicated-access (both ends) basis. AT&T offers H11 service, as well. MCI WorldCom also offers H0 and H11 service.

An even more recent development, ISDN multirate, also known as Nx64 or switched fractional T-1 service, lets users combine, on a call-by-call basis, between two and 24 B channels.

INVERSE MULTIPLEXERS

Although multirate ISDN becoming more available, it is not ubiquitous. An alternative is to use hardware to achieve variable-rate bandwidth, or *bandwidth on demand.* To dial up multiple 56 or 64 Kbps channels, a customer can use an inverse multiplexer (I-MUX). An I-MUX breaks a high-bandwidth videoconference into a number of lower-speed channels for transport across a switched digital network.

I-muxes were introduced in 1990. They break a high-speed data stream (such as that produced by a codec) into N (where 'N' typically indicates some number between 4 and 24) lower-speed switched digital channels. I-muxes use the EIA RS-366 standard to provide dialing commands to the network. They keep a signal synchronized so that a compatible device on the other end can rebuild a single high-speed signal from the multiple lower-speed signals it receives.

Synchronization is necessary because a switched digital network is a mesh of circuits. Many different paths can be taken to get between two points, and calls are routed across this mesh independently. If a high-speed videoconference were subdivided into lower-speed fragments, each fragment could take a different route to get to its destination. Routing disparities cause data stream synchronization problems.

I-muxes perform *delay synchronization*. In other words, they hold a frame open until all its fragments reach their destination. Once received, the I-MUX reconstructs the frame and presents it to the codec (or other high-bandwidth device). Depending on the configuration, I-muxes can perform additional tasks. Some are switches (hubs) that patch incoming channels to outgoing channels. Others receive ISDN PRI signals and convert them to T-1 or E-1/CEPT. An I-MUX may, among other things, convert protocols, perform overflow routing, and provide private line back-up service.

When I-muxes were first introduced, they could not interoperate—identical devices had to be installed on both ends. This presented another obstacle for inter-company videoconferencing. To address the problem, a consortium, which included almost 40 vendors, developed the BOnDInG standard; the first draft was approved on August 17, 1992.

BOnDInG stands for Bandwidth On Demand Interoperability Group. The BOnDInG specification describes how I-muxes can dial up channels across a network and combine them to create a single higher-speed connection. BOnDInG is discussed in more depth in Chapter 13.

FOLLOW THE MEGABIT ROAD

There may come a time when we will have as much bandwidth as we need. We draw closer to that day as the ISDN evolution takes its next step, from narrowband to broadband. Broadband ISDN (B-ISDN) offers all-in-one support for voice, data, image, and motion video. It delivers this service on a single high-speed network. At the bottom of the network (at the physical layer) will be DS-1, DS-3, and an optically-oriented technology known as the Synchronous Optical Network (SONET). Above the physical layer (but below the networking functions of the upper layer transport protocols) lies another technology known as asynchronous transfer mode (ATM). Above the ATM layer are two basic services: those that are designed for variable bit-rate (data-oriented) transmission and those that are aimed at constant bit-rate (streaming media—voice and video) traffic.

ATM is closely associated with SONET. It requires the speed that optical signaling can deliver; speed too great for metallic media to reliably support over long distances. SONET can carry DS-0 and its multiples, and thereby provide a bridge between the older, slower digital signaling hierarchy and ATM's faster (minimum 155 Mbps) data delivery rates.

Many books provide information on SONET and ATM. A very good one is William Flanagan's "Frames, Packets and Cells in Broadband Networking (which can be obtained by calling 800-LIBRARY)." It is not within the scope of this book to provide a tutorial on either SONET or ATM, but we can not conclude this section on circuit-switched networks without discussing them.

SONET and SDH

The North American digital hierarchy specification was developed for copper media. The aggressive deployment of fiber optic cable makes the digital signaling hierarchy (based on DS-0 multiples) highly-inefficient. Optical networks can transport data at speeds far in excess of 41.84 Mbps (DS-3). Synchronous optical network (SONET), an optical transmission interface originally proposed by Bellcore—and later standardized by ANSI—was conceived to replace the copper-oriented digital signaling (DS) interface over time, yet remain compatible with it throughout the upgrade process.

SONET resumes where the digital signaling hierarchy concludes. The SONET and SDH standards establish a standard multiplexing format that uses 51.84 Mbps channel multiples as building blocks. Lower level ANSI and ITU-T digital signaling hierarchies used a 64 Kbps (DSO, EO) building block. The 51.84 Mbps rate was specified because the overhead involved in framing precluded higher speeds from being exact multiples of the 64Kbps base speed. A 51.84 Mbps signal can carry a 44.84 Mbps DS-3 signal, with room left for overhead.

SONET line rates are referred to as Optical Carrier (OC) speeds. The electrical signal interfaces that correspond with these speeds (known as STS) have also been identified. The 51.84 Mbps base speed for SONET is known as OC-1/STS-1. Higher speeds are multiples of this rate. OC-3/STS-3 has a speed of 155.52 Mbps. It is expected to be an important speed level for establishing multimedia transmissions and, of the specified optical standards, it is the slowest one capable of 100 Mbps LAN speeds. SONET also includes a 622.08 Mbps, (or OC-12/STS-12), specification, and a 1.244 Gbps (OC/24/STS-24) specification. SONET's highest speed is the 2.48 Gbps OC-48/STS-48 specification.

SONET specifies not only line speeds, but also transmission encoding and multiplexing methods and establishes an optical signaling standard for interconnecting equipment from diverse suppliers. A synchronous multiplexing format carries DS-level traffic. The ITU-T developed a European-oriented version of SONET known as synchronous digital hierarchy (SDH). In short, SONET provides the physical infrastructure for a next-generation PSTN switching architecture. That architecture is known as B-ISDN and its most widely-known implementation is ATM.

ATM and B-ISDN

B-ISDN was developed by the CCITT to be a 155 or 622 Mbps public switched network service. In specifying B-ISDN, the goal of the ITU-T was to create a public network that is ideally suited to carrying the signals that are intrinsic to multimedia, which have a wide range of traffic characteristics.

The CCITT's "Task Group on Broadband Aspects of ISDN" looked at a variety of interactive broadband services that would be required in the public network. Of course, they considered video telephony and video and data conferencing, HDTV, and high-speed file transfer—all topics that we cover in this book. Indeed, the B-ISDN protocol stack, and its ATM layer, would not have been necessary were it not for Real-Time interactive data types that needed to share a public network with less time-sensitive traffic.

To reiterate, ATM is a layer in the B-ISDN model. Below it lies SONET. Above it lie various layers that adapt the ATM transport structure to meet the needs of different media types and applications. An ATM network switches data of all types in fixed-length cells (for that reason, its also called cell relay). The cell size is 53 bytes; of this, 48 bytes are filled with customer data and 5 bytes are used for cell header information. Cell relay works because information is "chopped" so finely that the network can easily fit many cells across one high-speed link. Although ATM has a great deal of overhead (more than 10%) it works well in fast network (155 Mbps and up) environments.

ATM user equipment connects to the ATM network via a user-network interface or UNI. Connections between ATM-provider networks are made via a network-network interface (NNI). Data contained in a cell header are used by the UNI, the NNI, and ATM switches during transport. Specifically, the first two fields in the ATM header at the NNI are the 12-bit virtual path identifier (VPI) and the 16-bit virtual circuit identifier. The 28-bit address formed by the VPI/VCI is used in switching a call, hop-by-hop, across the network. These 28-bits change as a call passes from ATM switch to another. The forwarding switch and the receiving switch track the VPI/VCI pairs (sender and receiver) locally, but only for a brief interlude, then the cell moves on.

Cells are arranged in logical connections called channels. This confuses some people who think ATM is designed to support both connection-oriented and connectionless services. Although it does support connectionless services, ATM is, over all, a *connection-oriented process*. A cell may not be sent until a channel has been established to carry it. ATM packages data into cells according to its type—e.g., datagram, voice sample, video frame. It does so in accordance with the layer above ATM in the B-ISDN protocol stack, the ATM adaptation layer or AAL. Five types of AALs have been identified in the B-ISDN model. The key ones are packet switching service adaptation and circuit switching service adaptation. In adapting non time-sensitive traffic for transport, it is possible to segment large packets into smaller ones and route them to be reassembled sequentially. However, time-sensitive traffic (voice and video) is processed differently, using buffers to keep data flowing in a smoothly paced stream.

When one ATM end-node needs to send data to another end-node, it requests a connection by transmitting a signaling request to the network. The network passes the *requested path* to the destination. If the destination node and the sender can negotiate a connection, a switched virtual circuit (SVC) is completed. When the devices are finished with their exchange, the SVC is *taken down* by all switching points originally engaged in setting it up.

The sender also arranges end-to-end quality of service by specifying call attributes such as type and speed. As discussed previously, audio and video transmissions are time sensitive, but are adequate with some inaccuracy. Data transmissions, in contrast, require absolute accuracy—e.g. no absence of information—but are not time sensitive. Because ATM establishes connectivity through switching rather than through a shared bus, it offers dedicated bandwidth per connection, high aggregate bandwidth, and explicit connection procedures.

ATM is, by definition, capable of providing isochronous service. End-nodes have a way of requesting specific network characteristics when they establish the call. For instance, a node can inform the network of the average bandwidth it will require and whether it will be bursting or sending Real-Time data. The network will condition a circuit based on this information. The network keeps a cumulative inventory of its bandwidth. As new requests for service arise, it decides, based on probabilities, whether it can service the new caller's request. If it cannot, it rejects the request until adequate bandwidth becomes available. For this reason, ATM is an ideal networking technology for interactive streaming media.

Although ATM and ISDN are mistakenly thought of as separate technologies, it is important to remember that ATM is a B-ISDN implementation. Cell switching is the protocol that is used to move packets across B-ISDN and ATM networks. B-ISDN, and its real-world manifestation, ATM, will provide a future in which distinctions between circuit- and packet-switching are moot.

Digital Subscriber Line (DSL)

Telcos have been using HDSL to conserve wire pairs while achieving T1 speeds for years. However, in 1989, Bellcore conceived an idea for transmitting video, audio, and data, at rates of more than one Mbps over ordinary twisted-pair telephone lines. The crux of the idea was to transfer information more quickly in one direction than in the other (asymmetrically), with downstream rates of 1.5 Mbps and upstream rates of 16 or 64 Kbps. Such asymmetry would match rate requirements for video on demand and information retrieval over data networks over much greater distances than symmetric means could. They termed this new technology Asymmetric Digital Subscriber Line (ADSL).

ADSL downstream speeds have increased nearly tenfold (albeit at the price of distance) and upstream speeds have increased at least tenfold. Major suppliers now mass-produce ADSL chip sets, and the footprint and power consumption of ADSL transceivers has significantly decreased. By summer 1998, the global ADSL modem installed base already included more than 100,000 of the 500 million residential telephone lines that existed at that time.

Bellcore conceived ADSL primarily for video at 1.5 Mbps, and early ADSL trials focused on Video on Demand (VOD) applications. However, the primary market is now Internet based interactive multimedia. Cable TV companies and telephone companies are furiously racing to develop infrastructure or to grow by acquisition so that they can win over users who desire high-speed Internet access from residences and remote offices. Data communications, to the Internet or to corporate LANs, is driving demand for ADSL and cable modem based network access. ADSL is only a method of moving bits from one end of copper wires to another; it depends upon access networks to perform network management, protocol conversion, data concentration, routing, multiplexing, and signaling between servers and personal computers.

Telcos had picked up only 30,000 DSL customers by the end of 1998. However, deployment of Digital Subscriber Line (DSL) reached nearly 250,000 lines in 1999, according to TeleChoice. Incumbent Local Exchange Carriers (ILEC) led the market, however Competitive Local Exchange Carriers (CLECs) installed enough DSL equipment in Central Offices to serve nearly 39 million customers, and allege that 26,950 lines are in service. With the Internet's popularity creating an insatiable hunger for bandwidth, and the Telecommunications Act of 1996 forcing (LECs) to prepare to compete with new competitors, LECs are seeking ways to leverage their infrastructure to provide broadband services to homes. They must move quickly if they are to deflect the assault from the cable television industry.

Sensing an imminent market boom, manufacturers started producing transceivers (modems) in summer 1996 that increased ADSL's downstream and upstream capabilities to as much as 9 Mbps and 640 Kbps, respectively. ADSL customers would connect exponentially faster (downstream) than they were connecting at the time with conventional V.34 modems. Perhaps more importantly, those customers would benefit from an always-on network connection. Since ADSL leverages existing POTS infrastructure, providers could implement it while interoperating with V.90 modems (for those who do not live close enough to a Telco CO—central office—to receive DSL service) and other existing technology.

The absence of standards presented a challenge. AT&T Paradyne defended its proprietary *Carrierless Amplitude and Phase Modulation* (CAP) DSL. The American National Standards Institute (ANSI) advocated Discrete Multitone (DMT) technology—the ASNI Working Group T1E1.4 approved DMT in its T1.413ADSL standard. Discrete Multitone divides the 1 MHz spectrum offered by a phone line into 256 4 kHz channels and varies the bit densities on each channel to overcome noise and interference that may be present in sections of that spectrum. Proponents contend that DMT is better than CAP on noisy lines because it maximizes throughput on good channels and minimizes use of channels that have significant interference. In contrast, CAP uses Quadrature Amplitude Modulation (much like V.90 modems) and relies on a combination of amplitude modulation and phase shifts to increase line capacity over a single line. AT&T integrated a feature of DMT, Rate Adaptive Digital Subscriber Loop (RADSL) to reduce each customer's bandwidth relative to their distance from their central office (CO) and their wire quality—at the cost, of course, of bandwidth.

To address the lack of interoperability between vendors, a consortium of organizations led by Intel, Microsoft, and Compaq announced the "Universal" Asymmetric Digital Subscriber Line (ADSL) Working Group. The group's stated purpose was to accelerate ADSL adoption and availability by proposing a simplified version that would deliver high-speed modem communications over existing phone lines to consumers, and would be based upon an open, interoperable ITU standard. By reducing the complexity of the on-site installation and eliminating the need for new wiring at the user's home, Universal ADSL promised to facilitate cost-effectively DSL deployment. Moreover, by leveraging existing rate adaptive ADSL (RAADSL or RADSL) technology, the standard promised to open the market to additional customers by automatically configuring itself for the fastest rate for any given line. In June 1999, the ITU-T approved the G.992.2 standard, widely known as *G.lite*.

Based on the same underlying technology as standard ADSL, G.lite provides a roadmap for vendor interoperability and eliminates the need to dispatch a technician to install a splitter at the customer premise. Once NSPs provision the central office equipment, the customer connects a G.lite modem as easily as she may have installed a conventional modem. G.lite modems began showing up in retail outlets in fall 1999. Unlike standard ADSL, G.lite works with Digital Loop Carrier, the local loop infrastructure that connects customers who are located more than 18,000 feet from the central office, and thereby opens the technology to a broader audience.

The new focus on the Internet and corporate LAN access has also forced changes in access network architectures. Because IP dominates the Internet and private networks, NSPs are constructing access networks to support IP to customer premises. However, recognizing ATM's inherent ability to support converged services, and QoS, NSPs are building access networks to relay IP via ATM multiplexing and switching. The first ADSL trials employed a router-based architecture in which ADSL modems perform MAC layer concentration by connecting to an IP router through an Ethernet hub or switch each Central Office (CO). Now, Digital Subscriber Line Access Multiplexers (DSLAM) displace the router by connecting CO modems directly to a shared high-speed backplane.

The multiplexing protocol in this scenario is Ethernet from the PC to the router, and IP for Multiplexing multiple connections into single PCs. NSPs can gradually migrate to this configuration from legacy equipment by integrating various pieces over time. Doing so involves no protocol conversion in the network, and is compatible with Internet and LAN protocols. However, this router-based architecture will not scale for the broad residential broadband market, and cannot be easily adapted for mixed services and switching. For instance, a user who desires to connect alternately to a NSP and to a corporate network requires two separate routers. Moreover, it does not support QoS or future path-oriented services for video and voice. Consequently, NSPs now deploy ADSL networks almost exclusively with ATM layer 2 multiplexing.

Currently, Network Service Providers are offering ADSL networks with Permanent Virtual Circuits (PVCs), and ATM-based paths between user terminals and NSPs or corporate LAN gateways. Users can not alter PVCs; they require network administrator intervention. A PVC to the Internet provides access to Internet resources through IP routing; a PVC to a corporate LAN provides access to corporate network resources the same way. Originally, ATM Switched Virtual Circuit (SVCs) were envisioned as the upgrade path as network size and capabilities grew. A SVC connection is established in Real-Time in response to signaling messages from the customer. SVCs would greatly reduce the effort to provision service to a new customer, and would permit customers to roam freely between Information Service Providers.

By switching all traffic through an ATM backbone, one gains high flexibility for connecting multiple services and provides the best compromise for convergence. By inserting a DSLAM with integrated ADSL modems for each subscriber at each end office, networks reach subscriber premises over existing copper lines. The ATM cloud resides within the ADSL access provider's access network. SVCs would allow sequential Network Service Provider (NSP) selection from a given client. Such premises may be comprised of an Ethernet connection between the ADSL modem and the PC, an ADSL modem that is integrated into a PC, or a premises network. To serve multiple PCs it might be necessary to install a small router at the premises.

PVCs do not scale as a network grows to millions of customers and thousands of circuit changes a day. SVCs allow users to connect and disconnect just as they make telephone calls, but are difficult and costly to implement. However, PPP over ATM simulates a limited form of customer-controlled switching that enables users to access numerous private networks in sequence.

NSPs have adopted Point-to-Point Protocol (PPP) over ATM because it is easy to integrate with existing protocols and operating methods. They use RADIUS (remote authentication of dial-in user services) servers for authentication, authorization, accounting (AAA) services that are dependent on PPP session establishment to end-users. By adopting the same service access protocol that dial-up users use, NSPs facilitate service convergence and leverage a mature service platform. In lieu of an end-to-end ATM network (or of IPv6), L2TP (Layer 2 Tunneling Protocol) Access Concentrators (LAC) map multiple PPP sessions within individual PVCs from the access network to PPP sessions within an L2TP tunnel. Multiple tunnels may exist between the LAC and an NSP where the tunnel used to convey a packet depends upon the priority assigned to the packet.

The NSP-gateway concept can also be deployed via a shared Broadband Access Server (BAS) with PPP Terminated Aggregation (PTA). The same BAS that a NSP would use to terminate PPP can be operated within the ADSL access network. Each AAA server manages sessions to the BAS through a RADIUS proxy interface to the BAS and thereby permits service autonomy. The BAS strips PPP encapsulation from the user packets before forwarding the packet to a NSP. The BAS serves as an IP router and participates in the IP domain of each NSP when IP is the L3 protocol. SVCs or the NSP gateway (LAC or BAS) permit users to alternate between service providers sequentially, and permit the network access provider and Internet service provider to efficiently provision service to large numbers of customers.

ADSL accommodates ATM transport with variable rates and compensation for ATM overhead. The ATM Forum recognizes ASDL as a physical layer transmission protocol. ADSL modems use forward error correction to reduce errors caused by impulse noise, and isolate POTS channels from digital channels to protect them from interruption as a result of a digital services failure. By 1998, Pacific Bell, Bell Atlantic, US West, and GTE all deployed commercial ADSL offerings. Providers expect to install neighborhood Optical Network Units (ONU) to provide virtual fiber to the curb (FTTC).

ADSL serves only customers who reside within 12,000–18,000 feet, or 2.25–3.4 miles, from their central office (CO) because signals on copper *attenuate*, or become corrupted over distance. Carriers who must install digital repeaters to provide users with ADSL service must charge more for services. Moreover, carriers who have enabled voice to transmit over longer distances by installing loading coils in the local loop must make expensive modifications to carry ADSL transmissions.

Cable is currently the greatest competition to G.lite, but except for the few areas where two-way service is available, cable modem service currently requires a telephone line for upstream transmission. Moreover, both performance and security are concerns because cable modems are a shared architecture. Finally, cable modems require technicians for installation. By contrast, G.lite and ADSL provide dedicated point-to-point connections and allow for consistent performance in a secure environment.

Cable Modems

At the time of that report, cable television carried only analog signals. Digital systems can deliver flawless images at a signal-to-noise ratio more than 1,000 times lower. Although, for example, DirectTV must send a signal 26,600 miles away to a satellite, and back down to an 18-inch dish on a roof, it outperforms analog video that simply travels down a coaxial cable. The reason is that digital pictures are constructed in the TV set rather than at the broadcasting station. Cable modems spread codes through numerous frequencies and thereby minimize the effect of interfering ones. In theory, cable television infrastructure can provide at least 8 Gbps of two-way bandwidth.

Cable modems seem to be beating DSL in the broadband race because their service is more widely available and it costs less. About 430,000 U.S. households subscribed to high-speed cable Internet services in 1998, and, according to the Yankee Group, that number may exceed 4.3 million by 2002. The phone companies had picked up only 30,000 DSL customers by the end of 1998. While the telcos are just getting started, cable companies are increasing their customer base by at least 200,000 homes every week.

Nevertheless, cable modem implementation has not been without its tribulations. Until recently, the massive infrastructure retrofitting that cable networks require, and an absence of cable modems standards have hampered their growth. Cable companies have invested in hybrid fiber-coaxial networks because, in 1997, no more than 10% of cable plants were equipped to handle two-way digital connectivity.

The IEEE *802.14 Cable TV Media Access Control (MAC) and Physical (PHY) Protocol Working Group* was formed in May 1994 to develop international standards for data communications over cable. Their charter was to submit a cable modem MAC and PHY standard to the IEEE in 1995, but the standards were delayed until almost 1998.

In January 1996, the *Multimedia Cable Network System Partners Ltd.* (MCNS), a limited partnership that was comprised of Comcast, Cox, TCI, and Time Warner, issued a RFP for a project management company to swiftly research and publish a set of high-speed cable data services interface specifications. The MCNS Data Over Cable Service Interface Specification (DOCSIS) RFP persuaded MediaOne, Rogers Cablesystems, and CableLabs to join the coalition and thereby constitute a provider organization that serves 85% of U.S. cable subscribers and 70% of Canadian subscribers. Consequently, more than 20 vendors announced plans to build products based on the MCNS DOCSIS standard in March 1997.

To reduce product costs and time to market, MCNS minimized technical complexity and developed a technology solution that, although, not ideal, was adequate. In contrast, the 802.14 group had been seeking to create a standard that would provide excellent quality and stand the test of time. At the physical layer, *modulation formats for digital signals*, the MCNS and IEEE specifications are comparable; both MCNS and the 802.14 upstream modulation standards incorporate QPSK (quadrature phase shift keying) and 16QAM. The 802.14 specification supports the ITU's J.83 Annex A (European DVB/DAVIC), B (MCNS), and C (Japanese) standards for 64/256 QAM modulation, and provides a maximum 36 Mbps of downstream throughput per 6 MHz television channel.

The media access control (MAC), which sets the rules for network access by users, is where the two significantly differ. The 802.14 group specified ATM as its default solution from the headend to the cable modem. MCNS specified a scheme that is based on variable-length packets and that favors the delivery of Internet Protocol (IP) traffic. Both specify a 10Base-T Ethernet connection from the cable modem to the PC. Because ATM is deterministic, it provides superior QoS for integrated delivery of video, voice, and data traffic to cable modem units (as long as the cable modem is an ATM device). The 802.14 group envisioned ATM as a long-term, flexible solution.

Cable operators, whose priority was to provide high-speed Internet services to consumers, believed that ATM would add unnecessary complexity and cost to cable modem systems. MCNS members' intent was to leverage the low costs of ubiquitous Ethernet and IP networking technologies. Standardized DOCSIS cable modems started shipping in limited quantities in the third and fourth quarters of 1998. DOCSIS defines MPEG-2 transport for the downstream transmission convergence sublayer. MPEG-2 allows both video and data signals to be carried in a single multiplexed bit stream that occupies one analog channel, and thereby preserve channel capacity.

The ITU recognition DOCSIS as an international standard in 1998, but the IEEE 802.14 continued its own work. In a token gesture to acknowledge the Working Group's work, MCNS indicated that it would implement IEEE 802.14's advanced PHY specification within DOCSIS. In meeting that commitment, MCNS asked the vendors whom the IEEE had selected to develop an advanced PHY for its own standard, to develop the advanced PHY for DOCSIS 1.2. Many believed that the IEEE 802.14 specification might become a standard for operators outside North America, or that the specification might apply to corporate data services, while DOCSIS would be deployed for residential services. These speculations now seem improbable. Despite good intentions and a better specification than that developed by MCNS, IEEE 802.14 was simply unable to complete a specification in time.

The existing set of DOCSIS specifications is known as DOCSIS 1.0, and supports high speed data services. DOCSIS 1.1, nearing completion at the time of this writing, will incorporate extensions for Quality of Service (QoS) and authentication to support telephony services. For the downstream physical layer, DOCSIS specifies ITU J.83B digital data distribution over existing North American cable TV networks using existing RF equipment. It combines 64 or 256 QAM modulation of the downstream signal, a variable length interleaver, trellis coding, and Reed-Solomon error correction coding. For the downstream transmission convergence sublayer, DOCSIS defines MPEG-2 transport to enable both video and data signals to be carried in a single multiplexed bit stream that occupy one analog channel. DOCSIS accommodates most cable network architectures because it uses a range of symbol rates including QPSK or 16 QAM modulation, Reed-Solomon error correction coding, and transmit power automatically adjusted by the MAC. The DOCSIS MAC enables initializing new modems on the network, sharing upstream bandwidth between active modems, periodic ranging and power adjustment to decrease the effects of temperature on the cable plant, and modem management. The DOCSIS standards for Baseline Privacy use 56-bit DES encryption of data traffic. It leverages the RSA public-key encryption algorithm for key management and distribution, with a key size of 768 bits for DOCSIS 1.0 and 1024 bits for DOCSIS 1.1. DOCSIS RF-return cable modems forward packets using IEEE 802.1D forwarding rules, as modified by the DOCSIS specifications. Telco return modems forward packets using IP forwarding rules. In both modes of operation, these modems are capable of layer 2 and layer 3 packet filtering, per operator-defined filter rules.

The DOCSIS specifications were developed to enable hardware and systems interoperability, and automated configuration and management. Cable Modems and Cable Modem Termination Systems (CMTS) from numerous vendors can use the DOCSIS specifications to operate on the same network. In the DOCSIS model, a CABLE MODEM is authorized by the CMTS for use on the network, and configures itself according to parameters that it receives from the headend, without user involvement. When the CABLE MODEM is powered up and logged on to the network for the first time (or if the data frequency has been changed), the CABLE MODEM automatically scans the downstream frequency spectrum to locate the data channel. If the CABLE MODEM has previously accessed the network, it will have stored the previous session frequency and will immediately tune to the data channel. Once the CABLE MODEM finds the DOCSIS data signal, it looks for a message that contains the basic parameters for the upstream channel (e.g., frequency, modulation, symbol rate, FEC parameters.). The CABLE MODEM then transmits a message to the CMTS with a request for additional information that will enable it to connect to the network. Through a series of messages and interactions, the CABLE MODEM establishes IP connectivity using DHCP, and then receives additional configuration parameters via TFTP so that it can configure itself. Once the CABLE MODEM is configured, it registers with the CMTS and becomes authorized to use the network. Optionally, the final step of the initialization is establishment of the parameters to use Baseline Privacy. Once the CABLE MODEM is configured and authorized, it is a standard Ethernet network device.

The DOCSIS downstream transmission specification is based upon ITU J.83B technology developed for digital TV applications, and supports 64 QAM and 256 QAM modulation methodologies. In 64 QAM mode, the maximum bandwidth available on a 6 MHz channel is approximately 27 Mbps after error correction. When running in 256 QAM mode, the system can support rates up to 38 Mbps. It uses ITU J.83-B variable-depth interleaving and Reed-Solomon forward error correction. It can be set anywhere in the DOCSIS downstream spectral range of 88-860 MHz. Upstream, the CABLE MODEM supports two modulation formats, QPSK and 16 QAM, and 5 different symbol rates. The spectral range for upstream transmission is 5-42 MHz.

The structure of the network is IP over Ethernet. The primary standards incorporated in the DOCSIS system architecture are IEEE Ethernet standards 802, 802.2, 802.3, and RFC-791 IP data standards. Once the transmission protocols have been established, the network operates transparently as an Ethernet network. DOCSIS cable modems are software upgradable during initialization or on command from the network operator via an SNMP command and a TFTP file transfer of the new software image. The upgrade process can fail at virtually any point without leaving the CABLE MODEM in an unusable state. The CABLE MODEM makes several checks of the new file to ensure that it is intended for that particular make and model of CABLE MODEM, since several different makes and models of CABLE MODEMS may be operating on a single network. There is an MD5 checksum on the new code image that is used to ensure that it has not been corrupted in transmission.

Despite the broad acceptance of DOCSIS in the US, the European community has not yet widely adopted it. A combination of standards bodies including DAVIC, IEEE 802.14, and the ATM Forum developed DVB-RCCL/DAVIC. DVB-RCCL/DAVIC is the preferred technology of ECCA (a consortium of European MSOs). As such, it is the only technology that rivals DOCSIS as a standard for international deployments. Vendor support for DVB-RCCL/DAVIC has been outstanding considering the emergence of DOCSIS as an ITU endorsed standard. Alcatel, COCOM, DiviCom, Hughes Network Systems, Nokia Multimedia Network Terminals, Sagem, Simac Broadband Technologies, Thomson Broadcast, and Thomson Multimedia have all announced that they will build to the specification. The leading cable modem suppliers are awaiting a European version of DOCSIS. Some big providers have chosen to deploy DOCSIS, and other providers may adhere to proprietary gear.

Although the cable companies have access to 65 million homes, they have little entry status into the business market. Cable television operators plan to drop fiber lines out of their network to reach them. Moreover, cable television networks are *shared networks*. Much like Ethernet LANs, they divide bandwidth between everyone on the network rather than denying access when they are overwhelmed (whereas Telcos provide busy signals when telephone circuits are all in use). In other words, each customer may have the potential to use a full 10 Mbps, but that much bandwidth will rarely be available to any single customer. Moreover, shared-media CATV provides little privacy. Security is an issue in any communication; it is especially so for business communications, or *electronic commerce.*

High Definition TV (HDTV)

The United States' commitment to Digital TV and the strength of its own semiconductor and computer technology stymied it ability to deploy HDTV. The United States, was the first nation to support digital high-definition technology, but was the last to broadcast HDTV. Europe shipped its Digital Video Broadcasting (DVB) standards for satellite, cable and terrestrial broadcasts years before the US. DVB is not high-definition, but the MPEG2-based technology was deployed while the US squabbled about digital HTDV. Meanwhile, Japan was broadcasting 13 hours of its analog (not digital) Hi-Vision programs every day by 1996. Japan significantly lowered the cost of its High-Definition TV equipment and quietly developed a digital replacement. By the end of 1999, Japanese consumers bought more than 746,000 Hi-Vision receivers.

The FCC reserved an extra 6 MHz of spectrum for HDTV and Standard Definition TV (SDTV), and the technology is spawning myriad data services and *datacasting* in the same TV-broadcast spectrum. However, no laws or regulations define how digital-TV licensees might use the new spectrum. Moreover, many people belittle the flexible standard, which the Grand Alliance developed and the Advanced Television Systems Committee (ATSC) recommended to the FCC, as a technology niche that affects TV manufacturers but not the computer industry.

The ATSC, a private-sector organization that develops voluntary standards for the entire spectrum of advanced-television systems, adopted two additional standards in 1996: a "program guide for digital television," and "system information for digital television." These specifications are part of the overall HDTV system on which the United States has standardized. They are important for fostering interoperability between different set-top boxes or TV systems for cable, satellite, multichannel/ multipoint distribution service (MMDS), and satellite master-antenna television systems. The system information defines the transmission parameters that a variety of digital decoders need for accessing and processing digital and analog transmissions. The program guide provides a common format that TV receivers and set-top boxes can decode.

The ATSC is in the process of developing extensions to the HDTV system, such as standards for data broadcasting and "non-Real-Time downloading of audio and video" to personal computers, TVs, and other consumer devices. The standard for data broadcasting will provide syntax and protocols to transfer computer files over the terrestrial broadcasting airwaves. The specifications for non-Real-Time downloading would allow any news clips, sports information, or multimedia programming to be transmitted and stored in PCs or other devices. Furthermore, during a typical digital-TV broadcast using a 6-MHz spectrum, at least 3 to 4 Mbps of data can be broadcast simply by using available vertical blanking intervals. That compares to the approximately 100 Kbps that is available in a vertical-blanking-interval space on an analog-TV broadcast.

On December 24, 1996, the United States Federal Communications Commission adopted the major elements of the ATSC Digital Television Standard (A/53) for the nation's next generation of broadcast television. Canada, South Korea, Taiwan, and Argentina have also adopted the ATSC DTV Standard for digital terrestrial broadcasts. Eventually, HDTV can be expected to provide users with an infinite number of combinations of digital high-definition programs, computer files, and Real-Time news, sports, and interactive multimedia via TV receivers, PCs, PDAs, mobile videophones or other innovative, convenient peripherals.

CHAPTER 10 REFERENCES

Thompson, Jim. "Move Over Cable, Here Comes G.lite." ISP News. June 23, 1999. http://www.internetnews.com/

Starr, Tom, Maxwell, Kim. "ADSL Access Networks," ADSL Forum, May 1998. http://www.adsl.com/

Carr, Jim. "Solving Asynchronous Transfer Mode," VARbusiness March 1, 1996 v12 n3 pp. 84-92.

Flanagan, William A. Frames, Packets and Cells in Broadband Networking Telecom Library, 1991.

King, T.J., et. al., "ATM-Practical Management Issues," British Telecom Technology Journal April 1991.

Meyer, Rich. AT&T Press Release, "AT&T announces plans to develop and deliver National ISDN-2 on the 5ESS-R switch," February 19, 1992.

Minoli, Daniel. Enterprise Networking: Fractional T-1 to SONET, Frame Relay to BISDN Artech House 1993 pp. 7, 11, 72-76, 552-553, 661.

Riggs, Brian. "ISDN ordering: not quite so EZ," LAN Times November 11, 1996 v13 n25 pp. 45-47.

Rockwell, Mark. "Carriers agree on ISDN service codes," CommunicationsWeek April 1, 1996 n603 p. 45.

Steinke, Steve. "Getting data over the telephone line," LAN Magazine April 1996 v11 n4 pp. 27-29.

The ATM Forum: W. El Camino Real, Suite 304 Mountain View, California 94040-1313

Thrasher, B. Holt., McNamara, Robert. "How merger mania has redefined the communications landscape," Telecommunications October 1996 v30 n10 pp. 42-44.

11

PACKET-SWITCHED NETWORKS

You could not step twice into the same rivers, for other waters are ever flowing on to you.
Heraclitus (c. 535–475 B.C).

NEW CHALLENGES FOR OLDER NETWORKS

Today, the typical large organization has multiple independent networks. These networks are usually optimized to carry unique types of traffic: voice, bursty or transaction-oriented data, and video. This might not be efficient, but, until recently, it was necessary because different data types have different characteristics and are, therefore, incompatible. Of course, this is changing. Whereas in the past, applications contained only one type of data, today they include Real-Time multimedia—at least we would like them to. The problems begin when streaming media moves onto the already-congested LAN or even worse, passes from the LAN to the WAN.

The buzz over new, faster network technologies continues but most companies are still making do with what they have. What they have is already straining under the weight introduced by changes in the network usage model. Traditional LANs and WANs began bog down when organizations moved from character-oriented host/terminal computing models to more interactive client/server architectures. Client/server computing, which splits a user level program into client processes and server processes, requires significant interaction between the two. Powerful CPUs on both sides of the exchange pump out data in a fashion that peppers a conventional LAN with 60–70 Mbps bursts.

Along with the shift to client/server (perhaps preceding it in many cases) came seemingly small differences in applications. For instance, in the early 1990s, users began to attach files to electronic mail messages. Large differences came next—organizations added Web browsers to the standard desktop configuration. Suddenly the network was bursting at the seams with media-rich information pulled down from the Internet. Along the way, network throughput steadily declined. And then came the deluge. Companies set out to build their own, internally-oriented versions of the Web—intranets became the rage.

In some enterprises, the term network management may be an oxymoron. Yet even as companies struggle to accommodate an overabundance of bits, the usage model is changing again. Early adopters are deploying MPEG-compressed playback and interactive video applications over their networks. This often introduces congestion to a LAN segment. When such dense traffic traverses WAN links, traffic jams are almost assured. Fortunately, most organizations, before launching new applications, adapt their LANs and WANs to cope with the load.

Adapting the network for streaming media means migrating toward infrastructures (hopefully enterprise-wide) that match service quality to traffic requirements. Before we talk about how this is done, we should review the differences between connection-oriented and connectionless networks.

Connection-Oriented Vs. Connectionless Networks

Phone calls and circuit-switched videoconferences establish a path between parties for the duration of an exchange. Until the communication concludes and the connection is dropped, no one else can use the circuit. A busy signal is returned to those who try. This type of arrangement is said to be *connection-oriented.* Connection-oriented networks work well for time-dependent transmissions—streaming media—that require a constant bit rate (CBR). Applications in this class not only require a CBR, they need a guarantee that they will receive it. The term used to describe this type of service is *isochronous*. Isochronous service provides predictable, unnoticeable delays, and regular delivery. Any LAN that is to carry Real-Time videoconferencing must furnish it.

Conventional packet-switched Ethernet and token-ring LANs are connectionless. This design is most effective with *bursty* or *transaction-oriented* data in which long lulls may occur between the transmission of associated bits. For the sake of efficiency, all devices are connected to a common medium. Busy signals are never returned in this scenario. Instead, connectionless networks react to increased traffic by slowing down. When they do, users tend to take 'corrective action' by twitching their cursor, reissuing commands and trying to open new applications. Of course, this only makes things worse. Eventually the congestion clears and throughput increases accordingly.

Even though users become annoyed, delays are usually acceptable in networked text and graphics applications. Real-time delivery is not critical to comprehension. To mediate congestion, frames of data are briefly buffered.

Buffering is not an option for interactive video exchanges. Human protocols, which have evolved over millions of years, are highly sensitive to timing. Regular and sequential delivery is mandatory. Speech must be *synched* to lip movement. Pauses are more than distractions. Delays in excess of 325 milliseconds are debilitating.

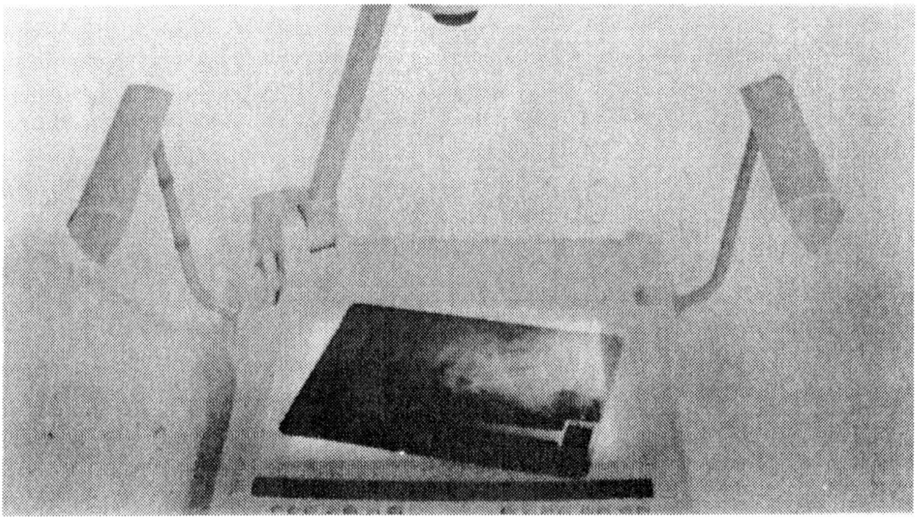

Figure 11-1. High-resolution Document Camera (courtesy of Canon).

Unfortunately, when streaming media moves over legacy networks, pauses are the norm, not the exception. One of the most prevalent of these legacy networks is Ethernet. In terms of LAN design, Ethernet still rivals higher-speed networking technologies such as ATM and Fiber Distributed Data Interface (FDDI). And, thanks to Ethernet's resilience and adaptability, there are several different approaches to modifying existing Ethernet LANs to make them more suitable for multimedia traffic.

When upgrading LANs, it is important to remember that multimedia communications will not be confined locally. The wide area network must also be considered. And, while intranets are very important, multimedia communications will not be confined to the populace of a single enterprise. Rather, an Internet or telephony (any-to-any) model, that allows almost infinite endpoints, is the goal. With this in mind we will look at the various ways that Ethernet (and token-ring, which is also addressed in this chapter) LANs can be adapted to multimedia traffic, including videoconferences and multicasts.

STREAMING MEDIA OVER ETHERNET

Ethernet was developed in the early 1970s to support laser printing. The Institute of Electrical and Electronic Engineers (IEEE), in their 802.3 specification, standardized the technologies that underlie Ethernet. Ethernet is founded on the Carrier Sense Multiple Access with Collision Detection (CSMA/CD) media access control (MAC) protocol. In CSMA/CD networks, nodes broadcast frames of data to all other stations on the same segment. Because the segment is shared, 802.3 LANs employ a listen-before-transmitting scheme. If a sending device hears no oncoming traffic, it transmits its data, which has been addressed to assure that only the intended node listens and responds to it. The system works smoothly unless two stations broadcast at precisely the same time (which is not uncommon when subnets support numerous devices). In that case, a collision occurs. Both devices, after hearing a jamming signal warn of the collision, must back off and wait a random period of time before retransmitting. Contention and collisions limit throughput on Ethernet and preclude any guarantee of timely signal delivery. Therefore, CSMA/CD is quite inadequate in real-time, interactive multimedia applications.

Since its invention, Ethernet deployment methods have continuously evolved. Ethernet began as 10Base-5. The name was descriptive: 10 refers to 10 Mbps, Base pertains to Ethernet's baseband method of transmission and the 5 reflects a network diameter of 500 meters. As time went on, 10Base-5 became known as Thick Wire Ethernet because the coaxial cable it required measured about one-half inch in diameter. After 10Base-5 came 10Base-2 that used coaxial cable about half as thick as 10Base-5. Thin-net cable, as it was also called, offered easier manipulation, and cleaner attachment to a workstation. A signal can be pushed a long way over coaxial cable. Thus older, 10Base-2/ 10Base-5 Ethernet LANs could daisy chain devices together to support an entire building or a campus. Some older Ethernet LANs supported as many as 300 devices. The problem with this approach (in addition to the obvious congestion implications) was that if any node had a problem (e.g., a bad cable connection or a faulty network adapter) it brought down the entire network.

In 1990, the introduction of 10Base-T Ethernet (also known as IEEE 802.3i) eliminated the need for coaxial cable altogether. Instead, it relies on unshielded twisted pair (UTP), using only two of the four pair of wires found in most UTP cable. 10Base-T is arranged in a star-hub topology, much as voice stations connect to a PBX. Hubs, which reside in floor-level equipment closets, are equipped with port. These ports are wired to individual nodes on a network. Data packets enter a hub through a single port and exit through all ports.

Unlike the coax-based Ethernet LANs of the past, 10Base-T LANs serve distinct workgroups or clusters of users. LAN segments today are much smaller, perhaps limiting the number of attached devices to 64 or 32. The maximum diameter of any 10Base-T collision domain is 2,500 meters, with five 500-meter segments allowed between repeaters, and four repeater hops allowed. Three of the five segments can contain Ethernet nodes other than the repeaters themselves, leaving two segments merely as links between repeaters. 10Base-T has met with strong acceptance in the marketplace. It is widely believed that over 70% of the LANs installed today rely on 10Base-T technology.

The problem with 10Base-T is that is operates at only 10 Mbps. More accurately, it operates at about 6 Mbps. The contention-oriented access methods Ethernet employs limit its throughput to about 60% of its true capacity. This means that an Ethernet segment can support only one or two stations that are concurrently running real-time multimedia applications. Even when only one multimedia station is active, the constant placement of video frames on a network designed for bursty traffic can severely impact network throughput.

How can Ethernet be adapted to videoconferencing and other bit-intensive multimedia applications? Because there is so much of it installed, the question is an important one, and one that has several answers.

ADAPTING ETHERNET FOR STREAMING MEDIA

LAN Microsegmentation

As applications become more complex and data-laden, network managers divide their LANs into smaller and smaller segments. This approach is known as microsegmentation. Whereas a LAN might have supported 64 devices in the past, hub bandwidth is now divided to serve segments that range from an individual port to several ports. A single hub might be capable of supporting as many as 30 different LAN segments. Individual hubs are connected via backbones that conform to one of two designs: collapsed or distributed.

In a collapsed backbone scenario, hubs are linked to multi-port bridges or routers that arrange connections between them. Each subnet served by the departmental hub is, typically, bridged to an Ethernet network that connects all devices to a campus or building hub (or series of hubs) and, from there, to other sites and to WAN services.

The packet switching technique that conventional routers use does not scale well. As traffic increases, the router's bus becomes saturated. Consequently, its switching logic can not keep pace and long delays are the result. It is important to note that a router must read an entire packet before it can switch that packet to its destination. These long delays spell doom for motion video applications.

The distributed backbone approach employs a faster backbone network (typically Fiber Distributed Data Interface—FDDI) to interconnect campus or building hubs. Hub-based LANs are bridged or routed to the fast backbone. In contrast to the collapsed backbone method of relying on one large router, distributed backbones rely on a number of moderately sized routers. The problem here is that FDDI itself is not always fast enough, especially when low latency is required. If segmentation is used as a method to increase speed, the network design becomes a collapsed backbone configuration.

In summary, microsegmentation has its consequences. Bridge ports and router ports are expensive. Moreover, microsegmentation is hard to administer. When clients and servers are not isolated on the same subnet, they must traverse LAN boundaries. This causes backbone networks to slow to unacceptable levels. Another drawback of traditional shared-media hubs is that everything connected to that hub competes for a slice of the hub's backplane bandwidth.

Microsegmentation offers a short-term solution that is worth consideration only if the objective is to introduce low-speed videoconferencing to the desktop in a very limited fashion. Eventually many organizations will abandon microsegmentation in favor of a new type of arrangement—switching hubs.

LAN Switches

The easiest and least expensive way to increase throughput for high-traffic desktop videoconferencing is to replace conventional Ethernet hubs with LAN switches. Switching allows the efficient interconnection of multiple LAN segments. Ethernet switches are hybrid internetworking devices that combine circuit switching with packet switching (layer-3 Ethernet switches are, in fact, high-performance routers). Network segments (or devices) are connected to switch ports. Traffic between ports is conveyed across the switch backplane. In this manner, large LANs can be constructed from many smaller LAN segments.

In a switched Ethernet environment, users contend for bandwidth only with other users on the same segment. The smaller the segment, the greater the average bandwidth available to each station. Because the switching device has much higher backplane speed than do individual segments, the aggregate capacity of the LAN is greatly increased.

Switching hub ports have an incoming packet cycle and an outgoing packet cycle, each of which operates at 10, 100, or 1000 Mbps. If the switch supports LAN segments, it is said to *segment switch* (since practically all switches do this, it is a fairly obsolete term). Switching hubs can also be arranged to "node switch," in which case individual desktops are provided with their own Ethernet segment. This is cost-effective only in instances where a workgroup requires very high-speed applications support, such as full-motion desktop videoconferencing.

Whether a switch is configured to segment switch or node switch, it operates as follows: During an incoming cycle a port opens up to accept a packet. As the packet enters the hub its MAC layer destination address is examined and it is briefly buffered until the outgoing hub port associated with the destination address opens to accept traffic. If the packet is destined for a node on the same segment as the sending device it does not cross the switch's backplane. If the packet is addressed to a node on a different segment, it must move across the high-speed backplane and through the silicon-based switching fabric. In this way, Ethernet switching hubs support multiple simultaneous 10/100/1000 Mbps connections between nodes, segments and combinations thereof.

In switching, only the sending and destination port are aware of the packet's existence. Hence, the network is not overwhelmed with extraneous packets. In effect, a switch changes Ethernet from a contention broadcast system to a direct delivery system. In a node-switched arrangement it creates the illusion that each station has its own private subnet that allows it to send and receive data at Ethernet's full 10 Mbps (for a total throughput of 20 Mbps). This same bandwidth can be sub-divided among a small group of stations in a segment switched arrangement. Thus, isochronous service is delivered to a user or group of users whose real-time applications drive the need for a LAN environment from destructive collisions.

Switches are available for 10, 100, and 1000 Mbps Ethernet. Numerous manufacturers offer products in each category. The 100 Mbps switches are most effective when positioned as traffic control points for the backbone. In this environment, a hub is attached to every port on the Ethernet switch. 100 Mbps Ethernet switches can also extend the diameter of a 100 Mbps Ethernet LAN beyond its 250-meter limit. The per-port price of the 1000 Mbps Ethernet switch limits its deployment to high-end applications. Switched 100 or 1000 Mbps Ethernet would most often apply to video applications in situations where multimedia servers store MPEG-2 encoded material that must traverse the LAN. In a few cases, 1000 Mbps is being extended directly to the desktop but, to obtain maximum value from this approach, supported nodes should be equipped with fast (PCI class or higher) buses.

The Ethernet switch is best suited for resolving throughput problems—for instance, where several nodes on the same subnet all try to deploy real-time audio-video applications at once. Throughput would decline accordingly and performance would be affected for everyone. To resolve the problem, an Ethernet switch might be installed. It would not necessarily have to replace a hub port-for-port (although switches are replacing hubs in most networks). It could be used to isolate a few high-powered desktops from the rest of the workgroup or to create smaller LAN segments with only a few nodes each. In this way, the switch divides the network into smaller collision domains.

Switched Ethernet is inexpensive enough to justify replacing hub ports with switch ports. With no modifications, category 3 cable plant is adequate for 10 Mbps Ethernet networks, and category 5 cable plant is adequate for 100 Mbps Ethernet networks. Gigabit Ethernet, originally designed to run only over fiber, will run over category 5 cable, but is best over category 7 cable. This allows a company to introduce more bandwidth with almost no downtime and very little cost.

Ethernet switches come either as chassis-based modules that support plug-in modules or as stand-alone stackable units. Chassis-based switches cost more, but they are highly scalable and generally offer redundant power supplies and central management. Stackable switches are more affordable and can be added incrementally. Port densities vary but most stand-alone switches offer between four and 48 ports, and each port will support a separate 10/100 Mbps Ethernet segment (in many cases, each port can not only switch, but also route). Some switches offer high-speed port (1000 Mbps) options, and most offer virtual LAN (VLAN) capabilities.

Switching hubs use two different techniques to handle frames. Cut-through switching begins to forward a packet to its destination port immediately after decoding its MAC address—before the entire frame is received. This approach reduces the device latency that is incurred when a packet is delivered from one port to another. However, errors are detected through the examination of the CRC (cyclic redundancy check) bits at the end of a packet. Although cut-through switching adds virtually no delay, retransmission of a packet is sometimes necessary after it reaches its destination, which consumes network bandwidth.

Store-and-forward switching receives the entire frame into a buffer before forwarding it to the destination port. In this approach the entire packet is checked before it is passed to its destination port. Although this method is highly reliable in terms of detecting and dealing with errors, it introduces a small amount of latency. Most store-and-forward switches comply with the Spanning Tree algorithm that discovers the best path to each destination and stores it in a look-up table. Subsequent packets that arrive for the same MAC address are sent out through the port specified in the table. Administrators can also use the table to create a redundant physical network for security.

Kalpana (which means imagination in Hindi) pioneered the concept of Ethernet switching in 1990. According to the results of a 1996 study performed by the Dell'Oro Group, U.S. switching/wiring hub revenues were $3.9 billion in 1994. In 1995 they grew to $6.1 billion. Revenues were expected to reach $9.8 billion in 1996 and to continue to grow throughout the remainder of the decade.

Given the advent of higher-layer switching (predominantly layer-3), store-and-forward switching is no longer much of an issue. Layer-3 switching is really *wire-speed* routing. So-called non-blocking switches execute routing in silicon rather than in software. By also offering backplanes with bandwidth capabilities that exceed the aggregate bandwidth of all ports, some manufacturers overcome the non-deterministic nature of Ethernet's collision-detection based architecture. One manufacturer, Extreme Networks combines 96-byte-wide data paths, non-blocking bandwidth, real-time filtering and forwarding, parallelism and pipelining to provide a sustained throughput rate of 1.5 million PPS concurrently on numerous Gigabit Ethernet switch ports. Such an architecture enables network designers to incorporate routing protocols such as RIP, RIPv2, OSPF, IGMP, DVMRP and PIM without introducing performance penalties.

100 Mbps Ethernet

Fast Ethernet is a general term for a number of technologies that conform to the IEEE 802.3u standard. 100Base-T is the technical designation for the standard. Under the 100Base-T umbrella exist specific implementations of 802.3u. These include 100Base-TX, 100Base-FX and 100Base-T4. To understand how these implementations compare, one must be familiar with various categories of cable plant and how their differences affect high-speed digital transmission.

EIA/TIA 568a

Cable plant plays a big role in allowing Ethernet to run at 100 Mbps speeds. In 1991, the Electronics Industries Association and Telecommunications Industry Association (EIA/TIA) introduced a cable-rating scheme. Knows as the Commercial Building Telecommunications Wiring Standards, EIA/TIA 568 (which has since been revised as EIA/TIA 568a) provides electrical performance specifications for Category 1 through Category 5 UTP. The EIA/TIA categories measure the resistance of the wire to frequency bleeding between pairs (also known as near-end crosstalk) and its ability to pass signals at different frequencies (known as the frequency attenuation curve).

The EIA/TIA 568a categories are as follows:

- Category 1 wiring is basic, low-grade UTP telephone cable that works well for low frequency transmissions such as voice service. By definition, it is not suitable for data transmission.
- Category 2 UTP is UTP that is certified for use as fast as 4 MHz (slower-speed token-ring).
- Category 3 is certified up to speeds of 10 MHz, and is the minimum quality cable required for 10Base-T. UTP in this category must have at least three twists per foot, with every twist conforming to a different pattern. Category 3 cable is the most common cable today, with over 50% of networks using it to support desktop devices.
- Category 4 is the lowest grade UTP suitable for use up to 16 MHz (e.g., for 16Mbps token-ring).
- Category 5 is certified up to 100 MHz. It is acceptable for FDDI over copper and 100Base-T.
- Category 6 offers twice the usable frequency spectrum for signal transmission of a category 5 or 5e system and twice the information carrying capacity. A category 6 channel provides additional signal bandwidth and about 10 dB of near-end crosstalk loss margin over a category 5e channel.
- Category 7 may offer as much as 1 GHz over twisted-pair cabling and thereby enable broadband video (with an upper frequency requirement of 862 MHz) to operate over class F cabling with concurrent connections to other networking applications. Category 7 cables include individually screened twisted-pairs and an overall shield. Pending category 7 specifications require connectors to provide at least 60 dB of crosstalk isolation between all pairs at 600 MHz.

Potential adopters of 100 or 1000 Mbps Ethernet should carefully examine their existing cabling to determine the necessary adjustments and require that the supplier certify that what is in place conforms to the specification in question. When it comes to EIA/TIA 568, every inch of cable plant—from the network adapter in the workstation to the wiring closet, and including punch-down blocks, patch cords and panels—must adhere to the standards. Customers that are not certain about how their cable plant conforms to EIA/TIA 568a should test it, using a cable tester from a company such as Tektronix, Fluke, or Scope. Without an accurate reading on conformance, a manager can not make an informed decision about what 100 or 1000 Mbps solution will work in his or her environment. When conducting a test, technical personnel (or subcontractors) should test *all* pairs. The reason is that if the plant turns out to conform only to Category 3 cable, all four pairs that make up a UTP bundle will have to be used to support 100VG or 100Base-T4 connections. Category 3 cable will not support 1000 Mbps Ethernet.

Fast Ethernet

In 1994 the Fast Ethernet Alliance completed a wiring specification that provides end users with interoperable 100 Mbps Ethernet products that can exist in a variety of cable plant environments. The completed specification, which includes three specifications, defines how 100Mbps Ethernet should run over Category 3, 4, and 5 UTP and over fiber optic cable.

The three specifications for 100Base-T Ethernet are 100Base-TX, 100Base-FX, and 100Base-T4. A slightly different specification, called 100VG-AnyLAN (IEEE 802.12) competes with 100-Base-T. The key difference among the 100-Mbps products is in the kind of cable they use and, in the case of 802.12, how well they cope with the needs of time-sensitive video packets.

Within the 100Base-T family the cabling differences are as follows 100Base-TX requires Category 5 UTP, 100Base-FX requires fiber optic cable, and 100Base-T4 uses Category 3, 4 or 5 UTP, but four pairs of wire are required for each node.

Over unshielded twisted pair cable, 100Base-T can support only two repeater hops (compared to 10Base-T's three to five hops) and its theoretical collision domain is limited to only 205 meters—less than one tenth that of 10Base-T. These limits can be overcome by deploying stackable hubs and switches.

Although estimates vary, it is safe to say that Category 3 UTP is installed in more than 50% of the telecommunications networks in North America. That simple fact makes 100Base-T4 a viable option for networks with pervasive Category 3 cable. 100Base-T4 needs four pair. In 100Base-T4 implementations, it is important that every wire and every connection in every cable is good. This is not always the case. Although 100Base-T4 is an easy step to take, the market shows little interest in it.

100Base-TX requires two pairs of Category 5 wires. The Category 5 requirement often forces organizations that select to pay for a new cable system. In various tests, 100Base-TX has been proved to handle increasing traffic loads much more effectively than 10Base-T. For instance, it is possible to run it at loads of up to70% before any signs of congestion begin to appear.

To lessen the impact of upgrading an entire network to Category 5 cable, many of the 100Base-TX vendors are shipping adapters and hubs that can support both 100Base-TX and 100-Base-T4. Because all 100Base-T solutions use the same Ethernet packets, no extra bridging hardware is necessary to mix 100Base-TX and 100Base-T4 hubs in the same stack. Some 100Base-T4 hubs will even integrate both 100Base-TX and 100Base-T4 ports to accommodate both technologies.

Fast Ethernet adapters, better known as 10/100 adapters, are designed with both 10-Mbps and 100-Mbps chips inside. A majority of Fast Ethernet adapters come with drivers and provide a single port with the capability to switch automatically between 10 Mbps and 100 Mbps connections without any modification on the client side. The availability of 10/100 adapters make it possible to buy incrementally and upgrade the LANs at some future date by merely replacing the hub or switch with one that supports 100Base-T. With pricing comparable to 10-Mbps adapters, buying Fast Ethernet adapters makes a great deal of sense.

With their double speed capability and competitive pricing, Fast Ethernet adapters are a no-brainer purchase for your network. The trick is to buy the right adapter. Look for one that provides a single port for automatic switching and make sure that it does not rely too heavily on the CPU. When it comes time to switch to Fast Ethernet, having this groundwork in place will make the transition easier. The fiber-based 100Base-FX systems are not vulnerable to radio frequency interference and can extend connections out to over a mile of cable.

FAST Ethernet and Gigabit Ethernet are the clear winners in high-bandwidth LAN infrastructure (although ATM keeps coming back like a bad cold). Nevertheless, we will describe 100VG-AnyLAN and ISOEthernet because readers may still encounter these technologies.

100VG-AnyLAN

100VG-AnyLAN will run over many different types of cable including Category 3 voice grade (VG stands for 'voice grade'). It will also support more repeater hops (five) than does 100Base-T. 100VG supports larger network diameters than 10Base-T—up to 4 kilometers when running on Category 5 wire. And, it can support both token-ring and Ethernet traffic. It is implemented as a segment-switched (or node-switched) solution, using a special hub to connect LAN segments.

Unfortunately it requires four pairs of wires (but so, too, does 100Base-T4). The four-pair requirement is the result of FCC radio frequency energy regulations, which require twice the number of wire pairs when operating at such high speeds.

Whereas Ethernet was never designed with demand-priority traffic (such as videoconferences) in mind, segment-switched 100VG was. Although it uses standard Ethernet frames, its designers made modifications to the MAC layer to replace stochastic CSMA/CD access with a deterministic token passing scheme that eliminates collisions. This approach also makes it compatible with Token Passing LANs.

It also introduces Demand Priority Architecture (DPA), a network access method in which nodes issue a request to the hub for priority treatment. DPA allows nodes to issue a request to the hub to send a packet on the network. Each request is labeled with either a normal priority level or a high priority level for packets supporting time-critical multimedia applications such as video. High-priority requests are granted access to the network before normal-priority requests (for instance, print or file packets), which helps time critical video frames to arrive at their destination in quick succession.

In unbiased tests, 100VG-AnyLAN has been found to perform better than 100Base-T in moving video packets across over congested networks that must concurrently support file and print services. It also compares favorably in terms of implementation cost (the cost to move to a 100 Mbps solution from an existing Ethernet network).

The creators of 100VG-AnyLAN were Hewlett-Packard and AT&T Microelectronics (now Lucent Technologies). They were able to get the technologies that underlie 100VG-AnyLAN approved by the IEEE as specification 802.12. Unfortunately, although its backers were heavyweights, 100VG-AnyLAN's biggest drawback is that it is supported by only a handful of vendors, chiefly HP. The other problem is that 100Base-T, with its CSMA/CD approach, is more backwards compatible. 100VG-AnyLAN is rarely seen anymore.

IsoEthernet

Another approach to providing isochronous service over Ethernet was developed by National Semiconductor and IBM. Isochronous Ethernet, or isoEthernet keeps voice, video and data separate but equal in their travels across the LAN. Since its introduction, the IEEE 802 Committee has standardized isoEthernet as 802.9a.

A transitional product, isoEthernet, can extend the life of 10Base-T until more powerful networking products such as Asynchronous Transfer Mode (ATM) come along. It extends 96 ISDN B-channels and native telephony call-control (D channel) signaling to each desktop along with traditional packet communications. Both B and D channels have a bandwidth of 64 Kbps. The 802.9s specification also includes a 96 Mbps M (maintenance) channel, used for network management.

IsoEthernet adapts traditional 10 Mbps Ethernet by adding 6.144 Mbps of bandwidth to it. Ethernet uses Manchester encoding to modulate data onto the wire. Manchester encoding is only 50% efficient in that it requires two signaling transitions for every binary bit of information transmitted. IsoEthernet employs the same modulation technique used by FDDI. Known as 4B/5B physical-layer signaling, it requires (on average) only 1.2 signal transitions for each bit transmitted. This is a 60% improvement over Manchester encoding in terms of signaling efficiency, allowing isoEthernet to squeeze an additional 6 Mbps of bandwidth.

IsoEthernet runs over Category 3 UTP cable, and thereby preserves 10Base-T's existing infrastructure. Moreover, the entire system is backward compatible with existing 10Base-T hardware and software, and does not degrade Ethernet's performance. The core 10 Mbps Ethernet channel remains a shared, packet-switched medium that can be used for data networking. The ISDN B channels provide isochronous service for time-sensitive applications, such as video conferencing and telephony.

The deployment of isoEthernet into an existing Ethernet LAN does not require an upgrade to routers, servers, software, or network management systems. It does require that traditional 10Base-T hubs be replaced, and that new isoEthernet network adapter cards be installed at each workstation.

An IsoEthernet hub port can support either conventional 10BaseT or isoEthernet devices. Hub ports can discriminate between the two device types and adapt accordingly. There are also special ports used to accept and pass on B channel traffic. Various ISDN BRI or PRI feeds (or DS-1 service) can terminate on these ports and run from there to a carrier's network.

By mingling the native framing mechanisms from circuit and packet-switched environments, isoEthernet can enable voice and video calls to utilize existing telephone system and user interfaces. To provide the circuit-switched interface, users must replace conventional NICs (network interface cards) with IsoEthernet NICs. IsoEthernet boards have an additional connector on the top. This connector is known as the Multivendor Interface Protocol (MVIP) interface. The MVIP captures data from connection-oriented devices (e.g., telephones and codecs) and combines it with Ethernet data. The merged stream travels across the computer's bus and is moved across the wire to the isoEthernet hub. There, the hub demultiplexes the two data streams, sending ISDN traffic to one type of port and Ethernet traffic to a different type.

Broad implementation of isoEthernet never happened in part because its cost was significantly higher than that of conventional 10Base-T components. ISOEthernet is elegant, but it arrived too late. The trend, right or wrong, seems to be to speed up packet-switched networks to accommodate traffic that has been traditionally circuit-switched—with an eye toward a longer-term ATM migration strategy. As it did 100VG-AnyLAN, 10/100/1000 Mbps Ethernet eclipsed ISOEthernet's hopes for mass implementation.

GIGABIT ETHERNET

A backbone's bandwidth must be greater than that of the nodes that connect to it, and greater even than the aggregate of all links that feed into it. Therefore, as 100 Mbps Ethernet extends to the desktop, faster standards such as Gigabit (1000 Mbps) Ethernet will become increasingly common on backbones. One need only consider the plummeting cost of 100 Mbps Ethernet network interface cards (NIC) to understand just how fast this migration is occurring.

Gigabit Ethernet (also known as 802.3z) was initially developed by the Gigabit Ethernet Alliance (GEA), that consisted of about 50 vendors including 3COM, Bay Networks (now Nortel Networks), Cisco Systems, Compaq, FORE Systems, Intel, Network Peripherals, Silicon Graphics and Sun Microsystems. The GEA's goal was to provide a low-cost and simple upgrade path for networks that already use Ethernet technology. The GEA presented their work to the IEEE, which formed the 802.3z Task Group to study the preliminary specification. On November 18, 1996, the 802.3z Task Group finalized a set of core proposals as the basis for writing the first draft of the standard. The first draft of the 802.3z specification was distributed in late January of 1997, and the standard was adopted in early 1998.

Gigabit Ethernet is based on the 10Mbps and 100Mbps Ethernet standards outlined in the 802.3 specification. It includes support for CSMA/CD (modifications must be made to maintain a half-duplex mode of operation) and uses the same frame format as Ethernet and Fast Ethernet. The first draft of the specification focuses primarily on physical media requirements. Gigabit Ethernet's physical (PHY) layer is a high-speed adaptation of Fiber Channel. An "Independent Interface" is also included in the draft that will allow the MAC protocol to be decoupled from the specifics of the lower layers—and thereby enable the independent development of other PHY types. Work is being done on adapting Gigabit Ethernet to operate over distances of up to 100 meters on unshielded twisted pair (UTP) cabling. Using LX (longwave length transceiver) GBICs and single-mode fiber, Gigabit Ethernet can span 5 kilometers with Gigabit Ethernet in 1999.

Modifications to CSMA/CD include two new features that enable efficient operation over a practical collision domain diameter at 1000 Mbps. These features are carrier extension and packet bursting and they will only affect operation in half-duplex mode. When Gigabit Ethernet is operating in full-duplex mode, it is identical to 802.3u (100Base-T) Ethernet, only faster. The 802.3z specification includes minor MAC changes, but frame length minimums and maximums and frame formats remain the same. Overall, 802.3z is very similar to its lower-speed predecessors.

As a result of raw speed and of cost reductions that companies such as Extreme Networks and Alteon WebSystems have achieved by adopting ASIC-based models, Gigabit Ethernet is dominating the backbone using switch-to-switch, switch-to-router or switch-to-server connections. Conventional router manufacturers have struggled to adapt their software-based architectures to achieve the high speed of low price of ASIC-based architectures. In a switch-to-switch scenario 1,000 Mbps pipes could be used to connect 100/1000 switches. Most such switches would, in turn, deliver 100Base-T to the desktop. In another scenario, a video or other high-performance server might be equipped with a Gigabit Ethernet NIC that connects it at 1,000 Mbps to a switch and, through the switch, to desktop video applications supported by 100Base-T. In yet another scenario, a shared FDDI backbone might be connected via a FDDI hub or an Ethernet-to-FDDI router with Gigabit Ethernet switches. In any case, Gigabit Ethernet has relegated FDDI to being a legacy technology; while many must accommodate FDDI, few are installing it.

The emerging specification will allow users or nodes to retain their existing NOS, NIC drivers and applications. Nodes will not be affected since Gigabit Ethernet is emerging primarily as a backbone technology for aggregating 10-Mbps and 100-Mbps end points at 1000 Mbps or for connecting fast switches or servers.

On July 28, 1998, the Gigabit Ethernet Alliance announced that balloting for the Gigabit Ethernet over copper proposed standard (1000BASE-T) had formally begun, and that the IEEE 802.3ab Task Force (that developed the draft standard) had resolved all outstanding technical issues. The Task Force in conjunction with the IEEE 802.3 Working Group (which oversees Ethernet Standards) voted unanimously to initiate a Working Group ballot for 1000BASE-T. The 1000BASE-T draft standard was intended to enable Gigabit Ethernet to extend to distances of up to 100 meters over Unshielded Twisted Pair Category 5 (Cat 5) copper wiring, the primary cabling medium inside buildings. Representatives from approximately 120 networking, computer, component and test equipment companies participated in the Alliance.

Concurrently, the group began work on an enhanced version of Category 5 wiring and Category 6 and Category 7 wiring standards. For most applications, Cat 5 will be adequate for the foreseeable future because it easily handles 10 Mbps Ethernet, and even 100 Mbps Ethernet. However, 1000B-T will require all four pairs of the Cat 5 cable rather than the two pairs that previous LAN technologies required. Enhanced Cat 5 was created to address this and to remedy crosstalk and line noise issues that are related to Gigabit Ethernet. Category 6 cabling can run at 200 MHz, twice as fast as Cat 5, and Category 7 would run at 600 MHz. These robust cables will have their places, but businesses that require a network faster than Gigabit Ethernet will adopt fiber optics.

ADAPTING TOKEN-RING TO STREAMING MEDIA

Ethernet relies on media access control methods that are contention oriented. Token-ring takes a different approach. Also known by its IEEE 802.5 designation, a token-ring LAN differs from an Ethernet LAN in how it arbitrates bandwidth among connected stations. In a token-passing LAN, each station is granted permission to send data only when it receives a special message called a *token*. The station accepts the token, changes it into a *frame*, embeds the data into the frame's information field, and transmits it.

In a token-ring environment, all stations act as *repeaters*. In other words, they rebroadcast a frame as it goes by. This allows a token-ring network's diameter to exceed that of a bus-oriented network (Ethernet). In addition to rebroadcasting a frame of data, each station examines its address to determine whether or not it is an intended recipient. If it is, it copies the data before rebroadcasting it.

Through a series of rebroadcasts, the frame works its way around the ring (which is both logical and topological) until it arrives back at the station where it originated. The originating station removes it from the ring and reissues a new token for use by the next downstream station with data to send. Following this protocol, all stations share access to the network in an orderly way. Collisions are avoided because there is only one token—in order to transmit, a station must secure it. For that reason, the access method used by a token-ring network is said to be *deterministic*.

Tokens can be used to flag transmissions as urgent. When a station has an urgent transmission (such as packets associated with a real-time media stream) it makes a *reservation* that converts a normal token into a priority-token. Only stations with priority requests can accept priority tokens; other stations must wait for a conventional token to circulate. Token-ring allows eight distinct levels of priority; each can be used to flag a different type of data. Although deterministic access treats continuous bit rate media streams better than do contention access methods, at speeds of 16 Mbps, even token-ring networks buckle under the weight of heavy multimedia traffic. This has led to the introduction of microsegmentation, switching and high-speed backbones.

Microsegmentation in a token-ring network is conceptually similar to the same approach in an Ethernet network. The 802.5 standard limits token-ring networks to 250 stations. In the real world, there are rarely more than 100 stations on a ring. This number can be progressively reduced to yield multiple segments with fewer stations in each. Combining this with the use of the priority capabilities inherent in the token-ring architecture results in increased bandwidth that is often sufficient to run time-critical multimedia sessions.

When the token-ring architecture was developed it was assumed that most transmissions (80%) would be between stations on the same ring. Two port bridges were developed to move the remaining 20% off one ring and on to the backbone. This led to hierarchical network structures consisting of workgroup rings attached to backbone rings. The 80/20 rule no longer applies—transmissions reflect changes in the enterprise environment. More and more traffic is moving between clients and servers on different networks. The result is that large amounts of information flood along the backbone in increasingly unpredictable traffic patterns. Eventually network managers have to address the congestion. Most do so by deploying token-ring switches.

Like Ethernet switches, token-ring switches can range from high-performance, low-cost workgroup-oriented products to higher-end backbone products with extensive management and integration capabilities. And, like switches developed for the Ethernet environment, token-ring switches use either cut-through switching or store-and-forward methods to speed packets on their way. These techniques were described in the section on Ethernet switching and are essentially the same for token-ring switching. The difference is that, in token-ring switching cut-through switching, a switch must sometimes buffer a packet until the destination ring's token is available. Buffering is also required when rings are operating at different speeds (e.g., 4 versus 16 Mbps). Store-and-forward token-ring switching is essentially identical to its Ethernet counterpart.

Like Ethernet switching, token-ring switching can be segment switched or node-switched. In a node-switched environment, a direct connection between a station and the token-ring switch is arranged, allowing the station to use the full capacity of the network rather than sharing it with others. This approach would work well in situations where there is a fairly constant need for interactive multimedia applications on the part of a few desktops. Of course, the cost of this approach rises with the number of desktops that require their own dedicated rings.

Token-ring networks are inherently half-duplex. There is only one token and data can be transmitted only when the ring is free of messages. In a dedicated network, there are only two transceiver entities on a ring—the station and the switch port to which it attaches. This allows a new operational mode, known as Transmit Immediate (TXI). When operating in the TXI mode, the requirement to capture a token before transmitting is eliminated and a station and switch port can achieve full-duplex transmission. This allows 4 or 16 Mbps transmission in each direction—plenty of bandwidth to meet the requirements of interactive high-resolution desktop conferencing. The IEEE 802.5 committee approved the TXI mode for dedicated token-ring in March of 1995.

There was a time when the death knell rang for token-ring. Today there appears to be a resurgence of interest in it. The ability to prioritize a packet through the use of priority tokens is well suited to the needs of videoconferencing. Switched token-ring, dedicated token-ring where use of made of the TXI mode and the use of high-speed backbone connections (FDDI or ATM) between switches assure it a place in addressing the demands of networked, interactive, high-resolution, full-motion applications. A study conducted by the Dell'Oro Group shows the token-ring switching market has plenty of upside potential. Dell'Oro estimates market revenue at $278.5 million in 1996, with sales jumping to $2 billion by the turn of the century. With Cisco Systems, Bay Networks, 3COM and IBM all selling into this market (not to mention dozens of other contenders) the range of token-ring networking options is both broad and deep. Those with IBM networks are still chained to Token Ring. However, few new Token Ring networks are being built.

FDDI AND CDDI

Fiber Distributed Data Interface (FDDI) is formally known as ANSI (American National Standards Institute) specification X3T9.5. The standard, which took eight years to develop, sets forth a 100 Mbps network that is logically implemented as dual counter-rotating rings. FDDI delivers IEEE-sanctioned 100-Mbps speeds. It is fast, highly reliable, clearly defined, and it boasts many tried-and-tested products from which customers can select. It can be used to make a backbone more able to support real-time interactive multimedia applications. Its disadvantages are complexity and, compared to the other 100 Mbps alternatives, high cost.

There are two versions of FDDI. The planners of the original FDDI, or FDDI-I, placed the emphasis on the transport of data packets, not on videoconferencing or voice data types. FDDI-II is intended to support the transmission of voice and videoconferencing as well via an overlay of synchronous services. As such, connections between nodes can be established in a circuit-switched fashion. Isochronous connections of varying speeds can be arranged using FDDI-II. The method is much the same as that used by isoEthernet. In both schemes, 6.144 Mbps channels are incorporated into the existing structure but, whereas isoEthernet offers only one 6.144 Mbps chunk, FDDI-II provides 16. With isoEthernet the additional bandwidth must be subdivided into 96 64 Kbps ISDN B channels. With FDDI-II, channels can be sized according to the bandwidth needed. Some of these channels might be 64 Kbps ISDN B channels, while others might be 1.544 Mbps T-1 channels or even connections consuming the entire 6.144 Mbps bandwidth.

FDDI has the reputation of being expensive because the fiber optic cable has been costly to splice and install. For that reason, FDDI has historically been used for backbone connections, but not extended to the desktop. With *connecterized* fiber cable now available, it is much less difficult to install fiber. Nevertheless, it is a fragile media, and one that is still more expensive than copper.

An alternative to fiber-based FDDI is copper-based FDDI (CDDI) which utilizes either Category 5 UTP or the Category 1 shielded twisted-pair (STP) used in Token Ring networks. The history of CDDI is convoluted. Several suppliers, in 1991, developed a method for running FDDI at 100 Mbps over STP that they called the Green Book specification. ANSI rejected it. Later, in 1992, IBM and about 10 other vendors came up with the SDDI specification, again running FDDI over STP. ANSI rejected it, too. Crescendo Communications, Incorporated (now owned by Cisco Systems of Menlo Park, California) introduced, in late 1991, yet another alternative known as the Copper Distributed Data Interface (CDDI) specification. Perhaps the third time was a charm; ANSI accepted portions of the CDDI specification and included it in a standard of its own that became the final word on how FDDI can be run over STP and UTP. ANSI calls it the TP-PMD (twisted-pair, physical-medium-dependent) specification. STP cable costs less than fiber or Category 5 UTP. Adapters for CDDI are also considerably less expensive than fiber-based ones. Nevertheless, because network managers strongly favor fiber over copper, CDDI has not been as widely deployed as has FDDI. Moreover, a great deal of FDDI is now being replaced with Gigabit Ethernet.

VIDEO SERVERS

Organizations are increasingly looking to *video servers* or *media servers* that permit centralized control of networked digital video resources. Although most of the video servers on the market in the early 1990s were designed for playback applications, video servers are now distributing resources between users who need to set up *interactive* videoconferences over a LAN. They are also supporting the store-and-forward video messaging requirements of *videomail* and video-enabled collaborative tools.

Emerging video-server technology addresses these low-end, intra-company applications, as well as the high-end requirements of interactive television and broadband cable networks discussed in Chapter 10. Subscribers will access video games and select movies on demand. They will even *go to school* from their living rooms, supported by networked video servers. Several computer companies, the major cable providers, and regional Bell operating companies are developing products that will deliver on-line video. The long-distance carriers use video servers to deliver desktop or interactive television-based videoconferencing services. Examples of such offerings include WorldCom's Media Manager and AT&T's Digital Video Services.

In the playback arena, Starlight Networks Incorporated (Mountain View, California) was one of the first developers to create video server software—they rolled it out in 1993. StarWorks combines a custom transport protocol tuned for video traffic with intelligent bandwidth management algorithms that run on Windows NT or UNIX-based servers. The server manages and distributes video broadcasts media clips so that multiple users can view/access them simultaneously. To tune in, users simply launch an application on their desktops that decodes and displays the feed. Starlight uses real-time networking protocols to guarantee the timely delivery of video and StarWorks software treats live media and video clips as streaming objects rather than as transactional data. The server supports a large number of concurrent video clients and offers many features, among which is the ability to deny requests for new video client sessions that will degrade existing ones. Starlight also offers StarWare, which runs as a Novell Incorporated NetWare Loadable Module on NetWare servers, as well as versions that run on other platforms, including Sun Solaris.

Other companies are pursuing the low-end video server market or its tributaries. These include Xing Technology Corporation of Arroyo Grande, California that offers Streamworks, and VDONet of New York, New York with its VDOLive. Xing builds its technology around the MPEG format, which allows wide-ranging compatibility but puts heavy demands on the client CPU. VDOLive can play video at high quality over low-bandwidth connections using a proprietary algorithm

At present, many manufacturers and service providers are re-deploying resources from interactive-television and video-on-demand markets to corporate applications for broadband networks. Uncertainty in the regulatory arena, relentlessness of new technology, and the risk of consumer markets make corporate applications such as distance learning, interactive and on-demand training, multimedia over the Internet, personal videoconferencing, collaborative computing, and collaborative workgroup systems more commercially appealing. Therefore, one can expect companies to increasingly support computer-based training with server-based video rather than distributing tapes and CD-ROMs.

ATM—THE NEXT ENTERPRISE NETWORK (?)

Enterprise networks are undergoing profound changes. Even as the bridged or routed LAN-based internetworking model is being assimilated, a new, switched architecture is emerging. Of course, we are referring to ATM.

Specifically designed to carry different types of traffic, ATM leverages the gigabit speeds offered by fiber-optic cable. It was designed to provide scalable, broadband, low-latency, cell switched services that fuses the LAN into the WAN and computer networks into telephone networks. The new ATM fabric will, at 622.08 Mbps, easily support high loads of data, voice, and video traffic—while solving many problems that organizations face as they try to put new media over old networks. Players large and small back it; these include 3COM, Apple, Cisco Systems, First Virtual, Fore Systems, IBM, Microsoft. Industry trade magazines devote space to it in almost every issue.

As First Virtual's CEO Ralph Ungermann is quick to point out, the standards for managing service quality, bandwidth allocation, network latency and data flows are already established for ATM. These same issues are still being addressed for conventional packet-switched networks. Solutions have been identified but none are widely deployed, and even trials (at the time of this writing) are limited. The irony here is that companies continue with their plans to adapt their packet-switched networks to carry time-sensitive media while ignoring a solution that was designed with it in mind. Why is it that, in spite of its myriad of benefits, one can only speculate as to when ATM will widely available?

Several things have prevented ATM technology from thus far entering the mainstream of enterprise networking—despite its obvious advantages. One is simply that it is different in concept and management from the packet-switched and routed networks that form the basis for current-day LANs and WANs. ATM is not only different, it is very complex (some assert that it is the most complex ever developed by the networking industry). Hardware-intensive switches require the overlay of a highly sophisticated, software intensive, protocol infrastructure. This infrastructure is required to both allow individual ATM switches to be linked into a network, and for such networks to internetwork with the vast installed base of extant LANs and WANs.

While it continues to draw many to seminars, where its mysteries are revealed and its benefits are extolled, there is always the hope that conventional network technology, once enhanced with switching and gigabit speeds, will rival ATM in the

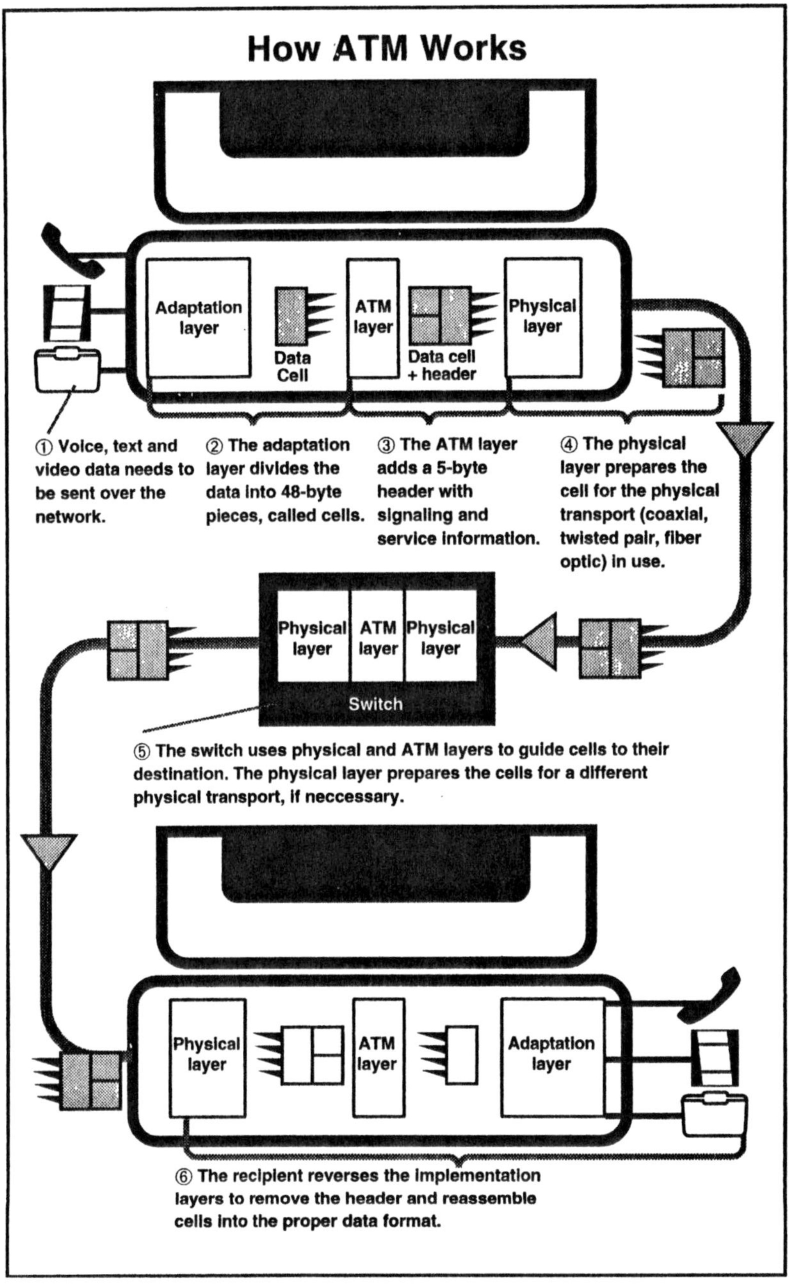

Figure 11-2. How ATM Works (Laura Long).

area of real-time multimedia delivery. This hope keeps network managers and their CFOs from making big investments in something as "revolutionary" as ATM.

ATM faces an even bigger problem. There is a gap between the LAN and the WAN. While it is only a matter of money that keeps companies from implementing ATM in the LAN, buying it for the WAN is a different story. Carriers may have announced support of ATM but they are not, at the time of this writing, aggressively selling it. Until they do, virtually all the traffic that flows across the carriers' networks will be carried over circuit-switched, time-division multiplexed 64 Kbps channels. Companies that try to plug in ATM LANs to the DS-3 WAN will find that multimedia data streams slow to a crawl. Since videoconferencing is distance-oriented (you can always walk across the campus for a meeting) the WAN component is critical to its enterprise-wide deployment.

CONCLUSION

The connection-oriented nature of ATM would seem to guarantee it a permanent quality advantage over connectionless networks, no matter how successful packet-switched QoS protocols become. On the other hand, high-overhead ATM compares less favorably to packet networks with regard to the efficient use of bandwidth. The tradeoffs of quality versus cost will ensure a role for both technologies in an increasingly large market for networked multimedia.

Over the years, there has been a shift in computing paradigms and applications. Clearly, the market is migrating from single protocol networks and toward the support of multiple protocols. It is abandoning proprietary internetworking schemes in favor of open ones. Peer-to-peer arrangements are displacing hierarchical schemes. Networks are becoming less application-specific as they service the enterprise's diverse needs. Moreover, fiber-optic cable is an alluring medium. Although it is still under-deployed in corporate networks, carriers and (generously-funded) network managers strongly prefer fiber.

Ethernet's various speeds (10/100/1000/10,000) are the most widely deployed architecture. However, to compensate for Ethernet networks' inability to truly guarantee service, network designers must offset with copious bandwidth. It is beyond the scope of this book to predict the future of internetworking. All that is certain is that, as bandwidth demands continue to grow and services are converged, the market will favor the arrangements that facilitate the most network control. ATM was designed for converged networks.

Chapter 11 References

Caruso, Jeff. "Beyond Category 5," Network World. July 1999. http://www.nwfusion.com/

Callaghan, Marilyn. "Proposed Standard for Gigabit Ethernet Over Copper Sent to Official Ballot." Gigabit Ethernet Alliance, July 1998. http://www.gigabit-ethernet.org/

"Special Report: Token-Ring Switching--The Next Generation," The Token Perspectives Newsletter January 1996 v14 n1 p. 11.

"Video Over ATM and Existing Networks," Cisco Systems, Incorporated.

Anthony Alles. "ATM Internetworking," Cisco Systems, Incorporated.

Barr, Christopher. "ISO What? (New 'Isochronous' Networking Technology)," PC Magazine November 9, 1993 p. 29.

Beck, Peter. "Twisted pairs challenge broadband signals," Electronic Engineering Times September 23, 1996 n920 pp. 54-60.

Cali, Paul D. and Deans, John D. "Installing fast Ethernet backbones," UNIX Review October 1996 v14 n11 pp. 46-50.

Cowtan, Mark. "Token-Ring switching applications," Telecommunications November 1996 v30 n11 pp. 113-118.

Karve, Anita, "Gigabit Ethernet prepares for the backbone," LAN Magazine October 1996.

Karve, Anita. "Switching on the Token-ring light," LAN Magazine September, 1996 v11 n9 p. 22.

Korzeniowski, Paul. "No end in sight to internetworking boom," Computer Reseller News October 21, 1996 n706 pS39-40.

Lipschutz, Robert P. "Power to the desktop," PC Magazine October 8, 1996 v15 n17 pNE1-6.

Merenbloom, Paul. "Boost your network with Fast Ethernet, fiber, switched hubs," InfoWorld October 28, 1996 v18 n44 p. 59.

Schnaidt, Patricia. "Plug in at 100," LAN Magazine March 1994 p. 12-30.

Sellers, Philip. "Gigabit Ethernet Flexes Its Muscles," Computing Canada October 10, 1996 v22 n21 pp. 1-2.

Serjak, Christopher W. "Migrating To ATM: Four Scenarios To Take Users From Today's Networks To Switched Gigabit 'Fabrics'," Distributed Computing Monitor September, 1993 pp. 3-19.

Simpson, David. "Making the trek to FDDI," Digital News & Review January 18, 1993 pp. 35-40.

Talley, Brooks, Broderick, John. "The Road To Bandwidthville," InfoWorld October 7, 1996 v18 n41 pp. 82-110.

Thryft, Ann R. "LAN Backbones Get Stronger—Gigabit Ethernet First Silicon Slated For 1997," Electronic Buyers Guide August 12, 1996 Issue 1019

Wilson, Tim. "With ATM, You Can Never Assume Anything," CommunicationsWeek, September 9, 1996 n627 p. 55.

PART FOUR

EVALUATING & BUYING VIDEO COMMUNICATION SYSTEMS

12

GROUP SYSTEMS

The engineering is secondary to the vision.
Cynthia Ozick

INTRODUCTION TO GROUP-SYSTEM VIDEOCONFERENCING

With the excitement over desktop videoconferencing, data collaboration, and document sharing, group systems, the staple of the videoconferencing market, are easy to overlook. This segment might lack the sizzle of desktop conferencing, but it has been, and still is, the industry's mainstay. The market research firm, Forward Concepts, asserts that set-top and compact appliances, and PC-based conference room systems are quickly dominating the entire videoconferencing industry. It forecasts that these systems will grow at a compound annual growth rate of over 40% to reach $639 million in sales in 2003. Set-top boxes are dominating the market segment, but PC-based systems will account for 28% of the business by 2004. Room videoconferencing system sales are exploding at the departmental, small office, and branch location level because the innovative technologies, useful operator features, extreme ease-of-set-up and ease-of-use, reduced support needs, and lower price points that these systems offer meet the needs of these business users.

Group systems differ from personal (desktop) conferencing products in that they are designed to accommodate multiple viewers. They differ from multicast products in that group-system viewers leave their desks and convene in conference rooms while multicast participants remain at their workstations. Furthermore, while desktop and multicast products can get by with software-only compression, group systems always rely on hardware-assisted compression.

At the heart of a group system is the *electronics module* that supports the codec. This module also includes audio and video plug-in jacks, and provides an interface to the network. It is usually integrated with other components (a monitor, camera, speakers and a microphone) and either cabinet- or cart-mounted, although it can be bought separately. Systems integrators usually buy just the codec and use their expertise to tie in monitors, cameras, audio, PC-graphics, presentation and projection systems.

Cabinet- or cart-oriented systems with wheels are known as roll-abouts. Many group systems today fall in this class. A roll-about's codec is mounted mid-cabinet and concealed behind doors. One or more monitors are placed above the codec. On top of the monitor is a camera. Some systems sandwich the camera in the middle, right between the monitor and the codec. Middle-mounted cameras are typically less obvious and, because of their placement, help seated participants to make better *eye contact* with the other end. Top mounted cameras, on the other hand, usually have a better field of view and can capture more of the room.

Group-oriented videoconferencing systems are broken into two categories: high-end/boardroom and low-end/small group. High-end systems are usually feature-rich and use top-of-the line components. It is typical to find them equipped with multiple microphones (wireless, wired or both), a stationary or *wireless remote* console unit, a high-performance audio sub-system (with echo cancellation) and dual monitors. Two monitors allow participants to view graphics on one while they talk face-to-face with conferees on another. The monitors of systems in this class measure at least 27-inches in diameter. Cabinets are either made of wood or industrial-grade plastic.

Small-group systems are either table-mounted or cart-based. They ship with a codec, a monitor, a fixed camera and all electronics. Monitors are no smaller than 17 inches; more usually, they are 20 inches. Features are limited; manufacturers take the "one size fits all" approach to reduce costs. Often small-group system installation is as simple as plugging in phone lines and power cables. ISDN or switched 56 service jacks can be extended to multiple conference rooms if systems are truly mobile. However, roll-abouts are not always moved; many vendors encourage a fixed installation that eliminates jostling of the delicate electronics.

DOMINANT PLAYERS IN GROUP-SYSTEM VIDEO

Until 1996, PictureTel, VTEL, and CLI dominated the videoconferencing market, and from 1994–1996, PictureTel Corporation of Danvers, Massachusetts assumed the lead. This dramatically changed in 1996 when VTEL acquired CLI, and Polycom expanded out of the audioconferencing market into the videoconferencing market with its ViewStation set-top products. PictureTel still boasts the largest installed base in the world, and VTEL is close behind. By perfecting the genre of videoconferencing products that PictureTel made popular with its SwiftSite products, Polycom shot to the forefront in terms of number of units sold. Behind the "big three" are a collection of mostly Japanese and U.S. manufacturers (Bosch, Fujitsu, Hitachi, ImageTel, Intelect, NEC, Panasonic, Sony, Tandberg, Toshiba, Verex and VSI). Some names may be missing from this list, but it is safe to say that, in the U.S., these companies provide 99 % of all systems shipped.

Figure 12-1. Roll-About System (courtesy of PictureTel).

CLI was founded in 1976. It was the first of the U.S. codec manufacturers to come up with a group system videoconferencing product: CLI's VTS 1.5 reached the market in September 1982. It provided very good picture quality, particularly considering that a single T-1 pipe was used to transport the signal. The VTS 1.5 was the first product to make heavy use of intraframe coding. In 1984, CLI tightened up the algorithm and rolled out a new codec: the VTS 1.5E. It compressed the signal down to bandwidths of 512 Kbps. The VTS 1.5E featured a new algorithm, Differential Transform Coding (DXC™). DXC was a remarkable breakthrough. When compared to previous compression techniques, it offered picture quality improvements so dramatic that it became the cornerstone of CLI's product line. A variation of DXC called discrete cosine transform went on to form the basis of three important image compression standards: JPEG, MPEG and H.261/H.263.

In 1984, PictureTel was formed. The company's research in low-bandwidth digital video signal compression led to the introduction, in 1986, of a compression technique dubbed Motion Compensated Transform (MCT). MCT became the basis of PictureTel's C-2000 codec that compressed video and audio signals down to transmission rates of 224 Kbps. In 1988, PictureTel introduced its C-3000 codec based on a new algorithm called Hierarchical Vector Quantization (HVQ). It compressed the signal down to 112 Kbps with acceptable quality. HVQ was well-timed. Switched 56 service was making its debut in the U.S. and ISDN BRI was emerging in Europe. In 1988, PictureTel shipped 150 C-3000 systems. In 1989, they sold over 600. Over the next five years (and still, today), the vast majority of room-system market growth comes from the low-bandwidth sector. By the early 1990s PictureTel had assumed the lead in the global marketplace.

In 1985, VTEL (formerly VideoTelecom Corporation) was founded in Austin, Texas. In 1986, it incorporated and began to develop a line of PC-based videoconferencing systems for the LAN environment. It did not take VTEL long to see that customers were not ready for LAN-based videoconferencing applications—it quickly shifted its attention to conferencing over the circuit-switched WAN. In 1989, VTEL began shipping two new products, the Conference System 200 and 300. Competing at the low end of the market (56 to 768 Kbps), these offered a new twist. VTEL used a 386-PC platform and based its products on DOS. For the first time, at least some videoconference system upgrades could be achieved by simply shipping customers a new set of floppy disks.

Through the years, VTEL wisely focused on several vertical markets. These include telemedicine, distance learning, legal/judicial and finance. VTEL has done particularly well in telemedicine and distance learning markets and sells more systems there than all other manufacturers combined.

In the early 1990s the videoconferencing industry began to experience upheaval. Standards were approved and codecs were being mass-produced. The popularity of low-end roll-abouts resulted in deep margin cuts. Intel announced ProShare in 1995. Overnight this new and well-funded player began to move the market toward the desktop. This is not to say that the room-system market is drying up, but many customers are rethinking their videoconferencing strategies. Finally, though the desktop market does offer great promise, much of the revenue generated by desktop sales will go to suppliers other than the high-end codec manufacturers. With

Figure 12-2. Set-top System (courtesy of Polycom).

contenders that include Corel, IBM, Intel, Lucent, Microsoft, and Netscape—to name just a few—the mix of suppliers is vastly different from what it was during the 1990-1993 timeframe. This is not to say that PictureTel, CLI and VTEL do not also sell into the desktop market; they do, and many testers count their products among the best. It is to say that the dominant room-system codec suppliers' commodious days are ending. While market growth is soaring, margins are being squeezed.

What is true is that a desktop-orientation has fueled the standards-effort, which extends across all classes of product. The "plug-and-play" approach makes a network administrator's life significantly less stressful and it protects the corporate investment. It is almost unheard of today to buy a group-oriented system that does not support the H.320 specification. Moreover, with the emergence of H.323 gateways, circuit-switched and packet-switched products are now co-mingling. To move the industry in that direction, many influential groups continue to push for interoperability. Standards have been good for the industry, specifically, the H.320 standard. Approved by the United Nation's ITU-T in the neutral environment of Geneva, Switzerland, it brought "peaceful coexistence" to the videoconferencing market.

Figure 12-3. CLI's VTS1.5E System (courtesy of CLI)

H.320's Impact On Group Videoconferencing Systems

The ITU-T's H.320 standard was approved on December 14, 1990. Beginning in 1991, "second tier" videoconferencing manufacturers (BT North America, GPT, Hitachi, Mitsubishi, NEC, Panasonic, and Toshiba) began building H.320-compliant products. The first major U.S. codec manufacturer to incorporate H.320 into its product was VTEL. VTEL provided free software upgrades to users of its newer systems (but charged users of older, hardware-oriented models $15,000 to upgrade).

In 1991, American videoconferencing manufacturers sold about 3,500 systems. Of that number, fewer than 5 % were shipped with Px64. Once the standard became well known in the U.S., customers began demanding that the two largest players, PictureTel and CLI, make it available on their products. CLI, early in the second quarter of 1992, announced H.261 upgrades for existing systems. These cost between $6,000 and $20,000. PictureTel was next, offering its standards-based Link-64 upgrades for $9,000. By 1992, over 70 % of the 6,500 codecs sold globally included the standard. Generally, products were shipped in a multi-algorithm arrangement where a proprietary scheme for single manufacturer conferencing was also included. In 1993 the number of products shipping with the standard increased to over 90 %. By year-end 1996, the number was almost 100 %.

Figure 12-4. Low-end System (courtesy of PictureTel).

Although suppliers did not like to see highly differentiated products become commodities overnight (a common result of strong standards), customers quickly realized the benefits of interoperability. Interactive multimedia is not simply limited to exchanges within a corporation. Since not all organizations select the same platform, standards are essential to moving visual communications in the same direction as the telephone. This is not to say that standards-based implementations always deliver identical results. Many group system manufacturers *enhance* standards, by adding improvements that are not specifically called out in a recommendation, but that are transparent to it. Such is the case with H.320.

Although it was not the only factor that caused changes in the videoconferencing industry, H.320 standardization certainly had an impact. Prices declined by 50 % almost overnight. Consequently, the videoconferencing industry is undergoing an evolution similar to the one experienced by the computer industry. The equivalent of computer mainframes is the boardroom system aimed at executive and customer applications. As is true of mainframes, it will take years for this segment of the market to go away, if it ever does. On the other hand, departmental videoconferencing, like departmental computing, will continue to grow rapidly because these systems offer affordable flexibility. They eliminate the requirement to contend for heavily used corporate facilities and can be rolled around from room to room. A parallel can be drawn between the desktop-based video systems covered in Chapter 14 and PCs.

Figure 12-5. High-end Codec (courtesy of PictureTel).

PC-based personal videoconferencing systems will exist alongside the room-based systems but will not replace them. Although room systems are sometimes derided as products that support "the meeting of two meetings," they offer considerable value. Meetings often have multiple people in a single room. What is the difference if there are two rooms involved and those rooms are separated by distance? Desktop products will address a different need, the need to work collaboratively, sharing data stored on PCs and workstations between individuals and groups. Group systems are including many features that started at the desktop such as applications sharing, file transfer, document viewing, and annotation (features that were first introduced to the group-system environment by VTEL).

Group-oriented Videoconferencing Systems Today

What are the components and features that one can expect to find in a group-oriented videoconferencing system? Of course all are built on the videoconferencing codec (or codecs, as today most systems include multiple silicon-based algorithms). As we have mentioned in earlier chapters, the codec converts analog information into a digital format and compresses the data for transmission over the telecommunications network. Codec manufacturers charge a premium for their high-performance proprietary algorithms—these can be the most expensive part of a group-oriented system, often accounting for as much as 25 % of system cost. The same does not hold true for standards-based codecs; standards led to mass production, which brought on dramatic declines in market price.

Set-top systems sell for $5,000–15,000. The cost for boardroom systems are about

$15,000–50,000. The additional for boardroom systems anymore primarily reflects aesthetics since most boardroom systems features are now available, or are becoming available in set-top units. Still, boardroom systems have an edge in features. The price spread reflects differences in the following areas:

- Number and type of audio and video compression algorithms supported (H.261, H.263, G.711, G.722, G.728, high-end proprietary, low-end proprietary)
- Picture resolutions supported (CIF, QCIF, proprietary high-resolution, other)
- Frame rates supported (30 fps for high-end, 8-15 fps for lower-end)
- Network interfaces offered (some products support ISDN BRI only, others provide multiple interfaces and may even build in ISDN NT-1 adapters, CSUs and inverse multiplexers)
- Transmission speeds supported (low-end systems almost never operate at data rates beyond 384 Kbps)
- Audio-related features (e.g., the number and type of microphones, echo cancellation).
- Cameras (number and type included, lines of resolution, sensitivity to light, features such as voice-activated camera movement)
- Monitors (size of and resolution)
- Execution of the operator's interface (e.g., touch-screen, push-button, wireless, electronic pen-tablet, Windows-oriented icon driven)
- Security provisions (password protection and encryption)
- Multipoint capabilities
- Peripherals (scheduling software, VCRs, document cameras, scan converters, inverse-multiplexers)
- Ongoing maintenance and support

We will devote the remainder of this chapter to discussing the subtleties of these system components and features. Understanding the differences will help prospective buyers make accurate systems comparisons.

AUDIO AND VIDEO COMPRESSION ALGORITHMS

Group-oriented systems today should support H.320 (including its G.728 compression algorithm for low-bandwidth audio encoding). Multipoint capabilities should incorporate the ITU-T's H.231/H.243 protocols. Group systems should be compatible with the T.120 data conferencing specification and, when complete, its T.130 companion.

Suppliers should be able to demonstrate that their H.320 system can successfully bridge through an H.323 gateway to conference with systems connected to packet-switched LANs and WANs. The H.323 standard is designed to facilitate point-to-point, multipoint, and broadcast calls among compliant LAN-, ISDN-, and room-based videoconferencing systems. H.323 also supports T.120, which provides a standard means of communication for collaborative tools such as whiteboard applications.

Standards-compliance does not preclude systems from shipping with a high-quality proprietary compression algorithm for connections between homogeneous systems. Moreover, for connections between like systems, proprietary compression techniques usually deliver superior results.

Group systems should offer automatic handshaking between codecs (performed to find the highest quality compatible algorithm). It is not acceptable to ask an end user to fumble through the process of finding a coding technique that is common to both (all) systems. In H.320 systems, the H.221 protocol performs this task. Successful implementations of H.221 can be tricky. It is widely acknowledged as the standard within the H.320 family that is the most difficult to implement, because it is the most complex.

PICTURE RESOLUTIONS

Picture resolution is a major differentiation between group systems. The number of horizontal and vertical pixels used to create a frame of video data expresses resolution. The smaller the monitor, the better a given resolution will appear to be because pixels are spread out over a smaller space.

Although image clarity is, to a limited degree, determined by screen size it is far more dependent on the processing techniques used by the codec to format the picture. There are standards-based image resolutions set forth in the H.320 Recommendation, specifically in its H.261 codec specification. These are known as QCIF and CIF and are described in Chapter 7. The QCIF image format delivers resolutions of about 26,000 pixels-per-screen. CIF produces four times the QCIF resolution (a little over 100,000 pixels per screen). Although the H.320 standard guarantees compatibility at some level, it is permissive. QCIF is mandatory, while CIF is optional. Using either format, a vendor can still truthfully claim standards-compliance.

In May of 1996 the ITU-T approved the H.263 Recommendation. It describes five picture formats. Along with QCIF (mandatory) and CIF (optional) there are Sub-QCIF, 4CIF and 16CIF (all optional and all covered in Chapter 7). Sub-QCIF or SQCIF is not applicable to group systems because it produces very low-resolution images. However, 4CIF delivers roughly the same resolution as NTSC television and 16CIF resolves an image with roughly the same clarity as the ATSC's (Grand Alliance) HDTV format. The H.263 algorithm is expected to replace H.261.

Besides standard resolutions, group-oriented systems may offer formats that are proprietary. These will be described (should a buyer inquire) using vertical and horizontal pixel counts. These may be compared to CIF (352 pixels by 288 lines) and QCIF (176 pixels by 144 lines).

FRAME RATES

The best compression techniques allow more frames of information to be sent in any given second, which results in better image and sound quality at lower bandwidths. To achieve the smooth motion handling of television, for example, images must be refreshed at 30 per second. At 30 fps, the eye cannot detect that the picture is being reassembled, so the brain "sees" continuous motion. A refresh rate as low as 12 fps yields an acceptable picture. Below that, almost any motion appears jerky. When distinguishing between group systems, frame rate comparisons can be made, but without sophisticated test equipment they will be subjective.

NTSC cameras capture video at speeds of 30 fps. What the codec does with those frames determines whether the motion on the screen will resemble a smooth waltz or the bunny hop. The H.320 standard does not specify a specific frame rate and, as we said in Chapter 7, some companies slow the frame rate down to improve resolution. Nevertheless all codecs (standards-based or proprietary) are optimized to deliver their best performance across a narrow range of network operating speeds. The discriminating evaluator will ask about the system's "sweet spot" (e.g., what operating bandwidth delivers the best picture resolutions and motion handling). It is unusual for a codec running at speeds below 384 Kbps to offer 30 fps on a continuous basis.

No matter what the transmission speed, a scene's "motion-component" will also affect the frame rate delivered by a codec. That is why a manufacturer will discuss frame rates in terms of a codec's average and maximum. If there is relatively little motion in a scene, a codec may come close to achieving its maximum. When large portions of the picture change, or if intricacies in the image require more rigorous computation, the codec must buffer the data while it performs intraframe compression. Often it falls behind; a new frame is presented while it is still coding a previous one. In cases such as this a codec will discard frames until it catches up.

A codec is sometimes called a compression engine. Like an automobile engine it has raw "horsepower" (speed) but it can also be tuned to use its power in special ways. Motion compensation represents one type of tuning. Motion compensation is based on interframe coding. It is optional in the H.320 specification. A H.320 decoder must interpret a motion-compensated stream of pixels if they are sent but a H.320 encoder does not have to create such a stream. Motion compensation is computation-intensive but it provides much better compression at comparable bandwidths (typically 30 % better than intraframe-only encoding).

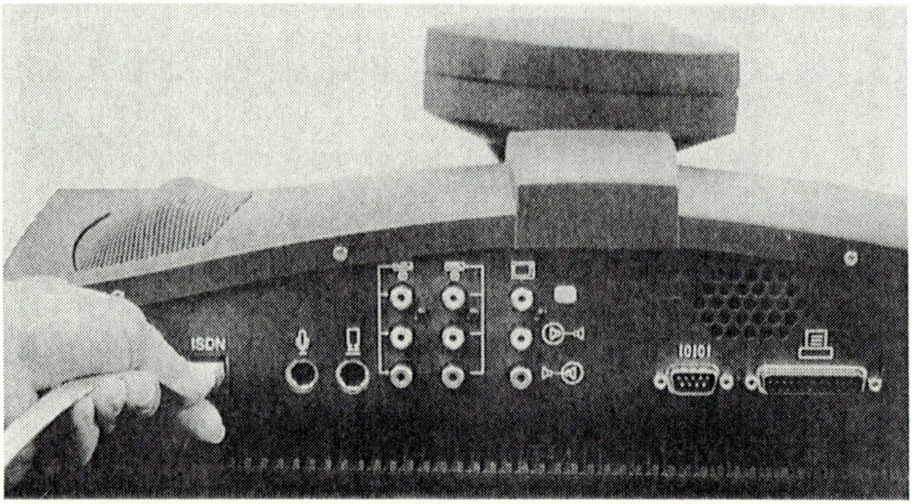

Figure 12-6. Back View of a Codec (courtesy of PictureTel).

Even when two codecs support all the same optional sections of the ITU-T's H.320 Recommendation, tuning can still make a difference in performance. In this case, 'tuning' refers to signal pre-processing and post-processing. Powerful codecs can take additional steps to *enhance* the H.261 process, preparing video frames for compression in a way that is transparent to a standards-compliant decoder. This is known as pre-processing. Post-processing is also performed, to make the most of the work done during pre-processing. When manufacturers contend that they enhance the standard, this is to what they are referring. There is a caveat. Dissimilar codecs are oblivious to pre- and post-processing steps so no advantage is gained. On the other hand, homogeneous codecs can make use of supplementary processing. That is why in a one-manufacturer H.320 demonstration (where codecs on both ends are identical) images are often "cleaner" and motion handling smoother.

NETWORK CONSIDERATIONS

Low-end group systems usually support transmission speeds of between 56 Kbps and 384 Kbps. Large systems sold in the U.S. and Japan usually support speeds between 56 Kbps and 1.536 Mbps. In the rest of the world, speeds range from between 64 Kbps to 1.920 Mbps (foreign PTTs do not offer switched 56).

Of course, bandwidth is only one aspect of signal transmission. How bandwidth is packaged is another. Standard transmission services include circuit-switched 56, ISDN (BRI and PRI), switched 384 Kbps (H0), switched 1.536 Mbps (H11), and DS0 multiples up to and including T-1/E-1. Some systems support packet-switched connections and almost all connect to POTS—but POTS is typically only used for audio-connections that allow participants without videoconferencing systems to hear and be heard.

Network Interfaces

When selecting a system, they buyer should already have determined the type of network arrangement that will support it. Information provided to a supplier should indicate whether the connection will be public or private, switched or dedicated, clear channel or bit robbed, and high-speed or low speed. If image quality-requirements will vary, multiple speeds may be required. For instance, in a meeting between two people who are discussing a project, the quality requirement may not be high. In a meeting between a sales team and a prospective customer high-bandwidth transmission will deliver more life-like results.

Many customers opt for the ability to select between transmission rates (often running their systems between 128 and 384 Kbps). The ability to deliver this flexibility will come from the codec itself (through H0 bonding) or from an external device (an inverse multiplexer). Some high-end group systems include a built-in inverse multiplexer, used to bond multiple B channels (or switched 56 circuits) together into higher bandwidth aggregates. Low-end roll-abouts do not bond beyond two channels. If speeds above 128 Kbps are required, bonding must be performed by a separate I-MUX.

All other things being equal, group system products that connect to the network in a highly flexible fashion should be favored. Systems that are data-rate agile (meaning that they function as a DTE device and so can follow the network clock) are preferable to those that are not. The ability to clock off the network allows the codec to detect changes and adjust its data rate accordingly.

During procurement, a customer should ask about the network (physical layer) interfaces that are offered. These might include Bell System interfaces (T-1); EIA (RS-449/422 and RS-366-A) and ITU-T (V.35, X.21 and ISDN). Typically ITU-T V.35 connections are used in the United States for circuit-switched digital connections (excluding ISDN). The V.35 specification defines a high-speed serial communications interface (an electrical connection) between a network access device (e.g., a multiplexer or a codec) and the network switching equipment. (In the U.S., CSUs also use V.35 plugs to connect to CPE.) V.35 makes its connection using a large rectangular connector with large hold-down screws. Although the ITU-T has formally stated that the V.35 specification is out of date, it is still widely used and provides a solid connection that is almost impossible to casually dislodge. X.21 connections are used for circuit-switched digital connections in Europe and the rest of the world. Like V.35 X.21 is a digital signaling interface, defined by the CCITT/ITU-T, and used to connect DCE to DTE. X.21 describes the names and functions of eight wires. The physical connector has 15 pins. X.21 connectors are almost never provided in the U.S. ISDN connections rely on an RJ-11C plug on the network side of the NT-1 and an RJ-45 connection on the CPE side (in other words, the side that connects to the codec). Besides determining which physical layer interfaces are provided by a system it is also important to specify whether the customer or the supplier will supply the CSU/DSUs, NT-1s and cables.

Transmission Speeds: Finding the "Sweet Spot"

As we just said, every codec is optimized for a particular bandwidth. H.261 is optimized to deliver its best performance at 384 Kbps. G.723 audio compression is optimized for transmissions between 5.3 and 6.3 Kbps. Proprietary codecs are optimized for a specific transmission rate, too. It is a good practice to ask what that rate is. For instance, if a product is optimized for 384 Kbps, running it at T-1 speeds will render little marginal improvement even though transmission costs will be four times higher. Furthermore, algorithms optimized at 712 Kbps may fall apart at speeds of 112 Kbps. Many high-end systems depend heavily on intraframe coding, which provides excellent results, but which consumes a great deal of bandwidth.

Packet- and Cell-Switched Interfaces

Group systems have long relied on circuit switching, but this is changing. Today, ITU-T standards address connections over LANs (IP and IPX) and ATM. These standards apply to group oriented systems, too, although most people construe them to be aimed solely at the desktop. Group systems with LAN (Ethernet or token-ring) interfaces facilitate multimedia exchanges (data collaboration). ATM interfaces (supporting transmission at 155.52 Mbps) provide support for *any* type of traffic. The provision of an OC-3 interface to an ATM switch makes it easy to directly aggregate data from the codec with data from PBXs, LANs and WANs.

AUDIO-RELATED FEATURES

Audio quality is critical to the success of a videoconference. For that reason, customers are advised to pay particular attention to the elements of the audio subsystem. These include microphones, speakers and echo cancellers.

Several recent advances in audio conferencing technology have greatly improved sound quality. Digital systems are clearer. Echo cancellation eliminates "clipping" (which causes sound to drop out when someone speaking from the other end cuts into the conversation). Today's systems are also more tolerant of poor room acoustics, ambient noise, and degradation caused by the transmission line. New room-system videoconferencing products integrate digital signal processing (DSP), echo control, noise reduction, and full duplex transmission to deliver high-quality audio.

Differences between the audio quality levels offered by different codec manufacturers have evened out substantially. There are significant differences between high- and low-end rollabouts, however. An even wider range of performance shows up in desktop systems, but we cover this issue in another chapter.

Audio Codecs

Digital audio is usually described in terms of its sampling rate, the number of bits per sample, the data rate (measured in bps) and the number of audio channels. The fundamentals of audio sampling, quantizing and encoding are covered in Chapter 6. The higher the audio bit rate, the less room will be left over for the video portion of the signal. Thus, it's important to look for efficient coding schemes.

Almost all audio codecs included in videoconferencing systems will comply with the ITU-T specifications described therein. The important ones for group-oriented systems are G.711, G.722 and G.728 audio. As we said earlier, G.728 audio compresses voice to 16 Kbps. G.711 and G.722 audio compress to 64 Kbps and, in an ISDN BRI connection use half the network bandwidth for voice. G.711/G.722 compression does make sense at higher-end transmission speeds (712 Kbps and above). The difference between the two is that G.722 samples at twice the frequency of G.711 (7 kHz versus 3.5 kHz) and, therefore, produces a more faithful representation of sounds other than simple speech.

There is also G.723 encoding, developed by the DSP Group of Santa Clara, California. G.723 audio was standardized by the ITU-T. G.723 uses Multipurpose-Maximum Likelihood Quantization (MP-MLQ) to squeeze voice down to about 6 Kbps. CELP predicts speech through a process of vocal tract modeling. It sends only the "error" (the difference between the model and real events). In low-bandwidth conferences the use of CELP allows significantly more bandwidth (about 50 Kbps) to be devoted to video signal transmission.

When inquiring about proprietary audio algorithms, ask the supplier to provide information on the range of frequencies encoded with each type and the data rates produced by this encoding. Also question suppliers on how bandwidth is assigned to audio. As with video, the more bits available for audio transmission, the better the quality. Some systems allow the end-user to specify the audio bandwidth, and others offer flexible bit-rate audio that changes with the amount of video information being transmitted. Another category uses schemes that are rigid (the same amount of bandwidth is assigned no matter how much video must be shipped). To find out what works best, analyze audio quality under different circumstances. Listen closely to audio quality during major scene changes (e.g., someone moves around) and compare what you hear to the quality delivered when there is little or no motion.

Audio Channels

All group-oriented systems offer at least two channels (stereo sound). Additional channels may be used in some systems. Some provide a center channel; others provide up to five channels (known as surround-sound). When a center channel is added to a group system videoconferencing unit it tends to "anchor" the sound field. As meeting participants move around the room, the audio portion of the conference appears to remain fixed. When only two channels are used (left and right speaker), it is possible to detect which speaker is producing which sounds by moving between them. A central loudspeaker also provides better frequency response matching across the stereo sound field and helps to match the action between the picture and the associated sound. When only two channels are used, the prominent an angular deviation between the sound and its picture can be detected by some listeners.

Microphones

A microphone is a *transducer* that converts sound into an electrical signal. Microphones vary in how they manage the ratio between signal and noise, how they avoid distortion and how they use companding (noise-reduction circuitry) to improve signal-to-noise ratios. Of course, there are many different types available and also many different qualities. Customers that try to cut corners by buying inexpensive microphones often regret it later. Microphones are not "big ticket items" in the overall scheme of things but good ones can make an enormous difference in the perceived quality of a system.

Customers should work with their supplier or consultant to identify the number and type of microphones that should be provided for a given installation. Some microphones are built in to the system control unit while others are independent of it, offering more flexibility. Microphones are not always table-mounted; they can be suspended from the ceiling, built into (and coordinated with) a camera or attached to a speaker's lapel. Lavaliere (lapel mounted) microphones can be wired or wireless. Wireless microphones are often preferred but speakers may forget to remove them before leaving the room and they are susceptible to RFI (radio frequency interference). A combination of microphones can be used in a single application, as long as they arranged such that they do not generate feedback.

The number of microphones supported by a system (e.g., the number of audio input ports) should be considered. To provide the best coverage, customers often order additional microphones and locate them strategically to maximize coverage. Moreover, when it comes to coverage, microphones should be evaluated in terms of their "direction." They can be unidirectional or omnidirectional. Unidirectional microphones have "dead spots" and speakers must be aware of where they are positioned in relation to them. Omnidirectional microphones can pull in sounds from all directions and are preferable for most applications.

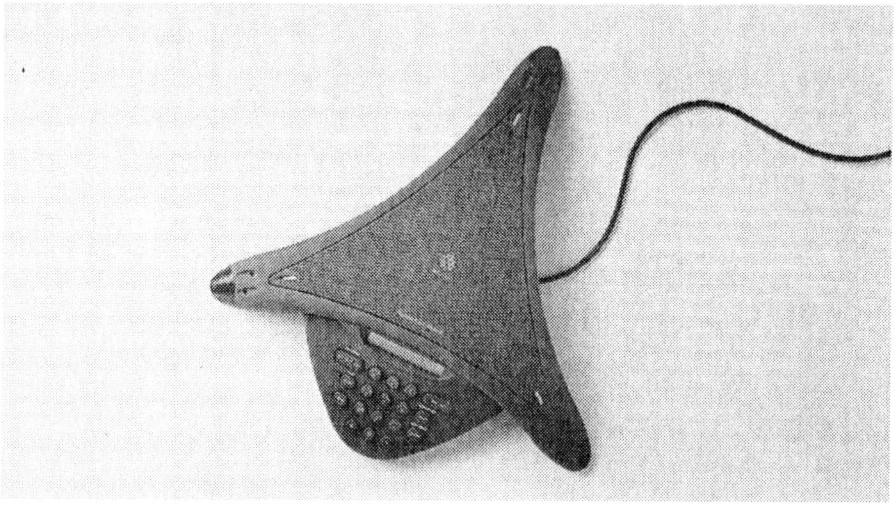

Figure 12-7. Conference Phone (courtesy of Polycom).

Audio Features

The audio-oriented features of videoconferencing systems vary. The most basic include audio-only bridging (the ability to bring people who do not have videoconferencing equipment into the conference) and audio out-dialing. Out-dialing is an important feature that should be supplemented through a dialing keypad. Audio call can be used to dial someone on the other end when there are problems with establishing the video component of a conference. If audio dial uses a line from a PBX or switchboard, it is helpful to have a *switchhook flash* key, used to access PBX features such as three-way audio conferencing. A recorder jack is also a nice-to-have feature.

Finally, all systems should include a mute button, which temporarily removes audio from the stream of bits sent to the distant end. Several embarrassing incidents have resulted from a misunderstanding of how muting works. When mute is activated, audio is removed from the information being transmitted to the far end site(s) but it is not generally removed from a taped recording of the proceedings. A story is told about the team that was videoconferencing with their manager, who was traveling in Asia. Mid-meeting, one team member muted and made a side comment about the manager that was mildly derogatory. Later, the group was reviewing a taped recording of the conference; the manager was present. It was then that they learned what many do not know: muting does not stop the microphone from receiving audio, nor does it stop the received audio from being recorded. It only stops the received audio from being transmitted. Fortunately the manager had a good sense of humor. The episode even had a positive aspect: the manager learned a little more about how to be effective in leading a team and team was able to educate their consultant about how muting really works in a videoconference.

Echo Cancellation

Echoes have always posed a sound quality problem in conferencing applications. Echo elimination is critically important in true roll-about applications because one can not depend on room treatment alone to address the problem. Customers in the market for group-oriented systems should inquire about how echoes are eliminated. There are two methods: echo suppression and echo cancellation. Echo suppression attenuates microphones and loudspeakers on an alternate basis to get rid of feedback. However, it causes *clipping*. Echo cancellation models an echo and subtracts it from an incoming signal, providing for smooth, natural exchanges.

Echo cancellation systems must "train themselves" to the room and network environments to operate effectively. Some units emit a burst of white noise to profile the room (sometimes called "whooshing the room"), which can be annoying to distant-end participants. Others use the voices of the meeting participants to train acoustic line-side echo cancellers. Some units automatically adapt to changing room and network conditions without losing stability. Still others become unstable when the unit is moved or when an object is sitting too close to the microphone. Increases or decreases in speaker volume may degrade performance; prospective buyers are advised to experiment.

When comparing echo cancellation equipment, compare convergence time, tail length, and acoustic echo return loss enhancement (AERLE) ratings. Convergence time is the measure of how long it takes for a canceller to model the acoustic characteristics of the room in which it is installed. The time, measured in milliseconds, should be as short as possible (less than 70 ms) because echoes will sneak through until the canceller completes its model of reality. Tail length is measured in milliseconds and corresponds to how long an echo canceller will pause after an original signal's echo has been modeled to wait for the return echo. The longer the tail length, the less acoustic treatment a room will require. AERLE, measured in decibels (dB), describes the maximum echo cancellation produced by the canceller. The higher the dB rating, the better equipped the system is to remove echo. Typical values range between 6 and 18 dB. It should be noted that the variable attenuator (also called the center clipper) should be disabled for a truly accurate measurement.

CAMERAS

Most group systems (high-end or low-end) come equipped with color cameras that can pan, tilt and zoom. Nearly all are based on integrated circuits called charge-coupled devices (CCDs). A CCD camera focuses a scene sample not on an imaging tube (which is used in older cameras) but on a solid state chip (the CCD). Cameras can be based on single-chip CCDs or multi-chip arrangements.

CCDs

A CCD is much smaller than an imaging tube. A single CCD chip is about the thickness of a quarter and may be as small as 1/3 inch square. The lens directs photons to strike the surface of the CCD chip, which is divided into individual elements (rather than the continuous photosensitive surface of an imaging tube). The surface of the CCD resembles a matrix of individual elements, which in turn define the spatial resolution capability of the camera. Each unique element samples the light that strikes it and converts that light to a charge. The charge is then read out to camera circuitry. The more chips, the more elements that can be used to resolve an image and the more sensitive a camera is to the visible spectrum.

In color video cameras, it is typical to sample the RGB components of a scene in order to reproduce color. Single chip CCD cameras place a color filter directly on adjacent rows of imaging elements, creating a series of "stripes." With three stripes (R, G, and B), it is possible to sample the scene directly through the same lens at precisely the same time on the same chip. Because components are not registered precisely in line (the red element is a row above the green, and so on), the result is mild optical distortion.

In a three-CCD camera, three separate chips the focused image is passed through a beam splitter, which allows each chip to sample the full scene in each respective color over the entire chip for full resolution. In addition, the optical performance of the system is superior because each color sample uses the same precise optical alignment. If each chip were the same specification of the single chip camera, then the spatial resolution in color could therefore be three times greater than that of the single chip.

Single CCD cameras are used for less demanding applications than three CCD cameras (which are used for broadcast and more performance-sensitive applications). In small-group roll-abouts, single CCD cameras are typically offered. In high-end group systems three CCD cameras are the norm. Cameras furnished with both categories usually offer automatic gain control, white balance. Most also include variable aperture ranges and focal lengths.

Technical Considerations

When evaluating cameras from a technical standpoint, the best are those that are most sensitive to light. Sensitivity is measured in lux; video cameras should have, at a minimum, a rating of 2-lux (3-lux is even better). This eliminates the need for special lighting and provides good depth of field, which keeps subjects in focus. Note that there is no standard method for measuring lux levels. However the camera's maximum aperture (f1.4, for instance) determines the lens' ability to capture light.

Typically, room system cameras focus best when objects are between five and 20 feet distant. Within this range people can move around freely without being concerned that image capture will be compromised. Zoom lenses are capable of variable focal lengths ranging from wide-angle to telephoto. A lens specified as 12:1 (12X), for example, has a maximum focal length ten times that of the minimum focal length. A large room requires a higher zoom ratio (with longer focal lengths available) than in a small room. In a small room, telephoto capabilities do not matter; the lens must zoom out for a wide angle of view. Note that angle of view is measured in degrees. Because both the focal length of the lens *and* size of the camera's imaging area determine the angle of view, one should not assume that two cameras with lenses of the same focal length will have the same angle of view.

A camera's arc of movement is described as its range. Range is measured in degrees, with 150° degrees being on the high-end of average. The time that it takes a camera to move from one point to another is described as its repositioning time. Moving the camera across its full range typically takes between one and two seconds. Some cameras move quietly while others are quite noisy. This may not seem important but recently a technician posted a question to an videoconferencing oriented Internet news group about how to muffle a noisy camera. The user noted that the motor used for camera panning and zooming was so loud on his system that he could not obtain a high quality recording of a conference.

Some cameras come equipped with gain control or automatic gain control (AGC). AGC boosts the video signal level during low light conditions. Most cameras calculate the required gain by averaging the levels in the overall image—this can cause problems in high contrast situations. AGC can also upset the levels and contrasts in an image when conference participants are wearing very bright (or white) clothing. These problems should not necessarily dissuade an organization from buying an AGC camera, but should considered, particularly in boardroom applications.

White balance is another camera feature. Various lighting conditions produce different color components. Cool-temperature lighting (see Chapter 13) casts a different tint on a room than does warm-temperature lighting. White balance adjusts the RGB components that, when combined, yield white in a video signal.

Auxiliary Cameras

Low-end videoconferencing systems usually come with a single camera. High-end systems typically have more than one. In addition to the camera built in to the system cabinet, high-end installations include one or more auxiliary cameras. Whereas system cameras work well to capture images of conferees seated at a table, auxiliary cameras perform better for other parts of the room. Some mount scissor-fashion on a wall while others are freestanding (usually mounted on a tripod).

Figure 12-8. Camera (courtesy of Panasonic Video).

Mobile auxiliary cameras are helpful in a large room or in cases when a speaker uses a whiteboard or lectern. They offer the flexibility that a cabinet- or wall-mounted camera can not provide.

Camera Control

A basic requirement of videoconferencing systems is camera control. Two important camera control features are far-end camera control, and camera presets. Far-end camera control is just that—it allows a person on one end of a videoconference to control a camera on the other end. It is useful when the participants on the other end are untrained in system operation or when they forget to move their camera to follow the action in the room. Near-end participants can step in to help, and thus assume responsibility for cameras on both ends. Multipoint far-end camera control is generally not offered. It can become confusing to control cameras in more than two sites.

Camera presets help speed camera movement. They are the camera-equivalent of telephone speed-dial. At the beginning of a meeting, a system operator frames key participants in the camera, makes any adjustments to zoom and/or centering that may be necessary, and then enters the position into memory. To recall the setting, the operator presses a button or touches an electronic pad and the camera moves to its preset position. When group discussion gets lively, presets allow an operator to capture most or all the action for the distant end.

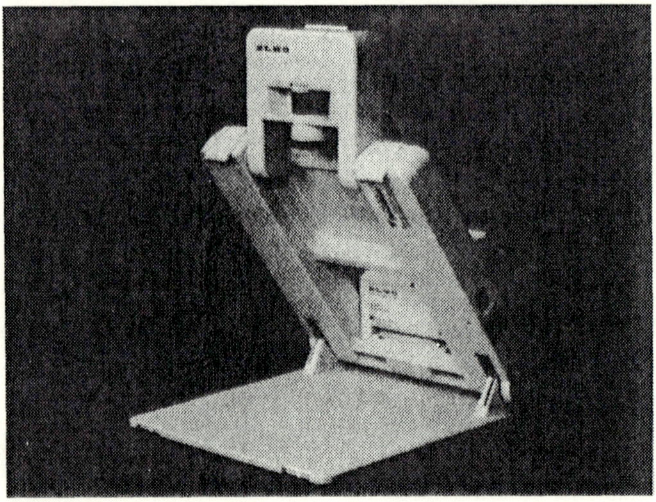

Figure 12-9. Elmo EV-274 Document Camera (courtesy of Elmo).

Most systems allow presets to be arranged for more than one camera (main and auxiliary, for instance). Some go farther to allow both near-end and far-end camera presets. The *number* of camera presets also varies between systems. Some offer only six camera presets; others offer sixteen. Six presets for each camera are adequate for most situations; more can become confusing.

Some group-oriented videoconferencing systems offer "follow me" camera features. In these systems, a software-controlled camera is synchronized with room or speaker microphones. Speech causes the camera to snap into position to follow the action.

Graphics Support And Subsystems

Documents and graphics are exchanged in most in-person meetings. Videoconferencing systems should provide some form of support for document transfer. At the most basic level there are document stands (more often called document cameras). Document cameras marry a small color video camera to an overhead projector. The camera points down at a baseboard with lighting to display physical objects, instructor's notes or transparencies, etc. They provide for standard resolution graphics exchange.

The capabilities of document cameras differ. Most systems offer single-chip CCD cameras. A three-chip CCD camera is required in cases where end-users want very high-quality graphics (remote inspection of parts, engineering applications, etc.). Some document cameras both focus automatically and offer manual adjustments. Others offer manual adjustments only. Controls are sometimes included as part of the videoconferencing system's operator console. More often the user must make

Figure 12-10. Picture-In-Picture (courtesy of Panasonic).

adjustments at the document camera itself.

Using a document camera or other image capture techniques, codecs may also deliver high-resolution display of "freeze-frame" graphics. Resolutions vary widely, from 2X to much higher definitions. Picture formats generally include JPEG, TIFF (Tagged Image File Format) or TARGA (Truevision Advanced Raster Graphics Adapter). Graphics systems often comply with the ITU-T's H.320 Recommendation H.261 Annex D that doubles the CIF horizontal and vertical resolution for television-quality graphics.

Most group-oriented videoconferencing systems provide the built-in ability to create and store images as slides. Program files can be retrieved during an interactive videoconference and used to make presentations. Participants can view these visual materials and annotate them independently. Collaborative computing tools (which let conference participants share keyboard control of a single computer file) vary in their power, as we discussed in Chapter 15. Almost all are now based on the ITU-T T.120 Recommendation; proprietary approaches should be avoided.

Even when a videoconferencing system does not integrate the ability to create, store, and retrieve documents and images, it can usually be equipped with a T.120 outboard system. This delivers similar functionality—at an additional cost, of course. These products run the gamut from simple telewriting terminal equipment to sophisticated PC-based systems.

Document and graphics subsystems vary enormously in sophistication. Nearly all allow conference participants to electronically annotate shared images in real time through the use of electronic tablets and stylus arrangements. Applications sharing

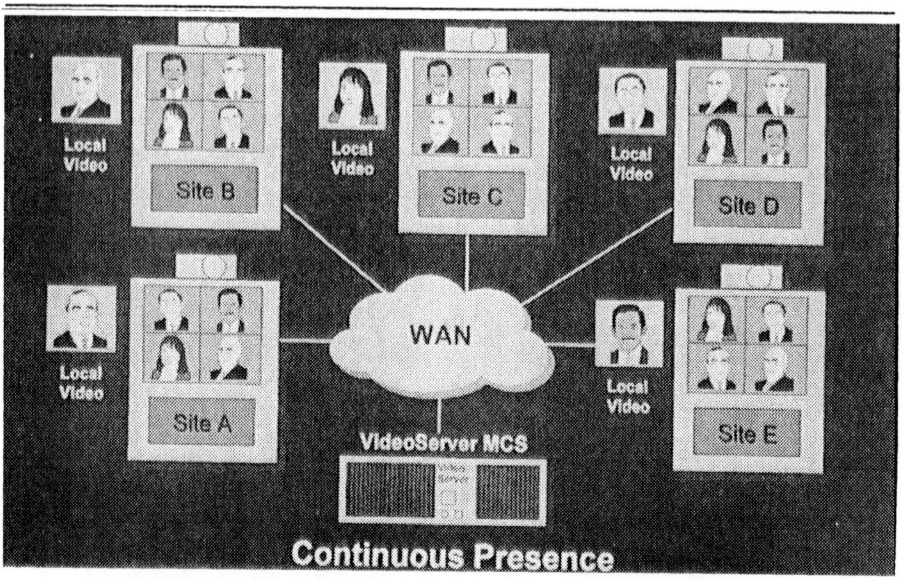

Figure 12-11. Continuous Presence (courtesy of VideoServer).

systems are more sophisticated. These permit users at different sites to interactively share, manipulate and exchange computer files (documents or spreadsheets), moving images (such as animation programs), and databases. Some systems offer very high-resolution graphics, including CAD support that allow engineers to collaborate on product designs, and to concurrently view computer simulations. Most are PC-based, and connect through data ports on the codec that allow them to share the audio/video data stream. Images can be scanned in, retrieved from files, or captured with cameras.

When photorealism is required (X-rays, medical images and cases when an entire typed page or detailed diagram must be transmitted) enhanced-resolution systems are required. These systems are available in monochrome or color and go beyond the PC VGA resolutions of 640H x 480V pixels to produce images containing between 3 and 13 times more pixels. Television cameras can not scan at such high levels of detail. In very high-resolution applications devices called scanners are required.

Flatbed scanners resemble small photocopiers. The image to be scanned is placed facedown on the clear-glass surface, and scanned from underneath. The scanning area or size of the bed can affect the price of the scanner, particularly when scanners have a bed size of 11-inches by 17-inches or larger. Within the scanner, one or more CCD converts incoming light into voltages with amplitudes that correspond to the intensity of the light. Four-bit gray-scale scanners can capture 16 shades of gray; eight-bit gray-scale scanners can capture 256 shades of gray, and are often used in medical applications. Color scanners are usually required in multimedia work; they typically make three scanning passes, one each for red,

Figure 12-12. Remote Control Unit (courtesy of CLI, Inc.).

green, and blue. A good scanner can resolve an image at about 300 dots-per-inch (DPI). Recently, 400 and 600 dpi scanners have started to proliferate. Images are either stored on hard disk (storage requirements for saving images add up quickly) or printed using laser printers.

MONITORS

Videoconferencing monitors come in various sizes and configurations. Obviously, monitor size is important. Beyond size, evaluating monitors is largely a subjective exercise. One should look for definition around the edges of the screen, crisp, clear images, true color, and straight horizontal and vertical lines.

A television monitor can be evaluated in terms of its dot pitch. The dot pitch is the distance between same color (R, G or B) dots, in any direction. A smaller dot-pitch provides a higher resolution on a given monitor, but a smaller dot-pitch does not necessarily mean that the picture quality will be better. Some monitors will look better with a larger dot-pitch. The goal is to match the dot-pitch with the pixels-per-inch delivered by the codec. Given that all monitors being compared are the same size (measured diagonally across the screen), a .28mm dot pitch is excellent; a 31mm dot pitch is good and a 51mm dot pitch is acceptable (although text will look fuzzy).

When looking at monitors remember that they use three electron guns (one each for R, G and B) to excite the phosphors that make up the pixels in an image. These guns must deliver signals of the same relative strength or "color balance" will be diminished. If the blue gun is adjusted to deliver a stronger signal the image will

Figure 12-13. Operator Interface (courtesy of VTEL).

look bluish. Nearly all monitors can adjust the relative strength of the three electron guns to correct most of the problem.

Some group-oriented systems use PC monitors as opposed to television monitors. PC monitors are evaluated according to their Video and Electronics Standards Association (VESA) rating. There are four standard VESA resolutions. These are VGA 640H x 480V; Super VGA (or SVGA) 800H x 600V; and two XGA resolutions: 1,024H x 768V and 1,280H x 1,024V. Some monitors even go higher, to resolve an image at 1,800H x 1,440V. The ultrahigh resolutions primarily suit professional-level work in fields such as desktop publishing and computer-aided design, not videoconferencing (where SVGA delivers an excellent image).

Picture In Picture

Although it is not really a monitor feature (it is a system feature), picture in picture is a very important in single monitor systems. Also known as quadrant display or windowing, PIP relies on a codec's receive circuitry to create and send two images to a monitor. One image occupies most of the screen except for a small corner where the second image, smaller but complete, can be inserted in a window.

The window can be closed when it is not needed. PIP provides a mechanism for monitoring near-end image capture in single monitor systems.

Continuous Presence

Again, continuous presence is not a function of the monitor itself but it relies on the monitor to display multiple images. It differs from PIP in that these images

Figure 12-14. Workgroup Application (courtesy of Intel).

describe far-end activity only. It differs from multipoint technology (where each conference site can see only one other site at a time) by allowing a conference site to see several other sites simultaneously (usually two or four) and hear the audio from all sites.

Continuous presence is described in the ITU-T's H.324 specification. It relies on a codec to deliver a single composite video stream composed of the video signals from up to four sites (or four cameras in a single site). Most the receiving codec "stacks" these discrete images on a single monitor, where each occupies one quadrant (in Hollywood Squares fashion), continuously and simultaneously.

Continuous presence also works well in point-to-point applications where a large group is seated around a table. In situations like this, a single camera can not capture everyone in one image, so two are used. One camera is focused on people on one side of the table; a second is aimed at those on the other side. Again, the two images are stacked for transmission and offered on a split screen basis (where one half of the table is displayed on the top half of the monitor and the other is displayed below) or in a *destack* mode where two monitors are used to display the images.

It should be noted that continuous presence requires double or quadruple the transmission bandwidth of single image applications. Hence, it works best at speeds of 384 and above (with 512 Kbps being the preferred minimum).

Figure 12-15. Multipoint Control Unit (courtesy of VideoServer).

OPERATOR'S INTERFACE

The videoconferencing operator's interface, also called the control unit, deserves much attention. It is critical because many people who would benefit most from videoconferencing are too busy to learn how to use it. A group system control unit should be menu-driven and as intuitive as possible. Most allow the operator to: dial calls using speed-call, switch between room and document cameras, activate the camera's pan, tilt and zoom features, control audio including volume and muting, and access peripherals such as slides projection systems, fax machines, and VCRs. Some systems allow the operator to move cameras at the remote site. This feature is called far-end camera control and is valuable when people on the distant end have not been trained on the use of the system.

Historically a desktop-mounted device, the control unit now takes many forms. In the desktop category there are control units that emulate a telephone, those that use an electronic template and stylus, and those that rely on a touch screen interface where mylar-covered electronics cause displays to change, depending on what part of the screen is pressed. This allows a great deal of control without a cluttered display. Wireless remotes are very common, particularly in small-group roll-about systems. These mimic a VCR or TV remote control device. Most provide an on-screen pointer and icon-driven controls. A user can move the pointer up and down by raising and lowering his hand. When he or she has selected a feature a button can be clicked to evoke it.

Different interfaces appeal to different people. Consider the sophistication of the end users in the evaluation. Assemble an evaluation team and have participants rate different system's ease-of-use. Some apparently "intuitive" commands stump users who are called upon to actively participate in a conference while managing its housekeeping functions. Finally, include the operator's instruction manual in the evaluation process. Documentation varies greatly.

SECURITY

When conferences rely on satellite transmission or include highly confidential content, companies often encrypt the signal. Within the U.S., the Data Encryption Standard (DES) standard is typically used. DES is an U.S. government-sanctioned (NIST) private key cryptographic technique in which only authorized personnel know the secret key. Unfortunately, U.S. law limits the export of DES products. Almost no videoconferencing systems offer DES encryption on systems bought overseas (except for specially engineered U.S. government installations). On the other hand, several codec manufacturers substitute proprietary algorithms. Since most confidential exchanges take place within a company this seems to work well for international applications. In addition, the ITU-T has specified H.233 and its companion H.KEY for protecting the confidentiality of H.320-compliant exchanges. This has rarely been implemented.

One other security measure provided by most systems is password protection for the operator's console. This prevents unauthorized use of a system and can even discourage theft.

For more on the subject of information security, see chapter 16.

MULTIPOINT CAPABILITIES

MCUs are something like a network depot where all compressed video and audio signals terminate. Also known as bridges they combine, exchange and manage inputs. Most MCUs can support multiple simultaneous bridged connections and are capable of supporting a variety of network interfaces and speeds. Not all systems support multipoint capabilities. For instance, low-end group systems often do not.

MCUs eventually find their way into most organizations. They generally appear after the company has been renting bridge space from service bureaus for some period of time; once it is possible to make a business case for the MCU. Most sell for between $4,000 and 10,000 per port, where one port is required for each site involved in the multipoint session.

The ideal multipoint conference would provide every location with access to all available speech, video and data coming from other locations. Unfortunately, 'continuous-presence' multipoint conferencing is not usually feasible because it requires bandwidth linking every site to all other sites. Fast switching provides an alternative to continuous presence. Video and data information are provided selectively using some criteria for determining which site should "have the floor." Selection can be made by humans (for instance, the facilitator of the conference) or can be fully automatic.

MCUs have different operations modes. Most allow chairperson control where a single conference manager determines who will be displayed on the screen. Others provide a rotating mode in which the MCU cycles through the conference sites, displaying each briefly on the screen. There is also a voice-activated mode in which the MCU fast-switches between sites based on who is speaking. In a voice-activated mode some systems offer speech-checking algorithms provided for voice-activation to prevent loud noises (sneezes, coughs and doors shutting, for instance) from diverting the camera from the site with the speaker to the site with the loud noise.

MCUs must support all the video and audio algorithms present in the conference and are often called upon to handle graphics and still-image annotation. This includes the full H.320 suite. Within that suite H.231 and H.243 address multipoint. G.728 audio support is also desirable. Some MCUs limit connection speeds to only some of the Px64 multiples and others do not support H0 multirate ISDN bonding. Nuances in how MCUs support the standards still exist and, are becoming more pronounced. Since the ratification of H.323 and H.324 an MCU will be called on to support H.263 and H.261 encoding. And, the new H.32X specifications went further in their definition of MCU capabilities. This is an area to investigate thoroughly.

MCUs are evaluated in terms of their size and capabilities. They are described in terms of the number of sites supported. Most low-end MCUs come equipped with four ports and can grow up to eight ports. Larger systems can group up to 72 ports and can be "cascaded" to link hundreds of sites. Some smaller systems can be expanded by adding modules while others "top-out" at six or eight ports and have to be cascaded or replaced. All systems have a maximum total aggregate bandwidth and, therefore, when called on to connect a large number of sites, may limit their transmission speeds. There is usually a perceptible end-to-end transmission delay in extensively cascaded conferences (three or more bridges).

There is usually a limit to the number of MCUs that can be cascaded. Cascading almost always consumes a port on the MCU (used to make the daisy-chain connection to other devices). In situations where a single organization will have many MCUs it is important to buy products that can be remotely managed.

MCUs generally support all common types of interfaces for public and private networks including T-1, F-T1, ISDN BRI or PRI, Switched 56 or private net connections. Most allow dial-in (meet-me), dial-out or dedicated-access connections in any combination. Most also allow connection arrangements to be mixed in a hybrid conference. Today's MCUs provide conference tones provided to signal conferee's entrance to, and exit from, a conference. They also permit conferees using a regular telephone to participate in the conference on a voice-only basis.

MCU management is another area where large differences still exist between products. Most are managed in a Windows environment but some are much easier to use, have richer diagnostics and offer many more administrative features. Administrative features include scheduling utilities. Some systems allow a conference to be scheduled in advance. Even more valuable is the ability for an MCU to automatically configure itself at a pre-determined time and, based on that configuration, to dial out to the sites involved in the conference. Also look for event logs and the ability to account for and bill back usage.

EVALUATION CRITERIA

Service and Support

Videoconferencing is, by nature, a dispersed application. It is critical that buyers make arrangements for comprehensive national and/or global product support. Support includes design, sales, installation, training and ongoing maintenance. Look for support that is "turnkey"; where the supplier also works with carriers to deliver an operational product. Also seek out national or global purchasing plans where volume discounts apply to purchases made anywhere within the organization.

Structured Procurement

One way to procure equipment is to divide the evaluation process into two categories: objective and subjective. Objective evaluations are usually performed as part of a structured procurement process. A Request for Proposal (RFP) or Request for Quote (RFQ) is issued to qualified suppliers. It describes exactly the features and capabilities that competing systems should include. When a customer does not know what they need, this becomes the second step of the process, where the first step begins with a Request for Information (RFI). An RFI lays out the application and asks suppliers for their solutions. Once the responses come back, the good ideas are combined into a more formal procurement document. For a summary of RFP questions, please refer to Appendix E.

Videoconferencing systems continue to inch toward commodity status, but they are not yet there. There are still differences in packaging and features, and especially between product categories. Most systems are similar within product categories but when comparisons are made cross-category big differences will exist. Small-group roll-abouts should be compared to each other, not to more fully-featured models—unless, of course, comparisons are being made within a manufacturer's product line.

Equipment Demonstrations and Trade Shows

A fast way to compare all codecs at the same time and in an identical environment is to visit an IXC's demonstration facility. Some have worked cooperatively with major codec manufacturers and/or distributors to set-up a videoconferencing system exhibit area. This is a useful way to investigate systems in quick succession. Of course, the carrier will promote its network services during the presentation;

performing such a valuable service for prospective codec buyers grants them such license. Listen to what they have to say, then reach a network decision with the same level of precision you have used to select the video equipment.

Trade shows provide good opportunities to view videoconferencing systems in a similar environment. The Telecon conference, organized by Applied Business teleCommunications of San Ramon, California is one of the oldest and most comprehensive of the videoconferencing-oriented trade shows. It is offered once a year in early winter and has, in the past, been located at the San Jose Convention Center. The International TeleConferencing Association (ITCA) in northern Virginia also hosts an annual conference (generally in May) in Washington DC. To obtain information on these shows please refer to Appendix H of this book.

CHAPTER 12 REFERENCES

"Corporate buyer demand for group videoconferencing systems is rising, while sales of desktop systems have yet to take off." Purchasing, Oct 21, 1999 v127 i6

"Videoconferencing: New Study Predicts over 40 Percent Growth for New Product Segment in Videoconferencing Industry." EDGE, March 1, 1999.

"Will IP Bring Videoconferencing into the Mainstream?" Newswire, July 19, 1999 p3797

"IDC predicts bright future for videoconferencing." Computing Canada, Oct 29, 1999 v25 i41 p7

"Lucent Technologies to offer industry-leading videoconferencing features; introduces release 4.0 of MultiPoint Conferencing Unit," Edge, on & about AT&T May 20, 1996 v11 p. 14.

Brown, Dave. "Bytes, Camera, Action!" Network Computing March 1, 1996 v7 n3 p. 46-59.

Frankel, Elana. "A Guide to Videoconferencing," Teleconnect September 1996 v14 n9 p. 66-82.

Judge, Paul C., Reinhardt, Andy. "PictureTel fights to stay in the picture," Business Week October 28, 1996 n3499 pp. 168-170.

Labriola, Don. "The next best thing," PC Magazine December 5, 1995 v14 n21 pp. NE1-9.

Lavilla, Stacy. "Video wares push multiconferencing," PC Week October 28, 1996 v13 n43 p. 125.

Leonhard, Woody. "Say it face-to-face," PC/Computing November 1996 V9 n11 pp. 340-345.

Miller, Brian L. "Videoconferencing," LAN Times November 11, 1996 v13 n25.

Molta, Dave. "Videoconferencing: the better to see you with," Network Computing March 15, 1996 v7 n4 pp. 11-17.

13

IMPLEMENTING GROUP-ORIENTED SYSTEMS

"What we anticipate seldom occurs; what we least expected generally happens."

Benjamin Disraeli

One should approach and manage the installation of a group-oriented videoconferencing system as a project. A good approach starts with setting an installation date and working backwards to determine the project timeline. One then expands the project plan through the inclusion of tasks (and their owners), dates by which these tasks will be accomplished, major milestones, and critical success factors. There are many different project management tools and methodologies. Project managers tend to use those endorsed by their particular organization; therefore we will not describe them here.

In this chapter, we assume that the project's goal is to develop a conventional group-oriented videoconferencing facility that is suitable for routine organizational use. We do not address special applications (e.g., telemedicine and distance learning) because they are unusual and, therefore, include considerations about which one can not generalize. Similarly, we do not address unique facilities—videoconferencing-equipped command centers (sometimes called "war rooms" that are used to manage crises such as natural disasters), mobile studios, and BTV broadcasting arrangements. For highly-specialized applications, it is best to hire a consultant or videoconferencing systems integrator.

Boardroom facilities are generally custom-engineered installations. Again, we recommend that customers secure the services of an engineering firm, consultant, or integrator. For a partial list, please refer to the Directory of Videoconferencing and Interactive Multimedia Suppliers included in Appendix H of this book. Customers can also work directly through suppliers; in some cases (particularly large installations) the supplier will manage the entire project.

As stated in Chapter 12, there are two types of group-oriented videoconferencing systems: those that are mobile, and those that are stationary installations. We make these distinctions independent of the fact that a one may equip a group-oriented system cabinet with wheels. High-end rollabouts are generally not moved from their original installation location; they are moved only in rare cases. They are heavy, and few come with wheels large enough to offer ample stability. Varying lighting and acoustical conditions result in inconsistent audio and video quality. When such systems are moved, peripherals such as VCRs, document and auxiliary cameras, and PC scan converters must be moved with them.

Low-end cart-based and set-top systems were designed to be more mobile. Moving them still entails risk; they contain delicate electronics, and jiggling often unseats boards and deteriorates wired connections. Nevertheless, some systems will be moved. If they are, it is important to develop a scheduling system that tracks not only conference rooms, but also equipment. Many such packages are available, and home-grown applications can also be created.

We will conclude the introduction to this chapter by summarizing some tasks that one may encounter during the process of implementing group-oriented videoconferencing and multimedia systems. Appendix F includes a summary of these. One should begin a project with site selection and site preparation. Early in the project, network services should be ordered. Shortly before equipment installation, network services should be brought into the building, extended to the equipment location, tested, and accepted. The installation of equipment and peripherals comes next, and is generally performed by a supplier or a system integrator. Before the actual production phase of the project, plans should be established for internal promotion and training. The project manager must also develop scheduling and confirmation systems, and consider how operational costs will be allocated across the range of system users.

A haphazard implementation can (and probably will) negate all the hours spent meticulously selecting videoconferencing and interactive multimedia equipment and network services. Suppliers can assume much of the burden but some tasks fall to the customer. System promotion is most effective when an insider, someone who understands the inner workings of an organization, coordinates it. Senior management support is the key differentiation between long-term failure and success.

SITE SELECTION

The acceptance of videoconferencing and interactive multimedia requires users to make some behavioral changes. To foster that behavior, conference facilities should be convenient and accessible. In a large campus, the system should be located centrally or placed near people who are expected to use it the most. Avoid, at all costs, putting a fixed-location system in a room also used for non-video meetings. The equipment will, from time-to-time, sit idle in a high-demand space, while potential users suffice with substitute alternative communications tools.

Figure 13-1. Roll-about System (courtesy of Panasonic Video).

Executives play a lead role in developing the "culture of use" so professional systems integrators often recommend putting group-oriented videoconferencing and interactive multimedia systems in places where senior managers can easily access them. Finally, strategically positioned signs can elevate awareness and help first-time users locate a facility.

Plan for back-to-back meetings. If possible, the videoconferencing facility should offer a lobby or an adjacent anteroom, used as a next-group gathering area. Be sure to put at least one telephone in this area—several are recommended. Some facilities provide a smaller companion room for "off-line" discussions (particularly important when executives use the facility). If there is to be a room coordinator, his or her workspace should be convenient—right outside the door if possible. The coordinator will also require a scheduling terminal, so cabling should be extended to this site.

Finally, the videoconferencing facility should be close to (or equipped with) a facsimile machine and a copier. The conference center should also be situated so that food, beverages, and restrooms are within easy reach; some meetings last all day.

Brokered Resale of Excess Capacity

The public can also share some corporate conferencing facilities. Public room network brokers seek out sites with excess capacity and resell blocks of time, taking a brokerage fee and passing on the remainder of the revenues to the organization that owns the room. Organizations that contemplate resale should plan accordingly. Reception facilities, break areas, parking, and site security may have to be modified if the public is to be allowed onto corporate premises on a routine basis.

The decision to go public is a complicated one. Once an organization begins to resell its excess capacity it may encounter conflicts of interest between internal and external users. It is hard to "bump" a customer when a critical need for an internal meeting pops up unexpectedly. It is even harder to bump an internal user. Organizations should carefully consider the implications of resale. Speak to others who have made the same decision to gain insight into what situations might arise and how they can be addressed. Finally, if resale is going to account for a significant portion of room activity, the technical support and training burden will probably be increased. This may offset a major portion of the revenue derived from resale.

Interior Design

The goal is to make a conference situation comfortable for a broad range of users. Try to make the environment virtually indistinguishable from a conventional conference room. Unless applications will be exclusively executive, avoid posh settings that may discourage others from using the facility. De-emphasize technology (cameras, monitors, microphones and cables) to avoid a "studio" feel. In all cases, exposed cables should be concealed in conduit, ducts, or raceways where they can not cause accidents. Conference tables are often modified to accommodate cables for microphones and wired control units.

Wall colors should be muted; grays and blues work best (system integrators generally recommend a light gray-blue). Many television backdrops are blue, because blue shades make skin tones appear warm and natural. Avoid stark white, creamy yellows and dark colors. These colors confuse the white balance functions performed by a camera. The result is skin tones that appear unnatural.

Try to minimize contrast ratios by using wall, ceiling and floor treatments that do not greatly differ in reflectance. Maintain acceptable effulgence values by avoiding highly reflective (chrome, polished metals or glass) or very light-color surfaces that cause glare. Wall coverings, carpets and upholstery fabrics should be minimally patterned. Stay away from surface textures or decorative details that show up as distractions when viewed through a camera.

It is important to develop a schematic drawing of the conference room, and include all equipment and furniture on the plan. This helps to arrive at room dimensions that can comfortably support the maximum anticipated number of participants. Do not forget to place tables, chairs, lecterns and, of course, the videoconferencing equipment itself on the floor plan. To accommodate the eye, a distance between viewers and monitors of no less than four times the height of the picture should be maintained. Most videoconferencing installation guides recommend separating the monitor from viewers by a distance of seven times the picture height. Monitors should be at least 26 inches off the floor for most viewing situations. This schematic can also show the coverage a camera affords with its lens set at the widest angle of view.

When large groups are expected to use the system, room designs are much more complex. Complete video coverage requires that auxiliary cameras be interspersed around a large room to capture different views. Monitors may be placed in corners or alcoves, mounted high on walls, or suspended from ceilings. Multiple microphones can be added to pick up sounds in various parts of the room. Sometimes they, too, are suspended from the ceiling.

Videoconferencing seating arrangements vary widely. The size of the group is a critical factor in determining table placement and shape. There are V- and U-shaped designs, trapezoid arrangements, ovals and triangles. Trapezoids, four-sided figures with only two of the sides being parallel are popular for small groups. The widest end of the trapezoid is placed at the end facing the cameras. Participants sitting around the table can see each other and interact; all can see and be seen by the distant-end viewers.

V-shaped tables also work well but require a larger room. Participants can face each other while swiveling slightly to see the screen.

One very difficult arrangement is to seat conferees in tiered rows, one behind the other. Conferees will turn their backs to the camera to converse with each other, excluding the distant end from the conversation. No amount of training seems to overcome human nature.

If possible, one should select sites that will minimize demolition and reconstruction costs. Avoid rooms that are dark and cavernous. It is just as bad to opt for rooms filled with windows because they cause lighting problems and, perhaps worse, echoes.

ACOUSTICS AND AUDIO

Video captures the imagination and as such, tends to occupy the minds of people in videoconferences. Audio can slip by unnoticed but do not minimize its importance. With audio only, one can still communicate. When audio is removed or impaired, communication is lost. Past experiments demonstrate that, when audio is better on one of two identical videoconferencing systems, users perceive that picture quality is also superior. Many do not notice differences in audio because they are preoccupied with video.

Achieving good audio can be challenging. Start the process by choosing a quiet location. Strive for minimal ambient (surrounding) noise. Ideally, room noise should be less than 50 dBa (where dBa refers to *decibels, adjusted*). Interior locations are best (street noise is very hard to control). Avoid high-traffic areas: reception lobbies, cafeterias, bullpen environments, and heavily-used adjacent corridors. Soundproofing walls and/or double-glazing the windows can block ambient noise. This is worth the effort in the case of a boardroom installation but may not be in the case of rollabout or set-top systems. Acoustic treatment does not have to be expensive. It can include simple techniques such as carpeting the room, hanging panels and drapes over windows, and placing screens in front of sound-generating equipment.

Poorly-designed HVAC (heating, venting and air conditioning) systems cause ambient noise; installations should be equipped with proper-sized fans and be physically isolated. Older fluorescent lights, computer fans, and vibrating objects represent other potential noise sources.

The acoustical properties of the conference room, combined with the selection and placement of microphones and speakers, have a significant effect on audio quality. Ideally, a loudspeaker should deliver signal strength sufficient for good reception with the loudspeakers' output directed only to the listener's ears. In practice, the sound waves travel outward and are picked up by the listener's microphone. This is direct acoustic coupling. The result is echo that is retransmitted back to the speaker as his or her own voice.

To combat echoes, unidirectional microphones are often used in videoconferencing applications. They respond differently, depending on the angle of a sound's approach. If the sound comes from the front (relative to the unit's primary axis), the microphone picks it up loud and clear. If it comes from behind, the microphone attenuates it (that is, it reduces the amplitude of the signal), and reduces the reverberation transmitted. Unidirectional microphones are acceptable as long as conferees remember to stay within their capture range. An omnidirectional microphone (one that picks up sounds from all sides) is superior if the system provides good echo cancellation.

Echo cancellation addresses problems caused by indirect acoustic coupling (also known as multipath echo), in which a microphone picks up sound waves that bounce off objects. Walls, ceilings and, especially, windows are launching pads for echoes. Indirect acoustic coupling cannot be controlled with a unidirectional microphone. Early methods of dealing with acoustic coupling relied on avoiding it altogether. Echo suppression, in which loudspeakers and microphones were attenuated on an alternating basis to prevent feedback, was the first real attempt to control indirect acoustic coupling. This caused words to be "clipped" as microphones switched back and forth. Interruptions, a natural part of any meeting, are not possible with echo suppression, which compromises the natural rhythm of speech.

Echo cancellation has largely replaced echo suppression. Speech is modeled to create a digitized replica of an echo. Using a digital signal processor (DSP) the synthesized echo of the signal is subtracted from the return echo. Modern echo cancellation systems are amazingly effective. With sophisticated echo cancellation systems, unidirectional microphones are no longer required. Continuous speech can be provided in both directions. Interruptions and side conversations (rude as they might be) are captured and transmitted. Audio is automatically adjusted to keep it from being too bright (too much residual echo) or too dead (no natural echo). Echo cancellation methods (because they are so processing-intensive) may introduce slight delays to interactive speech.

We advise that customers work closely with a supplier or multimedia systems integrator to develop a strategy for providing high-quality audio in a videoconferencing facility. Experiment with microphone types, quantities, and placements. One should be particularly careful if the conference room is large or if multiple microphones will be used. Background noise and reverberation (the reflection of sound waves) are cumulative if all microphones are "open" at once. One solution (although slightly cumbersome) is to use speak-listen control systems (sometimes called push-to-talk microphones). These do not allow interruption (resulting in a condition called *capture*). They do, however, provide good volume and are great in large, noisy rooms populated by big groups.

Systems are available that use automatic mixing techniques (for instance, noise adaptive threshold) to manage microphones. Speech detection circuitry provides a way to turn microphones on and off automatically, and preclude the necessity for manual adjustment. Systems of this type give the floor to the loudest sound even if it is a sneeze or ice clinking in a water pitcher. Auto adaptive techniques vary. Some provide outstanding coverage and feedback rejection, while others deliver mediocre performance. One should arrange major installations as 30-day money-back-if-not-satisfied trials.

Some speakers like the lavaliere microphones that are worn on lapels or collars, or looped around the neck with an attached cord. The lavaliere can be wired or wireless. Both types uniformly capture a speaker's voice but wireless versions can be susceptible to radio frequency interference. If a lapel microphone is used, it is important to keep the speaker away from the loudspeakers to avert feedback problems. If a wireless microphone is used, it is important to remind speakers to remove it before leaving the facility. Many organizations start out with wireless microphones only to revert to wired varieties after replacement costs begin to mount.

As an organization develops the audio portion of its conferenced multimedia strategy, attention should be paid to auxiliary inputs for audiotape units, external audio bridges for multipoint audio and voice-activated cameras. Finally, the audio component of a videoconferencing system should be tuned to provide acceptable privacy and security.

LIGHTING

To render a natural scene, a videoconferencing facility must offer light of the right level, angle, and color temperature. There must be enough light to provide a "noise-free" picture with adequate depth of focus. It must come from the proper direction to avoid undesirable facial shadows. On the other hand, lighting must also enhance image depth and contours by intentionally creating desirable shadows and highlights.

Light intensity is measured in foot-candles. One foot-candle offers illumination equal to the amount of direct light thrown by one candle on a square foot of surface. Most modern video cameras will operate at light levels between 50 and 200 foot-candles. High light levels (125 foot-candles and above) support improved camera performance and depth of field, making it easier to focus. High light levels also reduce "noise" in the video signal (which appears as fine-grained static in the displayed image). The problem with high light levels is they produce heat. This makes the room harder to cool and could necessitate noisy HVAC equipment.

A minimum illumination level of 75 foot-candles must be maintained for acceptable results. While low-light environments (under 80 foot-candles) generate less heat, they also wash out colors and accentuate shadows. Light levels between 75 and 125 foot-candles provide a good balance of comfort and camera performance.

Light angle is another factor to consider. Most conference rooms have overhead fixtures that direct light down on the surface of the conference table. This causes undesirable facial shadows (dark eye sockets, shaded areas under chins and noses) and excessive highlights (especially bad with bald heads). Keep light sources in front of the participants and above the eyes. An angle of 45 degrees above the subject is low enough to avoid shadows. Multi-source lighting helps to maintain a constant level throughout the room (a light meter can be used to detect large differences). When installing lighting, be careful not to direct any lighting at the camera's lens.

When professionals discuss room lighting, they talk in terms of a light's temperature, which is measured in degrees Kelvin (K). The whiter the light, the higher the temperature; lower temperatures take on a reddish cast. If fluorescent fixtures are used, avoid the exclusive use of warm-yellow tubes; they make people appear jaundiced and may introduce 60 Hz flicker. Cool white or blue-white bulbs are more flattering when placed overhead. Some facilities combine bulbs of different temperature. If mixed properly, the result will be rich, pleasing colors (rendered by using cool low Kelvin temperature lights with a yellow or orange cast) and bright light (achieved with hotter, higher Kelvin blue or white bulbs).

Videoconferencing Inputs And Outputs

Video sources can be cameras, 35mm slides, VCR, PC-to-video and PC-to-PC. Video cameras are the most common type of system input. A room camera is generally included with a videoconferencing group system, but it limits placement options. Most have a limited field of view, and can only capture a portion of a conference room. Limitations in the size of an area covered are a function of the camera lens itself and the distance between the camera and the conference participants. *Zooming* allows a camera lens to be moved in and out to accommodate different group sizes.

Auxiliary cameras can be used when the maximum viewing angle (measured in degrees) of a system's camera limits room coverage. They can be wall- or tripod-mounted. If conferees will do much writing on whiteboards, consider training an auxiliary camera permanently on the presentation space. Electronic whiteboards may be another requirement. If one will be installed, be certain that there is an interface port on the videoconferencing system to support it.

Most videoconferencing implementations include a VCR. Some systems also provide an interface to a 35mm slide projector, too. The ability to integrate computer graphics and documents into presentations is an important requirement. In the past, document cameras were used to capture printed images, blueprints and charts. Today, nearly all systems provide an interface to an audiographics subsystem; many build the subsystem directly into the videoconferencing group system.

Nearly all room systems should be equipped with input ports for audiographics equipment—the PC-based data collaboration and graphics subsystems discussed in Chapter 8. Audiographics capabilities should conform to the ITU-T T.120 specification so that any end-point can share graphics files and documents. Document annotation capabilities are generally included. The project manager may be called upon to provide space and wiring for the electronic tablets and/or workstations that provide the annotation interface.

If a document camera is needed, consider its placement. Some are mounted in the ceiling to secure the field of view necessary for handling large documents. Some could be termed as graphics consoles. They provide *backlighting* to illuminate slides and transparencies. Additional features such as graphic image preview monitors or special control panels are convenient, but they add to a system's cost.

If applications are scientific, a facility plan should accommodate microscopes, high-resolution cameras and other scientific equipment. If the goal is to accomplish engineering work over distance, the room may need CAD interfaces, as well as the ability to convey, and possibly incorporate, mechanical and electrical drawings, materials lists, specifications, and proposal preparation systems.

In addition, a phone interface for audio-only meeting participants is nearly always required. Audio add-on is usually provided as a feature of a videoconferencing system and requires a RJ-11 jack connection to a PBX or outside line.

Videoconferencing monitors must be selected according to the application. The greater the number of participants, the larger the monitor should be. Twenty-inch monitors will support only about four conference participants. A larger monitor (27-inches, for instance), can support six to eight participants. Where eight or more participants will be involved in a meeting, a 35-inch monitor is preferable.

Figure 13-2. Scan Conversion (courtesy of PC Video Conversion).

Although most monitors are CRTs, training environments in which there are many viewers and the room is large often require projection systems (front or rear). In that case, a RGB projection system will have to be procured. Systems in this category can use rear- or front-projection. As we said earlier, it is important to enlist the support of a professional for non-standard implementations of this nature.

SCAN CONVERTERS

Television monitors "paint the screen" using a technique known as interlace scanning. Interlace scanning divides a frame of video into two fields; one made up of odd lines and the other made up of even lines. To convey the frame, the field containing even lines is transmitted first, followed by the field containing odd lines. Sixty such fields are sent in a single second, which conforms to the 60 Hz electrical system used in the U.S. and Japan. This approach eliminates flicker, the shimmering effect that occurs when frames are delivered at a rate too slow to leverage human "persistence of vision."

PCs and workstations use video graphics adapter (VGA) and Super-VGA (SVGA) formatted signals—better known as progressive scanning. Computer monitors do not interlace a signal to deal with flicker. Their inherent frame rate runs at 60 fps and above—fast enough to fool the human eye. This difference in scan rate creates an incompatibility between computer and TV monitors.

Computers and television systems differ in resolution, too. As we said earlier in the book, resolution describes the number of horizontal and vertical pixels a monitor can display. The most commonly used formats in computing are 640-by-480 pixels

(VGA) or 1,024-by-768 pixels (SVGA). SVGA can be extended to accommodate larger (17-inch) monitors, in which case it uses 1,280-by-1,024 pixels (1.3 million pixels per screen).

In television systems, resolutions are either 525 vertical lines (NTSC) or 625 lines (PAL and SECAM). A viewer does not see all the 525 NTSC scan lines on a television monitor. Forty-two of them are "blanked" during vertical retrace leaving 483 visible lines. The horizontal resolution of an NTSC video image depends on the quality of the signal and monitor and generally ranges from about 300 to 450 dots per horizontal scan line. This brief explanation should serve to point out that the image quality of a picture displayed computer monitor will always be better than that displayed on a television monitor.

To display a computer-generated image on a television monitor, a scan converter is required. Scan converters are available from many sources (consult the Directory in Appendix H for a partial list). Scan converters also convert from composite to component video. With composite video, color is encoded using YIQ where the Y component describes luminance (a weighted average of the red, green and blue primaries of the image) and the I and Q components provide chrominance (color) information. VGA and SVGA monitors use a color encoding method called YUV in which luminance (Y) is stored separately from the chrominance (U and V).

CONNECTING TO THE NETWORK

Videoconferencing facilities should be located as close as possible to the network interface (demarc). This is important for several reasons: it keeps cabling costs to a minimum, makes troubleshooting more convenient, and eliminates the need for line drivers that are required to regenerate a digital signal when it needs to travel over extended distances. Plan and allow for power to avoid circuit overloads and minimize problems caused by *dirty power*. Make sure plugs and circuit locations are convenient.

Most videoconferencing group systems connect to a private or public circuit-switched digital network. If, instead, the system will connect to satellite service the project manager will need to work closely with a supplier or room integrator. Such installations are potentially very complex and are outside the scope of this book.

The type of circuit that will support the video application determines how a videoconferencing system connects to the network. Physical interfaces include EIA RS-449/422 and its associated dialing standard RS-366-A, the ITU-T V.35 (also able to support RS-366-A dialing), and X.21 interfaces. Interfaces also include RJ-11 or RJ-45 (ISDN) and DS-1 (T-1).

The most common transmission choice in America is switched 56, because ISDN deployment is not universally available. Switched 56 terminates in a CSU/DSU and interfaces to the network using V.35 or RS449/422 connection. V.35 is the most widely used physical interface, and is also used on the customer side of the network interface to take the signal from the demarc to the videoconferencing equipment.

EIA RS-449/422 is not widely used. This standard describes the functional and mechanical characteristics of an interface. It uses a 37-pin connector with an additional 9-pin extender. RS-449/422 allows for longer digital connection between the equipment and the network interface, or DTE (data terminal equipment), and DCE (data communications equipment) than most other interfaces. It will support transmission speeds up to 2.048 Mbps. Like V.35, RS-44/422 requires a CSU/DSU and cable connection to the network.

The ITU-T X.21 interface, which is used primarily in Europe, operates at bit rates between 56 through 384 Kbps and controls network dialing. One valuable feature of X.21 is its inherent dialing functions, which include the provision for reporting why a call did not complete. X.21 can be used to connect to both switched and dedicated networks.

ISDN BRI, the most complex network interface to arrange, requires an NT-1 interface. An RJ-11 plug from the network plugs into the NT-1. On the other side, connection to the equipment is made via an RJ-45 plug. The specific type NT-1 required depends upon which CO manufacturer's switch provides the connection. Several companies make an NT-1 that can interface to either Nortel's DMS-100 or AT&T's 5ESS. It is best to require the supplier to provide the NT-1 and take end-to-end responsibility for rendering the LEC interface operational. Provide the supplier with the LEC contact's telephone number and rely on them to resolve all issues related to ISDN connections.

Before moving forward with the purchase of ISDN-oriented interfaces, one should be certain that the LEC supports ISDN. Be certain to allow a month or so to get the ISDN service installed. Some LECs are notoriously slow. Some companies opt to use ISDN PRI, which is generally obtained from an IXC (see Chapter 11 for details). ISDN PRI terminates in an NT-2 interface, a PBX, or a specially-equipped network access device. Customers who buy PRI from an IXC in the U.S. can often use H0 and H11 bandwidth-on-demand service. This is true in some European countries as well—overseas high-speed dial up is offered as H0 and H12 and is obtained from a PTT.

Some organizations use PBX stations to provide network support for videoconferencing systems. Generally, ISDN BRI stations are used. On the "trunk" side of the PBX, connections are made to carriers or other corporate sites using T-1, fractional T-1, or ISDN PRI channels. Channels not used for video will probably carry inbound and outbound voice traffic. Putting videoconferencing behind a PBX allows an organization to move the system between conference rooms (equipped with the proper station jacks), as desired.

Finally, a videoconferencing codec may interface to the network via T-1 or fractional T-1. Connections of this type are made through a T-1 multiplexer (T-1

MUX) or inverse multiplexer (I-MUX). Multiplexers connect to a codec using either a V.35 or RS-449/422 interface (again, V.35 is most common). Carriers bring T-1 service into the building demarc, where it is connected to a CSU. As we said in another chapter, the CSU is used for signal shaping and equalization, longitudinal balance, voltage isolation, and loopback testing. More than one installation has been halted because a customer forgot to order the CSU (and all the required cables) prior to starting the job.

PROMOTING THE USE OF VIDEOCONFERENCING

At the same time that a videoconferencing system is being installed, plans should be in progress for getting people to use it. This task should be approached almost as if it were a "campaign." Many companies put up signs and banners announcing the arrival of videoconferencing. It is helpful to get on the agenda at executive staff meetings. Presentations, in all cases, should be applications-oriented (and not technical). At user presentations it is helpful to hand out small wallet cards with videoconferencing scheduling numbers and troubleshooting instructions and resources.

During the presentation, be sure to tell potential users how to find the corporate intranet Web page that describes how to arrange a videoconference. That site (or its paper-based equivalent) should cover the following subjects:

- A videoconferencing fact sheet that describes where systems are located and the equipment installed in each room. This sheet can also cover services (room coordinator available to operate the system) and equipment (VCR, document camera, electronic whiteboard) offered in support of the meeting. It is helpful to provide information about public rooms that are conveniently situated near corporate locations where videoconferencing equipment is not installed so that people get in the habit of thinking about videoconferencing before they consider traveling to a meeting.

- A map that can be used to find the videoconferencing room (appropriate in a campus environment, for instance).

- A simple set of instructions that lists whom to call to set up a reservation, and the lead-times required for simple and more complicated types of conferences (for instance, use of a public room or conversion service might require additional time to schedule).

- A brief overview of videoconferencing etiquette and tips for success. This should cover things like being on time and adhering to a schedule. It should include "protocol tips" for participants (speak naturally, look at the monitor, expect a slight audio/video delay, avoid coughing into the microphone, drumming fingers on the table or carrying on side conversations). It is helpful to include tips regarding what to wear (especially important if the system runs at low bandwidths where wild plaids and complicated patterns cause trouble for the system). Finally, the *tips sheet* should address meeting materials (how to prepare graphics including font sizes, landscape formatting and centering the text to leave ample white space around the edges). Provide a sample of a graphic to help people prepare visual aids.

❖ A brief clearly stated guide for multipoint conferencing etiquette. Developing a multipoint etiquette guide is very important, and all conferees should be briefed in advance of a multipoint about how they differ from point-to-point sessions. This etiquette guide might suggest keeping the microphone muted in voice-activated situations until the location has something to say. It might also explain how a director should control the camera in a chairperson-controlled multipoint, differences in features or functionality between point-to-point and multipoint systems, and how they affect conference participants. It might also detail how to dial into a bridge, and what to do if a site becomes disconnected during a multipoint conference.

❖ If a videoconferencing system provides perceptibly lower quality at lower bandwidths (most do), include a brief explanation of why multipoint conferences tend to offer lower quality images and sound. The decline in quality is related to a reduction in bandwidth—some is used for "overhead" so that multiple systems can coordinate their exchange.

Before developing a multipoint etiquette guide, sit through a few multipoint sessions. This helps the developer to pick up valuable tips.

❖ A sheet covering the cost of typical videoconferences. Some identify the cost for point-to-point, multipoint and public room conferences between corporate locations. This is a useful selling tool because many people are amazed when they find that a videoconference running at 112 Kbps costs between $16 and $25 per hour within the United States. Even costs for European and Asian calls seem inexpensive when compared to travel.

❖ A guide outlining questions to ask when attempting to arrange an inter-company videoconference. This document should provide a technical contact's name and number so that a scheduler from another company can call to arrange a test call. It should state the brand and type of codec (including the software revision) installed in each room. It should identify which ITU-T protocols are supported (H.320, H.323, H.324, G.728, etc.). The long distance carrier that provides transmission services should be identified. If switched digital access (ISDN BRI or switched 56) is used, mention this. Switched access supports any-to-any connections; dedicated access does not. State network speeds supported for each location and whether or not an I-MUX is available. If an I-MUX is used, describe the BOnDInG modes that are supported. If the organization is a member of a public room network or reservation service, provide information relative to this as well. This guide should not be handed out to first time users, but would be valuable for technical facilitators on both ends.

In disseminating information in meetings and on Web pages, there are several other ways an organization can promote this medium. One company temporarily installed its new videoconferencing equipment in cafeterias and lunchrooms at various sites. Employees could wander up to the system and speak to whoever was on the other end. This offered an excellent way to meet coworkers casually and stimulated a great deal of interest in the technology. After a week of this arrangement, the company moved the equipment to its permanent home. Several months after the implementation, the utilization rate of the equipment had reached 50 %.

Web pages and newsletters that publicize video success stories are also helpful. There are many samples on the Web. Finally, to stimulating videoconferencing use, the corporation may want to subsidize the cost of using the system for six months to a year. Once the system is fully integrated into a company's culture, charge-back may be acceptable. Hurrying to make everyone pay their fair share may result in reduced system use overall and a lower return on investment, company-wide.

THE SYSTEM ADMINISTRATOR, SITE COORDINATOR AND TECHNICIAN

Videoconferencing system users will expect a certain level of support at every videoconferencing site within an enterprise. Providing that support typically requires a coordinated team effort. Videoconferencing system administrators usually are the focal point for videoconferencing customer service activities. They, in turn, direct the activities of videoconferencing site coordinator assigned to each location.

The videoconferencing system administrator's role varies from organization to organization. Some are responsible for all aspects of event coordination, including logistics, meal planning, scheduling participants, preparing handouts, and hosting the event. In other companies, the videoconferencing system administrator provides scheduling support only. In most cases, system administrators schedule equipment. They also schedule services such as the use of public rooms, carrier gateway and conversion services, and equipment rental for special applications.

At larger corporate facilities (headquarters and regional locations, for instance), there is generally a dedicated videoconferencing system administrator. This individual trains system users, provides assistance in operating the equipment, schedules the rooms, coordinates with suppliers of equipment and network services, and manages all other videoconferencing-related activities at the site. A videoconferencing coordinator is often assigned to assist videoconferencing users at smaller sites (field or satellite locations) where a full-time person is not necessary. Some companies do not take this approach; rather, they rely on participants to handle most of the technical operations. Training and support are provided over the videoconferencing system. If an organization adopts this approach ease of use becomes even more important. Independent access to technical help must also be provided (e.g., a separate voice line used to request assistance in case of a videoconferencing system malfunction, and a serial line used by a technician for "modeming in" to remotely look at the system). It is also important to install back-up systems in videoconferencing rooms; for instance, high-quality speakerphones will support audio conferencing in case the video component fails.

Most experts agree that a single individual at each site should assume responsibility for the videoconferencing system installed there. That person does not have to be technical but does need to know the basics of system operation and troubleshooting. In locations where technical expertise is not strong, it is critical to have well-trained personnel ("key operator") and complete, accurate and easy-to-use system documentation. Documentation should indicate what type of equipment is installed, the software revision, initial equipment settings, how to interpret on-screen error messages, whom to call for technical support. It should also address how peripherals operate (document cameras, fax machines, VCRs, etc.). Finally, it should include a checklist covering the most commonly experienced problems and how to resolve them.

Technical support of videoconferencing is often more complex than suppliers lead their customers to believe. Vendors may not intentionally minimize the support burden associated with videoconferencing but, somehow, it usually seems to take on a life of its own after it is installed. Only set-top systems were designed to deliver true "plug-and-play" operation (although newer rollabouts have this level of simplicity as their goal). As additional components are added (inverse multiplexers, document cameras, VCRs, VGA-to-NTSC scan converters and the like) the support encumbrance increases. Technical support usually becomes an issue after the first important conference fails due to technical difficulties.

Technicians are generally responsible for the following: site set-up, troubleshooting and diagnostics, ongoing maintenance and upgrades, technical user training, and system fine-tuning. If technicians are local, they usually perform these tasks themselves. It they are remote, they may travel to the site to perform installation and training but, afterward, are usually able to assist a moderately knowledgeable site.

Job Duties	System Administrator	Technician	Field Site Coordinator
Developing & Presenting the Business Case	X		
Managing trials and demonstrations	X		
Project Management	X		
Installation Coordination	X	X	
Network Installation	X	X	
Scheduling Equipment	X		X
Scheduling Public Rooms	X		
Coordinating inter-company conferences	X		
Usage Tracking and Management Reporting	X		X
Applications Development	X		X
Training - Operational	X	X	X
Assisting with preparation of graphical materials	X		X
Confirming reservations	X		X
Setting Up Multipoints	X	X	X
Operating Equipment	X		X
Moving Rollabout or Set-Top systems		X	
Cost Allocation Tasks	X		
Supplier Management	X	X	X
Trouble Shooting	X	X	X
Etiquette Training	X		X
Procurements (Upgrades)	X	X	
Publishing Newsletters	X		
Promotional - Other	X		X
Track Maintenance Contr.	X	X	
De-installs and re-installs	X	X	
Developing migration path toward desktop apps.	X		
Developing business case for upgrades & expansion	X		
Supporting special applications	X	X	X

Figure 13-3. Position Responsibilities Of Videoconferencing Support Personnel.

It is useful for a technician to be familiar with voice communications and network operations. Usually technicians receive formal training from vendors, but a circuit-switched background is helpful. As videoconferencing migrates to the desktop, the skills required will broaden considerably. With these systems a more in-depth understanding of LAN technology becomes important.

The best time to develop a troubleshooting and system operation guide is immediately after providing system training—while details are fresh in the technician's mind. This guide should provide a list of steps that anyone can follow when troubleshooting a problem. The list might be organized as a problem/cause document. For example, 'can see but cannot hear participants' would be the problem and 'microphone not plugged in' might be the cause. It could also start out with a "top ten things to check" list suggesting steps to take that *usually* bring an out-of-service system back into operation (power-cycle the equipment, check that the monitor is turned on, check that you have the right video source selected, and so on).

As videoconferencing migrates toward the desktop, technical support will become increasingly important. Desktop applications are harder to install and maintain (there are many of them in a corporation, and not all users are sophisticated or practice good "PC hygiene"). There are issues regarding compatibility between desktop systems and room systems (standards, networks and applications). Once users become familiar with video, technical challenges will abound from people's aspirations to do more and more with it.

SCHEDULING VIDEOCONFERENCING SYSTEMS AND SERVICES

Videoconferencing represents a large investment by most organizations' standards. Even with costs for videoconferencing systems continuing to decline, it is desirable to have the system's potential maximized through frequent use. For that reason, the process and support tools that go into scheduling the use of a videoconferencing system should receive serious consideration.

Someone needs to assume overall responsibility for system scheduling. As usage increases, this task becomes increasingly more complex. Rather than trying to deal with scheduling issues on an *ad hoc* basis, it is a good practice to establish policies and procedures before system implementation.

The first scheduling issue to address is exclusivity of the videoconferencing room. Earlier in the chapter, we recommended installing videoconferencing equipment in a room that is not scheduled for non-video meetings. This is not always possible; some organizations simply do not have the space to devote to exclusive use. If use is not exclusive, management must establish whether a videoconference can *bump* a scheduled meeting that is not a videoconference.

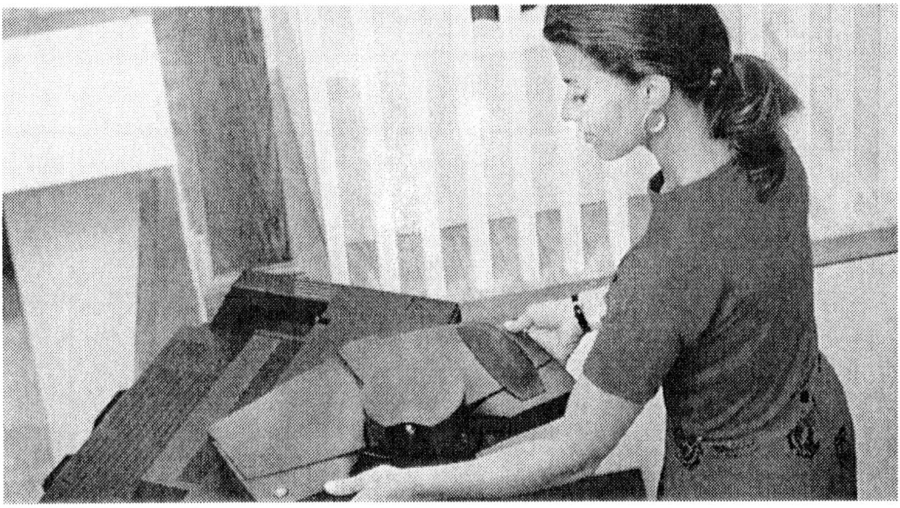

Figure 13-4. Installing a Videoconferencing System (courtesy of PictureTel).

Another issue to address is that of whom will have access to the system, and how usage will be prioritized. Installations with international sites often hold open hours when there is business-day overlap and reserve the remainder of the time for domestic connections when hours of business overlap to a greater degree. For instance, early morning room bookings might be reserved for European connections, and late afternoons held open for Asian conferences.

On the issue of access, some departments buy their own equipment and prioritize their own use over that of others. Some groups make excess capacity available to others at a price. In other cases, policy states that the system is to be used exclusively by the department that purchased it. Others can not use it even if it is sitting idle.

Other access issues center around whether excess corporate capacity can be "brokered" through a public room service. The decision to sell excess capacity introduces a host of priority-related issues. What if the room is scheduled for outside rental when an executive needs to conduct an urgent meeting? If the system is made available to outside groups, what is the cost, and how is the schedule arranged? Who is responsible for billing and collections?

What type of use is appropriate for the system? How does the "importance" of a meeting affect scheduling? Some companies allow important meetings to "bump" more routine meetings. This may or may not be a good idea. There is nothing wrong with asking a user who has previously scheduled a meeting if they would mind postponing their session; present them with the conflict and explain why the unscheduled user's need for a videoconference seems more urgent than their own. Nevertheless, most companies endow employees with the right to refuse the request.

It will discourage use if executives routinely "bump" scheduled meetings. Moreover, if they know they can get the room any time they want it, senior managers may be less likely to plan ahead.

Many organizations levy cancellation charges against users who decide, at the last minute, to call off a conference. These are generally charged to the cost center manager and frequently manifest as a one-half hour minimum "charge." It is advisable to forgo these charges if another group is successfully booked into the room.

Another issue has to do with multi-site scheduling conflicts. Some companies that have a number of rooms assign a coordinator to each local site. We suggest that the site coordinator work through a central system administrator to coordinate use of his/her own room. An alternative is to use a multi-user-scheduling package to manage multiple site reservations. Another issue that must be addressed is who schedules public rooms, codec conversion and IXC gateway services. This is typically done centrally but some companies delegate the responsibility on a site-by-site basis.

A great deal of consideration should be given to how conferences are scheduled in general. There are a number of companies that provide "service bureau" scheduling on behalf of their clients. A sampling of the companies that fall into this category are listed in Appendices H and I of this book.

Sprint offers an on-line tool that allows an organization to schedule not only its own sites but any other site also served by Sprint. Conferences can be arranged so that, at the appointed hour, all sites simply come up and are connected. Sprint has some unique accounting and cost allocation services as well and offers a wide range of management reports. AT&T and MCI WorldCom offer similar services.

If an organization chooses to *insource* scheduling there are a number of scheduling packages available that make the task easier. Nearly all are password protected with several levels of user privilege (view, schedule, and delete/change, for instance). All will schedule a conference based on a request for a specific date and time and, if that time is not available, will offer alternate times. All perform automatic conference scheduling. Nearly all can schedule repeat conferences for a given time across a range of dates (e.g., every second Tuesday from 8:00 - 9:00 between June 16 and September 23). Typically they show all available time slots for all sites for a full day, and many will "window" to allow a number of sites to be examined. All packages produce usage and cost-related management reports. Most will print out a list of conference participants and generate electronic messages that confirm participation.

Countless issues are involved in installing and supporting a videoconferencing system. One can best develop the comprehensive processes and policies that ensure success at the outset. The videoconferencing environment is involved, but not any more so than the realm of electronic messaging, telephony or computing.

The intricacies of inter-site communications have always existed, and will remain. An organization's best response to today's world is to put in place capable information technology tools that will allow it to do more with less, and do it faster. Videoconferencing is ideal for meeting, and transcending, the challenges of today's environment.

Chapter 13 References

Fritz, Jeffrey N. "From LAN to WAN with ISDN," Byte November 1996 v21 n11 p. 104NA3.

Hakes, Barbara T.; Sachs, Steven G.; Box, Cecelia; Cochenour, John. Compressed Video: Operations and Applications The Association for Educational Communications and Technology, a U.S. publication, 1993.

Noll, A. Michael. Television Technology: Fundamentals and Future Prospects Artech House Norwood, Massachusetts, 1988.

Portway, Patrick S. and Lane, Carla Ed.D. Technical Guide to Teleconferencing and Distance Learning. Applied Business teleCommunications, San Ramon, California. 1992.

Rossman, Michael and Brady, Kathleen. MediaConferencing Classroom Designs for Education, US West Communications, Business and Government Services, Portland, Oregon 1992.

14

Personal Conferencing

If we are always arriving and departing, it is also true that we are eternally anchored. One's destination is never a place but rather a new way of looking at things.
Henry Miller

The heretofore-separate worlds of computing and audio/visual communications are converging. One of the most powerful outcomes of this union is personal conferencing (also known as desktop conferencing). Personal conferencing applications center on a variety of distance-collaboration tools designed for use by an individual. They leverage components that are already part of the standard, multimedia desktop: a high-resolution monitor, a powerful microprocessor, speakers and perhaps, a microphone. They require software and (depending on the product) might include a camera, a video capture board, and a network adapter.

The personal conferencing usage model is, and will continue to be, somewhat different from group-oriented products. The culture and custom of boardroom videoconferencing emerged from a model that favored senior managers and executives. Although this is changing, it is still common for a group-system videoconference to be comprised primarily of senior executives. Moreover, it is common for executives who have an urgent need to use an important and limited resource to supersede a previously scheduled videoconference.

Personal conferences do not require a special room because they can be conducted from practically any networked PC. Moreover, since desktop tools operate within a singular domain, the range of applications is much broader. Individual contributors and members of a dispersed team are as likely to use personal conferencing as are senior managers, perhaps more so. It fits the needs of individual contributors: project managers, engineers, graphic artists, consultants and others who collaborate over distance. Some products offer features that allow one to establish a voice call first. After they establish the phone conversation, users can spontaneously agree to a videoconference. The option of impromptu usage (as opposed to the more prearranged model of the scheduled room system) is an important feature of personal conferencing.

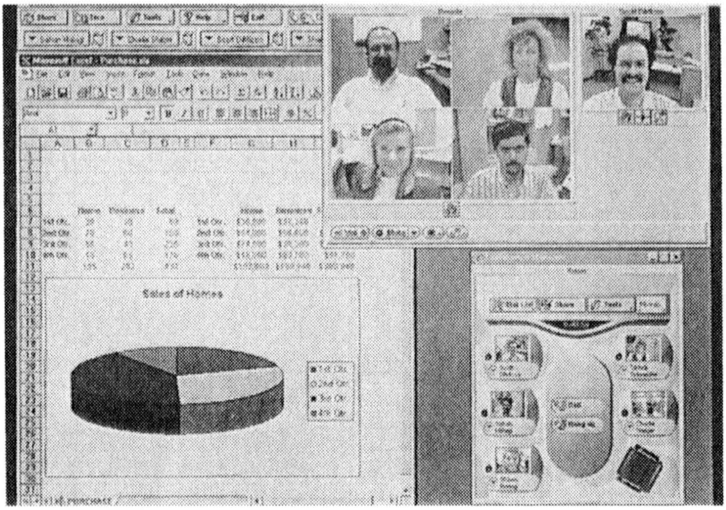

Figure 14-1. Board Sharing Screen Shot (courtesy of Intel).

Personal conferencing does have its more formal aspect. It comes as multipoint personal conferencing, an increasingly valuable tool for a distributed work group. Desktop staff-meetings, problem-solving discussions, and strategy planning sessions all get additional support from desktop conferencing.

Formal or informal, scheduled or impromptu, personal conferencing products come in many shapes and sizes. Most offer a toolbox of real-time collaborative utilities that enhance group work. Apart from that similarity, the variations in implementation are broad. Products can be software-only, software and hardware, bundled or build-your-own, business quality or consumer-focused, audiovisual or audiographics—a veritable cornucopia of options exist. When only software is added, most implementations do not support true "talking-head" interactive video. Instead these data-conferencing systems deliver capabilities that fall into five major categories:

- **Shared Whiteboard**
  Shared whiteboard tools are effective for geographically separated groups of individuals who need to brainstorm or collaborate. Products in this class work well for brainstorming sessions, project reviews, task force meetings, and product-design work. One might consider shared whiteboard tools if a group needs to collectively explore ideas, and to create a record of the proceedings. Most include an audio component although some require that participants set up a separate telephone call. Users rely on a mouse as a navigational tool. Typically, meeting participants can cut, copy and paste, highlight images, point to objects of interest, and type text-based messages. As changes are made, everyone can view the results. Products can be either object-oriented or pixel

oriented (object oriented products are preferable). Not all shared whiteboard products are oriented toward the desktop. For instance, LiveBoard, a meeting room-oriented whiteboard manufactured by LiveWorks, Incorporated (a Xerox Company), reside on a server, not on a desktop. It uses electronic markers and video feeds to create the illusion of a single site meeting across multiple sites. Electronic markers are much easier to draw with than a mouse.

- **Screen Sharing**
  Screen sharing products are presentation-oriented and, therefore, concentrate on manipulating "paper-like" text, graphic and still images. Systems in this call permit an "initiator" to launch an application for the benefit of a remote viewer or viewers. The initiator's machine is equipped with the conferencing software that allows the remote parties to view an application even though it is not running on their desktop. The role of the remote viewer is passive; they can not make changes to the application but they can provide verbal input over some type of audio connection. Screen sharing applications are applied in distance learning and remote presentations. They run very well over POTS networks although many products support screen sharing over the LAN.

- **Application Sharing/Document Collaboration**
  This class of personal conferencing product enables colleagues who are separated by distance to turn any off-the-shelf application into one that is shared. Activities including word processing, presentation development, and data entry into a spreadsheet can be performed on a collaborative basis. Typically, only one individual must have the application running on their machine. After launching the application, they can remotely transfer it to one or more team members (This ability is sometimes called jump- starting). At that point, all conferees can both see the shared document and make changes to it. Different products have different ways of characterizing who is making what changes. Some use a variety of colored fonts. Others append names or initials. And, a few products allow changes to be made only after the initiator "transfers" control. Application Sharing (apps sharing) differs from shared whiteboard. Document creation and refinement is the group's objective in apps sharing; brainstorming and idea capture is the focus of shared board applications. File transfer is also an applications sharing feature. Some products also offer chat tools that users can use to communicate common ideas, post comments to a conversation, or record meeting notes and action items as part of a collaborative process.

Figure 14-2. Document Conferencing Screen Shot (courtesy Intel).

- **Interactive Multimedia/Video Servers**
  Most interactive multimedia products support the need for just-in-time knowledge at the desktop. Some allow the recipient of the compressed audiovisual stream to interact with it (for instance, in a training application). Others deliver a one-way only stream of compressed digital video. Products in this class can take the form of audiovisual enhancements to Web-based applications. Interactive multimedia products typically compress the content MPEG-1 or MPEG-2 techniques. Stored material is transferred across a LAN or WAN in an on-demand environment. Interactive multimedia/video server products can be point-to-point or multipoint. They can be applied as integrated distance learning, performance support, and information management systems. Variations of this product class can be used in instructor-led situations; instructors often use these in course preparation and information presentation.

- **Multicast or Desktop Video Feeds**
  Products that fall in this category are almost always client/server based. They make it possible for individuals to use their PCs, workstations or network computers to receive "live material" as compressed digital broadcasts. Broadcasts can take the form of LAN-based retransmissions of television news programs. Products in this class include Intel's CNN at Work and Reuters Business Alert; there are others. Content can also be produced in-house; typical applications include dissemination of corporate information such as special announcements by the CEO, quarterly results updates, and new product updates. Some products allow viewers to send electronic messages to that presenters can retrieve and to which they can respond. Others are simply receive-only systems

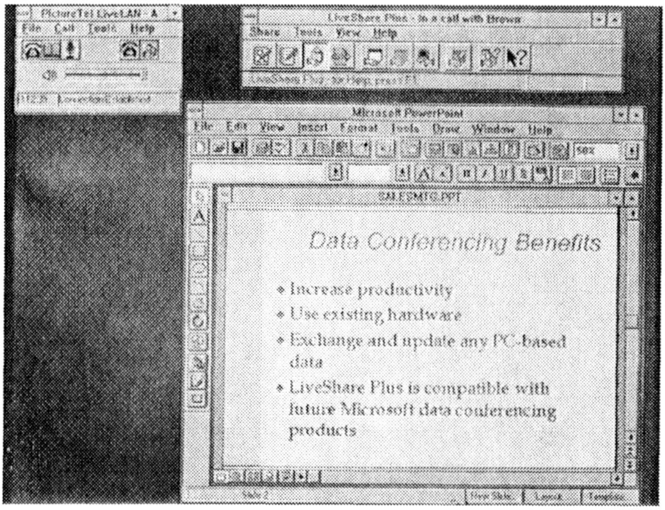

Figure 14-3. Document Collaboration Screen (courtesy of PictureTel).

that display motion video in a small window on their viewer's PC. Audio transmission relies on the soundboard in the user's machine; headsets are also an option.

Of the applications listed above, the one with the most collaborative value is application sharing. Almost anything one can do with a whiteboard or a screen-sharing product, one can do in an applications sharing environment. Presentation tools (e.g., Microsoft's PowerPoint) can function as a shared whiteboard; presentation software can also be placed in "slide show mode" to simulate screen sharing. Consumer-based personal conferencing products often include chat tools, too. Patterned after the Internet's relay chat spaces, chat utilities allow members of a group to post public messages. Chat can be used to communicate common ideas, post comments to a "threaded" conversation, or record meeting notes and action items as part of a collaborative process.

Desktop videoconferencing users often refer to the 80/20 rule to describe the value of adding a talking head to one's PC screen. Data sharing accounts for 80% of the information content; and the image of the participant on the other end accounts for the remainder. On the other hand, the video component of the application sucks up about 80% of the network's bandwidth. And equipping a desktop for talking-head videoconferencing can add another 80% to the cost of a data-conferencing product.

Figure 14-4. Video Phone Directory (courtesy of Corel Video).

That aside, if a camera, microphone and speakers are part of the microcomputer environment, a user can easily add the software and, possibly, the hardware necessary for desktop videoconferencing. Systems in this class display a remote meeting participant's head and shoulders. Generally, the image appears in a quadrant of the PC screen; other computer applications occupy the other 75% of the screen.

Face-to-face interactive videoconferencing applications fall into one of three categories: low-end videophones, desktop-to-desktop videoconferencing products, and desktop-to-room system arrangements. Products in the last two categories often overlap.

- **Videophones**
  Videophones are one of two things: special telephones that incorporate small video windows or software that runs on the PC. Almost all of today's products fall in the second category. Aimed at the consumer market, videophones use regular analog telephone lines for transmission and require a special type of high-speed modem to synchronize audio and video. Nearly all videophones conform to the ITU-T's H.324 standard, which makes them interoperable. Those that are not H.324-compliant should be viewed with skepticism. In nearly every case the greater the number of potential "end-points," the higher the value of a videophone. Therefore, proprietary solutions have limited value.

- **Desktop-to-Desktop Videoconferencing Systems**
  Desktop-to-desktop videoconferencing products are the personal conferencing equivalent of room-based systems. They may offer many of the same features such as picture-in-picture, speed dialing, and mute. Products in this class are

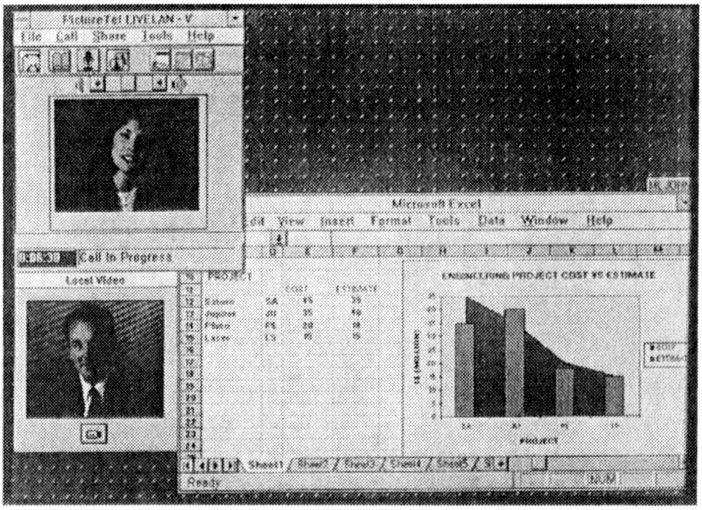

Figure 14-5. Application Sharing (courtesy of PictureTel).

either based on software-only codecs or incorporated additional hardware to assist in the compression process. Software-only compression designs warrant a "try it before you buy it" strategy to ensure that the quality of audio-video synchronization and the picture resolution and frame rate suit the applications. Moreover, one should never install software-only compression products on desktops with anything less than a 100 MHz processor. In business applications, it is best to adopt products that conform to one of the ITU-T's audiovisual standards (H.320, H.322 or H.323). H.320 systems use circuit-switched digital channels for transmission. H.323 systems use packet-switched LANs and WANs for signal transport. H.322 products use quality-assured LANs; in other words, a packet-switched 10Base-T Ethernet LAN that has been overlaid with 6 Mbps-worth of circuit-switched B channels (96 in all). There are very few H.322-compliant products on the market. Conversely, H.320 and H.323 products are abundant.

❖ **Desktop-to-Group System Videoconferencing Products**

When a desktop product is equipped with a H.320 compliant codec and has a network interface that allows it to establish circuit-switched videoconferencing connections, it can communicate with other H.320-enabled videoconferencing group systems. However, one should note that H.323-based products can also communicate with H.320 group-systems if they make the connection through a H.320-to-H.323 gateway or MCU. The applications for group-to-individual conferencing continue to expand. It is a good idea to trial desktop-to-group systems and to view the implementation from both ends, e.g., from the desktop and from the boardroom system. Remember, the quality of the picture and the

Figure 14-6. Desktop to Group Application (courtesy of CLI).

sound that a person perceives on one end largely reflects the capabilities of the system on the other end, where the compression takes place.

PERSONAL CONFERENCING MARKET DRIVERS

Several disparate technology trends have converged during the last few years, and thereby launched a renewed interest in personal conferencing. Currently the market is small (at least by computer industry standards). According to one market research firm, only about 30,000 desktop products shipped in 1995, during which time approximately 27 million minicomputers were sold. When compared to 1994 (the year Intel released ProShare) 1995 sales of personal conferencing products were relatively flat. But personal conferencing product sales appeared to increase by about 12% in 1996. Furthermore, many authorities expect 1997 to be the year when numerous favorable factors converge to produce double-digit (perhaps even triple-digit) growth.

The foundation for this growth is the PC-enhanced desktop. The sentiment today is that the PC is not an optional desktop appliance. One presumes it is existence in the corporate setting. The more current question centers on the desktop computer's processor speed and memory. The computing public seems always to be asking itself, " should I upgrade?"

Computers are more powerful when they are networked. Networking options of all types continue to abound but one rules supreme. Since the mid-1990s the Internet—and its graphical-oriented, hypertext-linked subset, the World Wide Web—has commanded our collective attention. Indeed, some market analysts called 1995 " the year of the Internet." Interest in the Net has not diminished. Magazines and newspapers of every type continue to publish pieces on the Web and the vast wealth of information it contains. Everyone seems to know the story of browser manufacturer Netscape's August 1995 initial public offering (IPO) and how, overnight, it turned its co-founders into multi-millionaires. And there is BBN's Internet division (BBN Planet), that grew 384% in the first three-quarters of 1996 before be acquired by GTE in 1997.

An interest in things technical is driving the acceptance of *new* computing applications. Personal conferencing, after repeated false starts and years of over-optimistic sales projections, is one that is nearly certain to take hold. Besides the huge installed base of networked microcomputers and Web-fever, other auspicious factors combine to ensure its success. These include:

- the abundance of multimedia-capable PCs and workstations
- applications suites that perpetuate demand through the addition of new utilities to each successive release
- GUI-tools and hypertext links that make applications easier to use
- the heightened sophistication of end-users
- the proliferation of fast LAN that can cope with latency-sensitive traffic
- advances in broadband WANs; increased implementation of SONET and ATM
- improved availability of digital local loop services (ISDN, ADSL)
- fast modems that make POTS lines more video capable
- a move by Congress to deregulate the telecommunications industry and thereby stimulate the construction of ubiquitous high-speed, end-to-end digital broadband services
- the increasingly dispersed enterprise and the acceptance of "tele-work"

The factors listed above have improved the acceptance of *many* desktop applications. Personal conferencing is no exception. But as we examine these factors from the perspective of personal conferencing, it is noteworthy how they contribute to its unique growth.

Workers today have the option of personal conferencing because of the microcomputer. Not only are PCs abundant (with a growth rate of 25% per year in 1994 and 1995 and 18% in 1996) but today's PCs are much easier to use. One of the most useful innovations in desktop computing was the introduction of the applications suite. Products such as Microsoft's Office 97, Lotus's SmartSuite 97, and Corel's OfficeJV 97 have a similar look and feel across applications. This sameness leads to an improved mastery of computing. Perhaps the greatest evidence of this collective expertise is the amazing growth of the Web. It took the GUI-based browser to make the Web accessible. Increasing numbers of erstwhile computer neophytes are now happily *webbing*.

Figure 14-7. Desktop Videoconferencing (courtesy of CLI).

As people become comfortable with computers, they get a better return on the time they invest learning to use them. In the past, the technical burden of personal computing was too great for the average user. Today mastering a new application is not difficult. GUI tools and browser-like interfaces make the process of setting up and managing desktop videoconferences much less daunting.

The next step is the fortification of the Internet. Designed in a time when traffic was character-oriented, the Net is buckling under the load of multimedia exchanges. In the early 1990s, Al Gore and other politicians began to plan for the Information Superhighway. Some describe the I-Way as the Internet on steroids. When completed, it will swiftly move the country's information-laden domestic product from place to place. Today it only partly does the job.

The I-Way will create new jobs, ensure economic superiority in the global marketplace, and improve the government's efficient delivery of public goods and services. Before it does, a significant obstacle must be overcome. The local loop—the twisted pair of copper wires that connects a subscriber to the telephone company—must be upgraded. It must quickly become broadband and digital. The process of enhancing the loop was plodding along until February 1996, when Congress passed the Telecommunications Deregulation Act. And, although it may not have been on the minds of the House and Senate members that voted to pass the Act, personal conferencing will greatly benefit from it.

The Deregulation Act will result in the construction of many new networks. In their rush to build, few new entrants will duplicate the phone companies' existing analog POTS arrangement. Instead, they will install high-bandwidth transmission service based on coax, fiber (and hybrid combinations of the two), wireless PCS and twisted pair-based digital subscriber line service. Completing this upgrade will take a decade or more but, by the year 2000, broadband local loop alternatives will be available to most urban areas. Increased bandwidth leads to better multimedia transmission. From the point of view of a networked desktop video user this translates to improved resolution, motion handling, audio quality, and audiovisual synchronization. Broadband transmission makes personal conferencing communications more realistic and natural.

Coincidental with the upgrade of the U.S. telecommunications infrastructure, a similar undertaking is in progress within organizations. The LAN is the corporate equivalent of the local loop. Although LANs are capable of moving data at millions of bits per second, they are limited because they are *shared* networks. Like the Internet, Ethernet was designed for character-oriented exchanges. Token ring LANs efficiently link office machines and machines on factory floors. Traffic trickles along these outdated LANs; today we must accommodate a multimedia flood.

One very popular trend is the construction of organizational intranets. These enterprise-wide, hypertext-linked, multimedia-enabled networks connect clients to server-based information caches. To achieve optimal performance, intranets require a new breed of LAN, one with abundant bandwidth. Many enterprises plan to install 100 Mbps service to the desktop within the next two years. LAN-based personal conferencing happens to be in the right place at the right time. This serendipity makes its future acceptance almost assured.

The 1990s will go down in history as the 'decade of the desktop.' It is no wonder that today's enterprises are becoming increasingly distributed. Why waste time traveling when one possesses the tools to work at a more convenient location than one's office? Although organizational dispersion is more practical than ever before, some aspects of it are complicated. Collaboration over distance requires fine-tuning and, therefore, requires special tools. Without them, achieving the synergy that can result from collective investigation and development of ideas is formidable. Personal conferencing, which conveys both audio and visual information, adds to the richness of human interaction. It does not exactly duplicate in-person interaction, but it is much better than a phone call. Yet, one can arrange a desktop conference as spontaneously as one places a phone call; accessibility of this type results in a dynamic and fluid teamwork environment.

Besides a generally favorable climate for all desktop applications, certain events boost the popularity of personal conferencing *specifically,* propelling its acceptance to new levels. These include:

- greater maturity of personal conferencing standards
- the trend toward building these standards in to operating systems and microcomputer motherboards
- advances in mathematics that result in more powerful compression algorithms
- software-only compression, which allows the dissemination of low-end

products
- greatly reduced cost of audiovisual peripherals (cameras, speakers, microphones)
- new IETF protocols and mechanisms designed for networked applications that require low-latency in an IP environment (RTP, RTCP, RSVP)
- joint marketing agreements and partnerships between videoconferencing suppliers as a group and between these suppliers and telecommunications carriers

The need for audiovisually-enhanced collaborative tools was anticipated with the invention of the Picturephone. Unfortunately, the installed base of Picturephones was so minute that none were useful. That could have been the situation faced by personal conferencing were it not for interoperability standards. The ability to casually call and be called, and to do this without distressing over compatibility limitations, will lead to the acceptance of desktop video products.

Harking back to Picturephone, its other great misfortune was that it needed a network that did not exist. Thirty years later, huge advances in video compression permit the use of much slower networks for signal transport. Chip manufacturers rush to set these new algorithms in silicon, to build them in to the PC operating system. And, the cost and availability of the other components that personal conferencing requires has plummeted. Today one can easily buy a consumer-oriented videophone for under $500, and a business-quality desktop videoconferencing system for under $1,000. Implementation choices abound.

Apart from a wide array of personal conferencing products, one can also have one's pick of transmission alternatives. Choose from circuit-switched ISDN and POTS, packet-switched LANs and WANs, and hybrid circuit/packet solutions such as isochronous Ethernet. Soon competitors will also offer ATM and wireless PCS options. And of course, there is the Internet and its enterprise-oriented relative, the intranet.

Personal Conferencing and the Internet

Streaming time-sensitive media (audio and video) over the Internet sends shivers, good and bad, down the spines of those most interested in such applications. On the plus side, IP-based streaming media tools hold tremendous promise. On the minus side, they present a colossal challenge because audiovisual communication, the most bandwidth-intensive of applications, is sure to take its toll on the Internet. Videoconferencing is challenging because there are many bits in a frame of video, because the delivery of this data must be smoothly paced, and because it involves multiple participants. In the worst-case scenario, everyone will want to interact with everyone else and, therefore, each participant will require a stream of synchronized audio and video. Not only will the additional traffic be hard on the Internet (or corporate intranet), traffic jams will also be hard on the users of IP-based videoconferencing.

The problem of streaming media over the Internet is being addressed. Protocols, both new and old, are adapting it to real-time traffic. In the category of " old" there is the User Data Protocol (UDP), which offers no guarantee of packet delivery and allows packets to be dropped when the network is busy. UDP may sound like a step backward when compared to the Transmission Control Protocol (TCP) which does guarantee delivery through the retransmission of dropped packets. However, there are two problems with TCP. First, it introduces overhead delay that interrupt the smooth flow of media streams during times of congestion. Second, TCP retransmits dropped packets. Retransmission works well in data communications, but it is detrimental in audiovisual exchanges. Streaming Media's pacing and sequence are quite sensitive. Moreover, an audience may hardly notice a dropped video frame.

There are also new protocols that have been developed to deal specifically with time-sensitive media streams. Three important ones are the Real-Time Transport Protocol (RTP), the Real-Time Transport Control Protocol (RTCP) and RSVP. The Internet Engineering Task Force (IETF) developed these protocols, specifically, the IETF's Audio Video Transport Working Group. The AVT group works to provide end-to-end network transport functions that are suitable for applications that transmit real-time data (streaming media) over multicast or unicast services.

In the IETF Request for Comments (RFC) 1889, the RTP described : RTP: A Transport Protocol for Real-Time Applications. It was developed to provide end-to-end network transport functions that are suitable for applications that transmit data with real-time properties, (e.g., audio and video) over multicast or unicast network services. Applications typically run RTP on top of UDP, although RTP can also be used with other underlying network or transport protocols.

The RTP, as a higher layer protocol, does not provide any mechanism to ensure that packets associated with a media stream arrive on time or in sequence: lower layer services take care of those tasks. However, the RTP does include a sequence number to allow the receiver to reconstruct packets in order. The sequence number can also be used to reconstruct a frame of video, for instance, an H.261 group of blocks (GOBs).

RTP is widely used on the MBONE (the Internet's multicast backbone) to transmit time-dependent media streams that take the form of "broadcasts." MBONE participants use class D (experimental use) Internet addresses that identify groups of hosts rather than individual machines. Now that the RTP is being used for videoconferencing, hosts are also identified through the use of regular (class A through C) IP addresses.

The User Location Service (ULS), developed in February 1996 by R. Williams of Microsoft Corporation, is a protocol for locating hosts and establishing real-time sessions between them. The ULS is a directory, a place in cyberspace where a client can publish connection information such as the transport address of an application or a person. The ULS enables communications between compatible applications by also allowing other clients to retrieve these addresses. The ULS also can be used to establish a connection.

The ULS is in no way part of the RTP—but the RTCP is. The RTCP, described along with the RTP in RFC 1889, is used to monitor the quality of service provided in a videoconference. It allows conference participants to convey quality information to the meeting's chair or other person responsible for the conference's usability. RTCP provides the option for a sender to receive feedback from the recipients of a multicast stream. The feedback provides insight into how successfully RTP packets are being delivered. This information can be used in several ways. Since all participants get the same information, a single site can determine whether problems in reception are unique to his site or are conference-wide. A sender can use the feedback from multiple recipients to make adjustments to the broadcast. That person can decide to scale back on video quality or to eliminate it entirely to reduce bandwidth requirements. Network administrators can use RTCP to see who is engaging in multicasts.

The RTP was adapted for use in videoconferences as RFC 1890: RTP Profile for Audio and Video Conferences with Minimal Control. RFC 1890 specifies a scheme to packetize the H.261 video stream for transport over a TCP/IP network. For instance, RTP packets identify the type of payload contained in the packet. And, depending on the type of information the packet contains, a timestamp may be included in the header. The header can also indicate encoding methods; i.e., whether formal or de facto standards (the ITU-T's G.728, or H.261, the ISO's MPEG, Sun's CellB) are being used to define the format of the media stream. The specification outlines the ports that are to be used for each payload encoding type and the port's clock rate. It also, on a per-port basis, defines whether the media stream consists of audio, video, or audio/video components and, when audio is present, how many channels are being used.

Another critical protocol for videoconferencing over the Internet is the Resource ReSerVation Protocol (RSVP). RSVP enables a user to reserve bandwidth at a specified time of day to provide a specified quality of service to a media stream called a *flow*. Routers that offer RSVP support can accommodate such requests and reserve capacity for audio and video streams at a given time, and thereby lessen the chances that unpredictable delays will cause bothersome degradation. Once all routers have granted the reservation, the stream can move over the TCP/IP network free from frame-freezes and audio break-up. The result is usable and natural voice and video, to the user's desktop.

In October 1996, T. Turletti and C. Huitema published RFC 2032, RTP payload format for H.261 video streams. In their publication, Turletti and Huitema defined a way for H.261 information to be carried as payload data within the RTP protocol. The RTP payload format described in RFC 2032 specifies a header that contains the start and end bits used to package image frames. It also includes information on whether the packet contains an image that has been exclusively intraframe encoded, and an indication of whether motion vectors are used in the bit stream. The header also includes bits used for decoding a group of blocks and its associated macroblocks, the value to be used during the quantization process, and horizontal and vertical motion vector data.

When writing about evolving Internet protocols it is very hard to stay current. The Internet standards track moves along and documents advance through it. An example of this is the Internet Draft that defines an *RTP Payload Format for H.263 Video Streams*. As is stated in the status section of the document, "It is inappropriate to use Internet-Drafts as reference material or to cite them other than as work-in-progress." The existence of the H.263 RTP payload format attests to the IETF's commitment to pursue techniques for adapting the Internet to videoconferencing. Since H.263 is the video coding method used by H.323, it will be particularly important to adapt it to the Internet and the Internet to it.

ADVANCING THE PERSONAL CONFERENCING INDUSTRY

The personal conferencing industry was made not born. Many large and influential companies decided that it was time for the multimedia industry to take off and did something about it. Key in this group are Intel and Microsoft, both of which have a stake in seeing successive generations of more powerful desktop applications. AT&T, MCI, Sprint, and the former Baby Bells all dream of the day when the average user will routinely present multi-megabit traffic to the network. In short, many different organizations are cooperating to provide the means for an interactive multimedia market. They are embracing existing standards. Led by the IMTC, they are engaging in operability tests. Driven by the requirement to simplify installations, they are bundling products into turnkey solutions.

The "one-stop shop" trend in personal conferencing might have started with Intel. The company had just introduced ProShare. Following that announcement came the news of an impressive partnership program that included five of the seven RBOCs, GTE, AT&T, and several other networking companies. Intel offered steep price reductions when ProShare customers bought their systems through these partners. The discounts were especially attractive when ProShare was bundled with multiple network offerings (LEC and IXC combinations). One key aspect of Intel's partnership was its creation of the "ISDN Blue" standard configuration. It allowed a LEC to deliver a standardized ISDN BRI service that was ideally configured for use with ProShare.

Another noteworthy event was the July 1996 announcement that Microsoft and Intel had reached accord in their effort to cross-license personal videoconferencing technology. Under the agreement, Intel provides its implementation of the H.323, RSVP, and RTP standards to Microsoft, and Microsoft, in turn, offers Intel its T.120 implementation, the ActiveX conferencing platform, and Microsoft's NetMeeting application. This will lead to a standard personal conferencing desktop endorsed by two industry giants.

Other partnerships and cooperative efforts include:

- 8x8, Incorporated and Amati Communications teamed to deliver television quality videoconferencing over ordinary telephone lines using Amati's ADSL technology and 8x8's DVC6 video codec
- Apple integrated Netscape Navigator's CoolTalk protocol into its QuickTime Conferencing technology and thereby allowed people to use a Navigator browser to audio conference and collaborate within and between Windows, UNIX, and Macintosh environments
- BBN Planet offered the world's first RSVP service in conjunction with Cisco Systems and content provider Worldwide Broadcasting Network, Incorporated
- Intel and MCI jointly developed technologies for delivering multimedia content over the Internet.
- Intel's ProShare Conferencing Video System 200 is supported by leading multipoint conferencing services including those available from AT&T, MCI, Sprint, Deutsche Telekom, France Telecom, PTT Telecom (Netherlands), and NTT PC Communications, Incorporated
- Lotus Real-Time Notes now includes Intel's ProShare Premier
- MCI WorldCom supports Microsoft's NetMeeting as part of its Media Manager conferencing service for business customers
- PictureTel and First Virtual are developing an ATM interface for PictureTel's desktop and group videoconferencing products
- Compaq and its competitors are adding Intel's Video Phone technology into the latest generation of Compaq desktop systems

The above information represents only a fraction of the companies who are actively partnering to pursue the personal conferencing market. This impressive list demonstrates that industry initiative is behind this market. But, as exciting as it might be, industry activity and technology events should never eclipse the all-important application. As always, the usage model should be the chief determinant of the type and brand of desktop conferencing system one selects. We provide tips for buying personal conferencing systems in the next chapter.

CHAPTER 14 REFERENCES

Braden, R., Zhang, L., Berson, S., Herzog, S., Jamin, S., "Resource ReSerVation Protocol (RSVP)—Version 1 Functional Specification," Internet Draft, November 1996.

Braden, R., Zhang, L., "Resource ReSerVation Protocol (RSVP)—Version 1 Message Processing Rules," Internet Draft, October 1996.

Czeck, Rita. "Desktop Videoconferencing: The Benefits and Disadvantages to Communication,"

DataBeam Corporation. "A Primer on the T.120 Series Standards," Published on the World Wide Web.

DataBeam Corporation. "T.120 Primer – Ratification of the T.120 and Future T.130 Standards," Published on the World Wide Web.

Dunlap, Charlotte. "Conferencing vendors seal alliances," Computer Reseller News June 3, 1996 n686 p. 72.

Edmonds, Roger. "Desktop Videoconferencing At The Open Access College,"

Earls, Alan R. "PCs bring people face to face," Computerworld April 29, 1996 v30 n18 p. 95.

"Videoconferencing: AT&T WorldWorx service adds support for new Intel product; AT&T delivers standards-based multipoint voice/video/data desktop videoconferencing service for ProShare Video System 200," EDGE, on & about AT&T May 6, 1996 v11 n407 p. 34.

"New video conferencing options from Microsoft, Compaq, Intel," Electronic News June 3, 1996 v42 n2119 p. 24.

Estrin, Judy; Casner, Stephen. "Multimedia Over IP," Data Communications on the Web August 1996.

Gill, B. "Presentation Tools Take Multimedia Center Stage," Gartner Group Multimedia Research Note--Markets November 25, 1996

Hamblen, Matt. "Desktop video surge forecast," Computerworld October 14, 1996 v30 n42 p. 85.

Johnson, Edward G. "Video Guidelines," Published on the World Wide Web.

McCall, Tom. "Desktop Videoconferencing Drives, Doesn't Run Over, Demand for Group Conferencing Systems Dataquest Study Indicates Strong Demand for Group and Rollabout Systems,"

"MCI, Microsoft Link For Internet Conferencing," Newsbytes May 29, 1996 pNEW05290051.

O'Brien, Jim. "New Interoperability Standards Anticipate Universal Internet Conferencing," Computer Shopper September 1996 v16 n9 p. 630.

Pappalardo, Denise. "BBN to test RSVP," Network World December 9, 1996 V13, n50, p. 1.

Rosen, Michele. PC sales defy predictions. MIDRANGE Systems June 14, 1996 v9 n9 p. 30.

Rupley, Sebastian, Levin, Carol. "Collaboration on call: videoconferencing takes a backseat to document sharing," PC Magazine September 10, 1996 v15 n15 p. 31.

Schroeder, Erica. "Fighting Problems of Interoperability; Groups Work on Conferencing Specs," PC Week February 5, 1996 v13 n5 p. 47.

Schulzrinne, H., et al. "RFC 1890: RTP Profile for Audio and Video Conferences with Minimal Control," January, 1996 Published on the World Wide Web.

Smith, Greg and Desmond, Michael. "What's Worse: Flying Coach or Setting Up An ISDN Videoconferencing System?" PC World November 1996 v14 n11 p. 630.

Sullivan, Kristina B. "Videoconferencing Arrives on the Internet," PC Week August 19, 1996 v13 n33 p. N10.

Taylor, Kieran and Tolly, Kevin. "Desktop Videoconferencing: Not Ready for Prime Time," Data Communications on the Web April 1995

Turletti, T, Huitema, C. RFC 2032 "RTP payload format for H.261 video streams," October 30, 1996 Published on the World Wide Web.

Waltz, Mitzi. "Netscape, Microsoft duel on conferencing," MacWeek October 28, 1996 p. 22.

Wayner, Peter. "New Videophones Starved for Bandwidth," BYTE May, 1996. Published on the World Wide Web.

Williams, R. "User Location Service," Microsoft Corporation. February, 1996. Published on the World Wide Web.

Zhang, L., Deering, S., Estrin, D., Shenker, S., and Zappala, D., "RSVP: A New Resource ReSerVation Protocol," IEEE Network September 1993.

Zhu, C. "RTP Payload for H.263 Video Stream," Internet Engineering Task Force; Audio-Video Transport Work Group. INTERNET-DRAFT. Published on the World Wide Web.

15

EVALUATING & BUYING A PERSONAL CONFERENCING SYSTEM

There is science and applications of science, bound together as the fruit of the tree which bears it.
Louis Pasteur

The successful application of personal conferencing technology starts with the question, "what are we trying to accomplish" and continues with the question, "what does success look (and sound) like?" Chapter 2 and the product categories in the previous chapter can be helpful in determining how one will use personal conferencing. Is the purpose to support communications between professionals and customers (e.g., graphic artists, architects, accountants, engineers)? If so, products should focus on the presentation of visual materials (screen sharing). If visual cues (facial expression and limited body language) will enhance the exchange, one might consider videoconferencing, particularly when the same parties work with each other on an ongoing basis. If the goal is to foster collaboration of group of people who are separated by distance, one should explore applications sharing/ document collaboration tools.

Most personal conferencing offerings are part of a product family. At the low end, the package may include whiteboard or screen sharing capabilities. The next step up might add a document collaboration utility. Moreover, by adding a camera, a microphone, speakers, and one or more PC boards, one might obtain videoconferencing functionality. Other enhancements might take the form of gateways that link LAN-video packages to circuit-switched digital systems or video servers for store-and-forward broadcast applications.

When developing an application, it is best to start with what is most necessary, then add features and capabilities as required. People will probably have to change their habits to use these tools. Consider phasing-in new skills.

Following is an example: if a service organization supports numerous customers, it may not be necessary to equip everybody with the hardware necessary for videoconferencing. However, the customers they support all have telephones. Most

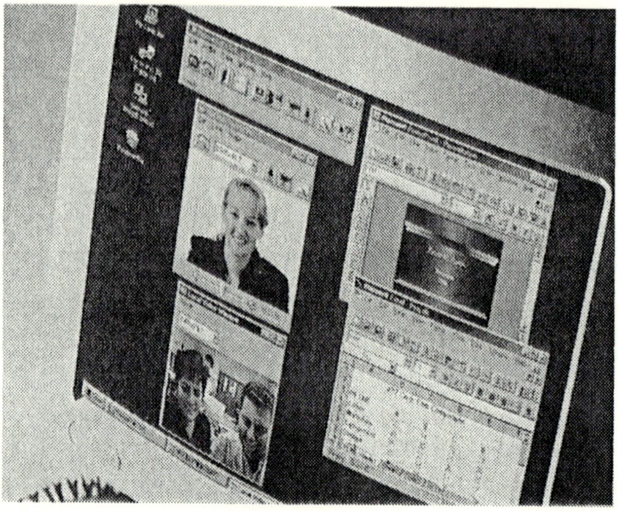

Figure 15-1. Application Sharing (courtesy of PictureTel).

probably have the high-speed (28.8 Kbps or faster) modems that shared screen applications require. After the workgroup masters the basics of document conferencing, they may find that certain individuals would benefit from more than passively viewing material. Should they decide to install collaboration tools, they can stay within the product family in which they made their initial investment.

For in-house applications in which there is a need to bolster the productivity of distributed workgroups, face-to-face communication becomes more practical. For one thing, one can standardize desktop configurations within a corporation or at the workgroup level. Distributed level. Distributed teams that use compatible videoconferencing tools can share a visual experience. Besides face-to-face conferencing, their cameras can capture blueprints or graphics or capture and exchange photos of objects.

The savvy decision-maker, will thoroughly perform her homework, and will let her application be her guide. To assist in this process, we include the following guide and a Personal Conferencing RFP Checklist in Appendix G.

Comparing Desktop Conferencing Products

The remainder of this chapter provides a step-by-step process that one can use to compare personal conferencing products. We have intentionally broadened the line of questioning to include all product categories. The reader may want to ignore questions that do not pertain to her particular application. Furthermore, the checklist omits many questions such as the financial position of a supplier, its ability to provide support, warranty considerations, and the hardware any particular application requires. For ideas on these questions, refer to Chapter 12 (Room Systems).

The number of desktop conferencing suppliers grows monthly. A partial list of suppliers appears in Appendix I, Product and Service Directory. We extend our apologies, in advance, to those whom we overlooked in our research. We do not intend to imply that one should limit one's research to manufacturers in our list.

Product And Manufacturer Background

Learn about the product's (and the supplier's) background, industry position, and direction:

- The desktop conferencing product's name and the date when it was first introduced.
- Description of the solution (client-side, server-oriented, client/server combination, etc.).
- Is it offered as a cross-platform solution? What computing environments does it support?
- The assumptions regarding personal conferencing that formed the foundation for the product's design and development. For a large installation (30 desktops or more), one might interview members of the product design/product marketing group. Consider signing non-disclosure agreements to obtain futures-information.
- The product's history, evolution to its present position, and market status. Is there a history of product-line backward compatibility? Have no-cost or minimal-cost upgrades been offered to ease the financial burden of staying current with standards and technology advances?
- The size of the installed base of product in North America, Europe, Asia, and other areas where an organization maintains, or plans to develop, operational interests. Languages supported?
- The supplier's position in the microcomputer industry. What other products does the supplier offer? How do these relate to the conferencing product? Has the manufacturer developed industry alliances and partnerships to assure that customers can fully exploit the power of personal conferencing? What is the nature of the partnership agreements?

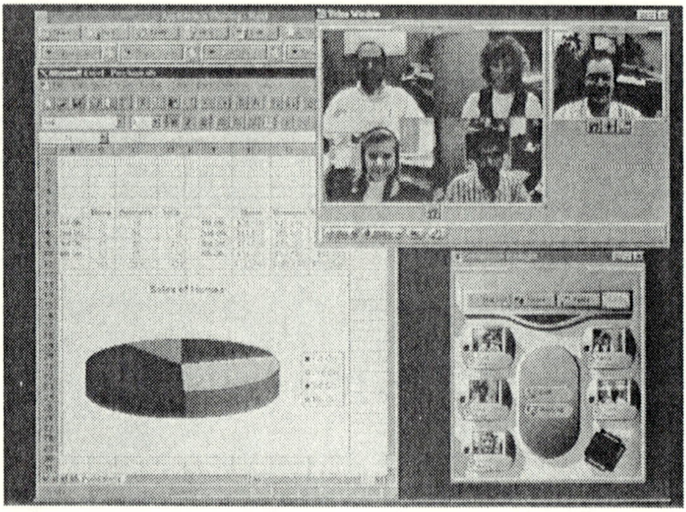

Figure 15-2. Document Collaboration (courtesy of Videoserver).

Product Family

Look at product families and how they inter-relate:

- How does the product fit within the desktop conferencing categories? Is it part of a family of products?
- Do members of the family interoperate across the entire offering? Can multiple conference types (e.g., point-to-point and multipoint videoconferencing, shared whiteboard, applications sharing) be part of the same conference?
- What is the upward migration path between the lowest-cost product in the family and the most expensive?
- What are the supplier's plans to continually enhance the product family?
- Is the user interface consistent across all members of the product family?

Network Considerations

Network infrastructure is probably the biggest barrier to widespread adoption of personal conferencing, particularly videoconferencing. – Ethernet, on the other hand, can handle compressed motion video rates of 128 Kbps with little problem, but does not offer isochronous service (guaranteed Real-Time delivery at a continuous bit rate). Various IETF protocols designed for IP networks (802.1Q,

802.1P, RTP/RTCP and RSVP) alleviate latency problems, but many networks incorporate routers and hubs that have not been configured to run these protocols. ISDN BRI to the desktop is fast enough for small screen applications, but it is only partially deployed. Again, a few questions might help in comparing products:

- What type of transmission system does the product require? Will it work adequately over analog POTS lines, switched and dedicated digital networks and LANs? Be specific about which LAN protocols the product supports.
- What switched digital network interfaces does the product support? In the case of ISDN, is the product N-ISDN-1 compliant? Does it ship with the network termination device (NT-1) and terminal adapter (TA)? In the case of switched 56, does the system include the data service unit (CSU/DSU) devices or must the customer provide them?
- Can videoconferencing, document conferencing or screen-sharing exchanges be conducted over the Internet? Provide detail.
- If the product works over POTS lines, what type of modem does it require? (Remember that H.324 conferences require a V.80 compliant modem; V.80 is an ITU-T standard for "video phone ready" V.34 modems).
- Can the same POTS line support voice and still-image transfer simultaneously? Does the manufacturer ship it with the product?
- If the product is designed for use on the Internet or intranets, does it use the services of a Web browser (Netscape, Exchange, etc.)?

Data Conferencing Capabilities

Ask about multiple capabilities (e.g., whiteboarding, screen and application sharing, chat, videoconferencing):

- Does the product offer shared workspace or whiteboard tools? How many users can share the whiteboard simultaneously? Can users capture the information developed within the whiteboard and store it for later reference?
- Does the product provide for presentation-oriented screen sharing (the remote end sees a bit mapped image of the original)? Are there any tools provided so that the distant end can point to objects, highlight them, etc? Can the remote end save the document locally as an image file?
- Does the product permit file transfers? During your performance testing (see the end of this chapter), time the file transfers and watch how they affect other applications that are running at the same time.

- Does the product offer 'chat' functionality?
- Can individuals or teams use the product to interactively share and annotate files and documents (such as Excel spreadsheets or Lotus Notes groupware tools) or entire suites of applications (e.g., Corel's OfficeJV 97, Lotus's SmartSuite 97, Microsoft's Office 97). Must both (or all) devices be running an application, or can sharing take place when only one desktop has it installed? How is the application controlled, and by whom?
- Does the product provide store-and-forward multimedia messaging or networked video-on-demand capabilities? If yes, what implications does this have for the system's configuration? Have the supplier describe the system's capabilities in terms of how many video segments can be stored, their maximum length/size, compression ratios, and algorithms used for compression, and other storage and playback-related attributes.
- Can the product be implemented as a multicast broadcast video arrangement? Have the supplier describe the environment. If the product captures and presents external content, what co-marketing agreements exist with content-providers (CNN, Dow Jones, etc.)?
- Does the product maintain a directory in which modem and LAN addresses can be stored?
- Does the product support call notification that allows users to accept or deny a conference attempt, based on who is calling?
- In what ways is the product unique in the marketplace? (Especially look for product differentiation that goes beyond the slick and the gimmicky to offer true business-oriented features and functionality).
- Has the product been customized for vertical market environments? If yes, which ones?
- Is the core technology licensable by third-party vendors such that they can create product enhancements?

Videoconferencing Product Capabilities

If a given application will benefit from the addition of live videoconferencing capabilities ask the following questions:

- Is the system capable of supporting face-to-face personal videoconferencing? Is it a videophone (operating over analog lines) or videoconferencing system that relies on digital transmission (circuit or packet-switched).
- Is compression performed in software only or is it hardware-assisted?

If the manufacturer includes hardware, can it be used to capture, compress and store video and audio for multimedia applications? In what file formats can video and audio be stored?

- If the product allows motion video images to be viewed in a PC window, what size is the window? Is the size adjustable? Can the user move the window between screen quadrants?
- How many video frames per second can be sent (maximum and average)?
- What is the image resolution range (expressed in pixels)? Can users make resolution/motion handling trade-offs during a conference? How are adjustments made?
- If the product is a videophone or a videoconferencing system, how does a user initiate a video call? Does the product offer an on-line directory? Can a decision to add video be made on the spot, during a voice-only call?
- Does the product provide dynamic channel management, and allocate available bandwidth depending on the type of communication being supported (data, audio, still-image, motion video)?
- Does the product depend on a separate telephone line for audio support? If so, how (and how well) is audio synchronized with video? Does the product offer an external speakerphone or a headset, to permit hands-free operation?
- With what type of camera does the product interoperate (e.g., digital proprietary, analog NTSC, PAL, S-Video, etc.). How is the camera's focus adjusted (e.g., manually, using a mouse, auto-focus)? Can the camera be panned, tilted and zoomed and if so, how? Can the camera swivel to act as a document camera?
- Does the product include simultaneous local and remote viewing capabilities? How are multiple windows managed on the PC screen?
- Identify the average and maximum frame rates (measured in fps) supported by the product and call them out separately for each network type and speed supported (for example, 14.4 Kbps modem, 112 Kbps, 384 Kbps, TCP/IP) and network type (such as serial lines, ISDN/switched 56, or LAN).
- Can the system capture a high-resolution still image? Can these images be stored for later use? What is the maximum number that can be stored and recalled? Describe the resolutions supported including the color-depth (8-bit, 24-bit, etc.). Describe, including both picture resolution information and line speed, the range of transmission times

required to transmit a still image. Can three-dimensional (3-D) objects be displayed, or does the system support video graphics only? Does the product take advantage of existing PC graphics accelerators or other PC hardware enhancements to enhance video quality?

- Can the system accept input from audio or digital video sources such that one can include pre-recorded clips or materials in a conference? Is time-based correction supported?
- Can the system be used by conferees who wish to see and converse with each other while simultaneously collaborating on PC documents?
- What type of camera is included? Is it color or monochrome? Will its range of focus provide a wide angle as well as close-up view? Where is it mounted on the device? Can it pan, tilt and zoom?
- Does the system include a microphone? Describe the type of microphone included. How is it muted (manual, software-controlled with an icon provided for activation and deactivation, etc)? Can a telephone or speakerphone be used with the system? Can the system operate using a headset or earpiece? Does the system require a separate telephone line for audio? How (and how well) is audio synchronized with lip movement? How are audio echoes controlled?
- Which video signals does the product accept (NTSC, PAL, SECAM, S-Video)?
- Can the videoconferencing hardware also be used for multimedia applications? Explain how video and audio input can be captured. Are additional boards required?

Standards Compliance And Openness

Look for signs that a supplier has complied, and will continue to comply, with standards. Since standards are not static, review the supplier's history of implementing the *original* standard and examine its ongoing efforts to stay current with *enhancements*. Has the supplier played a role in shaping a given standard? Here are a few sample questions that relate to standards:

- Are proprietary algorithms the *real* basis for the product or do standards provide the product's foundation? Is the product in transition, moving from a proprietary implementation to one that is standards-based? (Note: Most vendors with proprietary solutions are now migrating toward standards. If a supplier is in the conversion process, do not categorically disregard them. Rather, ask for contractual assurances that you will be able to migrate gracefully and economically).
- Does the product support the ITU-T's T.120 Transmission Protocols

for Multimedia Data (audiographics) suite?

- What are the supplier's plans to support the T.130 (ITU-T draft) Real-Time Architecture for Multimedia Conferencing (advanced network architectures) suite?
- Is the product compliant with the entire H.320 family of standards for videoconferencing over circuit-switched digital channels? What audio algorithms (e.g., G.711, G.722, and G.728) are supported? Does the product offer full CIF resolutions or merely support QCIF/SQCIF? Does it implement options such as error correction framing or motion prediction encoding?
- Does the product operate over a non-guaranteed quality-of-service packet-switched network (e.g., Ethernet, Token Ring, and the Internet)? If so, does it conform to the entire ITU-T H.323 Recommendation (H.225, H.245, H.261, H.263, G.711, G.722, G.723, G.728, and G.729)? Does it also support IETF protocols (RTP, RTCP, and RSVP)?
- Is the product designed for isochronous Ethernet and, if so, does it support the ITU-T's H.322 (draft) standard? (If the product is designed to run on isochronous Ethernet, the answer will usually be, "Yes." However, it is debatable whether IEEE 802.9 networks will be widely implemented. Most industry experts think " iso-E's" time has come and gone).
- What is the vendor's position relative to supporting PC industry standards (OLE, DDE, etc.). and standard application programming interfaces (APIs). Have the supplier list those that are supported.
- If the product offers still-image compression, does it compress and decompress using JPEG? If not, what does it use?
- If the product supports playback video, is it stored and decompressed in MPEG-1 format? If not, what compression techniques are used (remember that motion-JPEG is proprietary)?
- Does the manufacturer belong to any audiographics or videoconferencing consortiums (for instance, the IMTC) or ad hoc groups that cooperatively develop standards for distributed computing, networking and software development? If so, to which group(s) does the manufacturer belong and what is the history and extent of its involvement?
- Do employees of the manufacturer sit on standards bodies such as the ECMA, the IEEE, the ISO, the North American ISDN Users' Forum (NIUF) and others? Has the supplier successfully contributed its technology to the ITU-T for adoption?

Technical Considerations

- What hardware is required in order for the product to operate? Specify the platform (e.g., approved 486 or Pentium machines; Apple Macintosh, Sun SPARCstation, etc.). Describe (when applicable) the number of card slots required; specify the card size (half-size or full-size) and identify whether card slots must be adjacent. Define the type of monitor required (SVGA, etc.) and whether products such as graphics accelerator cards, video boards, audio boards are also required.
- If the product works over analog phone lines, describe the modem required to support it. What transmission speeds are supported? Who supplies the modem (considering the battles within this market, it may be a good idea to know who supplies the modem manufacturer with modem chips)? Is it part of the package or must it be purchased separately?
- Does the system include all cabling required for complete installation?

Ease-Of-Use

- What is the procedure for installing and configuring the system?
- Does the product offer speed-dialing menus and activity logs to track videoconferences?
- Does the product offer annotation tools (e.g., colored markers, highlighters, "notepads" and symbols)?
- What type of documentation is shipped with the product? Is an installation guide included? Does the product include context-sensitive on-line help menus and a tutorial?
- Does the product offer a consistent user interface across all products? If yes, explain.
- Does the supplier offer a Web page with installation and application tips, listing of known-bugs, information on product releases, etc.
- Does the supplier sponsor a user's group?

Cost

- How does the product's pricing compare to that of other products in the same group?
- How many users are covered by any software licenses that must be purchased?

CONCLUSION

By carefully defining objectives, characterizing the best possible scenario, and researching technology, one can ensure satisfaction in implementing a personal conferencing system. Appendices H and I of this book provide a (non-exhaustive) directory of manufacturers and Appendix G offers a helpful checklist. As a result of a thorough and thoroughly-conceived plan, screen sharing, videoconferencing, applications sharing, and document collaboration can facilitate the accomplishment of worthwhile work.

Chapter 15 References

DiCarlo, Lisa. "Vendors zoom in on inexpensive add-in card, chip," PC Week March 11, 1996

Hendricks, Charles E. and Steer, Jonathan P. "Videoconferencing FAQ,"

Rettinger, Leigh Anne. "DT5: Desktop Videoconferencing Product Survey," Cirriculum 21 Succeed

Rettinger, Leigh Anne. "Desktop Videoconferencing: Technology and Use for Remote Seminar Delivery," (Directed by Dr. Thomas K. Miller III.)

Schroeder, Erica. "Vendors sharpen desktop image," PC Week May 13, 1996

Sullivan, Kristina B. "Videoconferencing arrives on the Internet," PC Week August 19, 1996

16

INFORMATION SECURITY & VIDEO COMMUNICATIONS

"The only secure computer is one that is turned off, locked in a safe, and buried 20 feet down in a secret location... and I'm not completely confident of that one either."
Bruce Schneier

HACKING INTO A VIDEOCONFERENCE?

Video communications have always been vulnerable to eavesdropping. However, when the only two people on the call were a pair of maverick executives, and the only people who could eavesdrop were bored telephone company central office technicians or a few *phreakers*, not many people cared.

Hacking is not new. During the 1960s, the *blue box* became popular for stealing long-distance minutes. Telephone hacker or *phreaker* might nefariously place an 800 call from a pay telephone. While the number was ringing, he would press a button on the blue box to generate a 2600 Hz tone, and thereby disconnect the ringing at the far end and leave the phreaker connected to the long-distance network. By pressing a certain combination of keys on the touchtone pad, the phreaker could place long-distance calls at no cost. Not to be confused with the blue box, the *black box* is a device that phreakers would use to attach to an electromechanical central office (outside of rural independent Telcos, this stuff is long gone) to deceive the telephone company into thinking that a long-distance call had not been answered. Yet another device, the *red box* emulates the tones that are generated by coins dropping into a pay telephone.

Clearly, fraud has been around about as long as people have. However, it is much more sophisticated now. Moreover, more opportunities exist now for commiting fraudulent behavior. As we have chronicled in this text, video communications (both interactive and non-interactive) pervade a plethora of applications and communications media. Packet-switched interactive multimedia intruduces new liabilities. While packet-switched networks offer a single pipe over which data, voice, and video may travel, they also create more portals from which one can be comprimised. With the Internet, one can never know who else is sharing the network, or what they intend. It is not always possible even to know who actually requests, sends, or receives data. Consequently, as we converge video with data, we expose our video communications to all of the security threats that we associate with those scary data networks on which hackers lurk.

On any given day, one can easily find headlines about military agencies, educational institutions, or large corporations being comprimised. Much of this is the pastime of bored teens or *hacker-wannabes* who can simply point and click with any one of the countless hacking programs that are freely distributed on the Internet. Given what these folks have done to deface web pages, one can easily imagine what they might do to a live broadcast or videoconference.

However, hacking is increasing at a far slower rate than is corporate and governmental espionage or pirating. Disgruntled employees, professional spies, and pirates are increasingly responsible for information security breaches. In 1997, according to Dataquest, Corporate America spent $6 billion on network security, yet more than 40% of corporations reported security compromises. The cost of computer crime increased from $100,119,555 in 1997 to $360,720,555 in 1999. At least 30% of incidents that involved the Internet required evading a firewall. Computer crime losses are exceeding $10 billion each year. Surprisingly, A 1995 American Society for Industrial Security survey found that 24% of corporations have no procedures for safeguarding proprietary data. Any such numbers should be regarded conservative because, unfortunately, little incentive exists for companies to admit that they have been hacked. For instance, in 1994, Citibank discovered that Russian hackers had robbed it of $10 million in illegal transfers. The bank admitted the scandal to the media and consequently lost its top 20 customers to rival banks that claimed that they had more secure computer systems.

Piracy is also an issue. In November 1999, a 22 year old Public Policy major at an Oregon university became the first MP3 pirate convicted under the No Electronic Theft (NET) Act. For pleading guilty for illegally distributing about $70,000 worth of MP3 files, movie clips, and software, the court ordered a lenient sentence of two years probation with periodic urine tests, and a limit on access to the Internet. Video-on-demand only provides another source from which such people can steal and resell information assets.

Malicious code is a very serious threat. Although the Y2K bug dominated the headlines, the most common software bug of the 1990s was a form of malicious code known as a *buffer overflow*, that hackers use to control targeted computers. In a buffer overflow, a perpetrator floods an address bar or some other field with more characters than it can accommodate. She then activates the excess characters as executable code through means that firewalls may not be configured (or even able) to prevent. The demand for fast applications has resulted in sloppy computer programming (from large software providers) as a result of the elimination of quality control steps that could prevented such weaknesses.

So what does this have to do with videoconferencing? If it is packet-switched video (whether over the Internet or not), a lot! In a November 1999 posting on SecurityPortal, Ronald L. Mendell reported that U.S. Army special agents were showing their commanding officers how to turn user-installed microphones and cameras on Microsoft Windows NT Workstations into remote spying devices. Doing so allowed perpetrators to anonymously and remotely watch and listen to people who have no idea that they are being watched. This particular attack is initiated in the form of a Trojan horse (malicious software that carries executable code) concealed in an e-mail attachment. Once the attachment was opened, a perpitrator loaded a remote administration tool and ordered the Trojan horse to turn on the video and/or audio of the targeted machine. Victims of this type of comprimise may be oblivious of eavesdropping because many user-installed cameras and microphones lack any indications that they are in use other than a small tool bar icon. The same tactics can enable perpitrators to hijack videoconferencing sessions that leverage such products as Microsoft NetMeeting. Whether in the form of hijacking packets or performing sophisticated surveilance attacks such as this, videoconferences that occur across IP networks are as vulnerable to information security breaches as are any other traffic flows.

In this section, we will ouline the components of an information security strategy. We will neither provide an exhaustive text on this subject nor a detailed technical explanation of how the related technologies work. We will provide the reader with some basic steps for developing information security strategies.

Information Security Strategy

It is common for an organization to believe that they are secure because they have installed a firewall. However, simply installing a firewall is not in itself an information security strategy. Firewalls are important, but they are a single element in a strategy that should be built on a foundation of policies, guidelines, and procedures. An information security strategy can *mitigate* risk, but it can not eliminate risk. Every organization must determine its own risk tolerances… that is, to what extents they will go to protect various assets. An information security strategy should address three goals: confidentiality, integrity, and availability. In most cases, outside assistance is critical to establishing a strong security strategy, and to verifying the strategy is as effective in practice as it is in theory. As one works with a Certified Public Accountant (CPA) for financial accounting, one should work with a Certified Information Systems Security Professional (CISSP) to develop one's information security strategy.

To establish specific information security policies and guidelines, executive management must establish broad policies and standards regarding information assets, including use of its network(s). These constitute the foundation from which one builds an information security strategy. Nested under the overall security policy are a number of security policies. In the balance of this section we will highlight some of the areas for which the organization should establish specific sets of security policies and guidelines.

Security Management Practices

Every organization that possesses information assets should have a high-level security policy. We define an information security policy as an ***explicit set of prescribed practices that fosters protection of the enterprise network and of information assets***. That policy should state that all information assets are the organization's property, and it should define the criteria upon which the organization classifies those assets.

A key aspect of security management practices is that of privileges and responsibilities. The basic policy regarding privileges is that employees and officers should only be granted the privileges that they require to execute their jobs. This minimum access policy fosters diligent division of responsibilities. The organization's security policies should provide a methodology for identifying who is responsible for each information asset along with the scope of each information asset owner's responsibilities. That information asset owner is responsible for establishing and reviewing the asset's classification, confirming that adequate security controls are in place, establishing access rights and confirming appropriateness of access rights, determining the value of the asset, and mandating backup requirements.

Security Management Practices are the structure by which an organization determines its guidelines and operating procedures. The general security policy is the starting point for the various security policies that regulate file storage, data encryption, change management, backup and recovery, separation of responsibilities, access, auditing and testing, virus checking, and ongoing management. The highest possible organizational officials should express the importance or information security. These individuals should also support efforts to formalize security management practices because those practices are the foundation upon which the organization builds its information security strategy.

Law, Ethics, and Investigation

As important as any of an organization's assets is its ethical conduct. Ethical conduct warrants that the organization treat all employees equally. If an organization accuses an employee of improper conduct, it must demonstrate that it is not singling out that employee. It must demonstrate that whatever means it used to monitor that employee and build its case are a part of its policies and standard operating procedures, and that all employees are aware of and understand those policies. The implication is that an organization must establish and follow employee-monitoring policies.

If an organization believes anyone to be guilty of computer (or any other) crime, it must follow strict procedures regarding proper search and seizure, hearsay evidence (computer-generated evidence is generally considered hearsay evidence), and chain of custody. Moreover, an organization should specify procedures for returning confiscated assets.

Risk Assessment

As we have discussed previously, the business case for video communications is the support of the organization's business model. To be clear, video communications support the business model, not vice versa. The purpose of information security is, in turn, to support information technology applications such as videoconferencing. The first step in policy formulation is classification of information assets by value and by risk.

Not all information assets hold the same value. Moreover, the degree and nature of risk to each of those assets is most likely different. To implement an information security strategy, one must first assess the value of one's various information assets. One must also assess threats to any given asset, and the requirements of each asset in terms of confidentiality, integrity, and availability. A videoconference in which doctors are discussing a patient's medical history must remain highly confidential. A video message from a stockbroker's customers who is instructing him to buy a stock at a given price requires a high degree of integrity to confirm that the sender is who she says she is. A videoconference that involves a potential candidate who presently works for a competitor may require more confidentiality than a weekly company-wide report from the company president. The Information Security Officer is responsible to work with data owners to establish values and to identify risks. She should also identify any legal or regulatory obligations the organization has regarding any assets, and who the organization has assigned ownership for each asset.

With information asset classifications established, the ISO may prepare a high-level business impact analysis. This analysis should quantify the cost to the organization of the loss of each information asset, and whether that loss relates primarily to confidentiality, integrity, or availability. However, determining the organization's plans for protecting its assets requires a broad corporate information security policy that should include specific information security policies.

Physical Security

Physical security may be the least glamorous aspect of an information security strategy. However, it is too common to discover that a perpetrator could bypass an expensive firewall simply by jacking into an unprotected wall socket (e.g., in a lobby or commissary) or a port in an unlocked closet. It is often easier to steal a computer than it is to hack into the system from the Internet. Polls blame insider threats for 70–90% of information security breaches. One can conduct a simple physical security survey by observing whether office doors, desk drawers and file cabinets are locked, workstations are shut down or locked, and that sensitive papers and media are secured.

Distributed computing has complicated the job of physically securing data. Stories abound of competitors viewing an organization's strategy through a window and simply taking detailed notes. Moreover, it may be simpler to steal a computer from a telecommuter's home than to break in to corporate headquarters. Worse yet, a trusted friend may simply log on to the corporate network to obtain confidential information such as the date of a marketing campaign or an initial public stock offering.

Despite the need to protect information assets, the primary goal of physical security is the safety of people. Just as security policies begin with a risk analysis, a physical security strategy must begin with a business impact analysis. Such an analysis should list threats such as flood, loss of power, or earthquake, and rate each threat in terms of human impact, property impact, business impact, probability, and resources available in the case of such an event.

An important factor in physical security is physical access. Historically, access has been managed through locking important assets behind closed doors and by carefully managing keys. Many organizations now require picture ID. Challenge-response tokens that may require the use of a personal ID number (PIN), or challenge-response based smart cards are increasingly replacing or augmenting this level of security. State of the art methods include biometrics devices such as fingerprint scanners, retinal scanners, palm scanners, and hand geometry scanners.

Finally, organizations should carefully examine their policies regarding management of portable computing devices by both telecommuters and portable computer users. Although the latter may not apply to videoconferencing today, technology often evolves faster than corporate policy does. It is always better to design quality into a system than to retrofit it in after the fact. Organizations should also review processes for terminating employees to ensure that those employees do not exploit their knowledge and access at the expense of their new former employer.

Business Continuity & Disaster Recovery

As organizations increase reliance upon such applications as interactive multimedia, business continuity and disaster recovery become crucial components of an information security strategy. Without remote sites, there is little need for videoconferencing. The information security officer will always be challenged to keep up with both physical and information asset growth at numerous premises. For this reason, the organization should establish standards in acquisition, configuration, and management. If the organization determines what hardware components will comprise its various offices, how those hard assets will be configured, and how those assets and configurations will be managed, it will simplify the process, ensure uptime, and save money.

The basis of the business continuity and disaster recovery plan is the risk assessment and the security policies. Much as a Project Manager establishes critical paths by understanding task dependencies, the ISO can establish a business continuity and disaster recovery plan by establishing intradepartmental and interdepartmental dependencies. Steps to protect people include ensuring adequate emergency exits, emergency lighting, alarm systems, and fire suppression mechanisms. People should know where to meet to receive further instructions in an emergency evacuation. Bolting hardware to walls and floors may protect people from injury from falling machinery (even a monitor) that could result from such an event as an earthquake or a storm.

Hardware protection steps include implementation of redundant power (ensure that the redundant power does not follow the same path as the primary power), maintenance of spares, and installation of uninterruptible power supplies (UPS). UPS manufacturers such as American Power Conversion provide tools on their websites for determining the proper units for the hardware that one needs to protect. An information asset protection strategy should include both on-site and off-site data archives. Network connectivity is generally achieved through the incorporation of redundant network connections (again, these should follow diverse paths), and hardware that is programmed to failover to a secondary path in the event of a circuit failure. For Internet connectivity, it may even be a good idea to incorporate a secondary service provider.

Again, the highest priority in a disaster is the protection of people. A good business continuity and disaster recovery strategy will ensure the protection of people as well as information assets and network assets.

User Education

Users are the weakest link in a security strategy. They are also the reason a communications infrastructure exists. Of the 70–90% of breaches that occur from the inside, many result from the unintended consequences of poor operator practices. Users need to know the importance of such basics as regularly changing their password. Users also need to know that they should not share their password with anyone or write it down any place in which another may easily discover it. Moreover, users need to know what constitutes a good password (e.g., a combination of at least eight letters, numbers, and special characters).

Organizations should establish policies and inform users of such policies that prevent loading of unauthorized software, whether unlicensed software or *freeware*. Organizations should make those users aware of some basic forms of attack so that they can recognize them and act accordingly. Moreover, organizations should inform users of how to respond when they witness suspicious activity (e.g., a suspicious Email attachment or a program that acted different than usual). Explore.Zip and Melissa (both of which are technically classified as *worms*) are only two example of *malicious code* that began ravaging computer systems in 1999.

Melissa affected more than 100,000 computers in a matter of a few days. Organizations could have limited or prevented damage from either through good user education efforts.

It is important that an organization make users aware of its policies and guidelines through announcements from the highest possible executive level and through regular reminders.

Cryptography & Network Security

Cryptography can be difficult to implement for interactive multimedia applications because both encryption and decryption introduce latency. As we discussed in chapter seven, the H.323 standards family specifies security and encryption with the H.235 standard. Because we already addressed this topic, we will not reiterate the details of the H.235 standard. However, we will provide an overview of the standard's primary method of data encryption, the IPS Security Standard (IPSec).

IPSec is a framework of open standards that ensures interoperable establishment of secure private communications over the Internet. IPSec does this by establishing a virtual private network (VPN). A VPN is often referred to as a *tunnel*. Although this is a misnomer, it is helpful for conceptually understanding what a VPN does. VPN packets do not travel in a reserved spectrum of a packet-switched network. They are simply encrypted packets that are illegible between the time that they leave the sender or the sender's VPN gateway, and the time that they reach the desired recipient or VPN gateway.

IPSec is a security standard that operates at the network or packet-processing layer, rather than at the application layer as did previous security approaches such as SSL (Secure Sockets Layer). IPSec is a standard for implementing virtual private networks between networks or from users to networks. Although IPSec does require the installation of a client, it does not require changes to individual user computers.

IPSec defines Transport Mode and Tunnel Mode. Transport Mode protects only the (TCP, UDP, or ICMP) Payload. Tunnel Mode Protects both the Payload and the IP header. The elements of IPSec include the Authentication Header (AH), for source authentication, and Encapsulating Security Payload (ESP), for both source authentication and data encryption. Associated information is placed into the packet in a header that immediately follows the IP packet header. IPSec is not itself a security association, key distribution, or key management protocol. It relies upon other such protocols such as Internet Key Exchange (IKE) (RFC 2409) which, in turn, relies upon ISAKMP for security association and key management and Oakley for key exchange (Oakley is based upon Diffie-Hellman). IPSec can also be used in conjunction with a variety of encryption algorithms such as DES (data encryption standard) and triple-DES.

IPSec is a technology that enables secure packet transmission over the public Internet. Unfortunately, the Internet is not yet adequate as a videoconferencing network, and VPN encryption and decryption processes will add latency and only make things worse. However, it is clear that, as processors become faster, the Internet becomes more robust, and end-to-end QoS implementations become more reliable, VPN based videoconferences will become common.

CONCLUSION

An organization's information security strategy is as important as its information and network assets. Although hacking is not new, it has become much more sophisticated and common with the advent of the Internet. An information security strategy should begin with a broad security policy and a risk assessment. Its importance should be emphasized to all users at the highest possible executive level. Enforcement of the information security strategy requires periodic auditing and on-going auditing and monitoring.

CHAPTER 16 REFERENCES

Krause, Micki and Tipton, Harold F. "Handbook of Information Security Management," CRC Press 1999.

Bernstein, Terry, Bhimani, Anish B., Schultz, Eugene, Siegel, Carol A. "Internet Security for Business," John Wiley; 1996.

Pfleeger, Charles P. "Security in Computing," Prentice Hall; 1997.

Maitra, Amit K. "Building a Corporate Internet Strategy," Van Nostrand Reinhold 1996.

Mendell, Ronald L. "Covert Channels and Web Sites," Security Portal. November 22, 1999. http://www.securityportal.com/

Behar, Richard. "Who's Reading Your E-Mail?," Fortune Magazine. February 3, 1997

Staff. "E-Mail Virus Spreads," CNN Financial Network. March 29, 1999. http://www.cnnfn.com/

Sullivan, Bob. "Explore.Zip Worm Strikes Anew," MSNBC. November 30, 1999. http://www.msnbc.com/

Newton, Harry. "Newton's Telecom Dictionary," Miller Freeman. February 1999.

Sullivan, Jennifer. "MP3 Pirate Gets Probation," Wired Magazine. November 24, 1999. http://www.wired.com/news/

Festa, Paul. "Study Says "Buffer Overflow" Is Most Common Security Bug," CNET News.com. November 23, 1999. http://www.cnetnews.com/

Paller, Alan. "Security's Vicious Cycle." Computerworld, November 1999. http://www.computerworld.com

PART FIVE

THE FUTURE

17

THE FUTURE OF VIDEO COMMUNICATIONS

"We are looking at the dawning of the age of visual communications."

Dr. Norm Gaut

IT'S ABOUT TIME

Video communications have overcome many obstacles to become the practical tools they are today. Still, few of us have developed a habit and integrated video communications into our lives as we have telephones, radios, televisions, and personal computers. Inexpensive video-enabled PCs have eliminated hardware as an obstacle. However, until broadband always-on connectivity is common, PCs will not reach their potential. Even if we have such connectivity, we can not assmume that friend's or neighbor's PC to be ready were we to make an unplanned video call. In contrast, it is hard to imagine someone's telephone not being connected or turned on when we call. Surprising numbers of people still have not even accepted the PC. With PCs and dial-up Internet access so cheap, something other than cost must account for this phenomenon. Technology aversion may share the blame, but so must timing.

Technology, access, and culture thwarted AT&T's PicturePhone in 1964. In the dawn of the 21st century, however, the environment is drastically different. Our machines and our methods of interconnecting those machines have evolved. Equally important, *we* have evolved. AT&T introduced its PicturePhone in an environment in which telephones and color televisions were marvelled. Now, digital telephone services and personal computers are essential tools for executives, couriers, mechanics, cashiers, and practically all other working individuals.

Communications appliances are worthless without a means or a reason to connect. That too has evolved since 1964. Practically every city in the world now incorporates a compatible digital telecommunications system, and thereby contributes to a global communications network. Users are leveraging that network for messaging, research, entertainment, and commerce. Personal computers, and now handheld communications appliances, are displacing telephones as the preferred user interface to our global communications system. Notwithstanding the chasm between the *technology literate* and the *technology illiterate*, we have integrated personal computers into our lives. As a result, many of us have video communications tools on our desk… or in our pockets.

Just as this generation finds peculiar its parents' association with the telegram for sending an urgent message to someone in a distant location, this generation's children will find their parents' association with the *telephone* for only voice communications. Videoconferencing is living up to its promise to save time and money, and to make people more available, but it is still not widely accepted. It will be desktop and mobile communication appliance conferencing over the Internet that will make it so.

Moreover, if those such as the MPEG-7 Working Group succeed (and eventually they will), we will be able to search on virtually any criteria we can imagine through voice-activated systems. We could hum a tune to either buy recordings (in the form of on-demand files), lyrics, sheet music, or movies. Should we desire that image from about halfway through the movie Out of Africa, we would simply need to describe it to our handheld communications appliance / remote control device and it could appear on the living room wall. Should we be worried about the whereabouts of an elderly relation or a child, we do the same so that our handheld device can tap into a GPS system that links to another handheld system that has a miniature camera and screen. Is this as unlikely as AT&T's Picturephone? Yes. Is it more far-fetched? Probably not. That is why so much is being spent on such a small market.

Videoconferencing today presents such an enormous opportunity that countless equipment manufacturers and service providers continue to invest in it despite the relatively small size of the market. It is the potential to enable videoconferencing, complete with a camera and the network interface, on each of the over 100 million new PCs sold each year, and retrofitting the more than 300 million PC unit installed base that motivates them. Demand for online video, music, and software distribution will culminate in displacement of dial-up Internet connections with high-speed always-on services. Dial-up Internet services have sufficed for retrieving text and graphics information, but they will not suffice for these services.

This change will undermine the current business models of brick and mortar companies that physically distribute intangible goods such as videos, music, and software. With the firm entrenchment of the Internet, and the growth of DSL, cable modems, and handheld communications appliances, carriers must provide robust networks, and must be able to support practically any access to its networks. Sprint demonstrated its understanding of this in 1999 when it offered to buy People's Choice TV of Shelton Connecticut, American Telecasting, Inc., of Colorado Springs, Colorado, and Videotron USA, the wireless broadband subsidiary of Le Groupe Videotron of Montreal, Quebec. Sprint knew that its ION would need to support a variety of access technologies and methods to deliver broadband services, including wireless. Sprint (now MCI/WorldCom) acted to expand its already robust network of long-distance and Internet fiber infrastructure, local infrastructure, and PCS mobile voice telephone infrastructure.

Through the balance of this chapter, we will examine the technologies and the conditions that will transform video communications from a viable tool into an essential one. We will begin with a look at the changes going on in the area of computer operating systems.

THE OPERATING SYSTEM

With the raging popularity of Java, Linux, and the Palm OS, Microsoft is beginning to lose its grasp on the operating system. While Windows NT is stealing its way into carrier networks, Windows is neither stable nor secure enough to satisfy many IT managers. The fact that Linux is free and that the source code is available makes it a much better fit for many applications. The significance of this is reflected in the decisions of many companies such as Novell and Intel (the second half of Wintel) to support Linux. This was an especially significant move for Intel, whose products have become practically synonymous with Microsoft Windows systems. However, it seems unlikely that the market will simply transfer its dependence upon Microsoft to RedHat. Operating systems just may not be as significant in the future as directories become robust network device and service information repositories. With such protocols as X.500 and the Lightweight Directory Access Protocol (LDAP), file services are in the directory rather than in the operating system.

X.500 is an ISO and ITU standard that defines how global directories should be structured. X.500 directories are hierarchical and offer different levels for each category of information, such as country, state, and city. X.500 is an overall model for Directory Services within the OSI model that addresses the namespace and the Directory Access Protocol (DAP), the protocol for querying and updating it. DAP runs over the OSI network protocol stack. Because DAP is so extensive, participants at the University of Michigan worked in conjunction with the ISODE Consortium to develop the Lightweight Directory Access Protocol (LDAP). LDAP is an information model and a protocol for querying and manipulating that model. Its overall data and namespace model is fundamentally the same as X.500 except that the LDAP protocol is streamlined and is designed to run directly over the TCP/IP stack. X.500 is a directory web that defines a global directory structure much as http & html define & implement the global hypertext web (the WWW). Anyone with an X.500 or LDAP client may examine the global directory the way that they use a web browser to examine the WWW. Of course, merging disparate directories is not a trivial operation and will continue to instigate obstacles.

Java is the programming language of the WWW, and it, too, strikes a blow to Microsoft's domination (dare we say monopoly?) over the operating system. In 1999, the European Cable Communications Commission's (ECCA) decided to include a Java-based system within its standard digital set-top box specifications, and thereby formally fostered independence from Windows in the European digital cable market. The Eurobox 4.0 specification includes APIs (Application Programming Interface) from the Digital Video Broadcasting group's Multimedia Home Platform (MHP) that favors Sun Microsystems's JavaTV. MHP's 'open' API will enable cable operators to enjoy alternatives when choosing an operating system choice (previous Eurobox implementations have used OpenTV operating system).

Having opened the door to the topic of cable modems, we will discuss methods for connecting to the Internet in the next section.

The Network

The Internet

Whether to reach the content on the WWW or to avoid toll charges with VPNs, it is the Internet that people want to access with those desktop conferencing systems and handheld communications appliances that they are buying. When they are not trying to reach the Internet, workers are often accessing private Internet protocol (IP) based intranets (private websites) that emulate the Internet. In 1999, firms such as Alteon WebSystems created a new genre of products that make Web sites run better by distributing network loads between servers. Such devices distribute incoming data evenly between multiple servers, and thereby ensure that no single server is overwhelmed. The Internet Research Group expects the traffic management market to explode to $828 million by 2002 because all e-businesses must ensure that their websites are always available. The cost of this type of infrastructure and the cost to manage will push future businesses to delegate that work to specialists. That (and declining revenue from processors) explains why, in 1999, Intel expanded into the businesses of co-location, web hosting, database hosting, and application hosting business units.

With companies such as Intel entering the network services businesses and with cable providers waging war to keep their networks closed, ISPs will need to channel their resources into implementing innovative applications that solve targeted business needs. By 2002, approximately 80% of businesses will outsource major hosted services to application service providers. Initially, these are large-scale applications such as enterprise resource management or network security services. However, the field will grow and smaller applications will pervade the market... especially as portable communications appliances mature.

VON (Voice On the interNet) advocate Jeff Pulver asserts, "It will be the technologies surrounding *instant messaging* and *presence management* that will be the true 'killer app' for service providers who have invested in IP based communication networks." Such IP based technologies and applications will enable the new generations of handheld communications appliances because they provide services that users can customize and manage. For instance, one might be able to drag-and-drop a voice message into a task list on a PDA (e.g., a Palm Pilot) in which the voice-to-text conversion occurs automatically. Instant messaging, unified messaging, and presence management will justify the investments that worldwide service providers are making in their IP Communication Networks. In the future, although endpoints will remain the domain of H.323, carrier trunking switches are likely to rely upon SIP (session initiation protocol). SIP is the protocol for intelligence on the edge and for inter-domain communication between switches; it is ideal when bandwidth is ample and IT managers can mandate a particular client. Most carriers are integrating SS7 functionality, and the cable industry, having completed its PacketCable specifications in summer 1999, is strongly implementing VON to provide comprehensive PSTN interconnectivity.

VON's potential became clear when Hurricane Floyd disabled not only long distance service, but also Internet, wireless, and even automated teller machine connectivity in Northern New Jersey. Unlike San Francisco's 1989 earthquake, in which reporters could at least conduct their work over cellular telephones, Hurricane Floyd caused one million Northern New Jersey residents to completely lose connectivity to the outside world for several days. Presence management schemes enabled by VON, and the Internet's inherent redundancy might have reduced much of this. Although circuit switches are inherently more reliable, the overall design of the PSTN does not provide for redundant paths the way that presence management enabled IP networks can. VON technology's presence protocols provide the ability to determine when someone (or something) is available, and thereby fosters better call completion. A standardized methodology such as a *presence instant messaging* inter-domain protocol, that would provide its own signaling network, will be required. Such a protocol could leverage both SS7 and DNS (domain name service) for ubiquitous anytime-connectivity. The enterprise VON market will also require expanded SNMP support and proactive monitoring tools so that organizations can outsource portions of network management to application service providers.

High-bandwidth always-on connections are crucial for presence management, instant messaging and, of course, ubiquitous interactive video communications. In the next section, we will discuss some ways of establishing those connections.

DSL & Cable Modems

Worldwide ADSL modem shipments rose 74% in the last three months of 1999, and exceeded 1.2 million shipments by 2000, according to Cahners In-Stat Group. Mark Peden, ADSL Forum Ambassador and senior DSL technologist for Intel proclaimed, "Now that we can support DLCs, it's conceivable that within the next three to five years, the technology will serve 90–95 percent of all the homes in America."

Multi-line voice, Internet access and other enhanced services are about to revolutionize next-generation local loop growth. Companies like Netopia are designing voice over DSL (VoDSL) Internet devices to allow ISP and CLECs to offer small businesses a compelling, integrated solution that includes high-speed DSL Internet access and cost-effective voice services. Small businesses need cost-effective alternatives to LECs' expensive analog voice services. In 1999, the combination of speed and instant access allowed 1.5–7 Mbps SDSL services to drive the deployment of approximately 40,000 DSL lines in the U.S. Such routers deliver packetized voice traffic from customers to VoDSL gateways designed to connect to circuit switches and to extend call control features such as call forwarding, call waiting, and auto redial to customers' phones through VoDSL. Such services allow small business customers to avoid contracting with multiple vendors to provide integrated communications. Incumbent carriers are most vulnerable in the 4–16 line market segment that is comprised primarily of small businesses and high-end residential customers. The Yankee Group asserts that this market segment accounts for as much as 50% of incumbent carriers' revenues, and that it will increase to 1.44 million customers by 2002. To win this market, DSL providers will need to overcome challenges from cable providers.

IDC's 1999 study on the cable-TV broadband market indicated that about 1.3 million US households would subscribe to cable modem services by 2000, and that the number would increase to 9 million by 2003. At that point, IDC predicted that DSL will become consumers' preferred broadband access service. Cable providers will need to upgrade their networks and to improve their marketing execution to overcome the barriers of widespread deployment to the US consumer market, and to outperform DSL in attracting and retaining customers. IDC anticipates that cable providers will overcome these issues and that their revenues will increase from $421.9 million in 1999 to $2.6 billion by 2003. Cable TV operators report that they have installed more than a million cable modems in users' homes; that is still a small fraction of the over 38 million households that accessed online services by 2000. Internet access via cable modems will generate billions of dollars in additional revenues for the cable industry.

Through 1999, cable modems out-shipped ADSL modems with a stable growth rate of 27%. Motorola alone sold more than one million cable modems in 1999. About 430,000 U.S. households subscribed to high-speed cable Internet services in 1998, and, according to the Yankee Group, that number may exceed 4.3 million by 2002. In 1999, cable companies are increasing their customer base by at least 200,000 homes every week.

In October 1999, Arthur D. Little conducted a telephone survey of 495 men and 509 women 18 years and older living in private households in the continental US. Seventy-four percent recommended the service to a friend or relative, and 84% responding that the service "meets or exceeds their expectations." A total of 59% of current and 74% of prospective customers cited speed as the primary draw, and 97% considered unlimited online hours to be a "desirable benefit." Fifty-four percent said that they are "very or somewhat interested" in being able to connect more than one computer in their home to allow for simultaneous independent use. The study found that, at $40 per month, about 28% of U.S. households may subscribe to cable Internet access service. These approximately 28 million households represent as much as $13.4 billion in annual revenues. In the study, twice as many respondents favored cable than favored telephone for high speed Internet access. Half of households headed by persons age 18–24 are likely subscribers, versus only 9% of households that are headed by persons older than 64. The cable Internet access market is already huge, and it is just beginning.

Dial-up ISPs are lobbying for direct access to cable modem users because most users are not willing to pay an extra charge for the value-added services that they provide. While cable providers like AT&T battle with ISPs and regulators to maintain unconditional control of their networks, telephone companies will keep selling DSL service. Ironically, cable providers and established ISPs are a very good match. Cable providers provide the raw bandwidth, ISPs understand the Internet infrastructure and the market, and they provide value-added services that motivate customers to subscribe. Were ISPs to promote the cable network, telephone companies would find themselves with a formidable rival. Without such a reliance, customers will continue to cancel their dial-up service in favor of the most attractive high-bandwidth service available. Cable providers have an additional advantage in that many existing telephone lines will not support DSL services.

Cable providers will bolster both their revenues and the attractiveness of their services by increasingly offering voice and interactive video. In September 1999, Comcast and a few other cable providers began testing IP telephony over their networks and thereby confirmed that the future of cable modems is Voice over IP (VoIP). Significant goals of the trial included tracking QoS, interoperation with the PSTN for such crucial operations as provisioning and billing. In late 2000 or early 2001, Comcast expects to be the first multiple systems operators to implement CableLabs PacketCable specifications for transmitting multi-featured IP telephone calls over hybrid fiber-coax (HFC). Of course, a major obstacle will be that the DOCSIS (data over cable service interface specifications) standards have not been tested in the market. Other obstacles will include issues such as powering the network, defining network demarcation points, network termination, and plant environment. DOCSIS cable modems and CMTS equipment sales in North America will exceed $3 billion and service revenue will reach $11.9 billion through 2003. A total of 8.5 million subscribers will be served by cable operators versus only 2 million customers that will be served by DSL providers by 2003 according to Forrester Research.

Cable providers are essentially providing Ethernet networks while carriers are implementing ATM at the core. However, a newcomer with a partially familiar name may mix things up a bit.

Ten Gigabit Ethernet

If the IEEE 802.3 working group has its way, Ethernet, the de facto LAN protocol, will soon also become a WAN protocol. The group has set a short schedule for completing the 10-gigabit Ethernet specifications. Because it is simpler and less expensive to deploy, many municipalities have chosen to extend Ethernet from their LANs to their MANs (metropolitan area networks). Soon organizations may have the option to extend Ethernet to their WANs. Although the group has not progressed far enough to define a physical-layer interface, it is committing that 10 Gbps Ethernet will retain the same frame format and sizes as 10, 100, and 1,000 Mbps Ethernet. Ten Gbps Ethernet will enable Ethernet to rival optical transport, by exceeding the OC-192 protocol (9.58 Gbps). In addition, an 802.3 study group is reviewing proposals for 300-meter short-haul and 20-kilometer long-haul versions of a 10 Gbps Ethernet specification, and companies are investigating methodologies for extending Ethernet as far as 100 kilometers.

Initially, 10 Gbps Ethernet will most likely be used to aggregate 1 Gbps Ethernet links into the network core. However, carriers could eventually use it for connections over leased fiber-optic cables. Proponents say that the first draft of the 10 Gbps specifications is due in September 2000, and they hope to submit a final draft in March 2001, about the same time that products should appear. The group is considering several PHY chips, such as one that combines four 2.5 Gbps transceivers on a die, and aggregating their output via WDM (wave division multiplexing). Because interfaces to WAN edge equipment would be simplified, the cost of constructing access rings and metropolitan rings for Ethernet would be 4–5 times lower than the cost of meeting full SONet jitter specs. The question is whether Ethernet is reliable enough to supplant ATM in the PSTN.

Were Ethernet extended to the WAN, IEEE 802.1q and IEEE 802.1p could enable seamless end-to-end QoS (quality of service). IEEE 802.1q enables VLAN identification and QoS levels by adding four bytes to an Ethernet frame and thereby increasing the maximum frame size from 1518 to 1522 bytes. It uses three bits to identify eight priority levels and twelve bits to identify up to 4096 VLANs. Used in conjunction with IEEE 802.1q, IEEE 802.1p, enables QoS in 802-based networks. It defines three bits to permit switches to reorder packets based on priority level, and defines the Generic Attributes Registration Protocol (GARP) to allow client stations to request membership in a multicast domain, and the GARP VLAN Registration Protocol (GVRP) to enable them to register into a VLAN.

Because implementation and knowledge of Ethernet is widespread, and because of the end-to-end QoS that Ethernet offers, its extension into the WAN would only facilitate WAN and Internet desktop conferencing.

Satellite Networks

Next generation satellites are beginning to fill the gaps between terrestrial networks, and to change perceptions about the cost of communicating anywhere on the globe. Satellite based switches are poised to offer packet-based video, voice, and data as their terrestrial counterparts do, and in ways their terrestrial counterparts can not. A 1998 Pioneer Consulting study of global broadband access services identified 500 operational VSAT networks in the United States. By 2000, more than 10 million U.S. consumers subscribed to direct-to-home (DTH) satellite services such as direct broadcast service (DBS). Meanwhile, corporate subscribers were employing very small aperture terminal (VSAT) systems for remote access, distributed data, and private networking at rates as high as 2 Mbps. Industry experts expect broadband access subscriptions to swell from less than one million subscribers in 1999 to more than 137 million by 2005.

In 2001, the first generation of Ka-band satellites will enable the broadband multimedia satellite services, which generated $180 million in revenue in 1998, to overcome technology and launch limitations to grow to $44 billion by 2008. With fixed-dishes installed at the customer end and a sky-based Internet backbone, satellite network providers will be able to compete head-to-head with terrestrial network service providers. While the latter are just developing bandwidth-on-demand models, satellite networks offer such access inherently. The broadcast and broad coverage features of satellite technology already suit streaming IP multicast video as well or better than terrestrial methods do. By implementing cell-based technologies, broadband satellite systems portend wireless global Internet access, HDTV, video broadcast, and videoconferencing by 2003.

By 2002, a new generation of broadband Ka-band (18–30 GHz) data satellites will offer broadband bandwidth and global coverage to small, inexpensive ground antennas. Improved switching and on-board baseband processing technologies will transform satellites from primitive orbiting relay stations into high-tech switches-in-the-sky. By combining Ku-band satellite-to-user and Ka-band user-to-satellite transmission techniques, they will be capable of providing robust, highly reliable network communications. The system leverages geostationary satellites to deliver multiple spot beams and regional asymmetric broadband speeds as fast as 38 Mbps to the user and 2 Mbps from the user. Ka-band return channel will provide bandwidth-on-demand for collecting, processing, and distributing interactive multimedia. It is a standards-based technology that is already licensed globally and that can be implemented economically.

Satellite ground systems will need to support multiple networking services, and to enable service providers to quickly add new features and applications. Worldwide subscription will require low equipment costs and access service fees, and widely adopted standards. Once that occurs, however, DSL and cable modem systems, that are dependent upon cabling infrastructure, may have a tough time competing with satellites that can be deployed quickly and can beam signals thousands of miles.

Satellite networks offer the potential of a homogenous global network that offers standardized service offerings to any spot on the planet.

FROM THE OFFICE TO THE KITCHEN, AND BEYOND

Desktop Video Communications

Desktop videoconferencing (DVC) will not be constrained by the conventional videoconferencing paradigm. DVC's usefulness lies in combining videoconferencing, audio conferencing, file sharing, whiteboarding, and web browsing. In 1999, such combinations still relied on separate voice and data networks. However, IP-enabled conferencing is now becoming feasible over private networks (intranets), and desktop monitors will commonly integrate miniature cameras. Compression technology is decreasing the necessary bandwidth, and 802.1q and 802.1p standards are enabling QoS within Ethernet LANs and MANs. Gigabit and ten-gigabit Ethernet is even extending Ethernet to WANs (such distinctions are becoming unhelpful).

An ideal environment for videoconferencing is two groups of people who are gathered at two remote offices, using simple, effective technology. A videoconference can be a nice excuse to leave one's cubicle, stretch one's legs, become acquainted with people, and have a *bio break*. Personal interaction is the experience that videoconferencing only emulates, and video-enabled conference rooms are ideal meeting environments. Therefore, DVC (or mobile communications appliance conferencing) may not be the preference when alternatives exist, however alternatives do not always exist. Therefore, desktop video communications will drive the construction of LANs in both offices and homes. The reduction is systems and components pricing and the simplification of system use will facilitate this trend.

By 2001, 80% of the PC camera market should be USB; at that point, the market should move toward IEEE 1394 (Firewire). Consumer interest in digital video has already created a second generation of Firewire cards that are easier to use and cost less than $250. As the market increases, the price of a PC camera will decrease to about $40. Semiconductor pricing will continue to drop and, by 2002, most cameras will be based on single-chip solutions. In that same period, PC camera semiconductor revenue should grow by a factor of five. Through 2003, the PC camera market should see rapid growth as PC makers begin including cameras in the PC package. Once corporations begin deploying PC cameras at the desktop, the desktop video communications market will begin to meet its potential.

Overcoming substandard or nonexistent wiring will be a challenge that wireless networking technologies will address.

Wireless LANs

Many offices are still stuck with category three wiring, and are averse to re-wiring to support 100/1000 Mbps Ethernet. Significantly fewer households will install category five (much less category seven) wiring to support Ethernet networks. Consequently, the market for wireless LANs is abundant and growing. In fall 1999, Apple Computer debuted an iBook with wireless networking and thereby lit a fire under the PC industry. Shortly thereafter, Dell Computer began shipping Aironet Wireless Communications' 4800 series wireless LAN cards as a factory-installed option on its Latitude notebooks. The enabler for these wireless PCs is the 802.11 wireless Ethernet specification that supports 11 Mbps wireless connections at a maximum distance of 300 feet.

Commercial grade wireless Ethernet devices for PCs are generally comprised of a PC Card with a small antenna that connects to a base station. To avoid the cost and inconvenience of laying new wire, the education and health-care industries led the way in adopting these wireless networks, and mainstream corporations are following. In late 1999, Bluetooth- enabled devices hit the market and thereby offered an extension to wireless LANs. A variant of 802.11, Bluetooth uses the 2.45GHz radio-frequency range to establish 1 Mbps connections at ranges up to forty feet. It is targeted at the fast, simple connection of PDAs, wireless phones, and PCs. Intel expects its Bluetooth hardware modules and software drivers to be ready for production by mid 2000. Bluetooth may also play a role in home networking. However, the Home Phoneline Networking Alliance endorses a 10 Mbps solution that leverages existing home phone wiring for which 3Com, D-Link, Intel, and Netgear all offer products. The Yankee Group estimates that more than 17 million U.S. households want to network their PCs and peripherals.

Since many households can not justify the need and the cost for 802.11 wireless Ethernet, a simpler and less expensive alternative has evolved.

Home Networking

Presently, one of the biggest trends is home networking. Market-research firm Cahners In-Stat (conservatively) projects that the U.S. home-networking market will grow from $230 million in 1999 to $1.4 billion by 2003. The firm estimates that, by 2000, there were more than 21 million homes with more than one PC, and it expects this number to grow to approximately 31 million by 2004. The home networking market will top $1 billion by 2002. In January 1999, the HomeRF Working Group announced that it had ratified the Shared Wireless Access Protocol (SWAP) specification 1.0 and that thirteen companies had committed to build products based on that protocol. The SWAP specification established an open platform to enable a broad range of interoperable consumer devices for wireless voice and data communications in the home. Member companies that were actively developing SWAP-based products included Butterfly Communications, Compaq Computer Corporation, Hewlett-Packard, IBM, Intel, iReady Corporation, Microsoft,

Motorola, OTC Telecom, Proxim, Samsung, Symbionics, and Symbol Technologies. By 2000, numerous companies had shipped inexpensive kits that offered 10 Mbps throughput and that conformed to the Home Phoneline Networking Alliance's (HomePNA) HomePNA 2.0 specification. Netgear, a subsidiary of Nortel Networks, began shipping a family of compliant home networking products with a USB adapter that let users connect numerous Ethernet-ready desktops and laptops with ADSL devices or cable modems. Their PC-card kit began selling for $79. At about the same time, Intel introduced its HomePNA compliant AnyPoint Home Networking PCI adapter card, also for $79.

Consumer enthusiasm for video cameras and for anything that can be used in conjunction with the Internet, combined will make digital video cameras popular. In 1999, consumers could buy digital video cameras that offer higher resolution than their analog counterparts offer for less than $1,000. By 2001, that price should drop to as low as $200. By 2000, sales of 2–2.3 pixel digital still cameras rose dramatically, and costs fell to as low as $800. That trend should continue such that many will sell for as low as $200.

The choke point for home network is not in the home, but between the home and the broadband Internet access provider. Providers will employ satellites, DSL, cable modems, and combinations of these, to enable interactive video communications. The Internet and, subsequently, the concept that broadband cabling to the home is a good idea, is still fairly new. Therefore, whereas water and power are delivered in a predetermined manner, broadband Internet may be delivered in any of a number of ways, and the homeowner must make the choice. That is likely to change.

In the meantime, the box, referred to either as a *residential gateway* or a *SOHOware gateway*, that connects the wiring inside the home and the wiring outside the home is a critical point over which competition will rage. The Yankee Group anticipates that the first five million broadband adopters in the United States will do so primarily for data applications. The implication of this is that, in the early stages, the market will simply need a way to connect multiple PCs within a single home. Lucent Technologies forecasts the market for residential gateway products that are designed for multiple PC households, to reach 40 million in the United States by 2002. In contrast, IDC predicts that more smart communications-enabled appliances than PCs will be shipped in 2001. The implication of this is that the market would require ways to connect disparate devices such as game stations, PCS, and handheld communications appliances. To address this latter prediction, residential gateway manufacturers are beginning to design products that integrate all possible options into one device.

A residential gateway is a device that routes Internet traffic in the home to a specific PC or appliance. It may offer firmware-based features such as firewall protection, and parental content and access control. What distinguishes the first SOHOware gateways is that they are designed only for routing data traffic. The presumption is that voice and video applications are still futures, and that service providers will provide gateways that accommodate those needs when enough people ask for them.

Whatever the immediate implementation, users will eventually want options that integrate video, voice, and data communications over wired and wireless methods. They will probably also want to use the same devices to play games, program their microwaves and their DVDs, and to adjust both internal climate and the window shade height. Presently, cable providers are positioning themselves much better for handheld communications appliances than are telephone companies.

Handheld Communications Appliances

Most people now accept that portable digital wireless devices will eventually displace many of our stationary computing devices just as mobile telephones have displaced our old telephones. They have already started, but cost is an obstacle and no-one knows when they will become dominant. Approximately 90% of cellular-phone operators have standardized on the Wireless Application Protocol (WAP). With this obstacle out of the way, the wireless revolution is much closer. The magnitude of that revolution is hard to anticipate because the ability for almost anything to communicate with almost anything else creates myriad possibilities. The market for wireless handheld appliances became clear in 1999, when Palm Computing offered the PalmVII mobile Internet access, and Harmon/Kardon began offering its Take Control mobile handheld controller for audio components, window blinds, and lights. While the former exemplifies the direction of wireless handheld communications appliances, the latter exemplifies the market for adding control of any kind into such devices. Internet Telephony technologies are likely to become part of the embedded systems in future IP devices whether they are conventional network devices like routers or microwave ovens.

In December 1999, New World Mobility announced installation of the Nokia General Packet Radio Service (GPRS) solution. It was a major step toward what is being termed *third-generation mobile communications*, for which the company expected commercial offerings in mid 2000. GPRS offers data speeds of more than 100 Kbps, and enables always-on network connections for mobile phone users. This, in turn, will enable access to the Internet and corporate LANs. With rumors of mobile products that soar as fast as 384 Kbps, one can expect that videoconferencing will certainly be a strategic application in the family of advanced data services for these handheld communications appliances. That Nokia and Sony began licensing the Palm OS (not Microsoft's Windows CE) in 1999 provides insight about the companies' strategies in providing users with access to information anytime, anywhere. Three days after Nokia was recognized as Europe's second largest company (in December 1999), company executives proclaimed that, one year ahead of their earlier predictions, the worldwide market of wireless users would reach 1 billion. Nokia expects 1999 worldwide subscribership of more than 450 million to reach 1 billion by 2003.

To serve as interactive video communications devices, handheld communications appliances will require cameras. Pasadena based Photobit targets video cell phones and other hand-held or small format applications with its 352-by-288 pixels and 640-by-480 pixel sensors. These CMOS active-pixel image sensor technology based sensors (invented in NASA's Jet Propulsion Laboratory in 1993) offer full electronic pan, tilt and zoom, auto-exposure, and full programmability via a serial interface. The company considers these sensors cameras-on-a-chip. They offer the pixel array, the timing and control logic and the analog-to-digital converter on one chip. Photobit claims that these sensors offer a level of integration that is not possible with charged couple device (CCD) technology. The company claims that, by combining multiple functions on one chip, its CMOS sensors reduce the number of additional components that OEMs would have to buy using CCD sensors, and enable programming of frame size, exposure, and other parameters. Although CMOS sensors do not yet provide CCD level quality, numerous manufacturers are investing in the technology and should soon narrow the gap. Such devices not only facilitate desktop videoconferencing, they also enable video in new generations of handheld communications appliances.

Government & the Public Network

Government and the Internet

By 2002, metered, pay-per-use Internet access revenue models are likely to become quite common. The innovation that is resulting from today's decentralized model is largely incompatible with the desire for more stability. Furthermore, various agencies of the US Government would prefer a centralized, controllable, and taxable Internet. Under the guise of protecting children from harmful material, Congress could introduce legislation that would mandate a fundamental shift in philosophy within the US but, since Congress can not legislate outside of its own borders, this could lead to a disconnected network. A metered Internet is also likely to split users into business that pay by the cell, home users that pay a flat rate, and educational users for which taxes pay. Under this scenario, it is likely that the three groups would spawn three separate (but hopefully) interconnected networks. The American way would simply be to let advertising pay an increasing amount; the downside of that would be an increase in banner advertising. Paying by the byte would largely prohibit interactive video communications. This would be unfortunate. If, as George Gilder proclaims, "We live inside our televisions, computers, and telephones as much as we live inside our homes," such separation could undo much of the good that the Internet promises.

However, the elements are in place for it to happen. The existing Domain Name Service (DNS) system is decentralizing from a centrally controlled root server into a series of domain registers. Were those registers to make a case that they own the root servers, they could rescind the cooperation that now enables interconnectivity. Internet service providers (ISPs) could persuade users not to leave their cached Internet-emulating LANs by intentionally introducing latency. Such practices would inhibit interactive video communications. ISPs and municipalities such as the City of Portland, Oregon are fighting to open up cable provider networks. They contend that not doing so will lead to the monopolistic conditions that the 1996 Telecommunications legislation was enacted to overcome.

Not surprisingly, the cable industry claims that efforts to open up broadband Internet networks such as the "Internet Freedom Act," the measure, that U.S. Representatives Rick Boucher (D-Va.) and Bob Goodlatte (R-Va.) introduced in fall 1999, will end in disaster. The industry contends that such measures would limit competition in broadband services, require overarching government regulation, and consequently not serve consumers. The legislation would require cable operators that offer broadband networks to open those networks to unaffiliated competing ISPs, and it would invoke antitrust laws to prevent them from discriminating against ISPs. The cable industry alleges that requiring cable providers to share broadband capacity in which they have invested will discourage future network investment.

ISPs are at a distinct disadvantage. They did not exist when most of the existing telecommunications legislation was written and are, therefore, excluded from much of the legislative process. Such companies as AT&T, on the other hand, virtually (or perhaps literally) wrote the Telecommunications Act of 1996. The Internet will benefit as ISPs are included in legislative carrier definitions.

Government agencies have struggled to catch up to the Internet. More to the point, they have had a hard time controlling, regulating, and taxing it. While that may be a large part of the beauty and success of the Internet, it is a condition that will not be permanent. IT managers will be required to address privacy and ethics extensively. They are already responsible for email management, prevention of network breaches (that may lead to breaches of other networks), and forensics. They will be required to also address the content that is on their networks. Fortunately, network monitoring and enforcement tools are improving.

IT managers may need to address steganography, the hiding of information in seemingly unrelated files, if the federal government continues to vacillate or postpone eliminating prohibitions on encryption exportation. These encryption prohibition practices have allowed other countries to advance beyond the US in encryption technology, have forced US companies to move their encryption development offshore, and have deprived US companies and citizens the benefits of strong encryption.

Telecom Deregulation Act

Even before enactment of the Telecommunications Act of 1996, local phone companies contended that they needed to charge more to compensate for the universal service subsidies that provide cheap consumer service. Simultaneously, long-distance carriers were contending that they should pay less to connect to the local phone companies' equipment. The FCC was not sympathetic with the RBOCs; in 1996 it ordered all seven, and GTE, to extend 17-25% discounts on local call capacity to new entrants. The RBOCs immediately filed suits.

As a result of the Telecommunications Act, satellite companies, cellular operators, competitive access providers, and utility companies are pursuing new broadband market and service opportunities. The Act allows power companies to lease their excess capacity to ISPs and to forge partnerships with telecommunications firms. It has allowed a tremendous amount of industry consolidation. Although it is certainly not over, there are not many large players left standing alone.

Existing telecommunications players are expanding to capture new service revenues. Three of 1996's top mergers were between telecommunications companies: Bell Atlantic and Nynex ($22.1 billion), SBC Communications and Pacific Telesis Group ($16.7 billion), and US West and Continental Cablevision ($10.8 billion). Three of the biggest deals in history occurred in 1998. They included SBC Communications' $72.4 billion acquisition of Ameritech, Bell Atlantic's $71.3 billion acquisition of GTE, and AT&T's $69.9 billion acquisition of TCI. However, that was all eclipsed in 1999 when Qwest Communications bought US West for about $35 billion, and MCI WorldCom bought Sprint for $115 billion. Long-distance carriers want the local services market that the RBOCs and GTE dominate; the RBOCs want the long-distance markets. In November 1996, the FCC began the actual process of implementing the Telecom Act and establishing a national framework for telecommunications policy.

The Supreme Court struck down the Communications Act of 1934 statute that banned in-region video offerings by telephone companies. However, on May 18, 1996 the Federal Communications Commission and the Justice Department asked the Supreme Court to overturn that decision. For instance, should the FCC impose a dual regulation scheme on any telephone company that also delivers video programming? TCI Cable's new owner, AT&T, and Continental Cable's owner, Qwest (since it bought US West) would say it should not. However, these are the types of questions one can expect to see raised for the foreseeable future.

To foster competition, the FCC set rules to allow consumers to keep their phone numbers when they change local telephone carriers. Under the new rules, local telephone companies began deploying *number portability* technology in 1998. Until number portability is deployed throughout the nation (many rural customers still can not even receive anything but POTS), they must provide comparable functionality through call forwarding services.

Following the Telecom Act will be nearly impossible because shrewd business people, bureaucrats, and attorneys will dispute its interpretation for years (many refer to it as the Attorney Employment Act). It will foster innovation and competition, but it will not be a simple process.

CONCLUSION

We can no more predict what our networks will look like in the year 2040 than could the designers of AT&T's Picturephone have predicted the next generation of handheld communications appliances. However, we do know that our network appliances will become more powerful, more portable, and more reliable, and that our networks will become more robust. To quote William James, "Change is the only absolute."

In the final analysis, technology is not really what matters. In the context of this book, what is important is the extent to which technology can improve the quality of people's lives and break down barriers to worthwhile communications. Communications technologies are miraculous developments but, without people, they are meaningless.

Therefore, we foster the belief that only the noblest of desires could enable people to contribute such extraordinary achievements. Our small contribution, this text, is offered in the hope that people will put those achievements to good use.

Chapter 17 References

Schwartz, Steve. "Living Large In Year 2000: Three Likely Hardware Trends Will Help You Forget All Your Worries About Y2K." Computer Shopper, January 2000 p249.

Ozer, Jan. "Digital Video Face-Off.(Digital Origin's IntroDV and Pinnacle Systems' Studio DV)." PC Magazine, Jan 4, 2000 p60.

Masud, Sam. "Cable Operators Eye Telephony." Telecommunications, November 1999 v33 i11 p35

Sweitzer, John. "The Future of Broadband Satellite Networks." Satellite Communications, July 1999 v23 i7 p30(4)

Woods, Bob. "Cable Modems Leading DSL In Broadband War." Newsbytes, December 8, 1999.

"Internet Service Providers' Business Is Threatened by Cable High-Speed Internet Access." Cambridge Telecom Report, November 29, 1999.

"TI Announces Next-Generation, Cable Modem Solution Complies with Euro-DOCSIS Industry Standard." PR Newswire, October 18, 1999 p1840.

Bonisteel, Steven. "Cable Companies & ISPs Should Be Friends." Newsbytes, November 23, 1999.

Glick, Eric. "Open Net Could Spell Disaster." Cable World, October 18, 1999 v11 i42 p8

"Residential Gateways are the 'Golden Spike' of Broadband Communications, But Strategies Differ On Driving Force." Business Wire, December 16, 1999 p0325

" Modem Research." CableFAX, November 24, 1999 v10 i229.

"Market Research." CableFAX, November 2, 1999 v10 i213.

"Market Research." CableFAX, December 1, 1999 v10 i232.

"Key Decision On Euro Cable Box Specification." Screen Digest, September 1999 i335.

"Cable calls on IP voice: Comcast claims positive trial results." Telephony, November 22, 1999.

Emmerson, Bob. "Back In The Game.(Innovations On Videoconferencing)." Communications International, March 1999 v26 i3 p20(1).

Costa, Dan. "Faster, Better, Everywhere: New technologies will continue to boost the speed and ubiquity of networking, with or without the wiring." Computer Shopper, Jan 2000 p275.

Gaffin, Adam. "The future, courtesy of Network World." Network World, September 16, 1999. http://www.nwfusion.com/

Pulver, Jeff. The Pulver Report, October 21, 1999. http://www.pulver.com

Matsumoto, Craig. "IEEE Drafting 10-Gbit Ethernet Standard." Electronic Engineering Times, November 5, 1999. http://www.eet.com/

Fusco, Patricia. "Netopia Develops VoDSL For ISPs." InternetNews.com. June 17, 1999

Thompson, Jim. "Move Over Cable, Here Comes G.lite." ISP-Planet. June 23, 1999

Staff. "New World Mobility Partners With Nokia to Step Towards Third-Generation Mobile Services in Hong Kong." Business Wire, Dec 1, 1999 p1025

Faletra, Robert "The Wireless Opportunity." Computer Reseller News, November 29, 1999 p18.

Shapiro, Jeff. "The future of the Internet, Part II." Network World, November 15 1999. http://www.nwfusion.com/archive/1999b/1115shapiro.html.

Staff. "Market Darling Nokia Increases Growth Estimates." Communications Today, December 6, 1999 v5 i235.

Stroh, Steve. "Sprint Goes On A Broadband Wireless Buying Spree." Boardwatch, October 1999

Staff. "Targeting Cell Phone/Hand Held Market." Electronic News, Jan 18, 1999 v45 i2253 p22(1).

Staff. "Videoconferencing Forecast: PC Camera Market to Reach $1 Billion by 2003." EDGE: Work-Group Computing Report, April 19, 1999.

APPENDICES

A

INTERNATIONAL STANDARDS BODIES

Standards are published documents that describe, in useful detail, a technical specification. Competition, customer demand, and the convenience of developing interfaces that can be extended across multiple environments, are the driving forces that propel the adoption of standards.

Standards have value because they give governments and organizations the ability to reach beyond local implementations and conventions to construct unifying systems. The more widely-published a standard, the better its chances to make an impact on a technology or market. Wide publication is not enough, however. The organization that sponsors the publication of the standard, and its stature within a given 'community', is also of critical importance.

Standards can be established by law, formal recommendation, convention, or custom and are of two types; de jure and de facto. As the name denotes, a de jure standard is legitimized by a "jury" that assembles to develop it. A nationally- or internationally-recognized assembly, sanctioned by a government or governments, gathers in a series of formal meetings with the intention of developing a specification. These specifications become treaties between national governments that operate telecommunications networks.

De jure standards aren't actually *laws* but, rather, technical *covenants*. Issued as *recommendations*; they offer a prescribed approach to connecting disparate systems and management domains. The word recommendation was chosen in order to stress the sovereign right of countries to deviate from a standard. It is usually expected that countries that do will make their reasons known in the form of a publication—but compliance is strictly voluntary.

De facto standards are more accurately described as conventions that are well established in practice, and made legitimate by virtue of their wide acceptance. De facto standards are 'created' by industry associations or consortia, representing key suppliers and, possibly, customers. These interested parties convene to resolve compatibility issues and later publish their results.

THE INTERNATIONAL TELECOMMUNICATIONS UNION

The ITU operates under the auspices of the United Nations. Headquartered in Geneva, Switzerland it is a de jure treaty organization. Its membership consists of "administrations" (where each is a country). Nearly every nation in the world is represented in the ITU. National delegates usually come from the largest telecommunication service provider in a member country. Each ITU administration has one vote.

The State Department represents the U.S. in the ITU. Elsewhere in the world, where telecommunications networks are not yet privately owned, government-owned Post Telephone and Telegraph entities (PTTs) provide members. Other organizations (non-government-owned carriers, manufacturers, scientific organizations, etc.) can participate, but only the government administration can cast a vote in an ITU plenary session.

The "one country-one vote" approach is meant to achieve harmony. The ITU's goal is not to create telecommunications standards but to encourage international cooperation in order to arrive at an efficient international telecommunications infrastructure. It operates in six languages and must have consensus before it can ratify a recommendation. This used to take years (four to be precise) but the ITU has accelerated its standardization work. It can now approve a standard in 15 months. This quickening of pace resulted in the approval of over 900 specifications during the period between 1993 and 1996. These are published in at least three languages (French, German and English).

Within the ITU, two organizations promote recommendations that relate to multimedia and videoconferencing. These are the ITU's Telecommunications Standardization Sector and its Radiocommunications Sector. Until 1993, the ITU-T was known as the CCITT (Comité Consultatif International Téléphonique et Télégraphique) and the ITU-R as the CCIR (Comité Consultatif International Téléphonique des Radiocommunications).

The ITU-R generates recommendations that deal with the preparation, transmission, and reception of radio-based signals, with the term 'radio' being taken in the broadest sense, to include television and telephony. The ITU-R's contribution to multimedia primarily relates to television formats, specifically the CCIR Rec. 601-2 specification for digital video and the CCIR Rec. 709 –1 specification for HDTV.

The ITU-T is the largest body of the ITU. It generates functional and electrical specifications for telecommunications and data communications networks. Because standardization today is a global activity the ITU-T cooperates with other standards bodies. For instance, the Internet Engineering Task Force (IETF) is a member of the ITU-T and the European Telecommunications Standards Institute (ETSI) and International Standards Organization (ISO) also incorporate their protocols into the ITU standards.

The ITU-T has ratified two important groups of interactive multimedia standards: the H.32X and T.12X specifications. It also developed the G.7XX audio specifications and the V.80 modem specification. Along with its work on ISDN and B-ISDN, the ITU-T has laid the foundation international audiovisual exchanges.

In October of 1996 the ITU-T convened its second World Telecommunication Standardization Conference (WTSC 96) in Geneva. At the Conference, the Questions for the next ITU study period (1997-2000) were drafted and Study Group 16 was created. Known as "Multimedia Services and Systems", Study Group 16 is intended to formally coalesce the informally linked spheres of computing, telecommunications and audiovisual entertainment. This structured convergence, and the standards that result, can not help but have a profound effect on organizations, and society as a whole.

INTERNATIONAL STANDARDS ORGANIZATION (ISO)

The International Standards Organization was founded in 1947 to promote the development of international standards and activities that relate to the exchange of goods and services worldwide. Its membership consists of national bodies that are populated by representatives of relevant user and vendor communities. Members in a national body consist of corporations, companies, partnerships, and other firms that engage in industrial or commercial enterprises (or in education, research and testing). In the U.S. American National Standards Institute (ANSI) in the U.S.

The ISO is affiliated with the International Electrotechnical Commission (IEC). Like the ITU-T, the ISO/IEC is headquartered in Geneva, Switzerland. The ISO/IEC has developed many important standards including the Motion Pictures Experts Group (MPEG) and Joint Photographic Experts Group (JPEG) standards for high-resolution image compression.

JPEG is *the* international standard for still image compression. It begins with a digital image in the format YCbCr (such as is defined in CCIR-601-2) and provides several levels of compression. JPEG-1 is defined in ISO/IEC DIS 10918-1. MPEG (ISO/IEC 11172) outlines four different standards for handling tightly-compressed motion sequences: MPEG-1, MPEG-2, MPEG-3 and MPEG-4. MPEG is described in greater detail in Appendix B of this book.

According to ISO Internet information the term "ISO" is not an acronym. Rather, it is derived from the Greek word *isos*, which means equal. For example, isochronous transmission means "equal in length of time," and an isosceles triangle has two equal sides. Standards are great equalizers and the ISO intends that they remain so. The name ISO offers the further advantage of being valid in all the official languages of the organization (English, French & Russian), whereas if it were to be an acronym it would not work for French and Russian.

Internet Engineering Task Force (IETF)

In addition to the ITU-T and the ISO there is another important standards development "community" involved in crafting recommendations for internetworked multimedia handling systems: the Internet Activities Board (IAB) and, through that body, the IETF. Standards for communications across the Internet evolve through the IETF's rather informal (in comparison to the ITU-T and ISO) standards-setting process that relies on circulars called Request for Comments (RFCs). RFC contributors are mostly scientists and academicians having an interest in some aspects of internetworking including, but not restricted to, multimedia communications. Often these individuals are involved in research funded by various grants or contracts with private corporations. RFCs are also developed in cooperation with other organizations and consortia, by employees of private organizations and by academicians.

The IMTC

The IMTC is a non-profit corporation founded to promote the creation and adoption of international standards for multipoint document exchange and video conferencing. Its members promote a Standards First initiative to guarantee internetworking for all aspects of multimedia teleconferencing. The organization is open to all that support its goals.

The IMTC maintains an informative Web site that contains a wealth of information on the H.32X and T.12X Recommendations. See Chapter 8 for the URL.

The long-standing president of the IMTC is Neil Starkey of DataBeam, Inc.

B

MPEG Family of Specifications

The Moving Picture Experts Group (MPEG) is a committee of the ISO/IEC; more specifically the Joint Technical Committee 1, Sub-committee 29, Work Group 11. It has produced a series of four standards for lossy data compression and storage of full-motion video. These four standards are MPEG-1, MPEG-2, MPEG-3, and MPEG-4. MPEG-3 was originally planned, was later merged into MPEG-2, and has re-emerged as a popular format for music file storage on the Internet. Because that is the only common application for MPEG-3, we will not discuss it further in this text.

MPEG defines only the operations that a decoder must perform to interpret a compressed bit stream. It does not address what constitutes a valid bit stream (although it is implicit in the decoding process). Encoding is left up to the individual manufacturers. This allows a proprietary advantage to be obtained in spite of the fact that MPEG is a publicly available international specification.

The MPEG committee meets four times a year. During its meetings it reviews the work that has been accomplished during the quarter and plans its next steps. To ensure that harmonized solutions to the widest range of applications are achieved the committee works jointly with the ITU-T Study Group 15 and its successor, Study Group 16. MPEG also collaborates with representatives from other organizations including the ITU-R, the SMPTE, and the ATSC.

Work Group 11 began meeting in 1988. Its original goal was to define a format for compressing audiovisual sequences for CD-ROM storage and playback. As it turned out, its work engendered a great deal of international interest. Technical experts from all over the world (more than 200 participants by 1992) collaborated on the development of a *syntax* for MPEG-1.

To represent an object using compact and coded data, it is necessary to develop a language that is capable of dealing with abstraction. The ISO refers to a unique language (the specific bit codes used to represent objects—and their meaning) as syntax. For example, a few tokens can represent a large block of data. Syntax is also used to decode a complex string of bits and to map those bits from their compact representation back into their original form (or a semblance thereof). In video coding, syntax exploits common characteristics (block-oriented motion, spatial and temporal redundancy, color-to-brightness ratios, etc.).

By the end of 1990, the MPEG-1 syntax had emerged. It defines a standard input format (SIF) that can be used to produce audio and video samples that are coded and compressed at a bit rate that is not to exceed 1.86 Mbps. Image sizes can be no larger than 720 pixels by 576 lines (although it is syntactically possible to encode picture dimensions as high as 4095 lines by 4095 pixels). In fact, MPEG-1 images are almost always 352 pixels by 240 lines. They are captured using progressive scanning (such as is used by computer monitors). MPEG-1 samples two channels of audio, combines it with the video and delivers it (either over a direct connection to a CD-ROM storage device or via a telecommunications network connection).

After demonstrations proved that the syntax was flexible enough to be applied to bit rates and sampling frequencies much higher than those required for CD-ROM playback applications, a second phase (MPEG-2) was initiated within the committee. Its objective, to define a syntax for the efficient encoding of interlaced (broadcast) video, was more difficult to achieve than that of encoding progressive scanned images. Audio encoding also presented a challenge. MPEG-2 would introduce a scheme to decorrelate multichannel discrete surround sound audio.

In 1991 it appeared that HDTV had special needs that would require a separate syntax. Thus, plans were laid to define MPEG-3. Tests in late 1992 revealed that the MPEG-2 syntax would, with a small amount of fine-tuning, scale with the bit rate, obviating this third MPEG phase. As a result, MPEG-3 was merged into MPEG-2 in 1992. However, most music sites on the Internet now use MPEG-3 because its file sizes are approximately 30% smaller than are those of MPEG-2.

MPEG-4 (ISO/IEC 14496) was launched in late 1992 to explore the requirements of a more diverse set of applications. Its goal was to find a syntax that could be used to code very low bit rate (4.8–64 Kbps) audio and video streams. MPEG-4 encoding is aimed at videophone and small-screen terminal (176 pixels-by-144 lines) applications. Formal plans to pursue MPEG-4 were approved by unanimous vote of the ISO/IEC JTC1 in Brussels, Belgium in September 1993. A draft specification was delivered in 1997, and was approved in December 1999. In addition to videophones, MPEG-4 enables interactive mobile multimedia, remote sensing and sign language captioning.

In 1995, MPEG became virtually assured of dominance as a standard when Microsoft announced plans to bundle software MPEG-1 playback technology with its operating system, and Compaq announced that it would ship a motherboard with a hardware-based implementation of MPEG. In 1996, both IBM and LSI Logic announced large price reductions as a result of reduced number MPEG encoding chipsets. MPEG-2 is used for real time high-quality applications (e.g., digital-cable distribution systems and satellite broadcasts).

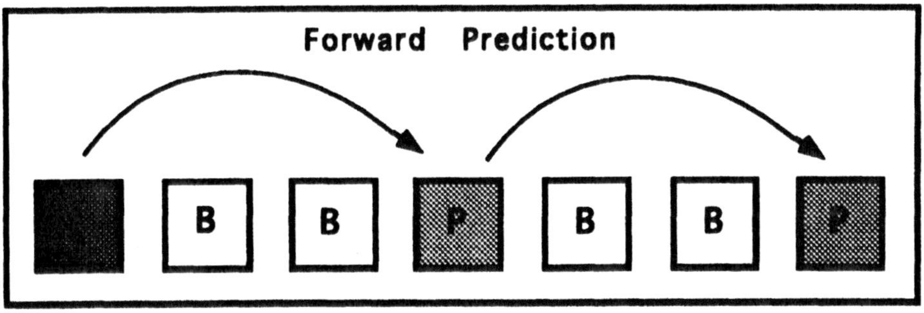

Figure Appendix B-1. Forward Prediction (Michel Bayard).

MPEG PICTURE CODING

MPEG manipulates motion video as image sequences. An image is divided into macroblocks. MPEG syntax identifies the three approaches that are used to code these macroblocks. MPEG manipulates motion video as image sequences. As such, a great deal of redundancy exists between frames. To achieve temporal compression, it is useful to compute some frames from other frames. Hence, MPEG defines three types of frames. The most basic type is the Intraframe or I-frame. I-frames are compressed using intraframe encoding (DCT). In addition there are Predicted frames (P-frames) and Bi-directional frames (B-frames).

I -frames are coded without reference to past or future frames and contain explicit information about every pixel in the image. I-frame coding generates significant amounts of data. A certain number of I-frames must be sent in an MPEG sequence (once every 400 ms is typical) to eliminate accumulated errors that result from interframe coding techniques. I-frames must also be sent for major scene changes. For highly efficient coding, the object is to send as few I-frames as possible.

P-frames are coded through a process of predicting the current frame using a past frame (an I-frame or another P-frame). The picture is broken into 16x16 pixel blocks. Each block is compared to a pixel block in the same horizontal and vertical position in a previous frame. The P-frame technique assumes all pixels in a block move together and does not describe each pixel individually. Only information about differences between pixels in the current frame and the previous frame is coded.

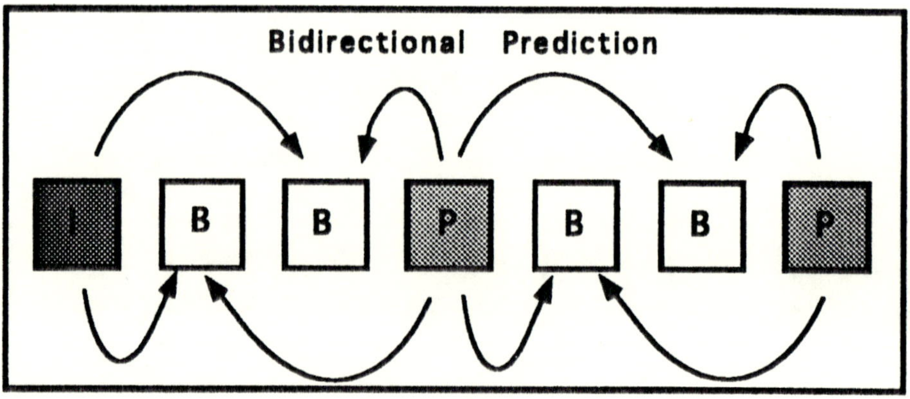

Figure Appendix B-2. Bi-Directional Interpolated Coding (Michel Bayard).

B-frame pictures use bi-directional interpolation coding. Interpolation is the process of determining that a given pixel is a certain color because a pixel in the same place in a prior frame was that color. B-frame coding uses hints to predict a current frame based on what was contained in a past and a future frame. B-frame coding includes background estimation—working with areas in the background that are uncovered as an object moves from side to side. B-frame coding also uses motion compensated prediction to guess at where a moving object will be, based on where it was in the prior frame.

The process of MPEG encoding always starts with an I-frame. After a time interval that is defined by each particular implementation another frame is sent, typically, a P-frame. The elapsed time between the transmission of frames (of any type) is often too great to permit the illusion of smooth motion. Thus, B-frames are computed (interpolated) by comparing a past frame to a present frame. These interpolated frames are used to fill in the gaps between I-frames and P-frames (or some combination thereof).

B-frames tend to make motion sequences smoother on playback while conserving bandwidth. Unfortunately, their use forces a decoder to buffer the P-frames from which they are computed. This buffering increases the cost of a decoder and, consequently, presents a problem for some low-end, mass-market applications. I-frames anchor picture quality, because ultimately P and B-frames are derived from them. P-frames are the least demanding of the three, in terms of their impact on a decoder.

MPEG 1 – ISO/IEC 11172

The official title of the ISO/IEC's MPEG-1 specification is, "Coding Of Moving Pictures And Associated Audio For Digital Storage Media At Up To About 1.5 Mbps." It was originally approved as a three-part specification in October of 1992. Later, two additional parts were added, one in 1994 and one in 1995.

MPEG-1 encoded video is optimized for playback on computers and set-top boxes. MPEG-1 uses progressive (non-interlaced) scanning to provide a typical picture resolution of 352H-by-240V pixels (although the resolutions can vary). Images are displayed at 30 fps (in North America and Japan only) and 25 fps. The MPEG-1 data rate is 150 Kbytes (not Kbps). This speed, which matches the data rate delivered by a single-speed CD-ROM player, is also compatible with T-1/E-1 network speeds.

Special MPEG-1 compliant chips provide near VHS-quality desktop video (with CD-ROM quality stereo sound) at data rates of 150 Kbytes. This data rate conforms to T1/E1 speeds and also matches the data rate from a standard, single-speed CD-ROM player).

The five MPEG-1 parts are as follows:

Part 1—SYSTEM (IS 11172-1). This part describes the syntax used to synchronize and multiplex audio and video signals. These signals can be transported over digital channels and/or stored as digital media. Part 1 also includes the syntax for synchronizing video and audio streams.

Part 2—VIDEO (IS 11172-2). This part describes compression of non-interlaced video signals. It specifies the header and bit stream elements for video and identifies the algorithms (semantics) used to code and compress video. Video handles the image by dividing it into nested layers. At the highest layer (the picture layer) frame rates and resolutions are defined. Below the picture layer comes slices, macroblocks, blocks, samples and coefficients. At each layer, coding and compression algorithms are defined. Methods are also described for synchronizing, accessing, buffering and error recovery.

Part 3—AUDIO (IS 11172-3). This part describes the compression of audio signals. It includes syntax and semantics for three compression methods (known as I, II, and III). These methods, or *classes*, define algorithms that vary in complexity and coding efficiency to produce streams of audio at different bit rates. Layer I (audio at 384 Kbps) is used for compact disc video. Layer II (audio at 224 Kbps) is used in satellite broadcasting and compact disc video. Layer III (128 Kbps audio) is used in ISDN, satellite and Internet audio applications.

Part 4—CONFORMANCE (IS 11172-4). This part describes the procedures for determining the characteristics of coded bit streams and how they are decoded. It also defines the meaning of MPEG-1 conformance for the first three parts of IS 11172 (Systems, Video, and Audio), and provides two sets of test guidelines for determining compliance in bit streams and decoders.

Part 5—SOFTWARE SIMULATION (IS 11172-5). This part contains a sample ANSI C language software encoder and compliant decoder for video and audio. It also provides an example of a systems codec, that can multiplex and demultiplex the separate video and audio streams that are used in computer files.

BRIEF EXPLANATION OF HOW MPEG-1 WORKS

MPEG-1 compresses relatively low-resolution source input format (SIF) video sequences (approximately 352-by-240 pixels) that are synchronized with relatively high-quality audio. The color images have been converted to the YUV space with the chrominance channels (U and V) further decimated to 176-by-120 pixels. MPEG-1 uses motion prediction (temporal compression) first and then follows it up with DCT (spatial compression). DCT acts on 8-by-8 pixel blocks while motion prediction operates on 16-by-16 pixel blocks. After temporal and spatial compression are complete MPEG-1 uses fixed-table Huffman encoding and differential PCM. As is true with all MPEG types, MPEG-1 uses I frames, P frames and B frames for temporal compression. MPEG-1 files are usually smaller than QuickTime or Video for Windows files, however the quality is not always as good.

MPEG 2 – ISO/IEC 13818

The official title of the ISO/IEC's MPEG-2 specification is, "Generic Coding of Moving Pictures and Associated Audio." It was formally approved in November 1994. MPEG-2 was produced in collaboration with the ITU-T, which also published it as Recommendation H.262. The full title of Recommendation H.262 is "Information Technology—Generic Coding of Moving Pictures and Associated Audio."

MPEG-2 is intended to provide compression for studio-quality video applications that include digital broadcast television, digital storage media, digital VCRs and video on demand. MPEG-2 compressed media is suitable for distribution over coaxial and fiber optic cable and satellite.

MPEG-1 was forced to compromise on video quality so that data could play on a single-speed CD-ROM in real time. These compromises manifest as picture *blockiness*. By contrast, MPEG-2 generates higher quality images when compared to previous video CD players that utilize MPEG-1.

MPEG-2 goes beyond MPEG-1 to address the need for higher-resolution images and interlaced video formats. It does so by compressing a full CCIR-601 digital video image (480 lines by 720 pixels) at a rate of 30 frames per second. It also supports multiple programs in a single stream, interlaced and progressive scan (whereas MPEG-1 supports only progressive), interactive data transmission (for applications such as home shopping and distance learning) and surround-sound audio. MPEG-2 also differs from MPEG-1 in that it can use symmetric compression (MPEG-1 uses asymmetric compression techniques only). MPEG-2 is backward compatible with MPEG-1 and can incorporate MPEG-1 encoded streams.

The digital versatile disk (DVD) *standard* for storing large quantities of digital video and audio specifies MPEG-2 video compression (although it supports Dolby AC-3 audio and *not* MPEG-2 audio). DVDs use laser technology to store up to 17 gigabytes (GB) of data, enough for nine hours of studio-quality audio and video.

MPEG-2 Parts

The MPEG-2 ISO/IEC 13818 volume consists of a total of eight parts, 1-7 and 9 (part 8 was withdrawn).

Part 1—SYSTEMS (13818-1). Part 1 addresses how one or more elementary streams of video, audio and data are combined into single or multiple streams suitable for storage and transmission. These streams take one of two forms, the Program Stream and the Transport Stream. Each is optimized for a different set of applications. The Program Stream is similar to MPEG-1 Systems Multiplex. It results from combining one or more Packetized Elementary Streams (PES), which have a common time base, into a single stream that run at between 3-15 Mbps. The Program Stream is used for DVD encoding. The Transport Stream combines multiple PES with one or more independent time bases into a single stream. Elementary streams sharing a common time base form a program. The Transport Stream is designed for use in environments where errors are likely (broadcast and telecommunications). Transport stream packets are 188 bytes long.

Part 2—VIDEO (13818-2). Part 2 builds on the video compression capabilities of the MPEG-1 standard to offer coding tools. These have been grouped in seven profiles to offer different functions. The first five were approved with the standard in November of 1994. The sixth profile (the 4:2:2 Profile) and the seventh (Multiview Profile) were added in 1996.

Part 3—AUDIO (13818-3). Part 3 is a backward compatible multi-channel extension of the MPEG-1 Audio standard.

Part 4—COMPLIANCE TESTING (13818-4). Part 4 of MPEG-2 corresponds to Part 4 of MPEG-1. It was approved in March 1996.

Part 5—SOFTWARE SIMULATION (13818-5). Part 5 of MPEG-2 corresponds to Part 5 of MPEG-1 and was also approved in March 1996.

Part 6—DIGITAL STORAGE MEDIUM COMMAND AND CONTROL (13818-6). This part defines a syntax for controlling VCR-style playback and random-access of bit streams encoded onto digital storage media (e.g., compact disc). Commands include fast forward, advance, still frame and go-to. Part 6 was approved in 1996.

Part 7—NON-BACKWARDS COMPATIBLE AUDIO (13838-7). This part

extends the two-channel audio of MPEG-1 (11172-3) by adding a new syntax to efficiently decorrelate discrete multi-channel surround sound audio. Part 7 of MPEG-2 was approved in 1997.

Part 9— REAL-TIME INTERFACE (RTI) (13838-9). This part defines a syntax for video on demand control signals between set-top boxes and head-end servers. Part 9 was approved as an International Standard in July 1996.

MPEG-2 Levels

Each MPEG-2 defines "quality classifications" that are known as levels. Levels limit coding parameters (sample rates, frame dimensions, coded bit rates, etc.). The MPEG-2 levels are as follows:

Level	Resolution Sampled	Frame rate	Pixels per Second	Maximum bit rate	Purpose
Low	352 x 240	30 fps	3.05 M	4 Mbps	Consumer Tape, CIF
Main	740 x 480	30 fps	10.40 M	15 Mbps	CCIR-601 Studio TV
High 1440	1440 x 1440	30 fps	47.00 M	60 Mbps	Commercial HDTV
High	1920 x 1080	30 fps	62.70 M	80 Mbps	Production SMPTE

Figure Appendix B-3. MPEG-2 Levels

The two most popular MPEG-2 levels are the Low (or SIF) Level and the Main (or CCIR-601) Level.

MPEG-2 Profiles

MPEG-2 consists of six different coding tools that are known as *profiles*. Profiles are a defined sub-set of the MPEG-2 specification's syntax (algorithms). Different profiles conform to different MPEG-2 levels and are aimed at different applications (e.g. high- or regular-definition television broadcasts over different types of networks). Profiles also provide backward compatibility with other specifications such as H.261 or MPEG-1.

	Simple Profile	Main Profile	SNR Scalable Profile	Spatially Scalable Profile	High Profile	4:2:2 Profile
Low Level		X				
Main Level	X	X		X	X	X
High 1440		X	X		X	
High Level		X	X		X	

Figure Appendix B-4. MPEG-2 Profiles

The MPEG-2 Video Main Profile conforms to the CCIR-601 studio standard for digital TV, and is implemented widely in MPEG-2 decoder chips and in direct broadcast satellite. It will also be used for the delivery of video programming over cable television. It is targeted at a higher encoded bit rate of less than 15Mbps and specifies a resolution of 720x480 at 30 fps, allowing for much higher quality than is typical with MPEG-1. It supports the coding parameters as set forth in MPEG-2's high, high 1440, main and low levels. It uses the 4:2:0 chroma format. The Video Main Profile also supports I, P, and B frames. The U.S. ATSC Digital Television Standard (Document A/53—HDTV) specifies MPEG-2 Video Mail Profile compression.

The Simple Profile is nothing more than the Main profile without B frames. As we said earlier, B frames require a set-top or other MPEG decoder to have a certain amount of integrated circuit (IC) memory; that becomes too costly for some applications.

The SNR Scalable and Spatially Scalable Profiles are very complex and are useful primarily for academic research. Scalability allows a decoder to divide a continuous video signal into two or more coded bitstreams that represent the video at different resolutions (spatial scalability) or picture quality (SNR scalability). Video is also scalable across time (temporal scalability). Equipment manufacturers do not generally pursue scalable profiles. They require twice as many integrated circuits as non-scalable profiles, that approximately doubles their cost.

The High Profile is aimed at high-resolution video. It supports chroma formats of 4:2:2 and 4:2:0, resolutions that range between 576 lines by 720 pixels and 1152 lines by 1920 pixels, and data transfer rates of between 20 and 100 Mbps. It also supports I, P, and B frames.

The 4:2:2 Profile (that was added to MPEG-2 Video in January of 1996) possesses unique characteristics more desirable in the professional broadcast studio and post-production environment. The 4:2:2 Profile uses a chroma format of 4:2:2 (or 4:2:0), uses separate luminance and chrominance quantization tables, allows an unconstrained number of bits in a macroblock and operates at 608 lines/frame for 25 fps or 512 lines/frame for 30 fps.

The Multiview Profile, that was completed in October 1996, uses existing video coding tools for the purpose of providing an efficient way to encode two slightly different pictures such as those obtained from two slightly separated cameras shooting the same scene. This allows multiple views of scenes, such as stereoscopic sequences, that are coded in a manner similar to scalable bit streams.

How MPEG-2 Differs from MPEG-1

MPEG-2 is not intended to replace MPEG-1. Rather, it includes extensions to MPEG-1 to cover a wider range of applications. MPEG-1 deals only with progressive scanning techniques where video is handled in complete frames. The MPEG-2 standard supports both progressive scanning and interlaced displays such as those used for televisions. In interlaced video, each frame consists of two fields (half frames) that are sent at twice the frame rate.

The MPEG-1 specification was targeted nominally at single speed CD ROMs (1.5 Mbytes per second). MPEG-2 is targeted at variable frame rates, including those many times higher than MPEG-1.

Each of the two standards, MPEG-1 and MPEG-2, is divided into parts. MPEG-1 has five parts (listed in this document); MPEG-2 has eight, of which five are either identical to or extensions of MPEG-1 parts and three are additions.

The MPEG-1 stream is made up of two layers, the system layer and the compression layer. The MPEG-2 stream is made up of program and transport streams. MPEG-2 streams are subdivided into packets for transmission. The MPEG-2 program stream is designed for use in relatively error-free environments. As such, it is similar to the MPEG-1 system stream. The MPEG-2 transport stream is designed for error-prone environments (broadcast). MPEG-1 does not have an equivalent to the MPEG-2 transport stream.

Both the MPEG-1 and MPEG-2 standards define a hierarchy of data structures in the video stream. There is a group of pictures (a video sequence). The next level down in the hierarchy is the picture (the primary coding unit of a video sequence). MPEG-2 only defines a slice (used to handle errors in a bit stream). Both MPEG-1 and MPEG-2 define a macroblock (a 16 pixel by 16 line selection of luminance components and its corresponding 8 pixel by 8 line chrominance components), and a block (an 8-pixel by 8-line set of luminance and chrominance values).

MPEG-1 handles only two channels of audio. MPEG-2 handles up to five channels (surround sound). Because of this difference, MPEG-1 and MPEG-2 use different techniques to synchronize audio and video.

In summary, MPEG-2 extends MPEG-1 to handle audiovisual broadcasts (whereas MPEG-1 was aimed at playback applications). It can deliver audiovisual material at higher speeds, with greater resolution, with surround sound audio and in interlaced scanned environments. MPEG-2 may eventually replace MPEG-1 but it was not intended to do so.

MPEG 4 – ISO/IEC 14496

The official title of the ISO/IEC's MPEG-4 specification is, "Very Low Bitrate Audio-Visual Coding." It was approved as a Working Draft in November 1994, was finalized in October 1998, and became an International Standard in 1999.

MPEG-4 is targeted at low bit rate applications with frame sizes of 176x144 or less, frame rates of 10Hz or less, and encoded bit rates of 4.8–64 Kbps. The promise of MPEG-4 is to provide fully backward compatible extensions under the title of MPEG-4 Version 2. MPEG-4 is designed to address digital television, interactive graphics applications that build on synthetic content, and interactive multimedia (e.g., distribution of, and access to, content). MPEG-4 provides standardized technological elements to enable the integration of the production, distribution, and content access paradigms of these three domains.

MPEG-4 enables extensive reusability of content across disparate technologies such as digital television, animated graphics, and World Wide Web (WWW) pages. It also offers manageability of content owner rights. Furthermore, MPEG-4 offers a generic QoS descriptor for dissimilar MPEG-4 media that can be interpreted and translated into the appropriate native signaling messages of each network. End-to-end signaling of the MPEG-4 media QoS descriptors enables transport optimization in heterogeneous networks. However, the exact translations from the QoS parameters set for each media to the network QoS are left to network providers. MPEG-4 offers end users higher levels of interaction with content, and allows the author to set those limits. It also extends multimedia to new networks, such as mobile networks and others that employ lower bit rates.

MPEG seeks to supercede proprietary, non-interoperable formats by providing standardized ways to represent units of aural, visual or audiovisual content, called *media objects*. These media objects could be recorded with a camera or microphone, or generated with a computer. MPEG describes the composition of these objects to create compound media objects that form audiovisual scenes. It multiplexes and synchronizes the data associated with media objects so that they can be transported over network channels and provide a QoS that is appropriate for the nature of the specific media objects, and it interacts with the audiovisual scene that is generated at the receiver's end.

Media objects may require streaming data that is conveyed in multiple elementary streams. Therefore, MPEG-4 defines an object descriptor that identifies all streams that are associated with one media object. This enables the handling of hierarchically encoded data, and the association of both object content and intellectual property rights information. Each stream is characterized by a set of descriptors for configuration information, (e.g., required decoder resources, or the required precision of encoded timing information). The descriptors may also describe the QoS it requests for transmission (e.g., maximum bit rate, bit error rate, or priority). MPEG-4 enables synchronization of elementary streams by time stamping individual access units within elementary streams. The synchronization layer manages the identification of access units and manages the time stamping. Independent of the media type, this layer allows identification of the type of access unit (e.g., video or audio frames, scene description commands) in elementary streams, and the recovery of the media object's or scene description's time base. It also enables synchronization among these.

The MPEG-4 ISO/IEC 14496 volume consists of four basic functions:

Delivery Multimedia Integration Framework (DMIF)

DMIF is a session protocol for the management of multimedia streaming over generic delivery technologies. It is similar to FTP except that, where FTP returns data, DMIF returns pointers toward (streamed) data. DMIF is both a framework and a protocol. The functionality provided by DMIF is expressed by an interface called DMIF-Application Interface (DAI), and translated into protocol messages that may differ based on any given network on which they operate.

MPEG-4 specifies an interface to the *TransMux* (Transport Multiplexing) models, the layer that offers transport services for matching the requested QoS. Any suitable existing transport protocol stack (e.g., RTP in UDP/IP, AAL5 in ATM, or Transport Stream in MPEG-2) over a suitable link layer may become a specific TransMux instance. The synchronized delivery of streaming data may require the use of different QoS schemes as it traverses multiple public and private networks. MPEG defines the delivery-layer FlexMux multiplexing tool to allow grouping of Elementary Streams (ES) with low multiplexing overhead. It may be used to group ESs with similar QoS requirements, to reduce the number of network connections, or to reduce end-to-end delay. The FlexMux layer may be empty if the underlying TransMux instance provides adequate functionality.

The DMIF framework enables control functions such as the ability to identify access units, to transport timestamps and clock reference information, and to recognize data loss. It also enables interleaving of data from different elementary streams into FlexMux streams. Moreover, it permits the conveyance of control information to indicate the required QoS for each elementary stream and FlexMux stream, translation of such QoS requirements into actual network resources, association of elementary streams to media objects, and conveyance of the mapping of elementary streams to FlexMux and TransMux channels.

Systems

MPEG-4 supports scene description for composition (spatio-temporal synchronization with time response behavior) of multiple media objects. The scene description provides a rich set of nodes for two-dimensional and three-dimensional composition operators and graphics primitives. It also supports text with international language support, font and font style selection, timing and synchronization. Moreover, MPEG-4 supports interactivity such as client and server-based interaction, an event model for triggering events or routing user actions, and event management and routing between objects in the scene, as a result of user or scene triggered events.

The FlexMux tool provides interleaving of multiple streams into a single stream, including timing information, and the TransMux provides transport layer independence through mappings to relevant transport protocol stacks. MPEG-4 also provides the initialization and continuous management of the receiving terminal's timing identification, synchronization and recovery mechanisms, as well as other receiving terminal buffers. It also recognizes data sets such as the identification of Intellectual Property Rights that relate to media objects.

Audio

MPEG-4 Audio permits a wide variety of applications that could range from simple speech to sophisticated multi-channel audio, and from natural sounds to synthesized sounds. In particular, it supports the highly efficient representation of audio objects consisting of:

Speech signals: Speech coding can be done at bitrates from 2 Kbps up to 24 Kbps using the speech coding tools. Lower bitrates, such as an average of 1.2 Kbps, are possible through variable rate coding. Low delay is possible for communications applications. When using the HVXC tools, speed and pitch can be modified under user control during playback. If the CELP tools are used, a change of the playback speed can be achieved by using an additional tool for effects processing.

Synthesized Speech: Scalable TTS coders bitrate range from 200 Bps to 1.2 Kbps that allows a text, or a text with prosodic parameters (e.g., pitch contour, phoneme duration,), as its inputs to generate intelligible synthetic speech.

General audio signals: Support for coding general audio ranging from very low bitrates to high quality is provided by transform coding techniques. With this functionality, a wide range of bitrates and bandwidths is covered. It starts at a bitrate of 6 Kbps and a bandwidth below 4 kHz, but also includes mono or multichannel broadcast quality audio.

Synthesized Audio: Synthetic Audio support is provided by a Structured Audio Decoder implementation that allows the application of score-based control information to musical instruments described in a special language.

Bounded-complexity Synthetic Audio: This is provided by a Structured Audio Decoder implementation that allows processing of a standardized wavetable format.

Examples of additional functionality include speed control, or change of the time scale without altering the pitch while decoding, and pitch change, or change of the pitch without altering the time scale while encoding or decoding. Audio Effects provide the ability to process decoded audio signals with complete timing accuracy to enable such functions as mixing, reverberation, and spatialization.

Visual

The MPEG-4 Visual standard will allow the hybrid coding of natural (pixel based) images and video together with synthetic (computer generated) scenes. This will, for example, allow the virtual presence of videoconferencing participants. To this end, the Visual standard will comprise tools and algorithms supporting the coding of natural (pixel based) still images and video sequences as well as tools to support the compression of synthetic 2-D and 3-D graphic geometry parameters (i.e. compression of wire grid parameters, synthetic text). The MPEG-4 visual standard will support bitrates typically between 5 Kbps and 10 Mbps, progressive and interlaced video, and resolutions ranging from SQCIF to DTV. Moreover, it supports compression efficiencies from *acceptable* to *near lossless*, and will allow for random access of video such as fast forward and reverse.

Spatial scalability allows decoders to decode a subset of the total bitstream generated by the encoder to reconstruct and display textures, images and video objects at reduced spatial resolution. For textures and still images, a maximum of 11 levels of spatial scalability is supported. For video sequences, a maximum of three levels is supported. Temporal scalability allows decoders to decode a subset of the total bitstream generated by the encoder to reconstruct and display video at reduced temporal resolution. A maximum of three levels is supported. Quality scalability allows a bitstream to be parsed into a number of bitstream layers of different bitrate such that the combination of only a subset of the layers can be decoded into a meaningful signal. The bitstream parsing can occur either during transmission or in the decoder. The reconstructed quality, in general, is related to the number of layers used for decoding and reconstruction.

MPEG-4 supports shape coding to assist the description and composition of conventional images and video as well as arbitrarily shaped video objects. Applications that benefit from binary shape maps with images are content based image representations for image databases, interactive games, surveillance, and animation. Error resilience assists the access of image and video over a wide range of storage and transmission media such as the useful operation of image and video compression algorithms in error-prone environments at low bit-rates (i.e., less than 64 Kbps). Tools are provided that address both the band-limited nature and error resiliency aspects for access over wireless networks. The Face Animation part of the standard allows sending parameters that calibrate and animate synthetic faces.

Tools	AAC main	AAC LC	AAC SSR	AAC LTP	AAC Scalable	TwinVQ	CELP	HVXC	TTSI	Main synthetic	Wavetable synthesis	General MIDI	Algorithmic Synthesis & Audio FX
MPEG-2 AAC Main	X												
MPEG-2AAC LC		X		X	X								
MPEG-2AAC SSR			X										
Noise Shaping	X	X	X	X	X								
Long Term Prediction				X	X	X							
Tools for Large Step Scalability					X								
TwinVQ						X							
CELP							X						
HVXC								X					
TTSI									X				
Structured Audio tools										X			X
SA Sample Bank Format										X	X		
MIDI										X	X	X	

Figure Appendix B-5. MPEG-4 Tools

MPEG-4 only standardizes the parameters of these models, not the models themselves.

MPEG-4 Parts

The MPEG-4 requirements have been addressed by the 6 parts of the MPEG-4 Version 1 standard:

Part 1: Systems - specifies scene description, multiplexing, synchronization, buffer management, and management and protection of intellectual property

Part 2: Visual - specifies coded representation of natural and synthetic visual objects

Part 3: Audio - specifies the coded representation of natural and synthetic audio objects

Part 4: Conformance Testing - defines conformance conditions for bitstreams and devices; this part is used to test MPEG-4 implementations

Part 5: Reference Software - includes software corresponding to most parts of MPEG-4 (normative and non-normative tools); it can be used for implementing compliant products as ISO waives the copyright of the code

Part 6: Delivery Multimedia Integration Framework (DMIF) - defines a session protocol for the management of multimedia streaming over generic delivery technologies

Parts 1–3 and 6 specify the core MPEG-4 technology; Parts 4 and 5 are *supporting parts*. Parts 1, 2 and 3 are delivery independent, leaving to Part 6 (DMIF) the task of dealing with the idiosyncrasies of the delivery layer. The MPEG-4 parts are fairly independent and can be used independently or in conjunction with proprietary technologies. However, they were developed to ensure that the maximum benefit results when they are used together.

Participants in MPEG-4 represent broadcasters, equipment and software manufacturers, digital content creators and managers, telecommunication service providers, publishers and intellectual property rights managers, and university researchers. Hundreds of experts, from organizations throughout the world, developed MPEG-4 for the next generation of multimedia products and services. MPEG-4 Version 1 became available at the end of 1998; MPEG-4 Version 2 extends the standard in a backward compatible way.

MPEG-4 Audio Object types

For coding natural sound, MPEG-4 includes the Advanced Audio Coding (AAC) and Twin Vector Quantization (Twin VQ) algorithms. The following object types exist:

1. The **Advanced Audio Coding (AAC) Main** object type is similar to—and compatible with—the AAC Main profile that the MPEG-2 (ISO/IEC 13818-7) defines. MPEG-4 AAC adds the Perceptual Noise Shaping tool and supports 5 channels plus a low frequency channel in one object.
2. The **MPEG-4 AAC Low Complexity** object type is a low complexity version of the AAC Main Object type.
3. The **MPEG-4 AAC Scalable Sampling Rate** object type is the counterpart to the MPEG-2 AAC Scalable Sampling Rate profile,
4. The **MPEG-4 AAC LTP** object type is similar to the AAC Main object type but replaces the MPEG-2 AAC predictor with the long term predictor to provide the same efficiency at a lower implementation cost.
5. The **AAC Scalable** object type allows a large number of scalable combinations such as combinations with TwinVQ and CELP coder tools as the core coders. It supports only mono or 2-channel stereo sound.
6. The **TwinVQ** (Transform domain Weighted Interleave Vector Quantization) object type is based on fixed rate vector quantization instead of AAC's Huffman coding. It operates at lower bitrates than AAC and supports both mono and stereo sound.
7. MPEG-4 includes two different algorithms for coding speech, each operates at different bitrates, plus a Text-to-Speech Interface.
   - The **CELP** (Code Excited Linear Prediction) object type supports 8 kHz and 16 kHz sampling rates at 4–24 Kbps. CELP bitstreams can be coded in a scalable way through bit rate scalability and bandwidth scalability.

- The **HVXC** (Harmonic Vector Excitation Coding) object type gives a parametric representation of 8 kHz, mono speech at fixed bitrates between 2–4 Kbps and less than 2 Kbps using a variable bitrate mode, and supports pitch and speed changes.

8. The **TTSI** (Text-to-Speech Interface) object type gives an extremely low-bitrate phonemic representation of speech. The actual text-to-speech synthesis is not specified; only the interface is defined. Bit rates range from 0.2 to 1.2 Kbps. The synthesized speech can be synchronized with a facial animation object (see below).
9. Lastly, a number of different object types exist for synthetic sound.
   - The **Main Synthetic** object type collects all MPEG-4 Structured Audio tools. Structured Audio is a way to describe methods of synthesis. It supports flexible, high-quality algorithmic synthesis through the Structured Audio Orchestra Language (SAOL) music-synthesis language, efficient wavetable synthesis with the Structured Audio Sample-Bank Format (SASBF), and enables the use of high-quality mixing and postproduction in the Systems Audio BIFS tool set. Sound can be described at '0 Kbps' (i.e., sound continues without input until it is stopped by an explicit command) to 3-4 Kbps for extremely expressive sounds in the MPEG-4 Structured Audio format.
   - The **Wavetable Synthesis** object type is a subset of the Main Synthetic object type that makes use of the SASBF format and the popular, widely used MIDI (Musical Instrument Digital Interface) wavetable format tools to provide simple sampling synthesis.
   - The **General MIDI** object type gives interoperability with existing content (see above). Unlike the *Main Synthetic* or *Wavetable Synthesis* object types, it does not provide completely predictable (i.e., normative) sound quality and decoder behavior.
10. The **Algorithmic Synthesis and AudioFX** object type provides SAOL-based synthesis capabilities for very low-bitrate terminals (*FX* stands for *effects*).
11. The **NULL** object type provides the possibility to feed raw PCM data directly to the MPEG-4 audio compositor to allow local sound enhancement at the decoder. Support for this object type is in the compositor, not in the decoder.

MPEG-4 Profiles

Although there are numerous object types in the audio area, there are only four distinct profiles (as defined below). Codec builders can claim conformance to profiles at a certain level, but can not claim conformance to object types.

Two levels are defined, determining whether either one or a maximum of 20 objects can be present in the (audio) scene.

The *Scalable* profile was primarily defined to allow good quality, reasonable complexity, low bitrate audio on the Internet (an environment in which bitrate varies between users and over time). Scalability enables optimal use of limited, and of varying, bandwidth without encoding and storing the material multiple times. The scalable profile has 4 levels that restrict the amount of objects in the scene, the total amount of channels, and the sampling frequency. The highest level employs the concept of complexity units.

The *Synthetic* profile groups the synthetic object types. The target applications are defined by the need for good quality sound at very low data rates. There are three levels that define the amount of memory for data, the sampling rates, the amount of TTSI objects, and some further processing restrictions.

The *Main* profile includes all object types. It is useful in environments in which processing power is available to create rich, highest quality audio scenes that may combine organic sources with synthetic ones. Two applications are the DVD and multimedia broadcast. This profile has four levels that are defined in terms of complexity units. There are two different types of complexity units: processor complexity units (PCU), that are specified in millions of operations per second, and RAM complexity units (RCU), that are specified in terms of the number of kWords. The standard also specifies the complexity units required for each object type. This provides authors with maximum freedom in choosing the right object types and allocating resources among them. For example, a profile could contain main AAC and wavetable synthesis object types, and a level could specify a maximum of two of each. This would prevent the resources reserved for the AAC objects to be used for a third and fourth wavetable synthesis object even though it would not break the decoder. Complexity units enable the author freedom to use decoder resources for any combination of profile-supported object types.

How MPEG-4 Differs from MPEG-2

The difference between MPEG-4 and MPEG-2 is not improvement in video or audio reproduction for a single application (as MPEG-2 specifically supports DTV). MPEG-4 represents the establishment of an adaptable set of tools for combining various types of video, audio, and interaction to provide environments beyond that anyone may now imagine. The essence of MPEG-4 is an object-based audiovisual representation model that allows authors to build scenes using individual objects that have relationships in time and space. It addresses the fact that no single coded representation is ideal for all object types. For instance, animation parameters ideally address a synthetic self-playing piano; an efficient representation of pixel values best suits organic video such as a dancer. MPEG-4 facilitates integration of these different types of data into one scene. MPEG-4 also enables interactivity through hyperlinking with the objects in the scene (e.g., through the Internet). Moreover, MPEG-4 enables selective bit management (pre-determining which bits will be forfeited if bandwidth becomes less than desirable), and straightforward re-use of content without transcoding.

Object Type	Speech	Scalable	Main	Synthetic
AAC Main			X	
AAC SSR			X	
AAC LC		X	X	
AAC LTP		X	X	
AAC Scalable		X	X	
TwinVQ		X	X	
CELP	X	X	X	
HVXC	X	X	X	
TTSI	X	X	X	
Main Synthetic			X	X
Wavetable Synthesis			X	X
General MIDI			X	X
Algorithmic Synthesis			X	X
Number of levels	2	4	4	3

Figure Appendix B-6. MPEG-4 Object Types

MPEG-4 benefits myriad applications in various environments. Whereas MPEG-2 is constructed as a rigid standard, MPEG-4 represents a set of tools, or *profiles* that address numerous settings, and countless combinations. MPEG-4 is less an extensive standard than an extensive collection of standards that authors can select and combine as they choose to improve existing applications or to deploy entirely new ones. It facilitates creation, alteration, adaptation, and access, of audiovisual scenes. With the advent of MPEG-4, one can expect richer virtual environments that will benefit such applications as conventional terrestrial multimedia entertainment, remote multimedia, broadcasting, and even surveillance. MPEG-4 is designed to enable convergence through the coalescence of such different service models as communication, on-line interaction, and communication.

To foster competition in the non-normative areas, MPEG-4 specifies normative tools only as interoperability necessitates. For instance, decoding is specified in the standard because it must be normative; video segmentation and rate control are not strictly specified because they can be non-normative. The MPEG-4 groups "specified the minimum for maximum usability." This strategy facilitates creativity and competition, and ensures that authors can make optimal use of the continuous improvements in the relevant technical areas. Competitors will continue to establish differentiation through the development of non-normative tools.

MPEG-7

Formally called "Multimedia Content Description Interface," MPEG-7 will be a standardized description of various types of multimedia information (it is worth noting that the group apparently arbitrarily chose the number seven; at the time of this writing, MPEG-5 MPEG-6 have not been defined). It will complement MPEG-1, MPEG-2, and MPEG-4. This description will be associated with the content itself to enable fast and efficient searching for material that is of interest to the user. The MPEG-7 Group is comprised of broadcasters, equipment manufacturers, digital content creators and managers, transmission providers, publishers and intellectual property rights managers, and university researchers who are interested in defining the standard. Participants include Columbia University, GMD-IPSI, Instituto Superior Técnico, Kent Ridge Digital Labs, KPN Research, Philips Research, Riverland, and Sharp Labs.

The purpose of MPEG-7 is to establish a methodology for searching for video and audio context on the Internet as one can search for text now. The group recognized the immense amount of audio and video content that may be accessible on the Internet, the interest in locating that content, and the current lack of any way to locate that content. The problem is that no methodology exists for categorizing such information. One can search on the basis of the color, texture, and shape of an object in a picture. However, one can not effectively search for *the moment in which the wicked witch melts* in The Wizard of Oz, or to search for ten minutes of video that meets my interests. Because the same limitations apply to audio, the group alluded to enabling a search based on humming a portion of a melody. It is not hard to understand how this applies to the ongoing cable television paradox of *500 channels but nothing worth watching* by allowing users to search on characteristics that suit their whim.

This newest member of the MPEG family, called "Multimedia Content Description Interface" (MPEG-7), may extend the limited capabilities of existing proprietary solutions in identifying content by including more data types. MPEG-7 will specify a standard set of descriptors to describe various types of multimedia information, ways to define other descriptors, and structures, or Description Schemes, for the descriptors and their relationships. The combination of descriptors and description schemes will be associated with the content itself to allow fast, efficient searching. MPEG-7 will also standardize a Description Definition Language (DDL) to specify description schemes. MPEG-7 will allow searches for AV content, such as still pictures, graphics, 3D models, audio, speech, video, and *scenarios* (combinations of characteristics). These general data types may include special cases such as personal characteristics or facial expressions.

The MPEG-7 standard builds on other representations such as analog, PCM, MPEG-1, -2 and -4. The intent is for the standard to provide references to suitable portions of such standard representations as a shape descriptor that is used in MPEG-4, or motion vector fields used in MPEG-1 and MPEG-2. However, MPEG-

7 descriptors are not dependent upon the ways the described content is coded or stored. One can attach an MPEG-7 description to an analog movie or to a picture that is printed on paper. Even though the MPEG-7 description does not depend upon the representation of the material, the standard builds on MPEG-4, which provides the means to encode audio-visual material as objects that have certain relations in time and space (either two- or three-dimensional). Using MPEG-4 encoding, it will be possible to attach descriptions to audio and visual objects within a scene. MPEG-7 will offer different levels of discrimination by allowing variable degree of granularity in its descriptions.

To ensure that the descriptive features are meaningful in the context of any given application, MPEG-7 will allow description of the same material using different types of features. In visual material, for instance, a lower abstraction level may describe shape, size, texture, color, movement (trajectory) and position (where the object can be found in the scene). In audio, the lower abstraction may describe pitch, timbre, tempo, or changes and modulations. The highest abstraction level would provide semantic information such as, "This scene includes a child playing a Mozart sonata on a piano, a gray and yellow cockatiel squawking in a gold cage, and an adult trying to calm the bird." All these descriptions would be coded to allow for searching. The level of abstraction is related to the way the features can be extracted: many low-level features can be extracted in fully automatic ways, whereas high level features may require human interaction. In addition to a description of the content, other types of information about the multimedia data may be required. Examples may include:

The form – Such as the coding scheme used (e.g. JPEG, MPEG-2), or the file size. This information helps determine whether the user can read the material.

Conditions for accessing the material – Such as copyright and price information.

Classification – Content sorting into pre-defined categories (e.g., parental rating).

Links to other relevant material - To assist the user in conducting a timely search.

Context - For recorded non-fiction content, it is important to know the occasion of the recording (e.g. Superbowl 2001, fourth quarter)

The Group seeks to make the descriptions as independent from the language area as possible, textual descriptions will be desirable in many cases — e.g., for titles, locations, or author's name. MPEG-7 data may be physically located with the associated AV material, in the same data stream, or on the same storage system. The descriptions may reside remotely. When the content and its descriptions are not co-located, mechanisms that link MPEG-7 will address applications that can be stored on-line or off-line, or streamed, and can operate in both real-time and non real-time environments. Digital libraries (e.g., image catalog or musical dictionary), multimedia directory services (e.g., yellow pages), broadcast media selection (e.g., radio or TV channel), and multimedia editing (e.g., personalized electronic news service or media authoring) will all benefit from MPEG-7.

MPEG-7 allows for any type of AV material to be retrieved by means of any type of query material. For example, video material may be queried using video, music, or speech. MPEG-7 does not dictate how the search engine may match the query data and the MPEG-7 AV description, but it may describe a standard programming interface to a search engine. A few query examples may include:

1. *Music-* Play a few notes on a keyboard to receive a list of musical pieces that contain the required tune or images that in some way match the notes.
2. *Graphics-* Draw a few lines on a screen and receive a set of images that contain similar graphics or logos.
3. *Image-* Define objects, including color patches or textures and receive examples from which to select.
4. *Movement-* On a given set of objects, describe movements and relations between objects and receive a list of animations that match the described temporal and spatial relations.
5. *Scenario-* For a given content, describe actions to receive a list of scenarios in which similar actions occur.
6. *Voice-* Using an excerpt of a given vocalist's voice, receive a list of that vocalist's recordings or video clips.

At the time of this writing, MPEG-7 is at an early stage and is seeking the collaboration of new experts in relevant areas. The preliminary work plan for MPEG-7 projects a committee draft in October 2000, a final committee draft in February 2001, a draft international standard in July 2001, and an international standard in September 2001.

C

CCIR-601

CCIR-601 is the ISO/IEC standard that defines the image format, acquisition semantic, and parts of the coding for digital "standard" television signals. Because many chips that support this standard are available, CCIR-601 is commonly used in digital video applications for computer systems and digital television. It is central to the MPEG, H.261, and H.263 compression specifications.

CCIR-601 is applicable to both NTSC and PAL/SECAM systems. In the U.S., CCIR-601 is 720x243 fields (not frames) of luminance information, sent at a rate of 60 per second. The fields are interlaced when displayed. The chrominance channels are 360x243 by 60 fields a second, again interlaced.

CCIR-601 represents the chroma signals (Cb, Cr) with half the horizontal frequency as the luminance signal, but with full vertical *resolution*. This particular ratio of subsampled components is known as 4:2:2. The sampling frequency of the luminance signal (Y) is 13.5 MHz. Cb and Cr are sampled at 6.75 MHz.

CCIR-601 describes the way in which analog signals are filtered to obtain the samples. Often RGB signals are converted to YCbCr. The formulas given for the CCIR-601 color conversion are for gamma corrected RGB signals. The gamma for the different television systems are specified in CCIR Report 624-4.

The encoding of the digital signal is described in detail in CCIR Rec. 656. The correspondence between the video signal levels and the quantization levels is also specified. The scale is between 0 and 255, the luminance signal provides for 220 quantization levels; for the color-difference signals, it provides for 225 quantization levels. The signals are only coded with 8-bits per signal.

D

World Television and Color Systems

Country	Television System	PTT Digital Service Network Interface
Abu Dhabi	PAL	No digital services
Afghanistan	PAL	No digital services
Albania	PAL	No digital services
Algeria	PAL	No digital services
Andorra	PAL	No digital services
Angola	PAL	No digital services
Antigua and Barbuda	NTSC	No digital services
Antilles	NTSC	No digital services
Argentina	PAL	No digital services
Australia	PAL	X.21
Austria	PAL	X.21
Azores	PAL	No digital services
Bahamas	NTSC	No digital services
Bahrain	PAL	No digital services
Bangladesh	PAL	No digital services
Barbados	NTSC	No digital services
Belgium	PAL	X.21
Bermuda	NTSC	No digital services
Bolivia	NTSC	No digital services
Bosnia	SECAM (V)	No digital services
Botswana	PAL	No digital services
Brazil	PAL	No digital services
Brunei	PAL	No digital services
Bulgaria	SECAM (V)	No digital services
Burma	NTSC	No digital services
Cameroon	PAL	No digital services
Canada	NTSC	V.35/V.25
Chile	NTSC	V.35
China	PAL	No digital services
CIS (formerly USSR)	SECAM (V)	No digital services

Columbia	NTSC	V.35
Congo	SECAM (V)	No digital services
Costa Rica	NTSC	No digital services
Croatia	SECAM (V)	No digital services
Cuba	NTSC	No digital services
Cyprus	SECAM	No digital services
Czechoslovakia	SECAM (V)	No digital services
Denmark	PAL	X.21/V.35
Diego Garcia	NTSC	No digital services
Djibouti	SECAM	No digital services
Dominican Republic	NTSC	No digital services
Dubai	PAL	No digital services
Ecuador	PAL	No digital services
Egypt	SECAM (V)	No digital services
El Salvador	NTSC	No digital services
Ethiopia	PAL	No digital services
Fiji	PAL	No digital services
Finland	PAL	X.21
France	SECAM (V)	X.21
Gabon	SECAM (V)	No digital services
Germany	PAL/SECAM	X.21
Ghana	PAL	No digital services
Gibraltar	PAL	No digital services
Greece	SECAM	No digital services
Greenland	PAL	No digital services
Guadeloupe	SECAM (V)	No digital services
Guam	NTSC	V.35
Guatemala	NTSC	No digital services
Guyana (French)	SECAM (V)	No digital services
Haiti	NTSC	No digital services
Honduras	NTSC	No digital services
Hong Kong	PAL	V.35
Hungary	SECAM (V)	No digital services
Iceland	PAL	No digital services
India	PAL	No digital services
Indonesia	PAL	V.35
Iran	SECAM (H)	No digital services
Iraq	SECAM (H)	No digital services
Ireland	PAL	X.21
Israel	PAL	V.35
Italy	PAL	X.21
Ivory Coast	SECAM (V)	No digital services

Jamaica	NTSC	No digital services
Japan	NTSC	X.21
Johnston Island	NTSC	No digital services
Jordan	PAL	No digital services
Kenya	PAL	No digital services
Korea, North	SECAM	No digital services
Korea, South	NTSC	V.35
Kuwait	PAL	No digital services
Lebanon	SECAM (V)	No digital services
Liberia	PAL	No digital services
Libya	SECAM	No digital services
Luxembourg	PAL/SECAM	X.21
Madagascar	SECAM	No digital services
Madeira	PAL	No digital services
Malaysia	PAL	V.35
Malta	PAL	No digital services
Martinique	SECAM (V)	No digital services
Mauritius	SECAM (V)	No digital services
Mexico	NTSC	V.35
Midway Island	NTSC	No digital services
Monaco	SECAM (V)	No digital services
Morocco	SECAM (V)	No digital services
Netherlands	PAL	X.21
New Caledonia	SECAM (V)	No digital services
New Zealand	PAL	X.21
Nicaragua	NTSC	No digital services
Nigeria	PAL	No digital services
Norway	PAL	X.21
Okinawa	NTSC	No digital services
Oman	PAL	No digital services
Pakistan	PAL	No digital services
Panama	NTSC	No digital services
Paraguay	PAL	No digital services
Peru	NTSC	No digital services
Philippines	NTSC	V.35
Poland	SECAM (V)	No digital services
Portugal	PAL	No digital services
Puerto Rico	NTSC	V.35
Qatar	PAL	No digital services
Reunion	SECAM (V)	No digital services
Rumania	PAL	No digital services
Sabah and Sarawak	PAL	No digital services

Samoa	NTSC	No digital services
Saudi Arabia	SECAM (H)	No digital services
Senegal	SECAM (V)	No digital services
Serbia	SECAM (V)	No digital services
Sierra Leone	PAL	No digital services
Singapore	PAL	V.35
South Africa	PAL	V.35
Soviet Union	SECAM (V)	No digital services
Spain	PAL	V.35
Sri Lanka	PAL	No digital services
St. Kitts	NTSC	No digital services
St. Pierre and Miquelon	SECAM	No digital services
Sudan	PAL	No digital services
Surinam	NTSC	No digital services
Swaziland	PAL	No digital services
Sweden	PAL	X.21
Switzerland	PAL	X.21
Syria	SECAM	No digital services
Tahiti	SECAM (V)	No digital services
Taiwan	NTSC	V.35
Tanzania	PAL	No digital services
Thailand	PAL	V.35
Tibet	PAL	No digital services
Togo	SECAM	No digital services
Trinidad and Tobago	NTSC	No digital services
Trust Isl. (Micronesia)	PAL	No digital services
Tunisia	SECAM (V)	No digital services
Turkey	PAL	No digital services
United Arab Emirates	PAL	No digital services
Uganda	PAL	No digital services
United Kingdom	PAL	X.21
Uruguay	PAL	No digital services
United States	NTSC	V.35
Venezuela	NTSC	V.35
Vietnam	NTSC	No digital services
Virgin Islands	NTSC	No digital services
Zaire	SECAM (V)	No digital services
Zambia	PAL	No digital services
Zanzibar	PAL	No digital services
Zimbabwe	PAL	No digital services

Note (1). Digital services can be obtained via private satellite services in some cases. Check with the PTT to determine which countries will allow private networks and what the conditions of service are.

E

VIDEOCONFERENCING RFP CHECKLIST

Define: Application and locations involved

√ Category of system requested for each location

√ Features required for each site

Ask: Basic System Specifications

√ Cameras (room, auxiliary, document)

√ Monitors (single, dual or other)

√ Algorithms (H.261, G.728, proprietary, other)

√ Network supported (ISDN, switched 56, T-1, IP)

√ Network interfaces (V.35, RS-449/422, X.21, etc.)

√ Network type (dedicated access, switched or hybrid)

√ If behind PBX, who provides interface components?

√ Who provides CSU/DSUs, cables & incidental equipment?

√ Who provides NT-1 (NT-2) in ISDN applications?

√ If an MCU is required, how is it configured?

√ If an inverse multiplexer is required, how is it configured?

Ask: History of manufacturer

√ Request financial data on supplier

√ Sign non-disclosure to determine mfg. future plans

√ Learn about manufacturer's/distributors partnerships

√ Examine distribution channels

√ Request information on users group

√ Determine desktop videoconferencing strategy

Ask: Characteristics of the system

√ Is the system desktop or room system product?

√ Is the product software-only or software and hardware?

√ Integrated into single package or component-based?

√ If component based is integration also proposed?

√ If PC is required for operation, who provides PC?

√ Product's dimensions and its weight (if hardware)

√ State system's environmental requirements.

√ What documentation is provided with the product?

Ask: Proprietary Algorithms Offered

√ Name compression algorithms employed for video?

√ Name compression algorithms employed for audio?

√ Backward compatibility with earlier algorithms?

√ Picture resolutions offered with each algorithm?

√ Average fps across range of network speeds offered?

√ Maximum fps across range of speeds offered?

√ Echo cancellation algorithms offered?

Ask: Standards Compliance

√ Ask about compliance with H.32X Recs. individually

√ Does product offer CIF/QCIF or QCIF only?

√ Average/maximum fps at various H.320 bandwidths?

√ T.120 standards compliance?

√ Does the product support JPEG and MPEG? How?

Ask: Network-Specific Issues

√ What network arrangements does product support?

√ Can system transmit images using only POTS lines?

√ What network interfaces are required for configuration as proposed?

√ Who supplies interface equipment and cables?

√ Does proposal offer turnkey installation including network connections?

√ For what network speed is the codec optimized?

√ How is the transmission speed changed? Describe.

√ What LAN interfaces are available for the product?

√ With which ITU-T network-oriented standards does the product comply?

√ Does the product offer a built-in inverse multiplexer?

√ If so, describe it. Does it comply with BOnDInG?

Ask: Videoconferencing System Features

√ Examine system documentation during procurement.

√ Compare system features relative to how well-documented they are for each product considered.

√ What type of system interface is provided with the system?

√ Is the control unit a push button-type device, a touch-screen based unit, a PC keyboard, wireless remote or electronic tablet and stylus based?

√ Can the document camera be controlled from the primary system control unit or operator's console?

√ If the system's primary control unit is not a PC, is a PC keyboard also used to activate or change any system features that a conferee would commonly need during a conference? Which ones?

√ Does the product offer camera presets?

√ Does it offer far-end camera control?

√ Does the product offer picture-in-picture? In a dual-monitor arrangement what can be seen in the window? A single-monitor arrangement?

√ Can audio-only conferees be part of conference?

√ How many audio-only conferees can be included?

√ How are conferences set up? Describe process.

√ Can frequently-dialed numbers be stored? How many speed dialing numbers can be stored? How are they activated?

√ Do codecs automatically handshake to determine compatible algorithm?

√ Can the system be placed in a multipoint mode, and support a multipoint conference?

√ Does the product offer on-line help?

√ Is it backward compatible with codec manufacturer's previous products? Describe fully.

√ Does the product offer continuous presence?

√ Does the product offer scheduling software?

√ Does the product offer applications sharing? What environments are supported (Windows)?

Ask: Audio considerations

√ List the names of proprietary audio algorithms offered and describe them.

√ What range of frequencies are encoded with the above?

√ Is bandwidth assignment flexible? How are adjustments made?

√ What method is used to eliminate echoes?

√ If echo cancellation is used is a burst of noise used to acquainted the system with the room? Or, does unit use voices to train acoustic line-side echo cancellers?

√ What is the echo cancellation system's convergence time measured in milliseconds?

√ What is the echo cancellation system's tail length measured in milliseconds?

√ What is the echo cancellation system's AERLE rating measured in dB?

√ How many and what type of microphones are provided?

√ Is audio input provided via a speakerphone or external microphone?

√ Where are speakers located on system?

√ Are microphones unidirectional or omnidirectional?

√ Are lapel, ceiling or wireless microphones included in system price?

√ Examine products to see how well audio is synched with video particularly in a desktop videoconferencing application.

Ask: Camera considerations

√ Is the camera color and does it offer pan/tilt/zoom?

√ What is the room camera's sensitivity (in lux)?

√ How many CCDs are used in the room camera?

√ What is the range of viewing angles of the room camera using the zoom?

√ Is a wide-angled lens provided? Can it be ordered optionally if not?

√ Does camera offer automatic gain control (AGC)?

√ Does camera offer white balance?

√ What type of auxiliary camera is used (light and CCD ratings, etc)?

Ask: Monitors

√ What size monitor is proposed? Single or dual?

√ What resolution does monitor offer?

√ What is the dot pitch and how does it correlate with the monitor's resolution?

Ask: Graphics Support and Subsystems

√ How is document transfer supported?

√ What document stand is included, is it backlit for slides, how large can documents be?

√ What standard resolutions are supported for still images?

√ Are high-resolution graphics supported? As what resolutions?

√ How are high-resolution (bit-mapped) graphics are compressed and formatted?

√ Do audiographics systems should comply with the ITU-T's T.120 Recommendation?

√ Does product offer the built-in ability to create and store images as slides (T.120)?

√ Is application sharing supported (T.130)?

√ Can participants electronically annotate shared images in real time (T.120)?

√ Can users at different sites interactively share, manipulate and exchange still images (T.120)?

√ Does system offer very-high-resolution graphics (including CAD support)?

√ Is graphics subsystem an integral component or is it an outboard product?

√ If external and PC-based, how does the graphics sub-system connect to the codec?

√ Can system support the need for photorealism? (X- rays, medical imaging applications)

√ Is a flatbed scanner included in price? (This is an application- driven requirement).

√ If scanner is included what is the size of the bed?

√ What is the scanner's color depth (4-bit grayscale, 24-bit color, etc.)?

Ask: Multipoint Control Unit

√ List proprietary video/ audio algorithms supported.

√ Are conference ports are universal?

√ State the MCU maximum port size. How many ports is it proposed with? Describe the expansion process.

√ Describe how the product can be upgraded to a more fully-featured model.

√ How can MCUs be cascaded to expand capacity?

√ Does cascading consume ports? Does it create delays in end-to-end transmission? Explain.

√ Describe MCU in terms of network interfaces (public, private and LAN).

√ What network speeds are supported?

√ How many simultaneous conferences can take place at any given speed and how are the MCU bridging capabilities subdivided?

√ Does system offer a director/chairperson control mode of operation? A voice-activated mode? A rotating mode? Other? Explain.

√ In voice-activated mode, how does the system prevent loud noises from diverting the camera?

√ Does the product offer full support of the ITU-T H.231/H.243 Recommendation? Explain fully.

√ How does the MCU provide graphics support and what limitations exist?

√ Does the MCU support H.261 Annex D graphics?

√ Does the MCU support G.728 audio?

√ Does the MCU operate in meet-me, dial-out and hybrid arrangements?

√ After a conference is arranged, state all limitations in terms of the user's ability to add conferees or change transmission speeds.

√ Are conference tones provided to signal a conferee's entry-to and exit-from a conference?

√ Can audio-only participants be included?

√ Does the system provide for voice and video encryption and if so, which methods are used?

How is the MCU managed? Provide detailed information on the administrative subsystem.

√ Can the MCU store a database of sites and the codecs installed at those locations as well as network information?

√ How does the network operator configure the MCU for a multipoint conference?

√ Can the administrative console be used to configure, test and diagnose problems with the MCU? Can it keep an event log and account for use?

√ What type of conference scheduling package is provided? Can conferences be scheduled in advance? Describe. At the appointed time does the MCU automatically configure itself? Can it dial out to participating sites? Does the MCU reservation system allow the user to control of videoconference rooms or is it used just to schedule bridge ports?

√ Is there an additional cost for the scheduling package?

Ask: Security-Related Features

√ Is the Data Encryption Standard (DES) supported?

√ What other encryption techniques are supported?

√ Are both audio and video encrypted?

√ How does encryption differ between point-to-point and multipoint conferences?

√ Is the operator's console password-protected?

Ask: Miscellaneous Questions

√ If system is sold through a distributor or value-added reseller, can you call the manufacturer directly?

√ Who will install the equipment? Do they have a local presence? Who will provide technician and end-user training?

√ What is the length of warranty and terms of service?

√ Where are spare parts stocked and what response time is guaranteed when the system fails? What are the terms of the second year service agreement? Cost? How is defective equipment or software repaired or replaced? Is immediate replacement in possible? In what time frame?

F

INSTALLATION PLANNING CHECKLIST

Physical space considerations

√ Acceptable and convenient location

√ Will excess capacity be brokered? Plan for it.

√ Dimensions adequate for group size

√ Minimal windows

√ Proximity to communications demarcation

√ Anteroom or next-group gathering space

√ Videoconferencing coordinator's work space

√ Sufficient electrical power and additional outlets

√ Conduit, ducts, etc. for concealing cables

√ Signage directing conferees to room

√ Sufficient privacy to meet application's needs

√ Security (locking door, card-key, punch-coded entry)

Interior Design

√ Carpeting

√ Wall color and treatments

√ Drapes, curtains or blinds

√ Facade wall and shelving (boardroom applications)

√ Table type, shape, surface and placement

√ Spectator seating for

√ Chairs and upholstery

√ Whiteboards

√ Clocks showing times at local and primary remote sites

√ Table sign identifying site and organization

Approaches to ambient noise control

√ HVAC system improvements

√ Acoustic panels and heavy draperies

√ Replacement, rearrangement or addition of lighting fixtures

√ Double-glazed windows

Network considerations

√ Network installed and tested

√ Necessary cables on hand

√ CSU/DSU or NT-1 installed and tested

√ Network documented at completion of project

Videoconferencing peripherals

√ Cameras (auxiliary)

√ Monitors (auxiliary)

√ Audio bridging

√ Still-video (graphics) components such as document cameras

√ Presentation graphics subsystems

√ PCs for file access and file sharing applications

√ NTSC-to-VGA (or SVGA) scan converters

√ Electronic whiteboards

√ Fax machines and copiers

√ VCRs

√ 35mm slide projector interfaces

√ RGB projection system interfaces (front or rear)

√ Interfaces to CAD and/or scientific equipment (scopes, etc.)

√ I-MUX installed and tested

√ Multipoint conferencing unit installed and tested

Promotional and Usage-Oriented Preparation

√ Select personnel in remote locations to support system

√ Develop and publish videoconferencing usage policy

√ Determining chargeback policy

√ Determining scheduling system

√ Address scheduling issues (prioritization, bumping, etc.)

√ Develop instruction sheet for scheduling

√ Develop etiquette tips for point-to-point and multipoint conferences

√ Develop tips for setting up inter-company conferences

G

Personal Conferencing Product Evaluation Criteria

Implementation

√ Client/server, server- only or client-only?

√ Point-to-point or multipoint?

√ Standards-based or proprietary?

√ Is the system offered as a cross-platform solution?

√ Product family? What capabilities are included in the family?

√ Do all applications in the product family have a similar look & feel?

√ Is the product offered in multiple languages?

Platforms Supported

√ Microsoft Windows 3.1x, Windows 95, Windows NT, Windows 2000

√ Mac OS

√ UNIX (Solaris, HPUX, OSF, AIX, Ultrix, other)

√ IBM OS/2

√ Proprietary / Other (Explain)

Hardware Configuration

√ What class of processor is required (minimum / recommended)?

√ Processor clock speed (minimum / recommended)?

√ How much RAM is required (minimum / recommended?

√ How much free space on the hard drive is required?

√ What number & type slots (ISA, EISA, PCI) does the system require?

Hardware Supplied with Product

√ V.80 (or other) modem

√ Camera

√ Sound card

√ Microphone

√ Speakers

√ Video capture board

√ Hardware-level codec

√ NT-1 for ISDN BRI

√ All required cables

Networks and Protocols Supported

√ POTS

√ Circuit-switched digital ISDN BRI

√ Circuit-switched digital, non-clear channel Switched 56

√ Other circuit-switched (T-1, E-1, ISDN PRI)

√ Multirate ISDN (Nx64, H0, H11, H12)

√ IP networks (TCP or UDP)

√ Novell IPX/SPX

√ Isochronous Ethernet (802.9)

√ NetBEUI / NETBIOS (not recommended)

√ ATM

Frame Rates, Data Transfer Rates

√ Range of operating data rates?

√ Optimal data rate?

√ Average frame rate at optimal data rate?

√ Maximum frame rate at optimal data rate?

√ Can users control bandwidth allocation between voice, video & data?

Standards Compliance

√ H.320 compatible?

√ H.261

√ H.263

√ H.320-based multipoint support?

√ H.321 ATM network support?

√ H.322 (Isochronous Ethernet) supported?

√ H.323 supported?

√ H.324 supported? If so, is V.80-compliant modem included?

√ H.323-compliant gateway between H.320 and packet network?

Picture Viewing and Resolution

√ What is the maximum / minimum size of viewing window?

√ Can the user scale the viewing window(s) using a mouse?

√ What video resolutions are supported (SQCIF, QCIF, CIF, other)?

√ Can the user adjust the picture resolution?

√ Can users make on-the-fly trade-offs between frame rate & resolution?

√ Does the product provide a local video window for self-view?

√ Can users control the viewing window screen quadrant?

√ Does the product offer far-end camera control?

Making and Receiving Calls

√ Does the product offer "voice-call first" (to add a video connection)?

√ Does an on-line directory permit "scroll & click" to place a video call?

√ Is an incoming caller's ID captured and displayed?

√ Is an incoming caller's # automatically stored for callback (ISDN)?

Audio Sub-system

√ In-band or out-of-band audio?

√ Are microphone and speakers included?

√ Is microphone built in to the camera?

√ Is a headset or handset included?

√ Audio/video synchronization (subjective evaluation of)

√ Audio-delivery quality (subjective evaluation of microphone)

√ Audio-receive quality (subjective evaluation of speakers)

Camera Features

√ Does the camera offer pan/tilt/zoom?

√ Can camera swivel in order to act as a document camera?

√ Choices of focal lengths?

√ Color or black and white?

√ Does the camera offer brightness, contrast, color, and tint adjustments?

√ Does the camera include an audio/video shutter for privacy?

Data Collaboration / Graphics / Document Conferencing Features & Support

√ T.120 compliance?

√ Document conferencing / data collaboration?

√ Application viewing / screen sharing?

√ Bit-mapped whiteboard (clipboard) capabilities?

√ File transfer?

√ Can the user control the flow of files during a file transfer? If so, how?

√ Can conferees prevent network floods during multipoint file transfers?

√ Chat (message pad) features?

√ Annotation tools (markers, highlighters, pens, etc.)?

√ Drawing tools (inclusion and sophistication of)?

√ Pointing tools?

√ Slide show capabilities?

√ Screen-capture and storage as "photo"?

√ Are full- or partial-screen video "freeze frame" snapshots offered?

√ What format are snapshots stored in?

Intranet / Internet Adaptations

√ Does the client use a Web browser for connection and control?

√ RTP and RTCP support?

√ RSVP client capabilities?

√ UDP (vs. TCP) sessions?

√ Does the system support the User Location Service (IP-network)?

√ Is a user automatically logged onto the ULS when they sign on to their computer?

Multipoint Capabilities

√ Does the system support multipoint conferencing? How many parties?

√ What conference management features are provided?

√ Multipoint Control Unit (bridge) required? Is it included?

√ Multipoint file transfers supported?

√ Multipoint capabilities – broadcast one-to-many

√ Multipoint capabilities – can all desktops interact with one another?

√ Multipoint capabilities – maximum number of simultaneous conferees?

√ Is a UNIX-based reflector required for multipoint?

√ Password protection?

√ Conference attendance control features

√ Standards supported

√ When one first signs on to a conference does the system display the number of meeting participants and the names of the other sites?

Miscellaneous Features

- √ Does the product offer traditional "voice" features (do-not-disturb, call forward, call waiting and hold)?
- √ Does the product offer video messaging? What compression method is used to compress audiovisual files?
- √ Context-sensitive on-line help or application "assistant" to guide user?
- √ Audio-only callers included in conference?
- √ Call center features?
- √ MPEG video file playback from video sources?

Cost

- √ Cost, per desktop
- √ Cost of server
- √ Concurrent-use licensing cost
- √ Other miscellaneous costs

Installation and Performance Tests

- √ Ease-of-installation, as rated by microcomputer-oriented trade press & surveys?
- √ Trial installation. How easy is the product to install?
- √ Does the product include a quick install feature?
- √ Does the package also include an uninstall feature?
- √ Is documentation adequate?
- √ Does the system minimize the transfer of non-essential data (e.g., mouse movements) in performance tests?
- √ How fast can the system transfer files?
- √ Did you encounter any bugs that crashed the application during performance tests?

Supplier Support / Commitment to Customer's Success

√ What support (applications, installation, testing) does the supplier provide?

√ On screen diagnostics and messages provided?

√ Are application and installation notes offered on line?

√ Does the manufacturer offer low-cost (no cost) upgrades to allow the installation to keep pace with product evolution?

√ Does the manufacturer publish a list of known bugs and product shortcomings and provide information on when and how these problems will be corrected?

√ Does the supplier provide a test-center that you can call when you are trying to get your application working?

H

INTERACTIVE MULTIMEDIA SUPPLIERS (BY CATEGORY)

AUDIO COMPONENTS

A.T. Products, Inc.
Audio-Technica U.S., Inc.
Autel Inc.
Coherent Communications Systems Corp.
Gentner Communications Corporation
IRP Professional Sound Products
Jabra
Polycom, Inc.
Rane Corporation
Shure Brothers, Inc.
Sound Control Technologies, Inc.
3Com

BOARD-LEVEL PRODUCTS

ABL Canada
Bitfield Oy
Boca Research
Digital Vision Inc.
Kenwood USA Corporation
Lucent Technologies
Philips Semiconductors
Toshiba America Electronic Components
VCON
VistaCom Inc.
Winnov L.P.
Zandar Technologies

CAMERAS, CAMERA CONTROL AND DOCUMENT CAMERAS

ACS Innovations, Inc.

Active Imaging, Inc.
Canon USA, Inc.
Connectix Corporation
Elmo Manufacturing Corp.
Hitachi Multimedia Systems
Howard Enterprises, Inc.
ParkerVision
Ricoh Corporation's Consumer Products Group
Silicon Vision, Inc.
Sony Electronics, Inc.
VideoLabs
Wolfvision, Inc.
Xirlink, Inc.

Carrier Services (Terrestrial, Satellite)

AT&T Tridom
AT&T
Bell Atlantic
Chanticleer Communications, Inc.
MCI Telecommunications Corp.
Microspace Communications Corp.
Sprint Conferencing
Starvision Multimedia Corporation
Vista Satellite Communications, Inc.

Component-Level Products

8x8, Inc.
Analog Devices, Inc.
C-Cube Microsystems
Chromatic Research
Cirrus Logic
DSP Group
General Instrument
Hewlett-Packard Company
IBM
National Semiconductor
Optivision, Inc.
Philips Semiconductors
Phylon Communications
Sanyo Semiconductor Corp.
Zoran

Data Collaboration (No Video)

DataBeam Corporation
Microfield Graphics, Inc. (personal and group)
Microsoft Corporation
Netscape Communications
Optel Communications Inc.
OutReach Technologies
Polycom, Inc.
Smart Technologies, Inc. (group-oriented)

Development Environments

DataBeam, Inc.
nCube
Tektronix-Video Networks Division
Zydecom, Inc.

Digital Networking Products and Inverse Multiplexers

Lucent Technologies
Bay Networks
Broadband Networks, Inc.
Canoga Perkins Corporation
Cisco Systems
First Virtual Corporation
Madge Networks Inc.
National Semiconductor
Orckit
Promptus Communications, Inc.
Tektronix-Video Networks Division

Distributors Specializing in Videoconferencing Products (Catalog Sales)

Global Videoconferencing Solutions, Inc.
Picturephone Direct

Freeware

CU-SeeMe (Cornell University)
Microsoft NetMeeting
Xing Technologies

Modems for Videoconferencing over POTS

Archtek America Corporation
Diamond Multimedia Systems
3Com

Multicasting Software and Streaming Media Products

CU-SeeMe (Cornell University)
Cisco Systems (Precept Software)
Vivo Software
White Pine Software
Xing Technology Corporation

Multipoint Conferencing Units

Accord Video Telecommunications
Creative Software Technologies (software-only MCU)
InView
Lucent Technologies
MultiLink, Inc.
PictureTel Corporation
Sony (integrated in its group-oriented videoconferencing system)
VideoServer, Inc.
VTEL

Personal Conferencing & Multimedia Software

AETHRA, Inc.
Apple Computer, Inc.
Casio Phonemate, Inc.
Cinecom Corporation
Compunetix, Inc.
Connectix
Corel Corporation (networked multimedia)
C-Phone (networked multimedia)
Datapoint NCP
Elsa Inc.
EyeTel
IBM (Lotus) VideoNotes
Intel Corporation
Intelligence at Large, Inc.
IPC Peripherals
Panasonic Matsushita Consumer Electronics Company
PictureTel

Radvislon
RSI Systems, Inc.
Sagem
Silicon Graphics, Inc.
Smith Micro Software, Inc.
Sony Electronics, Inc.
Sun MicroSystems
Target Technologies C-Phone
Teles Corporation
Vivitar Corporation
VocalTec
Winnov L.P.
Zydacron, Inc.

SCAN CONVERTERS, MONITORS & PROJECTION SYSTEMS

AverMedia (scan converters)
Barco Projection Systems (projection)
Digital Vision, Inc. (scan converters)
Electrohome Limited (projection)
Extron Electronics (scan conversion)
Focus Enhancements (scan conversion)
Folsom Research, Inc. (scan conversion)
In Focus Systems (projection)
Mitsubishi Electronics America, Inc. (monitors and projection)
Polaroid Corporation (projection)
Proxima Corporation (projection)
RasterOps (scan converter)
RGB Spectrum (projection)
Tektronix-Video Networks Division
TVOne (scan converters)
Umax Technologies (scan converters)
VideoLogic Inc. (scan converters)
Wolfvision, Inc. (projection)

SERVICES BUREAUS

1-800-Video-On! LLC
ACT Teleconferencing, Inc.
Affinity VideoNet, Inc.
ConferTech International (Global Crossing)
VideoLinx Communication, Inc.
Williams

Scheduling Software

AC&E Ltd.
PictureTel Corporation
VTEL

Video PBXs and Video Call Centers

Teloquent

Client/Server Videoconferencing Solutions

Avistar Systems
C-Phone Corporation
Corel Corporation
Datapoint Corporation
Lattitude Communications
RADVision Ltd.

Group-Oriented Videoconferencing Systems

Bosch Telecom Inc.
C-Phone
Dolch Computer Systems (makes platform)
Fujitsu Business Communication Systems, Inc.
Hitachi Multimedia Systems
ImageTel International, Inc.
Intelect Visual Communications
Lucent Technologies
NEC Corporation
Panasonic Matsushita Consumer Electronics Company
PictureTel Inc.
Sony Electronics, Inc.
Tandberg
Toshiba
VCON
VERREX Corporation
Videoconferencing Systems, Inc. (VSI)

VIDEOCONFERENCING FOR VERTICAL MARKETS

Andries Tek, Inc. (Telemedicine)
Convene International (Distance Learning)
LearnLinc (Distance Learning)
One Touch Systems, Inc. (Distance Learning)

MAGAZINES, TRADE SHOWS AND PROFESSIONAL ASSOCIATIONS

Advanstar (magazine, annual trade show)
IMCCA (professional association, annual trade show)
TeleConnect (magazine and annual trade show)
Telespan (newsletter)

SYSTEMS INTEGRATION AND ENGINEERING

AAC Inc.
Adcom Inc.
CritiCom, Inc.
Lucent Technologies
Peirce-Phelps, Inc.
VERREX Corporation
Videoconferencing Systems, Inc. (VSI)
ViewTech, Inc.
Winsted Corporation (security products)

I

INTERACTIVE MULTIMEDIA SUPPLIERS (BY COMPANY)

1-800-Video-On! LLC
5665 Flatiron Parkway
Boulder, CO 80301
Phone: 800-843-3666
Fax: 303-415-3540
URL: http://www.one800video-on.com
Product: 1-800-Video-on! Offers multipoint bridging services for videoconferencing and data collaboration.

3Com Corporation
5400 Bayfront Plaza
Santa Clara, CA 95052
Phone: (408) 326-5000
Fax: (408) 326-5001
URL: http://www.3com.com
Product: 3Com makes routers, hubs, switches, network interface cards, and V.80-compliant modems that can be used for videoconferencing over POTS. It also makes a conference speakerphone that provides 360° coverage.

8x8, Inc.
2445 Mission College Blvd
Santa Clara, CA 95054
Phone: 408-727-1825
Fax: 408-980-0432
URL: http://www.8x8.com/
Product: 8x8's family of products includes both silicon products and the software applications that implement various multimedia compression algorithms. Products include POTS video phone and a POTS video phone browser.

AC&E Ltd.
14101 Sullyfield Circle
Chantilly, VA 22021
Phone: 703-968-5700
Fax: 703-968-4331
URL: http://www.aceltd.com/
Product: AC&E's VC Wizard software schedules conference room resources, equipment and people.

Accord Video Telecommunications
Atlanta, Georgia
Phone: 770-641-4400
Fax: 770-641-4499
URL: http://www.accordtelecom.com
Product: Accord makes a standards-compliant MCU that supports T.120 & H.320.

ACT Teleconferencing, Inc.
1658 Cole Blvd, Suite 162
Golden, CO 80401
Phone: 303-233-3500
Fax: 303-238-0096
URL: http://www.acttel.com/
Product: ACT Teleconferencing is an international provider of videoconferencing services. Products include meet-me conferencing, dial-out conferencing, reservation scheduling.

Active Imaging, Inc.
P.O. Box 7879
Incline Village, NV 89650
Phone: 702-832-0792
Fax: 702-832-0778
URL: http://www.activeimaging.com
Product: Active Imaging Inc. makes small web server and a range of intelligent video cameras for Internet and intranet use.

Adcom Inc.
1 Westside Drive, Unit 9
Toronto, Ontario Canada, M9C 1B2
Phone: 416-251-3355
Fax: 416-251-3977
URL: http://www.adcom.com/
Product: ADCOM Inc. is a Canadian supplier of videoconferencing systems and services. Products include conference facilities, custom site engineering and facility design, and equipment maintenance.

AETHRA, Inc.
AETHRA Telecommunications
1221 Brickell Ave., Suite 1030
Miami, FL 33131-3258
Phone: 305-375-0010
Fax: 305-375-0655
URL: http://www.aethra.com/
Product: AETHRA makes a hardware/software bundled H.32X-compliant videophone and group workstations for use over ISDN.

Affinity VideoNet, Inc.
7 DeSoto Road
Essex, MA 01929
Phone: 508-768-7480 or 800-370-7150
Fax: 508-768-7474
URL: http://www.affinityvnet.com/
Product: Affinity provides public room rental service (predominantly PictureTel). It also coordinates multipoint bridging and offers system rentals.

Analog Devices, Inc.
3 Technology Way
Norwood, MA 02062
Phone: 510-417-6699
Fax: 510-462-5226
URL: http://www.analog.com/
Product: Analog Devices makes chips for use in multimedia computing.

Andries Tek, Inc.
4314 Medical Parkway, Suite 9
Austin, TX 78756
Phone: 512-453-6076
Fax: 512-453-8627
URL: Product: http://www.andriestek.com/
Andries Tek makes telemedicine-oriented products.

Apple Computer, Inc.
1 Infinite Loop
Cupertino, CA 95014
Phone: 408-996-1010
Fax: 408-996-0275
URL: http://www.apple.com/
Product: Apple makes QuickTime Conferencing software used for videoconferencing over the Internet, LANs, WANs, ISDN, and POTS.

Archtek America Corporation
4F,No.9, Lane 130,Min-Chyuan Rd.
Hsin-Tien Taipei,
231,Taiwan
Phone: +886-2-2188730
Fax: +886-2-2189283, +886-2-2183264
In the U.S. (City of Industry, CA)
Phone: 818-912-9800 or 888-272-4835
Fax: 818-912-9700
URL: http://www.archtek.com/
Product: Archtek makes a V.34-compliant multimedia modem which, when used with software, supports audio-enhanced data collaboration. It also makes switches, a WWW set-top box, and an external Ethernet adapter.

Spacenet Services, Inc. (formerly AT&T Tridom)
1750 Old Meadow Road
McLean, Virginia 22102
(703) 848-1000
URL: http://www.spacenet.com/
Product: SpaceNet sells business satellite network services that can be used for two-way videoconferencing or business television.

A.T. Products, Inc.
1600 S. Division St.
Harvard, IL 60033
Phone: 815-943-3590 or 800-848-2205
Fax: 815-943-3604
URL: http://www.atproducts.com/
Product: AT Products, Inc. is a designer and manufacturer of audio teleconferencing systems.

Audio-Technica U.S., Inc.
1221 Commerce Drive
Stow, OH 44224
Phone: 330-686-2600
Fax: 330-686-0719
URL: http://www.audio-technica.com/
Product: Audio-Technica makes speakers and related audio components for use in multimedia computing.

Autel Inc.
70 Walnut St
Wellesley, MA 02181
Phone: 617-239-8219
Fax: 617-239-7569
URL: http://www.autel.com/
Product: Autel specializes in the supply of automated audio conferencing solutions.

AVerMedia
47923A Warm Springs Blvd.
Freemont, CA 94539
Phone: 510-770-9899
Fax: 510-770-9901
URL: http://www.aver.com/
Product: AVerMedia makes computer-to-television scan converters and a desktop camera.

Avistar Systems
555 Hamilton Ave.
Palo Alto, CA 94301
Phone: 415-617-1350
Fax: 415-617-1351
URL: http://www.avistar.com/
Product: Avistar makes client/server oriented videoconferencing and collaboration software that runs on Sun Microsystems servers and which incorporates Macintoshes, PC and UNIX clients.

Barco Projection Systems
Noordlaan 5
8520 Kuurne
Belgium
Phone: + 32-56-36-82-11
Fax: + 32-56-35-16-51
URL: http://www.barco-usa.com/
Product: Barco makes high-end large-screen projection systems.

Bell Atlantic Video Services Company
1880 Campus Commons Drive
Reston, VA 20191
Phone: 703-708-4360
Fax: 703-708-4252
URL: http://www.bell-atl.com/
Product: Bell Atlantic offers commercial video-on-demand (VOD) services over its switched broadband network. It provides ISP, ISDN, and DSL services.

BellSouth Business Systems, Inc. (a subsidiary of BellSouth Telecommunications)
Atlanta, GA
Phone: 800-250-7272
URL: http://www.bellsouth.com/
Product: BellSouth offers a complete suite of voice, video and document conferencing bridging services.

Bitfield Oy
Espoo, Finland
Phone: +358-0-502-4220 or 310-322-2240 (El Segundo, CA)
Fax: +358-0-455-2240
URL: http://www.bitfield.fi/
Product: Bitfield sells a desktop conferencing system that includes codec, ISDN interface, camera and software. The product can be enhanced through the use of a daughterboard for high-performance desktop conferencing.

Boca Research
1377 Clint Moore Road
Boca Raton, FL 33487-2732
Phone: 407-997-6227
Fax Server: 561-994-5848
URL: http://www.bocaresearch.com/
Product: Boca Research makes board-level multimedia (video, telephony, sound, voice and data) products. It also sells H.324-compliant videophone software.

Bosch Telecom Inc.
9201 Gaither Road
Gaithersburg, MD 20877-1439
Phone: 301-670-9777
Fax: 301-670-3992
URL: http://www.bosch-telecom.dk/
Product: Bosch makes an H.320-compliant videoconferencing system.

Broadband Networks, Inc.
2820 E. College Ave., Suite B
State College, PA 16801
Phone: 814-237-4073
Fax: 814-234-2841
URL: http://www.bnisolutions.com/Site/home.html
Product: BNI designs, manufactures and integrates system solutions for video, voice and data networks.

C-Cube Microsystems
1778 McCarthy Blvd.
Milpitas, CA 95035
Phone: 408-944-6300
Fax: 408-944-6314
URL: http://www.c-cube.com/
Product: C-Cube makes various video- and multimedia-oriented compression chips.

C-Phone Corporation
6714 Netherlands Drive
Wilmington, NC 28405
Phone: 910-395-6100
Fax: 910-395-6108
URL: http://www.cphone.com/
Product: C-Phone makes an ISDN-based video PBX that turns networked desktop PCs into videophones with T.120 data collaboration capabilities. It includes all the desktop, server and network hardware and software needed for a complete solution.

Canoga Perkins Corporation
21012 Lassen St.
Chatsworth, CA 91311
Phone: 818-718-6300
Fax: 818-718-6312
URL: http://www.canoga.com/
Product: Canoga sells fiber-optic network products used for (among other things) videoconferencing.

Canon USA, Inc.
One Canon Plaza
Lade Success, NY 11042
Phone: 516-328-5956
Fax: 516-328-5959
URL: http://www.usa.canon.com/
Product: Canon makes a wide range of video cameras.

Casio Phonemate, Inc.
20665 Manhattan Place
Torrance, CA 90501
Phone: 310-618-9910
Fax: 310-212-6316
URL: http://www.casiophonemate.com/
Product: Casio makes a videophone that transmits color video images (with audio) over POTS and which has its own built-in camera and LCD screen.

Chanticleer Communications, Inc.
8760A Research Blvd., Suite 510
Austin, TX 78758
Phone: 512-338-0095
Fax: 512-338-1862
E-mail: http://www.chanticleercomms.com/chanticleer.htm
Product: Chanticleer produces business television programming.

Cinecom Corporation
15621 Neath Drive
Woodbridge, VA 22193
Phone: 703-680-4733
Fax: 703-680-1697
URL: http://www.cinecom.com/
Product: CINECOM makes Windows based software that supports desktop videoconferencing over POTS and IP-based networks. The product works with the Connectix QuickCam.

Cirrus Logic
Fremont, CA
Phone: 510-623-8300
Fax on demand: 800-594-6414
URL: http://www.cirrus.com/
Product: Cirrus Logic manufacturers multimedia chipsets including a 64-bit accelerator and a V.34/V.80-compliant chipset for H.324 videophone applications.

Cisco Systems
1835 Alexander Bell Dr. Suite 100
Reston, VA 22091
Phone: 703-716-9411
Fax: 703-716-9499
URL: http://www.cisco.com/
Product: Cisco is a global networking products company that sells (among other things) routers, switches, firewalls, and VoIP products.

Coherent Communications Systems Corp.
44084 Riverside Parkway
Leesburg, VA 20176
Phone: 703-729-6400
Fax: 703-729-6152
URL: http://www.coherent.com/
Product: Coherent designs, manufactures and markets audio components for conferencing applications.

Compunetix, Inc.
2000 Eldo Road, Monroeville Industrial Park
Monroeville, PA 15146
Phone: 800-879-4266
Fax: 412-373-6990
URL: http://www.compunetix.com/
Product: Compunetix makes an H.320-compliant multipoint conferencing unit that works with any videoconferencing hardware. Its MCU supports the H.320 and T.120 standards.

Connectix Corporation
2655 Campus Drive
San Mateo, CA 94403
Phone: 415-571-5100 or 800-950-5880
Fax: 415-571-5195
URL: http://www.connectix.com/
Product: Connectix makes the QuickCam camera for desktop videoconferencing and also sells Windows-based videophone software, which comes bundled with QuickCam. The bundled product runs over IP- and IPX-based LANs.

Convene International
250 Montgomery Street, 8th Floor
San Francisco, CA 94104
Phone: 415-782-0500 or 888-266-8363
Fax: 415-782-0505
URL: http://www.convene.com/
Product: Convene is a group-oriented distance learning tool used to create IP- or POTS-based conferencing networks that incorporate PCs and Macintosh computers.

Corel Corporation
1600 Carling Ave.
Ottawa, Ontario K12 8R7, Canada
Phone: 613-728-8200
Fax: 613-761-1061 or (fax-back) 613-728-0826, ext. 3080, document #1081
URL: http://www.corel.com/
Product: Corel makes an H.320/T.120-compliant videoconferencing system that runs over a LAN (IP, IPX, and NetBEUI) using Cat. 5 UTP. It includes a camera.

CritiCom, Inc.
4211 Forbes Rd.
Lanham, MD 20706
Phone: 301-306-0600
Fax: 301-306-0605
URL: http://www.criticom.com/
Product: CritiCom is a videoconferencing system integrator.

DataBeam Corporation
3191 Nicholasville Road
Lexington, KY 40503
Phone: 606-245-3500
Fax: 606-245-3528
URL: http://www.databeam.com/
Product: DataBeam makes a T.120-based, software-only server for hosting multi-point conferences. It also makes a T.120-based client. Its products run over LANs, WANs and POTS. DataBeam also offers a T.120 development environment.

Datapoint Corporation
8410 Datapoint Drive
San Antonio, Texas 78229
Phone: 800-DPT-MINX
Fax: 210-593-7518
URL: http://www.datapoint.com/
Product: Datapoint's multimedia conferencing software runs on Windows NT and UNIX to provide streaming video broadcast, videoconferencing, videomail, and MCU functions.

Diamond Multimedia Systems
San Jose, CA
Phone: 408-325-7000
Fax: 408-325-7070
URL: http://www.diamondmm.com/
Product: Diamond Multimedia makes a modem that supports the ITU-T's V.80 videophone technology. It also makes a home networking product.

Digital Vision Inc.
270 Bridge St.
Dedham, MA 02026
Phone: 617-329-5400 or 800-346-9090
Fax: 617-329-6286
URL: http://www.digitalvision.se/
Product: Digital Vision makes scan converters and video capture boards. It bundles its capture card & drivers, a capture utility, CU-SeeMe, a microphone, & a camera.

Dolch Computer Systems
3178 Laurelview Court
Fremont, CA 94538
Phone: 510-661-2220
Fax: 510-490-2360
URL: http://www.dolch.com/html/home_dolch.html
Product: Dolch makes custom, high-end portable computers.

DSP Group
3120 Scott Boulevard
Santa Clara, CA 95054-3317
Phone: 408-986-4300
Fax: 408-986-4323
URL: http://www.dspg.com/
Product: DSP holds the patent to the G.723 codec used in many H.323 implementations for videoconferencing over LANs. DSP licenses its codec to others—including Microsoft, Intel, Cirrus Logic and Creative Labs.

Edsson Software
P. O. Box 131201
Roseville, MN 55113
Phone: 612-638-9842
Fax: 612-636-8819
E-mail: http://www.edsson.com/
Product: Edsson makes inexpensive facility scheduling software.

Electrohome Limited
809 Wellington St., N.
Kitchener, ONT N2G 4J6, Canada
Phone: 519-744-7111
Fax: 519-749-3136
URL: http://www.electro.com/
Product: Electrohome develops and markets a high-brightness projector that can be integrated into boardroom conferencing solutions.

Elmo Manufacturing Corp.
New Hyde Park, NY 11040
Phone: 800-947-3566
Fax: 516-775-3297
URL: http://www.elmo-corp.com/
Product: Elmo makes document cameras for videoconferencing.

Extron Electronics
1230 S. Lewis St.
Anaheim, CA 92805
Phone: 714-491-1500
Fax: 714-491-1517
URL: http://www.extron.com/
Product: Extron makes computer/TV scan converters for NTSC and PAL, and a video equalizer.

EyeTel (Sales and Marketing)
Suite C210 - 501 Goodlette Road North
Naples, Florida 34102
Phone: 941-435-1079
Fax: 941-434-7613
URL: http://www.eyetel.com/
Product: EyeTel makes an H.261-based board that is packaged with a camera, a microphone, and software. EyeTel also makes a POTS-oriented videophone and Windows-oriented data collaboration software. EyeTel has also developed a series of secure video conferencing components.

Ezenia! Inc. (formerly VideoServer)
Northwest Park
63 Third Avenue
Burlington, MA 01803
Tel: 1-781-229-2000
URL: http://www.videoserver.com/
Product: Ensenia was the first company to ship an H.320-compliant MCU. Today it offers many fully-featured multimedia bridging products. All are fully standards (H.32X and T.120) compliant.

First Virtual Corporation
3393 Octavius Drive
Santa Clara, CA 95054
Phone 800-351-8539
Fax: 408-988-7077
URL: http://www.fvc.com/
Product: FVC makes ATM-based, networking products that deliver video collaboration to the desktop.

Folsom Research, Inc.
526 E. Bidwell St.
Folsom, CA 95630
Phone: 916-983-1500
Fax: 916-983-7236
URL: http://www.folsom.com/
Product: Folsom Research develops and markets high-end scan converters for broadcast quality PC-to-NTSC or PAL conversions.

Fujitsu Business Communication Systems, Inc.
3190 Miraloma Ave.
Anaheim, CA 92806
Phone: 602-921-4768
Fax: 602-921-4800
URL: http://www.fujitsu.com/
Product: Fujitsu makes a wide range of standards-based group-oriented and desktop videoconferencing systems and provides room design consulting services, engineering and systems integration (with an emphasis on distance learning applications).

General Instrument
6262 Lusk Blvd.
San Diego, CA 92121
Phone: 619-535-2408
Fax: 619-535-2485
URL: http://www.gi.com/
Product: GI offers a product family, which consists of MPEG-2 encoding and decoding products. GI bought this family (known as Magnitude) from CLI.

Gentner Communications Corporation
1825 Research Way
Salt Lake City, UT 84119
Phone: 800-945-7730
Fax: 801-794-3676
URL: http://www.gentner.com/index.html
Product: Gentner carries digital products for audio production, broadcast, communications and control including an audio system for videoconferencing.

Global Videoconferencing Solutions, Inc.
1455 Airport Blvd., West Bldg. Suite 200
San Jose, CA 95110
Phone: 800-909-4874
Fax: 408-280-1402
URL: http://www.globalvideoconf.com/
Product: Global Videoconferencing Solutions sells a wide variety of videoconferencing-oriented products, both on-line and through their catalog.

Hewlett-Packard Company
Test and Measurement Organization
5301 Stevens Creek Blvd.
Santa Clara, CA 95052-8059
Phone: 303-649-5637 or 800-452-4844
URL: http://www.hp.com/
Product: HP offers a full-service real-time encoder system that turns analog broadcast signals into network-ready digital data, sending it out as an MPEG-2 transport stream on ATM. The product is aimed at cable television or telephone companies that want to provide real-time live broadcast services to their subscribers over a digital network. It also offers its OpenView network management software.

Hitachi Multimedia Systems
3890 Steve Reynolds Blvd.
Norcross, GA 30093
Phone: 770-279-5600
Fax: 770-279-5696
URL: http://www.hitachi.com/
Product: Hitachi Multimedia systems makes cameras and monitors, and packages videoconferencing systems.

Howard Enterprises, Inc.
545 Calle San Pablo
Camarillo, CA 93010
Phone: 805-383-7444
Fax: 805-383-7442
URL: http://www.howent.com/
Product: Howard Enterprises makes color video cameras for videoconferencing. Some include a built-in microphone.

IBM
8999 Nelson Way
Burnaby, BC V5A 4B5, Canada
Phone: 604-293-6060
Fax: 604-293-6148
URL: http://www.ibm.com/
Product: IBM makes many video-oriented products including Lotus VideoNotes, Person to Person for Windows, OS/2 or AIX and a variety of DSPs.

In Focus Systems
27700 SW Parkway Avenue
Wilsonville, OR 97077
Phone: 503-685-8888 or 800-294-6400
Fax: 503-685-8631
URL: http://store.infocus.com/
Product: In Focus makes computer projection systems.

Intel Corporation
5200 N.E. Elam Young Parkway
Hillsboro, OR 97124
Phone: 800-538-3373
URL: http://www.intel.com
Product: Intel OEMs its ProShare family of videoconferencing and T.120-compliant data collaboration products, that operate over ISDN, Ethernet and POTS, to PictureTel. Intel also offers hubs, switches, firewalls and hosting services (not to mention processors).

Intelect Visual Communications
645 5th Ave. 17th Floor
New York, NY 10022
Phone: 212-317-9600
Fax: 212-317-9620
URL: http://www.videoconferencing.com/
Product: Intelect designs and manufactures desktop, rollabout and boardroom videoconferencing systems that support H.32X, MPEG and M-JPEG and work over circuit-switched (switched 56, ISDN, T-1) and packet-switched (IP-based) digital networks.

Intelligence at Large, Inc.
3508 Market St., Suite 230
Philadelphia, PA 19104
Phone: 215-387-6002
Fax: 215-387-9215
URL: http://www.beingthere.com/
Product: Intelligence at Large offers a software-oriented QuickTime-based desktop conferencing product that runs Macintosh computers over LANs (Ethernet, Token Ring, and LocalTalk) and WANs (analog dial-up, switched digital including ISDN BRI and switched 56, and dedicated digital services.)

InView
8420 W. Bryn Mawr, Suite 400
Chicago, IL 60631
Phone: 312-399-1604
Fax: 312-399-1588
URL: http://www.inview.net/
Product: InView offers multipoint video bridging services.

IPC Peripherals
48041 Fremont Boulevard
Fremont, CA 94538
Phone: 510-354-0800
Fax: 510-354-0808
URL: http://www.ipc.com/
Product: IPC makes desktop-oriented H.32X-compliant hardware/software combinations that work over various networks (ISDN, T-1, POTS, IP-based). Products come equipped with a codec, camera, telephone handset and software and support both videoconferencing and data collaboration.

IRP Professional Sound Products
1111Tower Lane
Bensenville, IL 60106
Phone: 800-255-6993
Fax: 630-860-1997
URL: http://www.irp.net/
Product: IRP manufacturers a variety of audio-oriented products including amplifiers, microphones, equalizers, and mixers. These can be integrated into various videoconferencing room implementations.

IMCCA
Phone: 516-818-8184
Fax: 516-922-2170
URL: http://www.imcca.org/
Product: The IMCCA is a professional organization that represents users and providers of collaborative communications by linking members with information, applications and solutions. The IMCCA offers an annual conference and exposition.

Jabra
San Diego, CA
Phone: 619-622-0764 or 800-327-2230
Fax: 619-622-0353
URL: http://www.jabra.com/
Product: Jabra makes a very small Ear PHONE, a DSP-based headset that fits into the ear to allow hands-free, full-duplex communication.

Kenwood USA Corporation
2201 E. Dominguez St.
Long Beach, CA 90810
Phone: 310-761-8214
Fax: 310-604-4487
URL: http://www.kenwoodcorp.com/
Product: Kenwood offers a PCMCIA card and accessories that allows laptop computer users to hold video conferences with each other in real time over local area networks, the Internet, or phone lines.

Lattitude Communications
2121 Tasman Drive
Santa Clara, CA 95054
Phone: 408-988-7200
Fax: 408-988-6520
URL: http://www.latitude.com/
Product: Lattitude makes a hardware/software-based conference server that uses e-mail, fax, pager and the WWW to schedule conferences, notify participants and distribute meeting materials.

LearnLinc
385 Jordan Rd.
Troy, NY 12180
Phone: 518-283-8799
Fax: 518-286-2439
URL: http://www.ilinc.com/
Product: LearnLinc develops self-paced multimedia learning tools.

Lucent Technologies
211 Mt Airy Rd., Room 2E105
Basking Ridge, NJ 07920
Phone: 908-953-6515
Fax: 908-953-6183
URL: http://www.lucent.com
Product: Lucent is a global provider of individual and group video systems equipment and services. It sells a full complement of equipment. Fee-based professional services include consultative planning, turnkey project management, equipment and network systems integration, and on-line basic user as well as advanced training courses. Lucent offers ongoing maintenance, reservations and scheduling software and services and complete video operations management services. With its acquisitions of Ascend, Livingston, Elemedia, and other companies, it is a prime source for virtually all networking products.

Macromedia, Inc.
600 Townsend Street, Suite 310W
San Francisco, CA 94103
Phone: 415-252-2000 or 800-326-2128
Fax: 415-626-0554
URL: http://www.macromedia.com/
Product: Macromedia makes a family of multimedia tools that support streaming media over the Internet.

Madge Networks Inc. (acquired Teleos)
210 N. First St.
San Jose, CA 95131
Phone: 408-955-0700
Fax: 408-955-0970
URL: http://www.madge.com/
Product: Madge Networks provides inverse multiplexers, video switches and video hubs that support group-oriented videoconferencing systems, desktop systems and MCUs. Additionally, it provides video networking among multiple video units on a global basis.

MCI WorldCom
8750 W. Bryn Mawr, Suite 900
Chicago, IL 60631
Phone: 800-480-3600
Fax: 312-399-4470
URL: http://www.wcom.com/

Product: MCI WorldCom Conferencing provides multipoint bridging, a single 800 number for reservations and support, and digital transmission and conferencing services for audio, video and documents. MCI WorldCom Media Manager is a server-based product for storage, management, retrieval, and distribution of multimedia content.

Microfield Graphics, Inc.
9825 SW Sunshine Court
Beaverton, OR 97005
Phone 503-626-9393
Fax: 503-641-9333
URL: http://www.microfield.com/
Product: Microfield makes two models of an electronic whiteboard: one that is mounted on a wall and one that can be rolled from room to room. Microfield also makes a whiteboard product for personal use.

Microsoft Corporation
One Microsoft Way,
Redmond, WA 98052
Phone: 800-426-9400
Fax: 206-936-7329
URL: http://www.microsoft.com
Product: Microsoft offers its freeware product NetMeeting, a T.120- and H.323-compliant collaboration tool. It is controlled via an Internet Explorer-style tool bar. It offers audio-enhanced application sharing and integrated audioconferencing as well as whiteboard, file transfer and chat features.

Microspace Communications Corp.
3100 Highlands Blvd.
Raleigh, NC 27604
Phone: 919-850-4550
Fax: 919-850-4554
URL: http://www.microspace.com/
Product: Microspace is a provider of satellite data and audio broadcast services.

Mitsubishi Electronics America, Inc.
5665 Plaza Drive
Cypress, CA 90630
Phone: 714-220-2250
Fax: 714-229-3854
URL: http://www.mitsubishi.com/
Product: Mitsubishi makes monitors (including touchscreen) and projectors that can be used for group-oriented videoconferencing applications.

MultiLink, Inc.
6 Riverside Drive
Andover, MA 01810
Phone: 508-691-2100
Fax: 508-691-2190
URL: http://www.multilink.com/
Product: Multilink makes a H.32X-compliant multipoint videoconferencing unit. The product supports a large number of video and audio ports and many different features. Multilink has focused on MCU management capabilities.

National Semiconductor
2900 Semiconductor Drive
Santa Clara, CA 95052-8090
Phone: 408-721-5000
Fax: 408-739-9803
URL: http://www.national.com/
Product: National Semiconductor makes various products that have applicability to videoconferencing and interactive multimedia. Among these are chipsets, isochronous Ethernet products, and audio and video amplifiers.

nCube
110 Marsh Drive
Foster City, CA 94404-1184
Phone: 415-593-9000
Fax: 415-508-5408
URL: http://www.ncube.com/
Product: nCube offers an application development environment that can be used to develop interactive multimedia applications that include video on demand and distance learning. NABLE includes software, hardware, networking capabilities and sample applications. It runs on nCube's mediaCUBE 30 server.

NEC Corporation
1555 W. Walnut Hill Lane
Irving, TX 75038
Phone: 214-751-7000
Fax: 214-751-4441
URL: http://www.nec.com/
Product: NEC makes a number of videoconferencing and video compression products. Their products include H.320 group-oriented and desktop-oriented videoconferencing implementations, an MCU, a telemedicine system and a distance learning system.

Netscape Communications
501 E. Middlefield Rd.
Mountain View, CA 94043
Phone: 415-528-2555 or 800-638-7483
Fax: 415-528-4140
URL: http://www.netscape.com
Product: Netscape, through its Communicator suite of applications, provides point-to-point voice communication and online collaboration integrated with a Web browser.

Nokia Networks Inc.
6000 Connection Drive
Irving, Texas 75039
United States
Phone: 972 894 5000
Fax: 972 894 5050
http://www.nokia.com/
Product: Nokia makes circuit switches, handheld communications appliances, firewalls, wireless Ethernet products, and VoIP products.

Nortel Networks
4401 Great America Pkwy P.O. Box 58185
Santa Clara, CA 95052-8185
Phone: 408-988-2400
Fax: 408-495-5525
URL: http://www.nortelnetworks.com/index.html
Product: Nortel Networks manufacturers PBXs, Telco switches, routers, switches, firewalls, and VoIP products.

One Touch Systems, Inc.
40 Airport Parkway
San Jose, CA 95110
Phone: 408-436-4600
Fax: 408-436-4699
URL: http://www.onetouch.com/
Product: One Touch makes video-enabled distance learning products that include a conferencing system, a response keypad and a site controller.

Optel Communications Inc.
50 Jackson Ave. 3rd Floor
Syosset, NY 11791
Phone: 516-921-3700
Fax: 516-921-3709
URL: http://www.optelusa.com/

Product: Optel makes Windows-based software that supports application screen sharing, storage, retrieval and real-time annotation of PC-generated information.

Optivision, Inc.
3450 Hillview Ave.
Palo Alto, CA 94304
Phone: 800-562-8934
Fax: 415-855-0222
URL: http://www.optivision.com/
Product: Optivision makes the OPTIVideo Low Latency Encoder for MPEG applications. It is targeted at distance learning and telemedicine applications, among others.

Orckit
38 Nahalat Yitzhak St.
Tel Aviv, 67448, Israel
Phone: + 972-3-696-2121.
Fax: +972-3-696-5678
URL: http://www.orckit.com/
Product: Orckit's product line includes HDSL, ADSL, and VDSL transmission systems that modify POTS lines to allow broadband delivery.

OutReach Technologies (a division of Communication Systems Technology Inc.)
8975 Guilford Rd. Suite 100
Columbia, MD 21046
Phone: 410-381-5087
Fax: 410-381-3589
URL: http://www.outreachtech.com/
Product: Outreach makes T.120-compliant hardware/software tools for audiographics conferencing. The products can run over POTS, include a video-ready modem and can support up to 72 conferees.

Panasonic Matsushita Consumer Electronics Company
One Panasonic Way
Secaucus, NJ 07094
Phone: 201-271-3405
Fax: 201-348-7209
URL: http://www.panasonic.com/
Product: Panasonic makes integrated videoconferencing group and desktop systems and offers monitors. It is also involved in the development and marketing of many other video and audio components.

ParkerVision
8493 Baymeadows Way
Jacksonville, FL 32256
Phone: 904-737-1367
Fax: 904-731-0958
URL: http://www.parkervision.com/
Product: ParkerVision specializes in automated camera control and user interface technology. The company's product allows a conference participant to press a button to move the camera to them so they can speak. The product supports up to 99 keypads and works well in distance learning applications.

Philips Semiconductors
811 East Arques Avenue
P.O. Box 3409
Sunnyvale, CA 94088-3409
Phone: 800-234-7381
Fax. 708-296-8556
URL: http://www.philips.com/
Products: Philips makes a number of digital audio and video products including chips and video capture boards. It also bundles its boards with cameras and software to deliver desktop videoconferencing products.

Phylon Communications
47436 Fremont Blvd.
Fremont, CA 95438
Phone: 510-656-2606
Fax: 510-656-0902
URL: http://www.philips.com/
Product: Phylon makes DSPs (chipsets) used in video and audio signal processing.

Picturephone Direct
200 Commerce Drive
Rochester, NY 14623
Phone: 716-334-9040 or 800-521-5454
Fax: 716-359-4999
URL: http://www.picturephone.com/
Product: Picturephone Direct is a reseller of full-motion desktop videoconferencing, still-video equipment, document conferencing software peripherals and accessories. They offer a catalog listing their products.

PictureTel Inc.
222 Rosewood Drive
Danvers, MA 09123
Phone 508-762-5000 or 800-716-6000
Fax: 508-749-2890
URL: http://www.picturetel.com/
Product: PictureTel offers a full line of videoconferencing and multimedia products. These range from high-end boardroom systems to desktop products to videophones and include everything in between. PictureTel's products are standards-compliant, and support the entire range of H.32X and T.120 protocols. PictureTel's products run on both digital circuit-switched and packet-switched network and over POTS.

Peirce-Phelps, Inc.
2000 N. 59th Street
Philadelphia, PA 19131
Phone: 215-879-7000 or 800-862-6800
Fax: 215-879-5427
URL: http://www.peirce.com/
Product: Peirce-Phelps is a full-service multimedia systems integrator. The company has worked with hundreds of Business Week 1000 companies to establish enterprise-wide videoconferencing and multimedia systems and networks.

Polaroid Corporation
549 Technology Square
Cambridge, MA
Phone: 617-386-2000
Fax: 617-386-3125
URL: http://www.polaroid.com/
Polaroid Corporation makes a variety of projection systems.

Polycom, Inc.
2584 Junction Ave.
San Jose, CA 95134
Phone: 408-526-9000
Fax: 408-526-9100
URL: http://www.polycom.com/
Product: Polycom makes high-quality set-top videoconferencing systems, audio conferencing products and a T.120-compliant audiographics product that transmits full-page, grayscale images of documents.

Proxima Corporation
San Diego, CA
Phone: 619-457-5500 or 800-447-7692
Fax (619) 457-9647
URL: http://www.proxima.com/
Product: Proxima makes projection systems.

Pyramid National Pressport
480 National Press Building
Washington, DC 20045
Phone: 202-783-5030 or 800-598-9260
Fax: 202-628-7228
URL: http://www.pressport.com/
Product: Pyramid National Pressport provides production, post production and satellite transmission services to the public relations, news gathering, cable, broadcast, business and corporate television industries.

Symantec Corporation (formerly Quarterdeck)
20330 Stevens Creek Blvd.
Cupertino, CA 95014
Phone: (408) 253-9600
Fax: (408) 253-3968
URL: http://www.symantec.com/
Product: Symantec offers a T.120-compliant data collaboration product for the Internet that allows users to share documents or applications in real time within a *conferencing channel.*

RADVision Ltd.
8 Hanehoshet St.
Tel-Aviv 69710, Israel
Phone: +972-3-645-5220
Fax: +972-3-647-6669
In the U.S. (Mahwah, NJ)
Phone: 201-529-4300
URL: http://www.radvision.com/
Product: RADVision makes an H.320 and H.323-compliant videoconferencing system that operates over LANs and WANs for point-to-point and broadcast applications. It also manufactures a video gateway that links LANs to remote sites.

Rane Corporation
10802 47th Ave. West
Mukilteo, WA 98275
Phone: 206-355-6000
Fax: 206-347-7757
URL: http://www.rane.com/
Product: Rane makes audio components that are used in professional studios and high-end videoconferencing production facilities.

RealNetworks, Inc.
2601 Elliott Avenue, Suite 1000
Seattle, WA 98121
Phone: 206-674-2700
http://www.realnetworks.com/
Product: Real Networks makes cross-platform streaming media client and server products that offer and support for IP Multicast (including MBONE) and RTSP.

RGB Spectrum
950 Marina Village Parkway
Alameda, CA 94501
Phone: 510-814-7000
Fax: 510-814-7026
URL: http://www.rgb.com/
Product: RGB Spectrum makes high-end scan converters.

Ricoh Corporation's Consumer Products Group
Sparks, NV
Phone: 702-352-1600 or 800-225-1899
Fax: 800-544-8246
URL: http://www.ricoh-usa.com/
Product: Ricoh makes a multimedia digital camera.

RSI Systems, Inc.
7400 Metro Blvd., Suite 475
Minneapolis, MN 55439
Phone: 612-896-3028
Fax: 612-896-3030
URL: http://www.rsisystems.com/
Product: RSI makes a stand-alone peripheral that plugs into a Macintosh SCSI port or a PowerBook PC card slot that houses a video codec. It also includes a full-duplex speakerphone and connections for POTS or ISDN. RSI also offers an H.320-based system for Windows, Macintosh, and Unix computers that works over circuit-switched digital lines to deliver videoconferencing and document sharing

Sagem (also known as Sat Sagem)
20370 Town Center Lane, Suite 255
Cupertino, CA 95014
Phone: 408-446-8690
Fax: 408-446-9766
URL: http://www.sagem.com/
Product: Sagem makes H.320 ISDN products for Macintosh platforms.

Sanyo Semiconductor Corp.
453 Ravendale Drive, Suite G
Mountain View, CA 94043
Phone: 415-960-8582, ext. 26
Fax: 415-960-8591
URL: http://www.sanyo.com/
Product: Sanyo develops digital signal processors for videoconferencing.

SGS-Thomson
Carrollton, TX
Phone: 214-466-7644
Fax: 214-466-6572
URL: http://us.st.com/
Product: SGS-Thomson makes DSPs and other multimedia devices such as MPEG decoders.

Shure Brothers, Inc.
222 Hartrey Ave.
Evanston, IL 60202
Phone: 708-866-2527
Fax: 708-866-2353
URL: http://www.shure.com/
Product: Shure manufacturers audio components including wired and wireless microphones, mixers and teleconferencing systems.

Silicon Graphics, Inc.
2011 N. Shoreline Blvd.
Mountain View, CA 94043-1389
Phone: 415-960-1980 or 800-800-7441
Fax: 415-961-0595
URL: http://www.sgi.com/
Product: Silicon Graphics Inc. makes an IP-based document and videoconferencing product and a multimedia development engine.

Smart Technologies, Inc.
1177 11th Ave., S.W., Suite 600
Calgary, AB T2R 1K9, Canada
Phone: 403-245-0333
Fax: 403-245-0366
URL: http://www.smarttech.com/
Product: Smart Technologies manufacturers the rear projection Smart Board, an interactive electronic whiteboard for meeting room environments. The product has a touch-sensitive screen and can integrate with videoconferencing systems.

Smith Micro Software, Inc.
51 Columbia
Aliso Viejo, CA 92656
Phone: 714-362-5800
Fax: 714-362-2300
URL: http://www.smithmicro.com/
Product: Smith Micro Software manufactures a point-to-point product that allows videoconferencing over POTS. It can also send video e-mail over the Internet.

Sony Electronics, Inc.
3 Paragon Dr. Maildrop S725
Montvale, NJ 07645
Phone: 800-686-7669
Fax: 201-930-6964
URL: http://www.sony.com/
Product: Sony manufactures a wide variety of videoconferencing systems including a group-oriented system (that integrates multipoint, I-MUX, continuous presence, and on-screen messaging). Sony also offers monitors, cameras and bundled desktop videoconferencing products.

Sound Control Technologies, Inc.
28 Knight St.
Norwalk, CT 06851
Phone: 203-854-5701
Fax: 203-854-5702
URL: http://www.soundcontrol.net/sct_downloads.ht
Product: Sound Control Technologies, Inc. manufactures and markets full duplex audioconferencing systems that can be used as stand-alone products or as enhancements to videoconferencing systems.

Sprint Conferencing
3065 Cumberland Circle
Atlanta, GA 30339
Phone: 800-669-1235
Fax: 404-989-1362
URL: http://www.sprint.com/
Product: Sprint offers a comprehensive set of video communication products and services, including switched and dedicated transmission, connectivity services, personal and group videoconferencing systems from various manufacturers, a customer education program and ongoing network management support.

Star Vision Multimedia Corporation
4260 Still Creek Drive, Suite 450
Burnaby, BC V5C 6C6, Canada
Phone: 604-205-5500
Fax: 604-205-5511
URL: http://204.174.242.174/
Product: Star Vision makes direct broadcast satellite digital TV and home theater audio/video systems.

Stardust Technologies
1901 S. Bascom Ave. Suite 333
Campbell, CA 95008
Phone: 408-879-8080
Fax: 408-879-8081
URL: http://www.stardust.com/
Product: Stardust Technologies is an independent Winsock interoperability testing center. Stardust also manages the IP Multicast Initiative.

Sun Microsystems
2550 Garcia Ave.,
Mountain View, CA 94043-1100
Phone: 415-336-5714 or 800-880-4786
URL: http://www.sun.com/
Product: Sun's integrated package provides a complete video, audio, shared whiteboard, and shared application system that runs on Solaris 2.3 UNIX systems and uses the Internet for transport.

Tandberg
2100 Reston Parkway, Suite 206
Reston, VA 20191
Phone: 703-715-9898
Fax: 703-715-9842
URL: http://www.tandberg.com/
Product: Tandberg makes group-oriented videoconferencing systems.

Tektronix-Video Networks Division
14180 S.W. Karl Braun Drive
P.O. Box 500
Mail Stop 58020
Beaverton, Oregon 97077
Phone: 800-547-8949
Fax: 503-627-1130
URL: http://www.tek.com/
Product: Tektronix VND makes a wide variety of video production, storage and transmission, editing and advanced hardware and software products for networked computing and multimedia.

Teleconnect Magazine
12 West 21st Street
New York, NY 10010
Phone: 212-691-8215
Fax: 212-691-1191
URL: http://www.telecomlibrary.com/
Product: TeleConnect Magazine is a source of information on all facets of the telecommunications and videoconferencing industry. It periodically publishes product round-ups that compare supplier's offerings.

Teles Corporation
1818 Gilbreth Rd. Suite 211
Burlingame, CA 94010
Phone: 415-652-9191
Fax: 415-652-9192
URL: http://www.telecomlibrary.com/
Product: Manufactures a full-range of H.32X-compliant desktop-oriented videoconferencing systems. Bundled products include hardware/software, cameras, audio and all other components required to deliver a turnkey system. The company also manufactures ISDN TAs that bring H.320 videoconferences to a PC-desktop.

Telespan Publishing Corporation
50 West Palm Street
Altadena, CA 91001
Phone: 818-797-5482
Fax: 818-797-2035
URL: http://www.telespan.com/
Product: Telespan (which publishes a newsletter) is considered to be one of the most informed sources on the videoconferencing industry. The publisher of Telespan is Elliot Gold.

Teloquent Communications Corp.
4 Federal Street
Billerica, MA 01821
Phone: 508-663-7570
Fax: 508-663-7543
URL: http://www.teloquent.com/main.html
Product: Teloquent makes video call center hardware.

Toshiba Computer Systems Division
9740 Irvine Blvd.
Irvine, CA 92713
Phone: 800-999-4273
URL: http://www.toshiba.com/
Product: Toshiba makes a number of video-oriented products including an H.324-compliant videophone, a variety of video-capable laptops, video and audio decoder chips and consumer electronics.

TVOne
1445 Jamike Dr., Suite 8
Erlanger, KY 41018
Phone: 606-282-7303
Fax: 606-282-8225
URL: http://www.tvone.com/
Product: TVOne makes PC-to-television scan converters.

Umax Technologies
3353 Gateway Blvd.
Freemont, CA 94538
800-562-0311; 510-651-9488
Fax: 510-651-8834
URL: http://www.umax.com/
Product: Umax makes PC-to-television scan converters.

VCON
17130 N. Dallas Parkway, Suite 210
Dallas, TX 75248
Phone: 214-735-9001
Fax: 214-735-9099
URL: http://www.vcon.com/
Product: VCON makes H.320-compliant add-in-boards, desktop videoconferencing products, and a small-group system.

VDOnet Corporation
4009 Miranda Ave. Suite 250
Palo Alto, CA 94304
Phone: 415-846-7710
Fax: 415-846-7900
URL: http://www.vdo.net/
Product: VDOnet makes a videophone that operates over the Internet. Microsoft owns an equity stake in VDOnet.

VERREX Corporation
1130 Rt. 22 W.
Mountainside, NJ 07092
Phone: 908-232-7000
Fax: 908-232-7991
URL: http://www.verrex.com/
Product: A multimedia systems integrator that provides turnkey solutions. It sells all major videoconferencing products and also offer their own—a multimedia presentation system built " in the round." It holds 8–24 participants.

Vic Hi-Tech Corporation, Advanced Hi-Tech
2221 Rosecrans Ave., Suite 237
El Segundo, CA 90245
Phone: 310-643-5193
Fax: 310-643-7572
URL: http://www.vic-corp.com/
Product: Vic Hi-Tech makes two videoconferencing products, one for remote surveillance and the other a desktop/laptop product that runs on numerous networks including ISDN, TCP/IP LANs, POTS. The second product is H.32X compliant, uses hardware-level compression and includes whiteboard sharing and data collaboration.

VideoLabs, Inc.
10925 Bren Rd. East
Minnetonka, MN 55343
Phone: 612-988-0055 or 800-467-7157
Fax: 612-988-0066
URL: http://www.flexcam.com/
Product: VideoLabs makes a color video camera for use in various videoconferencing applications.

VideoLinx Communication, Inc.
7857 Heritage Drive, Suite 200
Annandale, VA 22003
Phone: 703-658-5469
Fax: 703-658-5470
URL: http://www.videolinx.com/
Product: A global video communications service provider. It offers brokerage service to over 400 public and private videoconferencing facilities. Additionally, it operates an occasional-use data service between the U.S. and Venezuela with four public facilities located in that country. The VideoLinx PictureTel rental program allows customers to rent videoconferencing equipment weekly or monthly.

ViewCast.com
2665 Villa Creek Drive, suite 200
Dallas, TX 75234
Phone: 972-488-7200
Fax: 972-488-7199
http://www.viewcast.com
Product: ViewCast makes video communications components and systems. Products include video distribution and switching systems, video capture cards, and streaming products.

ViewTech, Inc.
101 Pacifica, Suite 100
Irvine, CA 92618
Phone: 714-789-8800
Fax: 714-789-8810
URL: http://www.viewtech.com/
Product: View Tech is a system integrator and engineering organization that focuses solely on videoconferencing and its components, and offers single-vendor sourcing for every aspect of the videoconferencing process, including the integration of video, data, and voice.

VistaCom, Inc.
20431 Stevens Creek Blvd., Suite 240
Cupertino, CA 95014
Phone: 408-253-5165
Fax: 408-253-5170
URL: http://www.vistacom.fi/
Product: VistaCom makes board sets that comply with ITU-T specifications. These boards mount in ISA/EISA slots. VistaCom's boards support network speeds up to 384 Kbps and are supported by a complete API library.

Vista Satellite Communications, Inc.
3111 University Drive, Suite 418
Coral Springs, FL 33065
Phone: 954-755-7995
Fax: 954-755-7996
URL: http://www.vistasat.com/
Product: Vista is a full turnkey production, transmission and videoconferencing company.

Vivitar Corporation
1280 Rancho Conejo Blvd.
Newbury Park, CA 91320
Phone: 805-498-7008
Fax: 805-498-5086
URL: http://www.vivitar.com/
Product: Vivitar makes a color video phone system that runs on a PC and transmits over POTS.

Vivo Software
411 Waverly Oaks Road
Waltham, MA 02154
Phone: 617-899-8900
Fax: 617-899-1400
URL: http://www.vivitar.com/
Product: Vivo makes software that enables organizations to place videostreams on the World Wide Web. It is used by CNN and the Weather Channel, does not require a special video server, and uses the HTTP protocol to transport video data over the Internet and the Web.

VocalTec (product formerly manufactured by Insitu Inc.)
35 Industrial Parkway
Northvale, NJ 07647
Phone: 201-768-9400 or 800-843-2289
Fax: 201-768-8893
URL: http://www.vocaltec.com/
Product: VocalTec offers a data collaboration product that runs over Internet/intranets and that includes a whiteboard, a telephone, and a built-in Web browser that conference participants use to simultaneously view a Web page.

Voyant Technologies
1499 West 121st Street
Westminster, CO 80234
Phone: 303 633-7950
Fax: 303 633-3010
http://www.confertechsystems.com
Product: Voyant offers browser based audioconferencing bridging systems.

VSI Enterprises, Inc.
5801 Goshen Springs Road
Norcross, GA 30071
Phone: 770-242-7566
Fax: 770-242-6898
URL: http://www.vsin.com/
Product: VSI offers a complete range of videoconferencing products (desktop, rollabout, boardroom). Its products are based on ITU-T standards and run over digital circuit-switched and packet-switched networks and ATM.

VTEL Corporation
108 Wild Basin Road
Austin, TX 78746
Phone: 512-314-2594 or 800-299-8835
Fax: 512-314-2748
URL: http://www.vsin.com/
Product: VTEL offers videoconferencing and multimedia products that run on PC platforms. Their products range from low-end desktop conferencing products to high-end boardroom systems and include an MCU. VTEL's products are all standards-compliant but can also run proprietary algorithms. Products run over a variety of network types including circuit-switched and packet-switched digital. VTEL has a major share of the distance learning and telemedicine market.

White Pine Software, Inc.
542 Amherst St.
Nashua, NH 03063
Phone: 603-886-9050
Fax: 603-886-9051
URL: http://www.whitepine.com/
Product: White Pine makes Enhanced CU-SeeMe software for desktop point-to-point or multipoint conferencing over the Internet.

Winnov L.P.
Sunnyvale, CA
Phone: 408-733-9500 or 888-494-6668
Fax: 408-733-5922
URL: http:// http://www.winnov.com/
Product: Winnov makes a videoconferencing add-in board for PCs that can also be used for video capture. Winnov bundles its product with a camera and White Pine's Enhanced CU-SeeMe software. It also makes a product that allows laptop users to conduct videoconferences over the Internet.

Winsted Corporation
10901 Hampshire Ave., S.
Minneapolis, MN 55438
Phone: 612-944-9050
Fax: 612-944-1546
URL: http://www.winsted.com/
Product: Winsted makes a line of multimedia and video security products.

Wolfvision, Inc.
655 Sky Way, Suite 119
San Carlos, CA 94070
Phone: 415-802-0786
Fax: 415-802-0788
URL: http://www.wolfvision.com/wolf/1.html
Product: Wolfvision manufactures and distributes a wide variety of optical equipment, including document cameras and projection systems.

Xing Technology Corporation
1540 W. Branch Street
Arroyo Grande CA 93420
Phone: 805-473-0145
Fax: 805-473-0147
URL: http://www.xingtech.com/
Product: Xing Technology makes technology for streaming audio and video delivery over the Internet.

Xirlink, Inc.
2210 O'Toole Ave.
San Jose, CA 9531
Phone: 408-324-2100
Fax: 408-324-2101
URL: http://www.xirlink.com/
Product: Xirlink makes an audio/video digital camera for videoconferencing.

Zandar Technologies
1 Comsat House, Northbrook Road
Ranelagh, Dublin 6, Ireland
Phone: +353-1-2808-945
Fax: +353-1-2808-956
URL: http://www.zandar.com/
Product: Zandar Technologies makes board-level multi-video display systems. Its multi-image or split-screen displays feature full-motion, real-time video. The products are used in the generation of custom mosaic television channels and for multi-video or multi-camera monitoring.

Zoran
2041 Mission College Blvd.
Santa Clara, CA 95054
Phone: 408-986-1314
URL: http://www.zoran.com/
Product: Zoran manufacturers VLSI chips for high performance low-cost digital video and audio compression applications. Its products are integrated in multimedia, video editing, digital camera, digital video disks, and digital audio systems. Zoran chips are oriented toward JPEG, motion JPEG and MPEG.

Zydacron, Inc.
7 Perimeter Road
Manchester, NH 03103
Phone: 603-647-1000
Fax: 603-647-9470
URL: http://www.zydacron.com/
Product: Zydacron makes an H.320-compliant videoconferencing package for desktop PCs. It includes an ISDN BRI network interface, a codec, a camera, a microphone, a telephone handset, software, and cabling.

Zydecom, Inc.
5220 Hollywood Ave.
Shreveport, LA 71109
Phone: 510 606-6407
Fax: 510 606-6427
URL: http://www.zydecom.com/
Product: Zydecom Inc. offers a real-time Java based operating system that enables high-speed videoconferencing and video-on-demand over high-bandwidth technologies, including cable modems, ISDN, ATM, and DSL.

Glossary of Terms

— 0 ...9 —

3-D — A way to visually describe an image using height, width and depth components so that the object appears to have physical depth in relation to its surroundings. 3-D modeling is the process of defining the shape and related characteristics of objects that can later be rendered in 3-D form.

4CIF — The ITUT's H.263 coding and compression standard specifies a common intermediate format to provide resolutions that are four times greater than that of CIF. Support of 4CIF in H.263 enables the standard to compete with higher bit-rate coding schemes such as MPEG. 4CIF specifies 576 non-interlaced luminance lines, that each contain 704 pixels. Support of 4CIF in H.263 is optional. 4CIF is also referred to as Super CIF, which was defined in Annex IV of H.261 in 1992.

16CIF — As is true with 4CIF, the ITU-T's H.263 standard specifies, but does not mandate, support of 16 CIF, a picture resolution that is composed of 1152 non-interlaced luminance lines, that each contain 1408 pixels. At this resolution, H.263 can provide resolutions about twice as good as NTSC television.

— A —

A/D conversion — Analog to digital conversion. A/D converters accept a series of analog voltages and describe them via a series of discrete binary-encoded values that approximate the original signal. This process is known as digitizing or sampling. D-to-A converters reverse the process.

absorption loss — The attenuation of an optical signal within a transmission system, specified as dB/km.

access	A method of reaching a carrier or a network. In the world of wide area networking, access channels (which may be copper, microwave, fiber) carry a subscriber to a carrier's point of presence (POP). In the world of local area networking access methods are used to mediate the use of a shared bus.
access method	The technique and protocols that govern how a communications device uses a local area network (LAN). The IEEE's 802 standards 802.3 through 802.12 specify access methods for LANs and MANs.
ACCUNET Services	AT&T's high-speed dial-up services offered via their switched digital network. Used for full-duplex digital transmission at speeds of between 56 Kbps (switched 56) and 1.536 Mbps (T-1). In between these speeds there are offerings of 64 Kbps and 384 Kbps (H0 dialing).
acoustic echo canceller	An AEC is used to eliminate return echoes in an acoustically-coupled tele-meeting. AEC's are used in full-duplex audio arrangements in which all microphones are active at all times. This situation causes an increase in ambient noise that an AEC is designed to mediate.
acoustics	The qualities of an enclosed space that define how sound is transmitted, its clarity and how the original signal will be distorted.
active video lines	The lines that convey information in a television signal, e.g., all except for those that occur in the horizontal and vertical blanking intervals.
additive color	Direct light that is visible directly from the source: the sun, light bulbs, video monitors. The wavelengths of direct light can be viewed in three primary colors, red, greed and blue (RGB). Combinations of these three frequencies (for that is what colors are) result in most perceivable color variations.
additive primaries	By definition, three primary colors result when light is viewed directly as opposed to being reflected: red,

green and blue (RGB). According to the tri-stimulus theory of color perception, blending some mixture of these three lights can adequately approximate all other colors. This theory is harnessed in color television and video communications.

addressable — The ability of a device to receive communications over a network whereby the unique destination of the device can be specified. Typically, an address is a set of numbers (such as a telephone number) that allows a message to be intercepted and interpreted for purposes of an application.

ADPCM — CCITT Recommendation G.721. Adaptive Differential Pulse Code Modulation. A technique for converting an analog signal into digital form. It is based on standard sampling at 8 kHz and generates a 32 Kbps output signal. ADPCM was extended in G.726, which replaces both G.721 and G.723, to allow conversion between 64 Kbps PCM and 40, 32, 24 or 16 Kbps channels.

ADSL — Asymmetrical Digital Subscriber Line. A method of sending high-speed data over existing copper-wire twisted pair POTS lines. ADSL, developed by Bellcore and deployed by the telephone companies, uses a modulation technique known as discrete multitone (DMT) to transmit multimegabit traffic at between 16 and 640 Kbps upstream and 6 to 8 Mbps downstream. ADSL will not work over portions of the network that attenuate signals above 4 kHz. It also can not be used where there is bridged taps and cross-coupled interference.

affine map — A function that identifies similar frequency patterns in an image and uses one to describe all that are similar.

AIN — Advanced Intelligent Network. A digital network architecture based on out-of-band signaling that maximizes the intelligence, efficiency, and speed of the PSTN. AIN relies on databases that store vast amounts of data about network nodes and end-points and which are accessed across a packet-switched network that is separate from the one that carries customer traffic. AIN allows moment-to-moment call routing, automatic number identification (ANI), customer call-control, and more.

algorithm — A computational procedure that includes a prescribed set of processes for the solution of a problem in a finite number of steps; the underlying numerical or computational method behind a code or process. Algorithms are fundamental to image compression (both motion and still), because they allow an information-intensive file or transmission to be squeezed to a more economical size.

alias — Unwanted signals generated during the A-to-D conversion process. Aliasing is typically caused by a sampling rate that is too low to faithfully represent the original analog signal in digital form; typically, this occurs at a sampling rate that is less than half the highest frequency to be sampled.

aliasing — A subjectively disturbing distortion in a video signal that manifests in different ways depending on the cause. When the sampling rate interferes with the frequency of program material, aliasing takes the form of artifact frequencies known as sidebands. Spectral aliasing is caused by interference between two frequencies such as the luminance and chrominance signals and appears as herringbone patterns, wavy lines where straight lines should be, and loss of color fidelity. Temporal aliasing is caused when information is lost between line or field scans. It appears when a video camera is focused on a CRT. The lack of scanning synchronization produces an annoying flicker on the receiving device's screen.

amplifier — A device that receives an input signal in wave form (analog) and gives a magnified signal as an output.

amplify — To increase the magnitude of a voltage or a waveform in order to increase the strength of the signal.

amplitude — The magnitude of a waveform or voltage. Greater amplitude results when waves are set in motion with greater force. The term amplitude is also used to describe the strength of a signal.

amplitude modulation — AM. A method of changing a signal by varying its height or amplitude in order to superimpose it on a carrier wave. Used to impress radio waves (audio or video) onto a carrier in analog transmissions.

analog — Representations of numerical values by physical variables such as voltage and amplitude. Analog signals are continuously varying; indeed, depending on the precision with which they are sampled/measured, they can vary infinitely. By this we mean that each sample can produce a value that corresponds to the unique magnitude of the variable. An analog signal is one that uses electrical transmission methods to duplicate an original waveform, and thereby capture and convey these unique magnitudes.

analog transmission — A method of sending signals whereby the transmitted signal is analogous to the original signal. Sending a stream of continuously varying electrical waves represents the original sine wave.

animation — The process used to link a series of still images to create the effect of a motion sequence.

Annex A — (To Recommendation H.261). Inverse Transform Accuracy specification that defines the maximum tolerable error thresholds for the DCT.

Annex B — (To Recommendation H.261). Sets forth a Hypothetical Reference Decoder.

Annex C — (To Recommendation H.261). Specifies the method by which the video encoder and decoder delays are established for a particular H.261 implementation.

ANSI — The *American National Standards Institute*. A non-governmental industry organization that develops and publishes voluntary standards for the US ANSI has published standards for out-of-band signaling, for voice compression, for network performance, and for various electrical and network interfaces.

antenna — An aerial or other device that collects and radiates electromagnetic energy.

API — *Application Programmer Interface* A set of formalized software calls and routines, which can be referenced by an application program to access underlying network or other services.

application — An application is software that performs a particular useful function for a user—e.g., a spreadsheet tool, a word processing facility. Examples include word processing, spread sheets, distance learning, document conferencing, and telemedicine.

application sharing — A collaborative conferencing feature that provides personal conference participants with read/write access to an application, even when one or more of these participants does not have the application running at their desktop. In application sharing, one user launches and controls the application. It appears to be running on all other desktops but generally is not. In some cases all participants can make changes to the application; others can view these changes in real-time and discuss the results. In other cases, the individual who launched the application also controls it, and allows others to view the data, but not to make adjustments to it.

application viewing — In personal conferencing, the ability of one system to screen-slave off another system. Every keystroke or mouse movement made by the user who runs the application can be seen by the user at the other end, even though he/she is not running the application and has no control over it.

architecture — The design guidelines, physical and conceptual organization, and principles that describe how a system or network will support an activity. Architecture discusses scalability, security, topology, capacity and other high-level attributes.

artifacts	Spurious effects introduced to a signal that result from digital signal processing. These effects manifest as jagged edges on moving objects and flicker on fine horizontal edges.
ASCII	American Standard Code for Information Interchange, a digital coding scheme that is capable of representing 256 characters. ASCII is a 7-level code for asynchronous character transmission over a network. It is a "universal" code; for instance, a file that uses another coding scheme can nearly always be saved as ASCII text so other systems that use other coding schemes can get at the data. With seven-level ASCII, an eighth bit can be used for parity checking that can be defined as odd or even.
ASIC	Application-Specific Integrated Circuit. A chip designed for a specific application or purpose.
aspect ratio	The ratio of the width to the height of an image or video displayed on a monitor. NTSC and PAL television uses an aspect ratio of 4 wide to 3 high, which is expressed 4:3.
asymmetrical compression	Techniques in which the decompression process is not the reverse of the compression process. Asymmetrical compression is more processing-intensive on the compression side so that video images can be easily decompressed at the desktop or in applications in which sophisticated codecs are not cost effective.
asynchronous	Lacking in synchronization. A method of transmitting data over a network using a start bit at the beginning of a character and a stop bit at the end. The time interval between characters may be of varying lengths. In video, a signal is asynchronous when its timing differs from that of the system reference signal.
ATM	Asynchronous Transfer Mode (also known as cell relay). ATM provides a single network interface for audio, video, image and text with sufficient flexibility for handling these different media types.

The ATM transport technique uses a multiplexing scheme in which data are divided into small but fixed-size units called cells. Each cell contains a 48-byte information field and five-bytes of header information for a total cell size of 53-bytes. Although it is a packet switching technique, ATM can achieve the integration of all types of traffic, including those that require isochronous service.

ATSC — The Advanced Television Systems Communications. This group was formed by the Joint Committee on Inter-Society Coordination (JCIC) to establish voluntary technical standards for advanced television systems, including HDTV. In April 1995, the ATSC approved the Digital Television Standard for HDTV Transmission.

ATSC A/53 — The digital television standard for HDTV transmission proposed by the Grand Alliance and approved by the Technical Subgroup of the Federal Communications Commission (FCC) Advisory Committee. The standard specifies the HDTV video formats, the audio format, data packetization, and RF transmission. New television receivers will be capable of providing high resolution video, CD quality multi-channel sound, and ancillary data delivery to the home.

attenuation — The decrease in the amplitude of a signal. In video communications this usually refers to power loss in electromagnetic signals between a transmitter and the receiver during the process of transmission. Thus, the received signal is weaker or degraded when compared to the original transmission.

ATV — Advanced TV. Any system of distributing TV programming that results in better video and audio quality than that offered by the NTSC standard. ATV is based on digital signal processing and transmission. HDTV can be considered one type of ATV but systems can also carry multiple pictures of lower quality.

audio — In video communications, electrical signals that

carry sounds. The term is also describes sound recording and transmission systems —speech pickup systems, transmission links that carry sounds, amplifiers.

audio bridge — Equipment that mixes multiple audio inputs and feeds back composite audio to each station after it removes the individual station's input. This equipment may also be called a mix-minus audio system.

auto focus — In a camera, a device for measuring the distance of the lens from a given object is included to automatically set the lens-film distance. In videoconferences when there is almost no set-up time and subjects may be moving around from time to time this is particularly valuable.

auto iris — A process of correlating aperture size to the amount of light entering the camera. Auto Iris produces unpredictable quality in video production because white backgrounds or clothing will cause a camera to close down the lens when a person's face would be the desired gauge for the f-stop. Although it is a good feature in a videoconferencing camera, auto iris is not as effective as manual adjustment of the camera's iris in video production.

AVI — Audio Video Interleaved. The filename extension for compressed video usually used under Microsoft Windows. AVI decompression usually takes place in software. AVI compression works on key frames to achieve the maximum possible entropy through redundancy elimination. After key frames are intra-frame compressed AVI then constructs subsequent delta frames by recording only interframe differences. AVI competes with MPEG-1 although MPEG-1 produces higher-quality video.

AVP-100 — Introduced in April, 1992, AT&T Microelectronics' three-chip AVP-100 set supports Px64, MPEG and JPEG schemes for full-motion video/audio, stored motion video and still image compression. Most of the chip set's 25 billion operations per second are consumed by motion estimation. Competition for this chip set's market is growing.

AVT — Audio Visual Terminal. A term used in the ITU-T's H.320 specification. It refers to a videoconferencing implementation that can deliver an audio and video signal.

AWG — American Wire Gauge, a standard measuring technique used for non-ferrous conductors (copper, aluminum). The lower the AWG the thicker the wire; 22 AWG cable is thicker than 26 AWG cable.

— B —

B — Blue (as in RGB).

B channel — The ISDN circuit-switched bearer channels, capable of transmitting 64 Kbps of digitized information.

B frame — In MPEG, the B frame is a video frame that is created using bi-directional interframe compression. Computationally demanding, B frames are created by using I frames and P frames. Through bi-directional encoding the P (predictive) frame, which is created by using a past frame as a model, is compared an I (intraframe coded) frame: a frame that has had the spatial redundancy eliminated from it, without reference to other frames. Using interpolation the codec uses hints derived by analyzing past and predicted events to develop a "best-guess" present frame.

back porch — The portion of a video signal that contains color burst information and which occurs between the end of the horizontal synch pulse and the start of active video.

back projection — When a projector is placed behind a screen (as it is in television and videoconferencing applications) it is described as a back projection system. The viewer sees the image via the transmission of light as opposed to reflection used in front projection systems.

backbone network — A transmission facility used to interconnect distribution networks of typically lower speed. A backbone network often connects major sites (hubs). From these sites, spoke-like tail circuits (spurs), emanate and, in turn, often terminate in minor hubs.

bandwidth — A term that defines the information carrying capacity of a channel—its throughput. In analog systems, it is the difference between the highest frequency that a channel can carry and the lowest, measured in hertz. In digital systems the unit of measure of bandwidth is bits per second.

bandwidth-on-demand — The ability to vary the transmission speed in support of various applications, including videoconferencing. In videoconferencing applications, an inverse multiplexer or I-MUX takes a digital signal that comes from a codec and divides it into multiple 56- or 64 Kbps channels for transmission across a switched digital network. On the distant end, a compatible I-MUX recombines these channels for the receiving codec, and, therefore, ensures that, even if the data takes different transmission paths, it will be smoothly recombined at the receiving end.

BAS — Bit-rate Allocation Signal. Used in Recommendations H.221 and T.120 to transmit control and indication signals, commands and capabilities.

baseband — In a Local Area Network (LAN) context, this means a single high-speed information channel available to and shared by all the terminals or nodes on the network. Because there is sharing of this resource, means have to be provided to control access to the channel and to minimize information "collisions" and distortions caused by more than one terminal transmitting at the same time. Different types of LANs use different access methods to avoid collisions. Baseband LANs present a challenge to companies that wish to put video over their networks because video requires isochronous service (i.e., the delivery of information is smoothly timed).

Baseline Sequential JPEG — The most popular of the JPEG modes. It employs the lossy DCT to compress image data as well as lossless processes based on DPCM. The "baseline" system represents a minimum capability that must be present in all Sequential JPEG decoder systems. In this mode, image components are compressed either individually, or in groups. A single scan pass completely codes a component or group of components. If groups of components are coded, the data is interleaved; it allows color images to be compressed and decompressed with a minimum of buffering.

Basic Rate ISDN — See BRI.

BBC — British Broadcasting Corporation, formed in 1923 as the monopoly radio and later television, broadcaster in the United Kingdom. Also used as an abbreviation of background color cancellation.

Bell Operating Company — Any of the 22 regulated telephone companies that were "spun off" from AT&T during divestiture. The BOCs (or regional bell operating companies—RBOC) are grouped into RBHCs—Regional Bell Holding Companies such as Nynex, BellSouth and others.

Bellcore — An abbreviation for Bell Communications Research. Bellcore is a resource for software engineering and consulting that created many public network architectures for the Regional Bell Holding Companies (RBHCs) over the years. Formed to take the place of Bell Labs, which, after divestiture, severed all formal ties with the BOCs, it was owned by all seven RBHCs until the fall of 1996. At that time the RBHCs sold it to Science Applications International Corporation (SAIC), a company that specializes in government consulting for the Defense Department's Advanced Research Projects Agency (DARPA) and other federal customers.

B-frame — A mandatory MPEG picture coding technique that

	provides bi-directional interframe compression and which uses interpolation to predict a current frame of video data based on a past frame and a "future" frame.
binary	A method of coding in which there are only two possible values, 0 and 1, for a given digit. Each binary digit is called a "bit."
binary large objects	BLOBs. Events on a network caused by the transmission of bit-intensive images that cause bottlenecks.
B-ISDN	Broadband ISDN. The ITU-T is developing the B-ISDN standard, incorporating the existing ISDN switching, signaling, multiplexing and transmission standards into a higher-speed specification that will support the need to move different types of information around the public switched network.
bit	Binary Digit. The basic signaling unit in all digital transmission systems.
bit plane	The memory used to represent, on a VDT, one bit per pixel. Multiple bit planes can be introduced to produce deeper color and, as the number of bit planes increase, so does the color resolution. One bit plane yields two colors (monochrome). Two yields four colors (00, 01, 10, 11), four can describe 16 colors, and so on.
bit rate	The number of bits of information transmitted over a channel in a given second. Typically expressed bps.
bit-block transfer	Bit-BLT. The movement of an associated group of pixels around on a screen. When a window is opened or moved around on a PC or X-terminal a Bit-BLT occurs.
bitmap	The total of all bit planes used to represent a graphic. Its size is measured in horizontal, vertical and depth of bits. In a one-bit (monochrome) system there is only one bit plane. As additional planes are added, color can be described. Two bit planes yield four

possible values per pixel, eight yield 256, and so on.

black level — The lowest luminance level that can occur in video or television transmission and which, when viewed on a monitor, appears as the color black.

blanking interval — Period during the television picture formation when the picture is suppressed to allow the electron gun to return from right to left after a line (horizontal blanking) or from top to bottom after each field (vertical blanking).

blanking pulses — The process of transmitting pulses that extinguish or blank the reproducing spot during the horizontal and vertical retrace intervals.

block — In H.261, a block consists of 8 pixels by 8 pixels. It is the lowest element in the hierarchical video multiplex structure, which, at the top of the hierarchy, includes the picture, then a group of blocks, then a macroblock and individual blocks that comprise the macroblock. A block can be of two types, luminance or color difference.

blue — One of three additive primaries and B in the RGB.

BNC — Refers to Bayonet Neill-Concelman. A twist-lock connector widely used for the connection of video cables.

board — Boards consist of a flat backing made of insulating material and inscribed with conductive circuits etched on their surface. A fully-prepared circuit board is meant to be permanently affixed into a system as opposed to a module that is meant to slide in although the terms are now used interchangeably.

BOC — See Bell Operating Company. Also referred to as Regional Bell Operating Company or RBOC.

BOnDInG — Bandwidth On Demand Interoperability Group. This consortium of over 30 vendors developed the standard for inverse multiplexing that carries their name. Version 1.0 of the standard, approved in

August 1992, describes four modes of inverse multiplexer interoperability. It allows inverse multiplexers from different manufacturers to subdivide a wideband signal into multiple 56- or 64 Kbps channels, pass these individual channels over a switched digital network and recombine them into a single high-speed signal at the receiving end.

bps — The speed at which bits are transmitted over a communications medium; in other words, the number of bits that pass a given point in a communications line in one second. The term "bps" is also used more generically to describe the information-carrying capacity of a digital channel.

branch — Part of a cable television distribution system. Branches in the network are analogous to tree limbs that attach to a main trunk. Branches provide separate locales or communities with cable television service. Branch and tree systems are being replaced with fiber-optic distribution systems in which the cable television head-end is connected via fiber optics to a local hub.

BRI — Basic Rate Interface. In ISDN there are two interfaces, the BRI and the PRI or Primary Rate Interface. The BRI offers two circuit-switched B (bearer) channels of 64 Kbps each and one packet-switched D (delta) channel that is used for exchanging signals with the network. Known in Europe as the Basic Rate Access or BRA.

bridge — In videoconferencing vernacular, a bridge connects three or more conference sites so that they can simultaneously communicate. Bridges are often called MCUs—multipoint conferencing units. In IEEE 802 parlance, a bridge is a device that interconnects LANs or LAN segments at the data-link layer of the OSI model to extend the LAN environment physically. They forward frames (as opposed to packets) of data between networks. They learn station addresses and they resolve problems with loops in the topology by participating in the spanning tree algorithm. Finally, the term bridge can be used in audio conferencing to refer to a device that connects multiple (more than two) voice calls so that all participants can hear and be heard.

brightness — The luminance portion of a television or video signal.

broadband — The term applied to networks that have bandwidths significantly greater than that found in telephony networks. Broadband systems can carry a large number of moving images or a vast quantity of data simultaneously. Broadband techniques usually depend on coaxial or optical cable for transmission. They utilize multiplexing to permit the simultaneous operation of multiple channels or services on a single cable. Frequency division multiplexing or cell relay techniques can both be used in broadband transmission.

broadcast — To send information to two or more receiving devices simultaneously. The term originated in farming in which it referred to the scattering of seeds. Now it is used to describe the transmission of radio and television signals. One may also encounter the word in data communications when discussing transmission methods used by LANs. In that context, it refers to a packet delivery method that sends a copy of a specified packet or series of packets to all computers attached to a given network or " tuned to a specific IP address."

broadcast quality — In the US this corresponds to the NTSC system's 525-line, 30 fps, 60 fields-per-second audio-video delivery system. It is also a subjective concept, used to describe an audiovisual signal that delivers quality that appears to be approximately as good as that of television.

broadcasting — A means of one-way, point-to-multipoint transmission. For our purpose, we will consider this word to have two meanings. First it is the relaying of audio/visual information across the frequency spectrum where it propagates in free space and is picked up by properly equipped antennas. Second, it

	is the placement of information on digital networks (LAN, MAN or WAN) which can support many different applications including cable television.
BTV	See business television.
buffer	A storage reservoir designed to hold digital information in memory. Used to temporarily store data when the circuit used to transmit it is engaged or when differences in speed are involved.
burst	To send a group of bits in data communications, typically in a baseband transmission scheme. A color burst is used for synchronization in the NTSC standard for color television.
bursty data	Information that flows in short intense data groupings (often packets) with relative long silent periods between each transmission burst.
bus	A common path shared by multiple input and output devices. In the computer world a bus can be the short cable link between terminals networked in an office; in the world of circuitry a bus can be a thin copper wire on a printed circuit board. In video production, there are program buses that determine what is sent to the record deck, preview buses that allow a video source to be shown on a separate monitor, and mixing buses which work with special effect generators and which allow separate video signals to be combined.
business television	Point-to-multipoint videoconferencing. Often refers to the corporate use of video for the transmission of company meetings, training and other one-to-many broadcasts. Typically incorporates satellite transmission methods and is migrating from analog to digital modulation techniques. Also known as BTV.
B-Y	One of the color signals of a color difference video signal—the blue minus luminance signal. The formula for deriving B-Y is -.30R, -.59G and -.89B.

byte — A group of eight bits usually the smallest addressable unit of information in a data memory storage unit. Also known as an octet.

— C —

cable — A number of insulated metallic conductors or optical fibers assembled in a group and covered by a flexible protective sheath. Sometimes used in a slang sense to refer to cable television.

Cable Act of 1984 — An Act passed by Congress that deregulated most of the CATV industry including rates, required programming and municipal fees. The FCC was left with virtually no jurisdiction over cable television except among the following areas: (1) registration of each community system prior to the commencement of operations; (2) ensuring subscribers had access to an A-B switch to permit the receipt of off-the-air broadcasts as well as cable programs; (3) carriage of television broadcast programs in full without alteration or deletion; (4) non-duplication of network programs; (5) fines or imprisonment for carrying obscene material; and (6) licensing for receive-only earth stations for satellite-delivered via pay cable. The FCC could impose fines on CATV systems violating the rules. The Cable Reregulation Act of 1992 superseded this Act.

cable modems — Cable modems are external devices that link PCs to cable television systems' coaxial networks. They work by modulating the Ethernet data that comes out of a PC, converting it a specific frequency in order to send it over the cable network. The cable modem also receives and demodulates incoming data, and re-converts it into Ethernet format. To the PC, a cable modem looks and acts just like an Ethernet-based connection. Cable modems are, at the time of this writing, scarce, expensive, and proprietary (e.g., specific to a given cable operator's network and not based on standards). They are also fast; they provide data transfer rates of between 1 and 30 Mbps.

Cable Reregulation Act Reregulation Bill 1515 that passed Congress in October of 1992, that forced the FCC to regulate cable television and cable television rates. A lengthy and extremely complex set of rules in which the FCC defined allowable monthly rates for Basic service, Expanded Basic service, equipment and installation. Rates must now conform to these FCC benchmarks and can be reduced if too high. Another provision of the Act requires cable television companies to sell cable programming to DBS operators and owners of home satellite dishes. The Act places a huge regulatory burden on the understaffed FCC. President Bush vetoed it in his last months of office but Congress overrode the veto.

camcorder Cameras and video recorder systems packaged as a whole that permanently integrate camera, recorder and microphone components. Camcorders are used for remote production work and consumer activities.

Cameo Macintosh-based personal videoconferencing system announced by Compression Labs in January of 1992. Developed jointly with AT&T and designed to work over ISDN lines and, most recently, Ethernet LANs. The Cameo transmits 15 fps of video and requires an external handset or headset for audio transmission.

camera In video, an electronic (or in the past electromechanical) device used to convert visual images into electrical impulses. The camera scans an image and describes the light that is present using an optical system and a light-sensitive pick-up tube.

carrier A term used to refer to various telephone companies that provide local, long distance or value added services; alternately, a system or systems whereby many channels of electrical information can be carried over a single transmission path.

carrier wave A single frequency that can be modulated by another wave that contains information. Thus, the information contained in the second wave form is superimposed on the carrier for the purpose of transmitting it.

cathode ray tube — Developed by a German Karl Ferdinand Braun, the CRT is a glass picture tube, narrow at one end and wide at the other. The narrow end contains a negative terminal called a cathode The cathode emits a stream of electrons. These electrons are focused or beamed with a "gun" to "paint" an image on a luminescent screen at the wide end. The inside of the wide end is coated with phosphors that react to the electron beam by lighting up, thus creating a picture. CRTs are used in TV receivers, oscilloscopes, PC monitors, and video displays. In video cameras, they are part of the scanning mechanism.

CATV — Community Antenna Television. Developed in 1958, this technology was first used to carry television programming to areas where television service was not available. The term is now used to refer to cable television; which is a method of distributing multi-channel television signals to subscribers via a broadband cable or fiber optics networks. Early systems were generally branch-and-tree types, with all programs transmitted to all subscribers, who used a channel selection switch to indicate which program they wanted.

CBR — Constant Bit Rate. A feature offered with isochronous service and required for real-time interactive video and voice communications.

CCD — Charge coupled device. Used in cameras and telecines as an optical scanning mechanism. It consists of a shift register that stores samples of analog signals. An analog charge is sequentially passed along the device by the action of stepping voltages and stored in potential wells formed under electrodes. The charge is moved from one well to another by the stepping voltages.

CCIR — Comité Consultatif International Radiocommunications. An organization, part of the United Nations, that sets technical standards for international television systems as part of its responsibilities. The CCIR is now known as the ITU-R.

CCIR Rec. 656 The international standard that defines the electrical and mechanical interfaces for digital TV that operates under the CCIR-601 standard. It defines the serial and parallel interfaces in terms of connector pinouts as well as synchronization, blanking and multiplexing schemes used in these interfaces.

CCIR Rec. 601 An internationally agreed-upon standard for the digital encoding of component color television derived from the SMPTE RP125 and EBU 324E standards. It uses a 4:2:2 sampling scheme for Y, U and V with luminance sampled at 13.5 MHz and chrominance (U and V components) sampled at 6.75 MHz. After sampling, 8-bit digitizing is used. The particular frequencies set forth in the standard were chosen because they work for both 525/60 (NTSC) and 625/50 (SECAM and PAL) television systems. In the US the system specifies that 720 pixels be displayed on 243 lines of video and that 60 interlaced fields be sent per second. Chrominance channels are sent with 360 pixels on 243 lines, again at 60 fields/second. CCIR Recommendation 601 is used in professional digital video equipment.

CCIS Common Channel Inter-Office Signaling. In this scheme, which is used for ISDN, the signaling information is carried out-of-band over a special packet-switched signaling channel.

CCITT Abbreviation of Comité Consultatif International Téléphonique et Télégraphique, an organization that sets international telecommunications standards. The CCITT is now called the International Telecommunications Union's Telecommunications Standardization Sector or ITU-T.

CCTV Closed circuit television. Typically used in security and surveillance applications and usually based on slow-scan technology.

CD A high-capacity optical storage device that measures

4.75-inch in diameter and which contains multimedia or audio-only information. Originally developed for sound, CD technology was quickly seen as a storage medium for large amounts of digital data of any type. The information on a CD is digitally encoded in the constant linear velocity (CLV) format, which replaced the older CAV (constant angular velocity) format.

CD-i — Philips Compact Disc-interactive specification, which embraces the same storage concept as CD-ROM and Audio CD, except that CD-i also stores compressed full-motion video.

CD-ROM — Compact Disc Read-Only Memory. A standard used to place any type of digital data onto a compact disc. Compact discs hold a huge amount of audio, textual or video data. On a single 4.7-inch disk, as much as 800 Mbytes of information can be stored—the equivalent of 400,000 pages of text. They can now be used in multimedia applications; all CD-ROM drives available today support the Multimedia PC or MPC standard. Other standards including CD-I and DVI rely on CD-ROM. However, CD-ROMs are slow in the area of transferring the data they store; they deliver it at transmission speeds between 1.2 to 1.8 Mbps.

CDV — Compression Labs Compressed Digital Video, a compression technique used in satellite broadcast systems. CDV is the technique used in CLI's SpectrumSaver system to compress a NTSC or PAL analog TV signal so that it can be transmitted via satellite in as little as 2 MHz of bandwidth.

CellB — A Sun Microsystems Computer Corporation-proprietary video compression encoding technique developed by Michael F. Speer.

cell relay — The process of transferring data by dividing all transmissions (voice, video, text, image, etc.) into 53-byte packets called cells. A cell has 48 bytes of information and 5 bytes of address. The objective of cell relay is to develop a single high-speed network based on a switching and multiplexing scheme that works for all data types. Small cells favor low-delay, a requirement of isochronous service.

CELP — Code-Excited Linear Prediction, a low-bit audio encoding method, a low-delay variation of which is used in the ITU-T's G.728 compression standard.

channel — A physical transmission path along which signals can be sent, e.g., a video channel.

charge-coupled device — CCD (full name Interline Transfer Charge-Coupled Device or IT CCD). CCDs are used as image sensors in an array of elements in which charges are produced by light focused on a surface. They are specialized semiconductors, based on MOS technology and consist of a rectangular array of hundreds of thousands of light-sensitive photo diodes (pixels). Light from a lens is focused onto the pixels, and thereby releases electrons (charges) which accumulate in the photo diodes. The charges are periodically dumped into vertical shift registers and moved by charge-transfer so they can be amplified.

chip — An integrated circuit. The physical structure upon which circuits are fabricated as components of systems such as memory systems, and coding and decoding systems.

chroma — The color information in a television or video signal composed of hue and saturation.

chromaticity — The quality of light, in terms of its color, as defined by its wavelength and purity. Chromaticity charts describe this combination of hue and saturation, independent of intensity. The relative proportion of R, G and B determines the color perceived.

chrominance — The combination of hue and saturation that, taken together with luminance (brightness), define color.

CIE — Commission Internationale de l'Eclairage, an international body that specifies colors based on their frequencies.

CIF — Common Intermediate Format, an optional part of the ITU-T's H.261 and H.263 standards. CIF specifies 288 non-interlaced luminance lines, that each contain 352 pixels and 144 chrominance lines that contain 176 pixels. CIF is to be sent at frame rates of 7.5, 10, 15 or 30 per second. When operating with CIF, the number of bits that result can not exceed 256 K bits (where K equals 1024).

Cinepak — A proprietary software-based compression method developed by Radius for use on Apple Macintosh computers. Cinepak video is sent at 15 fps, with a 240-pixel high by 320-pixel wide resolution.

circuit — In telecommunications, pair of channels, which together provide bi-directional communications. A circuit includes the associated terminal equipment at the carrier's switching center.

circuit switching — The process of establishing a connection for the purpose of communication in which the full use of the circuit is guaranteed to the parties or devices that are exchanging information. After the communication has ended, the connection is released for use by others.

CISSP — $(ISC)^2$ grants the *Certified Information Systems Security Practitioner* designation to information systems security practitioners for passing a rigorous CISSP examination and subscribing to the $(ISC)^2$ Code of Ethics. Additional information is available at http://www.isc2.org/welcome.html.

CIVDL — Collaboration for Interactive Visual Distance Learning. A collaborative effort by 10 leading US universities that uses dial-up videoconferencing technology for the delivery of engineering programs.

clear channel — The characteristic of a digital transmission path in which the circuit is entire bandwidth is available for information exchange. This differs from channels in which part of the channel is reserved for signaling, control or framing bits.

CLI Compression Labs, Incorporated, San Jose, California is one of the foremost codec manufacturers in the world. CLI was the developer of the first "low-bandwidth" codec in the US, VTS 1.5. This codec was one of the first two codecs (along with one from NEC from Japan) able to compress full-motion video to 1.5 Mbps transmission speeds.

client A service-requesting program in a client/server computing environment that solicits support (service/resources) from a server, using a network to convey its request. The client provides the important resources required by a user to interface with a server. The term 'client' has, however, strayed from this strict definition to become a catchall phrase. A client today is often assumed to be a front-end application that offers user-friendly GUI tools for such actions as setting up conferences, adding additional participants, opening applications, copying files, and storing files.

clock An oscillator. A PC's CPU clock regulates the execution of instructions. Clocks are also used to create timing reference signals in digital networks and systems for the purpose of synchronization.

CO Central office. A CO can be one of many types of switching systems, either analog or digital, which connect subscriber lines to other lines and network trunks on a circuit-switched basis. The two most common in the US are AT&T's 5ESS and Nortel's DMS-100, both of which are digital.

coaxial cable A cable with one central conductor surrounded by an insulator that is, in turn, surrounded by a cylindrical outer conductor and covered by an outer insulation sheath. The insulator next to the central conductor is typically polyethylene or air and the outer conductor is typically braided copper. Coaxial cables are used to carry very high-frequency currents with low attenuation; often in cable television networks.

codec — A sophisticated digital signal-processing unit that takes an analog input and converts it to digital on the sending end. At the receiving end, another codec reverses the by reconverting the digital signal back to analog. Codec is a contraction of code/decode (some experts in the video industry assert it also stands for compress/decompress).

codec conversion — The back-to-back transfer of an analog signal from one codec into another codec in order to convert from one proprietary coding scheme to another. The analog signal, instead of being displayed to a monitor, is delivered to the dissimilar codec where it is re-digitized, compressed and passed to the receiving end. This is obviously a bi-directional process. Carriers such as AT&T, MCI and Sprint offer conversion service.

color — That which is perceived as a result of differing qualities of the light reflected or emitted. Humans see color via the additive process in direct light (e.g., television in which the primary colors are red, green, and blue) and the subtractive process in reflected light (e.g., books, in which the primary colors are yellow, magenta, cyan, and black). The three basic color components are hue, saturation, and brightness. They are all represented in both color televisions and computer monitors, though different means are used to display them.

color burst — A few cycles (8 to 12) of sub-carrier frequency that serves as a color synch signal and communicates the proper hues to a video monitor or television. The color burst is part of an NTSC or PAL composite video signal. It provides a reference for the demodulation of the color information. The absence of color burst indicates black and white video or television.

color depth — The number of distinct colors that can be represented by a piece of hardware or software. The number of bits that are used to describe a color determine the system's color depth.

color difference signal — The first step in encoding the color television signal. Subtracting the luminance information from each primary color forms the color difference signals: red, green or blue. Color difference conventions include the Betacam format, the SMPTE format, the EBU-N10 format and the MII format. Color difference signals are NOT component video signals—these are, strictly speaking, the pure R, G and B waveforms.

color monitor — CRT that works on the principle of the additive primary colors of red, green and blue. The phosphors of these monitors are tinted with these hues so that they glow in unique colors when excited with electrons beamed by an electron gun. The phosphor dots inside the visible face of the screen are organized in tightly grouped trios of red, green and blue; each trio is a pixel.

color shift — The unwanted changing of colors caused when too few bits are used to express a color.

color space — The three properties of brightness, saturation and hue can be pictured as a three-dimensional color space. The center dividing line or brightness column is the axis where no color exists at all. Hues (colors) form circles around this axis. There is also a horizontal axis that describes the amount of saturation. Highly saturated colors are closest to the center and less saturated colors are arranged toward the outer edges.

color subcarrier — The NTSC color subcarrier conveys color information and has a frequency of 3.579545 MHz. Color saturation is conveyed via signal amplitude and hue (tint) is conveyed via signal phase.

color timing — The synchronization of the burst phase of two or more video signals to ensure that no color shifts occur in the picture.

comb filter — An electrical filter that separates the chroma (color) and luma (brightness) components of a video signal into separate parts. It does this by passing some frequencies and rejecting others in between. Using a comb filter reduces artifacts but also causes some resolution loss in the picture. S-Video permits a video signal to bypass a comb filter, and thereby results in a better image.

common carrier A telecommunications operating company that provides specific telephony services.

compact disc CD. Information is stored on a CD's surface so that when it is scanned the fluctuations in the surface create two states: on and off. See CD-ROM.

companding Like 'codec' or 'modem,' companding is a contraction, in this case, combining the words compressing and expanding. It refers to the reduction of the dynamic range of an audio or video signal in which the signals are sampled and transformed into non-linear codes.

component video Transmission and recording of color television with luminance and chrominance (red, green and blue picture components) treated as separate signals. Component video is not a standard but rather a technique that yields greater signal controls and image quality. Hue and saturation (chrominance) are considered a single component, as is luminance (brightness), which is recorded at a higher frequency than chrominance; this makes it possible to exceed 400 lines of resolution. Component video is also known as Y/C. In component video, synchronization information may be added with the G signal; it can also be a separate signal.

composite video A color television signal in which the chrominance signal is a sine wave that is modulated onto the luminance signal that acts as a subcarrier. This is used in NTSC and PAL systems.

compression The process of reducing the information content of a signal so that it occupies less space on a transmission channel or storage device and a fundamental concept of video communications. An uncompressed NTSC signal requires about 90 Mbps of throughput, greatly exceeding the speed of all but the fastest and shortest of today's networks. Squeezing the video information can be accomplished by reducing the quality (sending fewer frames in a second or displaying the information in a smaller window) or by eliminating redundancy.

conditional frame replenishment — A process of compression in which only the changes that are present in the current video frame, when compared to the past video frame, are transmitted.

conferencing — The ability to meet over distance in which meetings can include both visual and audible information. Typically videoconferencing systems incorporate screens that can show the faces of distant-end participants, graphics, close-ups of documents or diagrams and other objects.

connection — A path that is established between two devices and which provides reliable stream delivery service.

content — In the context of video, the information object or objects that are packaged for playback by a viewer.

continuous presence — A technique used in video processing and transmission in which the sending device combines portions of more than one video image and transmits those separate images in a single data stream to a receiver or receivers. The receiver displays these multiple images on a single monitor where they are arranged side-by-side or stacked vertically. Continuous presence images can also be displayed on multiple monitors.

contone — Continuous tone. Used to describe the resolution of an image, particularly photographic-quality images.

contrast — The range of light-to-dark values of an image that are proportional to the voltage differences between the black and white levels of the signal.

convergence — The trend, now that media can be represented digitally, for historical distinctions between the boundaries of key industries to blur. Companies from consumer electronics, computer and telecommunications industries are forming alliances and raiding each other's markets. Convergence will be accelerated with the coming of the much-heralded U.S. information superhighway.

CPU — Central processing unit: the chip in a microcomputer or printed circuit board in a mainframe or minicomputer in which calculations are performed.

cross connect — The equipment used to terminate and manage communications circuits in a premises distribution system. Jumper wires or patch cords are used to connect station wiring to hardware ports of various types.

CSMA/CD — Carrier Sense Multiple Access with Collision Detection. A baseband LAN access method in which terminals "listen" to the channel to detect an idle period during which they can begin the transmission of their own messages. They might also hear a collision occur when two devices attempt to send information across the same channel at the same time.

CSU — Channel Service Unit. A customer-provided device, a CSU provides an interface between the customer and the network. The CSU ensures that a digital signal enters a communications channel in a format that is properly shaped into square pulses and precisely timed. It also provides a physical and electrical interface between the data terminal equipment (DTE) and the line.

CU-SeeMe — CU-SeeMe is a free videoconferencing program (under copyright of Cornell University and its collaborators) available to anyone with a Macintosh or Windows and a connection to the Internet. CU-SeeMe allows a user to set up an Internet-based videoconference with another site anywhere in the world. By using a reflector, multiple parties at different locations can participate in a CU-SeeMe conference, each from his or her own desktop computer.

— D —

D-channel
In an ISDN network the D-channel is a signaling channel over which the carrier passes packet-switched information. The D channel can also support the transmission of low-speed data or telemetry sent by the subscriber.

D1
Digital Tape Component Format. The CCIR 601-approved digital standard for making digital video recordings. It records each component separately and employs the YCbCr coding scheme.

D2
Digital Tape Composite Format. A digital system that is considerably less costly than D1. It records a composite signal in an 8-bit digital format that is derived by sampling the video signal at a rate of four times the frequency of the subcarrier.

D2-MAC
One of two European formats for analog HDTV.

DACs
Digital-analog converters.

DAI
DMIF-Application Interface (DAI) is an expression (a protocol message) of the functionality provided by DMIF.

data
The much-misused term that indicates any representation, such as characters or analog quantities, to which meaning is or can be attached or assigned. Data is the plural of datum, which means "given information" or "the basis for calculations." In general usage, however, data usually means characters (letters, numbers, and graphics) that can be stored or transmitted over various types of telecommunications networks. Until recently, voice and video signals were not considered data but now that they are being converted to a digital format they are being referred to as data.

data compression
Reducing the size of a data file by reducing unnecessary information, such as blanks and repeating or redundant characters or patterns.

Data Over Cable Service Interface Specifications	A standard interface for cable modems, the devices that manipulate signals between cable TV operators and customer computers or TVs. DOCSIS specifies modulation schemes and the protocol for exchanging bi-directional signals over cable. Now known as *CableLabs Certified Cable Modems*, the ITU ratified DOCSIS 1.0 in March 1998.
dB	Decibel. One-tenth of a Bell and a logarithmic measure of electric energy. A decibel expresses the ratios between voltages, sound intensities, currents, the power (amplitude) of sound waves, and so on.
DBS	Direct broadcast satellite, a transmission scheme used for program delivery, most generally entertainment. There are several DBS providers; none of the systems that they use are, however, compatible. These systems provide downstream speeds of 400 Kbps to 30 Mbps or higher and upstream speeds of 28 Kbps or higher.
DC	Direct Current.
DCE	Data communications equipment. The network side of an equipment to network connection with DTE, data terminal equipment that plugs into DCE, which provides a means of network connection.
DCT	See Discrete Cosine Transform.
DCT coefficient	An expression of a pixel block's average luminance, as used in DCT. The value for which the frequency is zero in both the horizontal and vertical directions.
decode	A process that converts an incoming bitstream, that consists of digitized images and sounds, into a viewable and audible state.
decryption	Decryption reverses an encryption process to return an encrypted transmission into its original form. Decryption applies a special decoding algorithm (key) to the encrypted exchange; any party without access to the proper key required for decryption can

	not receive the transmission in an intelligible form.
dedicated access	A leased, private connection between a customer's equipment and a telephone company location, most often that of an IXC.
dedicated leased line	A transmission circuit leased by one customer for exclusive use around the clock. See also private line.
delay	The time required for a signal to pass between a sender and a receiver; alternately the time required for a signal to pass through a device or conductor.
demultiplex	The process of separating two or more signals previously combined for transmission over a shared channel. Multiplexing merges multiple channels onto one channel prior to transmission; de-multiplexing separates them again at an appropriate network node. Often shortened to *DeMUX*.
depth of field	The range of distances from the camera in which objects around a focal point (the distance from the surface of a lens or mirror to its subject)) will be in focus. Use of a smaller lens aperture increases depth of field.
DES	Data encryption standard developed by the National Bureau of Standards and specified in the Federal Information Processing Standard Publication 46, published in January 1977. The DES is used to secure data. It uses a 64-bit key to encipher and decipher data.
desktop	A term used to refer to a desktop computer or workstation used by an individual user. For instance, the term "client desktop" most often refers to the PC used by a person to provide support for a number of applications, one of which may be videoconferencing.
desktop video	Communications that rely either on videophones or personal computers that offer a video window.
Dense wavelength	Dense WDM transmits up to 32 OC-48 (2.5Gbps)

division multiplexing — signals over a single fiber, and offers the potential to transmit trillions of bits per second over one fiber.

dial-up — The ability to arrange a switched connection, whether analog or digital, by entering a terminating address such as a telephone number, in order that the call can be routed by the network. Differs from point-to-point services that can be used only to communicate between two locations.

digital — Information that is represented using codes that consist of zeros and ones (binary coding). Binary digits (bits) can be either zeros or ones and are typically grouped into "words" of various lengths—8-bit words are called bytes.

Digital Access Cross Connection System — DACS. A switch/multiplexer that permits DS0 cross connection from one T-1 transmission facility to another.

Digital Signal Hierarchy — A TDM multiplexed hierarchy used in telephone networks. DS0, the lowest level of the hierarchy, is a single 64 Kbps channel. DS-1 (1.544 Mbps) is 24 DS0s. DS-2 (6.312 Mbps) is four DS-1 signals multiplexed together; DS-3 (44.736 Mbps) is seven DS-2 signals multiplexed together. At the top of the hierarchy is DS-4, which is six DS-3 signals and which requires a transmission system capable of handling a 274.176 Mbps signal.

Digital Signal Processor — See DSP.

digital transmission — The conveyance over a network of digital signals by means of a channel or channels that may assume in time any one of a defined set of discrete values or states.

digitizing — The process of sampling an analog signal so that it can be represented by a series of bits.

digitizing tablets — Graphics systems used in conjunction with videoconferencing applications. Using a special stylus or electronic "pen" a meeting participant can write on the tablet and the message can be viewed by the distant end and, if desirable, stored on a PC. Photos and text can also be annotated electronically. These devices are unsettling to use, however, because no image appears on the tablet, thus it is difficult to orient the letters.

direct broadcast satellite The use of satellite to broadcast directly to homes or businesses. Subscribers are obliged to purchase and install a satellite dish. DBS service originated in Japan, which is composed of many islands and which has a harsh geography that includes mountains, rivers, valleys and ridges that made it very difficult to plan and execute a terrestrial broadcasting CATV system.

directional couplers In cable systems, multiple feeder cables are coupled with these devices to match the impedance of cables.

Discrete Cosine Transform DCT. A pixel-block based process of formatting video data in which it is converted from a three-dimensional form to a two-dimensional form suitable for further compression. In the process, the average luminance of each block or tile is evaluated using the DC coefficient. Used in the ITU-T's H.261 and H.263 videoconferencing compression standards and the ISO/ITU-T's MPEG and JPEG image compression recommendations.

Discrete Wavelet Transform DWT. Based on same principles as DCT, this method segregates the spectrum into waves of different lengths and then processes all frequencies to retain the image's sharp lines, which are partially lost in the DCT process.

distance learning The incorporation of video and audio technologies into the educational process so that students can attend classes and training sessions in a location distant from that where the course is being presented. Distance learning systems are usually interactive and are becoming a highly-valuable tool in the delivery of training and education to widely-dispersed students in remote locations or in instances where the instructor cannot travel to the student's site.

dithering — In color mapping, dithering is a method of representing a hue, not available in the color map, by intermingling the pixels of two colors that are available and letting the eye-brain team average them together into a single perceived median color.

Divestiture — In early 1982, AT&T signed a Consent Decree and thereby agreed to spin off the 22 local Bell Operating Companies (BOCs). These were grouped into seven Regional Bell Holding Companies that managed their business, coordinated their efforts, and provided strategic direction. Restrictions were placed on both the BOCs and AT&T. The US Department of Justice stripped AT&T of the Bell name (except in their Bell Labs operation), the authority to carry local traffic, and the option to discriminate in favor of their former holdings. BOCs were awarded Yellow Pages publishing and allowed to supply local franchised-monopoly services, but were not allowed to provide information services or to manufacture equipment. They could carry calls only within local access and transport areas (LATAs). This agreement funda-
mentally changed the composition of telephone service in the US on January 1, 1984 when it became effective.

document camera — A specialized camera that is mounted on a long adjustable neck for taking pictures of still images—pictures, graphics, pages of text and objects —for manipulation such as a video conference.

downlink — The communications path from a satellite to an earth station.

DMIF — Delivery Multimedia Integration Framework is a session protocol for the management of multimedia streaming over generic delivery technologies. It is similar to FTP except that, where FTP returns data, DMIF returns pointers toward (streamed) data.

DOCSIS — See *Data Over Cable Service Interface Specifications*.

DPCM Differential Pulse Code Modulation is a compression technique that sends only the difference between *what was* (a past frame of video information) and *what is* (a present frame). DPCM requires identical codecs on each, the transmitting and receiving ends to predict, from a past frame of pixels, what the present frame will be. The transmitting frame, after computing its prediction, compares the actual to its speculation and sends information on the difference. In turn, the receiving codec interprets these differences (called errors) and makes adjustments to the present video frame.

driver A driver is software that provides instructions for reformatting or interpreting software commands for transfer to and from peripheral devices and the central processing unit (CPU). Many printed circuit boards require a software driver in order for the other PC components to work correctly. In other words, the driver is a software module that drives the data out of a specific hardware port. Video drivers may be required for desktop video.

DS-0 Digital service, level zero or DS-zero. A single 64 Kbps channel in a multiplexing scheme that is part of the North American and European digital hierarchy and which results from the process of digitizing an analog voice channel through the application of time division multiplexing, pulse code modulation and North American or European companding.

DS-1 (T-1). A multiplexing scheme that is part of the North American digital hierarchy and which specifies how to subdivide 1.544 Mbps of bandwidth into twenty-four 64 Kbps channels using time division multiplexing, pulse code modulation and North American com-panding. Europe has a similar multiplexing hierarchy that produces a 2.048 Mbps signal (E-1/CEPT).

DS-3 Also called T-3. A multiplexing scheme that is part of the North American digital hierarchy and which specifies how to subdivide 45 Mbps of bandwidth into 28 T-1 (1.544 Mbps) carrier systems—a total of

672 channels. The techniques for accomplishing this include time division multiplexing, pulse code modulation and North American companding.

DSP — Digital signal processor. A specialized computer chip designed to perform speedy and complex operations on digitized waveforms. Useful in processing sound and video signals.

DSU — Data service unit. A device used to transmit digital data on digital transmission facilities. It typically interfaces to data terminal equipment via an RS-232-C or other terminal interface, connecting this device to a DSX-1 (digital system cross connect) interface.

DSX — Digital Signal Cross-Connect, a panel that connects digital circuits to allow cross-connections via a patch and cord system.

DTE — Data terminal equipment. The equipment side of an equipment to network connection with DCE, data communications equipment connecting the DTE to the network for the purposes of transmission.

dual 56 — Combination of two 56 Kbps lines (usually switched 56) to yield a 112 Kbps channel used for low-bandwidth videoconferencing. Dual 56 allows for direct dialing of a videoconference call and can be obtained from IXCs or LECs.

DVC — Digital Video Cassette. A DVC is a storage medium based on a ¼-inch-wide tape made up of metal particles. The DVC source is sampled at a rate similar to that of CCIR-601 but additional chrominance subsampling (4:1:1 in the NTSC 30 kHz mode) provides better resolutions. When the NTSC 30-fps signal is encoded, the image frame resolution is 720 pixels by 480 lines with 8 bits used for each pixel.

DVD — DVD (Digital Versatile Disk) is a type of CD. It has storage capacity of 17 gigabytes, which is much higher than CD-ROM's 600 Mbytes and a higher data delivery than that of CD-ROM. DVD uses

MPEG and Dolby compression algorithms to achieve its storage capacity.

DVE — Digital Video Everywhere was developed by InSoft Incorporated as a core software architecture for open systems platforms. It features a hardware-independent API for running multimedia collaborative and conferencing applications across LANs, WANs, and TCP/IP-based networks.

DVI — Digital Video Interactive. A proprietary compression and transmission scheme from Intel. Compression is asymmetric, requiring relatively greater amounts of processing power at the encoder than at the decoder. DVI played an important role in the PC multimedia market.

DWDM — See *Dense Wavelength Division Multiplexing.*

— E —

earth station — An antenna transmitter or receiver that accepts a signal from a satellite and may, in turn, be capable of transmitting a signal to a satellite.

EBIT — A three-bit integer that indicates the number of bits that should be ignored in the final data octet of a RTP H.261 packet.

EBU — European Broadcasting Union, an organization that developed technical recommendations for the PAL television system.

echo — The reflection of sound waves that results from contact with non-sound-absorbing surfaces such as windows or walls. Reflected signals sound like a distorted and attenuated version of the original sound that, in videoconferencing, would primarily be speech. Echoes in telephone and videoconferencing applications are caused by impedance mismatches, points where energy levels are not equal. In a four-wire to two-wire connection, the voice signal moving along the four-wire section has more energy than the two-wire section can absorb; consequently, the excess energy bounces back along the four-wire path. When the return-delay approaches 500 ms, speakers will hear their own words transmitted back at them.

echo cancellation — A process that uses a mathematical process to predict an echo and remove that portion of the signal from an audio waveform to eliminate acoustical echo.

echo modeling — A mathematical process whereby an echo is created from an audio waveform and, subsequently subtracted from that form. The process involves sampling the acoustical properties of a room, calculating approximately what form an echo might take, and then removing that information from the signal.

echo suppression — The insertion of mild attenuation in audio transmit and/or receive signal paths. Used to reduce annoying echoes in the audio portion of a videoconference, an echo suppresser is a voice-activated "on/off" switch that is connected to the four-wire side of a circuit. It silences all sound when it is on by temporarily deadening the communication link in one direction. Unfortunately, echo suppression clips the remote end's new speech as it stops the echo.

EIA — Electrical Interface Association, a standards-setting group in the US that defines standards for interfaces including jacks and other network connections.

EISA — Extended Industry Standard Architecture. The independent computer industry's alternative to IBM's Micro-Channel data bus architecture that IBM used in its PS/2 line of desktop computers. EISA is a 32-bit bus or channel that expands on the original Industry Standard Architecture (ISA) 16-bit channel. EISA capabilities are particularly important when a machine is being used for processor-intensive applications.

electromagnetic spectrum — The range of wavelengths that includes light, physical movement of air (sound) or water, radio

	waves, x-rays, etc. These wavelengths propagate throughout the entire universe.
electromagnetic waves	Oscillations of electric and magnetic forces that produce different wavelengths and which include light, radio, gamma, ultraviolet, and other forms of energy.
electron beam	A stream of electrons focused on a phosphorescent screen and fired from a "gun" to create images. Deflecting it from magnetic coils or plates so that it hits a precise location on the screen focuses the beam.
electrons	Negatively charged particles that, along with positively charged protons, allow atoms to achieve a neutral charge.
encoding	The process through which media content is transformed for the purposes of digital transmission.
encryption	The conversion, through the application of an algorithm, of an original signal into a coded signal in order to secure it from unauthorized access. Typically the process involves the use of "keys" that can unlock the code. The most common encryption standard in the US Bureau of Standard's is the DES (data encryption standard) which enciphers and deciphers data using a 64-bit key specified in the Federal Information Processing Standard Publication 46, published in January, 1977.
enhanced standard	Standards enhancement is a common practice of videoconferencing codec manufacturers. They begin with an algorithm that is compliant with a formal standard (typically the ITU-T's H.320 algorithm). However, they add capabilities that are transparent to dissimilar products that run the standard, but which improve implementation when operating exclusively in their proprietary environment.
entrance facilities	In a premise distribution system, entrance facilities are the point of interconnection between a building wiring system and a telecommunications network

outside the building.

entropy — A measure of the information contained in any exchange. Entropy is the goal of nearly every compression technique. If information is duplicated, the excess amount (that portion that is over and above what is necessary to convey) is redundant. The goal is to remove the redundant portion of whatever is being conveyed (for our purposes, motion, video, audio, text, and still images). The remainder is entropy—information.

envelope — The variations of the peaks of the carrier that contain the video signal information.

envelope delay — The characteristics of a circuit that result in some simultaneously transmitted frequencies reaching their destination before others.

ESS — AT&T's term for Electronic Switching System, a central office switch designed for "class five" or "exchange office" operations. The 5ESS is one of the more common CO switches in the US and, for that matter, the world.

ether — The medium that, according to one theory, permeates all space and matter and which transmits all electromagnetic waves.

Ethernet — The original CSMA/CD LAN as invented by Xerox in 1973 and standardized by Digital Equipment Corporation, Intel and Xerox. Also known as an IEEE 802.3 network, Ethernet is most commonly implemented as 10Base-T, a LAN based on unshielded twisted pair and arranged in a star topology. In Ethernet, all terminals are connected to a single common highway or bus.

Ethernet switch — A device that connects local area networks. Ethernet switching is viewed as one solution to deliver 10Base-T networks that are bandwidth-constrained because of a new requirement to carry multimedia messages and interactive videoconferencing communications. To qualify as an Ethernet Switch, a device must be capable of switching packets from one Ethernet segment to another "on the fly" and exhibit very low port-to-port latency.

ETSI European Telecommunications Standards Institute, a group charged with devising Europe-wide telecommunications standards. This group issues Common Technical Regulations (CTRs) some of which pertain to video communications.

exchange A telephone company's switching center or wire center where subscriber lines terminate at a central location and are switched to other lines and to trunks.

Exchange Microsoft's electronic messaging server.

— F —

fade The gradual reduction in the received signal that results in the disappearance of a picture to black or, in the case of fade in, the gradual introduction of light to an all-black image.

fast packet multiplexing The combination of TDM, packet and computer intelligence to allow multiple digital signals to share a high-speed network. Fast packet multiplexing assumes a clean network and, therefore, does not buffer information, but rather moves it along, and assumes it will arrive with little or no degradation. The two most common forms of fast packet multiplexing are cell relay and frame relay.

FCC Federal Communications Commission, a US regulatory body established by Congress in 1934.

FDDI Fiber Distributed Data Interface. An ANSI standard for a 100 Mbps token-ring-based fiber-optic LAN. It uses a counter-rotating token ring topology and is compatible with the physical layer of the OSI model.

FDDI II Emerging ANSI standard that incorporates both circuit and packet switching over fiber optics at 100

Mbps. Not compatible with the original FDDI standard.

FDM — Frequency Division Multiplexing. A method of transmitting multiple analog signals on a single carrier by assigning them to separate and unique frequency bands and then transmitting the entire aggregate of all frequency bands as a composite.

fiber optics cable — A core of fine glass or plastic fibers that has extremely high purity and is surrounded by a cladding of a slightly lower refractive index. Light or infrared pulses that carry coded information signals are injected at one end. They pass through the core using a method of internal reflection or refraction. Attenuation is low; pulses travel as far as 3,500 feet or more before needing regeneration.

field — A normal television image is comprised of interlaced fields—each field contains one-half of a video frame's information. Each field carries half the picture lines. In the NTSC video standard 60 fields/30 frames are sent in a second and in the European PAL and SECAM systems 50 fields/25 frames are sent in a second.

field interlacing — In television, the process of creating a complete video frame by dividing the picture into two halves with one containing the odd lines and the other containing the even lines. This is done to eliminate flicker.

field of view — The focal length combined with the size of the image area light is focused on. Field of view is measured in degrees and is not dependent on the distance from a subject.

field sequential system — The first broadcast color television system, approved by the FCC in 1950. It was later changed to the NTSC standard for color broadcasting.

file — A set of related records treated by a computer as a complete unit. Retrieving information from one computer memory storage facility to another is called a file transfer.

FireWire — A high-speed serial bus that Apple Computer and Texas Instruments developed that allows for the connection of up to 63 devices. Also known as the IEEE 1394 standard, it provides 100, 200, 400, 800, 1600, and 3200 Mbps transfer rates. FireWire supports isochronous data transfer, and thereby guarantees bandwidth for multimedia operations. It supports hot swapping and multiple speeds on the same bus. FireWire will be used increasingly for attaching video devices to the computer.

filter — An electrical circuit or device that passes a selected range of energy while rejecting all others that are not in the proper frequency range.

firmware — Programs or data that are stored on a semiconductor memory circuit, often a plug-in board. Firmware-stored memory is non-volatile.

FITL — Fiber in the loop. A Bellcore technical advisory, number 909, Issue 2, which addresses the ability of telephone companies to provide video services and delivery using optical fiber cable.

FlexMux — The synchronized delivery of streaming data may require the use of different QoS schemes as it traverses multiple public and private networks. MPEG defines the delivery-layer FlexMux multiplexing tool to allow grouping of Elementary Streams (ES) with low multiplexing overhead. It may be used to group ES with similar QoS requirements, to reduce the number of network connections, or to reduce end-to-end delay. Use of the FlexMux tool is optional, and the FlexMux layer may be empty if the underlying TransMux instance provides adequate functionality.

flicker — An unwanted video phenomenon that results when the screen refresh rate is too slow or when the two interlaced fields that make up a video frame are not identically matched. Flicker is also known as jitter and sometimes as jutter. In the early days of television, interlacing two video fields to create a single video frame was used to combat flicker and eliminated it fairly well at rates over 40 fields per second. Flicker is not a problem with non-interlaced video display formats (those used for computer monitors).

fluorescent lights	Used for illumination in many corporate and public settings. These lights produce spectral frequencies of a less balanced nature than incandescent lights, and cause problems in a videoconference or video production process. They may also cause 60 Hz flicker.
footprint	The primary service area covered by a satellite where the highest field intensity is normally in the center of the footprint, with intensity reducing toward the outer edges.
format	In television the specific arrangement of signals to compose a video signal. There are many different ways of formatting a video signal: NTSC, PAL, SECAM, component video, composite video, CD-I, QuickTime and so on.
forward motion vector	Used in motion compensation. A motion vector is a physical quantity with both direction and magnitude; a course of motion in which pixels are the objects that are moving. A forward motion vector is derived from a video reference frame sent previously.
forward prediction	A technique used in video compression. Specifically, compression techniques based on motion compensation in which a compressed frame of video is reconstructed by working with the differences between successive video frames.
fps	Frames per second. The number of frames contained in a single second of a moving series of video images. 30 fps is considered to be 'full-motion' video in Japan and the US, while 25 fps is considered to be full-motion video in Europe.
fractal compression	An asymmetrical compression technique that shrinks

an image into extremely small resolution-independent files and stores it as a mathematical equation rather than as pixels. The process starts with the identification of patterns within an image, and results in collection of shapes that resemble each other but that have different sizes and locations. Each shape-pattern is summarized and reproduced by a formula that starts with the largest shape, repeatedly displacing and shrinking it. Patterns are stored as equations and the image is reconstructed by iterating the mathematical model. Fractal compression can store as many as 60,000 images on one CD-ROM and competes with techniques such as JPEG, which uses DCT to drop redundant information. One disadvantage of fractal compression is that it requires considerable processing power. JPEG is much faster but fractal compression is more efficient; it squeezes information into smaller files. Applications using fractal compression center on desktop publishing and presentation creation.

fractal geometry — The underlying mathematics behind fractal image compression, discovered by two Georgia Tech mathematicians, Michael Barnsley and Alan Sloan.

Fractal Image Format — FIF. A compression technique that uses on-board ASIC chips to look for patterns. Exact matches are rare; the basis of the process is to find close matches using a function known as an affine map.

fractional T-1 — FT-1 or fractional T-1 refers to any data transmission rate between 56 Kbps and 1.544 Mbps. It is typically provided by a carrier in lieu of a full T-1 connection and is a point-to-point arrangement. A specialized multiplexer is used by the customer to channelize the carrier's signals.

frame — An individual television, film or video image. There are either 25 or 30 frames per-second sent with television, 24 are sent in moving picture films. A variable number, typically between 8 and 30, are sent in videoconferencing systems, depending on the transmission bandwidth offered.

frame buffer — Memory used for holding the data for a single and complete frame (or screen) of video. Some systems have enough memory to store multiple screens of data. Frame buffers are evaluated in terms of how many bits are used to represent a pixel. The more bits that are used, the "deeper" the color. The greater the number of buffers used to store captured video frames the higher the possible frame rate.

frame dropping — The process of dropping video frames to accommodate the transmission speed available.

frame grab — The ability to capture a video frame and temporarily store it for later manipulation by a graphics input device.

frame grabber — A PC board used to capture and digitize a single frame of NTSC video and store it on a hard disk.

frame rate — The number of frames that are sent in a second, and the equivalent of fps. NTSC video has a frame rate of 30 fps. PAL and SECAM send frames at a rate of 25 per second and motion picture (film) images are delivered at a frame rate of 24 per second.

frame store — A system capable of storing complete frames of video information in digital form. This system is used for television standards conversion, computer applications that incorporate graphics, video walls and various video production and editing systems.

freeze frame — A single frame from a video segment displayed motionless on a screen. Also, a method of transmitting video images in which less than one or two frames are sent in any given second. Sometimes known as slow-scan, still video or captured frame video. When freeze frame video is viewed, the viewer sees successive images refreshing a scene but they lack a sense of continuous motion. This technology is often used in security and graphics conferencing systems.

frequency — The number of times that a periodic function or oscillation repeats itself in a specified period of time, usually one second. The unit of measurement of frequency is typically hertz (Hz) which is used to measure cycles or oscillations per second.

frequency interleaving — The process of putting hue and color saturation information into the vacant frequency spectrum via a process of offsetting that chrominance spectrum exactly so that its harmonics are made to fall precisely between the harmonics of the luminance signal.

frequency Modulation — FM. A method of passing information by altering the frequency of the carrier signal.

front porch — With reference to a composite video signal, the front porch is the portion of the signal that occurs between the end of the active video on each horizontal scan line and the beginning of the horizontal synch pulse.

full-motion video — Generally refers to broadcast-quality video transmissions in which the frame rate is 30 per second in North American and Japan and 25 per second in Europe.

— G —

G — Green, as in RGB. The G signal sometimes includes synchronization information.

G.711 — CCITT Recommendation entitled, "Pulse Code Modulation (PCM) of Voice Frequencies." G.711 defines how a 3.1 kHz audio signal is encoded at 64 Kbps using Pulse Code Modulation (PCM) and either mu-law (US and Japan) or A-law (Europe) companding.

G.721 — CCITT Recommendation that defines how a 3.1 kHz audio signal is encoded at 32 Kbps using Adaptive Differential Pulse Code Modulation (ADPCM).

G.722 — CCITT Recommendation that defines how a 7.5 kHz audio signal is encoded at a data rate of 64 Kbps.

G.723	ITU-T Recommendation entitled, "Dual Rate Speech Coder for Multimedia Communications Transmitting at 5.3 and 6.4 Kbps." G.723 is part of the H.323 and H.324 families
G.728	ITU-T Recommendation for audio encoding using Low Delay Code Excited Linear Prediction (CELP). The bandwidth of the analog audio signal is 3.4 kHz whereas after coding and compression the digitized signal requires a bandwidth of 16 Kbps.
G.729	Coding of speech at 8 Kbps/s using conjugate-structure algebraic-code-excited linear-prediction (CS-ACELP). Part of the ITU-T's H.323 standard for videoconferencing over non quality-of-service guaranteed LANs.
gain	An increase in the strength of an electrical signal; measured in decibels.
gamma	A display characteristic of CRTs defined in the following formula: light = volts ^ gamma. Gamma values range in CRTs, with most ranging between 2.25 and 2.45.
gate	A digital logic component whose output state depends on the states of the logic signals presented to its inputs.
GBIC	Gigabit Interface Converter
generic	Applicable to a broad range of applications, i.e., application independent.
Genlock	Short for generator locking device, a genlock is a device that enables a composite video system (e.g., a television) to accept two signals simultaneously. A genlock holds on to one set of signals while it processes a second set. This allows the combination of signals (video and graphics) into a single stream of video. Traditionally, genlock allowed multiple devices (video recorders, cameras, etc.) to be used together with precise timing so that they captured a

	scene in unison.
geostationary satellite	A satellite whose orbital speed is matched or synchronized with respect to the earth's rotation so that the satellite remains fixed, relative to a specific point on the earth's surface.
geosynchronous orbit	A satellite orbit that is synchronous with a point on the earth's surface. An orbit, approximately 22,500 miles above the earth's equator, where satellites circle at the same speed as the rotation of the earth, and thereby appear stationary to an earth bound observer.
ghost	A duplicate shadowy image set off slightly from the primary picture image.
GIF	Graphical Interchange Format, a commonly-used graphics file format for transferring image files over a network.
giga	A prefix denoting a factor of 10^9, abbreviated GHz.
Gigabit Interface Converter	An interface for attaching network devices to fiber-based transmission systems (e.g., Fibre Channel or Gigabit Ethernet). GBICs convert serial electrical signals to serial optical signals and vice versa. GBIC modules contain ID and system information that a switch can use to assess network device capabilities, and are hot-swappable.
Global System for Mobile Communications	A TDMA-based digital cellular telephone technology that is used by PCS telephones.
GOB	Group of Blocks. The ITU-T's H.261 Recommendation process divides a video frame into a group of blocks (GOB). At CIF resolutions there are 12 such blocks and at QCIF there are three. A GOB is made up of 12 macroblocks (MB) that contain luminance and chrominance information for 8448 pixels. A GOB relates to 176 pixels by 48 lines of Y and the spatially-corresponding 88 pixels by 24 lines of CB and CR. Each GOB is divided in 33 macroblocks, in which the macroblocks are arranged

in three rows that each contain 11 macroblocks.

GPT — A codec manufacturer. GEC and Plessy combined their efforts to create an early video codec that depended on BT's compression algorithm. GPT codecs are prevalent in Europe.

Grand Alliance — The merger of four competitive HDTV systems, previously proposed to the FCC as individual standards, into a collaborative venture that is backed by all the supporters of the original four separate systems. The companies that comprise the Grand Alliance include AT&T, the David Sarnoff Research Center, General Instrument, MIT, North American Philips, Thomson Consumer Electronics, and Zenith Electronics. The new HDTV standard was approved in late 1996 after a compromise between the computer and broadcasting industries was reached.

graphical user interface — (GUI). A "point and click" computing environment that depends on a pointing device such as a mouse to evoke commands and move around a screen as opposed to a standard computer keyboard.

graphics — Artwork, captions, lettering, and photos used in programs, or the presentation of data of this nature, in a video communications system.

graphics accelerator — A video adapter with a special processor that can enhance performance levels during graphical transformations. A CPU can often become bogged down during an activity of this type. The accelerator allows the CPU to execute other commands while it takes care of the compute-intensive graphics processing.

graphics coprocessor — A programmable chip that speeds video performance by carrying out graphics processing independently of the computer's CPU. Among the coprocessor's common abilities are drawing graphics primitives and converting vectors to bitmaps.

gray scale — A range of luminance levels with incremental brightness steps from black to gray to white. The

	steps generally conform to a logarithmic relationship.
groupware	A term for software that runs on a LAN and allows coworkers to work collaboratively and concurrently. Groupware is now being enhanced with video capabilities and many of the new desktop conferencing products offer capabilities commonly associated with groupware.
GSM	See Global System for Mobile Communications
guardband	Unused radio frequency spectrum between television channels.
GUI	See Graphical user interface.

— H —

H.221	The framing portion of the ITU-T's H.320 Recommendation that is formally known as "Frame Structure for a 64 to 1920 Kbps Channel in Audiovisual Teleservices." The Recommendation specifies synchronous operation in which the coder and decoder handshake and agree upon timing. Synchronization is arranged for individual B channels or bonded H0 connections.
H.222	ITU-T Recommendation, ratified in July of 1995, that specifies "Generic coding of moving pictures and associated audio information. H.222.0 is entitled, "MPEG-2 Program and Transport Stream" and H.222.1 is entitled, "MPEG-2 streams over ATM."
H.223	Part of the ITU-T's H.324 standard that specifies a control/multiplexing protocol, it is formally called "Multiplexing protocol for low bitrate multimedia communication." Annexes, passed in February 1998, deals with video packetization with H.263, and with multimedia mobile communications over error-prone channels.

H.225 Part of the ITU-T's H.323 Recommendation. H.225 establishes specific messages for call control such as signaling, registration and admissions as well as the packetizing and synchronizing of media streams. Annex I addresses call signaling protocols and media stream packetization for packet-based multimedia communications systems.

H.226 Part of the ITU-T's H.32x Recommendation, H.226 establishes channel aggregation protocols for multilink operation on circuit-switched networks.

H.230 A multiplexing Recommendation that is part of the ITU-T family of video interoperability Recommendations. Formally known as "Frame-synchronous Control and Indication Signals for Audiovisual Systems," the Recommendation specifies how individual frames of audiovisual information are to be multiplexed onto a digital channel.

H.231 ITU Recommendation, formally known as "Multipoint Control Unit for Audiovisual Systems Using Digital Channels up to 2 Mbps," H.231 was added to the ITU-T's H.320 family of Recommendations in March 1993. It specifies the multipoint control unit used to bridge three or more H.320-compliant codecs together in a multipoint conference.

H.235 Formerly known as H.SECURE, H.235 was ratified in February 1998 to establish security and encryption protocols for H.323 and other H.245-based multimedia terminals. H.235 is not itself a method of encryption and security, but establishes a methodology for leveraging such protocol families as IPSec (that, in turn, leverages security association and key distribution protocols such as ISAKMP and Oakley).

H.242 Part of the ITU-T's H.320 family of video interoperability Recommendations. Formally known as the "System for Establishing Communication Between Audiovisual Terminals Using Digital

Channels up to 2 Mbps," H.242 specifies the protocol for establishing an audio session and taking it down after the communication has terminated.

H.243 ITU-T "System for Establishing Communication Between Three or More Audiovisual Terminals Using Digital Channels up to 2 Mbps."

H.245 Part of the ITU's H.324 protocol that defines control of communications between multimedia terminals. Its formal Recommendation name is "Control protocol for multimedia communication."

H.246 ITU recommendation to establish a method for interworking of H-Series multimedia terminals with H-Series multimedia terminals and voice/voiceband terminals on the PSTN (more accurately, GSTN, or General Switched Telephone Network) and ISDN.

H.247 ITU recommendation to establish a method for multipoint extension for broadband audiovisual communication systems and terminals.

H.261 The ITU-T's Recommendation that allows dissimilar video codecs to interpret how a signal has been encoded and compressed, and to decode and decompress that signal. The standard, formally known as "Video Codec for Audiovisual Services at Px64 Kbps," it also identifies two picture formats: the Common Intermediate Format (CIF) and the Quarter Common Intermediate Format (QCIF). These two formats are compatible with all three television standards: NTSC, PAL and SECAM.

H.262 ITU recommendation for using the MPEG-2 compression algorithm for compressing a videoconferencing transmission.

H.263 H.263 is the ITU-T's "Video Coding for Low Bit Rate Communication." It refers to the compression techniques used in the H.324 Recommendation and in other ITU-T recommendations, too. H.263 is similar to H.261 but differs from it in several ways. Its advance negotiable options enable implementations of the Recommendation that employ them to achieve approximately the same resolution quality as H.261 at half the data rate. H.263 uses half-pixel increments for motion compensation (optional in both standards) while H.261 uses full-pixel precision and specifies a loop-filter. In H.263, portions of the data stream hierarchy have been rendered optional. This allows the codec to be configured for enhanced error recovery or, alternatively, for very low data rate transmission. There are, in H.263, four options designed to improve performance. They are advance prediction, forward and backward frame prediction, syntax-based arithmetic coding and Unrestricted Motion Vectors. H.263 supports not only H.261's optional CIF and mandatory QCIF resolutions but also SQCIF (128x96 pixels), 4CIF (704x576 pixels) and 16CIF (1408x1152 pixels).

H.310

H.310 is an ITU-T draft standard for broadcast (HDTV) quality video conferencing. It describes how MPEG-2 video can be transmitted over high-speed ATM networks. The standard includes subparts such as H.262 (MPEG-2 video standard), H.222.0 (MPEG-2 Program and Transport Stream), H.222.1 (MPEG-2 streams over ATM) and a variety of G.7XX audio compression standards. H.310 takes H.320 to the next generation of networks (broadband ISDN and ATM).

H.320

An ITU-T standard formally known as "Narrow-band Visual Telephone Systems and Terminal Equipment." H.320 includes a number of individual recommendations for coding, framing, signaling and establishing connections (H.221, H.230, H.321, H.242, and H.261). It applies to point-to-point and multipoint videoconferencing sessions and includes three audio algorithms, G.721, G.722 and G.728.

H.321

H.321 adapts H.320 to next-generation topologies such as ATM and broadband ISDN. It retains H.320's overall structure and some of its components, including H.261 and adds enhancements to adapt it to cell-switched networks.

H.322 H.322 is an enhanced version of H.320 optimized for networks that guarantee Quality of Service (QoS) for isochronous traffic such as real-time video. It will be first used with IEEE 802.9a isochronous Ethernet LANs.

H.323 H.323 extends H.320 to Ethernet, Token-Ring, and other packet-switched networks that do not guarantee QoS. It will support both point-to-point and multipoint operations. QoS issues will be addressed by a centralized gatekeeper component that lets LAN administrators manage video traffic on the backbone. Another integral part of the spec defines a LAN/H.320 gateway that will allow any H.323 node to interoperate with H.320 products. In addition to H.320's H.261 video codec H.323 also H.263, a more sophisticated video codec. Also in the family are H.225 (specifies call control messages); H.245 (specifies messages for opening and controlling channels for media streams); and the G.711, G.722, G.723, G.728 and G.729 audio codecs.

H.324 H.324 defines a multimedia communication terminal that operates over POTS lines. It can incorporate H.261 or H.263 video encoding. The H.324 family includes H.223, for multiplexing, H.245 for control, T.120 for audiographics, and the V.90 modem specification.

H.332 ITU Recommendation for large multipoint H.323 conferences (defined as "loosely coupled conferences").

H.450.1 ITU Recommendation that defines a generic functional protocol for the support of supplementary services in H.323.

H.450.x ITU Recommendation that defines specific supplementary services to H.323 that leverage H.450.1.

H0 The switched 384 Kbps dialing standard as defined

by an ITU-T Recommendation.

H11 The switched 1.544 Mbps dialing standard as defined by an ITU-T Recommendation.

H12 The switched 1.920 Mbps dialing standard as defined by an ITU-T Recommendation.

handshake The electrical exchange of predetermined signals by devices in preparation of a connection. Once completed, the transmission begins. In video communications, handshake is a process by which codecs interoperate by seeking out a common algorithm.

hard disk A sealed mass storage unit that allows archival of large amounts of data and smaller amounts of video or audio information.

hardware The mechanical, magnetic and electronic components of a system. Examples are computers, codecs, terminals, and scanners.

harmonic distortion A problem caused by the production of nonlinearities in a communications channel in which harmonics of the input frequencies appear in the output channel.

harmonics In periodic waves, the component sine waves that are integer multiples—exponents—of the fundamental frequency.

HD *MAC* One of the two analog HDTV standards the EC's Council of Telecommunications Ministers promoted, and which was abandoned in favor of digital formats that were subsequently proposed.

HDTV High Definition Television. TV display systems with approximately four times the resolution of standard television systems. Systems labeled as HDTV typically offer at least 1,000 lines of resolution and an aspect ratio of 16:9.

header A string of bits in a coded bit stream that is used to convey information about the data that follows.

head-end — The originating point in a cable television system where all the television and telecommunication signals are assembled for transmission over a broadband cable system to the subscribers. Signals may be generated from studios, received from satellites or conveyed via land line or microwave radio trunks. Head-end sites can be located in the same building as the cable operator's business headquarters or they can be sited close to satellite receiving dishes. They are generally equipped with amplifiers or signal regenerators.

hertz — Hz. The unit of measurement used in analog or frequency-based networks named after the German physicist Heinrich Hertz. One hertz equals one cycle-per-second.

high frequency — Electromagnetic waves between 3 and 30 MHz.

high-pass filter — A device that attenuates the frequencies below a particular cut-off point, a high-pass filter is useful in removing extraneous sounds such as hum and microphone boom.

holography — The recording and representation of three-dimensional objects by interference patterns formed between a beam of coherent light and its refraction from the subject. The hologram is the holographic equivalent of a phonograph. A three-dimensional image is stored which, if broken apart, can still reconstruct a whole image, though at reduced definition. Holograms require laser light for their creation and, in many cases, for their viewing.

horizontal — H. In television signals, the horizontal line of video information that is controlled by a horizontal synch pulse.

horizontal blanking interval — The period of time during which an electron gun shuts off to return from the right side of a monitor or TV screen to the left side in order to start painting a new line of video.

horizontal resolution — Detail expressed in pixels that provide chrominance and luminance information across a line of video information.

host — A computer that processes data in a communications network.

hub — A network or system signal distribution point where multiple circuits convene and are connected. Some type of switching or information transfer can then take place. Switching hubs can also be used in Ethernet LAN environments in an arrangement whereby a LAN segment might support only one workstation. This relieves congestion through a process called micro-segmenting.

hue — The attribute by which a color may be identified within the visible spectrum. Hue refers to the spectral colors of red, orange, yellow, green blue and violet. A huge variety of subjective colors exist between these spectral colors.

Huffman encoding — A lossless, statistically based entropy-coding compression technique. Huffman encoding is used to compress data in which the most frequently occurring code groups are represented by shorter codes and rarely occurring code groups are represented by longer codes. The idea behind Huffman encoding is similar to that of Morse code in that short, simple codes are assigned to common characters and longer codes are assigned to lesser-used characters. Huffman coding, used in H.261 and JPEG, can reduce a test file by approximately 40%.

hybrid fiber/coax — Hybrid fiber-coax (HFC) is being used by the cable companies to provide local loop service. HFC uses fiber links from the central site to a neighborhood hub. Existing coax cable connects the hub to several hundred nearby homes. Once installed, HFC provides subscribers with telephone service over the cable and, in addition, interactive broadband signaling, which can support videoconferencing over the cable network.

— I —

IANA — See Internet Corporation for Assigned Names and Numbers

ICCAN — See Internet Corporation for Assigned Names and Numbers

I frame — Intraframe coding, as specified by the MPEG Recommendation in which an individual video frame is compressed without reference to other frames in the sequence. Also used in the JPEG compression method. I-frame coding generates much data and is used when there are major scene changes or as a reference frame to eliminate accumulated errors that result from interframe coding techniques.

I-Signal — In the NTSC color system, the I signal represents the chrominance on the orange-cyan axis.

IEC — International Electrotechnical Commission. Also synonymous with IXC—interexchange carrier.

IEEE — Institute of Electrical and Electronics Engineers; the organization that evolved from the IRE—the Institute of Radio Engineers.

IEEE 802 standards — Various IEEE committees that developed LAN physical layer standards and other attributes of LANs and MANs. IEEE 802.9 specifies the isochronous Ethernet communications protocol, which adds 6 Mbps of bandwidth to the same twisted pair copper wire that carriers 10 Mbps Ethernet. This additional bandwidth takes the form of 96 ISDN circuit switched B channels. IEEE P 802.14 is a protocol for "Cable-TV Based Broadband Communications Network," another IEEE 802.X standard that has relevance for video communications.

IETF — Internet Engineering Task Force. The standards body that adopted the MIME protocol for sending video-enabled e-mail and other compound messages across TCP/IP networks and one of two working bodies of the Internet Activities Board.

image — An image, for the purposes of this book, refers to a complex set of computer data that represents a picture or other visual data. Images can offer high-resolution (in other words, they can be composed of many pixels-per-square-inch that causes them to have a photographic quality) or low-resolution, (crude animation, sketches and other pictures that contain a minimal number of pixels-per-square-inch.

image bit map — Digital representation of a graphics display image as a pattern of small units of information that represents one or more pixels.

imaging — The process of using equipment and applications to capture visual representations and transmit them over telecommunications networks. Imaging can be used to move and store medical X-rays, for engineering and design applications that allow engineers to develop 3-D images of a products or components for the purpose of design-refinement, and to store large quantities of documents.

impedance — The ratio of voltage to current as it is measured along a transmission circuit.

in-band signaling — Networks exchange information between nodes through the use of signaling. In-band signaling uses the communications path to exchange such information as request for service, addressing, disconnect, busy, etc. In-band signaling has been largely replaced by out-of-band signaling, an example of which is the ITU-T's Signaling System Number 7 or SS7.

Indeo — Intel's proprietary lossy compression/decompression algorithm for video playback and CD-ROM applications. Indeo is similar to Motion JPEG. Indeo supports playback at rates of 15 frames per second. Frames can be viewed full-screen while maintaining the same playback rate.

input — The data or signals entering a computer or, more

	generally, the signal applied to any electronic device or system.
input selector	A switch or routing device that is used to select video inputs in a digital picture manipulator or keying device.
integrated circuit	An electronic device *IC*'s are made by layering semiconductive materials and packaging both active and passive circuits into a single multi-pin chip.
intelligent peripheral	In the AIN, the intelligent peripheral or IP collects information from designated "triggers" and issues SS7 requests based on that information.
inter-LATA	Communications that cross a LATA boundary and, therefore, must be carried by an IXC in accordance with the MFJ.
interactive	Action in more than one direction, either simultaneously or sequentially. In interactive video there is a bi-directional interplay between two or multiple parties, this is different from television, which is a send-only system that does not allow the receiver to respond to the signal.
interactivity	The ability of a video system user to control or define the flow of information, including the capability of communicating in return on a peer-to-peer basis.
interexchange carrier	IXC or IEC. The long distance companies in the US that provide inter-LATA telephony and communications services. This concept is going away as a result of the passage of the Telecommunications Deregulation and Competition Act of 1996.
interface	A shared boundary or point common to two or more systems across which there is a specified flow of information. If interfaces are carefully specified, it should be possible to plug in, switch on, and operate equipment purchased from different sources. Unfortunately, this is not always possible. Many standard specifications incorporate so many options

	that interoperation of multiple devices requires special engineering. *Interface* can also refer to a circuit that converts the output of one system or subsystem to a form suitable to the next system or subsystem.
interference	Unwanted energy received with a signal that scrambles it or otherwise degrades it.
interframe coding	A compression technique used in video communications in which the redundancies that can be found between successive frames of video information are removed. This type of compression is also referred to as temporal coding.
interlace	A technique for "painting" a television monitor in which each video frame is divided into two fields with one field composed of the odd-numbered horizontal scan lines and the other composed of the even-numbered horizontal scan lines. Each field is displayed on an alternating basis—this is called interlacing. It results in very rapid screen refreshment and is done to avoid visual flicker. Interlacing is not used on computer monitors and is not required as part of the US HDTV standard.
International Standards Organization	A non-treaty standards-making body that, among other things, helped to develop the MPEG and JPEG standards for image compression. See ISO.
International Telecommunications Union	One of the specialized agencies of the United Nations that is composed of the telecommunications administrations of roughly 113 participating nations. Founded in 1865, it was invented as a telegraphy standards body. It now develops international standards for interconnecting telecommunications equipment across networks. Known as the CCITT until early 1994, the ITU played a big role in developing audiovisual communications standards through its Telecommunications Standardization Sector (see ITU-T). In this book we refer to standards as CCITT Recommendations if they were ratified before 1994 and ITU-T Recommendations if they were adopted after 1994.

Internet — The Internet is a vast collection of computer networks throughout the world. Originally developed to serve the needs of the Department of Defense's Advanced Research Projects Agency (ARPA) the Internet is now used by everyone. After the development of a hypertext-linked subset of the Internet, the World Wide Web, it has become a common vehicle for electronic commerce and information exchange among individuals and businesses large and small. Videoconferencing now traverses the Internet, aided by the ITU-T's H.323 Recommendation and the real-time Transfer Protocol (RTP).

Internet Corporation for Assigned Names and Numbers — ICANN, the successor to the Internet Assigned Names Authority (IANA) is a not-for-profit organization with an international Board of Directors that oversees the operations of the necessary central coordinating functions of the Internet.

Internet reflector site — A multipoint technique used by Internet-based videoconferencing. A reflector is a server that bounces signals back to all parties of a multipoint connection, allowing any number of users to conference with each other.

internetworking — The ability of LANs to interconnect and exchange information. Bridges and routers are the devices that connect these LANs with each other, with WANs, and with MANs. Users can, therefore, exchange messages, access files on hosts other than those on their own LAN, and access and utilize various inter-LAN applications.

interoperability — The ability of electronic components produced by different manufacturers to communicate across product lines. The trend toward embracing standards has greatly furthered the interoperability process.

interpolation — A compression technique with which a current frame of video is reconstructed using the differences between it and past and future frames.

intra-LATA — A connection that does not cross over a LATA boundary, and that regulated LECs are allowed to carry on an end-to-end basis. Recently passed legislation may make this term obsolete.

intraframe coding — A compression technique whereby redundancies within a video frame are eliminated. DCT is an intraframe coding method. Interframe coding is also called spatial coding.

inverse multiplexer — Equipment that receives a high-speed input and breaks it up for the network into multiple 56- or 64 Kbps signals so that it can be carried over switched digital service. The I-MUX supports the need for dialing over this network. It also provides the synchronization necessary to recombine the multiple channels into a single integrated transmission at the receiving end. This is necessary because, once the transmission has been subdivided into multiple channels, some parts of the transmission may take a different and longer path to the destination than others. This results in a synchronization problem even though the difference may be measured in milliseconds. The job of the I-MUX is to make sure that the channels are recombined into a cohesive single transmission.

IP — Internet Protocol. Defined in RFC 791, the Internet Protocol is the network layer for the TCP/IP protocol stack. It is a connectionless, best-effort packet-switched delivery mechanism. By connectionless we mean that IP can carry data between two systems without first requiring their connection. IP does not guarantee the data will reach its destination; neither can it break large packets down into smaller ones for transmission or recover lost or damaged packets. For that it relies on the Transmission Control Protocol.

ISDN — Integrated Services Digital Network. ITU-T standard for a digital connection between user and network. A multiplicity of services, voice, data, full-motion video and image can be delivered. Two interfaces are defined, Basic Rate Interface, and Primary Rate Interface. Basic Rate Interface (BRI) provides two 64 Kbps circuit-switched bearer (B) channels for customer data and one 16 Kbps delta (D) or signaling channel that is packet-switched. The Primary Rate Interface (PRI) differs between the US and Europe: in Europe it provides thirty 64 Kbps B channels and two 64 Kbps D channels (one for signaling and the other for synchronization) and in the US there are twenty-three B channels and one 64 Kbps D channel, which is used for synchronization and signaling.

ISO International Standards Organization. Founded in 1946, ISO has approximately 90 member countries, including the US's ANSI and its British equivalent, the British Standards Institution (BSI). ISO members include the national standards bodies of most industrialized countries. The ISO, in conjunction with the ITU-T, continues to develop video communications standards. Their joint efforts have produced the Joint Photographic Experts Group (JPEG) and the Motion Picture Experts Group (MPEG) family of encoding techniques.

isochronous Channels that are capable of transmitting timing information in addition to the data itself, and which thereby allow the terminals at each end to maintain exact synchronization with each other (the term is pronounced 'I-SOCK-ron-us').

IsoENET An approach to providing isochronous service over Ethernet. It derives an additional 96 switched B channels from 10Base-T. National Semiconductor and IBM developed it.

ITCA International Teleconferencing Association, a professional association organized to promote the use of teleconferencing (audio and videoconferencing). Located in Washington D.C.

ITFS Antenna System Instructional Television Fixed Service. A type of local distance learning system that provides one-way over-the-air television service at microwave frequencies. These frequencies are reserved for educational purposes. The signals can be received only by television installations equipped with a converter that changes the signals to NTSC.

ITU — One of the specialized agencies of the United Nations, the International Telecommunications Union was founded in 1865, before telephones were invented, as a telegraphy standards body.

ITU-R — Formerly the United Nation's CCIR, the ITU-R sets international standards that relate to how the radio spectrum is allocated and utilized.

ITU-T — The International Telecommunications Union's Telecommunications Standardization Sector. The ITU-T (formerly the CCITT) is the telephony standards-setting arm of the ITU. The ITU-T developed the H.320, H.323 and H.324 protocol suites that define how videoconferencing codecs interoperate over various types of networks.

IXC — Interexchange carrier, long distance service providers in the US that provide inter-LATA service.

— J —

Jitter — Random signal distortion, a subjective effect caused by time-base errors. Jitter in a reproduced video image moves from left to right and causes an irregular. Jitter can be controlled by time-base correction.

JPEG — Joint Photographic Experts Group. The joint ITU-T/ ISO standard for still image compression.

— K —

K — A prefix that denotes a factor of one thousand or 10^3. This abbreviation is used frequently when discussing computer networks and digital transmission systems. In computer parlance, K stands for 1024 bytes as in 64K bytes memory. In transmission systems the K stands for 1000—e.g., 64 Kbps means 64 thousand bits per second bandwidth.

K-Band — In satellite communications a frequency band that ranges between 10.9 and 36 GHz.

Kbps — Kilobits per second. The transport of digitized information over a network at a rate of 1,000 bits in any given second.

kHz — Kilohertz. One thousand Hertz or cycles.

kilobyte — 1,024 bytes of data.

kiosk — A small structure, open at one or more sides located in a public place. Kiosks today can be designed and equipped with motion video-enabled and multimedia displays to enable even the least computer-literate people to access information on a particular topic or product. Typically they use point-and-click or single-press methods for video-enabled information retrieval.

Ku-Band — In satellite communications systems, this frequency band ranges between 10.9 and 11.7 GHz for Direct Broadcast Satellite (DBS) service.

— L —

LAN — Local Area Network. A computer network, usually within a single office complex and increasingly within a single department, that connects workstations, servers, printers and other devices, and thereby permits resource sharing and message exchange.

LAN segmentation — Splitting one large LAN into multiple smaller LANs. This technique is used to keep LANs from becoming congested with multimedia and desktop video applications.

laser — Light Amplification by the Stimulated Emission of Radiation. A device that produces optical radiation both in the range of visible light wavelengths and outside this range. Lasers are used in optical fiber networks to transmit signals through a process of oscillation.

LATA — Local Access and Transport Areas. The areas within which the Bell Operating and independent telephone companies can provide transport services. This distinction will change as a result of the Telecommunications Deregulation Act of 1996; but only after sufficient competition in local access has been achieved. At that point RBOCs will be able to sell inter-exchange service in any area and the concept of LATA will fade and eventually disappear.

latency — Latency refers to the transmission delays encountered in a packet-switched network. Latency refers to the tendency of packet-switched networks to slow down when they become congested. It is lethal for data types such as voice and video that require constant bit rates to ensure that these time-sensitive data types arrive with minimal and predictable delays.

lavaliere microphone — A small clip-on microphone, popular because it is unobtrusive and maintains a fixed distance to the speaker's mouth.

layer — Layering is an approach taken in the process of developing protocols for compatibility between dissimilar products, services and applications. In the seven-layer OSI model, layering breaks each step of a transmission between two devices into a discrete set of functions. These functions are grouped within a layer according to what they are intended to accomplish. Each layer communicates with its counterpart through header-defined interfaces. The flexibility offered through the layering approach allows products and services to evolve while accommodating changes made at the layer level, rather than having to rework the entire arrangement of Interoperability.

leased line — A transmission facility reserved from a communications carrier for the exclusive use of a subscriber. See private line.

LEC	Local Exchange Carrier. LECs include the Bell Operating Companies and independent telephone companies that provide the subscriber local loop.
Lempel-Ziv-Welch compression	LZW, a data compression method named after its developers. LZW techniques are founded on the notion that a given group of bytes can be compressed by substituting an index phrase.
lens	An optical device of one or more elements in an illuminating or image forming system such as the objective of a camera or projector.
level	The intensity of an electrical signal.
line	A facility between a subscriber and a telecommunications carrier, generally a single analog communications path physically composed of twisted copper wire.
line of sight	Some spectrum-based transmission systems need an unobstructed path between the transmitter and receiver. The ability for the receiver to "see" the sender is described as having a clear line of sight.
lip synch	The techniques used to maintain a precise coordination between the delivery of sound and the facial movements associated with speech. Lip synch is required because it takes much longer to process the video portion of a signal than the audio portion (the video part contains much more information and takes about sixty to 120 times as long to compress). To "take up the slack," a codec incorporates an adjustable audio delay circuit. This delay-equalizes sounds with faces, and allows talking-head images to look natural at the receiving end.
LiveBoard	LiveWork's group-oriented electronic whiteboard that allows users in different locations to interactively share information. A wireless pen is used to create documents or images viewed and edited in real-time over POTS lines. LiveBoard can also display full-motion color video and provide

audio for mixed media applications.

local loop — In telephone networks, the lines that connect customer equipment to the switching system in the central office.

local multipoint distribution service (LMDS) — Broadband wireless local loop service that offers two-way digital broadcasting and interactive service over a special type of microwave.

logarithm — An exponential expression of the power to which a fixed number or base must be raised in order to produce a given number. Logarithms are usually computed to the base of 10 and are used for shortening mathematical calculations—e.g., 10^3 = 1,000.

Logarithmic Quantization Step Encoding — A digital audio encoding method that yields 12-bit accuracy using only eight-bit encoding. It is a technique used in CCITT G.711 audio.

loop filter — H.261 codecs break an original video field into 8-x-8 pixel blocks, then filters and compresses each block. A loop filter is used to separate the images' spatial frequencies so that they can be uniquely compressed.

lossless compression — Techniques that, when they are reversed, yield data identical to the original.

lossy compression — A compression technique that, when reversed, contains less information than the original image. Techniques that, when reversed, do not yield data that is identical to the original. Lossy compression techniques are good at compressing motion video sequences and achieve much higher compression ratios than lossless techniques.

low-pass filter — A device that attenuates the frequencies above the cut-off point and which is used in sound synthesis and digital audio sampling.

LSI — Large Scale Integration. Refers to degree of miniaturization achieved in manufacturing complex integrated circuits.

luma — The brightness signal in a video transmission.

lumen — A measure of light emitted by a source.

luminance — The information about the varying light intensity of an image produced by a television or video camera. Also called brightness.

Lux — A contraction of luminance and flux and a basic unit for measuring light intensity. A Lux is approximately 10 foot candles.

LWZ — Lempel-Ziv-Welch coding developed by three mathematicians in the 1970s. LWZ looks at repetitive bit combinations and represents the most commonly occurring sequences with abbreviated codes.

— M —

MAC — Multiple Analog Component, one of the original European HDTV formats.

MAC — In data networking, media access controllers are the interface between an application and an output device.

Macintosh® — Apple® brand desktop computer that is capable of supporting motion video. Often referred to as a Mac.

macroblock — In H.261 encoding, a macroblock is made up of six 8x8-pixel blocks of which two contain chrominance information and four contain luminance information components. A macroblock contains 16x16 pixels-worth of Y (luminance) information and the spatially-corresponding 8x8 pixels that contain CB and CR information.

MAN — Metropolitan Area Network.

MBONE — Internet Multicast Backbone, a sub-set of the Internet that uses special routers (mrouters) to handle multicasting, (the process of sending one live message to more than one recipient, without duplicating the message prior to sending). Devices involved in an MBONE multicast use IP addresses that are allocated from the "Class D" portion of the IP addressing spectrum. They connect to the MBONE using encapsulated packets or *tunneling*. Tunneling provides a point-to-point channel for multimedia traffic. Packets with class D addresses are enclosed in packets with the normal IP addresses of an mrouter or a multicast recipient. The mrouter strips off the IP header and routes the packet to the appropriate class D destination.

Mbps — Megabits per second or approximately one million bits per second.

MCU — See multipoint conferencing (or control) unit.

media — Air, water, space and solid objects through which information travels. The information that is carried through all natural media takes the form of waves.

Media Access Control — MAC. The network protocol that controls access to a LAN's bandwidth and could include techniques that would reserve bandwidth for isochronous communications.

megabyte — 1,048,576 bytes—2^{20}.

Megastream — British Telecom's brand name for a digital system that offers the customer thirty 64 Kbps channels. Used in high-bandwidth video conferencing systems, whether point-to-point or dial-up (using the ITU-T's H0 dialing standard).

memory — A digital store for computer data that commonly consist of integrated circuits. There are two primary types: read-only memory or ROM and random-access memory or RAM.

Merged Gateway — A protocol for controlling media gateways. It is the

Control Protocol	combination of Level 3's IPDC and Bellcore's and Cisco's SGCP (Simple Gateway Control Protocol).
mesh topology	A networking scheme whereby any node can communicate directly with any other node.
MFJ	Modified Final Judgment. The out-of-court settlement that broke up the Bell System, severing the Bell Operating Companies from AT&T.
MGCP	See Merged Gateway Control Protocol.
microsegmenting	The process of configuring Ethernet and other LANs with a single workstation per segment using hubs and inexpensive wiring. The goal is to remove contention from Ethernet segments to guarantee enough bandwidth for desktop video and multimedia. With each segment having access to a full 10 Mbps of Ethernet bandwidth, users can avail themselves of applications that incorporate compressed video.
microwave	Radio transmission above 1 GHz used for transmitting communications signals, including video pictures, between various sites using dish aerials.
middleware	Middleware is a layer of software that provides the services required to link distributed pieces of an application across a network, typically in a client/server environment. Middleware is transparent, hiding the fact that components of an application are distributed. It helps developers to overcome the difficulties of interfacing application components into heterogeneous network environments.
MIME	Multipurpose Internet Mail Extension. Developed and adopted by the Internet Engineering Task Force, this applications protocol is designed for transmitting mixed-media files across TCP/IP networks.
mixing	The process of combining separate sound and/or visual sources to make a smooth composite.

modulation	Alteration of the amplitude, frequency or phase of an analog signal by a different frequency in order to impress a signal onto a carrier wave. Also can be used in digital signaling to make multiple signals share a single channel. In the digital realm, this is generally achieved by dividing a channel into time slots, into which each separate signal contributes bits in turn.
moiré	In a video image, a wavy pattern caused by the combination of excessively high frequency signals; the mixing of these signals results in a visible low frequency that looks a bit like French watered silk, after which it is named.
monitor	A precision display for viewing a picture. The word is now often applied to any TV set with video (as opposed to RF) input. A receiver-monitor is a set that is both a conventional TV used for viewing broadcast television but which also accepts video input from a computer. Also refers to computer displays.
monochrome	Reproduction in a single color, normally as a black and white picture.
motion compensation	An interframe coding technique that examines statistics of previous video frames to predict subsequent ones. In a motion sequence each pixel can have a distinct displacement from one frame to the next. From a practical point of view, however, adjacent pixels tend to have the same displacement. Motion compensation uses motion vectors and rate-of-change analysis to exploit inter-frame similarities. An image is divided into rectangular blocks and a single displacement vector to describe the movement of all pixels within the block.
Motion JPEG	A compression technique that applies JPEG compression to each frame of a video clip.
motion vectors	In the H.261 Recommendation this optional calculation can be included in a macroblock. Motion vector data consists of one code word for the

horizontal information followed by a code word for the vertical information. The code words can be of variable length and are specified in the H.261 standard. Performing motion vector calculations places more demand on a processor and many systems do not include this capability, which is optional for the source coder. If a source encoder performs the motion compensation processing, the H.261 Recommendation requires that the decoder use it during decompression.

motion video capture board — A device designed to capture, digitize and compress multiple frames of video for storage on magnetic or optical storage media.

MPEG — Motion Picture Experts Group JTC1/SC29/WG11 standard that specifies a variable rate compression algorithm that can be used to compress full-motion image sequences at low bit rates. MPEG is an international family of standards that are not used for videoconferencing, but are more generally used for video images stored on CD-ROM or video servers and retrieved in a computer or television application. MPEG compresses YUV SIF images. It uses the same DCT algorithm used in H.261 and H.263 but uses 16 by 16 pixel blocks for motion compensation.

MPEG-1 — Joint ISO/IEC recommendation known as "Coding of Moving Pictures and Associated Audio for Digital Storage Media at up to about 1.5 Mbps." MPEG-1 was completed in October 1992. It begins with a rather low image resolution; about 240 lines by 352 pixels per line. This image is compressed at 30 frames per second. It provides a digital image transfer rate up to about 1.5 Mbps and compression rates of about 100:1. The MPEG-1 specification consists of four parts: system, video, audio, and compliance testing.

MPEG-2 — The MPEG-2 is Committee Draft 13818, and can be found in documents MPEG93/N601, N602 and N603. This draft was completed in November 1993. Its formal name is "Generic Coding of Moving Pictures and Associated Audio." MPEG-2 is targeted

	for use with high-bandwidth applications aimed at digital television broadcasts. It specifies 720-by-408 pixel resolution at 60 fields-per-second with data transfer rates that range from 500 Kbps to more than 2 Mbps.
MPEG-4	"Very Low Bitrate Audio-Visual Coding." An 11/94 Call for Proposals by ISO/IEC resulted in a Working Draft specification in 11/96.
MS-DOS	A computer operating system developed by Microsoft and originally aimed at the IBM PC.
multicasting	Conferencing applications that typically use packet-switched transmission to broadcast a signal that can be received by multiple recipients, all of whom are listening on a single multicasting address.
multi-mode fiber	Optical fiber with a central core of a diameter sufficient to permit light-pulses to zig-zag from side to side as well as to travel straight down the middle of the core. Step-indexed fibers have a sudden change of refractive index where cladding meets core. Signals are reflected back at this boundary. Graded index fibers have a gradual change of refractive index with radial distance from the center of the core, pulses are refracted back by this change. Multi-mode fiber is often used in campus wiring plans.
multimedia	According to the Defense Information Systems Agency: "Two or more media types (audio, video, imagery, text, and data) electronically manipulated, integrated, and reconstructed in synchrony." Generally, multimedia refers to these media in a digital format for it is the digitization of voice and video information that is lending much of the power to multimedia communications.
Multiple Systems Operator	When one cable company runs multiple cable systems, it creates what is referred to as a Multiple Systems Operator. MSOs benefit from economies of scale in areas of equipment procurement, marketing, management and technical expertise. Local decisions

are left to the individual cable company operators.

multiplex A method of transmitting multiple signals onto a single circuit in a manner so that each can be recovered intact.

multiplexer Electronic equipment that allows multiple signals to share a single communications circuit. Multiplexers are often called "muxes." There are many different types of multiplexers including T-1 and E-1 that use time division multiplexing, statistical and frequency division multiplexers, etc. Some use analog transmission schemes, some digital. A compatible demultiplexer is required to separate the signal back into its components.

multiplexing The process of combining multiple signals onto a single circuit using various means.

multipoint control unit A device that bridges together multiple inputs so that more than three parties can participate in a videoconference. An MCU uses fast switching techniques to patch the presenters or speaker's input to the output ports representing the other participants. An ITU-T H.320-compliant MCU must meet the requirements of H.231 and H.243.

Multirate ISDN A Bandwidth-on-Demand scheme in which telephone customers access, and subsequently pay for, ISDN bandwidth on an as-needed basis.

multisensory Involving more than one human sense.

— N —

N-ISDN Narrowband ISDN. Another name for conventional ISDN that defines bandwidths between 64 Kbps and 2.048 Mbps.

narrowband Networks designed for voice transmission (typically analog voice), but which have been adapted to accommodate the transmission of low-speed data (up to 19.2 Kbps). Trying to get the existing narrowband public switched telephone network to transmit video is a significant challenge to the local telephone operating companies.

narrowcast — A cable television or broadcast program aimed at a very small segment of the market. Typically these are specialized programs likely to be of interest to a relatively limited audience.

National ISDN — In late 1992, Bellcore, the COS and the NIUF introduced National ISDN-1, a standard that aims to provide a consistent interface among LECs, IXCs and equipment manufacturers. The standard was introduced at a week-long event called the Transcontinental ISDN project, or TRIP '92. National ISDN is conceived as an evolving, dynamic, digital network architecture that can be uniformly implemented in a multi-supplier environment. The second step, National ISDN-2 got underway in late 1993. The third step, National ISDN-3 is, at the time of this writing, planned for initial introduction in the latter part of 1995.

needs-analysis — The process of determining what system or technical solution is required to meet a business communications need. In videoconferencing the needs-analysis is critical because the technology, while not unproved, is still new, relatively expensive and viewed with distrust by many senior managers and controllers.

NetMeeting — Microsoft NetMeeting is a real-time Internet-oriented videophone. The NetMeeting client includes support for the ITU's T.120 and H.323 standard and provides multi-user application sharing and data conferencing. NetMeeting also includes a whiteboard and a chat function. The product is included with Explorer 3.0, and thereby simplifies locating end-points and establishing conferences.

network — Interconnected computers or other hardware and software between which data can be transferred. Network transmission media can vary; it can be optical fiber, metallic media, or a wireless arrangement.

Nipkow disc — A disc with holes that, when rotated, permit some light reflected from a screen to hit a photo tube. This creates a minuscule current flow; it is proportionate to the light in the image being reproduced. This was the basis of early television as pioneered by John Logie Baird in England in the 1920s. Paul Nipkow, a German physicist invented it, in 1884.

NLM — Network Loadable Module. An application that resides in a Novell NetWare server and coexists with the core OS. NLMs are optimized to this environment and provide superior service to applications that run outside the core.

node — A concentration point in a network where numerous trunks come together at the same switch.

noise — Any unwanted element accompanying program material. This can take the form of snow, random horizontal streaks or large smears of varying color.

normative — That which can be expressed as a predictable or logical behavior pattern.

NT-1 — Network Termination 1, an ISDN standards-based device that converts between the U-Interface and the S/T-Interface. The NT-1 has a jack for the U-Interface from the wall and one or more jacks for the S/T Interface connection to the PC or videoconferencing system, as well as an external power supply

NTSC — National Television Standards Committee, the body formed by the FCC to develop television standards in the US. NTSC video has a format of 525 scan lines. Video is sent at a rate of 30 frames per second in an interlaced format, in which two fields comprise a frame (60 Hz). The bandwidth required to broadcast this signal is 4 MHz. NTSC uses a trichromatic color system known as YIQ. The NTSC signal's line frequency is 15.75 kHz. Finally, the color subcarrier has a frequency of 3.58 MHz.

NTT — Nippon Telephone and Telegraph.

Nx384 — N-by 384. The ITU-T's approach to developing a standard algorithm for video codec interoperability that was expanded into the Px64 or H.261 standard, and approved in 1990. It was based on the ITU-T's H0 switched digital network standard.

Nyquist's Theorem — A formula that defines the sampling frequency in analog to digital conversions that states that a signal must be sampled at twice its bandwidth in order to be digitally characterized without distortion. For a sine wave, the sampling frequency must be no less than twice the maximum signal frequency.

— O —

OC — Optical carrier, as defined in the SONET specification. OC-1 or Optical Carrier Level 1 is defined as 51.84 Mbps. OC-3 is defined as 155.52 Mbps.

octet — An eight-bit datum representing one of 256 binary values. Also known as a BYTE

open systems — A standards-based approach to building computer platforms. All system components conform, when possible, to standards. This allows end users to move applications between platforms supplied by diverse suppliers, and also allows equipment from different manufacturers to work together. The UNIX operating system figures prominently in open mainframe computing platforms; Microsoft's NT is expected to do the same in the client/server world. In any case, hardware, software and networking components are built, to the degree possible, to conform with existing standards.

operating system — A fixed program used for operating a computer. An OS accepts system commands and manages space in memory and on storage media.

optical disk drives Peripheral storage disks. Used in video communications to store and play back motion image sequences, often accompanied by sound.

optical fiber Very thin glass filaments of extremely high purity onto which light from lasers or LEDs is modulated in such a way that the transmission of digitally encoded information takes place at very high speeds. Fiber optics systems are capable of transmitting huge amounts of information. See fiber-optic cable.

OSI Open Systems Interconnection. An international standard that describes seven layers of communication protocols that allows dissimilar information systems and equipment to be interconnected.

out-of-band signaling Network signaling (addressing, supervision and status information) that traverses a network using a separate path, channel or network than the information (call or transmission) itself. One well-known type of out-of-band signaling is the ITU-T's Signaling System #7.

output devices Electrical components such as monitors, speakers, and printers that receive a computer's data.

— P —

P frame Predictive framing, as specified in the MPEG Recommendation. Pictures are coded by predicting a current frame using a past frame. The picture is broken up into 16x16 pixel blocks. Each block is compared to a the block that occupies the same vertical and horizontal position in a previous frame.

packet A unit of digital data that is switched as a unit. A packet consists of some number of bits (either a fixed number or a variable number), such as those that serve as an address. The packet can be sent over a packet switching network by the best available route (switched virtual circuit) or over a predetermined route (permanent virtual circuit). In a switched virtual circuit or TCP/IP networking environment packets from a single message may take many different routes. At the destination they are reunited with other packets that comprise the communication, re-sequenced and presented to the recipient in their original form.

packet switching — A technique for transmitting data in which the message is subdivided into smaller units called packets. These packets each carry the destination address and sequencing information. Packets from many users are then collated on a single communications channel.

PAL — Phase Alternate Line. The television standard used in most of Western Europe except France. PAL is not a single format however; variations are used in Australia/New Zealand, China, Brazil, and Argentina. PAL uses an image format composed of 625 lines. Frames are sent at a rate of 25 per second and each frame is divided into two fields to accommodate Europe's 50 Hz electrical system. PAL uses YUV, a trichromatic color system.

pan — To pivot a camera in a horizontal direction.

parallel communications — A multi-wire or bus system of communications. The bits that make up the information are transmitted separately, each assigned to a separate wire in the cable. Parallel communications are used frequently in computer-to-printer outputs in which the data must be transferred very rapidly but over a short distance. The opposite method of transmission is serial in which information travels over a single channel a bit at a time.

passband — A range of frequencies transmitted by a network or captured by a device.

Pay-Per-View — PPV. A type of CATV or DBS service whereby a subscriber notifies a provider that he or she is interested in receiving a program and is billed for the specific service on a one-time basis.

PC	A self-contained desktop or notebook computer that can be operated as a standalone machine or connected to other PCs or mainframes via telephone lines or a LAN.
PCM	Pulse Code Modulation. A method of converting an analog signal to a digital signal that involves sampling at a specified rate (typically 8,000 per second), converting the amplitude of the sample to a number and expressing the number digitally.
PCS 100	PictureTel Live PCS 100, a PC-based system that supports both PictureTel's proprietary SG3 algorithm and the industry-standard Px64 algorithm. Supports switched 56 and ISDN BRI interfaces.
pel	Picture element. Generally synonymous with pixel, the term pel is used in the analog world of television broadcasting. As television moves toward the digital world of HDTV the term pixel is being embraced by the broadcasting industry.
peripheral equipment	Accessories such as document cameras, scanners, disks, optical storage devices that work with a system but are not integral to it.
persistence	The time taken for an image to die away.
Personal Mobility	The ability of end users to originate and receive calls and access subscribed telecommunication services on any terminal in any location, and the ability of the network to identify end users as they move.
phase	The relationship between the zero-crossing points of signals. A full cycle describes a 360-degree arc; a sine wave that crosses the zero-point when another has attained its highest point can be said to be 90 degrees out of phase with the other.
phase modulation	The process of shifting the phase of a sine wave in order to modulate it onto a carrier.
Phoneme	An element of speech such as, "ch," "k," or "sh," that is used in synthetic speech systems to assemble words

for audio output.

phosphor — Substance that emits visible light of specific wavelengths when irradiated, as, for example, by an electron beam in a cathode ray tube or by ultra-violet radiation in a fluorescent lamp.

photo diode — A basic element that responds to light energy in a solid-state imaging system. It generates an electric current that is proportional to the intensity of the light falling on it.

picture-in-picture — PIP. A video display mode in which a small video image is superimposed on a quadrant or smaller area of a video screen. This small image or "window" can be opened in order to display a second video input on a monitor. This is a particularly valuable feature in a single monitor videoconferencing system; it allows the near-end to view themselves in a small window while simultaneously seeing the far end.

Picturephone — AT&T's video-telephone that was introduced at the 1964 World's Fair in Flushing Meadow, New York. The device incorporated a camera that was mounted on top of a 5.25" x 4.75" screen. Since audio signals were transmitted separately from video signals, the system required a transmission bandwidth of 6.3 Mbps and, therefore, could not use the PSTN. It never became popular.

PictureTel — One of the largest manufacturers of videoconferencing equipment (both desktop systems and room-based systems) in the world. PictureTel is headquartered in Danvers, Massachusetts.

pixel — The smallest element of a raster display. A picture cell with specific color and/or brightness.

POP — Point of presence. Typically the closest location of a carrier to a subscriber and the point at which that subscriber will be supplied with service from that carrier.

port — A multi-wire input/output to a computer or other electronic component. The number of ports

	determines the number of simultaneous users, the number of peripheral devices one can simultaneously connect with, or a combination of both.
POTS	Plain Old Telephone Service. Analog narrowband telecommunications service designed for transmitting voice calls.
prediction	A type of motion compensation in which a compressed frame of video is reconstructed by a receiving codec by comparing it to a preceding frame of video and making assumptions about what it should be.
PRI	The ISDN Primary Rate Interface. In the US the PRI consists of 23 64 Kbps bearer or "B" channels and one 64 Kbps delta or "D" channel. In Europe, the PRI-equivalent is known as Primary Rate Access or PRA. The PRA consists of 30 64 Kbps B channels and two 64 Kbps D channels.
prism	Crystalline bodies with lateral faces that meet at edges that are parallel to each other. A prism is used to refract light, often dispersed into component wavelengths.
private line	A telephone line rented for the exclusive use of a business and which connects two locations on a point-to-point basis. Communications can only be exchanged between these two locations, as opposed to switched services in which calls can be placed to any other addressable location with compatible service.
private network	A collection of leased, private circuits that link multiple locations of an enterprise or organization. May be used to transmit different combinations of voice, data and video signals between sites over the point-to-point lines that exist between sites.
proprietary	Systems that use techniques and processes that are closely-guarded trade secrets and which, because of these highly-individual approaches to achieving a result, cannot interoperate with other manufacturers' equipment without a great deal of difficulty.

protocol	A standard procedure agreed upon by regulating agencies, companies, or standards-setting bodies to regulate transmission and, therefore, to achieve inter-communications between systems or networks.
PSTN	Public Switched Telephone Network. The conventional voice telephony network as provided by Local Exchange Carriers.
PTT	Post Telephone and Telegraph company. A generic term for the telephony providers in Europe and other non-US countries.
public room	A commercial videoconferencing center that customers without a facility of their own can rent. By accessing a furnished public room, customers can conduct a videoconference without the major investment or concern that the equipment may not be compatible with that at the distant end.
Px64	Pronounced "P times 64." Another (early) name for the ITU-T's H.261 codec.

— Q —

Q-Signal	In the NTSC color system, the Q signal represents the chrominance on the green-magenta axis.
Q.920	One of the two ITU-T Recommendations in which the Link Access Protocol-D (LAPD) is formally specified.
Q.921	Along with Q.920, this ITU-T Recommendation specifies the LAPD protocol, an OSI layer-2 protocol. The connection-oriented service establishes a point-to-point D channel link between a customer and a carrier's switch. Data is sent over the link as Q.921 packets.
Q.931	Whereas the D channel is packet-switched, B channels are circuit-switched. They are established, maintained and torn down using ITU-T Recommendation Q.931 (also known as ITU-T I.451).

	In Q.931, the ITU-T specified how 'H' channels—multiple contiguous channels on T-1 or E-1/CEPT frames—can be bound together and switched across an ISDN network.
QCIF	Quarter Common Intermediate Format, a mandatory part of the ITU-T H.261 compression standard that requires that non-interlaced frames of NTSC video be sent with 144 luminance lines and 176 pixels. When operating in the QCIF mode the number of bits that result from encoding a single image can not exceed 64 K bits where K equals 1024.
QoS	Quality of Service (QoS) defines a level of performance in a communications network. For example, video traffic requires low delay and jitter; data traffic does not, but will burst and thereby impede the transmission of voice traffic. Any channel that transports both must, therefore, reserve and execute preferential treatment for video.
quality reduction	One way of compressing data in which some compromises are made in picture resolution, frame rate and image size in order to accommodate the bandwidth available for transmission.
quantization	Quantization is one step in the process of converting an analog event into its digital representation. It involves the division of a continuous range of signal values into contiguous parts, a unique value being assigned to each part. Prior to quantization the signal is sampled at regular intervals (typically at a rate that is least twice its highest frequency). The instantaneous amplitude of each sample is expressed as one of a defined number of discrete levels. These levels can then be assigned a digital value.
quantization matrix	A set of values used by a de-quantizer. The H.261 quantization matrix specifies 64 8-bit values.
QuickTime	Apple's video compression solution developed for the Macintosh product line. Decompression can be accomplished using nothing more than standard computer hardware although QuickTime accelerator cards with hardware decompression chips allows

much better results.

— R —

RAM	See random access memory.
Random Access Memory	RAM. A storage receptacle that is volatile, i.e., that it only retains information until a computer is turned off.
RAS	Protocol used in IP networks for Registration, Admission, and Status
RAS	A Remote Access Server is any gateway device that enables network access from remote computers via modem.
raster	The pattern of horizontal lines that form the image scanning of a television system.
raster scan	The process of continually scanning both vertically and horizontally using an electron beam to create moving images on a television screen.
RBOC	Regional Bell Operating Company. This term is used in a general sense today to refer to any of the original 22 Bell Operating Companies that were spun off parent AT&T as part of the MFJ (pronounced R-BOK).
RCA	Radio Corporation of America. First large commercial enterprise to wholeheartedly pursue television in the US under the direction of David Sarnoff.
Real-time	The time that elapses when events occur naturally. This term describes computing and electronic applications in which there is no perceived delay in the transmission of an interactive communication.
Real-time compression	Process of capturing and compressing video in one step so that it can be written to disk or other storage media.
Real-Time Transport	RTP. An IETF Draft, RTP adds a layer to IP in order

Protocol to address problems caused when real-time interactive exchanges such as audiovisual communications are transported over TCP/IP networks. Packet-switched networks were designed for data where latency is generally tolerable. In voice and video communications a constant bit rate is required for smooth delivery. RTP's approach is to give low-latency connection-oriented communications a higher priority than connectionless data. RTP also addresses the need for multicasting and compression over the Internet and other TCP/IP-based networks. TCP is a reliable transport but because of its efforts on behalf of reliability it can cause videoconferencing packet delivery problems. For instance, TCP re-sends packets of data that have not been correctly transmitted. In a time-sensitive environment like videoconferencing this causes problems because if packets did not arrive precisely on time they are no longer useful. RTP does not resend missed packets. Instead, it notifies a server that a packet was missed. If the threshold of missed packets reaches a certain level RTP will communicate with RSVP, another Internet protocol, to request that additional bandwidth be allocated.

redundant In the context of compression, redundant information is that which does not change over time (temporal) or space (spatial). Temporal redundancy manifests in a sequence of video frames in which successive frames contain the same information as those that preceded them. This information is, thus, redundant; e.g., not necessary to convey. Rather, it is only necessary to convey the areas of the frame that *did* change for that information is critical to the recipient's accurate interpretation of the new frame. Spatial redundancy manifests within a frame of video in which a group of similar pixels are clustered. The goal of video compression is to eliminate redundancy that, in turn, reduces the data rate required for transmission.

reference frames In video compression reference or intra-coded frames are sent periodically to eliminate the accumulated errors generated through the process of interframe coding.

refresh To recharge the cells of a volatile digital memory so that their contents are not lost. Alternately, to "paint" a new picture on the screen of a VDT is to refresh the screen.

repeater A device used to reprocess and amplify a weak signal in a transmission system. Used where the distance between the sender and receiver is too great for the signal to travel between the two without being boosted along the way. Radio signals, as they travel through free space, are attenuated; their power is gradually lost. Thus repeaters are needed to interpret the original signal and amplify it. They also often amplify background noise and interference in the process.

reproducing spot In television broadcasting, images are sent as a series of signals that describe a series of scan lines. A black and white television receiver captures these signals and reproduces the image on the screen using a *reproducing spot* that writes to the screen, varying in intensity in accordance with the instantaneous amplitude variations of the received signal.

Request in Progress Message H.323v3 feature that allows the receiver of a request to specify, when a message can not be processed before the initial timeout value expires, that a new timeout value should be applied.

resolution The ability of an optical or video system to produce separate images of objects very close together and, hence, to reproduce fine detail.

retrace The return of an electron beam to its starting place to prepare for sending a new field of information.

retrace interval The process of moving a scan line back to the left-most position in order to begin a new scan.

RF Radio frequency. Electromagnetic signals that travel from radios or other sources through free space.

R-Y A designator used to name one of the color signals in the color difference video signal, with a formula of

	.70R, -.59G, -.11G.
RFI	Radio frequency interference. Often manifests in television signals as vertical bars moving slowly across a picture. It can also take the form of diagonal or vertical lines or a pattern of horizontal bars.
RGB	Red, green, blue. The additive used in color video systems. Color television signals are oriented as three separate pictures: red, green and blue. Typically, they are merged together as a composite signal. However, for maximum quality, and in computer applications, the signals are segregated.
RIP	See Router Information Protocol
RIP	See Request in Progress Message
roadrunner	A digital multi-node network switching system, manufactured by ACTION/Honeywell. It allowed voice, data and video to share point-to-point digital bandwidth.
roll-about	A totally self-contained videoconferencing system that includes a codec, monitor(s), audio system, and network interfaces. These systems can, in theory, be moved from room-to-room. In fact, they are not portable because they include electronic equipment that is not durable enough for a great deal of jostling about and, moreover, is quite heavy.
router	Equipment that facilitates the exchange of packets between autonomous networks (LANs and WANs) of similar architecture. Connection is made at OSI layer 3 (network layer). A router responds to packets addressed to it by either a terminal or another router. Routers move packets over a specific path or paths based on the packet's destination, network congestion and the protocols implemented on the network.
Routing Information Protocol	Hop-count based interior gateway routing protocol. RIP is one of the oldest and, perhaps, still the most prevalent routing protocol.

RS-170A A specification for adding color to the NTSC television signal. It uses the YIQ method to add hue and saturation to a luminance subcarrier.

RS-232-C An EIA interchange specification specifying electrical characteristics and pin allocations in a 25-pin connection cable. The equivalent of the international V24 standard.

RS-366 An EIA interface standard for autodialing.

RS-449 A physical layer specification that defines a 37-pin data connector designed for high-speed transmissions. The signal pairs are balanced and each signal pin has its own return line instead of a common ground.

RSVP Resource-Reservation Protocol. An IETF specification that allows users of conferencing over the Internet to reserve bandwidth at a given time.

RTCP Real-Time Transport Control Protocol. A companion to RTP that will allow users to provide feedback on how an RTP session is working; how well packets are being delivered, etc.

RTP See Real-Time Transport Protocol.

rubber bandwidth Coined by I-MUX manufacturer Ascend, the term refers to an ability to support applications that require varying speeds by dividing a signal up into 56- or 64-Kbps chunks and sending them over a switched digital network.

run-length encoding Compression method that works at the bit level to reduce the number of repeating bits in a file. Sending only one example, followed by a shorthand description of the number of times it repeats, indicates a string of identical bits.

— S —

S-Video Super Video (as opposed to composite). S-Video is a hardware standard that defines the physical cable jack used for video connections. The connector takes the form of a 4-pin mini plug when separate channels are provided for luminance and chrominance. Also known as Y/C Video, S-Video is used in the S-VHS and Hi8 videotape formats.

sampling — The process of measuring an analog signal in time slices so that it can be quantized and encoded in a digital format. The sampling interval is specified in Nyquist's Theorem: it must be at least twice the highest frequency contained in the analog input. Thus, in an analog signal in which frequencies of 4,000 hertz are possible, the sampling rate must be 8,000 per second.

satellite — A man-made object designed to orbit the earth. Used to receive and retransmit telecommunications signals that originate at an earth station.

satellite delay — In satellite transmissions a signal must travel from the earth to a transponder placed in geosynchronous orbit, a distance of 22,300 miles above the equator. Radio waves, which travel at approximately the speed of light (186,000 miles per second) take about.24 seconds to make the round trip, and thereby induce perceptible delay in satellite communications that are particularly annoying in speech and interactive video transmissions.

satellite receiver — A microwave antenna that is capable of intercepting satellite transmitted signals, lowering the frequency of those signals and retrieving the modulated information. Provides a baseband output that takes the form of audio, video, graphics, images or text-based data.

saturation — In color reproduction, the spectral purity or intensity of a color. Adding white to a hue reduces its saturation.

SBIT — A three-bit integer that indicates the number of bits that should be ignored in the first data octet of a RTP H.261 packet.

scan converter
A device that converts computer images to a television display format. Used to convert the scan rates of VGA or SVGA to NTSC, PAL or SECAM scan rates.

scan line
During scanning, a number of nearly horizontal passes are made across an image and the light recorded by the image is converted into an electrical signal. Each pass across the image is called a scan line.

scanner
A device used to capture and digitize images. A scanner reads the light and dark areas of an image—whether it is a person, a page of text or a scene. It converts the light it registers into a coded signal. All video cameras contain scanners; scanners are also used in the capture of information contained on paper such as text, pictures, and photographs. Scanners designed for paper-based information capture are usually based on optical character reader (OCR) technology.

scanning
The process of analyzing the brightness and colors of an image, using a camera or other collection device, according to a predetermined pattern. In monitors, the number of scanning lines per frame gives an indication of the quality of the picture transmitted and displayed.

SCIF
Super CIF. A standard video exchange format made up of a square of four CIF images. SCIF specifies 576 lines, each of which contains 704 pixels. Also known as 4CIF.

screen
Devices that emit or reflect light to a viewer. Examples include the white or pale silver sheets of beaded vinyl or other reflective material upon which motion pictures or slides are projected, and monitors—typically CRTs and their associated display circuitry—used in desktop and room-based videoconferencing applications. A monitor screen is simply a panel of glass coated with phosphorescent dots called pixels. The phosphors glow when bombarded with electrons from the CRT's electron

gun.

SDP	See Session Description Protocol.
SECAM	Sequential Couleur Avec Memoire. The color television system that offers 625 scan lines and 25 interlaced frames per second. It was developed after NTSC and PAL and is used in France, the former Soviet Union, the former Eastern bloc countries and parts of the Middle East. Two versions of SECAM exist: horizontal SECAM and vertical SECAM. In this system, frequency modulation is used to encode the chrominance signal.
Security policy	An information security policy as an explicit set of prescribed practices that fosters protection of the enterprise network and of information assets.
security video	Video systems that are used to observe the events in a distant location, nearly always in a receive-only arrangement. Many such systems are slow-scan and use inexpensive cameras to capture images. The video signal. Typically not digitized or compressed.
serial communication	Used to connect computers with modems, printers and networks. Networks based on serial communication typically use the EIA's RS-232-C interface in which the pins that carry the electrical signal are arranged in a pattern that is understood by both the sending and receiving device.
serial interface	Refers to data being transferred between a computer and some type of peripheral device, often a printer, in a series of bits in which each bit is sent one at a time as part of a sequence.
server	In a network, a server is the device that allocates the activities of shared support resources between client workstations and/or PCs. Servers store files and databases; they provide access to printers and fax machines and they permit the client to access external communications networks and information systems. The X Window System, however, reverses the usual definition: the X display device runs a "server"

program that provides display services, and the application program is a "client" that runs locally or remotely and requests those services.

Session Description Protocol — Protocol for conveying information about streams in multimedia sessions to enable recipients of a *session description* to participate in a session. In a Multicast based session on the internet, SDP is a means to communicate the timing and existence of a session, and to convey sufficient information to enable recipients to join and participate in the session.

Session Initiation Protocol — Defined in IETF RFC 2543, SIP is an application-layer control (signaling) protocol for creating, modifying, and terminating sessions with one or more participants. Sessions can be Internet multimedia conferences, Internet telephone calls, or multimedia distribution. Members in a session can communicate via multicast, a mesh of unicast relations, or a combination of these. SIP is touted as a simpler alternative to H.323.

set-top box — In a CATV environment, the cable terminates in the subscriber's location on a decoder or set-top box, which is connected directly to the television receiver. Set-tops vary greatly in their complexity. Older models merely translate the frequency received off the cable into a frequency suitable for the television receiver; newer models can be addressable with a unique identity much like a telephone. Interactive set-tops will allow a CATV subscriber to communicate "upstream" to place orders, answer questions in a distance-learning environment, vote in elections, etc.

seven-layer model — See OSI (Open Systems Interconnection) model.

shadow mask — In a color monitor, this component is placed between the electron guns and the screen to ensure that the electron beams are restricted to their targeted dots.

shutter — A device that cuts off light in an optical instrument.

SIF — Source input format. Used in MPEG, and not to be confused with the Common Intermediate Format (CIF) used in the ITU-T's H.32X family of videoconferencing standards.

signal-to-noise	A ratio used to describe the clarity or degradation of a circuit. Signal-to-noise is measured in decibels. An acceptable signal-to-noise ratio is generally 200:1 or 46 dB.
SIP	See Session Initiation Protocol.
simplex	A circuit capable of transmissions in only one direction.
sine wave	The smooth, symmetrical curve that is created by natural vibrations that occur in the universe.
single mode fiber	Optical fiber with a central core of such small dimension that only a single mode of transmission is possible. Light travels straight down the middle of the fiber without zigzagging from side to side. Single mode fibers are able to transmit high bit rates over long distances.
slow-scan	Television or video scanning system in which a frame rate lower than normal is used to reduce the bandwidth required for transmission. Often associated with the transmission of video frames over the public switched telephone network.
SMATV	Satellite Master Antenna Television. A distribution system that feeds satellite signals to hotels, apartments, etc. Often associated with pay-per-view.
SMDS	Switched Multimegabit Digital Service. A public networking service based on the IEEE's 802.6 specification.
smear	The undesirable blurring of edges in a compressed image, often caused by the DCT that tends to eliminate the high-frequency portions of an image that represent sharp edges.
SMPTE	Society of Motion Picture and Television Engineers, the authors of the SMPTE time code used in video film and A/V production.

SMPTE Time Code	An 80-bit time code used in video editing. Developed by the SMPTE.
snow	Random noise or interference appearing in a video picture as white specs.
software	The programs, procedures, rules and routines used to extend the capabilities of computers.
SONET	Synchronous Optical Network.
sound waves	Naturally occurring oscillations that are created when objects vibrate at a certain frequency, and thereby compress the air molecules around them and cause these molecules to seek equilibrium by decompressing outward. During decompression dynamic energy is expended, thereby causing neighboring groups of molecules to compress. This starts a chain reaction. Compressed air is pushed in all directions from the source. If the resulting waves are between 50 and 20,000 Hz humans can hear them as sounds.
spatial	Compression/coding that is performed on a single frame of video data as opposed to temporal (time) coding that is performed by comparing successive video frames to each other.
spatial relationships	The physical world about us is embedded in our mental structure so that we tend to think in spatial terms and in analogy to them. Pictures and moving images are the best vehicle for quickly describing spatial relationships to humans. Because of this, video and graphics are highly useful in certain types of applications. Information-bearing pictures are usually spatially oriented; circuit diagrams, assembly drawings, blueprints, and other graphics show the spatial relationships of their sub-elements better than words could describe them, or at least more efficiently.
spectrum	A range of wavelengths or frequencies of acoustic, visible or electromagnetic radiation. Also refers to a display of visible light radiation that is arranged in

order of wavelength.

SpectrumSaver Compression Labs compression system designed to digitize and compress a full-motion NTSC or PAL analog TV signal so that it can be transmitted via satellite in as little as 2 MHz of bandwidth.

splitter In CATV networks, multiple feeder cables are attached to splitters that match the impedance of the cables.

square wave A term typically used to refer to a digital signal comprised of only two voltage values, that represent on and off (or one and zero).

SQCIF H.263, a scalable version of H.261, Sub-QCIF, a 128-by-96 pixel image resolution format. SQCIF was also added to the H.261 recommendation, to allow low-resolution picture coding.

S/T-Interface The ISDN Subscriber/Termination (S/T) Interface uses two pairs of wires to deliver an ISDN signal from a wall jack to an ISDN adapter or other ISDN equipment.

standards conversion The process of adapting a television or video production from one set of standards (e.g., NTSC) to another (e.g., PAL). This is necessary when programming that was developed for one part of the world (e.g., North America), is viewed in another (e.g., Europe).

star topology A network in which there is an individual connection between a switching point (or in the CATV world, a head-end) and a device or subscriber.

store-and-forward Systems in which messages (including video-enabled messages) are stored at an intermediate point for later retrieval.

streaking In video, shifting brightness across an image at the vertical location of a bright object.

streaming data Any transmission with a time component, such as video and audio signals.

Study Group — Groups of subject experts that are appointed by the ITU-T, an international standards-setting body that is part of the United Nations. Study Groups draw up Recommendations that are submitted to the ITU-T at the next plenary assembly for adoption.

subcarrier — A band of frequencies superimposed onto a main carrier frequency. In color television the color information is carried on the same subcarrier as the luminance signal by modulating it onto the upper frequencies of the luma waveform.

subjective evaluation — During the process of comparing videoconferencing systems, the portion of the comparison that is in the "eye-of-the-beholder" as opposed to being documentable and scientific.

subscriber — A customer of a carrier, service provider or utility.

subtractive color — Objects themselves have no actual color properties. Rather, their surfaces reflect certain wavelengths of light and absorb others. Those that are reflected correspond to the "colors" that we attribute to a given object. This concept of reflected light is described as subtractive color; the subtractive color primaries are magenta, cyan and yellow. Subtractive color differs from additive color. Additive color is the result of light viewed directly, in other words the actual wavelengths of radiation emitted by light sources. Additive color primaries, used in video, are red, blue and green (RGB).

Super CIF — A video format defined in the 1992 Annex IV amendment of the ITU-T's H.261 coding standard. Also known as 4CIF in the ITU-T's H.263 standard, it is comprised of 704 by 576 pixels.

super trunks — Large diameter coaxial or fiber-optic cables used to carry a signal from a head-end to various hub sites in a CATV network.

Super VGA — SVGA. A higher resolution version of the VGA

	standard that allows applications to use video resolutions of 1,024-by-768 pixels.
switch	A device that establishes, monitors, and terminates a connection between devices connected to a network.
Switched 56	Switched 56 service allows customers to dial up and transmit digital information up to 56,000 bits per second in much the same way that they dial up an analog telephone call. The service is billed like a voice line—a monthly charge plus a cost for each minute of usage. Nearly all LECs and IXCs offer switched 56 service and any switched 56 offering can connect with any other offering, regardless of which carrier offers the service.
switching	The process of setting up a connection between an input and an output. Switching takes place in many parts of a network: at a customer's PBX, at the local exchange, at a long distance carrier's office, in value-added networks such as X.25 or frame relay nets, etc. It allows a subscriber to establish communications with multiple parties by sending their address to the switch, which will then attempt to make a connection.
switching hub	An Ethernet switching device that examines a packet's MAC-layer destination to determine which hub port it will exit. Other ports are not aware of the packet's existence, thus a network is not bombarded with extraneous packets. These hybrid-internetworking devices provide a private network segment for end-stations attached to the hub's ports. Switching hubs, like telephone switches, use a circuit-switched technology in order to support parallel Ethernet conversations. Each station essentially has its own private subnet and can, therefore, send and receive data at Ethernet's full 10 Mbps. This is valuable for a user or group of users whose Real-Time videoconferencing or multimedia requirements demand isochronous service.
symmetrical	Techniques in which the decompression techniques are an exact reverse of the compression techniques. Used in Real-Time interactive video applications.

synch pulse

Oscillator circuits generate the horizontal and vertical sweep signals in a television receiver; they are controlled, in precise synchrony, by the movement of the scanning element at the camera. To achieve horizontal control, the camera sends synch pulses along with the luminance information. To control the vertical sweep oscillator, a synch pulse is sent at the end of each field.

synchronization

The process of controlling two or more systems so that they establish a time-based relationship with each other. Clocks are used to ensure precision in the sending and receiving of bits or other signals; characters are spaced by time, not bits.

system bus

Analogous to the nervous system in the human body, the system bus serves to interconnect the microprocessor with memory, storage devices, and input/output hardware.

— T —

T-1

Also known as DS-1 or T-carrier. High-speed digital transmission system characterized by a bit rate of 1.544 Mbps and subdivided, via time division multiplexing, into 24 channels. Each channel has a bit rate of 64 Kbps. Frames of data are created 8,000 times a second by combining each channel's 8-bit time slot into a group of 192 bits, a synchronization bit is added to the frame that makes it 193 bits wide. These 193-bit frames are sent 8,000 times a second and received by a channel bank or T-1 multiplexer.

T.120

The ITU-T's "Transmission Protocols for Multimedia Data," a data sharing/data conferencing specification that lets users share documents during any H.32x videoconference. Like H.32x specifications, T.120 is an umbrella Recommendation that includes a number of other Recommendations. Data-only T.120 sessions can be held when no video communications are required, and the standard also allows multipoint meetings that include participants using different transmission media. The mandatory components of

T.120 include recommendations for multipoint file transfer and shared-whiteboard implementation.

T.121 The T.120 family member that is formally known as "Generic Application Template." This template encompasses those operations that are common to most T.120 application protocols.

T.122 ITU-T Recommendation that is part of the T.120 family and which is known as "Multipoint Communication Service for Audiographics and Audiovisual Conferencing Service Definition." T.122 defines the multipoint services available to an applications developer while T.125 specifies the data protocol used to implement these services.

T.123 ITU-T Recommendation that is part of the T.120 family and which is known as "Protocol Stacks for Audiographic and Audiovisual Teleconference Applications." This protocol covers public switched telephone networks, ISDN, circuit switched digital networks, packet-switched digital networks, Novell NetWare IPX (via a reference profile) and TCP/IP.

T.124 ITU-T Recommendation that is part of the T.120 family and which is known as that allows "Generic Conference Control."

T.125 ITU-T Recommendation that is part of the T.120 family and which is known as "Multipoint Communication Service Protocol Specification."

T.126 ITU-T Recommendation that is part of the T.120 family and which is known as "Multipoint Still Image and Annotation Protocol." This standard defines a protocol for annotated shared whiteboard applications and still image conferencing. It uses services provided by T.122 and T.124. Remote pointing and keyboard data exchanges are covered, and therefore allow terminals to share applications, even if they are running on different platforms or operating systems.

T.127 ITU-T Recommendation that is part of the T.120 family and which is known as "Multipoint Binary

File Transfer Protocol." This allows participants in an interactive data conference to exchange binary files, and provides a means to distribute and retrieve one or more such files simultaneously.

T.128 — T.128 - Audio Visual Control for Multipoint Multimedia Systems. Now replaced with the T.130 family of ITU-T Draft Recommendations.

T.130 — The ITU-T's Draft Recommendation for "Real Time Architecture for Multimedia Conferencing. Provides an overview of how T.120 data conferencing will work in conjunction with H.32x videoconferencing.

T.131 — The ITU-T's Draft Recommendation for "Network-Specific Mappings." Defines how Real-Time audio and video streams should be carried over different types of networks including B-ISDN and ATM when used in conjunction with T.120 data conferencing.

T.132 — The ITU-T's Draft Recommendation for "Real Time Link Management." Defines how real time audiovisual streams can be routed between diverse multimedia endpoints.

T.133 — The ITU-T's Draft Recommendation for "Audio Visual Control Services." Defines how to control the source and link devices associated with real time information streams.

T.84 — ISO-JPEG standard.

T.RES — The ITU-T's Draft Recommendation for "Reservation Services." Defines how terminals, MCUs and reservations systems will interact to reserve a conference. Part of the T.130 family.

T.TUD — The ITU-T's Draft Recommendation for "User Reservation." Describes how to transport user defined bit streams between conferencing end-points. Part of the T.130 family.

T-3 — See DS-3.

talking head	The portion of a person that can be seen in the typical business-meeting-style videoconference; the head and shoulders. This type of image is fairly easy to capture with compressed video because there is very little motion in a talking head image and most occurs in facial expression and torso movement.
tap	In CATV systems the subscriber drop connects to feeder cables via taps; passive devices that isolate the feeder cable from the drop.
tariff	The terms and conditions of telecommunications or transmission service. Tariffs generally require approval by a regulatory body such as the FCC, PUCs or Often (UK).
TCP/IP	Transmission Control Protocol/Internet Protocol. A *de facto* standard and a set of internetworking protocols originally developed by the Department of Defense. Connects dissimilar computers across networks and is, therefore, widely used in the private sector. TCP/IP protocols work in the third and fourth layers of the OSI model to guarantee the delivery of data even in very congested networks.
TDM	Time Division Multiplexing. A technique for interleaving multiple voice, data and video signals onto a single carrier by assigning each signal its own separate time slot during which it can place a segment of its digitally-encoded transmission. At the distant end, the signals are separated so that each discrete signal can be re-oriented and recombined as an entire communication or message.
Telco	A generic name generally used to refer to local exchange carriers; telephone companies providing local exchange service.
telecommunications	The art and science of applying services and technologies in order to enable communications over distance. Uses technologies such as radio, terrestrial and cable-based services, wireless transmission and optical fiber networks.

Telecommunications Competition and Deregulation Act of 1996 — Passed by the 104th Congress and signed by President Clinton in February, 1996, the Telecommunications Competition and Deregulation Act of 1996 was a rewrite of the Communications Act of 1934. The stated goal of the act was to promote competition and reduce regulation to secure lower prices and higher quality, more robust, services for American telecommunications consumers by encouraging the rapid deployment of new telecommunications technologies. Unfortunately, it has resulted in industry consolidation. The Act allows long distance carriers to sell local access service, allows anyone to sell cable television service and, after sufficient competition can be demonstrated in local loop services, allows RBOCs and GTE to enter the long distance market.

telecommuting — The process of commuting to work electronically rather than physically. Telecommuting will find much greater acceptance as the public switched telephone network becomes more robust and digital and as videoconferencing and multimedia technologies arrive at the desktop.

teleconferencing — The use of telecommunications links to provide audio or audio/video/graphics capabilities. These systems allow distant workgroups or individuals to meet, and thereby reduce the administrative and opportunity costs of holding in-person meetings involving people from many different cities or countries.

telemedicine — The practice of using videoconferencing technologies to diagnose illness and provide medical treatment over a distance. Used in rural areas where health care is not readily available and to provide medical services to prisoners, among other applications.

telephony — The convergence of telephone and computer functionality. Specifically, the process of converting voice and other sounds into electrical signals that can be transmitted by wire, radio or fiber; stored and reconverted to audio upon receipt at the distant end.

teleport — A facility generally operated on a commercial basis, which is used for transmitting a video signal.

telewriting-based terminal equipment — An older term that refers to devices that use digitizing tablets and monitors to enable the sharing of text and graphics in video- and teleconferences. These devices were more evident in the very early 1990s. They used voice-grade circuits or required low data rates for transmission, typically about 9.6 Kbps. They were the predecessor to document conferencing systems.

temporal coding — Compression that is achieved by comparing successive frames of video over time to eliminate redundancies between them.

tile — See tiling. An individual pixel block that becomes visible on the viewer's monitor. Tiles, together, appear as a series of mosaic squares.

tiling — Video effect in which the image appears as pixel blocks. Can be caused by compression when the sampling rate or bandwidth is not adequate to fully describe the original image.

time division multiplexing — A way of enabling a single bearer signal to carry more than one information channel simultaneously. This is achieved by sharing the common transmission path on a cyclical basis. Each channel takes a turn using the path by entering the source data into a "time slot." Common TDM systems can support 24 channels in the US and 32 in Europe.

time slot — In TDM or TDSW, the slice of time that belongs to a digitized communication whether it be voice, data or video communication.

transcoding — Conversion from one format to another. This may be from one digital format into another, or between dissimilar formats such as from digital frames into analog video or from text into speech.

transform coding — A technique of video compression that requires VLSI chips with hundreds of thousands of gates. See DCT for a description of one type of transform coding.

TransMux — MPEG-4 specifies an interface to the *TransMux* (Transport Multiplexing) models, the layer that offers transport services for matching the requested QoS. Any suitable existing transport protocol stack (e.g., RTP in UDP/IP, AAL5 in ATM, or Transport Stream in MPEG-2) over a suitable link layer may become a specific TransMux instance.

transponder — A microwave repeater mounted on a satellite and used to receive communication from an uplink and retransmit it at a different frequency on a downlink.

tree and branch — A cable television arrangement in which large diameter coaxial cables (and, increasingly, fiber-optic cables) called super trunks radiate out from the head-end to various sectors of the franchise area to buildings acting as hub sites. From these hub sites smaller diameter coaxial cables branch out into the surrounding districts to be split and split again until cable runs along every street. A tapping point outside each residence enables the final connection to be made if the subscriber elects to have CATV service.

tripod — A three-legged camera stand that is usually adjustable and collapsible.

tuner — A piece of equipment or portion of a circuit used to select one signal or channel from amongst many signals or channels.

twisted pair — Two insulated copper wires twisted at regular intervals and normally covered by a protective outer sheath composed of PVC.

— U —

U-Interface — In the world of ISDN, the U-Interface carries ISDN formatted signals over a single pair of wires between a subscriber's location and a telephone company's central office.

UDP — User datagram protocol; an unreliable connectionless transport protocol that sends un-sequenced packets

	across a packet-switched network. UDP is defined in RFC 768.
UHF	Ultra High Frequency. The spectrum band that occupies frequencies from 470 to 890 MHz, within which television channels 14 through 83, are transmitted. CATV systems cannot transport these frequencies so they are converted for the purposes of cable transmission.
ULS	User Location Service. A white-pages directory that allows users of Internet videoconferencing and personal conferencing tools to refresh IP addresses dynamically and to determine who is logged on and available to have a conference. Microsoft and Intel led the ULS effort, along with various white page service providers.
unicast	Application of conferencing, usually over packet-switched networks, where only one user or site receives data. Contrast this with multicast in which data is received by more than one user or site.
up-link	The portion of a communications link used for the transmission of signals from a satellite earth station to satellite transponders in space.
upstream transmission	The ability for a CATV subscriber to communicate interactively with the head-end or a hub-site.
USB	Universal Serial Bus is a hardware interface for low-speed peripherals such as keyboards, mice, scanners, and telephony devices. USB supports MPEG-1 and MPEG-2 digital video. USB allows for 1–127 attached devices, and allows devices to use its full 12 Mbps bandwidth or a 1.5 Mbps subchannel (it also allows for hot-swapping). Low-power devices that might normally require a separate AC adapter can be powered through the cable because the USB bus distributes 0.5 amps of power through each port.
UTP	Unshielded Twisted Pair.

— V —

V.35 — An ITU-T standard interface between a network access device and a network.

V24 — An ITU-T list of interchange circuits for connecting a terminal device to a modem or one type of communications equipment to another.

VCR — Videocassette recorder—originally a trade name but now a generic term commonly used for a device that plays videotapes.

VDSL — Very-high-speed-digital subscriber line. VDSL will run up to 60 Mbps over distances up to 2 kilometers. LECs plan to use VDSL to distribute multiple TV channels to consumers, and thus to compete with cable.

vector quantization — A vector is a mathematical representation of a force (in video the force is a frequency, or a series of frequencies). In vector quantization blocks of pixels are analyzed to determine their vectors. Vectors are then used to select predefined equations that describe them in a more efficient way. These equations are expressed as codes, which might be only a few bits long. A decoder interprets these abbreviated codes and uses them to describe a frequency with a given hue and saturation.

vertical blanking — An interval that occurs at the beginning of each video field in which the reproducing spot is turned off during the process of retracing from the bottom right to the top left of the screen. After the vertical blanking period has ended the electron starts shooting electrons at the screen again, starting at the top and working toward the bottom.

vertical resolution — The total number of horizontal scan lines.

vertical sweep signal — The electrical signal that moves each horizontal scan line vertically.

VESA — Video Electronics Standards Association.

VGA Video Graphics Array. Developed by IBM, this has become the dominant standard for PC graphics. VGA provides two different graphics modes: 640 by 480 pixels at 4-bits per pixel or 320 by 200 pixels where 8 bits are used to describe a pixel.

VHF Very High Frequency. The frequency band used to transmit television channels two through 13.

video A sequence of still images that, when presented at a sufficiently high frame rate, give the illusion of fluid motion. In the US, full-motion video (television) is sent at 30 frames per second. In Europe and most of the rest of the world the frame rate is 25 per second. Motion pictures send video at 24 frames per second.

video capture board A PC circuit board that can capture the two fields that comprise a single video frame. Most 386SX PCs can support such boards. The best source of single-frame video images is a laser disk player that can pause and display a perfect frame of video without noise or jitter. Video cameras or camcorders aimed at a static image also work well. VCRs, which produce a jittery image when the tape is paused, are the poorest source. See also frame grabber.

Video For Windows An extension to Microsoft's Windows operating environment and an architecture for incorporating different media types into Windows applications.

video mail A multimedia version of electronic mail that includes moving or still images that are embedded into the message. Also known as v-mail.

video server A specialized file server with enormous hard disc capacities (often measured in terabytes or trillions of bytes). A video server stores MPEG compressed audio and video images for access by consumers, typically in a VOD application. Often called video juke boxes, these servers provide service to end-users over high-speed LANs and WANs (ATM, ADSL, MMDS, LMDS, hybrid fiber/coax arrangements). Applications that require video servers include entertainment, training/education and video-enabled databases.

video wall — Multi-screen video system in which a large number of video monitors or back projection modules together produce a very big, bright image. This is achieved by splitting the incoming video signal across many monitors. Used primarily for exhibitions and trade shows.

Video-On-Demand — VOD. The ability for subscribers to control when and how they view a movie. Homes are connected via high-speed links to CATV providers' facilities. VOD delivers features that mimic VCRs including rewind, pause, fast-forward and so on.

videoconferencing — A collection of technologies that integrate video with audio, data, or both and convey the aggregate signal, Real-Time, over distance for the purposes of a meeting between dispersed sites.

videophones — These products are aimed at the residential market and are typically low-end systems that provide transmission bandwidths between 64 and 128 Kbps. Most comply with the ITU-T's H.324 standard that was designed for video transmission over the analog POTS network. Most videophones compress and decompress in software only. Their screens are small (generally no larger than 6 inches square) and motion is sometimes slightly jerky.

videotex — An interactive data service that was designed to deliver visual information stored in a central location. Subscribers retrieve data on demand, over a public telephone network. Videotex became popular in the mid-1980s when France introduced the MiniTel system. MiniTel supports electronic yellow pages and air and rail reservation applications. In the U.K., British Telecom's PRESTEL service used a TV receiver as a data display terminal to support various services. Videotex was made obsolete by the World Wide Web, which serves the same function.

virtual circuit — A seemingly real connection between two points in a packet-switched network that, although it appears to

	be dedicated solely to the sender and receiver, is shared with others. In a virtual circuit, packetized data from multiple devices is placed on the same circuit.
virtual private network	Virtual private network technology allows an organization to use the Internet as a private network by employing tunneling or data encryption techniques in a firewall.
VLSI	Very Large Scale Integration.
voice-activated microphones	Microphones that automatically capture and transmit audio when a sound such as a voice triggers them to do so. Transmission ceases when the triggering sound stops. Videoconferencing system manufacturers effectively incorporate voice-activated microphones with cameras. These cameras capture and transmit images based on who is speaking.
voice messaging systems	Voice messaging systems store voices and sounds for retrieval at a later time. Long referred to as voicemail or phone mail, these systems are now being integrated with other messaging systems (electronic messaging or e-mail).
voltage	Electrical pressure caused by electrons repelling other electrons.
VSAT	Very Small Aperture Terminals. Small transportable satellite earth stations used in videoconferencing BTV applications.
VTS 1.5	Compression Lab's first codec that was introduced in 1982. It had an operating bandwidth requirement of 1.544 Mbps (T-1), remarkable for the time.

— W —

watts	A measure of the power or electrical energy of a signal or waveform.
wavelength division multiplexing	A technology that enables the existing fiber infrastructure of the telephone companies and other

	carriers to be dramatically increased. It uses lasers to transmit multiple light signals concurrently over a single optical fiber. With WDM, each signal travels within its own color band and is modulated by the data (video, voice, or data).
waveform	A presentation of the varying amplitude of a signal in relation to time.
WDM	See *Wavelength Division Multiplexing.*
white balance	A camera feature that adjusts the balance between the RGB components that yields white in the video signal. Various lighting conditions produce different color components. Cool-temperature lighting casts a different tint on a room than does warm-temperature lighting. White balance produces a uniform white regardless of room lighting.
white noise	Noise, containing energy, distributed uniformly over the frequency spectrum.
whiteboarding	The ability for multiple users to share a drawing space, generally a bit-mapped image that all conferees can make changes to. The ability to perform remote mark-up mimics the whiteboard in a physical conference room. Some whiteboarding applications allow the user to generate text that can be saved as such, while others convert text to a bit map.
wide area network	WAN, a collection of circuits that make up the public switched network and over which organizations communicate.
Windows™	A Microsoft tradesman for an applications package that incorporates a graphical user interface (GUI) that has tool bars, and offers the capability of displaying multiple applications.
workstation	Specialized terminal or computer targeted at technical users. Often found in a UNIX environment. Capable of high-resolution graphics and often used in CAD applications.

— X —

X.21 Used primarily in Europe, X.21 is a standard that operates at bit rates between 56 Kbps and 384 Kbps to control network dialing. A valuable feature of X.21 is its inherent dialing functions, including the provision for reporting why a call did not complete. X.21 can be used to connect to both switched and dedicated networks.

— Y —

Y The common nomenclature for the luminance signal.

Y/C In component video, the Y or luminance signal is kept separate from the C (hue and color saturation signal) to allow greater control and to enable enhanced quality images. The luminance is recorded at a higher frequency and therefore more resolution lines are available. Super-VHS and Hi8 systems use Y/C video.

YCbCr This term refers to the three different components that make up component video. Y represents the luminance portion of the signal. Cb and Cr represent the two different chroma components. CCIR-601 specifies 8-bit encoding for component video. White is luma code 235. Black is luma code 16.

YIQ A trichromatic color system used in NTSC color television systems. The luminance signal is the Y signal. There are two elements of color, hue and saturation. The color information is modulated onto the subcarrier with the phase of the sine wave describing the color itself and the amplitude describing the level of color saturation. Y uses 4.5 MHz, I uses 1.5 MHz and 1 uses 0.5 MHz.

YPbPr Part of the CCIR Rec. 709 HDTV standard that refers to three components (luma and two color components) that are conveyed in three separate channels with identical unity excursions. YPbPr is employed by component analog video equipment such as M-II and Betacam. In YPbPr, Pb equals (0.5/0.886) multiplied by Bgamma minus Y. Pr equals (0.5/0.701) multiplied by Rgamma minus Y.

YUV — The complete set of component signals, that comprise luminance (Y) and the two color difference signals, U (B-Y) and V (R-Y).

— Z —

Zigzag scanning — Used in the Discrete Cosine Transform, zigzag scanning results in the reordering of DCT coefficients from the lowest spatial frequency to the highest. Since the highest spatial frequencies have values that tend toward zero, reordering them through zigzag scanning results in long strings of zeros that can be abbreviated using run-length encoding.

Zoom — As applied to cameras with variable focal lengths, zooming provides the ability to take close-up and distant shots using the same lens.

INDEX

1

3

8

A

B

C

D

F

I

J

K

L

M

N

Q

R

U

V

W

X

Y

Z

Index

Printed in the United States
15930LVS00002B/28

9 781578 200542